TRAVELING SALESMAN PROBLEM, THEORY AND APPLICATIONS

Edited by **Donald Davendra**

Traveling Salesman Problem, Theory and Applications
Edited by Donald Davendra

Published by InTech

Janeza Trdine 9, 51000 Rijeka, Croatia

Publishing Process Manager Ana Nikolic

Technical Editor Teodora Smiljanic

Cover Designer InTech Design Team

Additional hard copies can be obtained from orders@intechopen.com

Traveling Salesman Problem, Theory and Applications, Edited by Donald Davendra
p. cm.
ISBN 978-953-307-426-9

For EU product safety concerns:
IN TECH d.o.o., Prolaz Marije Krucifikse Kozulić 3, 51000 Rijeka, Croatia,
info@intechopen.com or visit our website at intechopen.com.

Meet the editor

Dr. Donald Davendra's research background is in the fields of Evolutionary Algorithms, Chaotic Systems and their application to combinatorial optimization problems. He has a Bachelor of Science (BSc), Post Graduate Diploma (PGDip.) and Master of Science (MSc) in Computing Science and Engineering from the University of the South Pacific, Fiji Islands and has a Doctor of Philosophy (Ph.D.) in Technical Cybernetics from Tomas Bata University in Zlin for which he won the Siemens Award for outstanding Doctoral Dissertation in Czech Republic for 2009. His research profile includes being a book editor and author of journal papers, book chapters and conference proceeding in the field of evolutionary computation. Currently he holds the position of Assistant Professor at the Faculty of Electrical Engineering and Computing Science at the Technical University of Ostrava, Czech Republic

Contents

Preface

Computational complexity theory is a core branch of study in theoretical computing science and mathematics, which is generally concerned with classifying computational problems with their inherent difficulties. One of the core open problems is the resolution of P and NP problems. These are problems which are very important, however, for which no efficient algorithm is known. The Traveling Salesman Problem (TSP) is one of these problems, which is generally regarded as the most intensively studied problem in computational mathematics.

Assuming a traveling salesman has to visit a number of given cities, starting and ending at the same city. This tour, which represents the length of the travelled path, is the TSP formulation. As the number of cities increases, the determination of the optimal tour (in this case a Hamiltonian tour), becomes inexorably complex. A TSP decision problem is generally classified as NP-Complete problem.

One of the current and best-known approaches to solving TSP problems is with the application of Evolutionary algorithms. These algorithms are generally based on naturally occurring phenomena in nature, which are used to model computer algorithms. A number of such algorithms exists; namely, Artificial Immune System, Genetic Algorithm, Ant Colony Optimization, Particle Swarm Optimization and Self Organising Migrating Algorithm. Algorithms based on mathematical formulations such as Differential Evolution, Tabu Search and Scatter Search have also been proven to be very robust.

Evolutionary Algorithms generally work on a pool of solutions, where the underlying paradigm attempts to obtain the optimal solution. These problems are hence classified as optimization problems. TSP, when resolved as an optimization problem, is classified as a NP-Hard problem.

This book is a collection of current research in the application of evolutionary algorithms and other optimal algorithms to solving the TSP problem. It brings together researchers with applications in Artificial Immune Systems, Genetic Algorithms, Neural Networks and Differential Evolution Algorithm. Hybrid systems, like Fuzzy Maps, Chaotic Maps and Parallelized TSP are also presented. Most importantly, this book presents both theoretical as well as practical applications of TSP, which will be a vital tool for researchers and graduate entry students in the field of applied Mathematics, Computing Science and Engineering.

Donald Davendra

Faculty of Electrical Engineering and Computing Science
Technical University of Ostrava
Tr. 17. Listopadu 15, Ostrava
Czech Republic

donald.davendra@vsb.cz

1

Traveling Salesman Problem: An Overview of Applications, Formulations, and Solution Approaches

Rajesh Matai[1], Surya Prakash Singh[2] and Murari Lal Mittal[3]
[1]*Management Group, BITS-Pilani*
[2]*Department of Management Studies, Indian Institute of Technology Delhi, New Delhi*
[3]*Department of Mechanical Engineering, Malviya National Institute of Technology Jaipur, India*

1. Introduction

1.1 Origin

The traveling salesman problem (TSP) were studied in the 18th century by a mathematician from Ireland named Sir William Rowam Hamilton and by the British mathematician named Thomas Penyngton Kirkman. Detailed discussion about the work of Hamilton & Kirkman can be seen from the book titled Graph Theory (Biggs et al. 1976). It is believed that the general form of the TSP have been first studied by Kalr Menger in Vienna and Harvard. The problem was later promoted by Hassler, Whitney & Merrill at Princeton. A detailed dscription about the connection between Menger & Whitney, and the development of the TSP can be found in (Schrijver, 1960).

1.2 Definition

Given a set of cities and the cost of travel (or distance) between each possible pairs, the TSP, is to find the best possible way of visiting all the cities and returning to the starting point that minimize the travel cost (or travel distance).

1.3 Complexity

Given *n* is the number of cities to be visited, the total number of possible routes covering all cities can be given as a set of feasible solutions of the TSP and is given as $(n-1)!/2$.

1.4 Classification

Broadly, the TSP is classified as symmetric travelling salesman problem (sTSP), asymmetric travelling salesman problem (aTSP), and multi travelling salesman problem (mTSP). This section presents description about these three widely studied TSP.

sTSP: Let $V = \{v_1, ..., v_n\}$ be a set of cities, $A = \{(r,s) : r,s \in V\}$ be the edge set, and $d_{rs} = d_{sr}$ be a cost measure associated with edge $(r,s) \in A$.

The sTSP is the problem of finding a minimal length closed tour that visits each city once. In this case cities $v_i \in V$ are given by their coordinates (x_i, y_i) and d_{rs} is the Euclidean distance between r and s then we have an Euclidean TSP.

aTSP: If $d_{rs} \neq d_{sr}$ for at least one (r,s) then the TSP becomes an aTSP.
mTSP: The mTSP is defined as: In a given set of nodes, let there are m salesmen located at a single depot node. The remaining nodes (cities) that are to be visited are intermediate nodes. Then, the mTSP consists of finding tours for all m salesmen, who all start and end at the depot, such that each intermediate node is visited exactly once and the total cost of visiting all nodes is minimized. The cost metric can be defined in terms of distance, time, etc. Possible variations of the problem are as follows: *Single vs. multiple depots*: In the single depot, all salesmen finish their tours at a single point while in multiple depots the salesmen can either return to their initial depot or can return to any depot keeping the initial number of salesmen at each depot remains the same after the travel. *Number of salesmen*: The number of salesman in the problem can be fixed or a bounded variable. *Cost*: When the number of salesmen is not fixed, then each salesman usually has an associated fixed cost incurring whenever this salesman is used. In this case, the minimizing the requirements of salesman also becomes an objective. *Timeframe*: Here, some nodes need to be visited in a particular time periods that are called time windows which is an extension of the mTSP, and referred as multiple traveling salesman problem with specified timeframe (mTSPTW). The application of mTSPTW can be very well seen in the aircraft scheduling problems. *Other constraints*: Constraints can be on the number of nodes each salesman can visits, maximum or minimum distance a salesman travels or any other constraints. The mTSP is generally treated as a relaxed vehicle routing problems (VRP) where there is no restrictions on capacity. Hence, the formulations and solution methods for the VRP are also equally valid and true for the mTSP if a large capacity is assigned to the salesmen (or vehicles). However, when there is a single salesman, then the mTSP reduces to the TSP (Bektas, 2006).

2. Applications and linkages

2.1 Application of TSP and linkages with other problems

i. Drilling of printed circuit boards

A direct application of the TSP is in the drilling problem of printed circuit boards (PCBs) (Grötschel et al., 1991). To connect a conductor on one layer with a conductor on another layer, or to position the pins of integrated circuits, holes have to be drilled through the board. The holes may be of different sizes. To drill two holes of different diameters consecutively, the head of the machine has to move to a tool box and change the drilling equipment. This is quite time consuming. Thus it is clear that one has to choose some diameter, drill all holes of the same diameter, change the drill, drill the holes of the next diameter, etc. Thus, this drilling problem can be viewed as a series of TSPs, one for each hole diameter, where the 'cities' are the initial position and the set of all holes that can be drilled with one and the same drill. The 'distance' between two cities is given by the time it takes to move the drilling head from one position to the other. The aim is to minimize the travel time for the machine head.

ii. Overhauling gas turbine engines

(Plante et al., 1987) reported this application and it occurs when gas turbine engines of aircraft have to be overhauled. To guarantee a uniform gas flow through the turbines there are nozzle-guide vane assemblies located at each turbine stage. Such an assembly basically consists of a number of nozzle guide vanes affixed about its circumference. All these vanes have individual characteristics and the correct placement of the vanes can result in substantial benefits (reducing vibration, increasing uniformity of flow, reducing fuel consumption). The problem of placing the vanes in the best possible way can be modeled as a TSP with a special objective function.

iii. X-Ray crystallography

Analysis of the structure of crystals (Bland & Shallcross, 1989; Dreissig & Uebach, 1990) is an important application of the TSP. Here an X-ray diffractometer is used to obtain information about the structure of crystalline material. To this end a detector measures the intensity of X-ray reflections of the crystal from various positions. Whereas the measurement itself can be accomplished quite fast, there is a considerable overhead in positioning time since up to hundreds of thousands positions have to be realized for some experiments. In the two examples that we refer to, the positioning involves moving four motors. The time needed to move from one position to the other can be computed very accurately. The result of the experiment does not depend on the sequence in which the measurements at the various positions are taken. However, the total time needed for the experiment depends on the sequence. Therefore, the problem consists of finding a sequence that minimizes the total positioning time. This leads to a traveling salesman problem.

iv. Computer wiring

(Lenstra & Rinnooy Kan, 1974) reported a special case of connecting components on a computer board. Modules are located on a computer board and a given subset of pins has to be connected. In contrast to the usual case where a Steiner tree connection is desired, here the requirement is that no more than two wires are attached to each pin. Hence we have the problem of finding a shortest Hamiltonian path with unspecified starting and terminating points. A similar situation occurs for the so-called testbus wiring. To test the manufactured board one has to realize a connection which enters the board at some specified point, runs through all the modules, and terminates at some specified point. For each module we also have a specified entering and leaving point for this test wiring. This problem also amounts to solving a Hamiltonian path problem with the difference that the distances are not symmetric and that starting and terminating point are specified.

v. The order-picking problem in warehouses

This problem is associated with material handling in a warehouse (Ratliff & Rosenthal, 1983). Assume that at a warehouse an order arrives for a certain subset of the items stored in the warehouse. Some vehicle has to collect all items of this order to ship them to the customer. The relation to the TSP is immediately seen. The storage locations of the items correspond to the nodes of the graph. The distance between two nodes is given by the time needed to move the vehicle from one location to the other. The problem of finding a shortest route for the vehicle with minimum pickup time can now be solved as a TSP. In special cases this problem can be solved easily, see (van Dal, 1992) for an extensive discussion and for references.

vi. Vehicle routing

Suppose that in a city n mail boxes have to be emptied every day within a certain period of time, say 1 hour. The problem is to find the minimum number of trucks to do this and the shortest time to do the collections using this number of trucks. As another example, suppose that n customers require certain amounts of some commodities and a supplier has to satisfy all demands with a fleet of trucks. The problem is to find an assignment of customers to the trucks and a delivery schedule for each truck so that the capacity of each truck is not exceeded and the total travel distance is minimized. Several variations of these two problems, where time and capacity constraints are combined, are common in many real-world applications. This problem is solvable as a TSP if there are no time and capacity constraints and if the number of trucks is fixed (say m). In this case we obtain an m-salesmen problem. Nevertheless, one may apply methods for the TSP to find good feasible solutions for this problem (see Lenstra & Rinnooy Kan, 1974).

vii. Mask plotting in PCB production

For the production of each layer of a printed circuit board, as well as for layers of integrated semiconductor devices, a photographic mask has to be produced. In our case for printed circuit boards this is done by a mechanical plotting device. The plotter moves a lens over a photosensitive coated glass plate. The shutter may be opened or closed to expose specific parts of the plate. There are different apertures available to be able to generate different structures on the board. Two types of structures have to be considered. A line is exposed on the plate by moving the closed shutter to one endpoint of the line, then opening the shutter and moving it to the other endpoint of the line. Then the shutter is closed. A point type structure is generated by moving (with the appropriate aperture) to the position of that point then opening the shutter just to make a short flash, and then closing it again. Exact modeling of the plotter control problem leads to a problem more complicated than the TSP and also more complicated than the rural postman problem. A real-world application in the actual production environment is reported in (Grötschel et al., 1991).

2.2 Applications of mTSP and connections with other problems

This section is further divided into three. In the first section, the main application of the mTSP is given. The second part relates TSP with other problems. The third part deals with the similarities between the mTSP with other problems (the focus is with the VRP).

2.2.1 Main applications

The main apllication of mTSP arises in real scenario as it is capacble to handle multiple salesman. These situations arise mostly in various routing and scheduling problems. Some reported applications in literature are presented below.

i. **Printing press scheduling problem:** One of the major and primary applications of the mTSP arises in scheduling a printing press for a periodical with multi-editions. Here, there exist five pairs of cylinders between which the paper rolls and both sides of a page are printed simultaneously. There exist three kind of forms, namely 4-, 6- and 8-page forms, which are used to print the editions. The scheduling problem consists of deciding which form will be on which run and the length of each run. In the mTSP vocabulary, the plate change costs are the inter-city costs. For more details papers by Gorenstein (1970) and Carter & Ragsdale (2002) can be referred.

ii. **School bus routing problem:** (Angel et al., 1972) investigated the problem of scheduling buses as a variation of the mTSP with some side constraints. The objective of the scheduling is to obtain a bus loading pattern such that the number of routes is minimized, the total distance travelled by all buses is kept at minimum, no bus is overloaded and the time required to traverse any route does not exceed a maximum allowed policy.

iii. **Crew scheduling problem:** An application for deposit carrying between different branch banks is reported by (Svestka & Huckfeldt, 1973). Here, deposits need to be picked up at branch banks and returned to the central office by a crew of messengers. The problem is to determine the routes having a total minimum cost. Two similar applications are described by (Lenstra & Rinnooy Kan , 1975 and Zhang et al., 1999). Papers can be referred for delaited analysis.

iv. **Interview scheduling problem:** (Gilbert & Hofstra, 1992) found the application of mTSP, having multiperiod variations, in scheduling interviews between tour brokers and vendors of the tourism industry. Each broker corresponds to a salesman who must visit a specified set of vendor booths, which are represented by a set of T cities.

v. **Hot rolling scheduling problem:** In the iron and steel industry, orders are scheduled on the hot rolling mill in such a way that the total set-up cost during the production can be minimized. The details of a recent application of modeling such problem can be read from (Tang et al., 2000). Here, the orders are treated as cities and the distance between two cities is taken as penalty cost for production changeover between two orders. The solution of the model will yield a complete schedule for the hot strip rolling mill.

vi. **Mission planning problem:** The mission planning problem consists of determining an optimal path for each army men (or planner) to accomplish the goals of the mission in the minimum possible time. The mission planner uses a variation of the mTSP where there are n planners, m goals which must be visited by some planners, and a base city to which all planners must eventually return. The application of the mTSP in mission planning is reported by (Brummit & Stentz, 1996; Brummit & Stentz, 1998; and Yu et al., 2002). Similarly, the routing problems arising in the planning of unmanned aerial vehicle applications, investigated by (Ryan et al., 1998), can also be modelled as mTSP.

vii. **Design of global navigation satellite system surveying networks:** A very recent and an interesting application of the mTSP, as investigated by (Saleh & Chelouah, 2004) arises in the design of global navigation satellite system (GNSS) surveying networks. A GNSS is a space-based satellite system which provides coverage for all locations worldwide and is quite crucial in real-life applications such as early warning and management for disasters, environment and agriculture monitoring, etc. The goal of surveying is to determine the geographical positions of unknown points on and above the earth using satellite equipment. These points, on which receivers are placed, are co-ordinated by a series of observation sessions. When there are multiple receivers or multiple working periods, the problem of finding the best order of sessions for the receivers can be formulated as an mTSP. For technical details refer (Saleh & Chelouah, 2004).

2.2.2 Connections with other problems

The above-mentioned problems can be modeled as an mTSP. Apart from these above metioned problmes, mTSP can be also related to other problems. One such example is balancing the workload among the salesmen and is described by (Okonjo-Adigwe, 1988). Here, an mTSP-based modelling and solution approach is presented to solve a workload scheduling problem with few additional restrictions. Paper can be referred for detailed description and analysis. Similalry, (Calvo & Cordone, 2003; Kim & Park, 2004) investigated overnight security service problem. This problem consists of assigning duties to guards to perform inspection duties on a given set of locations with subject to constraint such as capacity and timeframe. For more comprehensive review on various application of mTSP authors advise to refer papers by (Macharis & Bontekoning, 2004; Wang & Regan, 2002; Basu et al., 2000).

2.2.3 Connections with the VRP

mTSP can be utilized in solving several types of VRPs. (Mole et al., 1983) discuss several algorithms for VRP, and present a heuristic method which searches over a solution space formed by the mTSP. In a similar context, the mTSP can be used to calculate the minimum number of vehicles required to serve a set of customers in a distance-constrained VRP (Laptore et al., 1985; Toth & Vigo, 2002). The mTSP also appears to be a first stage problem in a two-stage solution procedure of a VRP with probabilistic service times. This is discussed further by (Hadjiconstantinou & Roberts, 2002). (Ralphs, 2003) mentions that the VRP instances arising in practice are very hard to solve, since the mTSP is also very complex. This raises the need to efficiently solve the mTSP in order to attack large-scale VRPs. The mTSP is also related to the pickup and delivery problem (PDP). The PDP consists of determining the optimal routes for a set of vehicles to fulfill the customer requests (Ruland & Rodin, 1997). If the customers are to be served within specific time intervals, then the problem becomes the PDP with time windows (PDPTW). The PDPTW reduces to the mTSPTW if the origin and destination points of each request coincide (Mitrović-Minić et al., 2004).

3. Mathematical formulations of TSP and mTSP

The TSP can be defined on a complete undirected graph $G=(V,E)$ if it is symmetric or on a directed graph $G=(V,A)$ if it is asymmetric. The set V ={1, . . . , n} is the vertex set, $E=\{(i,j):i,j\in V,i<j\}$ is an edge set and $A=\{(i,j):i,j\in V,i\neq j\}$ is an arc set. A cost matrix $C=(c_{ij})$ is defined on E or on A. The cost matrix satisfies the triangle inequality whenever $c_{ij}\leq c_{ik}+c_{kj}$, for all i,j,k. In particular, this is the case of planar problems for which the vertices are points $P_i=(X_i,Y_i)$ in the plane, and $c_{ij}=\sqrt{(X_i-X_j)^2+(Y_i-Y_j)^2}$ is the Euclidean distance. The triangle inequality is also satisfied if c_{ij} is the length of a shortest path from i to j on G.

3.1 Integer programming formulation of sTSP

Many TSP formulations are available in literature. Recent surveys by (Orman & Williams, 2006; O¨ncan et al., 2009) can be referred for detailed analysis. Among these, the (Dantzig et al., 1954) formulation is one of the most cited mathematical formulation for TSP. Incidentally, an early description of Concorde, which is recognized as the most performing exact algorithm currently available, was published under the title 'Implementing the Dantzig–Fulkerson–Johnson algorithm for large traveling salesman problems' (Applegate et al., 2003). This formulation associates a binary variable x_{ij} with each edge (i, j), equal to 1 if and only if the edge appears in the optimal tour. The formulation of TSP is as follows.
Minimize

$$\sum_{i<j} c_{ij}x_{ij} \tag{1}$$

Subject to

$$\sum_{i<k} x_{ik}+\sum_{j>k} x_{kj}=2 \qquad (k\in V) \tag{2}$$

$$\sum_{i,j \in S} x_{ij} \leq |S| - 1 \qquad (S \subset V, 3 \leq |S| \leq n-3) \tag{3}$$

$$x_{ij} = 0 \text{ or } 1 \qquad (i,j) \in E \tag{4}$$

In this formulation, constraints (2), (3) and (4) are referred to as degree constraints, subtour elimination constraints and integrality constraints, respectively. In the presence of (2), constraints (3) are algebraically equivalent to the connectivity constraints

$$\sum_{i \in S, j \in V \setminus S, j \in S} x_{ij} \geq 2 \qquad (S \subset V, 3 \leq |S| \leq n-3) \tag{5}$$

3.2 Integer programming formulation of aTSP

The (Dantzig et al., 1954) formulation extends easily to the asymmetric case. Here x_{ij} is a binary variable, associated with arc *(i,j)* and equal to 1 if and only if the arc appears in the optimal tour. The formulation is as follows.
Minimize

$$\sum_{i \neq j} c_{ij} x_{ij} \tag{6}$$

Subject to

$$\sum_{j=1}^{n} x_{ij} = 1 \qquad (i \in V, i \neq j) \tag{7}$$

$$\sum_{i=1}^{n} x_{ij} = 1 \qquad (j \in V, j \neq i) \tag{8}$$

$$\sum_{i,j \in S} x_{ij} \leq |S| - 1 \qquad (S \subset V, 2 \leq |S| \leq n-2) \tag{9}$$

$$x_{ij} = 0 \text{ or } 1 \qquad (i,j) \in A \tag{10}$$

3.3 Integer programming formulations of mTSP

Different types of integer programming formulations are proposed for the mTSP. Before presenting them, some technical definitions are as follows. The mTSP is defined on a graph $G = (V, A)$, where V is the set of n nodes (vertices) and A is the set of arcs (edges). Let $C = (c_{ij})$ be a cost (distance) matrix associated with A. The matrix C is said to be symmetric when $c_{ij} = c_{ji}, \forall (i,j) \in A$ and asymmetric otherwise. If $c_{ij} + c_{jk} \geq c_{ik}, \forall i,j,k \in V$, C is said to satisfy the triangle inequality. Various integer programming formulations for the mTSP have been proposed earlier in the literature, among which there exist assignment-based formulations, a tree-based formulation and a three-index flow-based formulation. Assignment based formulations are presented in following subsections. For tree based formulation and three-index based formulations refer (Christofides et al., 1981).

3.3.1 Assignment-based integer programming formulations

The mTSP is usually formulated using an assignment based double-index integer linear programming formulation. We first define the following binary variable:

$$x_{ij} = \begin{cases} 1 & \text{If arc (i, j) is used in the tour,} \\ 0 & \end{cases}$$

Otherwise.

Then, a general scheme of the assignment-based directed integer linear programming formulation of the mTSP can be given as follows:

Minimize

$$\sum_{i=1}^{n}\sum_{j=1}^{n} c_{ij}x_{ij}$$

Subject to

$$\sum_{j=2}^{n} x_{1j} = m \tag{11}$$

$$\sum_{j=2}^{n} x_{j1} = m \tag{12}$$

$$\sum_{i=1}^{n} x_{ij} = 1, \quad j = 2,\ldots\ldots,n \tag{13}$$

$$\sum_{j=1}^{n} x_{ij} = 1, \; i = 2,\ldots\ldots,n \tag{14}$$

+ subtour elimination constraints, (15)

$$x_{ij} \in \{0,1\}, \; \forall (i,j) \in A, \tag{16}$$

where (13), (14) and (16) are the usual assignment constraints, (11) and (12) ensure that exactly m salesmen depart from and return back to node 1 (the depot). Although constraints (12) are already implied by (11), (13) and (14), we present them here for the sake of completeness. Constraints (15) are used to prevent subtours, which are degenerate tours that are formed between intermediate nodes and not connected to the origin. These constraints are named as subtour elimination constraints (SECs). Several SECs have been proposed for the mTSP in the literature. The first group of SECs is based on that of (Dantzig et al., 1954) originally proposed for the TSP, but also valid for the mTSP. These constraints can be shown as follows:

$$\sum_{i \in S}\sum_{j \in S} x_{ij} \leq |S| - 1, \qquad \forall S \subseteq V \setminus \{1\}, \qquad S \neq \varnothing \tag{17}$$

or alternatively in the following form

$$\sum_{i \notin S} \sum_{j \in S} x_{ij} \geq 1, \qquad \forall S \subseteq V \setminus \{1\}, \qquad S \neq \varnothing \tag{18}$$

Constraints (17) or (18) impose connectivity requirements for the solution, i.e. prevent the formation of subtours of cardinality S not including the depot. Unfortunately, both families of these constraints increase exponentially with increasing number of nodes, hence are not practical for neither solving the problem nor its linear programming relaxation directly. Miller et al. (1960) overcame this problem by introducing $O(n^2)$ additional continuous variables, namely node potentials, resulting in a polynomial number of SECs. Their SECs are given as follows (denoted by MTZ-SECs):

$$u_i - u_j + p x_{ij} \leq p - 1 \text{ for } 2 \leq i \neq j \leq n \tag{19}$$

Here, p denotes the maximum number of nodes that can be visited by any salesman. The node potential of each node indicates the order of the corresponding node in the tour. (Svestka & Huckfeldt, 1973) propose another group of SECs for the mTSP which require augmenting the original cost matrix with new rows and columns. However, (Gavish, 1976) showed that their constraints are not correct for m≥2 and provided the correct constraints as follows:

$$u_i - u_j + (n - m) x_{ij} \leq n - m - 1 \text{ for } 2 \leq i \neq j \leq n \tag{20}$$

Other MTZ-based SECs for the mTSP have also been proposed. The following constraints are due to Kulkarni & Bhave (1985) (denoted by KB-SECs):

$$u_i - u_j + L x_{ij} \leq L - 1 \text{ for } 2 \leq i \neq j \leq n \tag{21}$$

In these constraints, the L is same as p in (19). It is clear that MTZ-SECs and KB-SECs are equivalent.

3.3.2 Laporte & Nobert's formulations

(Laporte & Nobert, 1980) presented two formulations for the mTSP, for asymmetrical and symmetrical cost structures, respectively, and consider a common fixed cost f for each salesman used in the solution. These formulations are based on the two-index variable x_{ij} defined previously.

3.3.2.1 Laporte & Nobert's formulation for the asymmetric mTSP

Minimize

$$\sum_{i \neq j} c_{ij} x_{ij} + f_m$$

Subject to

$$\sum_{j=2}^{n} \left(x_{1j} + x_{j1} \right) = 2m \tag{22}$$

$$\sum_{i \neq k} x_{ik} = 1 \qquad k = 2, \ldots\ldots, n \tag{23}$$

$$\sum_{j \neq k} x_{ik} = 1 \qquad k = 2, \ldots\ldots\ldots, n \tag{24}$$

$$\sum_{i \neq j; i, j \in S} x_{ij} \leq |S - 1|$$

$$2 \leq |S| \leq n - 2, \qquad S \subseteq V \setminus \{1\} \tag{25}$$

$$x_{ij} \in \{0, 1\}, \qquad \forall i \neq j \tag{26}$$

$$m \geq 1 \text{ and integer} \tag{27}$$

This formulation is a pure binary integer where the objective is to minimize the total cost of the travel as well as the total number of salesmen. Note that constraints (23) and (24) are the standard assignment constraints, and constraints (25) are the SECs of (Dantzig et al., 1954). The only different constraints are (22), which impose degree constraints on the depot node.

3.3.2.2 Laporte & Nobert's formulation for the symmetric mTSP

Minimize

$$\sum_{i < j} c_{ij} x_{ij} + f_m$$

Subject to

$$\sum_{j=2}^{n} x_{1j} = 2m \tag{28}$$

$$\sum_{i < k} x_{ik} + \sum_{j > k} x_{kj} = 2 \qquad k = 2, \ldots\ldots\ldots, n \tag{29}$$

$$\sum_{i < j; i, j \in S} x_{ij} \leq |S - 1|$$

$$3 \leq |S| \leq n - 2, \qquad S \subseteq V \setminus \{1\} \tag{30}$$

$$x_{ij} \in \{0, 1\}, \qquad 1 < i < j \tag{31}$$

$$x_{1j} \in \{0, 1, 2\}, \qquad j = 2, \ldots\ldots\ldots, n \tag{32}$$

$$m \geq 1 \text{ and integer} \tag{32}$$

The interesting issue about this formulation is that it is not a pure binary integer formulation due to the variable x_{1j}, which can either be 0, 1 or 2. Note here that the variable x_{1j} is only defined for i <j, since the problem is symmetric and only a single variable is sufficient to represent each edge used in the solution. Constraints (28) and (29) are the degree constraints

on the depot node and intermediate nodes, respectively. Other constraints are as previously defined.

4. Exact solution approaches

4.1 Exact algorithms for the sTSP

When (Dantzig et al., 1954) formulation was first introduced, the simplex method was in its infancy and no algorithms were available to solve integer linear programs. The practitioners therefore used a strategy consisting of initially relaxing constraints (3) and the integrality requirements, which were gradually reintroduced after visually examining the solution to the relaxed problem. (Martin, 1966) used a similar approach. Initially he did not impose upper bounds on the x_{ij} variables and imposed subtour elimination constraints on all sets S= {i, j } for which j is the closest neighbour of i . Integrality was reached by applying the 'Accelerated Euclidean algorithm', an extension of the 'Method of integer forms' (Gomory, 1963). (Miliotis, 1976, 1978) was the first to devise a fully automated algorithm based on constraint relaxation and using either branch-and-bound or Gomory cuts to reach integrality. (Land, 1979) later puts forward a cut-and-price algorithm combining subtour elimination constraints, Gomory cuts and column generation, but no branching. This algorithm was capable of solving nine Euclidean 100-vertex instances out of 10. It has long been recognized that the linear relaxation of sTSP can be strengthened through the introduction of valid inequalities. Thus, (Edmonds, 1965) introduced the 2-matching inequalities, which were then generalized to comb inequalities (Chv´atal, 1973). Some generalizations of comb inequalities, such as clique tree inequalities (Grötschel & Pulleyblank, 1986) and path inequalities (Cornu´ejols et al., 1985) turn out to be quite effective. Several other less powerful valid inequalities are described in (Naddef, 2002). In the 1980s a number of researchers have integrated these cuts within relaxation mechanisms and have devised algorithms for their separation. This work, which has fostered the growth of polyhedral theory and of branch-and-cut, was mainly conducted by (Padberg and Hong, 1980; Crowder & Padberg, 1980; Grötschel & Padberg, 1985; Padberg & Grötschel, 1985; Padberg & Rinaldi, 1987, 1991; Grötschel & Holland, 1991). The largest instance solved by the latter authors was a drilling problem of size n =2392. The culmination of this line of research is the development of Concorde by (Applegate et al., 2003, 2006), which is today the best available solver for the symmetric TSP. It is freely available at www.tsp.gatech.edu. This computer program is based on branch-and-cut-and-price, meaning that both some constraints and variables are initially relaxed and dynamically generated during the solution process. The algorithm uses 2-matching constraints, comb inequalities and certain path inequalities. It makes use of sophisticated separation algorithms to identify violated inequalities. A detailed description of Concorde can be found in the book by (Applegate et al., 2006). Table 1 summarizes some of the results reported by (Applegate et al., 2006) for randomly generated instances in the plane. All tests were run on a cluster of compute nodes, each equipped with a 2.66 GHz IntelXeon processor and 2 Gbyte of memory. The linear programming solver used was CPLEX 6.5. It can be seen that Concorde is quite reliable for this type of instances. All small TSPLIB instances ($n \leq 1000$) were solved within 1 min on a 2.4 GHz ADM Opteron processor. On 21 medium-size TSPLIB instances ($1000 \leq n \leq 2392$), the algorithm converged 19 times to the optimum within a computing time varying between 5.7 and 3345.3 s. The two exceptions required 13999.9 s and 18226404.4 s. The largest instance now solved optimally by Concorde arises from a VLSI application and contains 85900 vertices (Applegate et al., 2009).

N	Type	Sample size	Mean CPU seconds
100	random	10000	0.7
500	random	10000	50.2
1000	random	1000	601.6
2000	random	1000	14065.6
2500	random	1000	53737.9

Table 1. Computation times for Concorde

4.2 Exact algorithms for the aTSP

An interesting feature of aTSP is that relaxing the subtour elimination constraints yields a Modified Assignment Problem (MAP), which is an assignment problem. The linear relaxation of this problem always has an integer solution and is easy to solve by means of a specialized assignment algorithm, (Carpaneto & Toth, 1987; Dell'Amico & Toth, 2000 and Burkard et al., 2009). Many algorithms based on the AP relaxation have been devised. Some of the best known are those of (Eastman,1958; Little et al., 1963; Carpaneto & Toth, 1980; Carpaneto et al., 1995 and Fischetti & Toth, 1992). Surveys of these algorithms and others have been presented in (Balas & Toth, 1985; Laporte, 1992 and Fischetti et al., 2002). It is interesting to note that (Eastman, 1958) described what is probably the first ever branch-and-bound algorithm, 2 years before this method was suggested as a generic solution methodology for integer linear programming (Land & Doig, 1960), and 5 years before the term 'branch-and-bound' was coined by (Little et al., 1963). The (Carpaneto et al., 1995) algorithm has the dual advantage of being fast and simple. The (Fischetti & Toth, 1992) algorithm improves slightly on that of (Carpaneto et al., 1995) by computing better lower bounds at the nodes of the search tree. The Carpanteo, Dell'Amico & Toth algorithm works rather well on randomly generated instances but it often fails on some rather small structured instances with as few as 100 vertices (Fischetti et al., 2002). A branch- and bound based algorithm for the asymmetric TSP is proposed by (Ali & Kennington, 1986). The algorithm uses a Lagrangean relaxation of the degree constraints and a subgradient algorithm to solve the Lagrangean dual.

4.3 Exact algorithms for mTSP

The first approach to solve the mTSP directly, without any transformation to the TSP is due to (Laporte & Nobert, 1980), who propose an algorithm based on the relaxation of some constraints of the mTSP. The problem they consider is an mTSP with a fixed cost f associated with each salesman. The algorithm consists of solving the problem by initially relaxing the SECs and performing a check as to whether any of the SECs are violated, after an integer solution is obtained. The first attempt to solve large-scale symmetric mTSPs to optimality is due to (Gavish & Srikanth, 1986). The proposed algorithm is a branch-and-bound method, where lower bounds are obtained from the following Lagrangean problem constructed by relaxing the degree constraints. The Lagrangean problem is solved using a degree-constrained minimal spanning tree which spans over all the nodes. The results indicate that the integer gap obtained by the Lagrangean relaxation decreases as the problem size increases and turns out to be zero for all problems with $n \geq 400$. (Gromicho et al., 1992) proposed another exact solution method for mTSP. The algorithm is based on a quasi-assignment (QA) relaxation obtained by relaxing the SECs, since the QA-problem is solvable in polynomial time. An additive bounding procedure is applied to strengthen the lower bounds obtained via different r-arborescence and r-anti-arborescence relaxations and this procedure is embedded in a branch-and-bound framework. It is observed that the additive bounding procedure has a significant effect in improving the lower bounds, for which the QA-relaxation yields poor bounds. The proposed branch-and-bound algorithm is superior to the standard branch-and-bound approach with a QA-relaxation in terms of number of nodes, ranging from 10% less to 10 times less. Symmetric instances are observed to yield larger improvements. Using an IBM PS/70 computer with an 80386 CPU running at 25 MHz, the biggest instance solved via this approach has 120 nodes with the number of salesman ranging from 2 to 12 in steps of one (Gromicho, 2003).

5. Approximate approaches

There are mainly two ways of solving any TSP instance optimally. The first is to apply an exact approach such as Branch and Bound method to find the length. The other is to calculate the Held-Karp lower bound, which produces a lower bound to the optimal solution. This lower bound is used to judge the performance of any new heuristic proposed for the TSP. The heuristics reviewed here mainly concern with the sTSP, however some of these heuristics can be modified appropriatley to solve the aTSP.

5.1 Approximation

Solving even moderate size of the TSP optimally takes huge computtaional time, therefore there is a room for the development and application of approximate algorithms, or heuristics. The approximate approach never guarantee an optimal solution but gives near optimal solution in a reasonable computational effort. So far, the best known approximate algorithm available is due to (Arora, 1998). The complexity of the approximate algorithm is $O\left(n(\log_2 n)^{O(c)}\right)$ where n is problem size of TSP.

5.2 Tour construction approaches

All tour construction algorithms stops when a solution is found and never tries to improve it. It is believed that tour construction algorithms find solution within 10-15% of optimality. Few of the tour construction algorithms available in published literature are described below.

5.2.1 Closest neighbor heuristic

This is the simplest and the most straightforward TSP heuristic. The key to this approach is to always visit the closest city. The polynomial complexity associated with this heuristic approach is $O\left(n^2\right)$. The closest approach is very similar to minimum spanning tree algorithm. The steps of the closest neighbor are given as:

1. Select a random city.
2. Find the nearest unvisited city and go there.
3. Are there any unvisitied cities left? If yes, repeat step 2.
4. Return to the first city.

The Closest Neighbor heuristic approach generally keeps its tour within 25% of the Held-Karp lower bound (Johnson & McGeoch, 1995).

5.2.2 Greedy heuristic

The Greedy heuristic gradually constructs a tour by repeatedly selecting the shortest edge and adding it to the tour as long as it doesn't create a cycle with less than N edges, or increases the degree of any node to more than 2. We must not add the same edge twice of course. Complexity of the greedy heuristic is $O\left(n^2 \log_2(n)\right)$. Steps of Greedy approach are:

1. Sort all edges.
2. Select the shortest edge and add it to our tour if it doesn't violate any of the above constraints.
3. Do we have N edges in our tour? If no, repeat step 2.

The Greedy algorithm normally keeps solution within 15- 20% of the Held-Karp lower bound (Johnson & McGeoch, 1995).

5.2.3 Insertion heuristic

Insertion heuristics are quite straight forward, and there are many variants to choose from. The basics of insertion heuristics is to start with a tour of a subset of all cities, and then inserting the rest by some heuristic. The initial subtour is often a triangle. One can also start with a single edge as subtour. The complexity with this type of heuristic approach is given as $O(n^2)$. Steps of an Insertion heuristic are:

Select the shortest edge, and make a subtour of it.

1. Select a city not in the subtour, having the shortest distance to any one of the cities in the subtour.
2. Find an edge in the subtour such that the cost of inserting the selected city between the edge's cities will be minimal.
3. Repeat step 2 until no more cities remain.

5.2.4 Christofide heuristic

Most heuristics can only guarantee a feasible soluiton or a fair near optimal solution. Christofides extended one of these heuristic approaches which is known as Christofides heuristic. Complexity of this approach is $O(n^3)$. The steps are gievn below:

1. Build a minimal spanning tree from the set of all cities.
2. Create a minimum-weight matching (MWM) on the set of nodes having an odd degree. Add the MST together with the MWM.
3. Create an Euler cycle from the combined graph, and traverse it taking shortcuts to avoid visited nodes.

Tests have shown that Christofides' algorithm tends to place itself around 10% above the Held-Karp lower bound. More information on tour construction heuristics can be found in (Johnson & McGeoch, 2002).

5.3 Tour improvement

After generating the tour using any tour construction heuristic, an improvment heuristic can be further applied to improve the quality of the tour generated. Popularly, 2-opt and 3-opt exchange heuristic is applied for improving the solution. The performance of 2-opt or 3-opt heuristic basically depends on the tour generated by the tour construction heuristic. Other ways of improving the solution is to apply meta-heuristic approaches such as tabu search or simulated annealing using 2-opt and 3-opt.

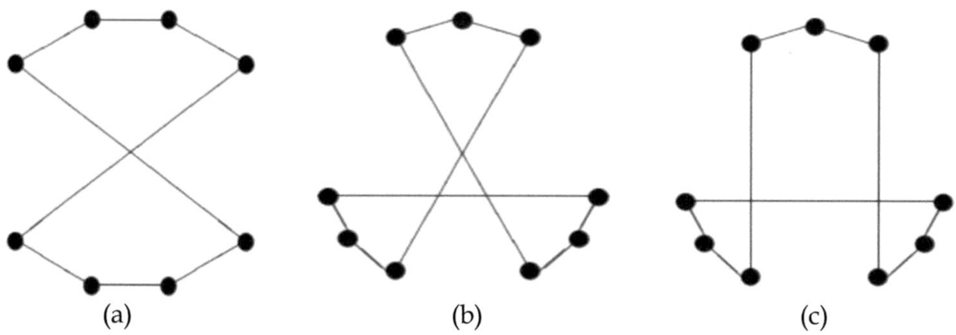

Fig. 1. A 2- opt move and 3-opt move

5.3.1 2-opt and 3-opt

The 2-opt algorithm removes randomly two edges from the already generated tour, and reconnects the new two paths created. This is refered as a 2-opt move. The reconnecting is done such a way to keep the tour valid (see figure 1 (a)). This is done only if the new tour is shorter than older. This is continued till no further improvement is possible. The resulting tour is now 2 optimal. The 3-opt algorithm works in a similar fashion, but instead of removing the two edges it removes three edges. This means there are two ways of reconnecting the three paths into a valid tour (see figure 1(b) and figure 1(c)). Search is completed when no more 3-opt moves can improve the tour quality. If a tour is 3 optimal it is also 2 optimal (Helsgaun). Running the 2-opt move often results in a tour with a length less than 5% above the Held-Karp bound. The improvements of a 3-opt move usually generates a tour about 3% above the Held-Karp bound (Johnson & McGeoch, 1995).

5.3.2 k-opt

In order to improve the already generated tour from tour construction heuristic, k-opt move can be applied (2-opt and 3-opt are special cases of k-opt exchange heuristic) but exchange heuristic having k>3 will take more computational time. Mainly one 4-opt move is used, called "the crossing bridges" (see Figure 2). This particular move cannot be sequentially constructed using 2-opt moves. For this to be possible two of these moves would have to be illegal (Helsgaun).

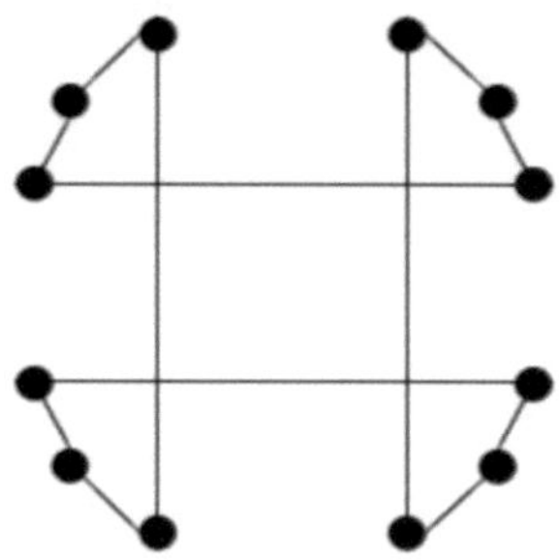

Fig. 2. Double bridge move

5.3.3 Lin-Kernighan

Lin & Kernighan constructed an algorithm making it possible to get within 2% of the Held-Karp lower bound. The Lin-Kernighan heuristic (LK) is a variable k-way exchange heuristic. It decides the value of suitable k at each iteration. This makes the an improvement heuristic quite complex, and few have been able to make improvements to it. The time complexity of LK is approximately $O(n^{2.2})$ (Helsgaun), making it slower than a simple 2-opt implementation.

5.3.4 Tabu search

It is a neighborhood-search algorithm which seacrh the better solution in the neighbourhood of the existing solution. In general, tabu search (TS) uses 2-opt exchange mechanism for searching better solution. A problem with simple neighborhood search approach i.e. only 2-opt or 3-opt exchange heuristic is that these can easily get stuck in a local optimum. This can be avoided easily in TS approach. To avoid this TS keeps a tabu list containing bad solution with bad exchange. There are several ways of implementing the tabu list. For more detail paper by (Johnson & McGeoch, 1995) can be referred. The biggest problem with the TS is its running time. Most implementations for the TSP generally takes $O(n^3)$ (Johnson & McGeoch, 1995), making it far slower than a 2-opt local search.

5.3.5 Simulated annealing

Simulated Annealing (SA) has been successfully applied and adapted to give an approximate solutions for the TSP. SA is basically a randomized local search algorithm similar to TS but do not allow path exchange that deteriorates the solution. (Johnson & McGeoch, 1995) presented a baseline implementation of SA for the TSP. Authors used 2-opt moves to find neighboring solutions. In SA, Better results can be obtained by increasing the running time of the SA algorithm, and it is found that the results are comparable to the LK algorithm. Due to the 2-opt neighborhood, this particular implementation takes $O(n^2)$ with a large constant of proportionality (Johnson & McGeoch, 1995).

5.3.6 Genetic algorithm

Genetic Algorithm (GA) works in a way similar to the nature. A basic GA starts with a randomly generated population of candidate solutions. Some (or all) candidates are then mated to produce offspring and some go through a mutating process. Each candidate has a fitness value telling us how good they are. By selecting the most fit candidates for mating and mutation the overall fitness of the population will increase. Applying GA to the TSP involves implementing a crossover routine, a measure of fitness, and also a mutation routine. A good measure of fitness is the actual length of the solution. Different approaches to the crossover and mutation routines are discussed in (Johnson & McGeoch, 1995).

5.4 Ant colony optimization

Researchers are often trying to mimic nature to solve complex problems, and one such example is the successful use of GA. Another interesting idea is to mimic the movements of ants. This idea has been quite successful when applied to the TSP, giving optimal solutions to small problems quickly (Dorigo & Gambardella, 1996). However, as small as an ant's brain might be, it is still far too complex to simulate completely. But we only need a small part of their behaviour for solving the problem. Ants leave a trail of pheromones when they explore new areas. This trail is meant to guide other ants to possible food sources. The key to the success of ants is strength in numbers, and the same goes for ant colony optimization. We start with a group of ants, typically 20 or so. They are placed in random cities, and are then asked to move to another city. They are not allowed to enter a city already visited by themselves, unless they are heading for the completion of our tour. The ant who picked the shortest tour will be leaving a trail of pheromones inversely proportional to the length of the tour. This pheromone trail will be taken in account when an ant is choosing a city to move to, making it more prone to walk the path with the strongest pheromone trail. This process is repeated until a tour being short enough is found. Consult (Dorigo & Gambardella, 1996) for more detailed information on ant colony optimization for the TSP.

5.5 The Held-Karp lower bound

This lower bound if the common way of testing the performance of any new TSP heuristic. Held-Karp (HK) bound is actually a solution to the linear programming relaxation of the integer formulation of TSP (Johnson et al. 1996). A HK lower bound averages about 0.8% below the optimal tour length (Johnson et al., 1996). For more details regarding the HK lower bound, paper by (Johnson et al., 1996) can be referred.

5.6 Heuristic solution approaches for mTSP

One of the first heuristics addressing TSP is due to (Russell, 1977). The algorithm is an extended version of the Lin & Kernighan (1973) heuristic. (Potvin et al., 1989) have given another heuristic based on an exchange procedure for the mTSP. (Fogel, 1990) proposed a parallel processing approach to solve the mTSP using evolutionary programming. Problems with 25 and 50 cities were solved and it is noted that the evolutionary approach obtained very good near-optimal solutions. (Wacholder et al., 1989) extended the Hopfield-Tank ANN model to the mTSP but their model found to be too complex to find even feasible soultions. Hsu et al. (1991) presented a neural network (NN) approach to solve the mTSP. The authors stated that their results are better than (Wacholder et al., 1989). (Goldstein, 1990) and (Vakhutinsky & Golden, 1994) presented a self-organizing NN approach for the mTSP. A self-organizing NN for the VRP based on an enhanced mTSP NN model is due to (Torki et al., 1997). Recently, (Modares et al., 1999 and Somhom et al., 1999) have developed a self-organizing NN approach for the mTSP with a minmax objective function, which minimizes the cost of the most expensive route. Utilizing GA for the solution of mTSP seems to be first due to (Zhang et al., 1999). A recent application by (Tang et al., 2000) used GA to solve the mTSP model developed for hot rolling scheduling. (Yu et al., 2002) also used GA to solve the mTSP in path planning. (Ryan et al., 1998) used TS in solving a mTSP with time windows. (Song et al., 2003) proposed an extended SA approach for the mTSP with fixed costs associated with each salesman. (Gomes & Von Zuben, 2002) presented a neuro-fuzzy system based on competitive learning to solve the mTSP along with the capacitated VRP. Sofge et al. (2002) implemented and compared a variety of evolutionary computation algorithms to solve the mTSP, including the use of a neighborhood attractor schema, the shrink-wrap algorithm for local neighborhood optimization, particle swarm optimization, Monte-Carlo optimization, genetic algorithms and evolutionary strategies. For more detailed description, papers mentioned above can be referred.

6. References

Ali, A.I. & Kennington, J. L. (1986). The asymmetric *m*-traveling salesmen problem: a duality based branch-and-bound algorithm. *Discrete Applied Mathematics*, Vol. No. 13, pp. 259–76.

Angel, R.D.; Caudle, W.L.; Noonan, R. & Whinston, A. (1972). Computer assisted school bus scheduling. *Management Science,* Vol. 18, pp.279–88.

Applegate, D.L., Bixby, R.E., Chv´atal, V. & Cook, W.J. (2003). Implementing the Dantzig-Fulkerson–Johnson algorithm for large scale traveling salesman problems. *Math Program Ser B* Vol. 97, pp. 91–153.

Applegate, D. L.; Bixby, R. E.; Chvátal, V. & Cook, W. J. (2006), *The Traveling Salesman Problem: A Computational Study,* Princeton University Press, ISBN 978-0-691-12993-8.

Applegate, D.L.; Bixby, R.E.; Chv´atal, V.; Cook, W.J.; Espinoza, D.G.; Goycoolea, M. & Helsgaun, K. (2009). Certification of an optimal TSP tour through 85900 cities. *Operations Reearch Letters.,* Vol. 37, No. 1, pp. 11–15.

Arora, S. (1998). Polynomial Time Approximation Schemes for Euclidian Traveling Salesman and Other Geometric Problems, *Journal of the ACM,* Vol. 45, No. 5, September 1998, pp. 753-782.

Balas, E. & Toth, P. (1985). Branch and bound methods. In: Lawler EL, Lenstra JK, Rinnooy Kan AHG & Shmoys DB (eds). *The Traveling Salesman Problem: A Guided Tour of Combinatorial Optimization,* Wiley: Chichester, pp. 361–401.

Basu, A.; Elnagar, A. & Al-Hajj, A. (2000). Efficient coordinated motion. *Mathematical and Computer Modelling,* Vol. 31, pp. 39–53.

Bektas, T. (2006). The multiple traveling salesman problem: an overview of formulations and solution procedures. *Omega,* Vol. 34, pp. 206-219.

Biggs N. L.; Lloyd E. Keith & Wilson Robin J. (1986). *Graph Theory 1736-1936,* Clarendon Press, Oxford, ISBN 978-0-19-853916-2.

Bland, R.E., & D.E Shallcross (1989). Large traveling salesman problem arising from experiments in X-ray crystallography: a preliminary report on computation. *Operations Research Letters,* Vol. 8(3), pp. 125-128.

Brummit, B. & Stentz, A. (1996). Dynamic mission planning for multiple mobile robots. *Proceedings of the IEEE international conference on robotics and automation,* April 1996.

Brummit, B. & Stentz, A. (1998). GRAMMPS: a generalized mission planner for multiple mobile robots. *Proceedings of the IEEE international conference on robotics and automation,* May 1998.

Burkard, R.; Dell'Amico, M. & Martello, S. (2009). *Assignment Problems.* SIAM: Philadelphia.

C. Song; K. Lee & W.D. Lee (2003). Extended simulated annealing for augmented TSP and multi-salesmen TSP. *Proceedings of the international joint conference on neural networks,* Vol. 3, pp. 2340–43.

Calvo, R.W. & Cordone, R. (2003) A heuristic approach to the overnight security service problem. *Computers and Operations Research,* Vol. 30, pp.1269–87.

Carpaneto, G. & Toth, P. (1980). Some new branching and bounding criteria for the asymmetric traveling salesman problem. *Management Science,* Vol. 26, pp. 736–743.

Carpaneto, G. & Toth, P. (1987). Primal-dual algorithms for the assignment problem. Discrete Applied Mathematics, Vol. 18, pp. 137–153.

Carpaneto, G.; Dell'Amico, M. & Toth, P. (1995). Exact solution of large-scale, asymmetric travelling salesman problems. *ACM Transactions on Mathematical Software,* Vol. 21, pp. 394–409.

Carter, A.E. & Ragsdale, C.T. (2002). Scheduling pre-printed newspaper advertising inserts using genetic algorithms. *Omega,* Vol. 30, pp. 415–21.

Christofides, N.; Mingozzi, A. & Toth, P. (1981). Exact algorithms for the vehicle routing problem, based on spanning tree and shortest path relaxations. *Mathematical Programming,* Vol.20, pp. 255–82.

Chv´atal, V. (1973). Edmonds polytopes and weakly Hamiltonian graphs. *Mathematical Programming,* Vol. 5, pp. 29–40.

Cornu´ejols, G.; Fonlupt, J. & Naddef, D. (1985). The travelling salesman problem on a graph and some related integer polyhedra. *Mathematical Programming,* Vol. 33, pp. 1–27.

Crowder, H. & Padberg, M.W. (1980). Solving large-scale symmetric traveling salesman problems to optimality. *Management Science,* Vol. 26, pp. 495–509.

D. Applegate; W. Cook & A. Rohe (2000). *Chained Lin-Kernighan for large traveling salesman problems,* July 27, 2000.

Dantzig, G.B.; Fulkerson, D.R. & Johnson, S.M. (1954). Solution of a large-scale traveling salesman problem. *Operations Research,* Vol. 2, pp.393–410.

Dell'Amico, M. & Toth, P. (2000). Algorithms and codes for dense assignment problems: The state of the art. *Discrete Applied Mathematics,* Vol. 100, No. 1-2, pp. 17–48.

Dorigo, M. & Gambardella, L.M. (1996). *"Ant Colonies for the Traveling Salesman Problem",* University Libre de Bruxelles, Belgium.

Dreissig, W. & W. Uebaeh (1990). *Personal communication.*

Eastman, W.L. (1958). *Linear programming with pattern constraints.* PhD thesis, Department of Economics, Harvard University, Cambridge, MA.

Edmonds, J. (1965). Maximum matching and a polyhedron with 0, 1-vertices. *J Res Natl Bur Stan, Vol.* 69B, p. 125–130.

Fischetti, M. & Toth, P. (1992). An additive bounding procedure for the asymmetric traveling salesman problem. *Mathematical Programming: Series A and B, Vol.* 53(2) , pp. 173–197.

Fischetti, M.; Lodi, A. & Toth, P. (2002). Exact methods for the asymmetric traveling salesman problem. In: Gutin G & Punnen AP (eds). *The Traveling Salesman Problem and Its Variations.* Kluwer: Boston. Pp 169–205.

Fogel, D.B. (1990). A parallel processing approach to a multiple travelling salesman problem using evolutionary programming. In: *Proceedings of the fourth annual symposium on parallel processing. Fullerton,* CA, pp. 318–26.

Gavish, B. (1976). A note on the formulation of the *m*salesman traveling salesman problem. *Management Science,* Vol. 22, No. 6, pp.704–5.

Gavish, B. & Srikanth, K. (1986). An optimal solution method for large-scale multiple traveling salesman problems. *Operations Research*, Vol. 34, No. 5, pp. 698–717.

Gilbert, K.C. & Hofstra, R.B. (1992). A new multiperiod multiple traveling salesman problem with heuristic and application to a scheduling problem. *Decision Sciences*, Vol. 23, pp.250–9.

Goldstein, M. (1990). Self-organizing feature maps for the multiple traveling salesmen problem. In: *Proceedings of the IEEE international conference on neural network.* San Diego, CA, pp. 258–61.

Gomes, L.D.T. & Von Zuben, F.J. (2002). Multiple criteria optimization based on unsupervised learning and fuzzy inference applied to the vehicle routing problem. *Journal of Intelligent and Fuzzy Systems,* Vol. 13, pp. 143–54.

Gomory, R.E. (1963). An algorithm for integer solutions to linear programs. In: Graves RL & Wolfe P (eds). *Recent Advances in Mathematical Programming*. McGraw-Hill: New York, pp. 269–302.

Gorenstein, S. (1970). Printing press scheduling for multi-edition periodicals. *Management Science,* Vol. 16, No. 6, pp.B373–83.

Grötschel, M. & Padberg, M.W. (1985). Polyhedral theory. In: Lawler E.L.; Lenstra J.K.; Rinnooy Kan AHG & Shmoys D.B. (eds). *The Traveling Salesman Problem: A Guided Tour of Combinatorial Optimization*. Wiley: Chichester, pp 251–305.

Grötschel, M. & Pulleyblank, W.R. (1986). Clique tree inequalities and the symmetric Travelling Salesman Problem. *Mathematics of Operations Research,* Vol. 11, No. 4, (November, 1986), pp. 537–569.

Grötschel, M. & O. Holland (1991). Solution of Large-scale Symmetric Traveling Salesman Problems. *Mathematical Programming,* Vol. 51, pp.141-202.

Grötschel, M.; M. Jünger & G. Reinelt (1991). Optimal Control of Plotting and Drilling Machines: A Case Study. *Mathematical Methods of Operations Research,* Vol. 35, No. 1, (January, 1991), pp.61-84.

Gromicho, J.; Paixão, J. & Branco, I. (1992). Exact solution of multiple traveling salesman problems. In: Mustafa Akgül, et al., editors. *Combinatorial optimization. NATO ASI Series*, Vol. F82. Berlin: Springer; 1992. p. 291–92.

Gromicho, J. (2003). *Private communication.*

Hadjiconstantinou, E. & Roberts, D. (2002). Routing under uncertainty: an application in the scheduling of field service engineers. In: Paolo Toth, Daniele Vigo, editors. *The vehicle routing problem. SIAM Monographs on Discrete Mathematics and Applications*, Philadelphia, pp. 331–52.

Hsu, C.; Tsai, M. & Chen, W. (1991). A study of feature-mapped approach to the multiple travelling salesmen problem. *IEEE International Symposium on Circuits and Systems,* Vol. 3, pp. 1589–92.

Johnson D.S. & McGeoch L.A. (1995). *The Traveling Salesman Problem: A Case Study in Local Optimization*, November 20, 1995.

Johnson, D.S; McGeoch, L.A. & Rothberg E.E (1996). Asymptotic Experimental Analysis for the Held- Karp Traveling Salesman Boun. *Proceedings of the Annual ACM-SIAM Symposium on Discrete Algorithms*, pp. 341-350.

Johnson, D.S. & McGeoch, L.A.(2002). Experimental Analysis of Heuristics for the STSP, *The Traveling Salesman Problem and its Variations*, Gutin & Punnen (eds), Kluwer Academic Publishers, pp. 369-443.

K. Helsgaun. *An Effective Implementation of the Lin-Kernighan Traveling Salesman Heuristic*, Department of Computer Science, Roskilde University.

Kim, K.H. & Park, Y. (2004). A crane scheduling method for port container terminals. *European Journal of Operational Research*, Vol. 156, pp. 752–68.

Kulkarni, R.V. & Bhave, P.R. (1985). Integer programming formulations of vehicle routing problems. *European Journal of Operational Research*, Vol. 20, pp. 58–67.

Land, A.H. (1979). *The solution of some 100-city traveling salesman problems*. Technical report, London School of Economics, London.

Land, A.H. & Doig, A.G. (1960). An automatic method of solving discrete programming problems. *Econometrica, Vol.* 28, pp. 497–520.

Laporte, G. & Nobert, Y. (1980). A cutting planes algorithm for the *m*-salesmen problem. *Journal of the Operational Research Society*, Vol. 31, pp.1017–23.

Laporte, G.; Nobert, Y. & Desrochers, M. (1985). Optimal routing under capacity and distance restrictions. *Operations Research*, Vol. 33, No. 5, pp.1050–73.

Laporte, G. (1992). The vehicle routing problem: an overview of exact and approximate algorithms. *European Journal of Operational Research*, Vol. 59, No. 3, pp. 345–58.

Laporte, G. (1992). The traveling salesman problem: An overview of exact and approximate algorithms. *European Journal of Operational Research*, Vol. 59, No. 2, pp. 231-247.

Lenstra, J.K. & A.H.G. Rinnooy Kan (1974). *Some Simple Applications of the Travelling Salesman Problem*. BW 38/74, Stichting Mathematisch Centrum, Amsterdam.

Lenstra, J.K,. & Rinnooy Kan, A.H.G. (1975). Some simple applications of the traveling salesman problem. *Operational Research Quarterly*, Vol. 26, pp. 717–33.

Little, J.D.C.; Murty, K.G.; Sweeney, D.W. & Karel, C. (1963). An algorithm for the traveling salesman problem. *Operations Research*, Vol. 11, pp. 972–989.

Lin, S. & Kernighan, B. (1973). An effective heuristic algorithm for the traveling salesman problem. *Operations Research*, Vol. 21, pp. 498–516.

Macharis, C. & Bontekoning, Y.M.(2004) Opportunities for OR in intermodal freight transport research: a review. *European Journal of Operational Research*, Vol. 153, pp.400–16.

Martin, G.T. (1966). *Solving the traveling salesman problem by integer programming*. Working Paper, CEIR, New York.

Miliotis, P. (1976). Integer programmi.ng approaches to the travelling salesman problem. *Mathematical Programming*, Vol. 10, pp. 376–378.

Miliotis, P. (1978). Using cutting planes to solve the symmetric travelling salesman problem. *Mathematical Programming,* Vol. 15, pp. 177–188.

Miller, C.E.; Tucker, A.W. & Zemlin, R.A.(1960). Integer programming formulation of traveling salesman problems. *Journal of Association for Computing Machinery,* Vol. 7, pp. 326–9.

Mitrović-Minić, S.; Krishnamurti, R. & Laporte, G. (2004). Double-horizon based heuristics for the dynamic pickup and delivery problem with time windows. *Transportation Research,* Vol. 28, No. 8, pp. 669–85.

Modares, A.; Somhom, S. & Enkawa, T.(1999). A self-organizing neural network approach for multiple traveling salesman and vehicle routing problems. *International Transactions in Operational Research,* Vol. 6, pp. 591–606.

Mole, R.H.; Johnson, D.G. & Wells, K. (1983). Combinatorial analysis for route first-cluster second vehicle routing. *Omega,* Vol. 11, No. 5, pp. 507–12.

Naddef, D. (2002). Polyhedral theory and branch-and-cut algorithms for the symmetric TSP. In: Gutin G & Punnen AP (eds). *The Traveling Salesman Problem and Its Variations.* Kluwer: Boston, pp. 29–116.

Okonjo-Adigwe, C. (1988). An effective method of balancing the workload amongst salesmen. *Omega,* Vol. 16, No. 2, pp. 159–63.

Orman, A.J. & Williams, H.P. (2006). A survey of different integer programming formulations of the travelling salesman problem. In: Kontoghiorghes E. & Gatu C. (eds). *Optimisation, Econometric and Financial Analysis Advances in Computational Management Science.* Springer: Berlin, Heidelberg, pp. 91–104.

O¨ncan, T.; Altınel, I.K. & Laporte, G. (2009). A comparative analysis of several asymmetric traveling salesman problem formulations. *Computers & Operations Research, Vol.* 36, pp. 637–654.

Padberg, M.W. & Grötschel, M. (1985). Polyhedral computations. In: Lawler EL, Lenstra JK, Rinnooy Kan AHG & Shmoys DB (eds). *The Traveling Salesman Problem: A Guided Tour of Combinatorial Optimization.* Wiley: Chichester, pp. 307–360.

Padberg, M.W. & Hong, S. (1980). On the symmetric travelling salesman problem: A computational study. *Mathematical Programming Study,* Vol. 12, pp. 78–107.

Padberg, M.W. & Rinaldi, G. (1987). Optimization of a 532-city symmetric traveling salesman problem by branch and cut. *Operations Research Letters,* Vol. 6, No. 1, pp. 1-7.

Padberg, M.W. & Rinaldi, G. (1991). A branch-and-cut algorithm for the resolution of large-scale symmetric traveling salesman problems. *SIAM Review,* Vol. 33, pp. 60–100.

Plante, R.D.; T.J. Lowe & R. Chandrasekaran (1987). The Product Matrix Traveling Salesman Problem: An Application and Solution Heuristics. *Operations Research,* Vol. 35, pp. 772-783.

Potvin, J.; Lapalme, G. & Rousseau, J. (1989). A generalized k-opt exchange procedure for the MTSP. *Information Systems* 1989;27(4): 474–81.

Ralphs, T.K. (2003). Parallel branch and cut for capacitated vehicle routing. *Parallel Computing,* Vol. 29, pp. 607–29.

Ratliff, H.D. & A.S. Rosenthal (1983). Order-Picking in a Rectangular Warehouse: A Solvable Case for the Travelling Salesman Problem. *Operations Research,* Vol. 31, pp. 507-521.

Ruland, K.S. & Rodin, E.Y.(1997). The pickup and delivery problem. *Computers and Mathematics with Applications,* Vol. 33, No. 12, pp. 1–13.

Russell, R.A. (1997). An effective heuristic for the *m*-tour traveling salesman problem with some side conditions. *Operations Research,* Vol. 25, No. 3, pp. 517–24.

Ryan, J.L.; Bailey, T.G.; Moore, J.T & Carlton, W.B. (1998). Reactive Tabu search in unmanned aerial reconnaissance simulations. *Proceedings of the 1998 winter simulation conference,* Vol. 1, pp . 873–9.

Saleh, H.A. & Chelouah, R. (2004). The design of the global navigation satellite system surveying networks using genetic algorithms. *Engineering Applications of Artificial Intelligence,* Vol. 17, pp. 111–22.

Schrijver, A. (1960). On the history of combinatorioal optimization.

Sofge, D.; Schultz, A. & De Jong, K. (2002). Evolutionary computational approaches to solving the multiple traveling salesman problem using a neighborhood attractor schema. *Lecture notes in computer science,* Vol. 2279, pp. 51–60.

Somhom, S.; Modares, A. & Enkawa, T. (1999). Competition-based neural network for the multiple traveling salesmen problem with minmax objective. *Computers and Operations Research,* Vol. 26, No. 4, pp. 395–407.

Svestka, J.A. & Huckfeldt, V.E. (1973). Computational experience with an *m*-salesman traveling salesman algorithm. *Management Science,* Vol. 19, No. 7, pp. 790–9.

Tang, L.; Liu, J.; Rong, A. & Yang, Z. (2000).A multiple traveling salesman problem model for hot rolling scheduling in Shangai Baoshan Iron & Steel Complex. *European Journal of Operational Research,* Vol. 124, pp. 267–82.

Torki, A.; Somhon, S. & Enkawa, T. (1997). A competitive neural network algorithm for solving vehicle routing problem. *Computers and Industrial Engineering,* Vol. 33, No. 3–4, pp. 473–6.

Toth, P. & Vigo, D. (2002). Branch-and-bound algorithms for the capacitated VRP. In: Paolo Toth, Daniele Vigo, editors. The vehicle routing problem. *SIAM Monographs on Discrete Mathematics and Applications,* Philadelphia, pp.29–51.

van Dal, R. (1992). *Special Cases of the Traveling Salesman Problem,* Wolters-Noordhoff, Groningen.

Vakhutinsky, I.A. & Golden, L.B. (1994). Solving vehicle routing problems using elastic net. *Proceedings of the IEEE international conference on neural network,* pp. 4535–40.

Wacholder, E.; Han, J. & Mann, R.C. (1989). A neural network algorithm for the multiple traveling salesmen problem. *Biology in Cybernetics,* Vol. 61, pp. 11–9.

Wang, X. & Regan, A.C. (2002). Local truckload pickup and delivery with hard time window constraints. *Transportation Research* Part B, Vol. 36, pp. 97–112.

Yu, Z.; Jinhai, L.; Guochang, G.; Rubo, Z. & Haiyan, Y. (2002). An implementation of evolutionary computation for path planning of cooperative mobile robots.

Proceedings of the fourth world congress on intelligent control and automation, Vol. 3, pp. 1798–802.

Zhang, T.; Gruver, W.A. & Smith, M.H. (1999). Team scheduling by genetic search. *Proceedings of the second international conference on intelligent processing and manufacturing of materials*, Vol. 2,. pp. 839–44.

2

The Advantage of Intelligent Algorithms for TSP

Yuan-Bin MO
College of Mathematics and Computer Science, Guangxi University for Nationalities, China

1. Introduction

Traveling salesman problem (TSP) means that a travelling salesman needs to promote products in n cities (including the city where he lives). After visiting each city (each city can be visited once), he returns to the departure city. Let's suppose that there is one road to connect each two cities. What is the best route to follow in order to minimize the distance of the journey?

TSP has been proven to be a NP-hard problem, i.e. failure of finding a polynomial time algorithm to get a optimal solution. TSP is easy to interpret, yet hard to solve. This problem has aroused many scholars' interests since it was put forward in 1932. However, until now, no effective solution has been found.

Though TSP only represents a problem of the shortest ring road, in actual life, many physical problems are found to be the TSP. Example 1, postal route. Postal route problem is a TSP. Suppose that a mail car needs to collect mails in n places. Under such circumstances, you can show the route through a drawing containing n+1 crunodes. One crunode means a post office which this mail car departures from and returns to. The remaining n crunodes mean the crunodes at which the mails need to be collected. The route that the mail car passes through is a travelling route. We hope to find a travelling route with the shortest length. Example 2, mechanical arm. When a mechanical arm is used to fasten the nuts for the ready-to-assembling parts on the assembly line, this mechanical arm will move from the initial position (position where the first nut needs to be fastened) to each nut in proper order and then return to the initial position. The route which the mechanical arm follows is a travelling route in the drawing which contains crunodes as nuts; the most economical travelling route will enable the mechanical arm to finish its work within the shortest time. Example 3, integrated circuit. In the course of manufacturing the integrated circuit, we often need to insert thousands of electrical elements. It will consume certain energy when moving from one electrical element to the other during manufacturing. How can we do to arrange the manufacturing order to minimum the energy consumption? This is obviously a solution for TSP. Except for the above examples, problems like route distribution of transportation network, choice of tourist route, laying of pipelines needed for city planning and engineering construction are interlinked with the problems of finding the shortest route. So, it is of significance to make a study on the problem of the shortest route. This renders us a use value.

As finding a solution for TSP plays an important role in the real life, since the TSP appeared, it has attracted many scholars to make a study on it.

2. Mathematical description for the TSP and its general solving method

2.1 Mathematical description for the TSP

According to the definition of the TSP, its mathematical description is as follows:

$$\min \sum d_{ij} x_{ij} \tag{2.1.1}$$

$$\text{s.t.} \quad \sum_{j=1}^{n} x_{ij} = 1 \qquad i = 1,2,\cdots n \tag{2.1.2}$$

$$\sum_{i=1}^{n} x_{ij} = 1 \qquad j = 1,2,\cdots n \tag{2.1.3}$$

$$\sum_{i,j \in S} x_{ij} \le |S| - 1 \quad 2 \le |S| \le n-2, S \subset \{1,2,\cdots n\} \tag{2.1.4}$$

$$x_{ij} \in \{0,1\} \quad i,j = 1,2,\cdots n \quad i \ne j \tag{2.1.5}$$

Where d_{ij} means the distance between the city i and city j; decision variable $x_{ij} = 1$ means the route the salesman passes through (including the route from city i and city j); $x_{ij} = 0$ means the route which isn't chosen by the salesman. Objective function (2.1.1) means the minimum total distance; (2.1.2) means that a salesman only can departure from the city i for one time; (2.1.3) means that a salesman only can enter the city j for one time; (2.1.2) and (2.1.3) only give an assurance that the salesman visits each city once, but it doesn't rule out the possibility of any loop; (2.1.4) requires that no loop in any city subset should be formed by the salesman ; $|S|$ means the number of elements included in the set S .

2.2 Traditional solving method for TSP

At present, the solving methods for TSP are mainly divided into two parts: traditional method and evolution method. In terms of traditional method, there are precise algorithm and approximate algorithm.

2.2.1 Precise algorithm for solving the TSP

Linear programming

This is a TSP solving method that is put forward at the earliest stage. It mainly applies to the cutting plane method in the integer programming, i.e. solving the LP formed by two constraints in the model and then seeking the cutting plane by adding inequality constraint to gradually converge at an optimal solution.

When people apply this method to find a cutting plane, they often depend on experience. So this method is seldom deemed as a general method.

Dynamic programming

S is the subset of the set $\{2,3,\cdots n\}$. $k \in S$ and $C(S,k)$ means the optimal travelling route (setting out from 1, passing through the points in S and ending to k). When $|S| = 1$, $C\{\{k\},k\} = d_{1k}$ and $(k = 2,3,\cdots n)$. When $|S| > 1$, according to the optimality principle, the dynamic programming equation of TSP can be written as $C(S,k) = \min_{j \in S-\{k\}} [C(S-\{j,k\},j) + d_{jk}]$ and the solution can be obtained by the iterative method based on dynamic programming. As the time resource (i.e. time complexity) needed for dynamic programming is $O(n^2 \cdot 2^n)$, and its needed space resource (i.e. space complexity) is $O(n \cdot 2^n)$, when n is added to a certain point, these complexities will increase sharply. As a result, except for the minor problem, this is seldom used.

Branch-bound algorithm

Branch-bound algorithm is a search algorithm widely used by people. It controls the searching process through effective restrictive boundary so that it can search for the optimal solution branch from the space state tree to find an optimal solution as soon as possible. The key point of this algorithm is the choice of the restrictive boundary. Different restrictive boundaries may form different branch-bound algorithms.

Branch-bound algorithm is not good for solving the large-scale problem.

2.2.2 Approximate algorithm for solving the TSP

As the application of precise algorithm to solve problem is very limited, we often use approximate algorithm or heuristic algorithm. The result of the algorithm can be assessed by $C / C^* \le \varepsilon$. C is the total travelling distance generated from approximate algorithm; C^* is the optimal travelling distance; ε is the upper limit for the ratio of the total travelling distance of approximate solution to optimal solution under the worst condition. The value of ε >1.0. The more it closes to 1.0, the better the algorithm is. These algorithms include:

Interpolation algorithm

Interpolation algorithm can be divided into several parts according to different interpolation criteria. Generally it includes following steps:

Step 1. Choose the insertion edge (i and j) and insertion point k through a certain way. Insert k into i and j to form $\{\cdots,i,k,j,\cdots\}$;

Step 2. Follow the process in an orderly manner to form a loop solution.

Interpolation algorithm mainly includes:

1. Latest interpolation effect $\varepsilon = 2$. Time complexity: $O(n^2)$.
2. Minimum interpolation effect $\varepsilon = 2$. Time complexity: $O(n^2 \lg n)$.
3. Arbitrary interpolation effect $\varepsilon = 21\mathrm{g}\, n + 0.16$. Time complexity: $O(n^2)$.
4. Farthest interpolation effect $\varepsilon = 2\lg n + 0.16$. Time complexity: $O(n^2)$.
5. Convex interpolation effect ε (unknown). Time complexity: $O(n^2 \lg n)$.

Nearest-neighbour algorithm

Step 1. Choose one departure point randomly;

Step 2. Choose the nearest point in an orderly manner to add to the current solution until the loop solution is formed.

Effect: $\varepsilon = (\lg n + 1)/2$. Time complexity: $O(n^2)$

Clark & Wright algorithm

Step 1. Choose one departure point P randomly to calculate $s_{ij} = d_{pi} + d_{pj} + d_{ij}$;

Step 2. Array s_{ij} in ascending order;

Step 3. Connect each (i,j) in an orderly manner upon arrangement to form a loop solution.

Effect: $\varepsilon = 2\lg n/7 + 2/21$. Time complexity: $O(n^2)$
Double spanning tree algorithm
Step 1. First determine the minimum spanning tree.
Step 2. Determine the Euler loop by adding a repetitive edge to each edge of the tree;
Step 3. Eliminate the repetitive point in the sequence of Euler loop point to form a loop solution.
Effect: $\varepsilon = 2$. Time complexity: $O(n^2)$
Christofides algorithm
Step 1. First determine the minimum spanning tree;
Step 2. Solve the minimum weight matching problem to all the singular vertexes of the tree;
Step 3. Add the matching edge to the spanning tree to determine its Euler loop;
Step 4. Eliminate the repetitive point in the sequence of Euler loop point to form a loop solution.
Effect: $\varepsilon = 2/3$. Time complexity: $O(n^3)$
$r-opt$ algorithm
This algorithm is a locally improved search algorithm and is put forward by Lin and other people (1965). Its thought is to improve the current solution by exchanging r edges each time according to the given initial loop. As for different r, we find from massive calculation that $3-opt$ is better than $2-opt$, and $4-opt$ and $5-opt$ are not better than $3-opt$. The higher the r is, the more time the calculation will take. So we often use $3-opt$.
Effect: $\varepsilon = 2$ $(n \geq 8, r \leq n/4)$. Time complexity: $O(n^r)$
Hybrid algorithm
Use a certain approximate algorithm to find an initial solution and then improve the solution by using one or several algorithms of $r-opt$.Usually, Hybrid algorithm will help you to get better solution, but it takes a long time.
Probabilistic algorithm
Based on the given $\varepsilon > 0$, this algorithm is often used to solve the TSP within the range of $1+\varepsilon$.Suppose that G is in the unit square and function $t(n)$ is mapped to the positive ration number and satisfies the following two conditions: (1) $t \to \log_2 \log_2 n$; (2) to all n, n/t is the perfect square, so the steps are as follows:
Step 1. Form the network by using $[t(n)/n]^{1/2}$ as size. Divide the unit square into $n/t(n)$ and G into several $n/t(n)$ subgraphs;
Step 2. Use dynamic programming to find the optimal loop for each subgraph;
Step 3. Contract $n/t(n)$ subgraph into one point. The distance definition is the shortest distance of the optimal sub-loop of the original subgraph. In addition, determine the minimum generation number T of the new graph;
Step 4. See T $\cup$ {the optimal sub-loop of each optimal sub-loop of } as the close loop with repetitive point and edge. According to the condition of the triangle inequality, reduce the repetitive points and edges to find a TSP loop.
Effect: $\varepsilon = 1+$ (give the positive number randomly). Time complexity: $O(n \lg n)$.
As these traditional algorithms are local search algorithms, they only help to find a local optimal solution when used for solving the TSP. It is hard to reach a global optimal solution and solve large-scale problem. So, people started to look for an evolution algorithm to solve the TSP.

3. Evolution algorithm for solving the TSP

As stated above, the traditional algorithms used to solve the TSP have some limitation. With the development of evolution algorithm, many numerical optimization algorithms appear. They are ACA, GA, SA, TS, PSO and IA, etc. These algorithms are, to some extent, random search algorithms. ACA and PSO are typical parallel algorithms. Though they cannot guarantee to help you to obtain an optimal solution within the limited time, they can give you a satisfactory solution within the affordable time range. To figure out the effect of the solution for TSP obtained by using optimization algorithm, we should consider the algorithm's search ability. Algorithm with strong optimization will produce better effect. Algorithm which is easy to trap in local extremum often helps you to obtain the local optimal solution for TSP.

3.1 Ant colony algorithm for solving the TSP

Ant colony algorithm (ACA) is a relatively new analogy evolution algorithm, which was put forward by scholars such as Italian scholar Dorigo. They called it ant colony system and used this ant colony to solve the TSP, achieving fairly good experimental result. As for ACA, n represents the number of cities for the TSP; m represents the number of ant in the ant colony; d_{ij} $(i,j=1,2,\cdots,n)$ represents the distance between city i and city j; $\tau_{ij}(t)$ represents the concentration of pheromone on the line of city i and city j at the time of t.At the initial time, the concentration of pheromone on each route is similar to one another. When $\tau_{ij}(0)=C$, C is a constant. During the moving process, ant $(k=1,2,\cdots,m)$ will determine which direction it will change according to the concentration of pheromone on each route. $P_{ij}^{k}(t)$ represents the probability for ant to move from city i to city j at the time of t. Its formula is

$$P_{ij}^{k}(t)=\begin{cases}\dfrac{\tau_{ij}^{\alpha}(t)\eta_{ij}^{\beta}(t)}{\sum\limits_{s\in \text{allowed}_k}\tau_{is}^{\alpha}(t)\eta_{is}^{\beta}(t)} & j\notin \text{tabu}_k\\ 0 & other\end{cases} \tag{3.1.1}$$

Wherein: tabu_k $(k=1,2,\cdots,m)$ means that ant k has passed through the set of the city. From the beginning, tabu_k has only one element, i.e. the departure city of ant k. With the process of evolution, the elements for tabu_k increase continuously; $\text{allowed}_k=\{1,2,\cdots,n\}-\text{tabu}_k$ means the next city that ant k is allowed to choose. η_{ij} represents the visibility, and is taken from the reciprocal of the length of the route (i,j); α,β regulates the relatively important degree of pheromone concentration τ and visibility η.

As time goes by, the pheromone on each route gradually disappears. Parameter $1-\rho$ is used to represent the volatility of pheromone. After ω time, the ants complete one circle. Pheromone concentration on each route can be adjusted according to the following formula:

$$\tau_{ij}(t+\omega)=\rho\cdot\tau_{ij}(t)+\Delta\tau_{ij} \qquad \rho\in(0,1) \tag{3.1.2}$$

$$\Delta\tau_{ij}=\sum_{k=1}^{m}\Delta\tau_{ij}^{k} \tag{3.1.3}$$

Wherein: $\Delta\tau_{ij}^{k}$ means the pheromone concentration left on the route (i,j) by the k ants during the process of this circle; $\Delta\tau_{ij}$ means the total pheromone concentration released on the route (i,j) by all the ants during the process of this circle.

ACA not only uses the positive feedback principle which may, to some extent, quicken the evolution process, but also is a parallel algorithm in nature. The ongoing process of information exchange and communication between individuals helps to find a better solution. It is easy to converge at a local extremum when there is only one individual. However, through cooperation, multiple individuals will help us to get a certain subset of the solution space, which provide a better environment for us to carry out a further exploration on solution space. The movement of multiple individuals in the ant colony is random. Actually, the measures taken to avoid the possibility of appearance of local extremum slow down the velocity of convergence. When the scale of ant colony expands, it will take a longer time to look for a better route.

In the light of the above problems, many scholars at home and abroad make an improvement of the basic ACA. Though some achievements have been made, they are not enough as a whole. Some principles are still needed to found to make a proof and test in practice.

3.2 Solve the TSP through particle swarm optimization

Ant colony algorithm is a discrete random number algorithm, which is suitable for solving the discrete optimization problem. TSP is a typical discrete optimization problem, so, since the appearance of ant colony algorithm, many scholars have used this algorithm to solve the TSP. However, as the travelling salesman problem is a NP, and the pheromone needs to be updated when ant colony algorithm is iterated each time, so, when solving the large-scale TSP, it will meet some problems such as slow searching speed. Though scholars at home and abroad have made some efforts to accelerate the searching speed, but what they've done is not enough as a whole. Some principles are still needed to found to make a proof and test in practice. Particle swarm optimization is a continuous algorithm. Its iteration formula is simple and easy to achieve. A slight improvement of this algorithm will help you to solve the discrete optimization problem of the travelling salesman. As its iteration formula is very simple, a use of this algorithm may help you to solve the slow searching speed problem found from the ant colony algorithm.

At present, different improvement algorithms for PSO have been provided to solve the TSP. In particular, great result has been made by Maurice who used discrete PSO algorithm to solve the TSP.A hybrid PSO algorithm which is used to solve the TSP is provided on the basis of GA, AC and SA. Application of PSO algorithm to solve the travelling salesman problem is a fresh attempt. However, as the traditional PSO will easily trap in the local optimal solution, we provide two improve strategies for the standard PSO and use them to solve the TSP.

4. Solve the TSP through improved PSO algorithm

4.1 Solve the TSP through DPSO algorithm

4.1.1 DPSO principle

Dynamic programming is a typical deterministic algorithm for solving the optimization problem. It is provided on the basis of the optimality principle and non-aftereffect and used for the algorithm of multistage decision process. Optimality principle: any truncation of the optimal decision still remains the optimal state; non-aftereffect: after truncation in any stage, the decision made in the later stage is only connected to the initial state of this stage and has no connection to others. Dynamic programming, through optimality principle and non-aftereffect, analyze the optimization problem in stages to simplify the problem, which greatly reduce the calculation steps.

PSO algorithm is an interactive parallel searching algorithm as well as a good attempt to look for global extremum. However, when solving the optimization problem of high dimensional function, as the mutual restraint exists between each dimensional variable, disadvantage has been found when the PSO algorithm is used to solve this problem. According to the numerical value test result, this algorithm is proven to be very effective when the dimension is low. The solving process of dynamic programming is to simplify the complex problem to obtain the solution. A combination of this with the property of PSO algorithm will surely improve the optimal performance of the PSO algorithm.

As for the solution of the problem $\min f(\mathbf{x}) = f(x_1, x_2, \cdots, x_n)$, *s.t.* $a_i \le x_i \le b_i$, $i = 1, 2, \cdots n$. (4.1.1.1), a strategy should be provided to fix some variables and change the remaining variables; i.e. partition the variable and approximate the optimal solution of the majorized function through partitioning to convert the high dimensional optimization problem into low dimensional optimization problem to get the condition optimal solution. Then fix the other part to get the other group of condition optimal solution. Use this information to carry out a comprehensive optimization process. Be aware that this strategy is different from the principle of dynamic programming, because aftereffect exists when partition optimization is applied. So, a strategy method concerning reasonable approximation of global extremum should be provided for the partition optimization of aftereffect.

It is hard to decide the order of fixed variable in the process of calculation. Different strategies can be used during the process of practical operation; after the algorithm traps in the local extremum, it may pick some components to be fixed randomly from the local optimal solution, or choose some components alternately; at the same time, transform the original problem into two problems after some components are picked randomly. If the dimension is too high, this problem can also be transformed into multiple problems to find a solution. See the following problem

$$\min f(x_1, x_2, x_3, x_4, x_5, x_6), \tag{4.1.1.2}$$

If PSO algorithm gives a local optimal solution $\mathbf{x}^{1*} = (x_1^{1*}, x_2^{1*}, \cdots x_6^{1*})$, the following two strategies can transform the high dimension optimization into low dimension optimization: (1) pick several components randomly, e.g. pick 3 components $x_1^{1*}, x_2^{1*}, x_4^{1*}$, then the result is

$$\min f(x_1^{1*}, x_2^{1*}, x_3, x_4^{1*}, x_5, x_6) \tag{4.1.1.3}$$

A local optimal solution $(x_1^{1*}, x_2^{1*}, x_3^{2*}, x_4^{1*}, x_5^{2*}, x_6^{2*})$ is given by using the PSO algorithm again. Then pick some components randomly or alternately (for example, if you pick components 1, 2 and 4 last time, you can pick components 3, 5 and 6 this time); in this way, a new optimal problem is found. Continue the run until you find a satisfactory result. (2) Pick some components randomly and divide the original problem into several problems, including: $\min f(x_1^{1*}, x_2^{1*}, x_3, x_4^{1*}, x_5, x_6)$ and $\min f(x_1, x_2, x_3^{1*}, x_4, x_5^{1*}, x_6^{1*})$. It may write down all the possible forms (i.e. $C_6^3 = 20$) of the three variables to divide the original problem into 20 optimization problems. If you think the dimension is too high, pick p (p is relatively high in number) components randomly and transform the original problem into several optimization problems. You can also list all the C_n^p optimization problems and use PSO algorithm to solve several optimization problems you get. Then compare the results of these optimization problems and pick the best one to use as the local optimal solution next step, and further analyze this solution until you find the satisfactory result.

4.1.2 Computational steps of the DPSO

As for the optimization problem of the formula (4.1.1.1), the key algorithm steps are as follows:

Step 1. Randomly generate the initial population m. Under normal circumstances, $m \geq 10$.

Step 2. After figure up certain algebras through PSO or after use PSO and find that the target values within several successive algebras remain the same, set the optimal solution as $\mathbf{x}^* = (x_1^0, x_2^0, \cdots x_n^0)$.

Step 3. Pick $[\frac{n}{2}]$ component randomly from the optimal solution $\mathbf{x}^*$ and set it as $x_{i_1}^0, x_{i_2}^0, \cdots x_{i_{[\frac{n}{2}]}}^0$.

Step 4. Use PSO to solve the following two optimization problems

$$\min f(\mathbf{x}) = f(x_1, x_2, \cdots, x_{i_1}^0, \cdots x_{i_2}^0, \cdots x_{i_{[\frac{n}{2}]}}^0, \cdots, x_n), \tag{4.1.2.1}$$

and

$$\min f(\mathbf{x}) = f(x_1^0, x_2^0, \cdots, x_{i_1}, \cdots x_{i_2}, \cdots x_{i_{[\frac{n}{2}]}}, \cdots, x_n^0). \tag{4.1.2.2}$$

In these two optimization problems, one is the function of $n - [\frac{n}{2}]$ dimension and the other is the function of $[\frac{n}{2}]$ dimension.

Step 5. Choose the best result from these two optimization problems to use as the current optimal solution $\mathbf{x}^*$ to see if it can reach a satisfactory result. If not, iterate the steps by starting from step 3; if a satisfactory result is obtained, terminate the computational process and get the optimal solution.

Note: Other strategies may be applied to Step 3, and here is only one of them. In order to ensure the rapid convergence of the algorithm, pick the optimal solution after each calculation to use it as a particle for the calculation next time.

4.1.3 Solve the TSP through DPSO

For the TSP with n cities ($a_1, a_2, \cdots a_n$), use $(a_{i1}, a_{i2}, \cdots, a_{in}, a_{i1})$ to represent the route (i.e. $a_{i1} \to a_{i2} \cdots \to a_{in}$). $a_{i1}, a_{i2}, \cdots, a_{in}$ is an array of $a_1, a_2, \cdots, a_n$ and is called solution sequence. As stated above, DPSO algorithm is applicable to the continuous problem. As TSP is a typical discrete problem, its solution is a sequence or loop rather than a point within the solution space. In order to apply DPSO to TSP, we introduce to you some definitions and algorithms of the solution sequence.

Definition 1 Exchange and exchange sequence Exchange the j point and k point of the solution sequence to form a new solution sequence. This is called exchange and is indicated with $E(j,k)$.Exchange a_{ij} and a_{ik} in the solution sequence of $T=(a_{i1},a_{i2},\cdots,a_{ij},\cdots,a_{ik},\cdots,a_{in})$. The new solution after exchange is $T+E(j,k)$. The ordered sequence $Q=(E_1,E_2,\cdots,E_m)$ after m times of exchanges is called exchange sequence. Exchange T through the exchange sequence in an orderly manner to generate a new solution. i.e.

$$T+Q=T+(E_1,E_2,\cdots,E_m)=[(T+E_1)+E_2]+\cdots+E_m \qquad (4.1.3.1)$$

When $m=0$, Q is equivalent to empty sequence. This means that formula (6.4.1.3.1) doesn't do any exchange for the solution sequence. Under such circumstances, you can add an exchange result to the exchange sequence and place this exchange result to the end of the sequence to form a new sequence.

Definition 2 Solution sequence difference As for any two solution sequences T_1 and T_2 of the same TSP, the exchange sequence Q always exists. As a result, $T_2=T_1+Q$ is formed. Q is the difference of the solution sequences T_2 and T_1, i.e. the result of T_2-T_1.When $T_1=(a_1,a_2,\cdots a_n)$ and $T_2=(b_1,b_2,\cdots b_n)$ are found, you can use the following procedure 1 to calculate $Q=T_2-T_1$.

```
Procedure 1        Q = empty sequence
    for j = 1 to n
    for i = 1 to n
    if a_i = b_j and i ≠ j then add E(i,j) to Q
        end
  end
```

In respect of T_1 and T_2, there are many Qs to be used in the formula $T_2=T_1+Q$.

Definition 3 Product of decimal and exchange sequence $\eta\in(0,1)$ and exchange sequence is Q which has an exchange of n_0. If $\frac{m_0}{n_0}\le\eta<\frac{m_0+1}{n_0}$ (m_0 is an integer from 0 to n_0-1), $\eta\cdot Q$ is the sequence formed by m_0 exchange before Q.

Through this operation, the above algorithm can be used to solve the discrete optimization problem like TSP.

4.1.4 Test and discussion of the performance of the algorithm

Use 14 points of the TSP provided by Huang Lan and other people to test the effectiveness of the algorithm. Description of the 14 points of the TSP is listed in table 1.

Point	1	2	3	4	5	6	7	8	9	10	11	12	13	14
X	16.47	16.47	20.09	22.39	25.23	22.00	20.47	17.20	16.30	14.05	16.53	21.52	19.41	20.09
Y	96.10	94.44	92.54	93.37	97.24	96.05	97.02	96.29	97.38	98.12	97.38	95.59	97.13	94.55

Table 1. Position data for 14 points

Use DPSO to carry out 8 times of tests and set the parameters as $\omega_1 = 0.53$, $\eta_1 = 0.35$ and $\eta_2 = 0.45$. The number of the initial population is 600. Set the maximum iterative number as 300. The result as follows:

Test serial number	1	2	3	4	5	6	7	8
Get the algebra of the optimum value 30.8785	58	30	58	58	58	58	93	196
Get the best route each time	6-12-7-13-8-11-9-10-1-2-14-3-4-5							

Tabela 2.

Algorithm analysis table

Number of the solution space	(14-1)!/2=3 113 510 400
Average iterative number	(58 $\times$ 5+30+93+196)/8=76.125
Average search space for each test	600+76.125 $\times$ 200=15825
Proportion of the search space to solution space	15825/3113510400=0.000508%

Tabela 3.

From the above test, we can see that DPSO may go beyond the local extremum to gen the final optimal solution for the problem. To achieve this, we should transform the high dimension optimization into low dimension optimization. We should optimize the remaining components while maintain some components unchanged; by doing this alternately, the ability for algorithm to optimize the high dimension problem will be strengthened. This improved algorithm only represents an improvement on the calculative strategy front. It does not add additional calculation and step to the algorithm, hence, maintaining the simplification of the PSO algorithm. At the same time, it helps to transform a high dimension optimization problem into several low dimension optimization problems, which will not complicate the calculation procedure.

4.2 Solve the TSP through MCPSO

When use MCPSO to solve the TSP, you also need to go through the relevant procedure which is used by continuous optimization algorithm to solve the discrete optimization problem; except for the above methods, MCPSO also has midpoint problem, so we introduce you the following definition:

Definition Midpoint solution sequence Set two solution sequences $T_1 = (a_1, a_2, \cdots a_n)$ and $T_2 = (b_1, b_2, \cdots b_n)$ for n cities of TSP and make the solution sequence as $T = (a_1, a_2, \cdots, a_{n_1}, b_{n_1+1}, b_{n_1+2}, \cdots, b_n)$ ($n_1 = [n/2]$).If repetitive point appears in the solution, adjustment can be made according to the procedure 2 to make it become a feasible solution sequence and call it a midpoint solution sequence of T_1 and T_2.

Procedure 2

Step 1. Search for the repetitive point of $a_1, a_2, \cdots, a_{n_1}$ from $b_{n_1+1}, b_{n_1+2}, \cdots, b_n$ and replace it with 0;

Step 2. Search for the points which are different from the points of $b_{n_1+1}, b_{n_1+2}, \cdots, b_n$ from $a_{n_1+1}, a_{n_1+2}, \cdots, a_n$ and replace the 0 point in an orderly manner.

4.2.1 Steps for MCPSO to solve the TSP

The steps for MCPSO algorithms to solve the TSP are as follows:

Step 1. Set relevant parameters l, β_1, β_2 and δ, and begin to conduct initialization complex. Each point is the solution sequence generated randomly and is indicated with $\mathbf{x}$;

Step 2. Pick l solution sequences, good and bad, for $\mathbf{x}_r$ and $\mathbf{x}_f$, and calculate the midpoint sequence $\mathbf{x}_m$ and ratio λ. Then determine the best solution sequence $\mathbf{x}_1$;

Step 3. Based on certain probability,

Pick formula $\mathbf{x}_p = \mathbf{x}_f + \phi_1(\mathbf{x}_r - \mathbf{x}_f) + \phi_2(\mathbf{x}_1 - \mathbf{x}_f)$ through probability β_1

Pick formula $\mathbf{x}_p = \mathbf{x}_r + \phi_1(\mathbf{x}_r - \mathbf{x}_f) + \phi_2(\mathbf{x}_1 - \mathbf{x}_f)$ through probability β_2

Pick formula $\mathbf{x}_p = \mathbf{x}_f + \phi_1(\mathbf{x}_f - \mathbf{x}_r) + \phi_2(\mathbf{x}_1 - \mathbf{x}_f)$ through probability $1 - \beta_1 - \beta_2$

to get m new solution sequences $\mathbf{x}_p$ to replace the bad solution sequence $\mathbf{x}_f$ to form a new complex;

Step 4. If the satisfactory result is reached, go to Step 5; otherwise, go back to Step 2;

Step 5. Show the optimal solution.

4.2.2 Test and discussion of the performance of the algorithm

Test the algorithm based on the 14 points of the TSP provided by Huang Lan and other people. The optimum value is 30.8785.We use this problem to test the optimal performance of MCPSO algorithm. Its parameters are $\delta = 0.85$, $\beta_1 = 0.675$, $\beta_2 = 0.175$ and $l = 50$. The pop-size is 600 and the upper limit of iterative number is 200. In order to facilitate comparison, we also use SGA and ACO to solve this problem. These two have the same pop-size and iteration upper limit as MCPSO. Each algorithm is run for 10 times. The parameter setting for these two algorithms are: SGA: multiplying probability $P_r = 0.2$,crossing probability $P_c = 0.6$ and mutation probability $P_m = 0.05$; ACO: constant $C = 20$, pheromone factor $\alpha = 1$, heuristic factor $\beta = 1$, and information keeping factor $\rho = 0.8$. The results of these algorithms are shown in the table 4.2.2.1 and the change curve of average mean fitness is shown in the figure 4.2.2.1.

ACO and integer-coded SGA can be directly used to solve the discrete optimization problems such as TSP. These algorithms have the ability to search for the global optimal solution, but the efficiency is relatively low as they can only make a change based on the probability. MCPSO is a continuous algorithm which introduces the group searching mechanism of PSO into the complex method. It considers the global property between solutions through geometry point, optimization and other principles so as to shorten the distance between the solution with poor adaptability and the solution with good adaptability. In order to avoid being trapped in the local extremum, certain probability will be considered. Shortening the distance between bad solution and good solution will help you to get the optimal solution in a more precise way within a short time, and greatly enhance the searching ability. The appearance of the algorithm targeted to TSP solution sequence not only helps to keep the above characteristics of MCPSO, but also guarantees the effective application of MCPSO to discrete problems. As for the 14 points of TSP, the running of MCPSO algorithm (7 out of 10 times) will help you to find the optimal solution with relatively low iterative number. However, after 10 times of running of ACO and SGA, no optimal solution is found. From this, we can see the advantage of MCPSO.

Algorithm	Number of times of reaching the optimum value	Minimum algebra for reaching the optimum value	Average algebra for reaching the optimum value	Best value	Average value	Standard deviation
ACO	0	N/A	N/A	31.8791	33.6888	3.7000
SGA	0	N/A	N/A	34.4509	35.9578	3.4209
MCPSO	7	35	143.57	30.8785	31.0262	0.7137

Table 4. Comparison of the results from three algorithms

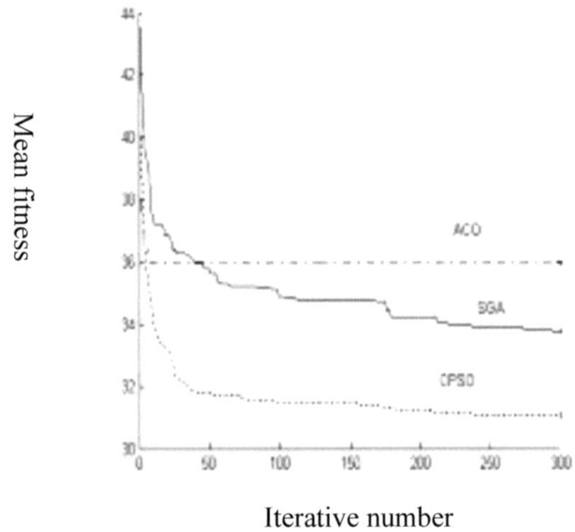

Fig. 1.

5. Application of the improved PSO algorithm for the TSP

PCB's digital control drilling problem can be described as follows: Process all the holes by starting from the tool changing point (repetition and omission are not allowed). After the processing, return to this point to do tool changing and processing for other aperture. In terms of digital control programming, we should consider the order of drill hole processing to minimize the time idle running, i.e. the best route problem of tool changing or the TSP problem in nature. With regard to the processing problem for a series of holes, the coordinate for these 20 holes has been listed in the figure 5.1. We use PCB-CAD software and PSO, SGA, ACO, DPSO and MCPSO to solve this problem. The parameter setting for PSO is: $\omega = 0.25$, $c_1 = 0.3$ and $c_2 = 0.45$. The speed will be indicated through exchange sequence. The parameters of the other three algorithms are the same as above. The tool changing routes generated are shown in figures 5.1 to 5.6. The latter five algorithms are run individually for 10 times with the upper limit of iterative number each time of 200 and pop-size of 600. The figures presented are their optimal structures. The path lengths for the tool changing routes generated from 6 algorithms are given in table 5.2.

No.	x	y	No.	x	y	No.	x	y
1	1	1	8	2.5	7.5	15	7	15.5
2	1	3	9	2.5	1	16	7	13.5
3	1	7	10	3.5	2	17	7	12.1
4	1	8	11	3.5	8.2	18	7	12
5	2.5	14	12	3.5	12.9	19	7	10
6	2.5	13.5	13	3.5	13.2	20	7	4
7	2.5	13	14	3.5	13.9			

Table 5. Position for 20 holes

Algorithm	PCB-CAD	ACO	SGA	PSO	MCPSO	DPSO
Average length	61.5555	60.5610	58.6334	59.4244	43.4923	44.4978
Minimum length	61.5555	56.7481	52.2687	53.2687	40.1203	40.1203

Table 6. Calculation result comparison

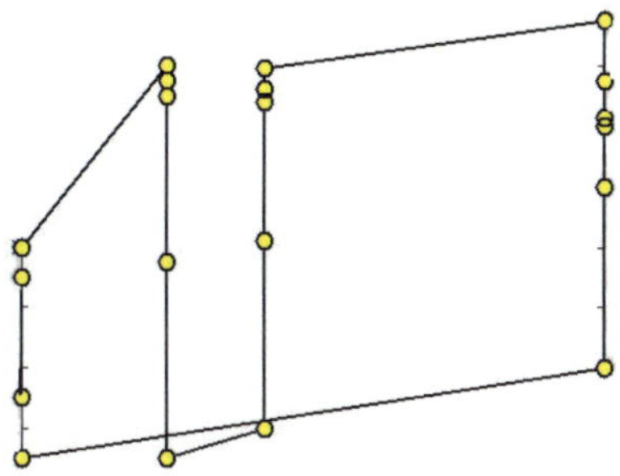

Fig. 5.1 Tool changing route chart generated from PCB-CAD

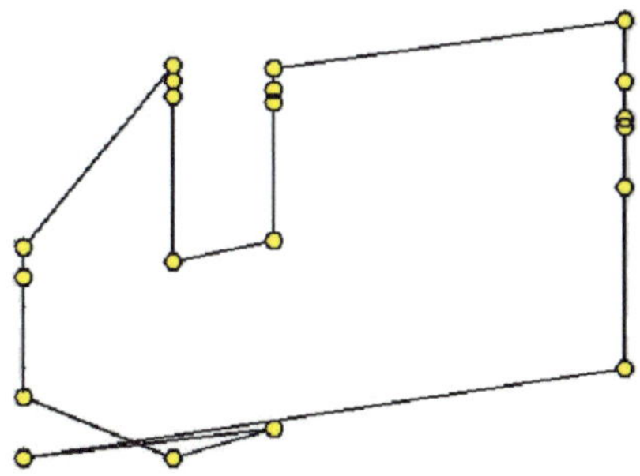

Fig. 5.2 Tool changing route chart generated from PSO

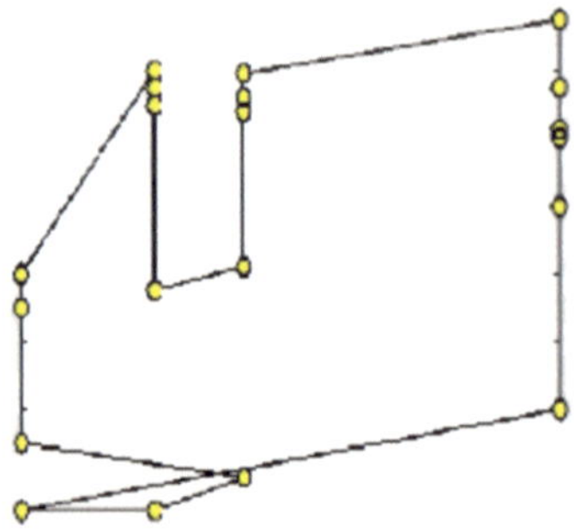

Fig. 5.3 Tool changing route chart generated from SGA

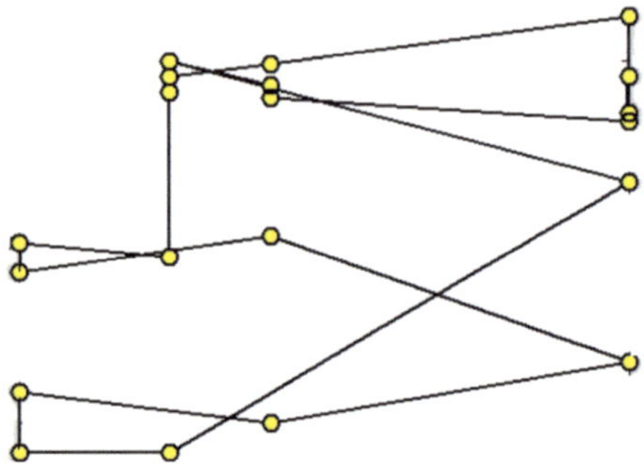

Fig. 5.4 Tool changing route chart generated from ACO

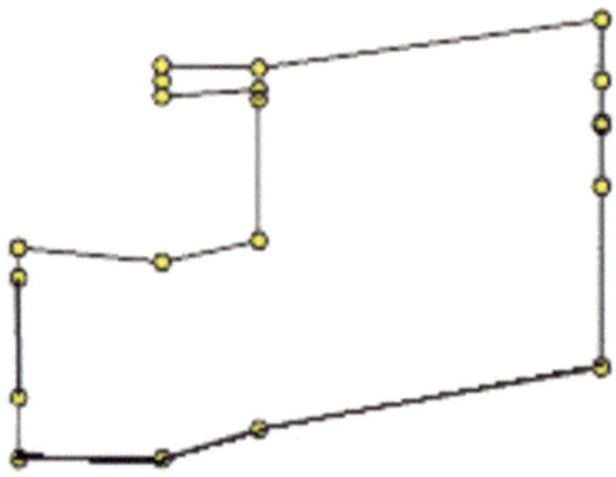

Fig. 5.5 Tool changing route chart generated from MCPSO

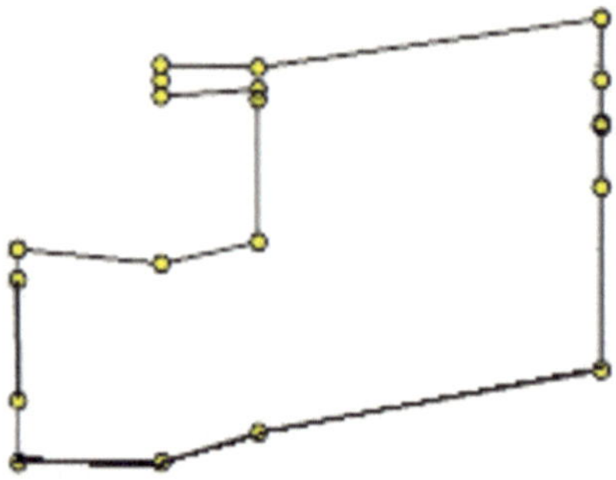

Fig. 5.6 Tool changing route chart generated from DPSO

From above, see can see that the lengths of tool changing routes generated from optimization algorithms are shorter than that generated from PCB-CAD software, of which the MCPCO enjoy the shortest length (about 29% shorter than others). Determination of the best route for PCB digital control drilling can effectively solve the optimization problem of the digital control programming in the course of PCB processing and develop a PCB automatic programming system.

6. Summary

This article consists of the definition of TSP, mathematical description methods, traditional solving methods for the TSP and problems existing in the traditional solving methods. At the same time, it introduces the evolution algorithms for solving the TSP. Based on this, two algorithms (MCPSO and DPSO) are provided. Finally, it shows us the best tool changing route for the digital control drilling by using the algorithms given.

7. References:

[1] Mo Yuanbin, Expansion and Application of PSO (D). Hangzhou: Zhejiang University. 2007

[2] Garey M R, Johnson D S. Computers and Intractabilitys: A Guide to the Theory of NP-Completeness [M]. San Francisco: Freeman WH , 1979.

[3] Maurice Clerc. Discrete Particle Swarm Optimization Illustrated by the Traveling Sales man Problem [DB/OL].
http: //www. mauriceclerc. net, 2000.

[4] Gao S , Han B,Wu X J . et al. Solving Traveling Sales2man Problem by Hybrid Particle Swarm Optimization Algorithm [J]. *Control and Decision*, 2004, 19 (11) :1286-1289.

[5] (US) Robert E. Larson (Writer). Chen Weiji (Translator). Dynamic Programming. 1st edition. Beijing: Tsinghua University Press, 1984

[6] (US) Leon Cooper and Mary W. Cooper (Writers). Zhang Youwei (Translator). Dynamic Programming. 1st edition. Beijing: National Defence Industrial Press, 1985

[7] Huang Lan and Wang Kangping, etc. Solve the Traveling Salesman Problem through PSO Algorithm [J]. Journal of Jilin University, 2003 (4): 477-480 ·

[8] Meng Fanzhen, Hu Yunchang and Xu Hui, etc. Genetic Algorithm of the Traveling Salesman Problem [J]. System Engineering Theory and Practice, 1997, 2 (7): 15-21.

[9] Conley WC. Programming an automated punch or drill[J]. International Journal of Systems Science, 1991, 22(11): 2039-2025.

[10] Wang Xiao and Liu Huixia. Modeling and Solving of the Best Tool Changing Route for PCB Digital Control Drilling [J]. Journal of Computer Aided Design and Graphics. 2001, 13 (7): 590-593.

[11] Colorni, A., Dorigo, M., and Maniezzo, V. Distributed optimization by ant colonies. Proceedings of the First European Conference on Artificial Life, Paris, France, Varela, F. and Bourgine, P. (Eds.), Elsevier Publishing, 1991, 134-142.

3

Privacy-Preserving Local Search for the Traveling Salesman Problem

Jun Sakuma[1] and Shigenobu Kobayashi[2]
[1]*University of Tsukuba*
[2]*Tokyo Institute of Technology*
Japan

1. Introduction

In this chapter, we specifically examine distributed traveling salesman problems in which the cost function is defined by information distributed among two or more parties. Moreover, the information is desired to be kept private from others.

As intuitive situations in which distributed private information appears in combinatorial optimization problems, we take problems in supply chain management (SCM) as examples. In SCM, the delivery route decision, the production scheduling and the procurement planning are fundamental problems. Solving these problems contributes to improvement of the correspondence speed to the customer and shortening the cycle time(Vollmann, 2005; Handfield & Nichols, 1999). In the process of forming the delivery route decision and production schedule decision, the combinatorial optimization plays an important role.

When the SCM is developed between two or more enterprises, information related to the stock, the production schedule, and the demand forecast must be shared among enterprises. Electronic Data Interchange (EDI), the standardized data exchange format over the network, is often used to support convenient and prompt information sharing[1]. Information sharing apparently enhances the SCM availability; however, all information related to the problem resolution must be disclosed to all participants to lay the basis for global optimization. Such information is often highly confidential and its disclosure would be impossible in many cases.

As more concrete examples, two scenarios are presented. These scenarios pose situations that appear to be unsolvable unless private information is shared.

Scenario 1: Let there be a server E_A that manages a route-optimization service and a user E_B who tries to use this service. The user's objective is to find the optimal route that visits points $F_1, \ldots, F_n$ chosen by himself. The user, however, does not like to reveal the list of visiting points to the server. The server manages a matrix of cost for traveling between any two points. The server does not like to reveal the cost matrix to the user, either. How can the user learn the optimal route without mutually revelation of private information?

Note that this problem is obviously solved as the Traveling Salesman Problem (TSP) if either of traveling cost or visiting points is shared. As more complicated examples, a multi-party situation is described next.

Scenario 2: Let there be two shipping companies E_A and E_B in two regions A and B. Client E_C requests that E_A deliver freight to point $F_1^A, \ldots, F_n^A$ in region A and also requests E_B to deliver

[1]United Nations Economic Commission for Europe, http://www.unece.org/trade/untdid/welcome.htm

freight to point $F_1^B,...,F_n^B$ in region B, separately. Now E_A, E_B and E_C are involved in the business cooperation and try to unify the delivery route to reduce the overall delivery cost. To search for the optimum unified route and to estimate the reduced cost, E_A and E_B must reveal their costs between any two points, but they would not reveal their delivery cost because they seek mutual confidentiality. How can these companies search for the optimal unified delivery route without revealing their confidential information?

In these scenarios, costs and visiting points are confidential information and participants would not reveal them. As shown, the difficulty of private information sharing sometimes thwarts problem resolution.

In our study, we specifically investigate a privacy-preserving local search to solve the traveling salesman problem. The easiest way to converting existing metaheuristics to privacy-preserving metaheuristics is to introduce an entity called a trusted third party (TTP). A TTP is an entity that facilitates interactions between two parties who both trust the TTP. If a TTP exists, then all parties can send their private information to the TTP; the TTP can find a local optimum using the existing metaheuristics and can return the optimized solution.

This idea works perfectly. However, preparation of a TTP is often quite difficult mainly in terms of cost. Needless to say, a protocol that works only between participants in the standard network environment (e.g. TCP/IP network) is preferred.

Secure function evaluation (SFE) (Yao, 1986; Goldreich, 2004) is a general and well studied methodology for evaluating any function privately, which allows us to convert any existing metaheuristics into privacy-preserving metaheuristics. However, the computational cost of SFE is usually quite large. The time complexity of SFE is asymptotically bounded by the polynomial of the size of the Boolean circuit of the computation. If the computation is primitive, SFE works practically; however, it can be too inefficient for practical use, particular when the large-scale computation is performed or large amount of datasets are taken as inputs and outputs.

In solving the traveling salesman problem by means of metaheuristics, not only the input size but the number of iterations can be quite large. Therefore, in our protocol, in order to solve TSP in a privacy-preserving manner, we make use of a public-key cryptosystem with homomorphic property, which allows us to compute addition of encrypted integers without decryption. Existing SFE solutions are used only for small portions of our computation as a part of a more efficient overall solution.

2. Problem definition

In this section, we introduce distributed situations of the traveling salesman problem (TSP). Then the privacy in the distributed traveling salesman problem is defined.

Let $G = (V, E)$ be an undirected graph and $|V| = n$ be the number of cities. For each edge $e_{i,j} \in E$, a cost connecting node i and node j, $\alpha_{i,j}$, is prescribed. Tours are constrained to be a Hamilton cycle. Then the objective of TSP is to find a tour such that the sum of the cost of included edges is as low as possible.

The permutation representation or the edge representation is often used to describe tours. In this chapter, we introduce the scalar product representation with indicator variables for our solution. Let $x = (x_{1,2}, ..., x_{1,n}, x_{2,3}, ..., x_{2,n}, ..., x_{n-1,n})$ be a tour vector where $x_{i,j}$ are indicator variables such that

$$x_{i,j} = \begin{cases} 1 & e_{i,j} \text{ is included in the tour,} \\ 0 & \text{otherwise.} \end{cases}$$

The cost can be written as an instance vector $\alpha = (\alpha_{1,2},...,\alpha_{n-1,n})$ similarly. The number of elements of the tour vector x and the cost vector α are $d = n(n-1)/2$. For simplicity, we respectively describe the i-th element of x and α as x_i and α_i. Then, using this representation, the objective function of TSP is written in the form of the scalar product:

$$f(x,\alpha) = \sum_{i=1}^{d} \alpha_i x_i = \alpha \cdot x. \tag{1}$$

The constraint function of the TSP is defined as

$$g(x;V) = \begin{cases} 1 & \text{If } x \text{ is a Hamilton cycle of } V, \\ 0 & \text{otherwise.} \end{cases}$$

Next, we consider distributed situations of the TSP. The instance of the TSP consists of city set V and cost vector α.

First, the simplest and typical two-party distributed situation is explained. Let there be two parties $P(1)$ and $P(2)$. Assume that city set V is publicly shared by $P(1)$ and $P(2)$. In such a case, $P(1)$ (referred to as *searcher*) arbitrarily chooses a city subset $V' \subseteq V$ and privately holds it. Here, V' represents the searcher's private list of visiting cities. The searcher can generate tour x that includes all cities in V' and aims to minimize the total cost of the tour.

In addition, $P(2)$ (referred to as *server*) privately holds cost vector α for all cities in V. The server works to support the optimization of the searcher.

We call this problem (1,1)-TSP or *one-server one-searcher TSP*. Here, (1,1)-TSP corresponds to the formal description of scenario 1 described in section 1.

Multi-party cases are explained as the extension of (1,1)-TSP. Assume a situation in which the cost vector α is distributed among k servers. Let $\alpha(i)$ be a vector that is owned by the i-th server such that $\alpha = \sum_{i=1}^{k} \alpha(i)$. As in the case of (1,1)-TSP, V' is chosen by the searcher. We designate this distributed TSP as $(k,1)$-TSP, which corresponds to the formal description of scenario 2 presented in section 1.

Next we explain $(1,k)$-TSP. Let $\{V'(1),...,V'(k)\}$ be city subsets that are chosen independently by k searchers independently. Let $V' = \cup_{i=1}^{k} V'(i)$. The server privately manages α.

See Fig. 1 for the partitioning patterns of these distributed TSPs. Apparently, (1,1)-TSP is a special case of these cases. The cost function is represented as the scalar product of two vectors in all situations. The constraint function is written as $g(x;V')$, which is evaluable by the searcher in (1,1) or (k,1)-TSP . However, $g(x;V')$ cannot be evaluated by any single party in $(1,k)$-TSP.

In our protocol presented in latter sections, we require that constraint function g is evaluable by a single party. For this reason, we specifically investigate (1,1)-TSP and $(k,1)$-TSP in what follows.

3. Our approach

In this section, we explain our approach for solving distributed TPSs with private information by means of the local search. For the convenience of description, we specifically examine (1,1)-TSP in the following sections. The extension to $(k,1)$-TSP is mentioned in Section 6.

Let $N(x)$ be a set of neighborhoods of solution x. Let $\in_r$ denote an operation which chooses an element form a given set uniformly at random. Then, the algorithm of local search without privacy preservation is described as follows:

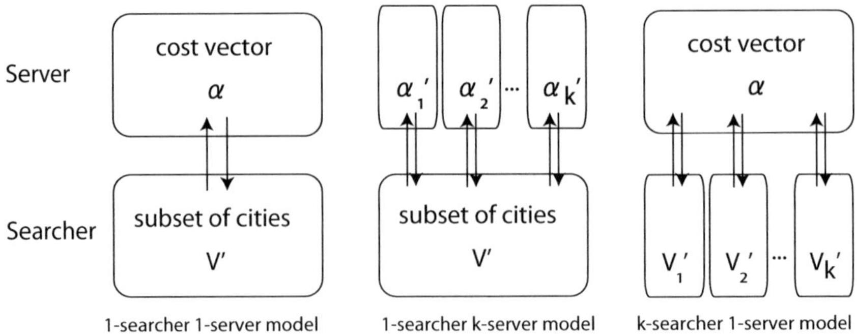

Fig. 1. Privacy model of the distributed TSP

[Local search]

1. Generate an initial tour x_0
2. $x \in_r N(x_0), N(x_0) \leftarrow N(x_0) \setminus \{x\}$.
3. If $f(x) < f(x_0), x_0 \leftarrow x$
4. If some termination conditions are satisfied, output x_0 as x^*. Else, go to step 2.

In the process of local search, cost values are evaluated many times. From the perspective of privacy preservation, if cost values are shared at each iteration, information leakage is likely to arise. For example, in (1,1)-TSP, the searcher might infer some elements of the server's private distance vector from a series of tours and cost values.

Fortunately, for many rank-based metaheuristics algorithms, including local search, cost values need not always be evaluated; the evaluation of a paired comparison of two cost values is sometimes sufficient. This fact is convenient for privacy preservation in optimization because the risk of information leakage from the result of paired comparison would be much smaller than the cost value itself.

Considering the matters described above, we consider a protocol that solves privacy-preserving optimization through a combination of local search and a cryptographic protocol that privately compares a pair of scalar products.

First, we define the private paired comparison of the scalar product. Let $x_1, x_2, \alpha \in Z_m^d (= [0, ..., m-1]^d)$. Also assume the the following inequalities.

- $\alpha \cdot x_2 - \alpha \cdot x_1 \geq 0$ be I_+
- $\alpha \cdot x_2 - \alpha \cdot x_1 < 0$ be I_-

Then, the problem can be stated as follows:

Statement 1 *(Private scalar product comparison) Let there be two parties: Alice and Bob. Alice has two private vectors x_1, x_2 and Bob has a private vector α. At the end of the protocol, Alice learns one correct inequality in $\{I_-, I_+\}$ and nothing else. Bob learns nothing.*

We call this problem *private scalar product comparison*. Assuming that there exist protocols that solve this private scalar product comparison, private scalar product comparison allows us to perform local search in a privacy-preserving manner as shown below:

In step one, the searcher generates an initial tour x_0. In step two, the searcher chooses a tour in neighborhood of x_0, $N(x_0)$, uniformly at random. These two steps can be executed by the

searcher solely. At step three, we make use of private scalar product comparison. Recall that $f(x) = \alpha \cdot x$ and $f(x_0) = \alpha \cdot x_0$. What we need here is to learn whether or not $\alpha \cdot x_0 - \alpha \cdot x < 0$. This problem is readily solved by means of private scalar product comparison without sharing the searcher's x, x_0 and the server's α. In step four, the searcher can terminate the computations after generating a prescribed number of individuals, or can terminate the serarch when he finds $N(x) = \emptyset$. In both cases, step four can be executed by the searcher solely.
As shown, assuming the existence of a protocol for private scalar product comparison, TSPs including private information can be securely solved. In next section, we introduce cryptographic building blocks required for solving private scalar product comparison. Then in Section 5, a protocol for solving the private scalar product comparison is presented.

4. Cryptographic building blocks

In this section, three cryptographic building blocks are introduced.

4.1 Homomorphic public-key cryptosystem

For our protocol, we use a public-key cryptosystem with a homomorphic property. A public-key cryptosystem is a triple (Gen, Enc, Dec) of probabilistic polynomial-time algorithm for key-generation, encryption, and decryption, respectively. The key generation algorithm generates a valid pair (s_k, p_k) of secret and public keys. The secret key and public key are used only for decryption and encryption. Then $Z_p = \{0, 1, ..., p-1\}$ denotes the plain text space. The encryption of a plain text $t \in Z_p$ is denoted as $\mathrm{Enc}_{p_k}(t; r)$, where r is a random integer. The decryption of a cipher text is denoted as $t = \mathrm{Dec}_{s_k}(c)$. Given a valid key pair (p_k, s_k), $\mathrm{Dec}_{s_k}(\mathrm{Enc}_{p_k}(t; r)) = t$ for any t and r is required.
A public key cryptosystem with additive homomorphic property satisfies the following identities.

$$\begin{aligned} \mathrm{Enc}(t_1; r_1) \cdot \mathrm{Enc}(t_2; r_2) &= \mathrm{Enc}(t_1 + t_2 \mod p; r_1 + r_2) \\ \mathrm{Enc}(t_1; r_1)^{t_2} &= \mathrm{Enc}(t_1 t_2 \mod p; r_1) \end{aligned}$$

In those equations, $t_1, t_2 \in Z_p$ are plain texts and r_1, r_2 are random numbers. These random numbers are used to introduce redundancy into ciphers for security reasons; encrypted values of an integer with taking difference random numbers are represented differently. These properties enable the addition of any two encrypted integers and the multiplication of an encrypted integer by an integer. A public-key cryptosystem is *semantically secure* when a probabilistic polynomial-time adversary cannot distinguish between random encryptions of two elements chosen by herself. Paillier cryptosystem is known as a semantically secure cryptosystem with homomorphic property(Pailler, 1999). We use the Paillier cryptosystem in experiments in section 6.

4.2 Secure function evaluation

As mentioned in the introductory section, secure function evaluation (SFE) is a general and well studied cryptographic primitive which allows two or more parties to evaluate a specified function of their inputs without revealing (anything else about) their inputs to each other (Goldreich, 2004; Yao, 1986).
In principle, any private distributed computation can be securely evaluated by means of SFE. However, although polynomoially bounded, naive implementation of local search using SFE can be too inefficient. Therefore, in order to achieve privacy-preserving local search efficiently,

we make use of existing SFE solutions for small portions of our computation as a part of a more efficient overall solution.

4.3 Random shares

Let $x = (x_1,...,x_d) \in Z_N^d$. When we say A and B have *random shares* of x, A has $x^A = (x_1^A,...,x_d^A)$ and B has $x^B = (x_1^B,...,x_d^B)$ in which x_i^A and x_i^B are uniform randomly distributed in $\mathbb{Z}_N$ with satisfying $x_i = (x_i^A + x_i^B) \mod N$ for all i. Random shares allow us to keep a private value between two parties without knowing the value itself. Note that if one of the party pass the share to the other, the private value is readily recovered.

5. Scalar product comparison

Before describing the protocol for scalar product comparison, we introduce a protocol which privately computes scalar products from privately distributed vectors. Goethals et al. proposed a protocol to compute scalar products of two distributed private vectors without revealing them by means of the homomorphic public-key cryptosystem (Goethals et al., 2004). For preserving the protocol generality, parties are described as Alice and Bob in this section. The problem of private scalar product is stated as follows:

Statement 2 *(Private scalar product) Let there be two parties: Alice and Bob. Alice has a private vector $x \in Z_\mu^d$; Bob also has a private vector $\alpha \in Z_\mu^d$. At the end of the protocol, both Alice and Bob learn random shares of scalar product $x \cdot \alpha$ and nothing else.*

Let Z_p be the message space for some large p. Set $\mu = \lfloor \sqrt{p/d} \rfloor$. In what follows, the random number used in encryption function Enc is omitted for simplicity. Then, the protocol is described as follows.

[Private scalar product protocol]

- Private Input of Alice: $\alpha \in Z_\mu^d$
- Private Input of Bob: $x \in Z_\mu^d$
- Output of Alice and Bob: $r_A + r_B = x \cdot \alpha \mod p$
  (Alice and Bob output r_A and r_B, respectively)

1. Alice: Generate a public and secret key pair (p_k, s_k).
2. Alice: For $i = 1,...,d$, compute $c_i = \mathrm{Enc}_{p_k}(\alpha_i)$ and send them to Bob.
3. Bob: Compute $w \leftarrow (\prod_{i=1}^d c_i^{x_i}) \cdot \mathrm{Enc}_{p_k}(-r_B)$ where $r_B \in_r Z_p$ and send w to Alice.
4. Alice: Compute $Dec(w) = r_A (= x \cdot \alpha - r_B)$

In step two, Alice sends the ciphertext of her private vector $(c_1,...,c_d)$ to Bob. Bob does not possess the secret key. Therefore, he cannot learn Alice's vector from received ciphertexts. However, in step three, he can compute the encrypted scalar product based on homomorphic properties without knowing Alice's x:

$$\begin{aligned} w &= (\prod_{i=1}^{d} c_i^{x_i}) \cdot \mathrm{Enc}_{p_k}(-r_B) = (\prod_{i=1}^{d} \mathrm{Enc}_{p_k}(\alpha_i)^{x_i}) \cdot \mathrm{Enc}_{p_k}(-r_B) \\ &= \mathrm{Enc}_{p_k}(\alpha_1 x_1) \cdots \mathrm{Enc}_{p_k}(\alpha_d x_d) \cdot \mathrm{Enc}_{p_k}(-r_B) \\ &= \mathrm{Enc}_{p_k}(\sum_{i=1}^{d} \alpha_i x_i - r_B) = \mathrm{Enc}_{p_k}(\alpha \cdot x - r_B) \end{aligned}$$

Then, in step four, Alice correctly obtains a random share of $\alpha \cdot x$ by decrypting w using her secret key: Bob's r_B is a random share of $\alpha \cdot x$, too. Assuming that Alice and Bob behave semi-honestly[2], it can be proved that the scalar product protocol is secure (Goethals et al., 2004). In the discussions of subsequent sections, we assume that all parties behave as semi-honest parties.

A protocol for the private scalar product comparison appears to be obtained readily using the private scalar product protocol. The difference of two scalar products $\alpha \cdot x_2 - \alpha \cdot x_1$ can be computed as

$$\prod_{i=1}^{d} c_i^{x_{2,i}} \cdot \prod_{i=1}^{d} c_i^{-x_{1,i}} = \mathrm{Enc}_{p_k}(\alpha \cdot x_2 - \alpha \cdot x_1). \tag{2}$$

By sending this to Alice, Alice learns $\alpha \cdot x_2 - \alpha \cdot x_1$. Equation 2 appears to compare two scalar products successfully and privately. However, it is not secure based on statement 1 because not only the comparison result but also the value of $\alpha \cdot x_1 - \alpha \cdot x_2$ is known to Alice. In the case of the TSP, tour vectors are $x_1, x_2 \in \{0,1\}^d$. Therefore, Bob's x_1 and x_2 are readily enumerated from the value of $\alpha \cdot x_2 - \alpha \cdot x_1$ by Alice. To block Alice's enumeration, Bob can multiply some positive random value r_B to the difference of two scalar products,

$$\prod_{i=1}^{d} c_i^{r_B x_{2,i}} \cdot \prod_{i=1}^{d} c_i^{-r_B x_{1,i}} = \mathrm{Enc}_{p_k}(r_B(\alpha \cdot x_2 - \alpha \cdot x_1)).$$

By sending this to Alice, Alice learns $r_B(\alpha \cdot x_2 - \alpha \cdot x_1)$. Since $r_B > 0$, Alice can know whether or not $\alpha \cdot x_2 > \alpha \cdot x_1$ from this randomized value; however, this is not secure, either. r_B is a divider of $r_B(\alpha \cdot x_2 - \alpha \cdot x_1)$ and is readily enumerated again. Alice can also enumerate the candidate of Bob's x_1 and x_2 for each r_B in polynomial time.

As shown, multiplying a random number does not contribute to hinder Alice's guess, either. In our protocol, we use the SFE for private comparison with scalar product protocol. Private comparison is stated as follows:

Statement 3 *(Private comparison of random shares) Let Alice's input be x^A and Bob's input be x^B, where x_i^A and x_i^B are random shares of x_i for all i. Then,* private comparison of random shares *computes the index i^* such that*

$$i^* = arg\max_i (x_i^A + x_i^B). \tag{3}$$

[2]A semi-honest party is one who follows the protocol properly with the exception that the party retains a record of all its intermediate observations. From such accumulated records, semi-honest parties attempt to learn other party's privte information (Goldreich, 2004).

After the protocol execution, Alice knows i^* and nothing else: Bob learns nothing.

When Alice has a cost vector α and Bob has two tour vectors x_1, x_2, the protocol for private scalar product comparison is obtained using SFE as follows:
[Private scalar product comparison]

- Private Input of Alice : $\alpha \in Z_m^d$
- Private Input of Bob : $x_1, x_2 \in Z_m^d$
- Output of Bob : An inequation $I \in \{I_-, I_+\}$ (Alice has no output)

1. Alice: Generate a private and public key pair(p_k, s_k) and send p_k to Bob.
2. Alice: For $i = 1, ..., d$, Alice computes $c_i = \mathrm{Enc}_{p_k}(\alpha_i)$. Send them to Bob.
3. Bob: Compute $w \leftarrow \prod_{i=1}^d c_i^{x_{2,i}} \cdot \prod_{i=1}^d c_i^{-x_{1,i}} \cdot \mathrm{Enc}_{p_k}(-r^B)$ and send w to Alice where $r \in_r Z_N$
4. Alice: Compute $r^A = \mathrm{Dec}_{s_k}(w) (= x_2 \cdot \alpha - x_1 \cdot \alpha - r^B)$.
5. Alice and Bob: Jointly run a SFE for private comparison. If $((r^A + r^B) \mod N) \geq 0$, I_+ is returned to Bob. Else, I_- is returned to Bob.

First, Alice encrypts her cost vector and send all elements to Bob. Then, Bob computes the encrypted difference of two scalar products with randomization as follows:

$$w = \prod_{i=1}^{d} c_i^{x_{2,i}} \cdot \prod_{i=1}^{d} c_i^{-x_{1,i}} \cdot \mathrm{Enc}_{p_k}(-r^B) \quad (4)$$

$$= \mathrm{Enc}_{p_k}\left(\sum_{i=1}^{d} \alpha_i x_{2,i} - \sum_{i=1}^{d} \alpha_i x_{1,i} - r^B \right) \quad (5)$$

$$= \mathrm{Enc}_{p_k}\left(\alpha \cdot x_2 - \alpha \cdot x_1 - r^B \right). \quad (6)$$

At step four, Alice obtains

$$r^A = x_2 \cdot \alpha - x_1 \cdot \alpha - r^B, \quad (7)$$

where r^A and r^B are random shares of $x_2 \cdot \alpha - x_1 \cdot \alpha$ over Z_N; both do not learn any from random shares. Then at the last step, Both jointly run SFE for private comparison to evaluate whether or not $(r^A + r^B) \mod N$ is greater than zero, which is the desired output.
In what follows, we describe the execution of this protocol as $(\alpha, (x_1, x_2)) \longrightarrow_{\mathrm{SPC}} (\emptyset, I)$.
Note that the input size for SFE is p regardless of the vector size m and dimension d. In principle, the computational load of SFE is large particularly when the input size is large. Although the computation complexity of this protocol in step two and step three is still $O(d)$, we can reduce the entire computational cost of private scalar product comparison by limiting computation of SFE only to comparison of random shares.

Theorem 1 *(Security of private scalar product comparison) Assume Alice and Bob behave semi-honestly. Then, private scalar product comparison protocol is secure in the sense of Statement 1.*

The security proof should follow the standardized proof methodology called simulation paradigm (Goldreich, 2004). However, due to the limitation of the space, we explain the

security of this protocol by showing that parties cannot learn nothing but the output from messages exchanged between parties.
The messages Bob receives from Alice before step five is $\mathrm{Enc}_{p_k}(\alpha_1),...,\mathrm{Enc}_{p_k}(\alpha_d)$. Because Bob does not have Alice's secret key, Bob learns nothing about Alice's vector. The information Alice receives from Bob before step five is only a random share $r^A = \alpha \cdot x_2 - \alpha \cdot x_2 - r^B$, from which she cannot learn anything, either. At step five, it is guaranteed that SFE reveals only the comparison result (Yao, 1986). Consequently, the overall protocol is secure in the sense of Statement 1.

6. Local search of TSP using scalar product comparison

Using the protocol for private scalar product comparison, local search is convertible to a privacy-preserving protocol. As an example, we introduce a Privacy Preserving Local Search (PPLS) for TSP using 2-opt neighborhood.
Because the local search described in Section 3 is rank-based, it is readily extended to a privacy-preserving protocol. Using the protocol for private scalar product comparison, PPLS is designed as follows:
[Privacy-Preserving Local Search]

- Private Input of Server: instance vector $\alpha \in Z_m^d$
- Private Input of Searcher: subset of instance $V' \subseteq V$
- Private Output of Searcher: local optimal solution x^*

1. Server: Generate a pair of a public and a secret key (p_k, s_k) and send p_k to the searcher.
2. Server: For $i = 1,...,d$, compute $c_i = \mathrm{Enc}_{p_k}(\alpha_i)$ and send them to the searcher.
3. Searcher: Generate an initial solution x_0 using V'
4. Searcher: $x \in_r N(x_0), N(x_0) \leftarrow N(x_0) \setminus \{x\}$
5. Searcher:
   a) Compute $(\alpha,(x,x_0)) \longrightarrow_{\mathrm{SPC}} (\emptyset, I)$ with probability 0.5. Otherwise, compute $(\alpha,(x_0,x)) \longrightarrow_{\mathrm{SPC}} (\emptyset, I)$.
   b) If I corresponds to $\alpha \cdot x - \alpha \cdot x_0 < 0$, then $x_0 \leftarrow x$
6. Searcher: If $N(x_0) = \emptyset$ or satisfies some termination condition, $x^* \leftarrow x_0$ and output x^*. Otherwise, go to step 4.

Step one and step two can be executed solely by the server. In step three, an solution is initialized. Step three and step four are also executed solely by the searcher.
Step five can be executed privately by means of private scalar product comparison. Note that the order of the inputs of private scalar product comparison is shuffled randomly in step 5(a). The reason is explained in detail in Section 6.2.
Readers can find multi-party expansion of private scalar product protocol in (Goethals et al., 2004). Multi-party expansion of private scalar product comparison is straightforward with a similar manner in the literature. This expansion readily allows us to obtain protocols of PPLS for $(k,1)$-TSP.

6.1 Communication and computation complexity

Communication between the server and the searcher occurs in steps one, two, and five. In (1,1)-TSP, we can naturally assume that the cost vector α is not changed during optimization. Therefore, transfer of $(c_1,...,c_d)$ occurs only once in steps one and two. The communication complexity of step 5(a) is $O(1)$. As shown, the communication complexity is not time consuming in this protocol.

The time consuming steps of PPLS are private comparison by SFE (step five of private scalar product comparison) and exponentiation computed by the searcher (step three of private scalar product comparison). The computation time of the SFE is constant for any d and cannot be reduced anymore. On the other hand, there is still room for improvement in the exponentiation step.

Using naive implementation, step three of private scalar product comparison costs $O(d)(= O(n^2))$. To reduce this computation, we exploit the fact that the number of changed edges by 2-opt is much smaller than d.

In vector $x - x_0$, only 2 elements are changed from 1 to 0 and the other 2 elements are changed from 0 to -1 when 2-opt is used as the neighborhood. The remaining elements are all 0 irrespective of the problem size. Since the exponentiation of 0 can be skipped in step three of private scalar product comparison, the time complexity is saved at most $O(1)$ by computing only in changing edges.

6.2 Security

Given a TTP, the ideally executed privacy-preserving optimization is the following.

Statement 4 *(Privacy-preserving local search for* $(1,1)$*-TSP (ideal)) Let the searcher's input be* $V' \subseteq V$*. Let the server's input be* $\alpha \in Z_m^d$*. After the execution of the protocol, the searcher learns the (local) optimal solution* x^**, but nothing else. The server learns nothing at the end of the protocol, either.*

Unfortunately, the security of the PPLS is not equivalent to this statement. We briefly verify what is protected and leaked after the protocol execution.

Messages sent from the searcher to the server are all random shares. Thus, it is obvious that the server does not learn anything from the searcher.

There remains room for discussion about what the searcher can guess from what it learns because this point is dependent on the problem domain. The searcher learns a series of the outcome of private scalar product comparison protocol in the middle of PPLS execution. Let the outcome of the t-th private scalar product comparison be $I(t)$.

In the case of TSP, $I(t)$ corresponds to an inequality, $\alpha \cdot x - \alpha \cdot x_0 \leq 0$ or $\alpha \cdot x - \alpha \cdot x_0 > 0$. Although the elements of the private cost vector α are not leaked from this, the searcher learns whether $\alpha \cdot (x - x_0) > 0$ or not from this comparison. This indicates that orders of cost values might be partially implied by the searcher because the searcher knows what edges are included in these solutions.

As long as the server and the searcher mutually interact only through the private scalar product comparison, the server never learns the searcher's V' and the searcher never learns the server's α. However, the security of PPLS is not perfect as a protocol with a TTP. A method to block the guess of the searcher from intermediate messages remains as a challenge for future study.

7. Experimental analysis and discussion

In this section, we show experimental results of PPLS for $(1,1)$-TSP in order to evaluate the computation time and investigate its scalability.

7.1 Setting

Five problem instances were chosen from TSPLIB(Reinelt, 1991). The city size is 195 – 1173. In the distributed TSP, the searcher can choose a subset of cities V' arbitrarily as the input. For our experiments, V' is set to V for all problems because the computation time becomes greatest when $V = V'$. PPLS was terminated when x_0 reaches a local optimum.
As a homomorphic cryptosystem, the Paillier cryptosystem(Pailler, 1999) with 512-bit and 1024-bit key was used. The server and the searcher program were implemented using java. Both programs were run separately on a Xeon 2.8 GHz (CPU) with 1 GB (RAM) PCs with a 100 Mbps Ethernet connection. For SFE, Fairplay (Malkhi et al., 2004), a framework for generic secure function evaluation, was used.
PPLS was repeated for 50, 100, and 300 times with changing initial tours (depicted as 50-itr, 100-itr and 300-itr).
Both the first and the second step of PPLS can be executed preliminarily before choosing city subset V'. Therefore, we measured the execution time from the third step to the termination of the protocol.

7.2 Results

Fig. 2 shows the estimated computation time required for optimization. With a 512-bit key, PPLS (1-itr) spent 19 (min) and 79 (min) to reach the local optimum of rat195 and rat575. Using a 1024-bit key, PPLS (1-itr) spent 21 (min) and 89 (min) for the same problems.
Table 1 shows the error index (=100× obtained best tour length / known best tour length) of PPLS (average of 20 trials). Note that privacy preservation does not affect the quality of the obtained solution in any way because the protocol does not change the behavior of local search if the same random seed is used.
Earlier, we set $V' = V$ for all problems. Even when the number of cities $|V|$ is very large, the computation time is related directly to the number of chosen cities $|V'|$ because the number of evaluations is usually dependent on the number of chosen cities.
Although the computation time is not yet sufficiently small in large-scale problems, results show that the protocol completes in a practical time in privacy-preserving setting when the number of cities are not very numerous.

8. Related works

A few studies have been made of the *Privacy-Preserving Optimization* (PPO). Silaghi et al. proposed algorithms for distributed constraint satisfaction and optimization with privacy enforcement (MPC-DisCSP)(Silaghi, 2003)(Silaghi & Mitra, 2004). Actually, MPC-DisCSP is based on a SFE technique (Ben-Or et al., 1988). Yokoo et al. proposed a privacy-preserving protocol to solve dynamic programming securely for the multi-agent system (Yokoo & Suzuki, 2002; Suzuki & Yokoo, 2003). (Brickell & Shmatikov, 2005) proposed a privacy-preserving protocol for single source shortest distance (SSSD) which is a privacy-preserving transformation of the standard Dijkstra's algorithm to find the shortest path on a graph. These studies are all based on cryptographic guarantees of security.

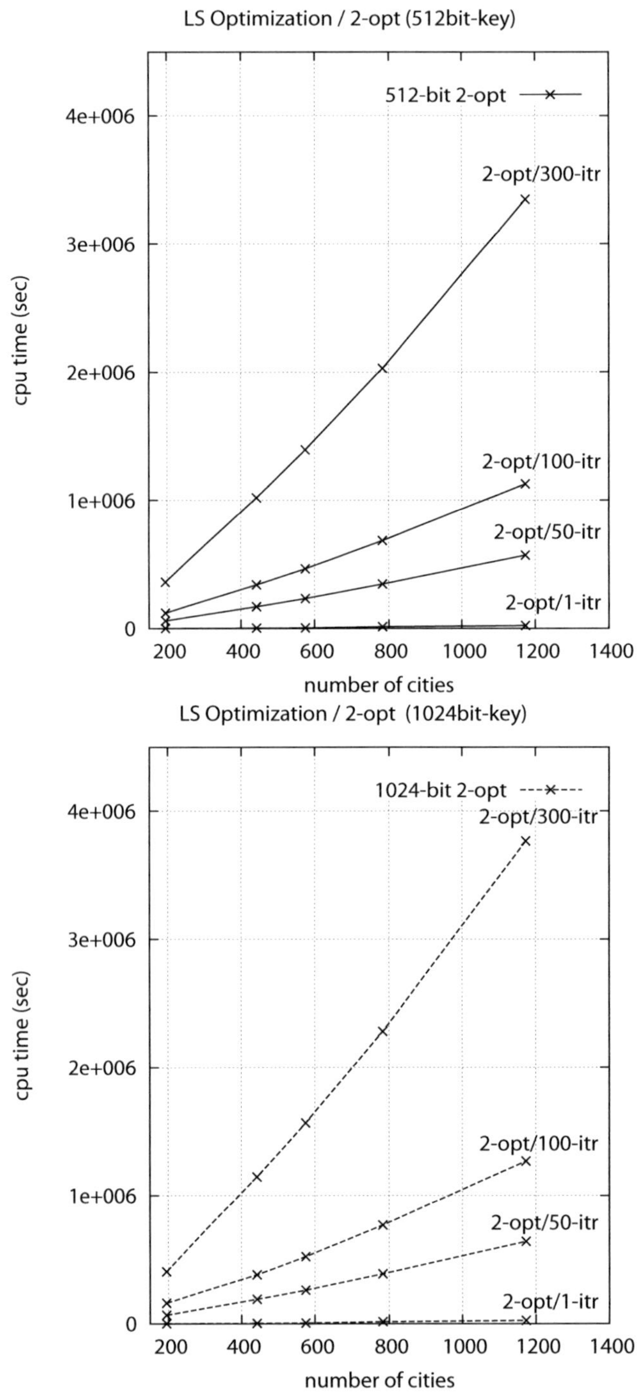

Fig. 2. Computation time of PPLS. Estimated time required for the completion of PPLS optimization (left: 512-bit key, right: 1024-bit key).

	PPLS (2-opt)			
	1-itr.	50-itr.	100-itr.	300-itr.
rat195	13.3	9.16	8.73	8.65
pcb442	16.4	8.88	8.88	8.88
rat575	11.6	9.96	9.96	9.90
rat783	12.2	10.8	10.8	10.3
pcb1173	15.4	12.9	12.9	12.3

Table 1. The error index of PPLS (2-opt).

To the best of authors' knowledge, this study is the first attempt for privacy-preserving optimization by means of meta-heuristics. As discussed earlier, private scalar product comparison allows us to compare two scalar products. It follows that our PPLS is available for any privacy-preserving optimization problems provided that the cost function is represented in the form of scalar products. In addition, private scalar product comparison can be incorporated into not only local search but more sophisticated meta-heuristics, such as genetic algorithms or tabu search, as long as the target algorithm uses only paired comparison for selection.

9. Summary

We proposed and explained a protocol for privacy-preserving distributed combinatorial optimization using local search. As a connector that combines local search and privacy preservation, we designed a protocol to solve a problem called private scalar product comparison. The security of this protocol is theoretically proved. Then, we designed a protocol for privacy-preserving optimization using a combination of local search and private scalar product comparison. Our protocol is guaranteed to behave identically to algorithms that do not include features for privacy preservation.

As an example of distributed combinatorial optimization problems, we specifically examined the distributed TSP and designed a privacy-preserving local search that adopts 2-opt as a neighborhood operator. The result show that privacy-preserving local search with 2-opt solves a 512-city problem within a few hours with about 10 % error. Although the computation time is not yet sufficiently small in a large-scale problem, it is confirmed that the protocol is completed in a practical time, even in privacy-preserving setting. Both the searcher's and the server's computation can be readily paralleled. The implementation of parallel computation is a subject for future work. Application of PPLS to distributed combinatorial optimization problems such as the distributed QAP, VRP, and Knapsack problem is also a subject for future work.

10. References

Ben-Or, M., Goldwasser, S. & Wigderson, A. (1988). Completeness theorems for non-cryptographic fault-tolerant distributed computation, *Proceedings of the Twentieth Annual ACM Symposium on Theory of Computing (STOC)*, ACM, pp. 1–10.

Brickell, J. & Shmatikov, V. (2005). Privacy-preserving graph algorithms in the semi-honest model, *Proceedings of ASIACRYPT, LNCS*, Springer-Verlag, pp. 236–252.

Goethals, B., Laur, S., Lipmaa, H. & Mielikäinen, T. (2004). On private scalar product computation for privacy-preserving data mining, *Proceedings of Seventh International Conference on Information Security and Cryptology (ICISC), LNCS*, Springer, pp. 104–120.

Goldreich, O. (2004). *Foundations of Cryptography: Volume 2, Basic Applications*, Cambridge University Press.

Handfield, R. & Nichols, E. (1999). *Introduction to supply chain management*, Prentice Hall Upper Saddle River, NJ.

Malkhi, D., Nisan, N., Pinkas, B. & Sella, Y. (2004). Fairplay - a secure two-party computation system, *Proceedings of the thirteenth USENIX Security Symposium*, pp. 287–302.

Pailler, P. (1999). Public-Key Cryptosystems Based on Composite Degree Residuosity Classes, *Proceedings of Eurocrypt, Lecture Notes in Computer Science*, Vol. 1592, pp. 223–238.

Reinelt, G. (1991). TSPLIB-A Traveling Salesman Problem Library, *ORSA Journal on Computing* **3**(4): 376–384.

Silaghi, M. (2003). Arithmetic circuit for the first solution of distributed CSPs with cryptographic multi-party computations, *Proceedings of IEEE/WIC International Conference on Intelligent Agent Technology (IAT)*, IEEE Computer Society Washington, DC, USA, pp. 609–613.

Silaghi, M. & Mitra, D. (2004). Distributed constraint satisfaction and optimization with privacy enforcement, *Proceedings of IEEE/WIC/ACM International Conference on Intelligent Agent Technology (IAT)*, IEEE Computer Society Washington, DC, USA, pp. 531–535.

Suzuki, K. & Yokoo, M. (2003). Secure Generalized Vickrey Auction Using Homomorphic Encryption, *Proceedings of Seventh International Conference on Financial Cryptography (FC)*, Springer, pp. 239–249.

Vollmann, T. (2005). *Manufacturing Planning and Control Systems for Supply Chaing Management*, McGraw-Hill.

Yao, A. C.-C. (1986). How to generate and exchange secrets, *IEEE Symposium on Foundations of Computer Science (FOCS)*, pp. 162–167.

Yokoo, M. & Suzuki, K. (2002). Secure multi-agent dynamic programming based on homomorphic encryption and its application to combinatorial auctions, *Proceedings of the First International Joint Conference on Autonomous Agents and Multiagent Systems (AAMAS)*, ACM Press New York, NY, USA, pp. 112–119.

4

Chaos Driven Evolutionary Algorithm for the Traveling Salesman Problem

Donald Davendra[1]*, Ivan Zelinka[1],
Roman Senkerik[2] and Magdalena Bialic-Davendra[3]
[1]*Department of Informatics, Faculty of Electrical Engineering and Computing Science, Technical University of Ostrava, Tr. 17. Listopadu 15, Ostrava*
[2]*Department of Informatics and Artificial Intelligence, Faculty of Informatics, Tomas Bata University in Zlin, Nad Stranemi 4511, Zlin 76001*
[3]*Department of Finance and Accounting, Faculty of Management and Economics, Mostni 5139, Zlin 76001*
Czech Republic

1. Introduction

One of the most studied problem in operations research and management science during the past few decades has been the Traveling Salesman Problem (TSP). The TSP is rather a simple problem formulation, but what has garnered it much attention is the fact that it belongs to a specific class of problems which has been labelled as "non-deterministic polynomial" or NP. What this implies is that no algorithm currently exists which can find the exact solution in "polynomial time". A number of current engineering applications are formed around this premise; such as cryptography.

TSP manages to capture the imagination of theoretical computer scientists and mathematicians as it simply describes the complexity of NP Completeness. A number of resources exists on the internet such as the TSPLIB , which allow any novice user to understand and incorporate the TSP problem.

Since no concrete mathematical algorithm exists to solve the TSP problem, a specific branch of research, namely evolutionary science, has been applied rather effectively to find solutions. Evolutionary science itself is divided into many scopes, but the most effective ones have been the deterministic approaches and random approaches. Deterministic approaches like Branch and Bound (Land & Doig, 1960) and Lin-Kernighan local searches (Lin & Kernighan, 1973) have proven very effective over the years. Random based approaches, incorporated in heuristics have generally provided a guided search pattern. Therefore the most effective algorithms have been a hybrid of the two approaches.

This research introduces another approach, which is based on a chaotic map (Davendra & Zelinka, 2010). A chaotic system is one which displays a chaotic behavior and it based on a function which in itself is a dynamical system. What is of interest is that the map iterates across the functional space in discrete steps, each one in a unique footprint. What this implies is that the same position in not iterated again. This provides a great advantage as the number

*donald.davendra@vsb.cz

generated in unique and when input into an evolutionary algorithm, it provides a unique mapping schema. The question that remains to be answered is that whether this system improves on a generic random number generator or not.
This chapter is divided into the following sections. Section 2 introduces the TSP problem formulation. Section 3 describes the algorithm used in this research; Differential Evolution (DE) and Section 4outlines its permutative varient EDE. The chaotic maps used in this research are described in Section 5 whereas the experimentation is given in Section 6. The chapter is concluded in Section 7.

2. Travelling salesman problem

A TSP is a classical combinatorial optimization problem. Simply stated, the objective of a traveling salesman is to move from city to city, visiting each city only once and returning back to the starting city. This is called a *tour* of the salesman. In mathematical formulation, there is a group of distinct cities $\{C_1, C_2, C_3, ..., C_N\}$, and there is given for each pair of city $\left\{C_i, C_j\right\}$ a distance $d\left\{C_i, C_j\right\}$. The objective then is to find an ordering π of cities such that the total time for the salesman is minimized. The lowest possible time is termed the optimal time. The objective function is given as:

$$\sum_{i=1}^{N-1} d\left(C_{\pi(i)}, C_{\pi(i+1)}\right) + d\left(C_{\pi(N)}, C_{\pi(1)}\right) \tag{1}$$

This quality is known as the *tour length*. Two branches of this problem exist, symmetric and asymmetric. A symmetric problem is one where the distance between two cities is identical, given as: $d\left\{C_i, C_j\right\} = d\left\{C_j, C_i\right\}$ for $1 \leq i, j \leq N$ and the asymmetric is where the distances are not equal. An asymmetric problem is generally more difficult to solve.
The TSP has many real world applications; VSLA fabrication (Korte, 1988) to X-ray crystallography (Bland & Shallcross, 1989). Another consideration is that TSP is *NP-Hard* as shown by Garey (1979), and so any algorithm for finding optimal tours must have a worst-case running time that grows faster than any polynomial (assuming the widely believed conjecture that $P \neq NP$).
TSP has been solved to such an extent that traditional heuristics are able to find good solutions to merely a small percentage error. It is normal for the simple 3-Opt heuristic typically getting with 3-4% to the optimal and the *variable-opt* algorithm of Lin & Kernighan (1973) typically getting around 1-2%.
The objective for new emerging evolutionary systems is to find a guided approach to TSP and leave simple local search heuristics to find better local regions, as is the case for this chapter.

3. Differential evolution algorithm

Differential evolution (DE) is one of the evolutionary optimization methods proposed by Price (1999) to solve the Chebychev polynomial fitting problem. DE is a population-based and stochastic global optimizer, and has proven to be a robust technique for global optimization.
In order to describe DE, a schematic is given in Figure 1.
There are essentially five sections to the code. Section 1 describes the input to the heuristic. D is the size of the problem, G_{max} is the maximum number of generations, NP is the total

Canonical Differential Evolution Algorithm

$$
\begin{array}{l}
1.\text{Input}: D, G_{\max}, NP \geq 4, F \in (0,1+), CR \in [0,1], \text{and initial bounds}: x^{(lo)}, x^{(hi)}. \\
2.\text{Initialize}: \left\{ \begin{array}{l} \forall i \leq NP \wedge \forall j \leq D : x_{i,j,G=0} = x_j^{(lo)} + rand_j[0,1] \bullet \left(x_j^{(hi)} - x_j^{(lo)}\right) \\ i = \{1,2,...,NP\}, j = \{1,2,...,D\}, G = 0, rand_j[0,1] \in [0,1] \end{array} \right. \\
\left\{ \begin{array}{l}
3.\text{While} \quad G < G_{\max} \\
\forall i \leq NP \left\{ \begin{array}{l}
4. \quad \text{Mutate and recombine}: \\
4.1 \quad r_1, r_2, r_3 \in \{1,2,....,NP\}, \\
\quad \text{randomly selected, except}: r_1 \neq r_2 \neq r_3 \neq i \\
4.2 \quad j_{rand} \in \{1,2,...,D\}, \text{randomly selected once each } i \\
4.3 \quad \forall j \leq D, u_{j,i,G+1} = \left\{ \begin{array}{l} x_{j,r_3,G} + F \cdot (x_{j,r_1,G} - x_{j,r_2,G}) \\ \text{if} \quad (rand_j[0,1] < CR \vee j = j_{rand}) \\ x_{j,i,G} \quad \text{otherwise} \end{array} \right. \\
5. \quad \text{Select} \\
x_{i,G+1} = \left\{ \begin{array}{l} u_{i,G+1} \text{ if } \quad f(u_{i,G+1}) \leq f(x_{i,G}) \\ x_{i,G} \quad \text{otherwise} \end{array} \right.
\end{array} \right. \\
G = G + 1
\end{array} \right.
\end{array}
$$

Fig. 1. Canonical Differential Evolution Algorithm

number of solutions, F is the scaling factor of the solution and CR is the factor for crossover. F and CR together make the internal tuning parameters for the heuristic.
Section 2 outlines the initialization of the heuristic. Each solution $x_{i,j,G=0}$ is created randomly between the two bounds $x^{(lo)}$ and $x^{(hi)}$. The parameter j represents the index to the values within the solution and i indexes the solutions within the population. So, to illustrate, $x_{4,2,0}$ represents the second value of the fourth solution at the initial generation.
After initialization, the population is subjected to repeated iterations in section 3.
Section 4 describes the conversion routines of DE. Initially, three random numbers r_1, r_2, r_3 are selected, unique to each other and to the current indexed solution i in the population in 4.1. Henceforth, a new index j_{rand} is selected in the solution. j_{rand} points to the value being modified in the solution as given in 4.2. In 4.3, two solutions, $x_{j,r_1,G}$ and $x_{j,r_2,G}$ are selected through the index r_1 and r_2 and their values subtracted. This value is then multiplied by F, the predefined scaling factor. This is added to the value indexed by r_3.
However, this solution is not arbitrarily accepted in the solution. A new random number is generated, and if this random number is less than the value of CR, then the new value replaces the old value in the current solution. Once all the values in the solution are obtained, the new solution is vetted for its fitness or value and if this improves on the value of the previous solution, the new solution replaces the previous solution in the population. Hence the competition is only between the new *child* solution and its *parent* solution.
Price (1999) has suggested ten different working strategies. It mainly depends on the problem on hand for which strategy to choose. The strategies vary on the solutions to be perturbed, number of differing solutions considered for perturbation, and finally the type of crossover used. The following are the different strategies being applied.

Strategy 1: DE/best/1/exp: $u_{i,G+1} = x_{best,G} + F \bullet (x_{r_1,G} - x_{r_2,G})$
Strategy 2: DE/rand/1/exp: $u_{i,G+1} = x_{r_1,G} + F \bullet (x_{r_2,G} - x_{r_3,G})$

Strategy 3: DE/rand−best/1/exp: $u_{i,G+1} = x_{i,G} + \lambda \bullet (x_{best,G} - x_{r_1,G}) + F \bullet (x_{r_1,G} - x_{r_2,G})$
Strategy 4: DE/best/2/exp: $u_{i,G+1} = x_{best,G} + F \bullet (x_{r_1,G} - x_{r_2,G} - x_{r_3,G} - x_{r_4,G})$
Strategy 5: DE/rand/2/exp: $u_{i,G+1} = x_{5,G} + F \bullet (x_{r_1,G} - x_{r_2,G} - x_{r_3,G} - x_{r_4,G})$
Strategy 6: DE/best/1/bin: $u_{i,G+1} = x_{best,G} + F \bullet (x_{r_1,G} - x_{r_2,G})$
Strategy 7: DE/rand/1/bin: $u_{i,G+1} = x_{r_1,G} + F \bullet (x_{r_2,G} - x_{r_3,G})$
Strategy 8: DE/rand−best/1/bin: $u_{i,G+1} = x_{i,G} + \lambda \bullet (x_{best,G} - x_{r_1,G}) + F \bullet (x_{r_1,G} - x_{r_2,G})$
Strategy 9: DE/best/2/bin: $u_{i,G+1} = x_{best,G} + F \bullet (x_{r_1,G} - x_{r_2,G} - x_{r_3,G} - x_{r_4,G})$
Strategy 10: DE/rand/2/bin: $u_{i,G+1} = x_{5,G} + F \bullet (x_{r_1,G} - x_{r_2,G} - x_{r_3,G} - x_{r_4,G})$

The convention shown is DE/x/y/z. DE stands for Differential Evolution, x represents a string denoting the solution to be perturbed, y is the number of difference solutions considered for perturbation of x, and z is the type of crossover being used (exp: exponential; bin: binomial).

DE has two main phases of crossover: binomial and exponential. Generally, a child solution $u_{i,G+1}$ is either taken from the parent solution $x_{i,G}$ or from a mutated donor solution $v_{i,G+1}$ as shown : $u_{j,i,G+1} = v_{j,i,G+1} = x_{j,r_3,G} + F \bullet \left(x_{j,r_1,G} - x_{j,r_2,G}\right)$.

The frequency with which the donor solution $v_{i,G+1}$ is chosen over the parent solution $x_{i,G}$ as the source of the child solution is controlled by both phases of crossover. This is achieved through a user defined constant, crossover CR which is held constant throughout the execution of the heuristic.

The *binomial* scheme takes parameters from the donor solution every time that the generated random number is less than the CR as given by $rand_j[0,1] < CR$, else all parameters come from the parent solution $x_{i,G}$.

The *exponential* scheme takes the child solutions from $x_{i,G}$ until the first time that the random number is greater than CR, as given by $rand_j[0,1] < CR$, otherwise the parameters comes from the parent solution $x_{i,G}$.

To ensure that each child solution differs from the parent solution, both the exponential and binomial schemes take at least one value from the mutated donor solution $v_{i,G+1}$.

3.1 Tuning parameters

Outlining an absolute value for CR is difficult. It is largely problem dependent. However a few guidelines have been laid down by Price (1999). When using binomial scheme, intermediate values of CR produce good results. If the objective function is known to be separable, then $CR = 0$ in conjunction with binomial scheme is recommended. The recommended value of CR should be close to or equal to 1, since the possibility or crossover occurring is high. The higher the value of CR, the greater the possibility of the random number generated being less than the value of CR, and thus initiating the crossover.

The general description of F is that it should be at least above 0.5, in order to provide sufficient scaling of the produced value.

The tuning parameters and their guidelines are given in Table 1.

4. Enhanced differential evolution algorithm

Enhanced Differential Evolution (EDE) (Davendra, 2001; Davendra & Onwubolu, 2007a; Onwubolu & Davendra, 2006; 2009), heuristic is an extension of the Discrete Differential Evolution (DDE) variant of DE (Davendra & Onwubolu, 2007b). One of the major drawbacks

Control Variables	Lo	Hi	Best?	Comments
F: Scaling Factor	0	1.0+	0.3 – 0.9	F $\geq$ 0.5
CR: Crossover probability	0	1	0.8 – 1.0	CR = 0, seperable CR = 1, epistatic

Table 1. Guide to choosing best initial control variables

of the DDE algorithm was the high frequency of in-feasible solutions, which were created after evaluation. However, since DDE showed much promise, the next logical step was to devise a method, which would repair the in-feasible solutions and hence add viability to the heuristic. To this effect, three different repairment strategies were developed, each of which used a different index to repair the solution. After repairment, three different enhancement features were added. This was done to add more depth to the DDE problem in order to solve permutative problems. The enhancement routines were standard mutation, insertion and local search. The basic outline is given in Figure 2.

4.1 Permutative population

The first part of the heuristic generates the permutative population. A permutative solution is one, where each value within the solution is unique and systematic. A basic description is

1. **Initial Phase**
   (a) *Population Generation*: An initial number of discrete trial solutions are generated for the initial population.
2. **Conversion**
   (a) *Discrete to Floating Conversion*: This conversion schema transforms the parent solution into the required continuous solution.
   (b) *DE Strategy*: The DE strategy transforms the parent solution into the child solution using its inbuilt crossover and mutation schemas.
   (c) *Floating to Discrete Conversion*: This conversion schema transforms the continuous child solution into a discrete solution.
3. **Mutation**
   (a) *Relative Mutation Schema*: Formulates the child solution into the discrete solution of unique values.
4. **Improvement Strategy**
   (a) *Mutation*: Standard mutation is applied to obtain a better solution.
   (b) *Insertion*: Uses a two-point cascade to obtain a better solution.
5. **Local Search**
   (a) *Local Search*: 2 Opt local search is used to explore the neighborhood of the solution.

Fig. 2. EDE outline

given in Equation 2.

$$
\begin{aligned}
P_G &= \{x_{1,G}, x_{2,G}, ..., x_{NP,G}\},\ x_{i,G} = x_{j,i,G} \\
x_{j,i,G=0} &= (\text{int})\left(rand_j\,[0,1] \bullet \left(x_j^{(hi)} + 1 - x_j^{(lo)}\right) + \left(x_j^{(lo)}\right)\right) \\
&\qquad if\ x_{j,i} \notin \left\{x_{0,i}, x_{1,i}, ..., x_{j-1,i}\right\} \\
i &= \{1,2,3,...,NP\}, j = \{1,2,3,..,D\}
\end{aligned}
\tag{2}
$$

where P_G represents the population, $x_{j,i,G=0}$ represents each solution within the population and $x_j^{(lo)}$ and $x_j^{(hi)}$ represents the bounds. The index i references the solution from 1 to NP, and j which references the values in the solution.

4.2 Forward transformation

The transformation schema represents the most integral part of the DDE problem. Onwubolu (Onwubolu, 2005) developed an effective routine for the conversion.
Let a set of integer numbers be represented as in Equation 3:

$$x_i \in x_{i,G} \tag{3}$$

which belong to solution $x_{j,i,G=0}$. The equivalent continuous value for x_i is given as $1 \bullet 10^2 < 5 \bullet 10^2 \leq 10^2$.
The domain of the variable x_i has length of 5 as shown in $5 \bullet 10^2$. The precision of the value to be generated is set to two decimal places (2 d.p.) as given by the superscript two (2) in 10^2 . The range of the variable x_i is between 1 and 10^3. The lower bound is 1 whereas the upper bound of 10^3 was obtained after extensive experimentation. The upper bound 10^3 provides optimal filtering of values which are generated close together (Davendra & Onwubolu, 2007b). The formulation of the forward transformation is given as:

$$x_i' = -1 + \frac{x_i \bullet f \bullet 5}{10^3 - 1} \tag{4}$$

Equation 4 when broken down, shows the value x_i multiplied by the length 5 and a scaling factor f. This is then divided by the upper bound minus one (1). The value computed is then decrement by one (1). The value for the scaling factor f was established after extensive experimentation. It was found that when f was set to 100, there was a tight grouping of the value, with the retention of optimal filtration′s of values. The subsequent formulation is given as:

$$x_i' = -1 + \frac{x_i \bullet f \bullet 5}{10^3 - 1} = -1 + \frac{x_i \bullet f \bullet 5}{10^3 - 1} \tag{5}$$

4.3 Backward transformation

The reverse operation to forward transformation, backward transformation converts the real value back into integer as given in Equation 6 assuming x_i to be the real value obtained from Equation 5.

$$\text{int}\,[x_i] = \frac{(1 + x_i) \bullet (10^3 - 1)}{5 \bullet f} = \frac{(1 + x_i) \bullet (10^3 - 1)}{500} \tag{6}$$

The value x_i is rounded to the nearest integer.

4.4 Recursive mutation

Once the solution is obtained after transformation, it is checked for feasibility. Feasibility refers to whether the solutions are within the bounds and unique in the solution.

$$x_{i,G+1} = \begin{cases} u_{i,G+1} \text{ if } \begin{cases} u_{j,i,G+1} \neq \left\{u_{1,i,G+1}, ..., u_{j-1,i,G+1}\right\} \\ x^{(lo)} \leq u_{j,i,G+1} \leq x^{(lo)} \end{cases} \\ x_{i,G} \end{cases} \tag{7}$$

Recursive mutation refers to the fact that if a solution is deemed in-feasible, it is discarded and the parent solution is retained in the population as given in Equation 7.

4.5 Repairment

In order to repair the solutions, each solution is initially vetted. Vetting requires the resolution of two parameters: firstly to check for any bound offending values, and secondly for repeating values in the solution. If a solution is detected to have violated a bound, it is dragged to the offending boundary.

$$u_{j,i,G+1} = \begin{cases} x^{(lo)} \text{ if } u_{j,i,G+1} < x^{(lo)} \\ x^{(hi)} \text{ if } u_{j,i,G+1} > x^{(hi)} \end{cases} \tag{8}$$

Each value, which is replicated, is tagged for its value and index. Only those values, which are deemed replicated, are repaired, and the rest of the values are not manipulated. A second sequence is now calculated for values, which are not present in the solution. It stands to reason that if there are replicated values, then some feasible values are missing. The pseudocode is given in Figure 3

Three unique repairment strategies were developed to repair the replicated values: *front mutation, back mutation* and *random mutation*, named after the indexing used for each particular one.

Algorithm for Replication Detection

Assume a problem of size n, and a schedule given as $X = \{x_1, .., x_n\}$. Create a *random* solution schedule $\exists! x_i : R(X) := \{x_1, .., x_i .., x_n\}; i \in Z^+$, where each value is unique and between the bounds $x^{(lo)}$ and $x^{(hi)}$.

1. Create a partial empty schedule $P(X) := \{\}$
2. For $k = 1, 2, ..., n$ do the following:
   (a) Check if $x_k \in P(X)$.
   (b) **IF** $x_k \notin P(X)$
       Insert $x_k \rightarrow P(X_k)$
   ELSE
       $P(X_k) = \emptyset$
3. Generate a missing subset $M(X) := R(X) \backslash P(X)$.

Fig. 3. Pseudocode for replication detection

Algorithm for Random Mutation

Assume a problem of size n, and a schedule given as $X = \{x_1, .., x_n\}$. Assume the missing subset $M(X)$ and partial subset $P(X)$ from Figure 3.

1. For $k = 1, 2, ..., n$ do the following:
   (a) **IF** $P(X_k) = \emptyset$
   Randomly select a value from the $M(X)$ and insert it in $P(X_k)$ given as $M(X_{Rnd}) \rightarrow P(X_k)$
   (b) Remove the used value from the $M(X)$.
2. Output $P(X)$ as the obtained complete schedule.

Fig. 4. Pseudocode for random mutation

4.5.1 Random mutation

The most complex repairment schema is the random mutation routine. Each value is selected randomly from the replicated array and replaced randomly from the missing value array as given in Figure 4.
Since each value is randomly selected, the value has to be removed from the array after selection in order to avoid duplication. Through experimentation it was shown that random mutation was the most effective in solution repairment.

4.6 Improvement strategies

Improvement strategies were included in order to improve the quality of the solutions. Three improvement strategies were embedded into the heuristic. All of these are one time application based. What this entails is that, once a solution is created each strategy is applied only once to that solution. If improvement is shown, then it is accepted as the new solution, else the original solution is accepted in the next population.

4.6.1 Standard mutation

Standard mutation is used as an improvement technique, to explore random regions of space in the hopes of finding a better solution. Standard mutation is simply the exchange of two values in the single solution.
Two unique random values are selected $r_1, r_2 \in rand[1, D]$, where as $r_1 \neq r_2$. The values indexed by these values are exchanged: $Solution_{r_1} \overset{exchange}{\leftrightarrow} Solution_{r_1}$ and the solution is evaluated. If the fitness improves, then the new solution is accepted in the population. The routine is shown in Figure 5.

4.6.2 Insertion

Insertion is a more complicated form of mutation. However, insertion is seen as providing greater diversity to the solution than standard mutation.
As with standard mutation, two unique random numbers are selected $r_1, r_2 \in rand[1, D]$. The value indexed by the lower random number $Solution_{r_1}$ is removed and the solution from that value to the value indexed by the other random number is shifted one index down. The removed value is then inserted in the vacant slot of the higher indexed value $Solution_{r_2}$ as given in Figure 6.

Algorithm for Standard Mutation

Assume a schedule given as $X = \{x_1, .., x_n\}$.

1. Obtain two random numbers r_1 and r_2, where $r_1 = rnd\left(x^{(lo)}, x^{(hi)}\right)$ and $r_2 = rnd\left(x^{(lo)}, x^{(hi)}\right)$, the constraint being $r_1 \neq r_2$
   (a) Swap the two indexed values in the solution
      i. $x_{r_1} = x_{r_2}$ and $x_{r_2} = x_{r_1}$.
   (b) Evaluate the new schedule X' for its objective given as $f(X')$.
   (c) **IF** $f(X') < f(X)$
      i. Set the old schedule X to the new improved schedule X' as $X = X'$.
2. Output X as the new schedule.

Fig. 5. Pseudocode for standard mutation

4.7 Local search

There is always a possibility of stagnation in evolutionary algorithms. DE is no exemption to this phenomenon.

Stagnation is the state where there is no improvement in the populations over a period of generations. The solution is unable to find new search space in order to find global optimal solutions. The length of stagnation is not usually defined. Sometimes a period of twenty generation does not constitute stagnation. Also care has to be taken as not be confuse the local optimal solution with stagnation. Sometimes, better search space simply does not exist. In EDE, a period of five generations of non-improving optimal solution is classified as stagnation. Five generations is taken in light of the fact that EDE usually operates on an average of a hundred generations. This yields to the maximum of twenty stagnations within one run of the heuristic.

Algorithm for Insertion

Assume a schedule given as $X = \{x_1, .., x_n\}$.

1. Obtain two random numbers r_1 and r_2, where $r_1 = rnd\left(x^{(lo)}, x^{(hi)}\right)$ and $r_2 = rnd\left(x^{(lo)}, x^{(hi)}\right)$, the constraints being $r_1 \neq r_2$ and $r_1 < r_2$.
   (a) Remove the value indexed by r_1 in the schedule X.
   (b) For k=r_1,.....,$r_2 - 1$, do the following:
      i. $x_k = x_{k+1}$.
   (c) Insert the higher indexed value r_2 by the lower indexed value r_1 as: $X_{r_2} = X_{r_1}$.
2. Output X as the new schedule.

Fig. 6. Pseudocode for Insertion

To move away from the point of stagnation, a feasible operation is a neighborhood or local search, which can be applied to a solution to find better feasible solution in the local neighborhood. Local search in an improvement strategy. It is usually independent of the search heuristic, and considered as a plug-in to the main heuristic. The point of note is that local search is very expensive in terms of time and memory. Local search can sometimes be considered as a brute force method of exploring the search space. These constraints make the insertion and the operation of local search very delicate to implement. The route that EDE has adapted is to check the optimal solution in the population for stagnation, instead of the whole population. As mentioned earlier five (5) non-improving generations constitute stagnation. The point of insertion of local search is very critical. The local search is inserted at the termination of the improvement module in the EDE heuristic.

Local search is an approximation algorithm or heuristic. Local search works on a *neighborhood*. A complete *neighborhood* of a solution is defined as the set of all solutions that can be arrived at by a move. The word solution should be explicitly defined to reflect the problem being solved. This variant of the local search routine is described in Onwubolu (2002) and is generally known as a 2-opt local search.

The basic outline of a local search technique is given in Figure 7. A number α is chosen equal to zero (0) ($\alpha = \emptyset$). This number iterates through the entire population, by choosing each progressive value from the solution. On each iteration of α, a random number i is chosen which is between the lower (1) and upper (n) bound. A second number β starts at the position i, and iterates till the end of the solution. In this second iteration another random number j is chosen, which is between the lower and upper bound and not equal to value of β. The values in the solution indexed by i and j are swapped. The objective function of the new solution is calculated and only if there is an improvement given as $\Delta(x,i,j) < 0$, then the new solution is accepted.

The complete template of EDE is given in Figure 8.

Algorithm for Local Search

Assume a schedule given as $X = \{x_1, .., x_n\}$, and two indexes α and β. The size of the schedule is given as n. Set $\alpha = 0$.

1. **While** $\alpha < n$
   (a) Obtain a random number $i = rand[1,n]$ between the bounds and under constraint $i \notin \alpha$.
   (b) Set $\beta = \{i\}$
      i. **While** $\beta < n$
         A. Obtain another random number $j = rand[1,n]$ under constraint $j \notin \beta$.
         B. **IF** $\Delta(x,i,j) < 0; \begin{cases} x_i = x_j \\ x_j = x_i \end{cases}$
         C. $\beta = \beta \cup \{j\}$
      ii. $\alpha = \alpha \cup \{j\}$

Fig. 7. Pseudocode for 2 Opt Local Search

Enhanced Differential Evolution Template

$$\text{Input}: D, G_{\max}, NP \geq 4, F \in (0,1+), CR \in [0,1], \text{and bounds}: x^{(lo)}, x^{(hi)}.$$

$$\text{Initialize}: \begin{cases} \forall i \leq NP \wedge \forall j \leq D \begin{cases} x_{i,j,G=0} = x_j^{(lo)} + rand_j[0,1] \bullet \left(x_j^{(hi)} - x_j^{(lo)}\right) \\ if\ x_{j,i} \notin \left\{x_{0,i}, x_{1,i}, ..., x_{j-1,i}\right\} \end{cases} \\ i = \{1,2,...,NP\}, j = \{1,2,...,D\}, G = 0, rand_j[0,1] \in [0,1] \end{cases}$$

$$\text{Cost}: \forall i \leq NP : f\left(x_{i,G=0}\right)$$

$$\begin{cases} \text{While } G < G_{\max} \\ \forall i \leq NP \begin{cases} \text{Mutate and recombine}: \\ r_1, r_2, r_3 \in \{1,2,....,NP\}, \text{randomly selected, except}: r_1 \neq r_2 \neq r_3 \neq i \\ j_{rand} \in \{1,2,...,D\}, \text{randomly selected once each } i \\ \forall j \leq D, u_{j,i,G+1} = \begin{cases} \left(\gamma_{j,r_3,G}\right) \leftarrow \left(x_{j,r_3,G}\right) : \left(\gamma_{j,r_1,G}\right) \leftarrow \left(x_{j,r_1,G}\right) : \\ \left(\gamma_{j,r_2,G}\right) \leftarrow \left(x_{j,r_2,G}\right) \quad \text{Forward Transformation} \\ \gamma_{j,r_3,G} + F \cdot \left(\gamma_{j,r_1,G} - \gamma_{j,r_2,G}\right) \\ \quad \text{if } \left(rand_j[0,1] < CR \vee j = j_{rand}\right) \\ \left(\gamma_{j,i,G}\right) \leftarrow \left(x_{j,i,G}\right) \quad \text{otherwise} \end{cases} \\ \left(u'_{i,G+1}\right) = \begin{cases} \left(\rho_{j,i,G+1}\right) \leftarrow \left(\varphi_{j,i,G+1}\right) \text{Backward Transformation} \\ \left(u_{j,i,G+1}\right) \overset{mutate}{\leftarrow} \left(\rho_{j,i,G+1}\right) \text{Mutate Schema} \\ \text{if} \left(u'_{j,i,G+1}\right) \notin \left\{\left(u_{0,i,G+1}\right), \left(u_{1,i,G+1}\right), .. \left(u_{j-1,i,G+1}\right)\right\} \end{cases} \\ \left(u_{j,i,G+1}\right) \leftarrow \left(u'_{i,G+1}\right) \text{Standard Mutation} \\ \left(u_{j,i,G+1}\right) \leftarrow \left(u'_{i,G+1}\right) \text{Insertion} \\ \text{Select}: \\ x_{i,G+1} = \begin{cases} u_{i,G+1} \text{ if } f(u_{i,G+1}) \leq f(x_{i,G}) \\ x_{i,G} \quad \text{otherwise} \end{cases} \end{cases} \\ G = G + 1 \\ \text{Local Search} \quad x_{best} = \Delta\left(x_{best}, i, j\right) \quad \text{if stagnation} \end{cases}$$

Fig. 8. EDE Template

5. Chaotic systems

Chaos theory has its manifestation in the study of dynamical systems that exhibit certain behavior due to the perturbation of the initial conditions of the systems. A number of such systems have been discovered and this branch of mathematics has been vigorously researched for the last few decades.

The area of interest for this chapter is the embedding of chaotic systems in the form of *chaos number generator* for an evolutionary algorithm.

The systems of interest are *discrete dissipative* systems. The two common systems of Lozi map and Delayed Logistic (DL) were selected as mutation generators for the DE heuristic.

5.1 Lozi map

The Lozi map is a two-dimensional piecewise linear map whose dynamics are similar to those of the better known Henon map (Hennon, 1979) and it admits strange attractors.
The advantage of the Lozi map is that one can compute every relevant parameter exactly, due to the linearity of the map, and the successful control can be demonstrated rigorously.
The Lozi map equations are given in Equations 9 and 10.

$$y_1(t+1) = 1 - a\,|y_1(t)| + y_2(t) \tag{9}$$

$$y_2(t+1) = by_1(t) \tag{10}$$

The parameters used in this work are $a = 1.7$ and $b = 0.5$ as suggested in Caponetto et al. (2003). The Lozi map is given in Figure 9.

5.2 Delayed logistic map

The Delayed Logistic (DL) map equations are given in Equations 11 and 12.

$$y_1(t+1) = y_2 \tag{11}$$

$$y_2(t+1) = ay_2(1 - y_1) \tag{12}$$

The parameters used in this work is $a = 2.27$. The DL map is given in Figure 10.

6. Experimentation

The experimentation has been done on a few representative instances of both symmetric and asymmetric TSP problems. The chaotic maps are embedded in the place of the random

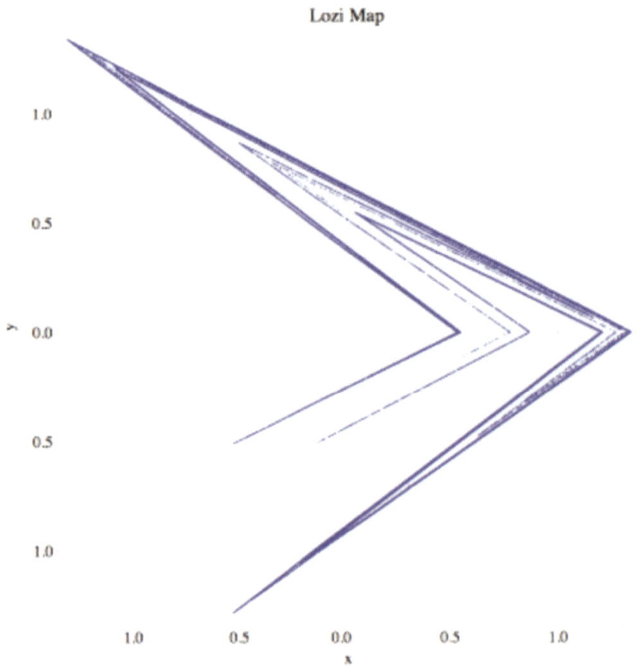

Fig. 9. Lozi map

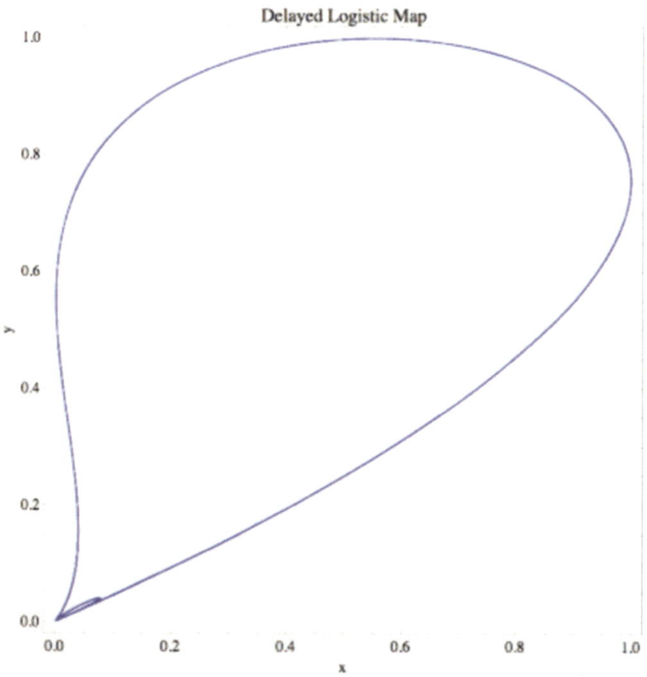

Fig. 10. Delayed Logistic

number generator in the EDE algorithm and the new algorithm is termed EDE_C. Five repeated experimentation of each instance is done by the two different chaotic embedded algorithms. The average results of all the ten experimentation is compared with EDE and published results in literature.

6.1 Symmetric TSP

Symmetric TSP problem is one, where the distance between two cities is the same *to* and *fro*. This is considered the easiest branch of TSP problem.

The operational parameters for TSP is given in Table 2.

Experimentation was conducted on the *City* problem instances. These instances are of 50 cities and the results are presented in Table 3. Comparison was done with Ant Colony (ACS) (Dorigo & Gambardella, 1997), Simulated Annealing (SA) (Lin et al., 1993), Elastic Net (EN) (Durbin & Willshaw, 1987), Self Organising Map (SOM) (Kara et al., 2003) and EDE of Davendra & Onwubolu (2007a). The time values are presented alongside.

In comparison, ACS is the best performing heuristic for TSP, and EDE_C is second best performing heuristic. On average EDE_C is only 0.02 above the values obtained by ACS. It

Parameter	Value
Strategy	5
CR	0.8
F	0.5
NP	100
Generation	50

Table 2. EDE_C TSP operational values

Instant	ACS	SA	EN	SOM	EDE	EDE_C
City set 1	5.88	5.88	5.98	6.06	5.98	5.89
City set 2	6.05	6.01	6.03	6.25	6.04	6.02
City set 3	5.58	5.65	5.7	5.83	5.69	5.61
City set 4	5.74	5.81	5.86	5.87	5.81	5.78
City set 5	6.18	6.33	6.49	6.7	6.48	6.21
Average	5.88	5.93	6.01	6.14	6	5.9

Table 3. Symmetric TSP comparison

must be noted that all execution time for EDE_C was under 10 seconds. Extended simulation would possibly lead to better results.

6.2 Asymmetric TSP

Asymmetric TSP is the problem where the distance between the different cities is different, depending on the direction of travel. Five different instances were evaluated and compared with Ant Colony (ACS) with local search (Dorigo & Gambardella, 1997) and EDE of Davendra & Onwubolu (2007a). The results are given in Table 4.

Instant	Optimal	ACS 3-OPT best	ACS 3-OPT average	EDE average	EDE_C average
p43	5620	5620	5620	5639	5620
ry48p	14422	14422	14422	15074	14525
ft70	38673	38673	38679.8	40285	39841
kro124p	36230	36230	36230	41180	39574
ftv170	2755	2755	2755	6902	4578

Table 4. Asymmetric TSP comparison

ACS heuristic performs very well, obtaining the optimal value, whereas EDE has an average performance. EDE_C significantly improves the performance of EDE. One of the core difference is that ACS employs 3−Opt local search on each generation of its best solution, where as EDE_c has a 2−Opt routine valid only in local optima stagnation.

7. Conclusion

The chaotic maps used in this research are of dissipative systems, and through experimentation have proven very effective. The results clearly validate that the chaotic maps provide a better alternative to random number generators in the task of sampling of the fitness landscape.

This chapter has just introduced the concept of chaotic driven evolutionary algorithms. Much work remains, as the correct mapping structure has to be investigated as well as the effectiveness of this approach to other combinatorial optimization problems.

8. Acknowledgement

The following two grants are acknowledged for the financial support provided for this research.

1. Grant Agency of the Czech Republic - GACR 102/09/1680
2. Grant of the Czech Ministry of Education - MSM 7088352102

9. References

Bland, G. & Shallcross, D. (1989). Large traveling salesman problems arising fromexperiments in x-ray crystallography: A preliminary report on computation, *Operation Research Letters* Vol. 8: 125–128.

Caponetto, R., Fortuna, L., Fazzino, S. & Xibilia, M. (2003). Chaotic sequences to improve the performance of evolutionary algorithms, *IEEE Transactions on Evolutionary Computation* Vol. 7: 289–304.

Davendra, D. (2001). *Differential evolution algorithm for flow shop scheduling*, Master's thesis, University of the South Pacific.

Davendra, D. & Onwubolu, G. (2007a). Enhanced differential evolution hybrid scatter search for discrete optimisation, *Proc. of the IEEE Congress on Evolutionary Computation*, Singapore, pp. 1156–1162.

Davendra, D. & Onwubolu, G. (2007b). Flow shop scheduling using enhanced differential evolution, *Proc.21 European Conference on Modeling and Simulation*, Prague, Czech Rep, pp. 259–264.

Davendra, D. & Zelinka, I. (2010). Controller parameters optimization on a representative set of systems using deterministic-chaotic-mutation evolutionary algorithms, *in* I. Zelinka, S. Celikovsky, H. Richter & C. G (eds), *Evolutionary Algorithms and Chaotic Systems*, Springer-Verlag, Germany.

Dorigo, M. & Gambardella, L. (1997). Ant colony system: A co-operative learning approach to the traveling salesman problem, *IEEE Transactions on Evolutionary Computation* Vol. 1: 53–65.

Durbin, R. & Willshaw, D. (1987). An analogue approach to the travelling salesman problem using the elastic net method, *Nature* Vol. 326: 689–691.

Garey, M. (1979). *Computers and Intractability: A Guide to the Theory of NP-Completeness*, W. H. Freeman, San Francisco.

Hennon, M. (1979). A two-dimensional mapping with a strange attractor, *Communications in Mathematical Physics* Vol. 50: 69–77.

Kara, L., Atkar, P. & Conner, D. (2003). Traveling salesperson problem (tsp) using shochastic search. advanced ai assignment, *Carnegie Mellon Assignment* Vol. 15213.

Korte, B. (1988). Applications of combinatorial optimization, *13th International Mathematical Programming Symposium*, Tokyo.

Land, A. & Doig, A. (1960). An automatic method of solving discrete programming problems, *Econometrica* Vol. 28(3): 497–520.

Lin, F., Kao, C. & Hsu (1993). Applying the genetic approach to simulated annealing in solving np- hard problems, *IEEE Transactions on Systems, Man, and Cybernetics - Part B* Vol. 23: 1752–1767.

Lin, S. & Kernighan, B. (1973). An effective heuristic algorithm for the traveling-salesman problem, *Operations Research* Vol. 21(2): 498–516.

Onwubolu, G. (2002). *Emerging Optimization Techniques in Production Planning and Control*, Imperial Collage Press, London, England.

Onwubolu, G. (2005). Optimization using differential evolution, *Technical Report TR-2001-05*, IAS, USP, Fiji.

Onwubolu, G. & Davendra, D. (2006). Scheduling flow shops using differential evolution algorithm, *European Journal of Operations Research* 171: 674–679.

Onwubolu, G. & Davendra, D. (2009). *Differential Evolution: A Handbook for Global Permutation-Based Combinatorial Optimization*, Springer, Germany.

Price, K. (1999). An introduction to differential evolution, *New ideas in Optimisation*, US.

5

A Fast Evolutionary Algorithm for Traveling Salesman Problem

Xuesong Yan, Qinghua Wu and Hui Li
School of Computer Science, China University of Geosciences,
Faculty of Computer Science and Engineering, Wu-Han Institute of Technology,
China

1. Introduction

The traveling salesman problem (TSP)[1] is one of the most widely studied NP-hard combinatorial optimization problems. Its statement is deceptively simple, and yet it remains one of the most challenging problems in Operational Research. The simple description of TSP is: Give a shortest path that covers all cities along. Let G = (V; E) be a graph where V is a set of vertices and E is a set of edges. Let C = (cij) be a distance (or cost) matrix associated with E. The TSP requires determination of a minimum distance circuit (Hamiltonian circuit or cycle) passing through each vertex once and only once. C is said to satisfy the triangle inequality if and only if cij + cjk $\geqq$ cik for all i, j, k V.

Due to its simple description and wide application in real practice such as Path Problem, Routing Problem and Distribution Problem, it has attracted researchers of various domains to work for its better solutions. Those traditional algorithms such as Cupidity Algorithm, Dynamic Programming Algorithm, are all facing the same obstacle, which is when the problem scale N reaches to a certain degree, the so-called "Combination Explosion" will occur. For example, if N=50, then it will take 5×10^{48} years under a super mainframe executing 100 million instructions per second to reach its approximate best solution.

A lot of algorithms have been proposed to solve TSP[2-7]. Some of them (based on dynamic programming or branch and bound methods) provide the global optimum solution. Other algorithms are heuristic ones, which are much faster, but they do not guarantee the optimal solutions. There are well known algorithms based on 2-opt or 3-opt change operators, Lin-Kerninghan algorithm (variable change) as well algorithms based on greedy principles (nearest neighbor, spanning tree, etc). The TSP was also approached by various modern heuristic methods, like simulated annealing, evolutionary algorithms and tabu search, even neural networks.

In this paper, we proposed a new algorithm based on Inver-over operator, for combinatorial optimization problems. In the new algorithm we use some new strategies including selection operator, replace operator and some new control strategy, which have been proved to be very efficient to accelerate the converge speed. At the same time, we also use this approach to solve dynamic TSP. The algorithm to solve the dynamic TSP problem, which is the hybrid of EN and Inver-Over algorithm.

2. Tradition approaches for travel salesman problems

2.1 Genetic algorithm (GA)

Genetic Algorithm is based on the idea of Darwin evolutionism and Mendel genetics that simulates the process of nature to solve complex searching problems. It adopts the strategy of encoding the population and the genetic operations, so as to direct the individuals' heuristic study and searching direction. Since GA owns the traits of self-organization, self-adaptation, self-study etc, it breaks away from the restriction of the searching space and some other auxiliary information. However, when facing different concrete problems (e.g. TSP), it's always necessary for us to seek better genetic operators and more efficient control strategy due to the gigantic solution space and limitation of computation capacity.

Use GA solve the TSP, including the following steps:

Chromosome Coding: In this paper, we will use the most direct way to denote TSP-path presentation. For example, path 4-2-1-3-4 can be denoted as (4, 2, 1, 3) or (2, 3, 1, 4) and it is referred as a chromosome. Every chromosome is regarded as a validate path. (In this paper, all paths should be considered as a ring, or closed path).

Fitness value: The only standard of judging whether an individual is "good" or not. We take the reciprocal of the length of each path as the fitness function. Length the shorter, fitness values the better. The fitness function is defined as following formula:

$$f(Si) = 1 \Big/ \sum_{i=1}^{N} d[C_{n(i)}, C_{n(i+1) \bmod N}] \tag{1}$$

Evolutionary Operator or Evolutionary Strategy: they are including selection operator, crossover operator and mutation operator.

Selection Strategy: After crossover or mutation, new generations are produced. In order to keep the total number consistent, those individuals who are not adjust to the environment must be deleted, whereas the more adaptive ones are kept.

Probability of mutation: In order to keep the population sample various, and prevent from trapping into local minimum, mutation is quite necessary. But to seek higher executing speed, the probability of mutation must be selected properly.

Terminal conditions: The stop condition of the algorithm.

2.2 A fast evolutionary algorithm based on inver-over operator

Inver-over operator has proved to be a high efficient Genetic Algorithm[2]. The creativity of this operator is that it adopts the operation of inversion in genetic operators, which can effectively broaden the variety of population and prevent from local minimum and lead to find the best solutions quickly and accurately. GT algorithm[2] is be perceived as a set of parallel hill-climbing procedures.

In this section, we introduce some new genetic operators based on GT. And there are also some modifications on some details, which aim to quicken the convergence speed. Numerical experiments show the algorithm can effectively keep the variety of population, and avoid prematurely in traditional algorithms. It has proved to be very efficient to solve small and moderate scale TSP; particularly, larger-scale problem can also get a fast convergence speed if we choose a small population that involves the evolution.

Selection Operator: Randomly select two chromosomes $S1, S2$ from population {P}, let f ($S2$)>f ($S1$); randomly select a gene segment $\Delta s1$ from $S1$, then judge if there is gene segment $\Delta s2$ in $S2$ that meets the conditions below: it has the same length (number of cities) and the starting city with $\Delta s1$. If $\Delta s2$ exists, replace $\Delta s1$ by $\Delta s2$ in chromosome $S1$, then the rest genes are adjusted follow the partly mapping rules.

Replace Operator: Randomly select two chromosomes $S1, S2$ from population {P}, let f ($S2$)>f ($S1$), let $S1$ be the parent, then randomly select a gene segment $\Delta s1$ in $S1$, then judge if there is a gene segment $\Delta s2$ exists in $S2$ that meets the conditions below: it has the same length (number of cities) and cities with $\Delta s1$, only the sequence of cities varies. If it exists, judge the distance of the two segments $\Delta s1$, $\Delta s2$. If $\Delta s2$ is shorter, replace $\Delta s1$ by $\Delta s2$ in $S1$; else quit.

The new algorithm mainly involves crossover operator, but crossover relies strongly on the current population and may be easily trapped into local minimum. So mutation is introduced and can effectively solve the problem. But mutation itself is blind; it can act efficiently at the beginning of the algorithm, but when it's converged round to the approximate best solution, the probability of successfully optimize the chromosome turns out to be very low. So Dynamically alter the probability of selecting mutation operator is necessary. We use the formula below to alter the probability of selecting mutation operator:

$$p = p \times (1 - GenNum \times 0.01 / \max Gen) \quad (2)$$

p is the probability of mutation, GenNum is the current evolutionary times; maxGen is the max evolutionary times when algorithm stops. Fig.2 provides a more detailed description of the whole algorithm in general.

```
Random initialization of the population P
While (not satisfied termination condition) do
i=0
Begin
  for each individual S_i ∈ P do
  begin (if i!=N)
{S' ← S_i
Select (randomly) a City C from S'
repeat
{begin
  if (rand() ≤ p_1)
    {select the city C' from S'
    invert the gene segment between C and C'
    }
  else
   {select (randomly) an individual S'' in P
assign to C' the next city to the city C in the select individual
}
  if (the next city or the previous city of city C in S' is C')
  exit repeat loop
```

```
  else
  {invert the gene segment between C and C'
   calculate d
   if(d<0 and evolutionary speed< critical speed)
   exit repeat loop
   }
   C ← C'
end
}
if (eval(S') ≤ eval(S_i))
   S_i ← S'
  i = i +1}
  end
calculate evolutionary speed and update the probability of mutation
if (evolutionary speed< critical speed and (rand() ≤ p_2)
 {select (randomly) S_1 , S_2 from P
  select (randomly) gene segment Δs1 from S_1
  if ( Δs1 = Δs2 and the starting city is same) // Δs2 in S_2
   replace Δs1 with Δs2
 }
Select the better gene segments from those adaptive chromosomes
if (eval(g_1) ≤ eval(g_2))
 g_1 ← g_2
end
```

In this section we present the experimental results of the proposed algorithm. All experiments are performed on PIV 2.4GHz/256M RAM PC. In the experiments all test cases were chosen from TSPLIB (http://www.iwr.uni-heidelberg.de/groups/comopt/software/TSPLIB95). The optimal solution of each test case is known. The parameters for algorithm are as Table.1.

Size of Population	100
Mutation Probability	0.02
Selection Probability	0.05
Critical Speed	5000

Table 1. Parameters for the algorithm

We list the test cases and their optimal solutions in Fig.1.

The above results demonstrate clearly the efficiency of the algorithm. Note that for the seven test cases the optimum was found in all ten runs. The number of cities in these test cases varies from 70 to 280. Note also, that the running time of the algorithm was reasonable: below 3 seconds for problems with up to 100 cities, below 10 seconds for the test case of 144 cities, below 40 seconds for the test case with 280 cities.

Instance	Result in TSPLIB	Optimum in TSPLIB	Our Result	Time
st70	675	678.597	677.109	0.67
eil76	538	545.387	544.369	1.16
kroA100	21282	21285.443	21285.443	1.69
rd100	7910	7910.396	7910.396	2.14
Pr136	96772	96772	96770.924	7.11
Pr144	58537	58537	58535.221	7.97
a280	2579	2856.769	2856.769	33.47

Fig. 1. Results of the algorithm

3. Information dynamic traveling salesman problem

Most research in evolutionary computation focused on optimization of static, no-change problems. Many real world optimization problems however are actually dynamic, and optimization methods capable of continuously adapting the solution to a changing environment are needed. The main problem with standard evolutionary algorithms used for dynamic optimization problems appears to be that EAs eventually converge to an optimum and thereby loose their diversity necessary for efficiently exploring the search space and consequently also their ability to adapt to a change in the environment when such a change occurs. Since Psaraftis [11] first introduced DTSP, some research works have touched on this area [3,4, 6,7,9,10]. However the research is just at the initial phase and quite a few crucial questions.

3.1 The elastic net method to TSP

The elastic net was first proposed as a biologically motivated method for solving combinatorial optimization problems such as the traveling salesman problem (TSP) [1]. In the method, let the coordinates of a city, i, be denoted by the vector ci, and let the coordinates of the route point (or unit), u, be tu. Define the TSP in terms of a mapping from a circle to a plane. The TSP consists of finding a mapping from a circle, h, to a finite set of points, C=ci…cN, in the plane, which minimizes the distance:

$$D = \oint_h f(s)ds \tag{3}$$

where the circle, h, is parameterized by arc-length, s, and f(s) provides a unique mapping from each point on h to a point on the plane. The locus of points defined by f(s) forms a loop, l, in the plane which passes through each city exactly once.

The loop, l, is modeled as finite set, t1..tM, of points, or units. Due to the difficulty in obtaining a one-to-one mapping of units to plane points (cities) it is customary to set M > N in order that each city can become associated with at least one unit.

The energy function to be minimized is:

$$E = -\alpha \sum_{i=1}^{N} \ln \sum_{u=1}^{M} \Phi(|c_i - t_u|, K - k \sum_{u=1}^{M} \ln \sum_{i=1}^{N} \Phi(|c_i - t_u|, k) + \beta \sum_{u-1}^{M} (|t_u - t_{u+1}|)^2 \tag{4}$$

where φ(d,K)=exp(-(d2/2K2)), and K is the standard deviation of the function, φ.
Differentiating E with respect to tu, and multiplying through by K, gives the change $(=-K\partial E/\partial t_u)$, Δt_u, in the position of a unit, u:

$$\Delta t_u = (\alpha \sum_{i=1}^{N} f_{ui} + k \sum_{u=1}^{M} b_{ui})(c_i - t_i) + \beta K(t_{u+1} - 2t_u + t_{u-1}) \tag{5}$$

where fui is like follow:

$$f_{ui} = \frac{\Phi(|c_i - t_u|, K)}{\sum_{v=1}^{M} \Phi(|c_i - t_v|, K)} \tag{6}$$

This term ensures that each city become associated with at least one unit. It is the Gaussian weighted distance of tu from ci expressed as a proportion of the distances to all other units from ci. In contrast, the term bui ensures that each unit becomes associated with at least one unit. It is the Gaussian weighted distance of ci from tu, expressed as proportion of the distances to all other cities from tu:

$$b_{ui} = \frac{\Phi(|c_i - t_u|, K)}{\sum_{v=1}^{M} \Phi(|c_i - t_v|, K)} \tag{7}$$

The EN method [8] is analogous to laying a circular loop of elastic on a plane containing a number of points (cities) and allowing each city to exert an attractive force on the loop. (In practice the EN method models this loop as finite set of points). Each city is associated with a Gaussian envelope which (using our physical analogy) effectively means that each city sits in a Gaussian depression on the plane. The standard deviation of the Gaussians associated with all cities is identical. Each city attracts a region on the elastic loop according to the proximity of that region to a given city and the standard deviation of the Gaussian. Initially the standard deviation is large, so that all regions on the loop are attracted to every city to the same extent (approximately) as every other region. As the standard deviation is decreased a city differentially attracts one or more nearby regions on the loop, at the expense of more distant loop regions. These loop-city interactions are modulated by the elasticity of the loop, which tends to keep the loop length short; the elasticity also tends to ensure that each city becomes associated with only one loop region. For a given standard deviation the integral of loop motion associated with each city is constant, and is the same for all cities, so that each city induces the same amount of motion of the loop. By slowly decreasing the standard deviation each city becomes associated with a single point on the loop_ Thus the loop ultimately defines a route of the cities it passes through. If the standard deviation is reduced sufficiently slowly then the loop passes through every city; and therefore defines a complete route through all cities.

3.2 The elastic net method to dynamic TSP

Dynamic TSP (D-TSP)[4] is a TSP determined by the dynamic cost (distance) matrix as follows:

$$D(t) = \{d_{ij}(t)\}_{n(t)\times n(t)} \tag{8}$$

where dij(t) is the cost from city(node) i to city j, t is the real world time. This means that the number of cities n(t) and the cost matrix are time dependent that's (1)some cities may appear, (2)some may disappear and (3)the locations of some may be modified with time going on. These are the three types of actions to a D-TSP.
The D-TSP solver should be designed as solutions of a two-objective optimization problem. One is to minimize the size of time windows:

$$s_k = t - t_k \tag{9}$$

where t tk. The other is to minimize the length of $\pi(t_k) = (\pi_1, \pi_2, ..., \pi_{n(t_k)})$:

$$d(\pi(t_k)) = \sum_{i=1}^{n(t_k)} d_{\pi_i, \pi_{i+1}}(t_k) \tag{10}$$

where $\pi_{n(t_k)+1} = \pi_1$.
The two objectives mean that the solver is to find the best tour in the minimal time window. If this aim cannot be satisfied, we can make some tradeoffs between the two objectives.
We introduce the thought of the EN method into dynamic TSP. First, suppose we have already attained the maximum optimum of static TSP. Second, add a dynamic point. When the dynamic point moves to a position, we can use the EN method to attain the maximum optimum route. The whole processing like Fig.2 shows.

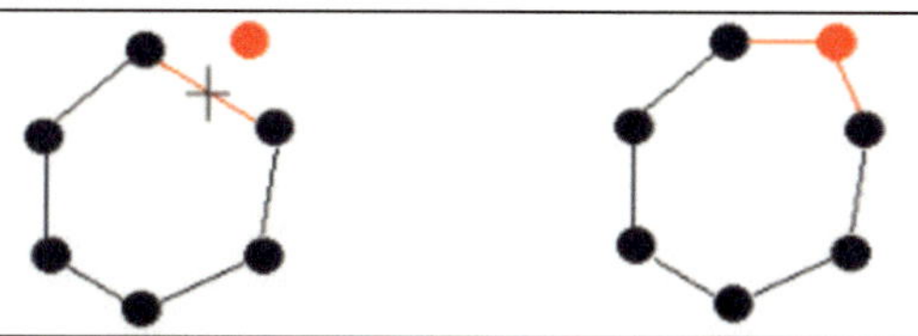

Fig. 2. The processing of EN method to dynamic point

Because the dynamic TSP needs give the maximum optimum in real-time, so the computation speed very high. Gou's algorithm [2] with Inver-Over operator is a very efficient evolutionary algorithm for static TSP with high speed and more details about this algorithm can be got in [5]. We convert it with EN method to solve dynamic TSP. The algorithm code like following shows.

```
DEN Algorithm ()
{
 Initiate parameter;
 Initiate population {Pi};
 While true do
 {
   Attain dynamic point position (x', y');
   Inver-Over (x [], y [], path [], M);
   EN (x [], y [], path [], x', y');
 }
}
```

3.3 Experiments and results

We have evaluated the algorithm and test it with the data set from TSPLIB (http://www.iwr.uni-heidelberg.de/groups/comopt/software/TSPLIB95). Fig.3 is the example of the DEN algorithm to KeroA150 in different time. In the example, the red point is the dynamic point and it moves around circle. From the example, we can see in different time, the dynamic point in different position and has the different distance. It shows this example is a dynamic problem. Through the experiment, we find the DEN algorithm cannot guarantee the route to be the maximum optimum, but this algorithm can move the dynamic point and confirm it to the new route very fast. So, it is very valid to solve dynamic TSP problem.

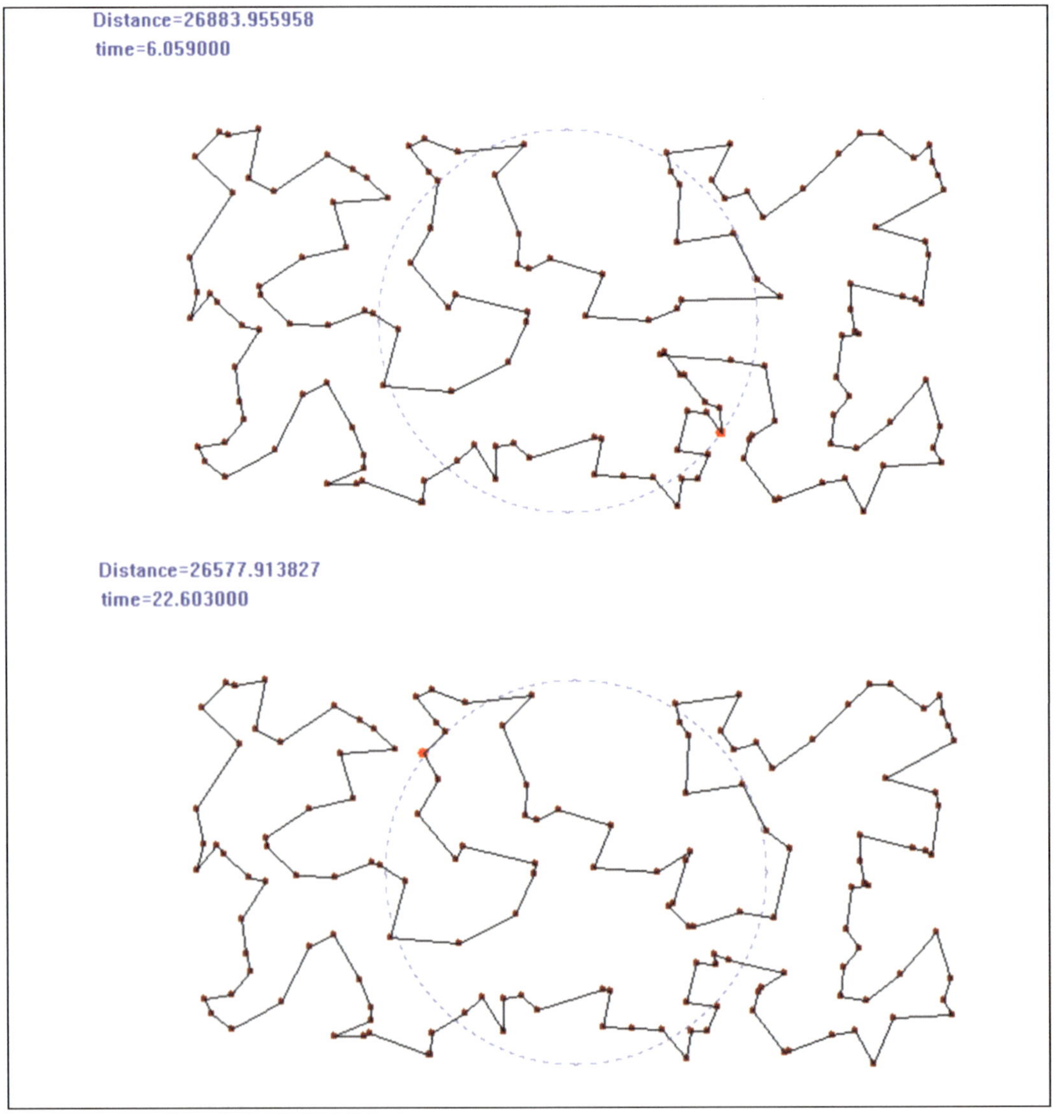

Fig. 3. DEN algorithm to KeroA150 in different time

4. Conclusion

In this paper, we introduce a fast evolutionary algorithm for combinatorial optimization problem. This algorithm is based on Inver-over operator, in the algorithm we use some new strategies including selection operator, replace operator and some new control strategy, which have been proved to be very efficient to accelerate the converge speed. The new algorithm shows great efficiency in solving TSP with the problem scale under 300. Particularly, if we choose a comparatively smaller population scale that involves evolution, the algorithm is also efficient to get the approximate best solution in a short executing time. In this paper, we also introduce an approach to solve dynamic TSP-- Elastic Net Method. A dynamic TSP is harder than a general TSP, which is a NP-hard problem, because the city number and the cost matrix of a dynamic TSP are time varying. And needs high computation speed. We propose the algorithm to solve the dynamic TSP, which is a hybrid of EN method and Inver-Over. Through the experiment, we got good results. Some strategies may increase the searching speed of evolutionary algorithms for dynamic TSP, forecasting the change pattern of the cities and per-optimizing, doing more experiments including changing the city number, and etc. These will be our future work.

5. References

Durbin R, Willshaw D. (1987). An Anlaogue Approach to the Traveling Salesman Problem Using an Elastic Net Approach. Nature, 326, 6114, pp. 689-691.

T.Guo and Z.Michalewize. (1998). Inver-Over operator for the TSP. In Parallel Problem Sovling from Nature(PPSN V),Springer-Verlag press, pp. 803-812.

Z.C.Huang, X.L.Hu and S.D.Chen. (2001). Dynamic Traveling Salesman Problem based on Evolutionary Computation. In Congress on Evolutionary Computation(CEC'01), pp. 1283-1288, IEEE Press.

Aimin Zhou, Lishan Kang and Zhenyu Yan. (2003). Solving Dynamic TSP with Evolutionary Approach in Real Time. In Congress on Evolutionary Computation(CEC'03), pp. 951-957, IEEE Press.

H.Yang, L.S.Kang and Y.P.Chen. (2003). A Gene-pool Based Genetic Algorithm for TSP. Wuhan University Journal of Natural Sciences 8(1B), pp. 217-223.

X.S.Yan, L.S.Kang et.al: (2004). An Approach to Dynamic Traveling Salesman Problem. Proceedings of the Third International Conference on Machine Learning and Cybernetics, pp. 2418-2420, IEEE Press, Shanghai.

X.S.Yan, A.M Zhou, L.S Kang et,al; (2004). TSP Problem Based on Dynamic Environment. Proceedings of the 5th World Congress on Intelligent Control and Automation, pp. 2271-2274, IEEE press, Hangzhou, China.

J.V.Stone. (1992). The Optimal Elastic Net: Finding Solutions to the Traveling Salesman Problem. In Proceedings of the International Conference on Artificial Neural Networks, pp. 170-174, Brighton, England.

J.Branke. (2002). Evolutionary Optimization in Dymnamic Environments. Kluwer Academic Publishers.

C.J.Eyckelhof and M.Snoek. (2002). Ant Systems for a Dynamic TSP -Ants caught in a traffic jam. In 3rd International Workshop on Ant Algorithms (ANTS2002), pp. 88-99, Springer Press, Brussels, Belgium.

H.N.Psaraftis. (1998). Dynamic vehicle routing problems. In Vehicle Routing: Methods and Studies, B.L.Golden and A.A.Assad(eds), pp. 223-248, Elsevier Science Publishers.

X.S.Yan, Hui Li et.al: (2005). A Fast Evolutionary Algorithm for Combinatorial Optimization Problems. Proceedings of the Fourth International Conference on Machine Learning and Cybernetics, pp. 3288-3292, IEEE Press.

6

Immune-Genetic Algorithm for Traveling Salesman Problem

Jingui Lu[1] and Min Xie[2]
Nanjing University of Technology,
P. R. China

1. Introduction

The Traveling Salesman Problem (TSP), first formulated as a mathematical problem in 1930, has been receiving continuous and growing attention in artificial intelligence, computational mathematics and optimization in recent years. TSP can be described as follows: Given a set of cities, and known distances between each pair of cities, the salesman has to find a shortest possible tour that visits each city exactly once and that minimises the total distance travelled.

The mathematical model of TSP is described below:

Given a set of cities C = {C1, C2, C3… Cn}, the distance of each pair of cities is d(Ci,Cj). The problem is to find a route （C1,C2,C3…Cn） that visits each city exactly once and makes $\sum_{i=1}^{n} d(Ci, Ci+1) + d(Cn, C1)$ to have a minimum value.

TSP is the problem of the permutation of n cities. For n cities, there should be n! different permutations. For the symmetric TSP, each route has two different ways to represent. Therefore, the size of its search space is: S =n!/2n= (n-1)!/2. As TSP is an 'NP-hard' problem, researchers all over the world try to solve the problem with various algorithms. Genetic Algorithm (GA), with the advantages of robustness, flexibility and versatility, has been widely studied to solve large-scale combinatorial and optimization problems. However, Genetic Algorithm has some significant drawbacks, for instance, the pre-mature convergence of computations, the poor use of system information during computational evolutions, expensive computation from evolutional procedures and the poor capability of "local" search (Potvin, 1996) (Jin et al., 1996) (Wei & Lee, 2004) (Lu et al., 1996).

Although TSP itself seems very simple, as the number of visited cities increases, the computation of the problem can be extremely time-consuming (in the order of exponential growth) or even results in no optimal solution in the worst case. Developing effective algorithms for the TSP has long been a topic of interest in both academic research and engineering applications, ranging from transportation optimization to the sequencing of jobs on a single machine.

The methods commonly employed to solve the TSP include simulated annealing algorithm, artificial neural networks, tabu search algorithm, genetic algorithm (GA), and so on. Each method has different advantages and disadvantages. For example, GA combines many positive features (such as robustness, flexibility, and versatility), leading to its widespread applications in engineering optimization. However, GA also has some significant drawbacks, for instance, the pre-mature convergence of computations, the poor use of system information during computational evolutions, expensive computation from evolutional procedures, and the poor capability of local search.

The immune system, which is made up of special organs, tissues, cells and proteins, is the body's defence against infectious organisms and other invaders (Liu, 2009). The immune system detects and attacks antigens that invade the body through different types of lymphocytes. Artificial immune systems are adaptive systems inspired by the functions, principals and models of the vertebrate immune system. When artificial immune systems are attacked, the immune mechanisms are started to guarantee the basic functions of the whole intelligent information system. Researches on artificial immune systems aim to set up engineering models, algorithms and advanced intelligent information system through intensive study on the information processing mechanisms of biological immune systems.

In the 1970s, Jerne first propounded the hypothesis of the immune network system and founded the basic theories of the artificial immune systems, Jerne's idiotypic network model. Perelson studied on a number of theoretical immune network models proposed to describe the maintenance of immune memory, which accelerated the development of artificial immune systems in computer science. In 1986, Farmer built a dynamic model of the immune system and brought in the concept of learning. Farmer's work contributed to turning artificial immune systems to practical application. One important aspect of the research on artificial immune systems is to develop effective learning and optimization algorithms. Immune algorithms are one of heuristic search algorithms inspired by immune principals. In 1990, Bersini put immune algorithms into practice for the first time. By the end of the 20th century, Forrest et al. started to apply immune algorithms to computer security field. At the same time, Hunt et al. began to use immune algorithms in machine learning.

Immune algorithms (IAs), mainly simulate the idea of antigen processing, including antibody production, auto-body tolerance, clonal expansion, immune memory and so on. The key is the system's protection, shielding and learning control of the attacked part by invaders. There are two ways considered to design an immune algorithm: one is to abstract the structure and function of the biological immune system to computational systems, simulating immunology using computational and mathematical models; the other is to consider whether the output of the artificial immune systems is similar with that of the biological immune system when the two systems have similar invaders. The latter doesn't focus on the direct simulation of the process, but the data analysis of the immune algorithm.

As the immune system is closely related to the evolutionary mechanism, the evolutionary computation is often used to solve the optimization problem in immune algorithms. The research on artificial immune systems lays a foundation for further study on engineering optimization problems. On the one hand, it aims to build a computer model of biological immune system, which contributes to the study of the immune system operation. On the other hand, it supplies an effective way to solve many practical problems.

Immune Algorithms inspired by biological immune mechanism, can make full use of the best individuals and the information of the system, and keeps the diversity of the population. In the optimization process, Immune Algorithms take the useful ideas of existing optimization algorithms, combine random search with deterministic changes, reduce the impact of the random factors to the algorithm itself and can better eliminate the premature convergence and oscillation.

One kind of immune algorithms is immunity based neural method, such as the neuro-immune network presented in (Pasti & De Castro, 2006), which is a meta-heuristics for solving TSP based on a neural network trained using ideas from the immune system. In addition, an immune-inspired self-organizing neural network proposed by Thiago is showed to be competitive in relation to the other neural methods with regards to the quality (cost) of the solutions found (Thiago & Leandro, 2009).

Combining GA with immune algorithms is another kind of method in TSP solving, such as an immune genetic algorithm based on elitist strategy proposed in (Liang & Yang, 2008). A genetic algorithm based on immunity and growth for the TSP is also showed to be feasible and effective, in which a reversal exchange crossover and mutation operator is used to preserve the good sub tours and to make individuals various, an immune operator is used to restrain individuals' degeneracy, and a novel growth operator is used to obtain the optimal solution with more chances (Zeng & Gu, 2007).

Besides, Clonal Selection Algorithm is widely used to solve TSP. For example, a Hyper-mutation Antibody Clone Selection Algorithm (HACSA) shows the advantage of enhancing the local search performance of the antibody in solving TSP (Du et al., 2009). A novel Clonal Selection Algorithm(CSA), which extends the traditional CSA approach by incorporating the receptor editing method, is proved to be effective in enhancing the searching efficiency and improving the searching quality within reasonable number of generations (Gao et al., 2007).

Moreover, a number of improved artificial immune algorithms are studied and show the capability for TSP solutions. For example, an immune algorithm with self-adaptive reduction used for solving TSP improves the probability that it finds the global optimal solution by refining the reduction edges which gradually increase in the number and enhance in the forecasting accuracy (Qi et al., 2008).

To partially overcome the above-mentioned shortcomings of GA, an immune-genetic algorithm (IGA) is introduced in this book chapter, and then an improved strategy of IGA for TSP is also discussed. Section 3 is related to a selection strategy incorporated into the conventional genetic algorithm to improve the performance of genetic algorithm for TSP. The selection strategy includes three computational procedures: evaluating the diversity of genes, calculating the percentage of genes, and computing the selection probability of genes. The computer implementation for the improved immune-genetic algorithm is given in section 4, and finally the computer numerical experiments will be given in this book chapter.

2. The immune-genetic algorithm

2.1 Immune algorithms

Immune Algorithms can be divided into Network-based immune algorithm and Population-based algorithm.

Immune Network theory was first proposed by Jerne in 1974. Currently the most widely used is Jerne's network based thinking: immune cells in the immune system link each other through the mutual recognition. When an immune cell recognizes an antigen or another immune cell, it is activated. On the other hand, the immune cell is inhibited when it is recognized by other immune cells.

There are two kinds of Immune Network models: the continuous model and the discrete model. The continuous Immune Network model is based on ordinary differential equations. The typical models include the model proposed by Farmer et al. in 1986 and the model

proposed by Varela and Coutinho in 1991. These models have been successfully applied to continuous optimization problems, automatic navigation system and automatic control field.
However, the equations of continuous immune network model can not always be solved and usually it needs numerical integration to study the behavior of the system. To make up the drawbacks of continuous immune network model, the discrete immune network model is produced, which is based on a set of differential equations or an adaptive iteration.
Population-based Immune Algorithm mainly includes Negative Selection Algorithm and Positive Selection Algorithm. Negative Selection Algorithm, proposed by Forrest et al. from the University of Mexico, is a kind of selection Algorithms used to test data change. The algorithm embodies the ideas of the ideological principles of negative selection (Ge & Mao, 2002). The immune system works out mainly by successfully detecting abnormal changes of the system. Negative selection refers to the identification and deletion of self-reacting cells, that is, T cells that may select for and attack self tissues (Forrest et al., 1994). The immune system removes the immune cells that response to autologous cells to realize self-tolerance through Negative selection algorithm. There are mainly two procedures contained in Negative selection algorithm: tolerance and detection. The task in tolerance procedure is to produce mature detector. In the detection phase, the detector detects the protected system. Negative selection Algorithm does not directly use self-information, but generates testing subset by self-assembly through Negative selection. The algorithm is robust, parallel, distributed detected and easy to implement. However, as its computational complexity increases exponentially, Negative selection algorithm is not conducive to handling complex problems. Positive selection algorithm is very similar to Negative selection algorithm. But it works contrary to the Negative selection algorithm. Negative selection algorithm removes the self-reacting immune cells, while Positive selection algorithm keeps them.
Besides, Clonal Selection Algorithm is also a widely used immune algorithm. It is inspired by the clonal selection theory of acquired immunity that explains how B and T lymphocytes improve their response to antigens over time. The algorithm solves problems through the mechanisms of cell cloning, high-frequency variation, clonal selection and dying. It is high parallel and can be used in machine learning, pattern recognition and optimization domains. Standard Clonal selection algorithm achieves population compression and ensures the quality of antibody population in the optimal solution through local search. But Positive selection algorithm requires the system to be static. To make up that defect, Kim and Bentley proposed Dynamic Clonal algorithms in 2002, mainly for Network Intrusion Detection, to meet the real-time network security requirements.

2.2 The immune-genetic algorithm

The Immune-Genetic Algorithm (IGA) is an improved genetic algorithm based on biological immune mechanisms. In the course of immune response, biological immune system preserves part of the antibodies as memory cells. When the same antigen invades again, memory cells are activated and a large number of antibodies are generated so that the secondary immune response is more quickly than the initial response. In the meanwhile, there are mutual promotion and inhibition between antibodies. Therefore, the diversity and immune balance of the antibodies are maintained. That is the self-regulatory function of the immune system. The Immune-Genetic Algorithm simulates the process of adaptive regulation of biological antibody concentration, in which the optimal solution of the objective function corresponds to the invading antigens and the fitness f(Xi) of solution Xi corresponds to the antibodies produced by the immune system. According to the concentration of antibodies, the algorithm adaptively regulates the distribution of the search direction of solutions and greatly enhances the ability to overcome the local convergence.

In general, the Immune-Genetic Algorithm includes:

1. Antigens definition: Abstract the problem to the form of antigens which the immune system deals with and the antigen recognition to the solution of problem.
2. Initial antibody population generation: The antibody population is defined as the solution of the problem. The affinity between antibody and antigen corresponds to the evaluation of solution, the higher the affinity, the better the solution.
3. Calculation of affinity: Calculate the affinity between antigen and antibody.
4. Various immune operations: The immune operations include selection, clone variation, auto-body tolerance, antibody supplementation and so on. The affinity and diversity are usually considered to be the guidance of these immune operations. Among them, select Options usually refer to the antibody poputlation selected from the population into the next operation or into the next generation of the immune antibody population. Clone variation is usually the main way of artificial immune algorithm to generate new antibodies. Auto-body tolerance is the process of judging the rationality of the presence of the antibodies. Antibody supplementation is the accessorial means of population recruitment.
5. Evaluation of new antibody population: If the termination conditions are not satisfied, the affinity is re-calculated and the algorithm restarts from the beginning. If the termination conditions are satisfied, the current antibody population is the optimal solution.
6. Evolution of the antibody using standard Genetic Algorithm: crossover and mutation.

This model makes the immune system learn to identify the antibodies that are helpful to the antigen recognition. Moreover, the introduction of fitness further improves the immunogenicity, ensuring the diversity of antibody population in Genetic Algorithm.

Immune-Genetic Algorithm introduces the "immune operator", genes inoculation and selection, and simulates the specific auto-adaption and artificial immune of the artificial immune system, possessing good properties of fast global convergence. The specific workflow of Immune-Genetic Algorithm is described in figure 1.

Step 1. Randomly generate μ individuals of parent population. The search space of those quasi-optimal values x^* is composed of mesh points in R^n. Each part of these points is an integral multiple of Δ . Each individual in the population is presented as (x,σ), where $x=(x_1,x_2,\cdots,x_n)\in X\subset R^n$, is a solution to the problem. $x^*\in X$ is the expected solution. $f(x^*)=\max f(x)(x\in X)=f$, where f^* is the max fitness of X.

Step 2. Generate the intermediate population by crossing, with the size 2μ. The specific process is that for each individual (x,σ) of parent population, select another individual (x',σ') to crossover with (x,σ) in a crossover-point to generate y and y'.

Step 3. Mutate on the individual (x,σ) and generate a new one (x',σ')

Step 4. Inoculate genes. Inoculating the individual (x,σ) means to modify the value of x and σ in the range of variation or the restrictions in some parts of the optimal individuals. The inoculation process satisfies: if $f(x)=f^*$, (x,σ) turns to itself with probability l.

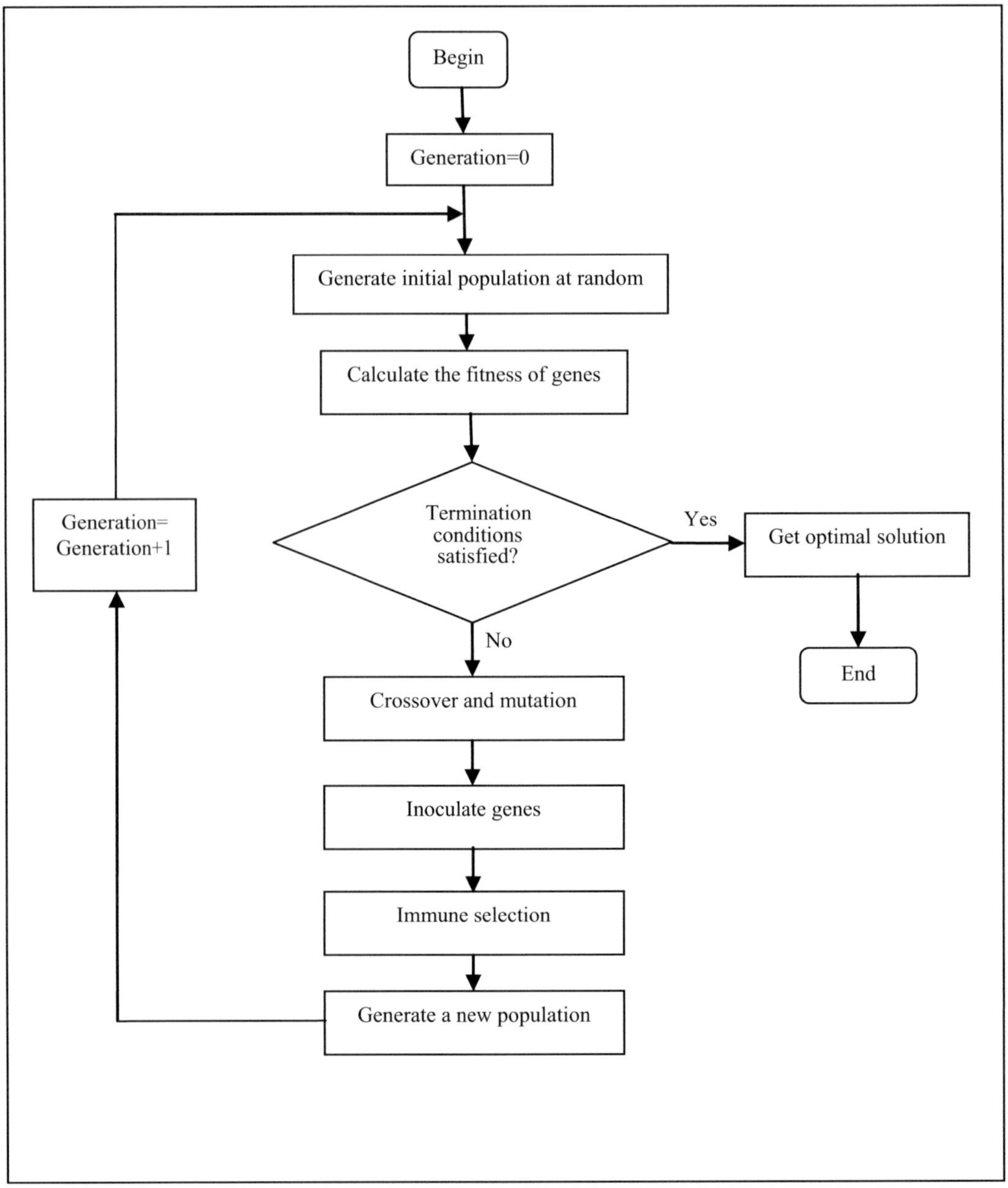

Fig. 1. Immune-genetic algorithm workflow

Step 5. Immune selection. It consists of two procedures: Immunity testing and selection. The first procedure is to test the inoculated individuals. If its fitness is smaller than its parent's fitness, there has been a serious degradation on the inoculated individual and its parent individual is used instead for the next competition. Immune Selection is to select μ individuals from 2μ individuals according to their fitness to compose a new parent population.

Step 6. If the termination conditions are not satisfied, generate a new generation and go back to step 2.

IGA has two advantages: 1. inoculating genes and adding a priori knowledge can effectively accelerate the convergence speed and improve the quality of the solution; 2. Concentration based immune selection method can prevent premature phenomenon and make sure the optimization process toward the global optimum direction. The disadvantage is that the selection of genes and inoculation approach should be analyzed according to specific situations.

3. The Improved immune-genetic algorithm for TSP

This section is related to improvements on the standard immune-genetic algorithm for TSP. An improved immune-genetic algorithm of the author's research work (Lu et al., 2007) for TSP is introduced in this section. The algorithm effectively integrates immune algorithm into GA (Jiao & Wang, 2000) using an improved strategy of IGA and applies a new selection strategy in the procedure of inoculating genes. The computer implementation for the improved algorithm is also discussed in this section.

3.1 The Improved immune-genetic algorithm

The improved immune-genetic algorithm uses a sequential representation to present the visited cities listed in the order (Lu et al., 2007). For example, the journey (5-7-8-9-4-3-2-6-1) can be expressed as (578943261). The path based coding method requires that the genetic code in the chromosome of an individual (a route) is not repeated. That is, any city should be visited once and only once.

The Roulette Wheel selection is employed where parents are selected according to their fitness (Lu et al., 2007). The individuals are generated using the Greedy crossover algorithm, which selects the first city of one parent, compares the others left in both parents, and chooses the closer one to extend the traveling way. If one city has been chosen, another city will be selected. And if both cities have been chosen, a not-yet-selected city will be randomly selected.

A swapping method is used for the TSP in IGA instead of the conventional mutation method. The method selects a binary code in random, which represents two cities from two individuals. The binary code is then swapped if the distance (length) of the traveling way for a new individual is shorter than that of the old one. (Lu et al., 2007)

In the procedure of developing and inoculating genes, the quality of genes has decisive influence on the convergence speed of the immune algorithm. Therefore, we make full use of prior knowledge and first develop a good gene pool that includes different genes representing the shorter traveling way of the TSP. After that, genes are randomly selected from the gene pool and finally inoculated into individuals.

In solving TSP, if the coordinates of 10 cities are in a circle for example, the route along the circle is the optimal solution and the optimal gene. The prior knowledge is applied to develop a gene pool. The gene pool is a two-dimensional 10 x 2 matrix. Having been calculated and optimized the gene pool can be the best, showed in table 1.

from	0	1	2	3	4	5	6	7	8
to	1	2	3	4	5	6	7	8	9

Table 1. The Gene Pool

When inoculating genes, a new selection strategy is applied to keep the excellent genes included in the population of individuals within a reasonable percentage. Those excellent genes are further used to generate other individuals. The selection strategy is developed based on the evaluation of the diversity of genes that are involved in the population of individuals. There are three computational procedures included in the strategy (Lu et al., 2007): 1) evaluating the diversity of genes included in the population of individuals, 2) calculating the percentage of genes included in the population of individuals, 3) computing the selection probability of genes. The details of the procedures are explained as follows.
1. Evaluating the diversity of genes
The diversity of genes is first evaluated by comparing the information entropy of every two genes. For example, giving two bit strings, each one has two alternative letters in its alphabet, thus the information entropy for the N genes is given by:

$$H(N) = \frac{1}{M}\sum_{i=1}^{n} H_i(N) \tag{1}$$

where Hj=Σi=1s- Pij logPij; Hj(N)is the information entropy of the jth binary bit of two genes, Pij is the probability of the jth binary bit of two genes being equal to ki. Pij is equal to 0 if the binary bits of two genes are the same; otherwise Pij is equal to 0.5. M is the number of genes.
The affinity of genes shows the similarity between the two genes. The affinity of gene v and gene w is:

$$ay_{v,w} = \frac{1}{1 + H(2)} \tag{2}$$

2. Calculating the percentage of genes
The percentage of gene v is Cv, given by:

$$c_v = \frac{1}{N}\sum_{w=1}^{N} ac_{v,w} \tag{3}$$

Where $ay_{v,\omega}$ is the affinity of gene v and gene ω :

$$ac_{v,w} = \begin{cases} 1, & ay_{v,w} >= Tac1 \\ 0, & \text{otherwise} \end{cases} \quad \text{,Tac1 is a predefined threshold} \tag{4}$$

If C_v is bigger than a predefined threshold, the gene will be inhibited (removed from the population), otherwise it remains. This step is to remove the extra candidates.
3. Computing the selection probability of genes
The selection probability of gene v is:

$$e_v = \frac{ax_v \prod_{s=1}^{N} (1 - as_{v,s})}{c_v \sum_{i=1}^{n} ax_i} \tag{5}$$

$$\text{where } as_{v,s} = \begin{cases} ay_{v,s}, & ay_{v,s} >= Tac2 \\ 0, & \text{otherwise} \end{cases} \text{ ,Tac2 is a predefined threshold} \tag{6}$$

$$ax_v = fitness(v) \tag{7}$$

$$\sum_{i=1}^{n} ax_i = sum\,fitness \tag{8}$$

This formula controls the concentration and diversity of genes. The genes with high affinity to the antigen will be selected to regenerate. The genes with high percentage are inhibited. The improvement of the improved genetic algorithm is mainly reflected in that: 1) Improve the fitness of individual genes and the quality of the individual by inoculating genes. This way the convergence rate is significantly sped up. 2) Concentration based immune selection method not only encourages the solution with high fitness, but also inhibits the solution with high percentage, ensuring the convergence of the algorithm and the diversity of the solution population. It's also suitable for multimodal function optimization.

3.2 Computer implementation for improved immune-genetic algorithm

The workflow of the improved immune-genetic algorithm is showed in figure 2.

The Computational Flow of the improved immune-genetic algorithm is showed in the following:

```
Begin
    Initiation: develop a gene pool using prior knowledge; select genes from the gene
    pool randomly;
    Repeat
            Calculate the fitness of each gene;
            Calculate the probability that genes are selected;
            Generate individuals using the Greedy crossover;
            Gene mutates;
        Inoculate genes using inoculation algorithm;
        Select genes using the selection strategy based on the evaluation of the
```

diversity of genes: Calculate the information entropy, the percentage and the selection probability of genes;
Replace the removed genes with the new developed genes to produce a new generation of genes;
Until (the genes satisfy the termination conditions)
End

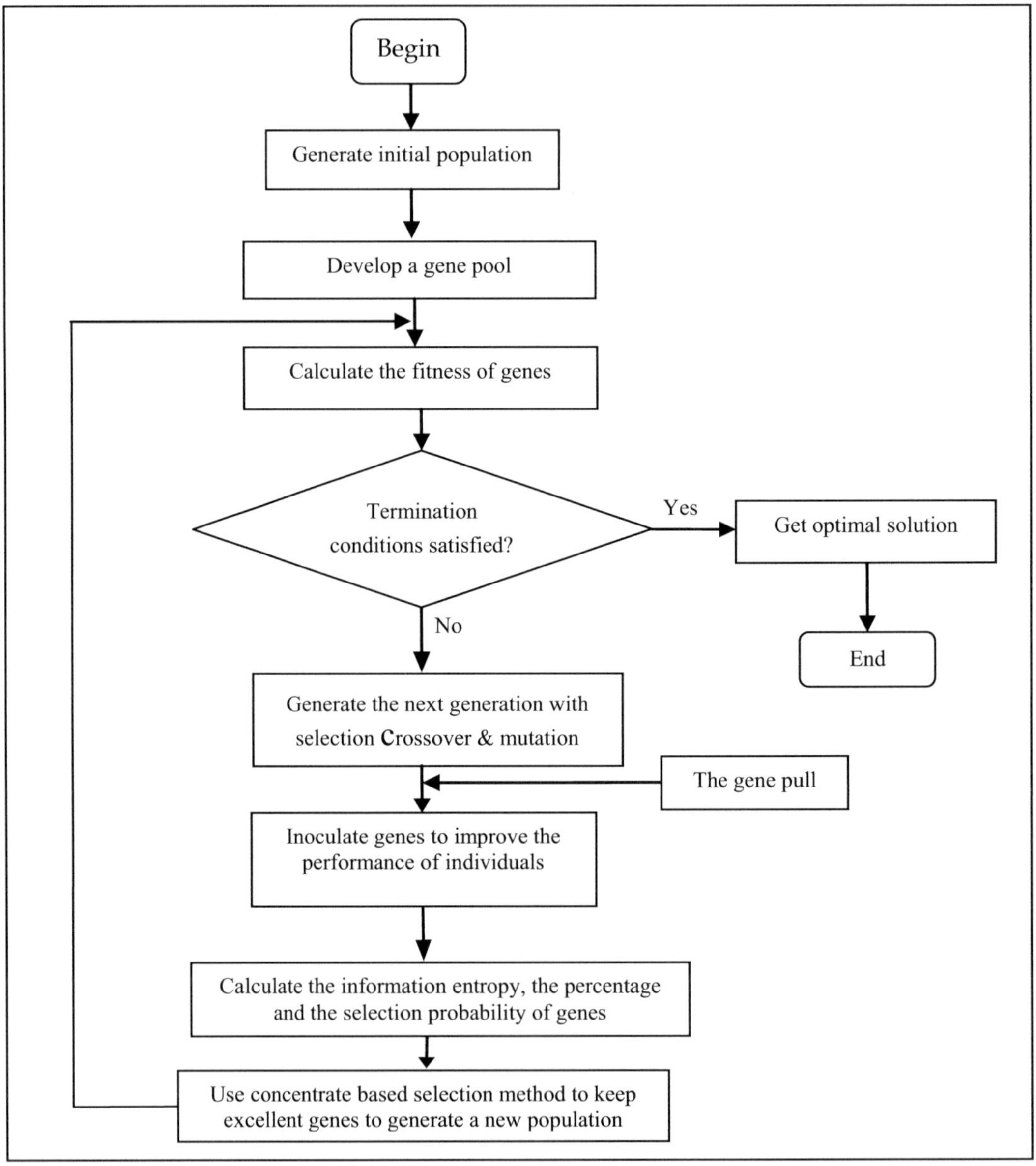

Fig. 2. The Improved Immune-Genetic Algorithm

The information of a gene individual includes gene chromosomes, chromosome length, individual fitness and the individual's corresponding variable. In the program, the structure of a gene individual is defined as follows.

```
typedef struct individual{
        int chrom[n];           /* chromosomes */
        float fitness;          /* individual fitness */
        int totaldistance;
        int lchrom;             /* chromosome length */
        double varible;         /* individual's corresponding variable */
};
```

The fitness function employed is showed as equation (9).

$$\mathrm{Fit}(x) = \frac{1}{\sum_{i=1}^{n} d(Ci, Ci+1) + d(Cn, C1)} \tag{9}$$

The probability that genes are selected is calculated using the roulette wheel selection with standard genetic algorithm
A swapping method is used for gene mutation. In the swapping method, a binary code that represents two cities from two individuals is randomly selected, and is then swapped if the distance (length) of the traveling way for a new individual is shorter than that of the old individual (Lu et al., 2007). The figure 3 shows an example of gene mutation: two locations are randomly selected to mutate. The probability of mutation is between 0.5 and 0.1;

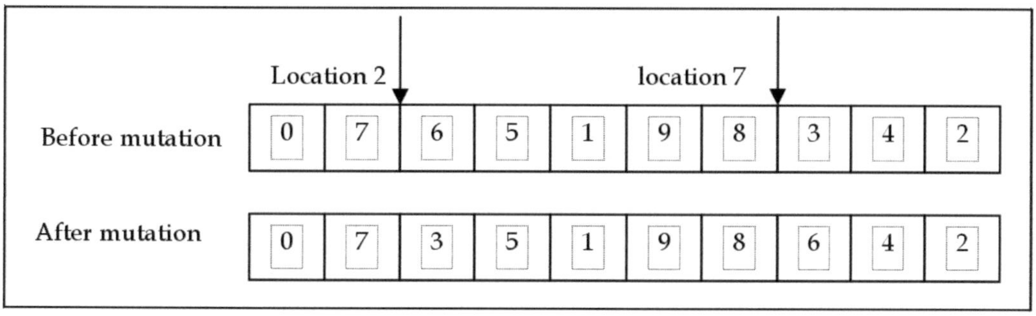

Fig. 3. Gene mutation

The computational flow of the gene mutation is as follows.

```
Begin
        Select locations to mutate at random;
        If (mutation probability< predefined value) swap the codes on the locations;
End;
```

The inoculation process is:

```
Begin
        Select a gene randomly from the gene pool;
```

Find a reasonable inoculating location;
Find and modify the conflict location of the gene to be inoculated;
Inoculate to the location of the gene;
End;

The process of the selection strategy based on the evaluation of the diversity of genes is:
Begin
Calculate the affinity of gene ν and ω according to the equation (2), where the diversity of two genes $H(2)$ is calculated using the equation (1);
Calculate the percentage C_ν of each gene in the population according to the equations (3) and (4),
If (C_ν >= Tac1) remove the gene from the population;
Else the gene remains;
Calculate the selection probability e_ν of genes according to the equations (5) and (6):
If(e_ν >= Tac2) the gene is selected to regenerate;
Else the gene is inhibited;
End;

4. Numerical experiments

Two case studies on 21-city and 56-city traveling salesman problems are given in this section to compare the solutions genetated by IGA and the conventional GA.
The comparisons of the number of evolutional iterations in IGA and conventional GA of two cases are showed in Figures 4 and 5 respectively. In both figures, the upper curve shows the evolutionary process of IGA and the lower one shows the evolutionary process of GA. Figures 6 and 7 show the optimal path for the TSP in the two case studies.
The results prove that the number of evolutional iterations is significantly reduced by using IGA. As seen from Figure 4, IGA takes only five iterations to reach the optimal solution while GA takes about 30 evolutional iterations.The selection strategy and the procedure of inoculating genes used by the improved immune-genetic algorithm proposed are effective to improve the performance of the individuals.
Therefore, the improvement on the performance of the individuals of IGA is helpful in acceleating the iterative process of GA. Althrough the convergence of the algorithm proposed need to be investigated, the computer numerical experiments on two case studies demonstrate preliminarily that the improved strategy of IGA is helpful for improving the evolutional iterations of genetic algorithms for traveling salesman problem (Lu et al., 2007).
The main data of IGA:

1. The probability of crossover is 0.8~0.9.
2. The probability of mutation is 0.05~0.2.
3. The size of the population is100.
4. The probability of inoculating is 0.85~1.
5. The evolutional generation is 200.

Seen from Figure 4, the optimal solution has been reached in the first 2 generations. Inoculating genes significantly improves the convergence speed of the algorithm.

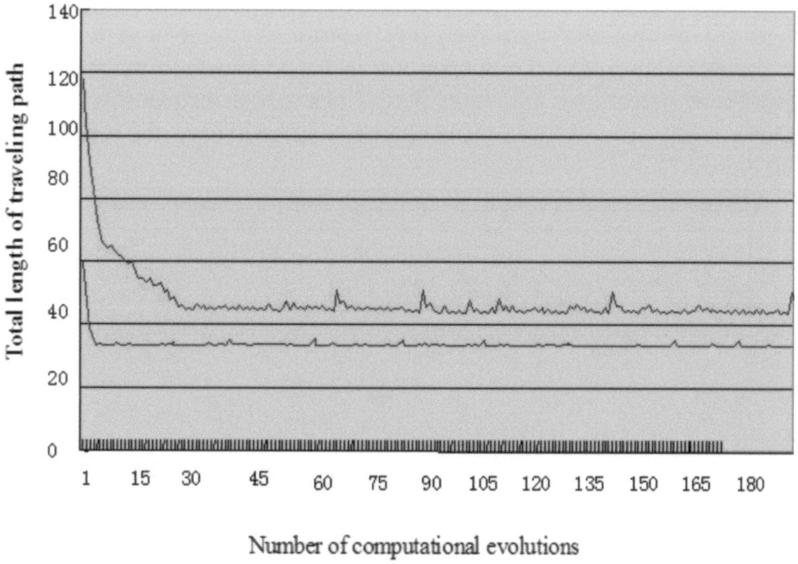

Fig. 4. Comparison of the number of evolutional iterations in IGA and the conventional GA: 21-city case

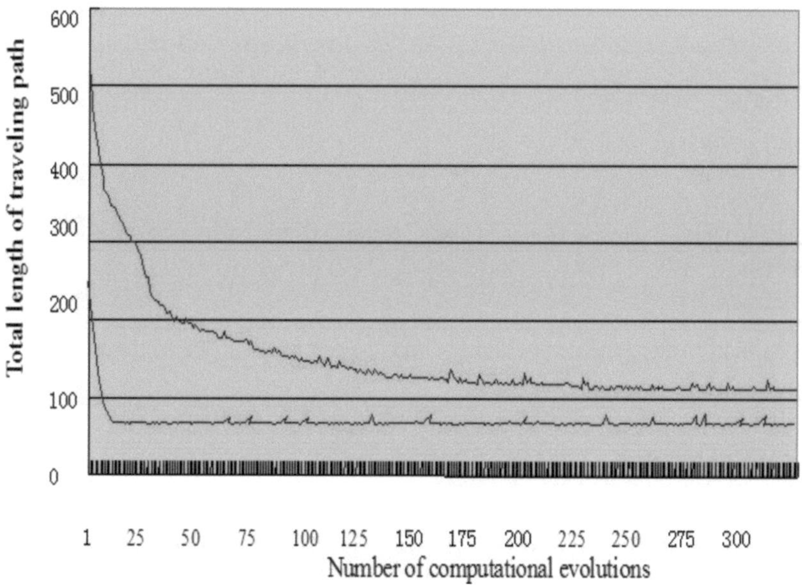

Fig. 5. Comparison of the number of evolutional iterations in IGA and the conventional GA: 56-city case

The main data of IGA:

1. The probability of crossover is 0.8~0.9.
2. The probability of mutation is 0.05~0.2.
3. The size of the population is100.
4. The probability of inoculating is 0.85~1.

5. The evolutional generation is 300.

Inoculating genes significantly improves the individual fitness and is conducive to the evolution of the population. As the concentration based selection mechanism is used, the individual with low percentage and high fitness has a high probability to regenerate. Its genes will then rapidly spread throughout the population. That's the reason why there is a steep slope in Figure 7.

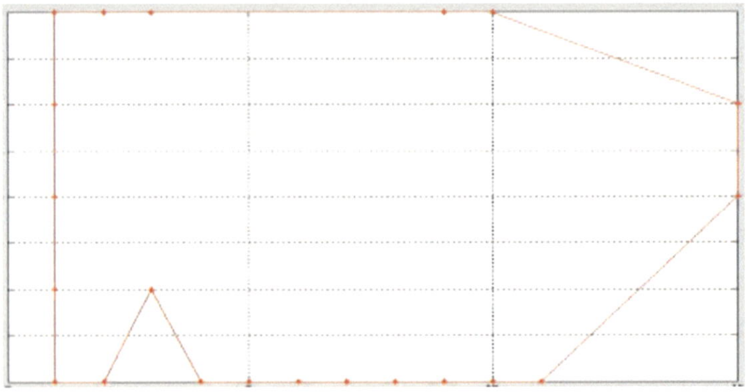

Fig. 6. Optimal path for the 21-city TSP

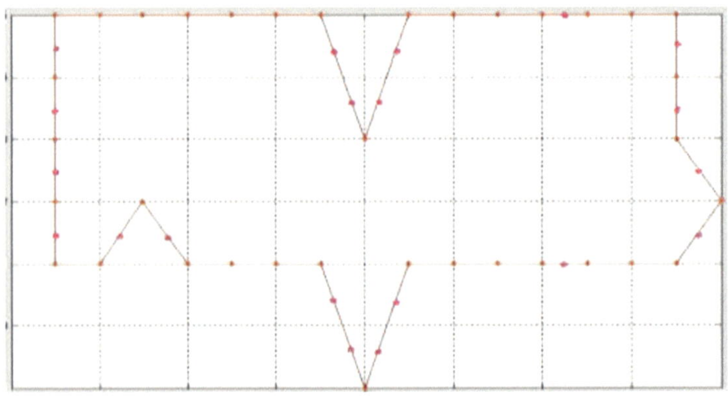

Fig. 7. Optimal path for the 56-city TSP

5. Concluding remarks

The immune-genetic algorithm integrating the advantages of artificial immune algorithm into genetic algorithm for TSP is introduced in this chapter. It retains a strong global random search capability of genetic algorithm, introduces gene inoculation and improves the convergence speed and accuracy of genetic algorithm. Meanwhile, immune-genetic algorithm borrows the idea of the antibody diversity from artificial immune system to ensure the diversity of population, which avoids the disadvantage of premature convergence and poor local search capabilities of genetic algorithm and improves the search efficiency.

The selection strategy of IGA discussed in this chapter includes three computational procedures: evaluating the diversity of genes, calculating the percentage of genes, and computing the selection probability of genes. Numerical experiments performed on 21-city and 56-city TSPs show that IGA significantly reduces the number of evolutional iterations for reaching an optimal solution.

6. References

Aarts, E. H. L.; Korst, J. H. M. & Laarhoven, P. J. M. (1988). A quantitative analysis of the simulated annealing algorithm: a case study for the traveling salesman problem, *J. Stats. Phys*, vol. 50, pp. 189-206

Aarts, E. H. L. & Stehouwer, H. P. (1993). Neural networks and the traveling salesman problem, *Proc. Intl. Conf. on Artificial Neural Networks*, Berlin Heidelberg: Springer Verlag

Applegate, D.; Bixby, R. E.; Chvatal, V. & Cook, W. (1998). On the solution of traveling salesman problems, *Documenta Mathematica* (Extra Volume, ICM III), pp. 645-658

Barnhart, C.; Boland, N. L.; Clarke, L. W.; Johnson, E. L.; Nemhauser, G. L. & Shenoi, R. G. (1998). Flight string models for aircraft fleeting and routing, *Transportation Science*, vol. 32, pp. 208–220

Choi, B. K. & Yang, B. S. (2001). Optimal design of rotor-bearing systems using immune-genetic algorithm, *Transactions of the ASME Journal of Vibration and Acoustics*, vol. 123, pp. 398-401

Du, Wei; Du, Haifeng & Li, Maolin (2009). Hyper-mutation antibody clone algorithms for TSP, *Journal of Xidian University*,vol.36, pp.527-534, ISSN: 10012400

Fiechter, C. N. (1994). A parallel tabu search algorithm for large traveling salesman problems, *Discrete Applied Mathematics*, vol. 51, pp. 243-267

Forrest, S.; Perelson, A.S.; Allen, L. & Cherukuri, R. (1994). Self-nonself discrimination in a computer, *Proceedings of the 1994 IEEE Symposium on Research in Security and Privacy*, Los Alamitos, CA. pp. 202–212

Gao, Shangce ; Dai, Hongwei ; Yang, Gang & Tang, Zheng (2007). A novel Clonal Selection Algorithm and its application to Traveling Salesman Problem, *Proceedings of IEICE Transactions on Fundamentals of Electronics, Communications and Computer Sciences*, pp. 2318-2325, ISSN : 09168508, Maruzen Co., Ltd., Tokyo, Japan

Ge, Hong & Mao, Zongyuan (2002). Improvement for Immune Algorithm, *Computer Engineering and Applications*, pp. 47-49, ISSN: 1002-8331-(2002)14-0047-03, Beijing

Gilmore, P. C. & Gomory, R. E. (1964). Sequencing a one state-variable machine: a solvable case of the traveling salesman problem, *Operations Research*, vol. 12, pp. 655-679

Jiao, L. C. & Wang, L. (2000). A novel genetic algorithm based on immunity, *IEEE Transactions on Systems, Man, and Cybernetics*, Part A – Systems and Humans, vol. 30, pp. 552-561

Jin, H. D. ; Leung, K. S. ; Wong, M. L. & Xu, Z. B. (2003).An efficient self-organizing map designed by genetic algorithms for the traveling salesman problem, *IEEE Trans. on Systems, Man, and Cybernetics Part B: Cybernetics*, vol. 33, pp. 877-888

Laarhoven, P. & Aarts, E. H. L. (1987). Simulated Annealing: Theory and Applications, MA: Kluwer Academic Publishers, Norwell

Lawler, E. L.; Lenstra, J. K.; Kan, A. H. G. R. & Shmoys, D. B. eds. (1985), The Traveling Salesman Problem, *Chichester: John Wiley*

Li,Tao (2004). Computer immunology , Publishing House of Electronics Industry, ISBN: 7-120-00107-8,Beijing

Liang, Yan & Yang, Kongyu (2008). Immunity genetic algorithm based on elitist strategy and its application to the TSP problem, *Proceedings of 2nd 2008 International Symposium on Intelligent Information Technology Application Workshop, IITA 2008*

Workshop, pp. 3-6, ISBN-13: 9780769535050, Shanghai, China, January 21, 2008 - December 22, 2008, Inst. of Elec. and Elec. Eng. Computer Society, Piscataway

Liu, C. Y. (2006) . Immune genetic algorithm and its application on TSP, *Technical Report of Nanjing University of Technology*, Nanjing

Liu,Jinkun (2009). *Intelligent control*, Second Edition, Publishing House of Electronics Industry, ISBN: 9787121011184, Beijing

Lu, J. G. ; Ding, Y. L. ; Wu, B. & Xiao, S. D. (1996). An improved strategy for GAs in structural optimization, *Computers & Structures*, vol. 61, pp. 1185-1191

Lu, Jinggui ; Fang, Ning ; Shao, Dinghong & Liu, Congyan (2007). An Improved Immune-Genetic Algorithm for the Traveling Salesman Problem, *Proceedings of Third International Conference on Natural Computation (ICNC 2007)*, vol. 4, pp.297-301, ISBN: 0-7695-2875-9, Haikou, Hainan, China, August 24-August 27,2007

Pasti, Rodrigo & De Castro, Leandro Nunes (2006). A neuro-immune network for solving the traveling salesman problem, *Proceedings of IEEE International Conference on Neural Networks*, pp.3760-3766, ISSN : 10987576, Vancouver, BC, Canada, July 16, 2006 - July 21, 2006, Institute of Electrical and Electronics Engineers Inc., Piscataway

Plante, R. D.; Lowe, T. J. & Chandrasekanran, R. (1987). The production matrix traveling salesman problem: an application and solution heuristic, *Operations Research*, vol. 35, pp. 772-783

Potvin, J. V. (1996). Genetic Algorithms for the Traveling Salesman Problem, *Annals of Operations Research*, vol. 63, pp. 339-370

Qi, Yutao ; Liu, Fang & Jiao, Licheng (2008). Immune algorithm with selfadaptive reduction for large-scale TSP, *Journal of Software*, vol. 19, pp. 1265-1273, ISSN: 10009825

Thiago A.S. Masutti & Leandro N. de Castro(2009). A self-organizing neural network using ideas from the immune systemmto solve the traveling salesman problem, *Information Sciences* 179 (2009), W. Pedrycz (Ed.), pp. 1454–1468, ISSN: 0020-0255

Timmis, J.; Neal, M. & Hunt, J. (2000). An artificial immune system for data analysis, *BioSystems* 55 (1), pp. 143–150

Wei, J. D. & Lee, D. T. (2004). A new approach to the traveling salesman problem using genetic algorithms with priority encoding, *Proc. 2004 IEEE Congress on Evolutionary Computation, Portland*, pp. 1457-1464

Wu, Jianhui ; Zhang, Jin & Liu Zhaohua (2009). Solution of TSP problem based on the combination of ant colony algorithm and immune algorithm, *Journal of Hunan University Natural Sciences*, vol. 36, pp. 81-87, ISSN: 16742974

Zeng, Congwen ; Gu, Tianlong (2007). A novel immunity-growth genetic algorithm for traveling salesman problem, *Proceedings of Third International Conference on Natural Computation, ICNC 2007*, pp. 394-398, ISBN-10: 0769528759, Haikou, Hainan, China, August 24, 2007 - August 27, 2007

Zheng, J. G. ; Wang, L. & Jiao, L. C. (2001). Immune algorithm for KDD, *Proc. SPIE*, vol. 4553, pp. 215-220

7

The Method of Solving for Travelling Salesman Problem Using Genetic Algorithm with Immune Adjustment Mechanism

Hirotaka Itoh
*Nagoya Institute of Technology,
Japan*

1. Introduction

Genetic Algorithm (GA) is widely used to find solutions to optimization problems (Goldberg, 1989). One optimization problem using GA is Travelling Salesman problem (TSP) (Lawler et al., 1985). The disadvantages of using GA are premature convergence and poor local search capability. In order to overcome these disadvantages, evolutionary adaptation algorithms based on the working of the immune system have been devised. One such algorithm is Genetic Immune Recruitment Mechanism (GIRM) (Bersini & Varela, 1991) (Tazawa et al., 1995). By incorporating the immune recruitment test and concentrating the search for a solution in the vicinity of a high-fitness solution, GIRM improves local search capability. However, narrowing the search range risks conducting to local solutions. In contrast, Immune Algorithm (IA) (Mori et al., 1997) (Honna et al., 2005) (Matsui et al., 2006), using production of various antibodies by the immune system and its mechanism of their adjustment, primarily avoids convergence to local solutions. Its local search capability is not as good as that of GIRM, but it allows efficient searches for multiple local solutions. GIRM and IA incorporating the workings of the immune system take more computation time than GA. Thus, they must be performed with a smaller population size.
To that end, the author devised an algorithm to overcome these GA's disadvantages with the small population size. The immune system has two features, the capacity to adapt to mutations in antigen and a mechanism to balance the generation of antibodies via other antibodies, and the author developed Genetic Algorithm with Immune Adjustment Mechanism (GAIAM) incorporating these features in GA. GAIAM maintains the diversity of the population as a result of the mechanism to adjust antibodies in a group of antibodies, so it avoids narrowing of the search range. In addition, its local search capability also improved as a result of the capacity to adapt to mutations in antigen. GAIAM provides effective results even with a small population size.
Using the TSP, the author compared the performance of GAIAM to that of GA, GIRM, and IA. First, an experiment was performed using eil51 from the TSPLIB. TSBLIB has benchmark data of TSP. Eil50 is one of the data in TSPLIB. Because it incorporates two features of the immune system even with a small population size, the GAIAM allows a more efficient search over the entire search range without succumbing locally. Moreover, its local search capability was found to be better than that of other techniques. Furthermore, experiments

ware performed using data with 100 cities or more, and GAIAM was found to be effective even in large-scale problems.
This paper first offers an overview of the GAIAM. In addition, differences between it and GA, GIRM and IA are described. Next, the experiments were performed using the TSP, and GAIAM's performance was compared to that of other algorithms. Last, GAIAM's effectiveness is set forth.

2. GAIAM

2.1 Feature of immune system

Various antibodies are present in the human body. As antigens invade the body, antibodies for these antigens are generated to eliminate the antigens. The immune system has the following two features:
[Feature 1] Capacity to adapt to mutations in antigens
It is difficult to produce antibodies for each and every antigen beforehand. When there is no antibody adapted for an antigen, genes of the antibodies with the best specificity respond by mutating. Through repeated mutations, these genes produce antibodies that can adapt to the antigens.
[Feature 2] Mechanism to balance the generation of antibodies via other antibodies
The generation of antibodies for a given antigen is not a continuous process. Antibodies recognize each other on the basis of their structure, and when a given antibody is generated in excess, other antibodies that identify it as an antigen and are also generated to inhibit its growth, and a balance is maintained.

2.2 GAIAM algorithm

The GAIAM algorithm is shown in Fig.1. The GAIAM algorithm is following.

Step 1. Generation of an initial group of antibodies
N antibodies are generated initially. These antibodies are similar to the individuals in GA and are helpful in solving optimization problems.

Step 2. Calculation of affinities
The affinities ax_i (i = 1,…, N) for antigens are calculated. The ax_i is set in accordance with the problem being dealt with. The affinity for an antigen is similar to the concept of fitness in GA.

Step 3. Calculation of expected values
The expected value e_i (i = 1,…, N) of antibodies that can survive into the next generation is calculated as

$$e_i = \frac{ax_i}{C_i} \tag{1}$$

Where C_i is the density of antibodies of type i (i = 1,…, N).

$$C_i = \frac{1}{N}\sum_{j=1}^{N} ay_{i,j} \tag{2}$$

Here, $ay_{i,j}$ is the similarity between antibodies of type i and j ($i = 1,\ldots,N$, $j = 1,\ldots,N$) and is set in accordance with the problem. $N/2$ antibodies with low expected values are eliminated,

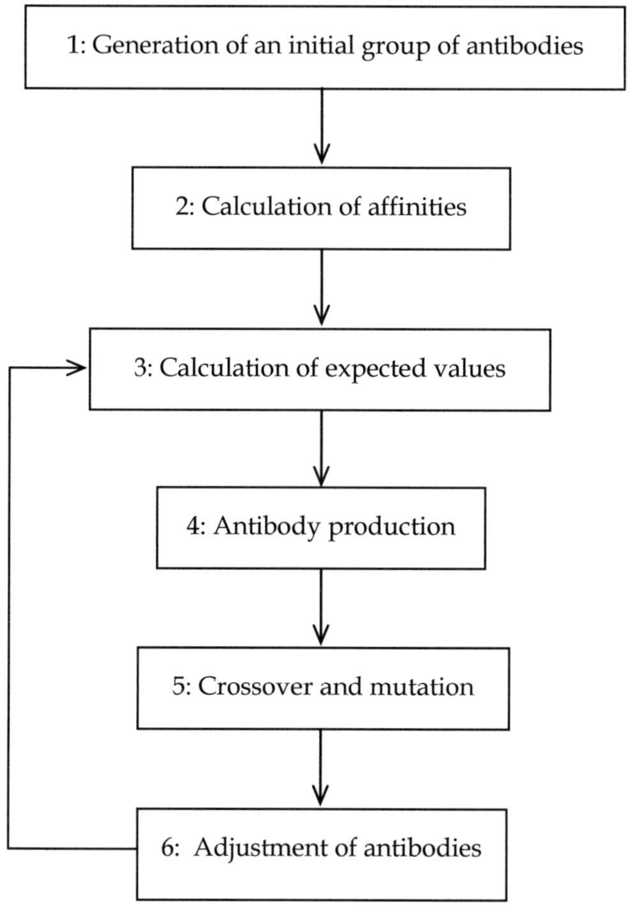

Fig. 1. The GAIAM algorithm

however, among these, 10% of the antibodies with high affinities for antigens are excluded from elimination.

Step 4. Antibody production

New antibodies are generated to replace the antibodies eliminated in Step 3. $N/2$ antibodies are selected from the surviving antibodies on the basis of the expected values. These selected antibodies are mutated, after which their affinities for antigens are calculated.

Step 5. Crossover and mutation

Antibodies are randomly selected (duplication permitted) from N antibodies, they undergo crossover depending on crossover probability P_c, thereby generating $N/2$ antibodies. The generated antibodies undergo mutation depending on mutation probability P_m, after which their affinities for antigens are calculated.

Step 6. Adjustment of antibodies

With respect to each antibody i of the $N/2$ antibodies generated in Step 5, an antibody j with the greatest affinity for i is sought from among the existing N antibodies. Among antibodies i and j, the one with the higher affinity for an antigen survives into the next generation, while the other is eliminated.

Step 7. Repetition of Steps 3 to 6 for a determined number of generations.

Step 4 models [Feature 1] of the immune system and Step 6 models [Feature 2] of the immune system. In GAIAM, antibodies with low density and high affinity for an antigen tend to survive in order to maintain diversity. Moreover, such antibodies are generated in GAIAM; antibodies with a high affinity for an antigen are produced through mutation. In terms of GA, local search capability is improved. Moreover, narrowing of the search range is eliminated through Step 6. Thus, the narrowing of the search to the vicinity of a single local solution in GA is eliminated.

3. Comparison of GA, GIRM and IA to GAIAM

3.1 The GA algorithm

Here, the GA algorithm is briefly explained. The GA algorithm is shown in Fig.2.

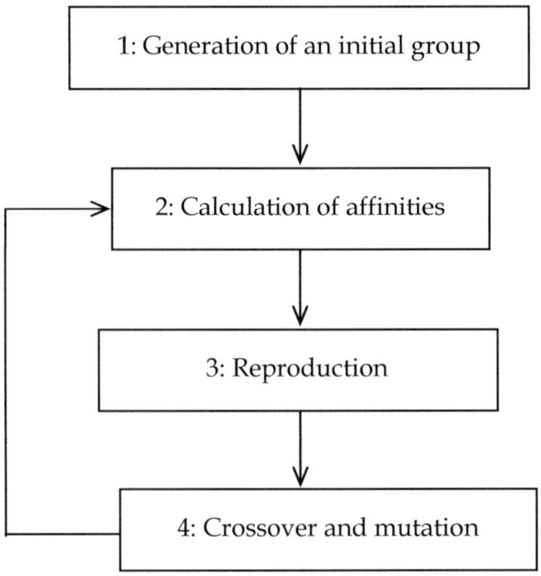

Fig. 2. The GA algorithm

Step 1. Generation of an initial group

Same as Step 1 in the GAIAM

Step 2. Calculation of affinities

Same as Step 2 in the GAIAM

Step 3. Reproduction

N antibodies are selected from antibodies group to surviving next generation on the basis of the affinity.

Step 4. Crossover and mutation
Same as Step 5 in the GAIAM
Step 5. Repetition of Steps 2 to 4 for a determined number of generations.
The disadvantages of using GA are premature convergence and poor local search capability.

3.2 The GIRM algorithm

Here, the GIRM algorithm is briefly explained. The GIRM algorithm is shown in Fig.3.

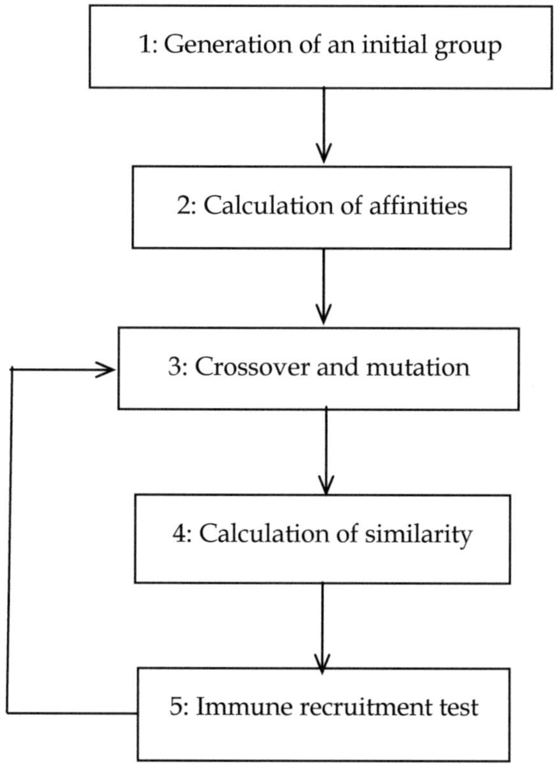

Fig. 3. The GIRM algorithm

Step 1. Generation of an initial group
Same as Step 1 in the GAIAM
Step 2. Calculation of affinities
Same as Step 2 in the GAIAM
Step 3. Crossover and mutation
Same as Step 5 in the GAIAM
Step 4. Calculation of similarity
Same as similarity for GAIAM
Step 5. Immune recruitment test
An immune recruitment test is performed on antibodies obtained in Step3; antibodies passing the test are added to the group. Alternatively, antibodies with

the lowest fitness in the group are removed. For details, see references (Bersini & Varela, 1991) and (Tazawa et al., 1995) .

Step 6. Repetition of Steps 3 to 5 for a determined number of generations.

With GIRM, highly fit antibodies in the group and similar antibodies increase as a result of the immune recruitment test, so searching in the proximity of a solution, i.e. highly fit antibodies, becomes more vigorous. That is, local searches are intensive. When, however, GIRM succumbs to a high-fitness local solution, it has difficulty escaping.

3.3 The IA algorithm

Here, the IA algorithm is briefly explained. The IA algorithm is shown in Fig.4.

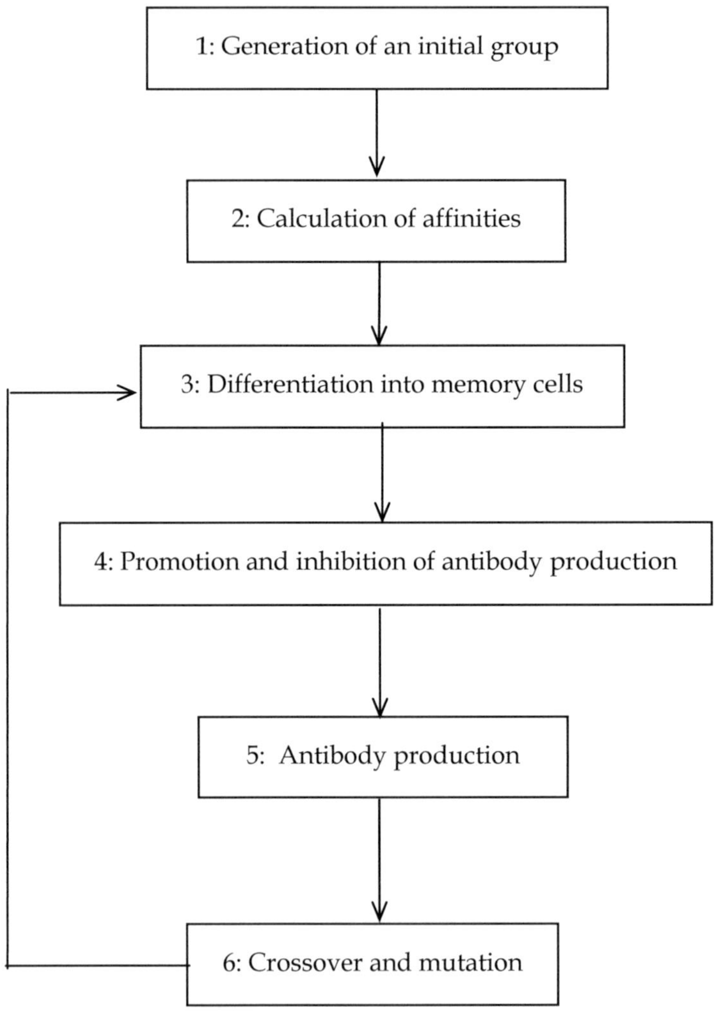

Fig. 4. The IA algorithm

Step 1. Generation of an initial group
Same as Step 1 in the GAIAM

Step 2. Calculation of affinities
Same as Step 2 in the GAIAM

Step 3. Differentiation into memory cells
For details, see reference (Mori et al., 1997).

Step 4. Promotion and inhibition of antibody production
Same as Step 3 in the GAIAM

Step 5. Antibody production
New antibodies are produced to replace $N/2$ antibodies eliminated in Step 4. New antibodies are produced by randomly determining their genes.

Step 6. Crossover and mutation
Same as Step 5 in the GAIAM

Step 7. Repetition of Steps 3 to 6 for a determined number of generation.

Because of Step 5, the IA avoided narrowing the search to local solutions. However, its local search capability was not as good as that of the GIRM, because new antibodies were randomly produced in Step 5.

3.4 Comparison of GA, GIRM and IA to GAIAM

The disadvantages of using GA are premature convergence and poor local search capability. GIRM has enhanced local search capability but easily conducts to local solutions. IA allows efficient searches for multiple local solutions, but its search capability in the vicinity of individual local solutions is poor. GAIAM has improved local search capability because of its capacity to adapt to mutations and avoids narrowing of the search range because of its mechanism to adjust antibodies via antibodies; in short, it allows efficient searches.

4. Use in the TSP

4.1 Path representation

Path representation is used for the coding of antibodies. Path representation is shown in Fig.5. Path representation orders cities by number in the order they are visited. The method in which initial antibodies are generated will now be explained. First, city numbers are randomly ordered. Next, antibodies are generated using the 2-opt method (Johnson, 1991).

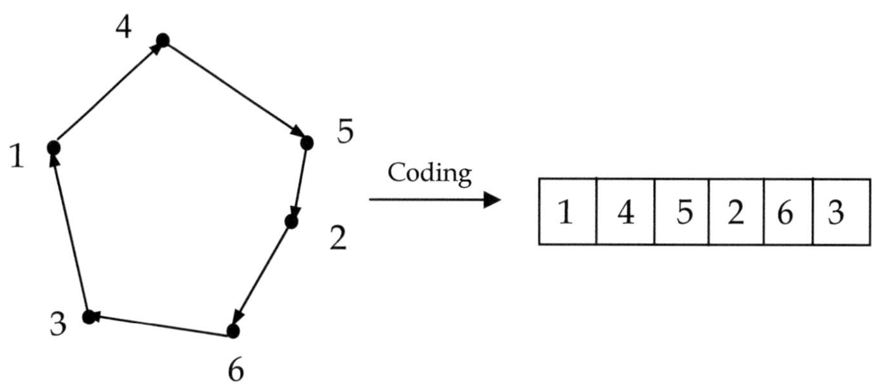

Fig. 5. Path representation

4.2 Affinity of antibody and antigen

The affinity ax_i of antibody i and the antigen is the inverse of the tour length d.

$$ax_i = \frac{1}{d} \quad (3)$$

4.3 Crossover and mutation

Various studies have been conducted on crossover methods used in the TSP (Nagata et al., 1999). The current work, however, sought to assess the performance of an algorithm, so OX crossover was used instead of a well-performing crossover method (Davis, 1985).

With regard to mutation, antibodies first undergo substitution or inversion once. Next, the 2-opt method was used. Substitution is shown in Fig.6 and inversion in Fig.7. For substitution, the positions of 2 random cities in the antibodies are switched and for inversion, the order of 2 random cities is reversed.

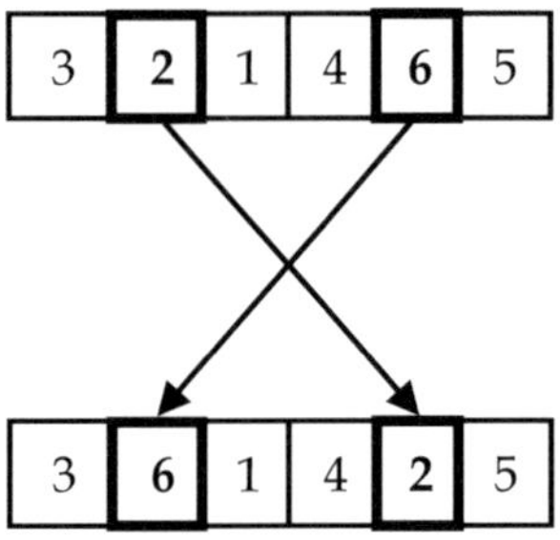

Fig. 6. Substitution

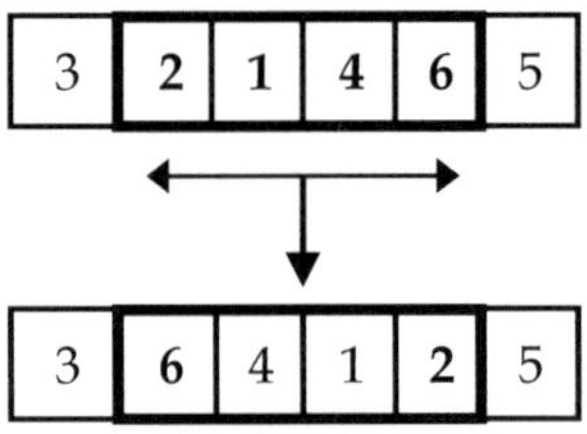

Fig. 7. Inversion

4.4 Similarity for antibodies

Similarity $ay_{i,j}$ for antibodies i and j is represented by the following equation.

$$ay_{i,j} = 1.0 - \frac{\sum_{a=1}^{L}\sum_{b=1}^{L}(-p_{a,b}) * \log(p_{a,b})}{-L * 2.0 * \log(1.0/2.0)} \quad (4)$$

$$p_{a,b} = \frac{N_{ab}}{2} \quad (5)$$

L is the number of cities.

N_{ab} is, for antibodies i and j, the number of branches connecting city a and city b on the tour. Similarity $ay_{i,j}$ was normalized; as they approached 0, i and j were dissimilar while they were similar as they approached 1.

5. Experiments

5.1 Experiment using eil51 from the TSPLIB

An experiment was performed using eil51 from the TSPLIB to assess the performance of GAIAM. A Linux machine was used. The shortest tour for eil51 is shown in Fig.8. The shortest tour length is 426. Parameters used in the experiment were generations of G=500, a crossover probability of P_c=0.8, and a mutation probability of P_m=0.2. There were 4 population sizes of 20, 30, 50, and 100. The experiment was performed 30 times each.

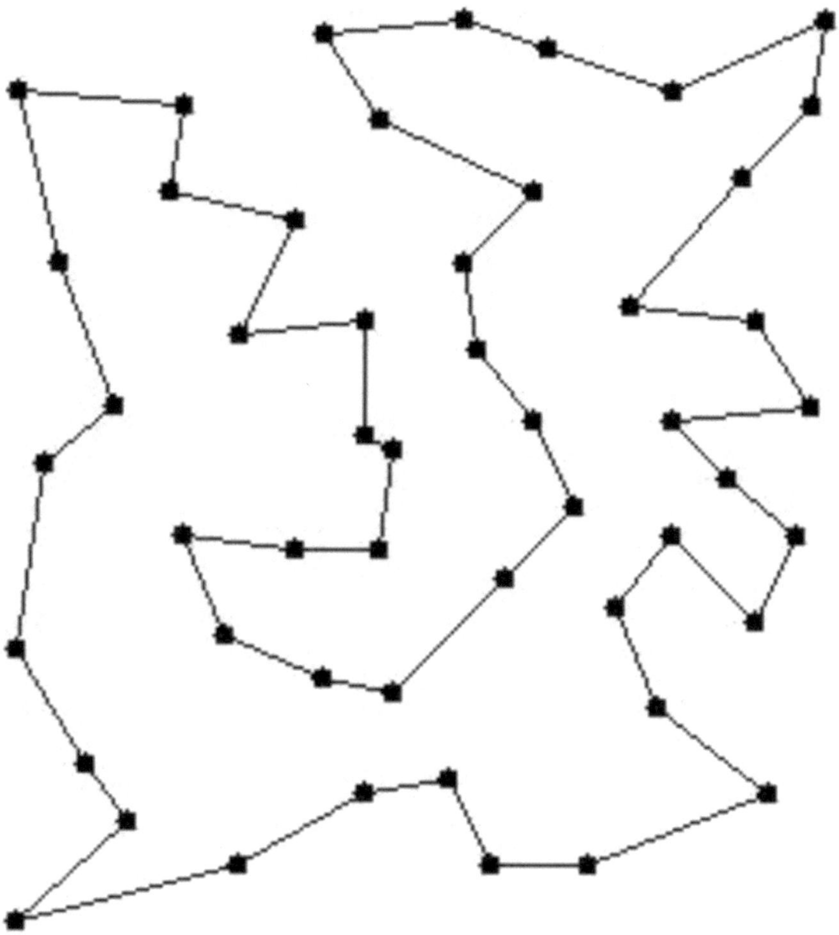

Fig. 8. The shortest tour length of eil51 (length=426)

Results are shown in Table.1. In Table.1, d_m is the shortest route length found as a result of 30 individual attempts. *avg* is the average of d_m for 30 iterations, *min* is the minimum of d_m for 30 iterations, *max* is the maximum of d_m for those iterations, and *std* is the standard deviation. N_o is the number of times the shortest tour length of 426 was found out of 30 attempts.

	N	d_m				N_o
		avg	*min*	*max*	*std*	
GAIAM	20	426.83	426	428	0.64	9
	30	426.70	426	428	0.75	14
	50	426.67	426	428	0.55	11
	100	426.60	426	427	0.50	12
GA	20	428.87	426	432	1.45	1
	30	428.77	426	432	1.43	1
	50	428.57	426	431	1.17	2
	100	428.47	427	430	0.97	0
GIRM	20	429.73	426	435	2.38	1
	30	428.77	426	434	2.03	2
	50	428.03	426	432	1.96	5
	100	426.83	426	431	1.15	13
IA	20	429.90	426	433	1.86	1
	30	428.53	426	431	1.25	1
	50	428.27	426	432	1.50	2
	100	427.60	426	429	1.00	4

Table 1. The result of the experiment

Generational changes in entropy when N = 100 are shown in Fig.9. Entropy is the average similarity of individual antibodies and other antibodies; the average for 30 attempts is shown in Fig.9. It indicates that there are more similar antibodies in the group as entropy approaches 1.

In Table 1, GAIAM yielded the best results. GAIAM yielded consistent results regardless of the population size. Even when N=20, *avg* is markedly better than that of other techniques. Both the *max* and *std* were smaller than those with other techniques, and the shortest tour length was found numerous times. With a smaller population size, results for GIRM and IA were poorer than those for GA. With a larger population size, results were better. When N=100, GIRM yielded results similar to those from GAIAM, but comparison of results for GAIAM when N=20 indicate that GAIAM yielded better results overall.

GIRM and IA are modifications of GA, but somewhat larger population size is required for them to perform well.

In Fig.9, maximum entropy recorded with the GIRM. In Table.1, the *avg* for GIRM was better than that for GA and IA, but the *max* and *std* were poor. As is apparent from Fig.9 and Table.1, GIRM has enhanced local search capability but once it conducts to a search in the

vicinity of high-fitness local solutions it cannot escape, and the search range narrows. Thus, if the vicinity of optimal values is searched in the search process, optimal values will be found, but when the search shifts to the vicinity of local solutions away from local values escape is difficult, and optimal values will not be reached. In Fig.9, the entropy of IA is the lowest. In Table.1, for IA, the *avg* was poorer than that for GIRM but better than that for GA. The *max* and *std* were better than with GIRM. For IA, the local search capability was not as good as with GIRM, but it allowed an efficient search for multiple local solutions. In Fig.9, entropy for GAIAM remained about 0.67. This is almost midway between entropies for GIRM and IA. Similarly, GAIAM is superior to other techniques in Table.1 as well.
GAIAM did not conducts to local values and allowed the efficient search over the entire search range, and its local search capability was also enhanced. In addition, GAIAM provided viable results even with the small population size.

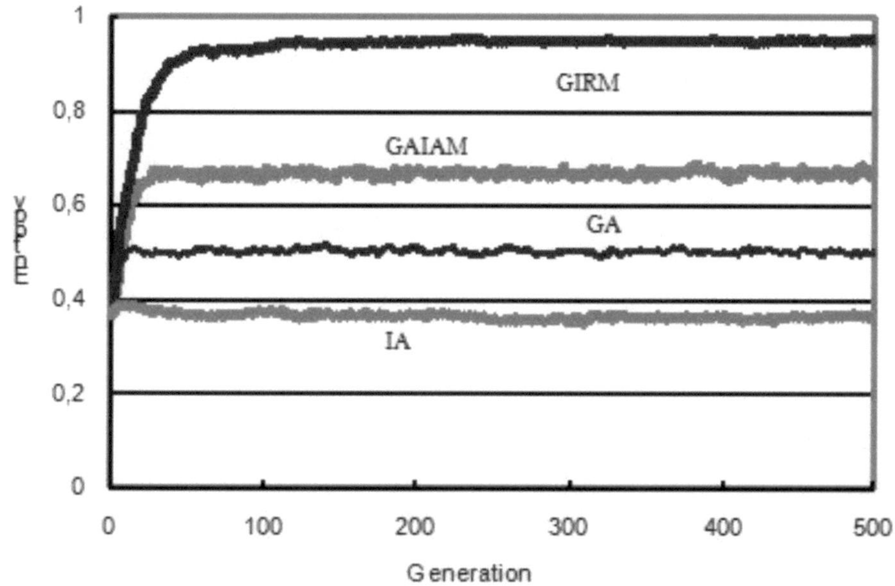

Fig. 9. Generation transition of entropy

5.2 Experiments using ch150, a280, and pcb442

Experiments were performed using ch150, a280, and pcb442 from the TSPLIB to assess the performance of GAIAM in large city problems. Outlines of ch150, a280, and pcb442 are shown in Table.2. Parameters are shown in Table.3. The shortest routes for ch150, a280b, and pcb442 are shown in Fig.10, Fig.11 and Fig.12. Results of the experiments are shown in Table.4, Table.5 and Table.6 As expected, GAIAM offered the best results. Trends in results were the same as when eil51 was used. GAIAM's *max* was better than the *min* for GA and IA. In addition, GAIAM found the shortest route for ch150 in 7 iterations, which is much better than other techniques. It found a unique shortest route for a280. Following GAIAM, GIRM had the best of *avg* , but its *max* was roughly worse than that of IA and it had the worst *std*. As expected, it had enhanced local search capability, but when it conducted to local values it lacked the ability to escape them. The above results indicate that GAIAM is able to provide viable results with the small-size population size even in large-scale problems. GAIAM allows efficient searches without conducting to local solutions and also provides enhanced local search capability.

6. Conclusion

GAIAM has faithfully incorporated the two features of the immune system, i.e. the capacity to adapt to mutations in antigens and the mechanism to adjust antibodies in a group of antibodies, into GA, and its effectiveness increased as the optimization technique.
Results of experiments with GA, GIRM, and IA were compared to those with GAIAM and GAIAM's performance was assessed via use of GAIAM in the TSP.
According to the results, GAIAM was found to offer more efficient and balanced searches in the population than IA and GIRM. Consequently, GAIAM sought optimum values from the entire search range and also displayed enhancement in local search capability. It also provided viable results with the small population size in large-scale problems as well. GAIAM is superior to GA, GIRM, and IA in finding solutions for TSP. GAIAM is efficient as solving method of TSP.

	Number of city	The shortest length
Ch150	150	6528
a280	280	2579
Pcb442	442	50778

Table 2. The outlines of ch150, a280 and pcb442

	Number of trials	Generation number	Antibody size
ch150	20	1000	30,50
a280	20	2000	30,50
pcb442	10	2000	30,50

Table 3. The parameters of the experiments

	N	d_m				N_o
		avg	*min*	*max*	*std*	
GAIAM	30	6548.85	6528	6584	17.55	7
	50	6544.50	6528	6570	16.53	7
GA	30	6668.35	6604	6759	41.73	0
	50	6691.60	6568	6766	45.80	0
GIRM	30	6589.40	6528	6662	38.21	1
	50	6572.65	6528	6696	43.29	2
IA	30	6659.80	6625	6709	18.88	0
	50	6639.50	6571	6707	37.75	0

Table 4. The result of ch150

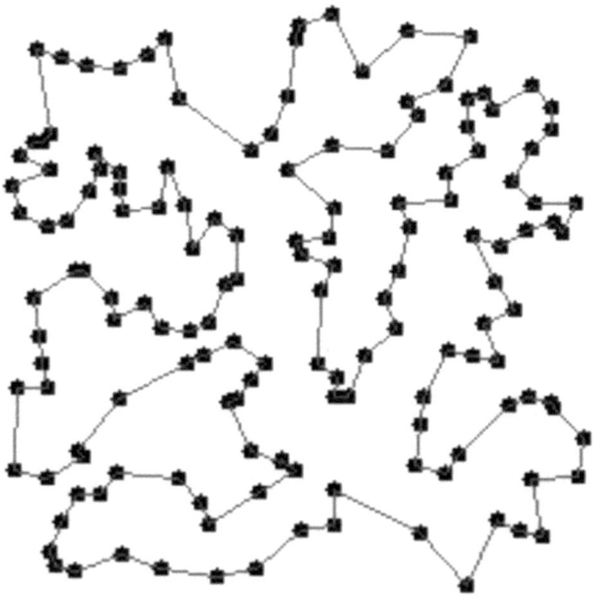

Fig. 10. The shortest route of ch150

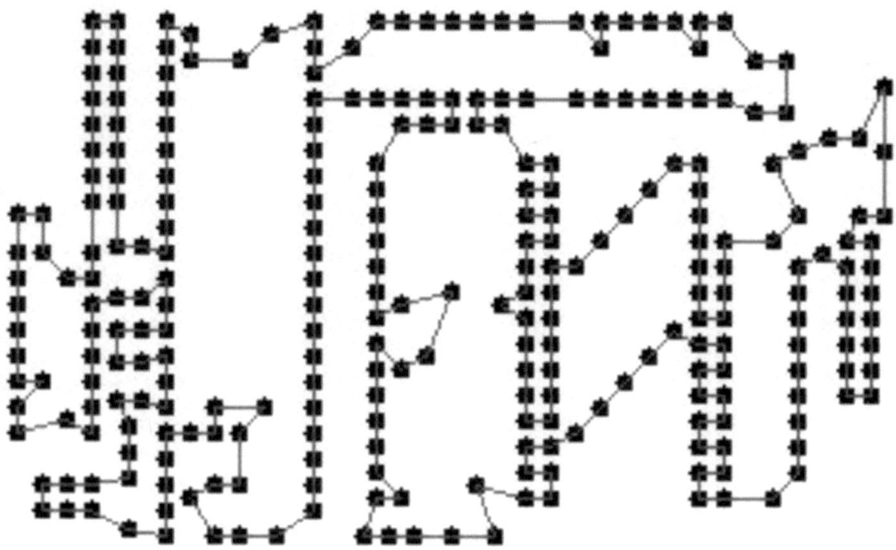

Fig. 11. The shortest route of a280

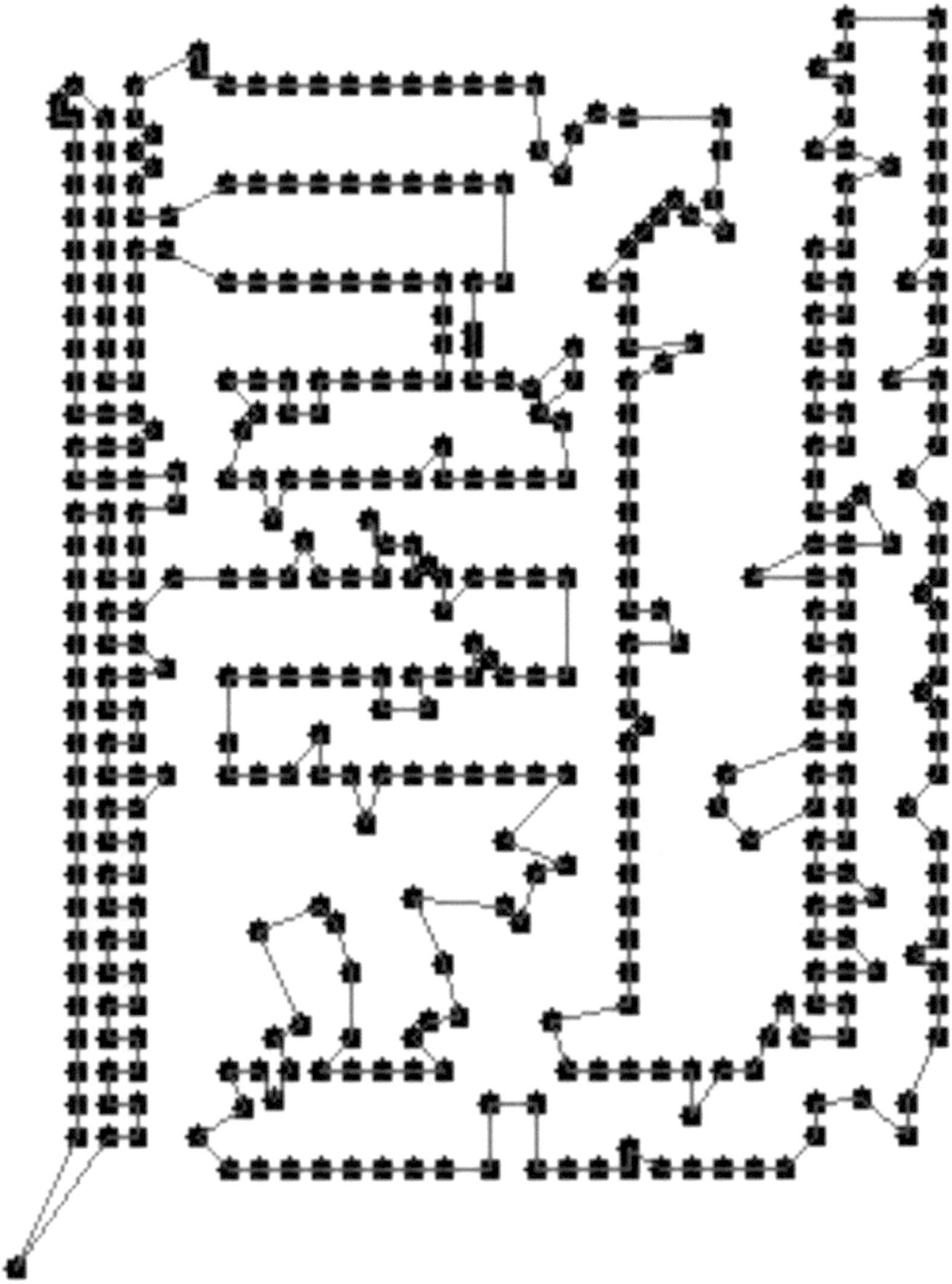

Fig. 12. The shortest route of pcb442

	N	d_m				N_o
		avg	*min*	*maxx*	*std*	
GAIAM	30	2591.3	2579	2616	11.41	3
	50	2588.5	2579	2611	12.87	9
GA	30	2670.5	2637	2702	17.82	0
	50	2678.4	2651	2720	16.82	0
GIRM	30	2640.8	2592	2715	38.14	0
	50	2621.3	2583	2667	27.26	1
IA	30	2655.6	2633	2683	15.28	0
	50	2655.7	2634	2666	11.61	0

Table 5. The result of a280

	N	d_m				N_o
		avg	*min*	*max*	*std*	
GAIAM	30	51406.3	51141	51587	122.81	0
	50	51353.6	51069	51879	277.07	0
GA	30	53351.3	53133	53740	211.59	0
	50	53274.1	52972	53772	219.23	0
GIRM	30	52878.0	52048	54036	648.81	0
	50	51856.7	51426	52332	314.42	0
IA	30	52886.5	52466	53456	311.54	0
	50	52692.7	52470	52892	125.50	0

Table 6. The result of pcb442

7. References

Goldberg, D.E. (1989). *Genetic Algorithms in Search, Optimization, and Machine Learning*, Addison Wesley,

Bersini, H. & Varela, F. (1991). The Immune Recruitment Mechanism : A Selective Evolutionary Strategy, *Proceedings of 4th International Conference on Genetic Algorithms*, pp. 520-526, San Diego, 1991

Tazawa, I.; Koakutsu, S. & Hirata, H. (1995), A VLSI Floor Design Based on Genetic Immune Recruitment Mechanism, *Transactions of the Society of Instrument and Control Engineers*, Vol.31, No.5, (5,1995), pp. 615-621

Mori, K.; Tsukiyama, M. & Fukuda, T. (1997). Immune Algorithm with Searching Diversity and its Application to Resourse Allocation Problem, *The Transactions of the Institute of Electrical Engineers of Japan,* Vol.113C, No.10, (10,1997), pp. 872-878

Mori, K.; Tsukiyama, M. & Fukuda, T. (1997). Application of an Immune Algorithm to multi-optimization problems, *The Transactions of the Institute of Electrical Engineers of*

Japan, Vol.117C, No.5, (5,1997), pp. 593-598

Honna, T.; Kaji, H. & Tosaka, N. (2005). Optimization of structure system by using an Immune algorithm and diversity of solutions, *Journal of structural and construction engineering Transactions of AIJ*, No.588, (2005), pp. 103-110

Matsui, H.; Ishiwaka, Y.; Kobayashi, J. & Konishi, O. (2006). Optimization of Catalyst Composition Using an Immune Algorithm, *Journal of Computer Aided Chemistry,* Vol.7, 2006, pp. 48-56

Lawler, E.L.; Klenstra, J.; Rinnooy A.J.K. & Shmoys, D.B. (1985). *The Travelling Salesman problem*, (1985), John Wiley

Johnson, D.S. (1991). Local optimization and the traveling salesman problem, Proceedings of 17th Colloquium on Automata, Languages, programming, pp. 446-461, England, (1991)

Nagata, Y. & Kobayashi, S. (1999). The proposal and Evaluation of a Crossover for Traveling Salesman Problems Edge Assembly Crossover, *Transactions of the Japanese Society for Artificial Intelligence*, Vol.14, No.5, (5,1999), pp. 848-859

Davis, L. (1985). Job shop scheduling with genetic algorithms, Proceedings of 1st International Conference on Genetic Algorithms, (1985), pp.136-140

8

A High Performance Immune Clonal Algorithm for Solving Large Scale TSP

Fang Liu, Yutao Qi[1], Jingjing Ma[2], Maoguo Gong[3], Ronghua Shang[4], Yangyang Li[5] and Licheng Jiao[6]
Xidian University, China

1. Introduction

Traveling Salesman Problem (TSP) is one of the most challenging combinatorial optimization problems. As the city number of TSP grows, the feasible solution space size increases factorially. For the small to mid-size TSP, the Lin-Kernighan (D. S. Johnson, 1990) (LK) and Lin-Kernighan Heuristic (C. Walshaw, 2001) (LKH) algorithms are very effective. However, these two algorithms are local search methods which find the best TSP tour in the k-change neighborhoods of the given initial TSP tour. Thus, they can only find a local optimal tour for TSP with complex solution space. Accordingly, the LK and LKH algorithms become very sensitive to the initial solution and often fail to find the global optimal tour within a reasonable time for solving large scale TSP. To remedy this problem, we make use of the global search ability of the immune clonal algorithm. Especially, we combine the two types of approaches (i.e. LK and immune clonal algorithm) to achieve high performance of the immune clonal algorithm, which can be run on loose-coupled computing environment for solving the large scale TSP.

The immune clonal algorithm inspired by biological immune system is a type of evolutionary random search algorithms. More and more research achievements indicate that immune clonal algorithm can maintain good population diversity and strong global search capability. Under the searching framework of the immune clonal algorithm, heuristic search strategies can be conveniently employed to enhance its local search capability. Such combinations take into account both global and local search strategies, and thus can realize a good tradeoff between effectiveness and efficiency. Moreover, the parallelizability of the biological immune system ensures the immune clonal algorithm can be run on loose-coupled computing environment which is advantageous to solve massive optimization problems such as the large scale TSP.

Simulation and analysis results show that the edges in the intersection set of several local optimal tours obtained by LK approach appear in the global optimal tour with high probability and the probability increases rapidly as the amount of local optimal tours increases. Using this phenomenon, an intersection set based vaccination strategy is designed in this chapter to accelerate the convergence speed of the immune clonal algorithm for TSP. In the immune clonal algorithm, vaccine is a set of genes which are estimations of the genes expected to appear in the global optimal antibody. The proposed approach in this chapter takes the intersection gene set of several memory antibodies as vaccine and injects the set into antibody populations which are distributed on different computing nodes. This information-delivery approach between antibody populations, which take vaccine as carrier, not only accelerated the procedure of the evolution but also promoted the co-evolution between antibody populations.

The main content of this chapter is arranged as follows. Section 2 provides a brief description of the related background including the development of the immune inspired optimization algorithm and its general flow chart. Section 3 describes the main loop of the proposed high performance immune clonal algorithm for TSP. Section 4 gives a detailed description of the intersection set based vaccination strategy for TSP. Section 5 investigates the experimental study of the proposed approach. Finally, concluding remarks are made in Section 6.

2. Immune optimization

Immunization is a physiological function of biological immune systems, which identify and remove the invading "non-self" antigen, mutated and damaged cells to maintain the bodies' physiological balance and stability. Human immune system is a complex system consists of organs, cells and molecules with immune functions that can protect the body against pathogens, harmful foreign bodies and other disease factors. The same as neurological and endocrine systems, immune system has its own operation mechanism and can mutual cooperate and restraint with other systems, common to maintain the bodies' physiological balance in the life processes. Since 1940s, with the development of medical research on the biological immune systems, people's awareness and understanding of the immune system has been continuously improved, a complete biological immune science system had gradually formed (Jiao Licheng et al., 2006).

2.1 Some inspiring biological mechanism of immune system

Inspired by the biological immune systems, the model and algorithm of artificial immune systems are proposed. The key inspiring biological mechanism of immune system includes: immune recognition, immune memory, immune diversity, immune tolerance, parallelism and other biological immune mechanism.

1. Immune recognition

Modern immunology believes that immune function is a response to stimulation from antigens, which is shown as the immune systems' ability of identifying themselves and excluding non-self materials. Identification is an important prerequisite in the process of immune system functions. For the phenomenon of immune recognition, clonal selection theory believes that because of the differentiation of embryonic cell, the body has formed many lymphocytic series, each lymphocyte cell's surface has a specific set of antigen receptors. When antigens enter the body, they select the corresponding lymphocytes and specifically bind to the antigen receptors of their surfaces, led to the lymphocyte activation, propagation, differentiation, and thus lead to specific immune response. In addition, the antibody itself has antigen determinant, which can be recognized by other internal antibodies and lead to a reaction with them. So, antibodies have the dual nature of recognizing antigens and being recognized by other antibodies (F.M. Burnet,1978).

2. Immune memory

Immune memory is another important feature of the immune system. Experimental results show that it can produce not only B memory cells but also TH memory cells during the immune response process. Immune memory can be explained as the phenomena of the increasing of the number of lymphocytes which have responses to specific antigens. When immune system first encounters an antigen, lymphocytes have to take some time to adjust themselves to identify antigens and save the memory information of the antigen after recognizing. When body meets the same antigen again, the effect of the associative memory, the Incubation Period of the appearance of antibodies reduced clearly and the content of antibody increased substantially, Erju duration Chang. Such phenomenon is called immunological memory (A. Tarakanov & D. Dasgupta, 2000).

Simulation on the immune memory is an important feature of artificial immune algorithms that distinction from other classic evolutionary algorithms. Farmer first presented an artificial immune model with memory which regards immune memory mechanism as an associative memory (J. D. Farmer et al, 1986). Smith compared the immune memory model and the sparse distributed memory model (SDM) and indicated that initial response corresponds to the procedure of information storage in SDM, the second response and the cross-immune response correspond to the procedure of reading memory (D. J. Smith et al,1998). Immune memory mechanisms can greatly accelerate the searching process of the optimization, speed up the learning process and improve the quality of learning. The introduction of immune memory mechanisms is an effective means to improve the efficiency of artificial immune system algorithm.

3. Immune diversity

In biological immune system, the number of antibody type is much larger than that of known antigen. There are two types of theories to explain the mechanism of immune diversity, the germlinetheory theory and the somatic mutation hypothesis. According to these theories, immune diversity may lies in the diversity of the connection of gene segments and it may be influenced by the complex pairing mechanism of the heavy chain and light chain. The immune diversity mechanism can be used for the searching procedure of optimization, it does not try global optimization, but deal with different antigens evolutionary, so as to enhancing the global search ability and keep the algorithms from falling into local optimum.

4. Immune tolerance

Immune tolerance is another important type of immune response and also one element of immunoregulation. Its performance is contrary to the positive immune response, and also different from a variety of non-specific immune suppressions which have no antigen specific, and can response or low response to various antigens. Immune tolerance is a phenomenon of body fail to response to a certain antigen which is caused by the lost function or death of specific antigen-induced lymphocyte. The general characteristics of immune tolerance are mainly in the following aspects: 1) For T or B cells were excluded or inhibited, immune tolerance is specific. 2) It's easier to introduce immature lymphocyte tolerance than mature cells. 3) The tolerance induction and maintenance of tolerance need the persistence of toleragen.

5. Parallelism

Biological immune system is a complex parallel system. Lymphoid organs, lymphoid tissue within other organs, lymphocytes cells and antigen presenting cells distribute to all parts of the body. Lymphocytes travel around the body by the blood, from one lymphoid organ or lymph tissue to another, so as to scattered the lymphoid organs and lymphoid tissue together all around the body into a functional whole. Various components of the immune system work in parallel and coordinated jointly, achieve all the features of the immune system. Simulation of biological immune system is very important to taking full advantage of loosely coupled computing resources and improving the efficiency of immune system.

2.2 Artificial immune system model

Compared with other intelligent computing systems, a complete set of mathematical theory has not yet developed in the research areas of artificial immune system. Since the immune system itself is rather complicated, there are relatively a few research findings on artificial immune system model. In 1973, Jerne proposed the idiotypic network model (N. K. Jerne, 1973) and initiated the study of artificial immune system model in 1980, Herzenberg, etc. presented a loose-coupled network architecture which is more suitable for distributed problems (L. A. Herzenberg & S. J. Black, 1980). In 1986, Hoffmann put forward symmetric network model (G. W. Hoffmann,1986) based on the immune neuron model according to the similarity between immune system and nervous system. In 1989, Perelson presented a probability model of unique type network based on previous studies. (A. S. Perelson, 1989). In 1990, Farmer proposed dynamic system model (J. D. Farmer, 1990) based on connectionism, after compared and analyzed the similarities, differences and characteristics among the immune system, neural network and genetic system.. In 1995, Ishiguro etc. presented coupled immune network model. In 1997, Tang proposed multi-valued immune network model based on the mechanism of interaction between B cells and T cells (Z. Tang et al, 1997). In 1997, borrowing ideas from the mechanism that the system balance can be maintained by the interaction between B cells, Mitsumoto proposed immune response network model, which is used for scheduling and controlling the distributed autonomous robots group (N. Mitsumoto & T. Fukuta, 1997). In 2000, Zak proposed an immune system stochastic model, according to the principle of response under stress.

At present, two influential artificial immune network models are the Resource Limited Artificial Immune System (RLAIS) proposed by Jonathan Timmis etc.(J. Timmis & M. Neal, 2001) and the aiNet proposed by De Castro etc. (L. N. De Castro & F. J. Von Zuben,2000). Timmis put forward RLAIS on the basis of Cook and Hunt's research. He also presented the concept of Artificial Recognition Ball (ARB). Timmis considered that the role of ARB and B cell function is similar, artificial immune system is composed by a fixed number of ARB. Further more, by analogy with the natural immune system,, he thought that the stimulation from which ARB suffered includes the main stimulation, the stimulation and restrain from adjacent antibody. In addition, the capability of cloning can be determined by the stimulation given to ARB. De Castro's aiNet algorithm which simulates the stimulation process of the stimulation from the immune network to antigens, mainly includes the antibody-antigen recognition, immune cloning proliferation, affinity maturation and network suppression Immune network is considered as an enabling undirected graph, and is not fully connected. However, the current prevalence of adaptive immune network model is rather poor, contains more parameters, and over-reliance on changes in the network nodes to maintain network dynamics, the lack of the understanding of immune network of nonlinear information processing capacity are also weak points.At the same time, the design of the algorithm generally starts from focusing on data compression, therefore, the scope of the application of the algorithm is limited. It should be noted that the relevant mechanism in the immune network has been widely used in computer networks, particularly network security study, but these applications are mostly ideological. There are still no specific algorithms.

In addition to the network models described above, there are also two different non-network models presented respectively by Alexander Tarakanov (A. Tarakanov & D. Dasgupta, 2000) and Nohara (B. T. Nohara & H. Takahashi, 2000) in 2000.Alexander Tarakanov etc. tried to establish the form of protein models based on artificial immune system for the establishment of a formal model. After that, they indicated that the improved model can be used for the evaluation of the complex calculations of Kaliningrad's Ecological Atlas. In their works,much attention was paid to the interaction between the immune function of cells, and the network was not much involved. Based the feature of antibody units, Nohara etc. presented a non-network model of artificial immune system.

2.3 Artificial immune system algorithm

As the understanding of the mechanism of the immune system is not yet very deep, there is not much research on the artificial immune system algorithm. Common artificial immune algorithms include the following four types: artificial immune network algorithm, negative selection algorithm, immune evolutionary algorithm and immune clonal selection algorithm.

1. Artificial immune network

The simulation researches of the immune network mainly focus on the application of computer network security, while the study on immune algorithm is rarely seen at present. Now two typical artificial immune network algorithms are the Resource Limited Artificial Immune System Algorithm proposed by Timmis etc. (J. Timmis & M. Neal, 2001) and the aiNet algorithm proposed by De Castro etc. (L. N. De Castro & F. J.Von Zuben, 2000). However, the current prevalence of adaptive immune network model is rather poor, contains more parameters, and the over-reliance on changes in the network nodes to maintain network dynamics, the lack of the understanding of immune network of nonlinear information processing capacity are also weak points.At the same time, the design of the algorithm generally starts from focusing on data compression, therefore, the scope of the application of the algorithm is limited.

2. Negative selection algorithm

Computer security problems and immune system problems encountered with striking similarities, they both have to be constantly changing environment to maintain system stability. Distribution, flexibility, adaptively and robust solution of the immune system are exactly what the field of computer security expects. According to self / non-self distinction principle of the immune system, Forrest etc. proposed a negative selection algorithm which can detect changes in computer system (S. Forrest et al, 1994). The algorithms simulate the "negative selection" principal of T cell maturation process: randomly generated detectors, remove detectors which detect themselves and preserve those detect non-self. Negative selection algorithm has laid a theoretical foundation for the application of the immunity in computer network security areas.

3. Immune evolutionary algorithm

As a kind of random search optimization method, evolutionary algorithm has been widely used. However, it still needs improving in practice. For example, evolutionary algorithm can not guarantee grantee getting the globally optimal solution, it may lose the best individual in the population and it also has the problems of premature convergence. More effective optimization algorithms will be got if evolution and immunity are combined. Under the framework of evolutionary algorithm, researchers have introduced many features of the immune system and developed a number of immune optimization algorithms. Such as immune optimization algorithm with vaccination (Jiao Licheng & Wang Lei, 2000), immune optimization algorithm with self-regulation mechanism (Zhang Jun et al., 1999), immune optimization algorithm based on immune response (J. S. Chun et al., 1998), and immune optimization algorithm with immune memory (S. Endoh et al., 1998). These improved algorithms can quickly find the optimal solution meeting the requirements of certain accuracy and are useful to solve engineering problems (Jiao Licheng &Du Haifeng, 2003).

4. Immune clonal selection algorithm

Clonal selection algorithm is an important type of immune optimization algorithm, and it has been widely used in the artificial immune system. In 2000, De Castro etc. concentrated the clonal selection mechanism of immune system with the help of previous studies, and proposed a clonal selection based immune algorithm, which was successfully used to solve pattern recognition, numerical optimization and combinatorial optimization problems (L. N. De Castro & F. J. Von Zuben, 2000). In 2002, Kim etc. proposed a dynamic clonal selection algorithm and it was used to solve the anomaly detection problem in the continuous changing environment (J. Kim & P. J. Bentley, 2002) In 2005, Jiao Licheng, Du Haifeng etc. proposed Immune polyclonal Strategy based on the work of predecessors, and what was more they proposed Immune clonal selection algorithm for solving the problem about high dimensional function optimization (Du Haifeng et al, 2005), which achieved good results. Jiao Licheng and others have also presented some other high-level algorithm, Such as the Immune Memory Clonal Programming Algorithm (Du Haifeng et al, 2004), Adaptive chaos clonal evolutionary programming algorithm (Du Haifeng, 2005) and so on.

2.4 Artificial immune optimization algorithm

Engineering Optimization technology is a technology for solving various engineering optimal problems. As an important branch of science, engineering optimization technology has been attracting widespread attention, and been applied in many engineering fields, such as system control, artificial intelligence, pattern recognition, production scheduling, VLSI technology, fault diagnosis, computer engineering and so on. Engineering process optimization plays an important role in improving the efficiency and effectiveness and saving resources. Theoretical study of optimization algorithms also plays an important role in improving performance of algorithm, broadening the application field of algorithm, improving algorithms system. Therefore, study of the optimization theory and algorithm is important both theoretically and practically.

As science and technology continues to progress and the computer technology has been widely used, the scale and complexity of engineering optimization problems are increasing. Because of some inherent limitations and shortcomings, traditional optimization methods fail to meet such requirements to solve complex optimization problems. Researchers have to find new ideas to solve problems. Since the 1980s, a number of novel optimization algorithms have been proposed, such as artificial neural networks, simulated annealing, tabu search, evolutionary algorithms, ant colony optimization, particle swarm optimization, artificial immune algorithms, EDA algorithms and hybrid optimization strategy. These algorithms develop through simulating or revealing certain natural phenomena or a process, and the ideas and content relate to mathematics, physics, biological evolution, artificial intelligence, neuroscience and statistics, so it provides new methods to solve the complex problems. These new algorithms can often get rid of the limitations of traditional optimization algorithm, using heuristic optimization strategies to explore the optimal solution, and has been used in a large number of practical applications and achieved encouraging results. With the development of interdisciplinary research, new intelligent optimization algorithms are emerging and bring new solutions to the optimization problems.

Artificial immune system is an adaptive system for solving the complex problems by simulating the function and principle of biological immune system. Immune algorithm retains many intelligent features of the biological immune system, so it has great diversity maintaining mechanisms, global search capability and robustness, and enables parallel search. Artificial immune algorithm is getting more and more attentions from researchers, and it is widely used for numerical optimization (Gong Maoguo et al, 2007), combinatorial optimization, multicast routing (Liu Fang et al, 2003), job shop scheduling (Z.X. Ong et al, 2005) multi-objective optimization (Shang Ronghua et al, 2007) and other engineering optimization problems.

2.5 The concept of immunology used in immune optimization algorithm

Immune optimization algorithm simulates immune mechanisms of biological immune system to deal with engineering optimization problems. Before Immune optimization algorithm is constructed, we need to map the various elements in engineering optimization problems to related concepts in immunology. As the biological immune system is very complex, it is impossible and unnecessary to completely apply biology definition in the artificial immune system. In order to better describe the artificial immune system algorithm, the following will briefly explain a few common used immune academic terms and their meaning in immune optimization algorithms.

1. Antigen

In the artificial immune system, it generally refers to the problem and its constraints, which is similar with fitness function in evolutionary algorithm. Specifically, it is a function of the objective function, and is the initiating factor and the important metrics of artificial immune algorithms.

2. Antibody

In the artificial immune system, it generally refers to candidate solutions of the problem, which is similar with individual in evolutionary algorithm. Collection of antibodies is called antibody group. In practice, the antibody generally appears in the form of coding.

3. Antibody-antigen affinity

It shows that the Antibody's binding capacity to Antigen, and reflects the binding site of a single antibody and the binding force of the unit antigen (or epitopes). In artificial immune system, it is used to show how the antibody at different locations (code) affects the antigen (or objective function).

4. Vaccine

Vaccine is defined as the estimate of the best individual gene, resulting from evolutionary environment or prior knowledge of the unknown problem.

5. Memory unit

In the artificial immune system, memory unit is an antibody group composed by specific antibody, which is used to maintain species diversity and the optimal solution in the process of solving problem.

6. Clone

Clone is the proliferation processes of biological Immune systems. In the artificial immune system cloning operator, based on clonal selection theory, clone is a composite operator which is a combination of selection, expansion, mutation and crossover operators.

3. Parallel immune memory clonal selection algorithm for large scale TSP

Traveling salesman problem (TSP) is a classical combinatorial optimization problem, with a strong engineering background and extensive application. TSP problem can be formally described as: given N cities $\mathbf{C} = \{C_1, C_2, \cdots, C_N\}$, and the distance between any two cities $d(C_i, C_j)$, find a closed path $\mathbf{C}_\pi = \{C_{\pi(1)}, C_{\pi(2)}, \cdots, C_{\pi(N)}\}$, through all cities in C only once, making minimal total distance $\sum_{i=1}^{N-1} d(C_{\pi(i)}, C_{\pi(i+1)}) + d(C_{\pi(N)}, C_{\pi(1)})$ (D.S.Johnson and L.A.McGeoch, 1997). The solution space of TSP problem increases rapidly as the size of the problem increases, as a result, traditional methods (such as the exhaustive method, dynamic programming, branch and bound, etc.) have been powerless. It has proven that TSP problem is NP-hard combinatorial optimization problem, and it is difficult to find an effective algorithm to obtain the optimal solution in polynomial time. Therefore for Large-scale problems, people are more inclined to seek an algorithm that can find acceptable approximate solution in a limited time. Approximation algorithm for solving TSP is divided into two categories: tour construction algorithm and loop improved algorithm. Tour construction algorithms start from an illegal solution and gradually change the path until to get up a legitimate path. Such algorithms include: nearest neighbor algorithm, greedy algorithm, Clarke-Wright algorithm, Christofides algorithm (D.S.Johnson & L.A.McGeoch, 1997) and so on. After given an initial legitimate solution, circle improved algorithm uses a certain strategy to find solutions of better quality. Such algorithms include: local search strategy (r-Opt, LK, LKH, cycle LK (D. S. Johnson & L. A. McGeoch, 2002), etc.), tabu search (D.S.Johnson & L.A.McGeoch, 1997), simulated annealing (D.S.Johnson & L.A.McGeoch, 1997), genetic algorithm (T. Guo & Z. Michalewicz, 1998), ant colony algorithm (X.M. Song et al., 1998), particle swarm optimization (X.X.He et al., 2006), multi-level algorithms (C. Walshaw, 2001), immune algorithms (Wang Lei et al., 2000) and so on.

For large search spaces of massive TSP, the computing power of single computer is far from being able to satisfy the search algorithm on the request of the time. At the same time, with the development of network technology, there exists a large number of loosely coupled idle computation resource. It is practicable that cluster these computing resources to handle large and complex problems. Therefore, the research on parallel algorithms running in a loosely coupled environment has a very important significance. Parallel algorithms for solving large-scale TSP have attracted more and more attention. There has been some research results about parallel ACO (Lv Qiang et al., 2007), however currently just in its infancy. This chapter attempts to design a parallel immune algorithm to solve this complex problem.

At present, the achievements of parallel artificial immune system research are mostly parallel immune algorithms that have been existed. Artificial immune system model on parallel research is still rare. However, the parallel algorithm is not simply the only existing serial algorithm using multiple processors in parallel to achieve. In the parallel genetic algorithm results, many mature parallel modes are in emergence, such as: Master (Master-Slave) model, fine-grained (Fine-grained) model, coarse-grained (Coarse-grained) model, mixed (Hybrid) model (Erick Cantú-Paz, 2000) and so on. Especially, the coarse-grained parallel model which is widely used can not only speed up the speed of algorithm for large-scale complex problems, and a variety of groups in the search can make the algorithm more stable, avoid local optima.

In this chapter, based on the successful experience of the Parallel genetic algorithm, artificial immune system, TMSM and PIMCSA are designed to solve the large-scale TSP problem according with the features of artificial immune system. TMSM is a coarse-grained two parallel artificial immune model, which stimulate the distributed immune memory and immune response mechanisms based on TMSM of PIMCSA. the migration of vaccines instead of individual migration in PIMCSA, not only reduces the cost of communication greatly, but also accelerate the convergence. Either the simulations of the symmetric or asymmetric TSP problem show that, PIMCSA compared with the most effective one of the local search algorithm cycle LK(D. S. Johnson, 1990) algorithm and the pure random search algorithm Guo Tao evolutionary algorithm (T. Guo & Z. Michalewicz, 1998) whose performance is best recognized , is much better. Meanwhile PIMCSA has good scalability.

3.1 Towerlike master-slave model

Coarse-grained parallel model of genetic algorithm is on the basis of the model of multi-populations evolution (Fig. 1), that is, each sub-population evolves independently, and sub-populations do the individual migration to a certain interval. On the research of coarse-grained parallel genetic algorithm, sub-species topology (X.M. Song et al., 2006), chromosome migration strategies (X.X. He et al., 2006), sub- population division strategy(C. Walshaw, 2001) and so on are key points of the algorithm design.

When designing a parallel artificial immune system, we should not only consider the division and organizational structure of sub-population antibody along with the way to information interactions of sub-populations of antibodies. The proposed tower master-slave model (TMSM) is a coarse-grained two parallel artificial immune system model, which is not only parallel but also embodies the distributed characteristics of antibodies populations and immune memory characteristics.

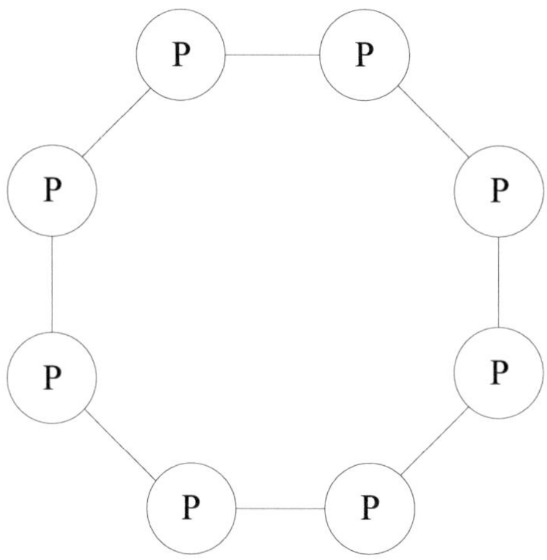

Fig. 1. Coarse-grained parallel genetic algorithm model

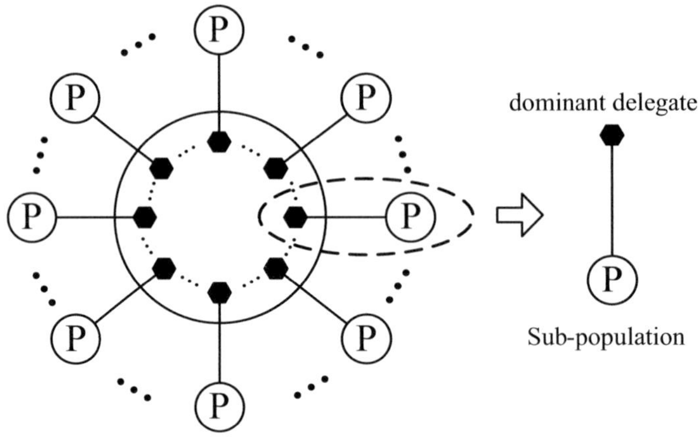

Fig. 2. Tower-like master-slave model

Definition 1: The towerlike master-slave model (TMSM), as shown in Fig. 2, is a two layer coarse-grained parallel model. The model consists of two types of populations organized as in Fig. 2, including a memory population M and several antibody populations P.
The top layer of the TMSM is the memory population $\mathbf{M} = \left(\hat{\mathbf{A}}_1, \hat{\mathbf{A}}_2, \cdots, \hat{\mathbf{A}}_m\right)$ formed by m memory antibodies. Each memory antibody of M corresponds to an antibody sub-population. The under layer of TMST are m sub-populations of antibodies with size n.
Definition 2: Each memory antibody in memory population M, $\hat{\mathbf{A}}_i$ ($i = 1,2,\cdots,m$), is mapped to a sub-population $\mathbf{P}_i$. We call $\hat{\mathbf{A}}_i$ is the dominant delegate of population $\mathbf{P}_i$.
TMSM inherits the advantage of the evolution of a variety of groups of a coarse-grained parallel model, while with modifies according to the characteristics of the immune system. In TMSM, the antibody population is divided into a memory and several sub-populations. Moreover, a one to one map between antibody in memory and sub-population is established. Such a design not only makes the immune system get the memory function, but also produce the distributed immune memory with the below driven algorithm used to a distributed population of antibodies. Meanwhile, the corresponding immune mechanism, the self adaptive extraction and inoculation mechanism o f the immune vaccine and can be expanded with this model.
As the memory population served to initiate and terminate the process of calculation, as well as schedule the task of information exchange between sub-populations of antibodies, the concept of primary and secondary comes out. Memory population is the "primary" and the sub-species antibody is "secondary." This is essentially different from the primary-secondary parallel model of the parallel genetic algorithm (Erick Cantú-Paz, 2000).

3.2 PIMCSA for solving TSP

To solve the TSP problem, Parallel Immune Memory Clonal Selection Algorithm (PIMCSA) adopted the encoding method of path representation. The antibody affinity A, is defined as:

$$\text{Affinity}(\mathbf{A}) = \left(\text{Length}(\mathbf{A}) - HKB\right) / HKB \tag{1}$$

$\text{Length}(\mathbf{A})$ indicates the path length after antibody A decoded, HKB indicates Held-Karp Bound of TSP problem which is the estimation of optimal path length of TSP.

In accordance with the description of the general framework of PIMCSA, PIMCSA includes two parts: the memory population immune algorithm (Memory Immune Algorithm, MIA) and sub-populations of antibody immune algorithm (Population Immune Algorithm, PIA). MIA and PIA process were designed to solve large-scale TSP problems.

3.2.1 Immune algorithm of memory population

Memory population immune algorithm (MIA) is running in memory antibody population driven algorithm of TMSM. MIA is the initiator of the parallel algorithm and termination of immune persons, not only in the memory to complete the memory antibody population evolution that is self-learning and memory mature operation, while responsible for extraction and distribution of vaccines to the antibody sub-populations. The pseudo code of memory immune algorithm population is described as follows:

Memory population immune algorithm (MIA):

Set algorithm termination conditions, and let evolution generations r=0；
Initialize population of memory antibodies randomly $\mathbf{M}(r)$ and calculate of affinity, then set Collection of vaccines $\mathbf{V}(r)$ to be Empty set;
While (algorithm termination conditions are not satisfied)
{
Try to receive every antibody $\bar{\mathbf{A}}_i$ which is sended from $\mathbf{P}_i$ to $\mathbf{M}(r)$.If $\bar{\mathbf{A}}_i$ is received and it's affinity is larger than $\hat{\mathbf{A}}_i$,
Then $\hat{\mathbf{A}}_i$ is replaced by $\bar{\mathbf{A}}_i$;
Run mature implementation of memory: $\mathbf{M}(r+1) = \text{Maturation}(\mathbf{M}(r))$;
Run Dynamic vaccine extraction operation: $\mathbf{V}(r+1) = \text{Extraction}(\mathbf{M}(r+1))$;
Run vaccine distribution operation: $\text{Dispatch}(\mathbf{P}_1, \mathbf{P}_2, \cdots, \mathbf{P}_m)$;
r=r+1;
}
Count, output the result, and send termination signal of the algorithm to each sub-population.

Mature implementation of memory: Cyclic LK algorithm process is adopted in the mature implementation of memory. For each memory antibody population, $\hat{\mathbf{A}}'_i$ is got after local search 4-Opt is done firstly, then after optimizing $\hat{\mathbf{A}}'_i$ through LK algorithm, we can get local optimal solution $\hat{\mathbf{A}}''_i$. If the affinity of $\hat{\mathbf{A}}''_i$ is greater than $\hat{\mathbf{A}}_i$, the alternative $\hat{\mathbf{A}}_i$ with $\hat{\mathbf{A}}''_i$, otherwise $\hat{\mathbf{A}}_i$ is retained. Mature memory populations in post-operation is $\mathbf{M}(r+1)$.

The strategy of the extraction of dynamic memory antibody vaccines will be divided into two parts, Vaccine is extracted from a part and is inoculated to another part of the memory of antibody sub-populations corresponding antibodies. Therefore, the moving into sub-populations of antibody vaccine is the evolutionary experience concluded from the representative of their own advantages other than some good memories antibodies. Extraction and distribution of this vaccine strategy is conducive to the exchange between the antibody sub-populations experience and accelerates the evolution of species.

Meanwhile, when the vaccine is extracted each time, it will be re-divided into two groups of memory. This will prevent too many antibodies being assigned to the sub-populations, so as to prevent the algorithm prematurity which is caused by the loss of diversity. The operation of dynamic extraction and distribution of vaccines will be given in detail in the next section.

3.2.2 Immune algorithm of antibody population

The immune algorithm of antibody sub-populations (PIA) is a driven algorithm running on every sub-population of antibodies in TMSM. PIA receives two kinds of information from the immune algorithm of memory populations in the process of iteration: Algorithm termination information and vaccines information.

Immune algorithm of antibody sub-populations maintains the iterative evolution of antibody sub-populations. The operation process of clonal selection can be adopted in the iterative evolution. The immune genetic operation to Sub-population of the antibodies is composed by the vaccination operation and Inver-over operator. It will be given in detail in the next section. The pseudo-code of the immune algorithm which runs in the sub-populations of antibody $\mathbf{P}_i (i = 1,2,\cdots,m)$ is given as follows:

Immune algorithm of antibody sub-populations(PIA):

Let iteration times t=0, set termination signal Halt=False;

Initialize the population of memory antibodies $\mathbf{P}_i(t) = (\mathbf{A}^i{}_1(t), \mathbf{A}^i{}_2(t), \cdots, \mathbf{A}^i{}_n(t))$ randomly, and calculate of affinity;

Assume $\bar{\mathbf{A}}_i(t)$ to be optimal antibody in $\mathbf{P}_i(t)$, Set current optimal antibody affinity: *CurrentBest*=Affinity$(\bar{\mathbf{A}}_i(t))$;

Send $\bar{\mathbf{A}}_i(t)$ to the population of memory M;

Set current vaccine $v(t)$ to be Empty.

While (Halt is not True)

{

Try to receive the termination signal algorithm from the population of memory M, If received, Set Halt=True. Otherwise, jump out of the loop;

Try to receive the vaccine from the population of memory M, If received, replace v with the new vaccine;

Run clonal operation: $\mathbf{P}_i'(t) = \mathrm{CL}(\mathbf{P}_i(t))$;

Run immunity operation: $\mathbf{P}_i''(t) = \mathrm{IG}(\mathbf{P}_i'(t))$;

Run clonal selection operation: $\mathbf{P}_i(t+1) = \mathrm{SL}(\mathbf{P}_i''(t))$;

Find the optimal antibody from $\mathbf{P}_i(t+1)$,If Affinity$(\bar{\mathbf{A}}_i(t+1)) >$ *CurrentBest* , then set *CurrentBest*=Affinity$(\bar{\mathbf{A}}_i(t+1))$ and send $\bar{\mathbf{A}}_i(t+1)$ to M;

t = t+1;

}

Cloning operation: cloning operation CL is defined as follows,

$$\mathrm{CL}\left(\mathbf{P}_i(t)\right)=\left(\mathrm{CL}\left(\mathbf{A}^i{}_1(t)\right),\mathrm{CL}\left(\mathbf{A}^i{}_2(t)\right),\ldots,\mathrm{CL}\left(\mathbf{A}^i{}_n(t)\right)\right) \tag{2}$$

In the formula, $\mathrm{CL}\left(\mathbf{A}^i{}_j(t)\right)=\vec{\mathbf{I}}_j\times\mathbf{A}^i{}_j(t)$ $(j=1,2,\cdots,n)$, $\vec{\mathbf{I}}_j$ is Unit row vector with q_j dimensions), which is called the q_j colon of antibody $\mathbf{A}^i{}_j(t)$. Clone size q_j and the antibody affinity $\mathbf{A}^i{}_j(t)$ are related. q_j is greater while affinity is greater.
Let $\mathbf{Y}_j'(t)=\mathrm{CL}\left(\mathbf{A}^i{}_j(t)\right)=\left\{y'_{j1}(t),y'_{j2}(t),\ldots,y'_{jq_j}(t)\right\}$, then the sub-populations of antibodies after the CL operation can be written as:

$$\mathbf{P}_i'(t)=\left\{\mathbf{Y}_1'(t),\mathbf{Y}_2'(t),\ldots,\mathbf{Y}_n'(t)\right\} \tag{3}$$

Immune gene action: immune genetic operation is defined as follows，

$$\mathrm{IG}\left(\mathbf{P}_i'(t)\right)=\left(\mathrm{IG}(\mathbf{Y}_1'(t)),\mathrm{IG}(\mathbf{Y}_2'(t)),\cdots,\mathrm{IG}(\mathbf{Y}_n'(t))\right) \tag{4}$$

Assume $\mathbf{Y}_j''(t)=\mathbf{IG}\left(\mathbf{Y}_j'(t)\right)=\left\{y''_{j1}(t),y''_{j2}(t),\ldots,y''_{jq_j}(t)\right\}$, then the sub-populations of antibodies after the IG operation can be written as:

$$\mathbf{P}''(t)=\left\{\mathbf{Y}_1''(t),\mathbf{Y}_2''(t),\ldots,\mathbf{Y}_n''(t)\right\} \tag{5}$$

Immune genetic manipulation IG acts on the antibody with the operator which is chosen with equal probability between vaccination operator Vaccination and Inver-over operator .Inver-over operator which is famous for Guo Tao algorithm designed for TSP problems an effective operation of the genetic evolution. Vaccination operator is designed according to the dynamic vaccine extracted from the memory population M. Detailed operational procedures will be written in the next section.
Inver-over operator is the local search which runs in the encoded space around with antibody, using the heuristic information within the sub-populations of antibodies. Vaccination operator will introduce the knowledge learned from the memory population M to the antibodies, in the use of heuristic information from other sub-populations of antibodies.
Clonal selection operation: clonal selection operation are defined as follows,

$$\mathrm{SL}\left(\mathbf{P}_i''(t)\right)=\left(\mathrm{SL}\left(\mathbf{Y}_1''(t)\right),\mathrm{SL}\left(\mathbf{Y}_2''(t)\right),\cdots,\mathrm{SL}\left(\mathbf{Y}_n''(t)\right)\right) \tag{6}$$

If $\mathbf{A}^i{}_j(t+1)=\mathrm{SL}\left(\mathbf{Y}_j''(t)\right)$ ($j=1,2,\cdots,n$),then the population in SL post-operation is ,

$$\mathbf{P}_i(t+1)=\left(\mathbf{A}^i{}_1(t+1),\mathbf{A}^i{}_2(t+1),\cdots,\mathbf{A}^i{}_n(t+1)\right) \tag{7}$$

The process of the operation $\mathrm{SL}\left(\mathbf{Y}_j''(t)\right)$ acted on $\mathbf{Y}_j''(t)$ is as follows: the antibody with maximum optimal affinity chosen from $\mathbf{Y}_j''(t)$ can be written as,

$$y_j''(t)=\left\{\mathbf{y}''_{jk}(t)\mid \max \mathrm{affinity}(\mathbf{y}''_{jk}(t)),k=1,\cdots,q_j\right\} \tag{8}$$

If $\text{Affinity}\left(y''_j(t)\right) > \text{Affinity}\left(\mathbf{A}^i{}_j(t)\right)$, then let $\text{SL}\left(\mathbf{Y}''_j(t)\right) = y''_j(t)$. Otherwise, $\text{SL}\left(\mathbf{Y}''_j(t)\right) = \mathbf{A}^i{}_j(t)$.

4. Dynamic vaccination

In artificial immune system, the vaccine is an estimate of the best individual gene on the basis of evolution environment or the apriori knowledge of unknown problem. Vaccine is not an individual, which can not be decoded to a solution of a problem as antibodies can be done. It just has the characteristics on some places of the genes. Therefore vaccine can be regarded as a single gene or a set of gene sequences fragment. The right choice for the vaccine will have a positive role in promoting population evolution, and thus have a very vital significance to the operating efficiency of algorithm. But, the quality of selection of vaccine and generated antibodies will only affect the function of the vaccination of immune operator, but will not involve to the convergence of algorithm.

4.1 Selection and distribution of vaccine

For TSP problem and PIMCSA algorithm, we design a dynamic vaccine extraction (Dynamic Vaccination, DV) strategy and a vaccine allocation strategy as described below.

Dynamic vaccination strategy will first divide current memory antibody population into two antibody sets: the set of vaccines extraction $\mathbf{M}_1(r+1)$ and the vaccination set $\mathbf{M}_2(r+1)$. Let k is the largest positive integer less than or equal to m/2 (m is the size of memory population), then randomly select k memory antibodies to compose $\mathbf{M}_1(r+1)$, and the remaining antibodies compose $\mathbf{M}_2(r+1)$.Then, do intersection operation for all the memory antibodies, and get the set $\mathbf{E}(r+1)$ of the public sides on the k paths. And next, we merge the sides with public cities into public sub-paths, and store the received public sub-paths and the rest of public sides as a multi-gene vaccine group and single-gene vaccine respectively into vaccine set $\mathbf{V}(r+1)$. In $\mathbf{V}(r+1)$, a single gene vaccine with length 1 represents an edge of the path and its storage form is city sequences of the end of a edge. Vaccine group represents a section of sub-paths such that a sequence of the edges of the head-to-serial, and its storage form is the sorted arrangement of a number of cities, and its length is the number of edges that sub-paths include.

After producing the vaccines, we will distribute them to the antibody sub-populations. We design the following vaccine distribution operation. First of all, randomly choose a vaccine v_i from the vaccine set $\mathbf{V}(r+1)$, which may be a single gene vaccine or a multi-genes vaccine group. Then, randomly choose a memory antibody $\hat{\mathbf{A}}_j$ from the vaccination set $\mathbf{M}_2(r+1)$ and send the vaccine v_i to the antibody sub-population $\mathbf{P}_j$ that $\hat{\mathbf{A}}_j$ corresponds to.

4.2 Vaccination

As the vaccination operations will bring the loss of population diversity when accelerating the convergence of algorithm. In Section 1.2 where we will operate it as part of immune genes operation rather than independent step, will help alleviate the loss of the diversity of antibody population. For the TSP problem, we take the implementation of the Inver-over operator and vaccination operator in equal probability, which jointly constitute the immune genes operators. The immune genes operation process of the antibody sub-population $\mathbf{P}'_j(t)$ (j = 1, 2,..., m) is described as follows:

The operation process of $\mathrm{IG}\left(\mathbf{P}_j'(t)\right)$:

```
for each antibody A'_i(t) in P'_j(t)
{
if ( Rand(0,1) ≤ 0.5 )
   Viccination(A'_i(t));
else
 Inver_over(A'_i(t));
}
```

Here, $\mathrm{Rand}(0,1)$ is a random number between 0 and 1. The vaccination $\mathrm{Viccination}(\mathbf{A})$ on antibody A is described as follows:

The operation process of $\mathrm{Viccination}(\mathbf{A})$:

```
Viccination(A)
{
 If (the current vaccine v of antibody sub-population is not empty)
{
c is the first city in v , c' is the next city of c in v ;
While ( c is not the last city in v )
{
    turn the city between the next city of c and c' in A'
    c = c';
    c' =The next city of c' in v
}
}
}
```

Here, the process of vaccination operation using Inver-over operator plant the edges of a single-gene vaccine into the operated antibody or plant the edges of multi-genes vaccine group into the operated individuals.

5. Simulating results and analysis

The simulating software of the proposed approach PIMCSA was developed by C&MPI and ran on the HPC (Cluster) parallel computing platform. We got several typical symmetric and asymmetric TSP instances from TSPLIB and tested them.

As the memory mature operation of PIMCSA used steps of ILK, and immune genetic manipulation of antibody sub-population introduced the Inver-over operator, we compare the performance of PIMCSA with iterated Lin-Kernighan (ILK) algorithm (D. S. Johnson, 1990) and GuoTao (GT) algorithm (T. Guo & Z. Michalewicz, 1998). ILK algorithm is one of the most effective algorithms based on local search, and GT algorithm is the best pure evolutionary stochastic searching algorithm. In PIMCSA, antibody sub-population number m is set as 8, antibody sub-population size n is set as 30. Population size of ILK and GT algorithm are both set as 30. Termination condition of these three algorithms is that current optimal path length of memory population is less than the best known path length or equal to it, or the current optimal path remains unchanged in 50 iterations. All the experimental data are statistical results of 20 independent runs.

5.1 Performances on symmetric TSP instances

Table 1 shows the performances of compared algorithms on symmetric TSP problems with different type and size. In the table, "Percent over Opt" refers to the percentage of difference between path length and the optimal path length, and "Running Time (seconds) "refers to the average time of computing.

Instance	Cities	Opt	Percent over Opt (mean)			Running Time (mean)		
			ILK	GT	PIMCSA	ILK	GT	PIMCSA
ATT532	532	27686	0.086	0.114	**0**	127.5	83.5	**17.4**
GR666	666	294358	0.061	0.176	**0.003**	292.1	102.4	**59.6**
DSJ1000	1000	18659688	0.133	0.152	**0.008**	418.6	372.4	**52.2**
PR2392	2392	378032	0.142	0.357	**0.006**	102.5	87.3	**16.6**
RL5915	5915	565530	0.163	0.879	**0.047**	293.7	**226.9**	239.1
PLA7397	7397	23260728	0.059	0.356	**0.007**	8843.2	8221.1	**1762.4**
RL11849	11849	923288	0.191	0.824	**0.105**	6311.3	5352.8	**2581.3**
USA13509	13509	19982859	0.163	1.209	**0.067**	10352.3	8931.5	**3520.7**
PLA33810	33810	66050499	0.184	1.813	**0.152**	76315.8	53356.6	**18137.4**
PLA85900	85900	142382641	0.246	1.115	**0.214**	214307.5	113755.9	**29883.2**
Average			0.1428	0.6995	**0.0609**	31736.45	19049.04	**5626.99**

Table 1. Performance comparisons on Symmetric TSP Instances

As it can be seen from Table 1, for symmetric TSP problems, both the tour quality and computing time of the proposed PIMCSA are superior to other two compared algorithms. With the increase of problem scale, the advantage of PIMCSA is getting more obvious. ILK can obtain TSP solution tour with higher quality, but the time cost of ILK is large, so it needs too long computing time for solving large scale TSP instances. GT expenses little computing time at each generation, however, it is easy to fall into local optimum. The running time of GT is shorter, but the quality of solution tour is not very good. PIMCSA combines the strengths of these two types of methods, it use the random search with small time cost for global search, and then it use the heuristic search with large time cost for local search. Experimental results indicate that PIMCSA achieves a good trade off between solution quality and computing time.

5.2 Performances on asymmetric TSP Instances

For asymmetric TSP with N cities, we use Jonker and Volgenant's method to transform it into symmetric TSP with 2N cities (Noda E et al., 2002).
Note $\mathbf{C} = \left[c_{ij}\right]_{N\times N}$ as the cost matrix of asymmetric TSP problem, we can use equation (9) to transform it into $\mathbf{C}' = \left[c'_{ij}\right]_{2N\times 2N}$ which is the cost matrix of the transformed symmetric TSP instance. L is a sufficiently large real number. In this paper, we set $L = \max\left(c_{ij}\right)$.

$$c'_{N+i,j} = c'_{j,N+i} = c_{ij} \quad i,j = 1,2,\cdots N \text{ and } i \neq j$$
$$c'_{N+i,i} = c'_{i,N+i} = -L \quad i = 1,2,\cdots N \qquad (9)$$
$$c'_{ij} = L \qquad \textit{otherwise}$$

Instance	Cities	Opt	Percent over Opt (mean)			Running Time (mean)		
			ILK	GT	PIMCSA	ILK	GT	PIMCSA
BR17	17	39	0	0	**0**	2.14	3.57	**0.12**
P43	43	5620	0.082	0.372	**0.002**	33.2	**21.7**	25.3
RY48P	48	14422	0.037	0.506	**0.015**	23.6	24.2	**1.34**
FTV70	71	1950	0.132	0.358	**0.039**	42.9	38.1	**2.33**
KRO124P	100	36230	0.031	0.114	**0.007**	72.3	55.6	**1.15**
FT53	106	6905	**0**	0.037	**0**	31.2	63.4	**1.85**
FTV170	171	2755	**0.018**	0.326	0.044	69.3	42.7	**1.03**
RBG358	358	1163	0.139	1.977	**0.006**	137.5	114.6	**36.6**
RBG 403	403	2465	0.082	0.973	**0**	291.7	174.3	**59.4**
RBG 443	443	2720	0.074	0.661	**0**	372.5	351.1	**84.9**
Average			0.0595	0.5324	**0.0113**	107.634	88.927	**21.402**

Table 2. Performance comparisons on asymmetric TSP problems

Table 2 shows asymmetric TSP simulation experiment results. Every term's meaning is as same as Table 1. According to the data of table 2, we can come to the same conclusions as that of table 1.

5.3 Performances on Large Scale Art TSP Instances

Robert Bosch has created a fascinating series of instances of the traveling salesman problem (TSP) that provide continuous-line drawings of well-known pieces of art. In this part, large scale art TSP instances with sizes from 100,000 to 200,000 were adopted to verify the efficiency of the proposed PIMCSA.

Fig. 3, Fig. 4 and Fig.5 are the city location and TSP tour obtained by the proposed PIMCSA. It can be seen that the obtained tours have no road crossing which indicates the tour is of good quality.

Table 3 is the numerical results of PIMCSA on six large scale art TSP instances. The best known tour lengths (BT) in table 3 are given by Keld Helsgaun and published on the website TSP Homepage (http://www.tsp.gatech.edu/data/art/index.html).

Instance	Cities	Best Known Tour Lengths (BT)	Tour Lengths	Percent over BT
Monalisa100K	100K	5,757,199	5,758,769	0.0273
Vangogh120K	120K	6,543,643	6,5455,94	0.0298
Venus140K	140K	6,810,730	6,812,641	0.0281
Pareja160K	160K	7,620,040	7,622,486	0.0321
Curbet180K	180K	7,888,801	7,891,518	0.0344
Earring200K	200K	8,171,733	8,174,864	0.0383
Average				0.0317

Table 3. Experimental results of PIMCSA on large scale art TSP instances

(a) City Location of Monalisa100K Instance (b) Part of the obtained Tour

Fig. 3. Performance of PIMCSA on Monalisa100K Instance

(a) City Location of Venus140K Instance (b) Part of the obtained Tour

Fig. 4. Performance of PIMCSA on Venus140K Instance

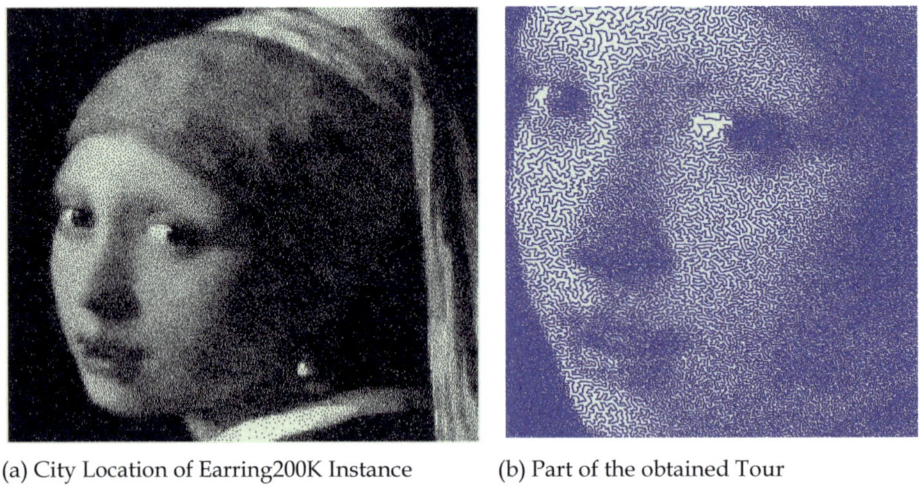

(a) City Location of Earring200K Instance (b) Part of the obtained Tour

Fig. 5. Performance of PIMCSA on Earring200K Instance

5.4 Effectiveness of the vaccine extraction strategy

This part of experiments is used to verify the effectiveness of PIMCSA vaccine strategy. Fig. 6 and Fig.7 shows the percentage of the edges' appearance in the known best tour. The higher the percentage the more superior the vaccine is. These data are statistic results of 20 independent runs.

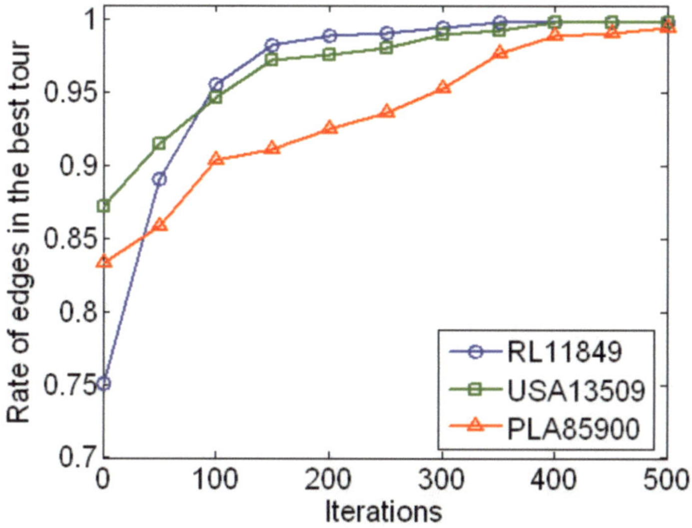

Fig. 6. Vaccine prediction accuracy for symmetric TSP

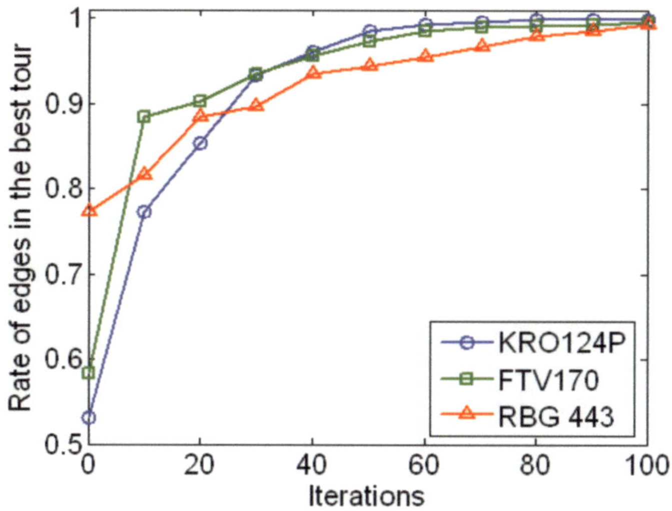

Fig. 7. Vaccine prediction accuracy for asymmetric TSP

Whether the problem is symmetrical or asymmetrical, the prediction accuracy of the vaccine increases rapidly along with the iteration times and the percentage is gradually close to one. It indicates that heuristic information of vaccine is helpful to speed up the algorithms' convergence. Further more, when the scale of the problem is large, the initial prediction accuracy of vaccine becomes high, however, the increasing rate of prediction accuracy is slow. When problem size is small, the initial vaccine prediction accuracy is low, but it increased rapidly along with iterations.

5.5 Scalability of parallel algorithm

Speedup ratio is an evaluation of the time gain of parallel algorithms. For a given application, speedup ratio of parallel system indicates how many times parallel algorithm is faster than serial algorithm. If T_S is the time that we need from start of algorithm to the last on a serial computer and T_p is the time we need on a parallel computer, the speedup ratio S is defined as:

$$S = \frac{T_s}{T_p} \tag{10}$$

We use the efficiency to measure the rate of a processor's effectively used computing power. If the CPU number is p, the efficiency E is defined as:

$$E = \frac{S}{p} \tag{11}$$

If W is the total computation of problem, $T_0(W,p)$ is additional expenses (which is a function of W and p), then T_p can be expressed as:

$$T_p = \frac{W + T_0(W,p)}{p} \tag{12}$$

Thus, the speed-up ratio S and efficiency E can be expressed as:

$$S = \frac{W}{T_p} = \frac{pW}{W + T_0(W,p)} = \frac{p}{1 + T_0(W,p)/W} = \frac{p}{1+\Omega} \tag{13}$$

$$E = \frac{S}{p} = \frac{1}{1 + T_0(W,p)/W} = \frac{1}{1+\Omega} \tag{14}$$

From equation (13) and (14) we can see that $\Omega = T_0(W,p)/W$ is the key factor affect the efficiency of algorithms and processor. If W is certain, $T_0(W,p)$ is only associated with p, it can be written as $T_0(p)$. This function is determined by the algorithm. $T_0(p)$ increase more slowly, the scalability of algorithm is better, otherwise be worse. From equation (14) we can deduce:

$$\Omega = \frac{T_0(W,p)}{W} = \frac{p}{S} - 1 = \frac{1}{E} - 1 \tag{15}$$

Fig. 8 and Fig. 9 show the relationship between Ω and p. Antibody sub-population size is 30, memory population size is p-1. The data are average results of 20 independent runs.

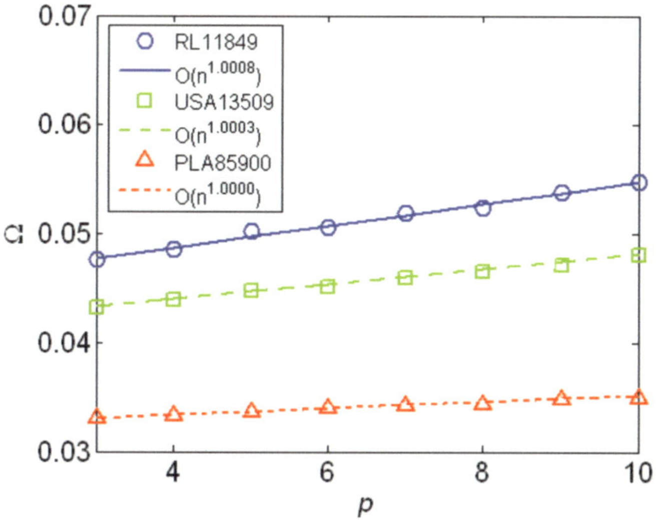

Fig. 8. Scalability of symmetric TSP

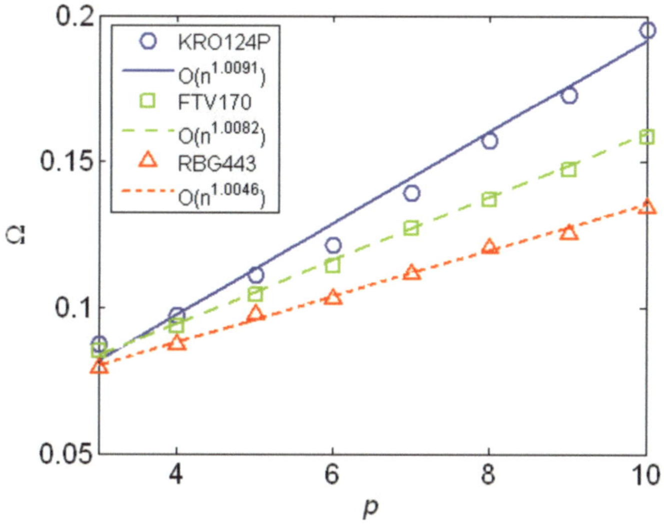

Fig. 9. Scalability of asymmetric TSP

When the scale of problem is certain, as the number of processors (p) increases, Ω shows linear increasing trend, it indicates that PIMCSA has good scalability. When problem becomes larger, Ω becomes smaller and increases more slowly, it indicates that the scalability of PIMCSA is better on large scale TSP problems.

These results above are reasonable. Additional expenses mainly include three parts: the expense of communication (denoted as C_1), vaccine producing of memory population (denoted as C_2) and vaccine delivery costs (denoted as C_3). C_1 will linearly increase when p increase under certain scale of problem. C_2 will linearly increase with the increase of p too. p has no influence on C_3. C_1 and C_2 are the major overhead costs for large-scale TSP problem. Compared to C_1 and C_2, C_3 can be neglected. Therefore, if the scale of problem is certain,

$T_0(W,p)$ will increase linearly with the increasing of p. When the scale of problem becomes larger, the total computation of problem (W) will increase, so Ω will increase more slowly.

6. Conclusion

This chapter first introduces the immune system and immune optimization algorithm, and then proposes the parallel immune memory clonal selection algorithm (PIMCSA) for solving large scale TSP problem. In the proposed PIMCSA, a dynamic vaccine extraction (DV) strategy is designed for solving large-scale TSP problem. Based on the general framework of PIMCSA, a special designed memory population immune algorithm (MIA) and a specific antibody sub-populations immune algorithm (PIA) are also proposed for solving TSP problems. Simulating results on the symmetric and asymmetric TSP instances in TSPLIB indicate that PIMCSA has good performance on both tour quality and running time. We also verify the validity of PIMCSA vaccine extraction strategy. Experimental results show that the rate of accuracy increases rapidly with the process of iteration and gradually close to 1. In addition, this chapter also analyses in theory that speedup ratio of parallel algorithms and the processor efficiency are related to variables Ω (the ratio of the extra overhead of algorithm and the total calculated amount of the problems). Experimental results show that, the parameter Ω of PIMCSA generally tends to enlarge linearly with the increase of the number of processors p, indicating that PIMCSA have good scalability.

It can be seen that the dynamic vaccine strategy designed in this chapter is very effective for the combinatorial optimization problems just as TSP problem. PIMCSA is a parallel artificial immune algorithm suitable for solving large-scale and complex optimization problems. For the parallel artificial immune algorithm, it is an important direction for further research that how to determine the size, quantity of the antibody sub-populations, and the relationship between them and the number of processors, computing power.

7. References

L.C. Jiao, H.F. Du, F. et al. (2006). *Immune optimization calculation, learning and recognition.* Science publishing Company, Beijing.

F. M. Burnet. (1978). Clonal selection and after, In: *Theoretical Immunology*, 63-85, Marcel Dekker Inc, New York.

L. N. de Castro, F. J. Von Zuben. (2000). *Artificial Immune System: Part I basic theory and applications*. Technical Report DCA-RT.

J. D. Farmer, S. Forrest, A. S. Perelson. (1986). The Immune System, Adaptation and Machine Learning. *Physical*, Vol. 22(D), 187-204.

D. J. Smith, S. Forrest, A. S. Perelson. (1998). Immunological memory is associative, In: *Artificial Immune System and their Applications*, Dasgupta, (Ed.), 105-112., Springer, Berlin

N. K. Jerne. (1973). The Immune System. *Scientific American*, Vol. 229, No.1, 52-60.

L. A. Herzenberg, S. J. Black. (1980). Regulatory circuits and antibody response. *European Journalist of Immune*, Vol. 10, 1-11.

G. W. Hoffmann. (1986). A Neural Network Model Based on the Analogy with the Immune System. *Journal of Theoretic Biology*, Vol. 122, 33-67.

A. S. Perelson. (1989). Immune Network Theory. *Immunological Review*, Vol. 1, No. 10, 5-36.

J. D. Farmer. (1990). A Rosetta Stone for Connectionism. *Physical*. Vol. 42 (D), 153-187.

Z. Tang, T. Yamaguchi, K. Tashima, et al. (1997). Multiple-Valued immune network model and its simulation, *Proceedings of the 27th International Symposium on multiple-valued logic*, Best Western, Autigonish, Canada, 1997.5.

N. Mitsumoto, T. Fukuta. (1997). Control of Distributed Autonomous Robotic System Based on Biologically Inspired Immunological Architecture, *Proceedings of IEEE International Conference on Robotics and Automation*, Albuquerque Convention Center, Albuquerque, NM, USA, 1997.4.

M. Zak. (2000). Physical Model of Immune Inspired Computing. *Information Sciences*, Vol. 129, 61-79.

J. Timmis, M. Neal. (2001). A resource limited artificial immune system for data analysis. *Knowledge Based Systems*, Vol. 14, No.3-4, 121-130.

L. N. De Castro, F. J.Von Zuben. (2000). An Evolutionary Immune Network for Data Clustering. *Proceedings of Sixth Brazilian Symposium on Neural Networks*, Rio de Janeiro, Brazil.

A. Tarakanov, D. Dasgupta. (2000). A formal model of an artificial immune system. *Bio-Systems*, Vol. 5, No.5, 151-158.

B. T. Nohara, H. Takahashi. (2000). Evolutionary Computation in Engineering Artificially Immune System, *Proceedings of the 26th Annual Conference of the IEEE Industrial Electronics Society*.

S. Forrest, A. Perelson, R. Cherukuri. (1994). Self non-self discrimination in a computer. *Proceedings of 1994 IEEE Computer Society Symposium on Research in Security and Privacy*, Oakland, CA, USA.

L.C. Jiao, L. Wang. (2000). A novel genetic algorithm based on immunity. *IEEE Transactions on Systems, Man and Cybernetics, Part A*, Vol. 30, No. 5, 552-561.

J. S. Chun, H. K. Jung, S. Y. HaHn. (1998). A study on comparison of optimization performance between immune algorithm and other heuristic algorithms. *Magnetics*. Vol. 34, No. 5, 2972-2975.

S. Endoh, N. Toma, K. Yamada. (1998). Immune algorithm for n-TSP. *IEEE International Conference on System, Man, and Cybernetics*.Vol 4, 3844-3849.

L.C. Jiao, H.F. Du. (2003). Development and Prospect of the Artificial Immune System. *Acta Electronica Sinica*, Vol. 31, No. 10, 1540-1548.

L. N. De Castro, F. J. Von Zuben. (2000). The Clonal Selection Algorithm with Engineering Application, *Proceedings of Workshop on Artificial Immune System and Their Applications*, 36-37.

J. Kim, P. J. Bentley. (2002). Towards an Artificial Immune System for Network Intrusion Detection: An Investigation of Dynamic Clonal Selection. *Proceedings of Congress on Evolutionary Computation*, 1015-1020.

H. F. Du, M. G Gong, L. C. Jiao, R. C. Liu (2005). A novel artificial immune system algorithm for high-dimensional function numerical optimization. *Progress in Nature Science*. Vol. 15, No. 5, 463-471.

F. Du, M. G Gong, L. C. Jiao. (2004). A immune memory clonal programming algorithm for high-dimensional function optimization. *Progress in Nature Science*. Vol. 14, No. 8, 925-933.

H. F. Du, M. G Gong, R. C. Liu (2005). Adaptive chaos clonal evolutionary programming algorithm. *Science In China, Ser. E*, Vol. 35, No. 8, 817-829.

M. G Gong, L. C. Jiao, H. F. Du, W. P. Ma (2007). A Novel Evolutionary Strategy Based on Artificial Immune Response for Constrained Optimizations. *Chinese Journal of Computers*, Vol. 30, No. 1, 37-46.

Y.Y. Li, L. C. Jiao (2007).Quantum-Inspired Immune Clonal Algorithm for SAT Problem. *Chinese Journal of Computers*. Vol. 30, No. 2,176-182.

F. Liu, X. J. Feng. (2003). Immune Algorithm for Multicast Routing. *Chinese Journal of Computers*, Vol. 26, No. 6, 676-681.

Y. T. Qi, L. C. Jiao, F. Liu (2008). Multi-Agent Immune Memory Clone based Multicast Routing. *Chinese Journal Electronics*. Vol. 17, No. 2, 289-292.

Z.X. Ong, J.C. Tay, C.K. Kwoh. (2005). Applying the Clonal Selection Principle to Find Flexible Job-Shop Schedules. *Proceedings of the 4th International Conference on Artificial Immune Systems*, Banff, Canada.

J. Chen, M. Mahfouf (2006). A Population Adaptive Based Immune Algorithm for Solving Multi-Objective Optimization Problems. *Proceedings of the 5th International Conference on Artificial Immune Systems*, Portugal, 2006.

R. H. Shang, L. C. Jiao, M. G. Gong, W. P. Ma (2007). An Immune Clonal Algorithm for Dynamic Multi-Objective Optimization. *Journal of Software* . Vol. 18, No. 11, 2700-2711.

D.S.Johnson, L.A.McGeoch. (1997). *The Traveling Salesman: A Case Study in Local Optimization. Local Search in Combinatorial Optimization*.

D. S. Johnson, L. A. McGeoch. (2002). Experimental analysis of heuristics for the STSP. In: *The Traveling Salesman Problem and its Variations*. G. Gutin, A. Punnen, (Ed.), 369-443, Kluwer Academic Publishers, Boston.

T. Guo, Z. Michalewicz. (1998). Inver-over operator for the TSP. In: *Proc of the 5th Parallel Problem Solving form Nature*, 803-812, springer, Berlin.

X.M. Song, B. Li and H.M.Yang. (2006). Improved Ant Colony Algorithm and its Applications in TSP. In: *Proc of Intelligent Systems Design and Applications*. 1145 – 1148.

X.X.He et al.. A New Algorithm for TSP Based on Swarm Intelligence. (2006). In: *Proc of Intelligent Control and Automation*, 3241–3244.

C. Walshaw. (2001). A Multilevel Lin-Kernighan-Helsgaun Algorithm for the Travelling Salesman Problem. *Computing and Mathematical Sciences*, University of Greenwich, Old Royal Naval College, Greenwich, London, SE10 9LS, UK.

P. Zou, Z. Zhou, G. L. Chen, J. Gu (2003). A Multilevel Reduction Algorithm to TSP. *Journal of Software*, Vol. 14, No. 1, 35-42.

L. Wang, J. Pan, L. C. Jiao (2000). The Immune Programming. *Chinese Journal of Computers*, Vol. 23, No. 8, 806-812.

Erick Cantú-Paz. (2000). Efficient and Accurate Parallel Genetic Algorithms. *Kluwer Academic Publishers*, Holland.

D. S. Johnson. (1990). Local optimization and the traveling salesman problem. *Proceedings of the 17th Colloquium on Automata, Language, and Programming, Lecture Notes in Computer Science 443*, 446-461, Springer-Verlag, Berlin.

E. Noda, A. L. V. Coelho, I. L. M. Ricarte, A. Yamakami and A. Freitas. (2002). A Devising adaptive migration policies for cooperative distributed genetic algorithms. *Proceedings of Congress on Systems, Man and Cybernetics*, vol.6.

9

A Multi-World Intelligent Genetic Algorithm to Optimize Delivery Problem with Interactive-Time

Yoshitaka Sakurai and Setsuo Tsuruta
Tokyo Denki University,
Japan

1. Introduction

Due to the complicated road network, the efficiency of product distribution remains on a lower level in Japan compared to that of the USA, which disadvantages the productivity of Japanese industries. This inefficiency also causes social problems and economical losses. Namely, we are facing the necessity of urgently reducing the volume of car exhaust gases to meet environmental requirement as well as curtailing transport expenses in Japan.
There are many distribution systems that should be optimized, including the delivery of parcels, letters and products supply/distribution across multiple enterprises. In order to improve the efficiency of these distributions, it is necessary to optimize the delivery routes, or the delivery order of multiple delivery locations (addresses). One round delivery comprises more than several tens or hundreds of different locations. Thus, the optimization of a delivery route can be modelled as such a large-scale of Traveling Salesman Problem (TSP). However, TSP is a combinatorial problem that causes computational explosion due to n! order of combinations for n-city TSP. Therefore, to practically obtain the efficient delivery route of such a distribution system, a near optimal solving method of TSP is indispensable. Yet, the practical use of such a solving method on an actual site needs human confirmation (which is difficult to formulate) of the solution, since social and human conditions are involved. Namely, human users should check to understand that the solution is practical. Users sometimes should correct manually or select the alternative solution.
Therefore, the TSP solving methods are required to ensure the response time necessary for the above human interaction.
By the way, solutions generated by domain experts may have 2~3% of deviation from the mathematical optimal solution, but they never generate worse solutions which may cause practical problems. On the other hand, conventional approximate TSP solving methods (Lawer et al., 1985; Kolen & Pesch, 1994; Yamamoto & Kubo, 1997) may generate even mathematically optimal solutions in some cases but cannot ensure the amount of errors below 2~3%. Such errors possibly discourage user, which makes those conventional methods not practically useful, especially for the above-mentioned applications.
Strict TSP solving methods, such as the branch and cut method (Grotschel & Holland, 1991) and Dynamic Programming (DP) (Bertsekas, 1987) or approximate solving methods using Simulated Annealing (SA) (Kirkpatrick et al., 1983; Ingber, 1993; Miki et al., 2003) and Tabu

Search (TS) (Glover, 1989; 1990; Hooker & Natraj, 1995; Fang et al., 2003), take much time for calculation. Therefore, they cannot guarantee the above-mentioned real-time conditions. The Lin-Kernighan (LK) method and its improved version (Lin & Kernighan, 1972) are also proposed as solving methods of the TSP. However, they cannot constantly guarantee expert-level accuracy (Kubota et al., 1999).

Thus, we developed a method which efficiently solves the TSP, using Genetic Algorithm (GA) (Onoyama et al., 2000). This method enables to guarantee the responsiveness by limiting the number of generations of GA and by improving genetic operations (initial generations, mutation, and crossover). However, in some distribution patterns, this solving method fell into a local minimum and could not achieve expert-level accuracy. Therefore, we needed further improvement of our solving method to guarantee expert-level accuracy for all cases.

The chapter is organized as follows: In the next (second) section, the delivery route optimization problem and its technical problems are described. In the third section, the method for solving the problem is proposed. Then, in the fourth section, experiments to validate its effect and its results are shown. In the fifth section, the effectiveness of the solving method will be proved based on the experiments, and in the sixth section, we will compare it with other methods. And in the last seventh section, the results will be concluded.

2. Problems in delivery route optimization

In this section, firstly, two kinds of actual distribution systems are depicted. And, in 2.2, the optimization problems of these distribution systems are formally and technically described.

2.1 Delivery route optimization problem

A distribution network across multiple manufacturing enterprises is outlined in Fig. 1. Parts for production are delivered from parts makers (suppliers) to factories directly or through depots. Parts are not delivered to a factory or a depot independently by each parts maker, but a truck goes around several parts makers and collects parts. This improves the distribution efficiency, which contributes to the curtailment of distribution expenses and to the reduction of the volume of car exhaust gases.

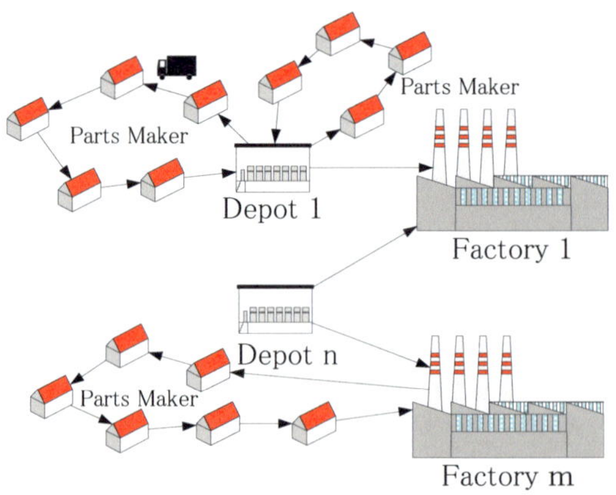

Fig. 1. Large-scale distribution network

In order to optimize the above-mentioned large-scale distribution network, we need to grasp the total cost of distribution under various conditions by repeating the simulation process as shown in Fig. 2. First, the conditions have to be set up manually, concerning locations of more than ten factories (parts integration points for production), locations of dozens of depots (intermediate depositories of parts), and allocation of trucks to transport parts. To calculate distribution cost in each simulation, it is necessary to create delivery routes. However, there are several hundreds of parts makers, dozens of depots and more than ten factories. Therefore, there are about 1000 distributing routes on each of which a truck goes around dozens (max. 40) of parts makers starting from one of the depots or factories. Thus, in each simulation, a delivery route creation is repeated about 1000 times for a set of conditions manually set up, the total delivery cost is calculated, and a person in charge globally decides the network optimality as shown in Fig. 2. To globally evaluate these results, human judgment is indispensable and interactive response time (less than tens of seconds) is required. Thus, the system needs to create about 1000 or several hundreds of distribution routes within at least tens of seconds. Therefore, one route has to be created within tens of milliseconds.

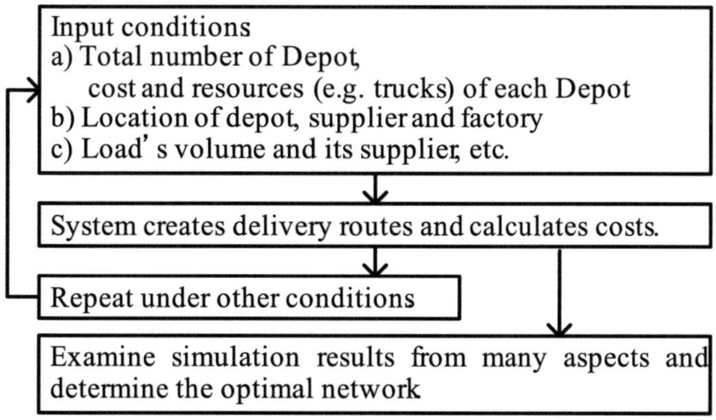

Fig. 2. Simulation process

Meanwhile, as to the delivery route optimization problem for parcels and letters, a round delivery is carried out 1-3 times a day with a small vehicle such as a motorcycle or a small truck.. Delivery zone that is covered by one vehicle is different according to the region. Delivery locations are comparatively overcrowded in the urban area, whereas scattered in the rural area. Therefore, the number of locations (addresses) for delivery differs - over several tens or hundreds - depending on the region and time zone. It is necessary to make and optimize a new delivery route for each round delivery since delivery locations change every day and every time. Though human or social factors should be considered, this is a problem to search the shortest path or route, modelled as a famous "Chinese Postman Problem" or "Traveling Salesman Problem (TSP)". The computer support by near optimal solving method is quite useful to reduce the burden and loss time of workers as well as car exhaust gases in such distribution networks or parcels / letters delivery.

2.2 Technical problems

The delivery route optimization problem of these distribution systems is formulated as follows:

The delivery network is represented by weighted complete graph $G=(V,E,w)$. V is node set. A node v_i $(i=1,\ldots,N)$ represents a location (address) for delivery. N is the number of nodes. E is edge set. A edge e_{ij} represents a route from v_i to v_j. w is edge weight set. A edge weight d_{ij} represents a distance from node v_i to node v_j, $d_{ij} = d_{ji}$. The problem to find the minimal-length Hamilton path in such a graph $G=(V,E,w)$ is called Traveling Salesman Problem (TSP).

Thus, to improve the delivery efficiency of such distribution systems, it is required to obtain an approximate solution of a TSP within an interactive length of time (max. tens of milliseconds). Yet, expert-level accuracy (less than 3% of the deviation from the optimal solution) is always necessary, since domain experts may have such errors in their solutions but never generate worse solutions which may cause practical problems.

We developed an efficient method for solving the TSP by elaborating a random restart method. The developed method enables to guarantee the responsiveness by limiting the number of repetitions and by devising component methods and heuristics (Kubota et al., 1999). However, to meet the required guarantee of expert-level accuracy (below 3% of errors), it took more than 100 milliseconds to solve one TSP, which caused the time to solve one TSP should be significantly decreased.

Therefore, in order to improve the real time behavior, we proposed a GA that uses heuristics for the crossover and the mutation, and yet whose generation number is limited (Onoyama et al., 2000).

However, for some kinds of delivery location patterns, obtained solutions had more than 3% of errors. To overcome these weaknesses of the solving method, other heuristics were applied. Nevertheless, these heuristics were not effective again for some patterns, and the above-mentioned accuracy was still not guaranteed for all kinds of patterns (as is described in detail in section 5.1).

In the next section, an intelligent approximate method to solve above-mentioned problems is proposed.

3. A multi-world intelligent genetic algorithm

As stated in the foregoing sections, the delivery routing problem in the above distribution systems can be formalized as a TSP. Especially a symmetrical (non-directed) Euclidean TSP (Lawer et al., 1985; Yamamoto & Kubo, 1997) is assumed in this chapter.

3.1 Concept of the proposed method

In order to solve problems mentioned above (in section 2), the following multi-world intelligent GA (MIGA) method is proposed. This guarantees both real-time responsiveness and accuracy for various kinds of delivery location patterns. At the initial phase of GA, groups of individuals (population) that become the candidates of the solution are generated. And, based on the population, new individuals (solution candidates) are generated by the crossover and the mutation operator, and individuals are improved by the evaluation and the selection. With our GA, each individual (chromosome) represents the tour, namely the delivery route in TSP. Each gene of the chromosome represents the node number (identification number of the address for delivery). A chromosome is a sequence of nodes whose alignment represents a round order as shown in Fig. 3.

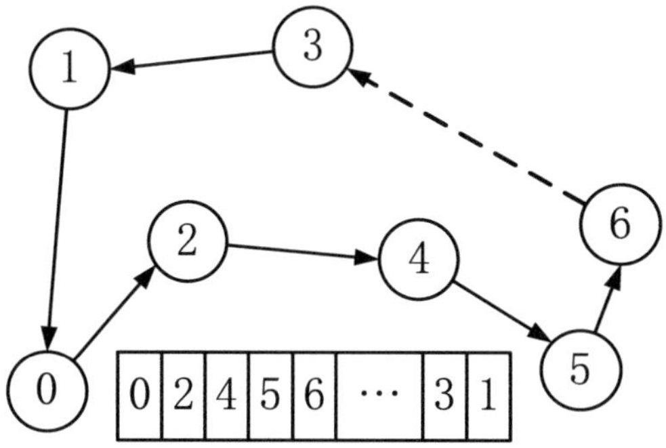

Fig. 3. Chromosome

3.1.1 Multi-world intelligent GA

It is difficult to find an effective search method that always guarantees expert-level optimality as well as the required real-time behavior for various distribution location patterns. Heuristics, that are effective to particular patterns, are not necessarily useful to other patterns. Yet, the application of excessively complicate algorithms or heuristics makes the responsiveness worse. Therefore, a high-speed GA that mainly uses simple general heuristics is combined with an intelligent GA, into which knowledge for handling particular problems is incorporated. In this way, we could avoid local minima for various delivery location patterns.

Concretely speaking, a 2opt-type mutation is used for the high-speed GA. This 2opt-type mutation quickly improves tours. Therefore, good solutions are usually expected to be obtained within a short length of time. However, it also takes risks of falling into a local minimum. Our experiments revealed that this high-speed GA (called 2opt-type GA) computes some inefficient tours for certain delivery location patterns.

Thus, a multi-world intelligent GA method is proposed. In this method, there are two kinds of GA worlds; (1) an intelligent GA world (called block-type GA) holding the knowledge to meet the particularities of problems as well as (2) the high-speed GA world (called 2opt-type GA). Both kinds of worlds are independently executed. Such execution is repeated. The same kind of worlds can be repeated. And they are collaborated through integrating the results.

In the intelligent GA world, the following rather problem-oriented knowledge about the neighborhood conditions or their relaxation is incorporated into operations of the block-type GA so that these operations can be controlled through utilizing the knowledge.

a. **Multi-step NI method**

   This is particular heuristics that constructs the initial tour by using step-by-step the NI (Nearest Insertion) method to globally consider adjacent delivery locations, where the adjacency is defined by problem-oriented knowledge as mentioned later.

b. **Block-type mutation**

   This mutation selects a node randomly out of a tour, and mutates it together with its neighbor nodes in order to avoid local minimum solutions.

3.1.2 Limiting the generation number of GA

In this method, the computation time necessary for processing the GA is calculated as follows.

Let

- *n* be the the population size,
- *l* be the length per individual,
- *T(X)* be the computation time of X,
- *Prob(X)* the probability of X, and
- *Ave(X)* the average of X.

So the computation time can be estimated as
computation time =
*T(initialize) + number of generations * T(one generation of GA) + margin constant C*
with

- $T(initialize) = n * C_{ini} * f_{ini}(l)$
- *T(one generation of GA)* = *T(crossover stage) + T(mutation stage) + T(evaluation) + T(selection)*
- *T(crossover stage) = n * Prob(crossover) * Ave(T(crossover))*
- $Ave(T(crossover)) = C_{cros} * f_{cros}(l)$
- *T(mutation stage) = n * Prob(mutation) * Ave(T(mutation))*
- $Ave(T(mutation)) = C_{mut} * f_{mut}(l)$
- $T(evaluation) = C_{fit} * f_{fit}(l, n)$, $T(selection) = C_{sel} * f_{sel}(n)$

As the parameters of GA, *n*, *l*, *Prob(crossover)* and *Prob(mutation)* are given. $f_{ini}(l)$, $f_{cros}(l)$, $f_{mut}(l)$, $f_{fit}(l, n)$ and $f_{sel}(n)$ are respectively computational complexity of each operation (initialization, crossover, mutation, fitness evaluation, and selection) that basically does not depend on hardware details such as the CPU architecture. These are derived through analyzing the algorithm. For example, since "quick sort" is used in the selection operator, $f_{sel}(n)$ *is* calculated as follows:

$$f_{sel}(n) = n^{*}(\log n) + C_1^{*}n + C_0 \tag{1}$$

Here, C_1 and C_0 are the coefficients for the minor dimension to calculate the complexity of the quick sort algorithm. C_{ini}, C_{cros}, C_{mut}, C_{fit}, C_{sel}, are coefficients to obtain computation time from the complexity of each operation mentioned above. These coefficients are hardware dependant but can be identified using the result of experiments. More precisely, these can be calculated using the number of steps of each program, and identified/adjusted using the result of experiments to take detailed factors such as the CPU architecture into account. The computation time for one generation of GA changes stochastically.

However, the estimation error can be suppressed within allowable ranges, through

1. dividing the computation time into that of fundamental components and
2. calculating the computation time using each component's computational complexity and the experimental results to determine the coefficient.

Furthermore, to absorb this estimation error, and to guarantee the interactive real-time responsiveness, a *margin constant* C can be set by the user as a safety margin.

Using this computation time, the number of generations repeatable within the required response time can be calculated.

3.2 Components of the proposed method

In this method, a gene represents a (traveling) node, and an individual represents a tour.

3.2.1 Method for generating initial individuals

In order to obtain a highly optimized solution by avoiding the convergence into a local minimum, the randomness of the initial individuals is important. However, the speed of convergence slows down, if totally random initial solutions are generated as is done by a random method. Thus, the other methods are devised as shown below.

a. **Random method**

Construct a tour by putting nodes in a random order.

b. **Random NI method**

Put nodes in a random order and insert them into a tour by using the NI method according to the randomized order.

c. **Multi-step NI method**

In case experts generate a tour (a traveling route), they usually determine the order of delivery locations, globally considering the whole route, so that the nearest location from the present one can always be the next location to deliver. On the model of such global consideration of experts, a multi-step NI method is proposed which enables to generate a tour similar to the tour generated by experts.

In detail, this method constructs a tour through the following steps:

1. *Que(nodes)* is a queue of nodes with their *check count* of each node initialized as zero. $tour_{gen}$ is the tour generated. w is a real type variable that meets the requirement $1 <= w$. Its initial value is decided by problem-oriented knowledge. For example, w is decided based on the position of the entire node as follows:

$$w = (Dist_{ave} + d * \sigma) \ / \ Dist_{ave} \tag{2}$$

   $Dist_{ave}$ is an average of the distance between each node and a depot. σ is a standard deviation of the distance among nodes. The initial value of d is 1.0.
2. Enqueue all nodes to *Que(nodes)* at random order.
3. Dequeue a node ($node_{add}$) from *Que(nodes)*.
4. Temporally add a $node_{add}$ to $tour_{gen}$ by the NI method.
5. Evaluate L_{pre} and L_{after}. L_{pre} is the length of $tour_{gen}$ before its addition. L_{after} is the length of $tour_{gen}$ after its addition. ... (*)
6. If $L_{after} < (L_{pre} * w)$, then $node_{add}$ is inserted (actually added) into $tour_{gen}$ and w is returned to an initial value. Else enqueue $node_{add}$ to *Que(nodes)*, with *check count* of $node_{add}$ incremented.
7. f the *check count* of the top node of *Que(nodes)* is not zero, then w is increased, and the *check count* of every node in *Que(nodes)* is initialized zero. Here, the quantity of this increase is also decided by problem-oriented knowledge, for example, $d_{new} = d_{old} + 0.5$ of the equation (2).
8. If *Que(nodes)* is empty, then it ends. Else it returns to step (3) and repeat.

* Distances between two points are calculated for all their combinations by the Dijkstra method beforehand.

3.2.2 Method for crossover (NI-combined crossover)

To inherit good features of parents by crossover and to realize the quick convergence in GA, a crossover operation using the NI method is proposed. This crossover operation called NI-combined crossover comprises the following steps (Fig. 4):

1. $tour_{par1} = \{x_1, x_2, \ldots, x_n\}$ and $tour_{par2} = \{y_1, y_2, \ldots, y_n\}$ are parent tours and $tour_{chi}$ is a child tour.
2. Determine a crossover point x_i from $tour_{par1}$.
3. Copy a sub-tour $\{x_1, x_2, \ldots, x_i\}$, representing a group of nodes located before the crossover point in $tour_{par1}$, to $tour_{chi}$.
4. Change the order of remaining nodes $\{x_{i+1}, \ldots, x_n\}$, according to the order of nodes in $tour_{par2}$.
5. Insert the remaining nodes into $tour_{chi}$, using the NI method in the order that is changed in (4). When all nodes of $tour_{par1}$ are inserted to $tour_{chi}$, the crossover processing ends.

In this way, the generated tour is represented as a new child. Through applying this NI-combined crossover, the order of nodes contained in parents is inherited to their children to increase the convergence speed.

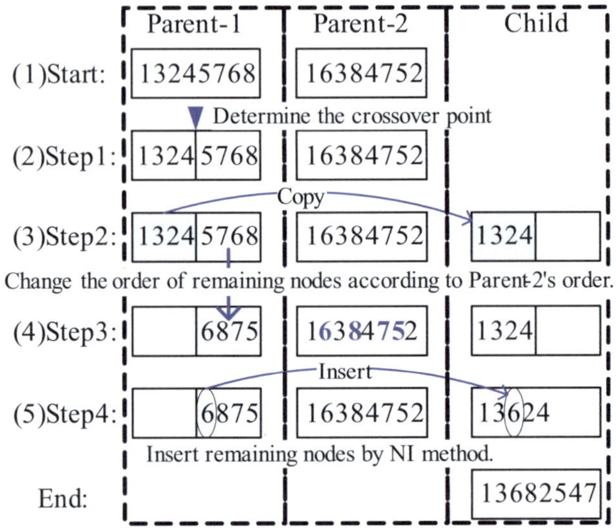

Fig. 4. NI-combined crossover

3.2.3 Method for mutation

Mutation of GAs often did not have much impact on the convergence of solutions without combining local search methods or without embedding problem-oriented knowledge. Thus, the following two mutation methods are proposed.

a. 2opt-type mutation

This method enables to improve the convergence speed by combining a 2opt-like simple local search heuristic method with GA's mutation operation. This consists of the following steps :

1. $tour_{par} = \{x_1, x_2, \ldots, x_n\}$ is a parent tour and $tour_{chi}$ is a child tour.
2. Copy the contents of $tour_{par}$ to $tour_{chi}$.
3. Select a node x_i randomly from $tour_{chi}$.
4. Select another node x_j randomly from $tour_{chi}$ except $\{x_i, x_{i+1}\}$.
5. Generate $tour_{gen}$ $\{x_1,\ldots, x_i,x_j, \ldots , x_{i+1},x_{j+1},\ldots, x_n\}$ by reversing sub-tour $\{x_{i+1}, \ldots , x_j\}$ of $tour_{chi}$ $\{x_1,\ldots, x_i,x_{i+1}, \ldots , x_j,x_{j+1},\ldots, x_n\}$

6. If $L_{chi} < L_{gen}$ (tour length is not improved), then it ends. Else copy the contents of $tour_{gen}$ to $tour_{chi}$. Until such link exchanges are all checked, return to step (4) and repeat. L_{gen} is the length of $tour_{gen}$. L_{chi} is the length of $tour_{chi}$.

b. Block-type mutation

2opt-type mutation easily improves tours, and good solutions are expected to be obtained within a short length of time. However, it also takes risks of failing into a local minimum. To obtain a solution closer to the optimum, it is desirable to escape from a local minimum by destroying a block of a tour at a time. For this purpose, the following block-type mutation is proposed. This consists of the following steps:

1. $tour_{par} = \{x_1, x_2, ..., x_n\}$ is a parent tour. $tour_{chi}$ is a child tour.
2. Select a node x_i randomly from $tour_{par}$.
3. Move the nodes, except $\{x_{i-r}, \dots, x_{i+r}\}$ namely except x_i and its neighbor nodes of $tour_{par}$, to $tour_{chi}$. The size of neighborhood r is specified as problem-oriented knowledge, for instance, a random number from *0* to *B * (the distance to the node farthest from a depot). B* is a constant number specified as problem-oriented knowledge.
4. Insert $\{x_{i-r}, \dots, x_{i+r}\}$ into $tour_{chi}$ using the NI method. When all nodes have been inserted to $tour_{chi}$, the mutation processing ends.

3.2.4 Method for selection

In order to get highly optimized solutions and realize quick convergence in GAs, individuals are selected out of the population including both parents' and children's. And, 10% of individuals in a new generation are selected randomly from the above populations to give the chance of reproduction to even inferior individuals. Furthermore, to enhance the evolution efficiency, only one individual is selected when the same individuals are generated.

3.3 Proposed solving method

Through integrating above components, the following three kinds of GA methods are proposed to ensure both real-time responsiveness and accuracy for various kinds of delivery location patterns.

3.3.1 2opt-type GA (high-speed GA)

This method is shown in Fig. 5. This method makes it possible to guarantee quick convergence of solutions through improving initial solutions due to the random NI method and through applying the NI-combined crossover and the 2opt-type mutation.
The computational complexity of the NI-combined crossover is $O(n^2)$. On the other hand, the computational complexity of the 2opt-type mutation is much smaller. Indeed, the computational complexity of the 2opt-type mutation is $O(n^2)$ in worst cases, but it hardly occurs for highly optimized individuals generated in the initial population phase by the random NI method and improved in later phases by the NI-combined crossover.
In more detail, the probability of improvement by link exchanges of the 2opt method is small, since the NI method inserts each node so that the difference, between

1. the sum of the length of both links with both sides' neighbors and
2. the length of the link among both neighbors before its insertion,

can be minimized. Thus, the computation time of the 2opt-type mutation is expected to be much smaller than that of operations using the NI method such as the NI-combined crossover.

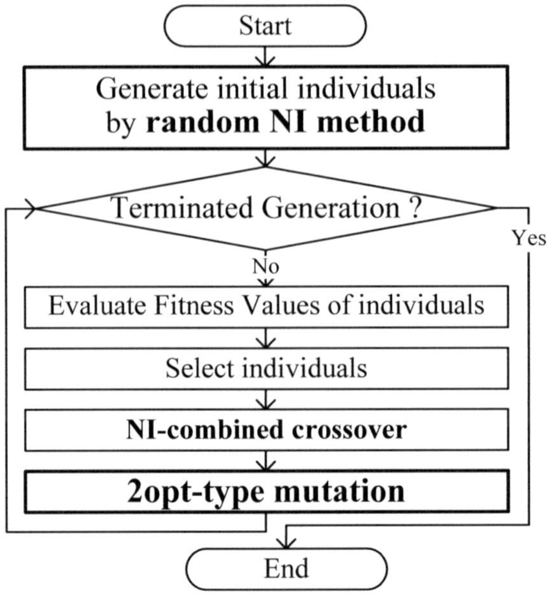

Fig. 5. 2opt-type GA

3.3.2 Block-type GA (intelligent GA)

This method is shown in Fig. 6. This method is expected to obtain highly optimized solutions through avoiding local minima. This can be attained through (1) constructing highly optimized initial solutions by means of the multi-step NI method, and (2) reconstructing a large part of a locally optimized tour by means of block-type mutation to avoid falling into a local minimum.

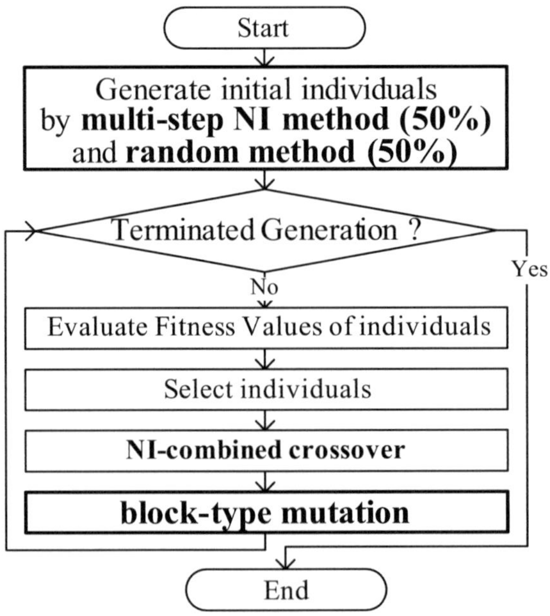

Fig. 6. Block-type GA

3.3.3 Multi-world intelligent GA

The finally proposed method is called "Multi-world intelligent GA (MIGA)". This comprises the 2opt-type GA method (world) and the block type GA method (world) that follows the former. MIGA selects the better one out of the solutions obtained in these two GA worlds. This raises the probability to have highly accurate solutions for various types of delivery location patterns within an interactive real-time context, because of the following reasons:

1. As is explained in 3.3.1, though the computation time of the NI-combined crossover is $O(n^2)$, the computation time of the 2opt-type mutation in the 2opt-type GA method (world) is much smaller than the former. Furthermore, the NI method checks just links among neighbors but all links among neighbors in the tour to be inserted. Meanwhile, though not all links, the 2opt operation in the 2opt-type mutation checks links between nodes that are not neighbors. Thus the 2opt-type mutation in the 2opt-type GA world but not being in the block type GA world can have the possibility to search other optimal solutions than the NI method, namely the block type GA method where only NI method is used effectively as heuristics.
2. On the other hands, the block type GA world can have the possibility to search other optimal solutions than 2opt-type GA, owing to the Multi step NI method and the block-type mutation, both of which exploits the power of the NI method enforced by problem oriented knowledge mentioned previously in (c) of 3.2.1 and in (b) of 3.2.3.

Yet, to guarantee real-time responsiveness, both of these two GAs finish their processing within the limited length of time through offline calculation of the number of generations repeatable within the time limit (e.g. 15 milliseconds for each GA).

4. Experiment and results

4.1 Experiment

In this section, the experiment to evaluate the proposed method is explained. The program codes are written by C language. A computer equipped with Intel Pentium II (450MHz) processor and 256MB memory is used for this experiment.

As explained by the footnote in the introduction, 40 cities TSPs were used for this experiment. Yet, various combinations of 40 delivery locations are possible. Thus, randomly selected 20000 different patterns of 40 delivery locations were prepared. Then, to evaluate three kinds of GA methods described in 3.3, each solving method solved 20000 test patterns, 100 times per pattern, and the probability to obtain solutions within 3% of errors was calculated.

In this experiment, the population size is 100 and each crossover rate and mutation rate are 10% respectively. These parameters were determined by the way of comparative experiments with many sets of parameters.

4.2 Results

To guarantee the real-time responsiveness, the time necessary for processing one generation is calculated, and based on this value, the number of generations of the GA is determined. Table 1 shows an example of the number of generations to respond within 30 milliseconds when the population size is 100. Then, the tests were repeated 100 times per pattern for three kinds of GAs.

Each test used 20000 kinds of delivery location patterns. The probability to obtain solutions within 3% of errors compared to the optimal solutions was checked. Furthermore, the probability to obtain the optimal solutions within 30 milliseconds was also checked. These results are shown in Table 2.

#	Method	Generating Initial Individuals	Mutation	Number of Generations
1	2opt-type	Random NI	2opt-type	24
2	Block-type	Random + Multi step NI	Block-type	20

Table 1. The number of generations of each method repeatable within 30 milliseconds

#	Method	Optimal	Below 3%
1	2opt-type GA	84.45%	99.885%
2	Block-type GA	83.75%	99.785%
3	MIGA	92.05%	100.0%

Table 2. The solution optimality

5. Evaluation

5.1 Effect of the proposed TSP solving method

Table 2 shows the usefulness of the proposed MIGA quite convincingly. Only MIGA method could solve a 40 cities TSP with less than 3% of errors with 100% of probability within 30 milliseconds.

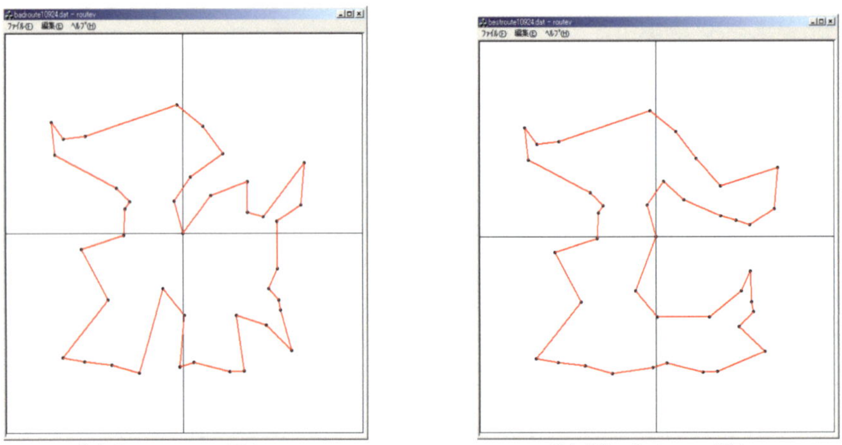

(a) 2opt-type GA (Tour length:259) (b) Block-type GA (Tour length:249)

Fig. 7. Difference of tour shape in a special location pattern

5.1.1 Effect of block-type GA (intelligent GA)

Tour shapes were examined as to solutions generated by the 2opt-type GA and leaving more than 3% errors. As a result, most of these shapes were like gear wheels as shown in Fig. 7 (a). Experts usually generate more straight routes as shown in Fig. 7 (b). If experts find inefficient routes such as shown in Fig. 7 (a), they reject to use the system since they consider it as an unreliable one.

In case of using a block-type GA (intelligent GA), tours similar to Fig. 7(b) were generated even for such delivery location patterns. The reason is why the intelligent GA has the block-type mutation in order to avoid falling into a local minimum.

5.1.2 Effect of multi-world intelligent GA

According to our experiment, in case of the 2opt-type GA, 43 cases out of 20000 tests had more than 3% errors. In case of the block-type GA method, 23 cases had more than 3% errors.

However, the multi-world intelligent GA (MIGA), namely, the 2opt-type GA subsequently followed by the block-type GA could generate solutions below 3% of error within 30 milliseconds, for every case in 20000 tests. The reason is that, coping with various delivery location patterns, either the 2opt-type GA or the intelligent GA can avoid falling into a local minimum (over 3% errors). Thus, MIGA method could guarantee the responsiveness as well as the expert-level accuracy, namely, below 3% errors.

5.2 Applicability of the proposed solving method

To evaluate the applicability of our proposed solving method, we applied it to a simulation of a parts supply logistics network which consists of one (assembly) factory, 7 depots, and 30 part makers (suppliers). This simulation needs to optimize the distribution area allocation of each truck, as well as to optimize each truck route. This simultaneous optimization of each truck area allocation and each truck route is classified as the Vehicle Routing Problem (VRP) (Laporte, 1992).

To apply our proposed methods to the VRP, we modified the chromosome structure and the NI method which is used in GA operations (initial construction, mutation, and crossover). Namely, the chromosome structure is extended to represent multiple trucks' routes instead of one truck's route, and the extended NI method puts a new node into the best position out of all truck routes instead of only one truck route.

We simulated the above-mentioned logistics network in 3 cases, which have the same simulation conditions except the amount of loads, as shown in table 3. The resultant number of trucks in table 3 is verified as optimal. Moreover, the total tour length deviation from the optimal solution is less than 3 %.

Consequently, our proposed GA methods such as the multi-step NI method and the block-type mutation are applicable not only to the TSP but also to more general problems such as the VRP. That is to say, these methods are effective in solving the problems defined over metric space such as the TSP and the VRP. Moreover, the concept of the block type mutation is applicable to the problems defined over topological space which does not have metric system but only neighborhood system.

#	Condition (number of loads)	Number of trucks	Total tour length (Deviation)
1	700	29	1015km (2.6%)
2	900	41	1345km (2.8%)
3	1000	48	1612km (2.8%)

Table 3. VRP simulation result

6. Comparisons

A lot of methods to solve TSP are proposed for practical applications. In this section, our methods are compared with other methods.

Three types of the proposed methods (multi-world intelligent GAs) are tested, each of which has different stopping condition. MIGA1 (multi-world intelligent GA type 1) stops searching when it stops improving the solution. The computation time of MIGA2 is one tenth of that of MIGA1. The computation time of MIGA3 is 30 milliseconds. Experiments were conducted under the following computation environment. Namely, CPU is AMD Athlon 64 X2 3800+ 2GHz processor. It is almost the same performance as Athlon 64 3200+ 2GHz because of its execution on the single core mode with 1GB memory. The programs were written in C language, compiled by Microsoft Visual C++ .NET 2003 ver. 7.1.3091 with /O2 option (directing the execution speed preference), and executed on Windows XP Professional.

Yet, since other solution methods to be compared are executed on machines with different performance specification, it is necessary to take the difference into account. Therefore, referring to the statistical results of tests using RC5-72 benchmark (JLUG, 2008) for measuring the arithmetic processing speed, we obtained the spec difference correction coefficient (SDCC). This can be obtained by dividing the resultant value of the benchmark test executed on the experimental environments of other solution methods, by the resultant value of the benchmark test on our experimental environment. Through multiplying SDCC to the execution time of other solution methods, we calculated an assumed execution time on the same specification machine as ours.

As for the strict optimization method, Branch-and-cut and Dynamic Programming (DP) are proposed. These methods require long computation time though they can obtain optimal solutions. Some algorithms using DP can search very near-optimal solutions for the Euclidean TSP in polynomial time (Arora, 1998). However, even these algorithms take too long time for practical applications such as ours, and it seems too hard for ordinary system developers to modify or adjust them for coping with various particular requirements.

As for the approximate solution technique, various techniques are proposed. LK is famous as the heuristics search technique for TSP. However, LK and its improving methods (Lin & Kernighan, 1972; Yamamoto & Kubo, 1997) also take a long computation time though the optimality of obtained solutions is high and these methods are often incorporated with the meta-heuristics search such as SA, TA and GA.

Simulated Annealing (SA) and Tabu Search (TS) are known as the meta-heuristics search technique. Theoretically, SA (Kirkpatrick et al., 1983; Ingber, 1993; Miki et al., 2003) is said to be able to search very near-optimal solutions by decreasing the risk of falling into a local minimum. But practically, it is very difficult to adjust SA's parameters such as cooling speed for coping with various location patterns. Furthermore, SA usually takes a long computation time to get above-mentioned theoretical near-optimal solutions.

TS (Glover, 1989; 1990; Hooker & Natraj, 1995; Fang et al., 2003) usually needs a long computation time to get practically optimal solutions. Worse still, TS is said to be weak in maintaining solution diversity though it has strong capability for local search. However, TS is improved in these weaknesses by Kanazawa & Yasuda, 2004.

So-called random restart methods (Yanagiura & Ibaraki, 2000), which apply local search such as 2-opt for improving random initial solutions, can obtain near-optimal solutions. These include GRASP (Feo et al., 1994) or the elaborated random restart method (Kubota et al., 1999) that can guarantee responsiveness by limiting the number of repetitions. However, according to our experiments, the above-mentioned elaborated random restart method needed about 100 milliseconds to solve 40 cities TSP and to guarantee less than 3% errors (Kubota et al., 1999).

As for the Genetic Algorithms (GA) to efficiently solve TSP, various techniques are proposed. GA applied solving methods using the edges assembly crossover (EAX) (Nagata & Kobayashi, 1999) and the distance-preserving crossover (DPX) (Whiteley & Starkweather, 1989) could get highly optimized solutions in case of very-large-scale TSPs (with 1000-10000 cities) (Tamaki et al., 1994; Baraglia et al., 2001; Tsai et al., 2004; Nguyen et al., 2007). These crossover methods examine characteristics of parent's tour edge to strictly inherit to children. However, since these crossover operations take long computation time for analyzing edges, using it for not-very -large-scale TSP is often inefficient.

In reference (Baraglia et al., 2001), two kinds of methods are compared in many cases. It shows that Cga-LK is advantageous to 300-10000 cities TSP, but Random-LK is advantageous to 198 cities TSP. Therefore, the solution that can efficiently solve TSP of 1000 cities or more can not necessarily efficiently solve TSP of about 100 cities. As to TSP of our intended scale (with 10s to 100 cities), in reference (Baraglia et al., 2001), a TSP lin105 is solved with 1.77% average error rate in 231seconds. The performance specification of this experimental environment is 200-MHz PentiumPro PC running Linux 2.2.12. Since this SDCC is 0.048, the solving time on our experimental environment is 11.088 seconds. Moreover, in reference (Cheng et al., 2002), the performance comparison experiments were conducted using various crossover operators. Even when the best crossover operator is used, average error rate is 3.1% and computation time is 750 seconds by SUN SPARC Ultra-5 10 machine. Since this SDCC is 0.065, the solving time on our environment is 48.75 seconds. Meanwhile, our MIGA1 obtains the optimal solution within 1.11 seconds, and MIGA2 obtains a solution with average error rate 0.31% in 0.15 seconds.

A GA method with the same purpose as ours (aiming to obtain high quality approximate solution as fast as possible for 10s - 100s cities TSPs) is proposed by Yan et al., 2007. To compare the proposed methods with GA by Yan and TS by Kanazawa, the proposed methods are tested on nine benchmark problems in TSPLIB whose number of cities ranges from 70 to 280. Each problem is solved 100 times.

Table 4 presents the SDCC of each method. And Table 5 presents the experimental results obtained by applying MIGA to the above nine benchmark problems and results corrected by using SDCC. The mark "-" on the Table 5 indicates no data. The digits (e.g. 70) contained in the name (e.g. st70) of TSP indicate the number of cities.

Results of GA by Yan are compared with those of MIGA. Results for the problem st70 indicate MIGA can obtain the solution having almost the same accuracy as GA by Yan, while the computation time is 20%. Results of problem eil76 indicate MIGA can obtain always optimal solution though the average error rate of GA by Yan is 1.184% within the same computation time. Specific results of problem a280 indicate MIGA can obtain solutions whose average error rate is 4% which is lower than that of GA by Yan and the computation time is 7% compared with that of GA by Yan.

Next, results of TS by Kanazawa and MIGA are compared. Results indicate MIGA obtained almost the same accuracy solutions as TS by Kanazawa, while the computation time is 19% for the problem pr107, 63% for pr144, 45% for pr152, and 5% for pr226.

Overall results show that MIGA is more effective than GA by Yan and TS by Kanazawa in solving the above mentioned nine TSP benchmark problems whose number of cities ranges from 70 to 280.

Results of MIGA3 show the average error rate is around 1% and even the worst case error is under 3.5%, to solve, within 30 milliseconds, eight TSP benchmark problems whose number of cities ranges from 70 to 226.

	GA by Yan	TS by Kanazawa
Spec of computing machines	CPU：Pentium4 2.4GHz, メモリ：256MB	CPU：Pentium4 2.55GHz, メモリ：1GB (DDR266)
Spec Difference Correction Coefficient (SDCC)	0.519	0.590

Table 4. Spec Difference Correction Coefficient (SDCC)

Name of TSP	Average error rate from optimal solution [%] (Average execution time [sec])					
	GA by Yan	TS by Kanazawa	MIGA1	MIGA2	MIGA3	
					Average	Worst
st70	0.312 (0.348)	-	0 (0.750)	0.370 (0.074)	0.400 (0.030)	1.333
eil76	1.184 (0.602)	-	0 (0.844)	1.914 (0.080)	2.193 (0.030)	2.974
kroA100	0.016 (0.877)	-	0 (0.937)	0.176 (0.131)	0.873 (0.030)	1.588
pr 107	-	0.290 (0.826)	0.086 (0.985)	0.256 (0.156)	0.449 (0.030)	0.899
pr 136	0 (3.690)	0.190 (4.378)	0.624 (2.016)	1.067 (0.233)	2.460 (0.030)	3.481
pr 144	0 (4.136)	0.019 (4.685)	0 (2.625)	0.149 (0.284)	1.665 (0.030)	2.896
pr 152	-	0.120 (7.558)	0.153 (3.375)	0.551 (0.338)	1.175 (0.030)	2.77
pr 226	-	0.510 (12.685)	0 (3.125)	0.515 (0.652)	1.854 (0.030)	2.566
a280	10.770 (17.371)	-	3.180 (10.453)	6.572 (1.100)	-	-

Table 5. Results compared with related works on TSPLIB

7. Conclusion

In this chapter, an intelligent GA method for solving the TSP was proposed and evaluated. This is applicable to the optimization of various distribution systems such as the parcel and letter delivery as well as large-scale distribution networks that requires repetitive interactive simulations. This kind of application requires responsiveness as well as optimality, for example, solving a TSP with expert-level accuracy within 30 milliseconds.

In order to guarantee expert-level solutions for various kinds of delivery location patterns, the high-speed GA world was combined with the intelligent GA world. The high-speed GA world comprises the random NI method and the 2opt-type mutation. And this high-speed GA mainly uses simple general heuristics. The intelligent GA world includes the random method, the multi-step NI method, and the block-type mutation. And particular knowledge was incorporated in this intelligent GA to overcome the weakness of the high-speed GA. Namely, to cope with delivery location patterns for which the high-speed GA cannot guarantee expert-level solutions, this intelligent GA has rather problem-oriented knowledge.

According to our experiment, in case of using the former high-speed GA, 23 test cases out of 20000 test cases had more than 3% of errors compared to the optimal solution. However, our proposed multi-world intelligent GA method (which comprises the high-speed GA world and the intelligent GA world) could solve each of all 20000 test cases within 30 milliseconds at expert-level accuracy (less than 3% errors).

Our experimental results showed that the proposed methods enable to solve TSPs with responsiveness and optimality necessary for a large-scale distribution network's interactive simulation.

8. References

Arora, S. (1998). Polynomial Time Approximation Schemes for Euclidean TSP and Other Geometric Problems, *Journal of the ACM*, Vol. 45, No. 5, pp. 753-782

Baraglia, R.; Hidalgo, J.I. & Perego, R. (2001). A hybrid heuristic for the traveling salesman problem, *IEEE Transactions on Evolutionary Computation*, Vol. 5, Issue 6, pp. 613-622

Bertsekas, D. P. (1987). *Dynamic Programming: Deterministic and Stochastic Models*, Englewood Cliffs, NJ: Prentice-Hall

Cheng, C.; Lee, W. & Wong, K. (2002). A genetic algorithm-based clustering approach for database partitioning, *IEEE Transactions on Systems, Man and Cybernetics*, Part C, Vol. 32, Issue 3, pp. 215-230

Fang, Y.; Liu, G.; He, Y. & Qiu, Y. (2003). Tabu search algorithm based on insertion method, *Proc. of the 2003 International Conference on Neural Networks and Signal Processing*, pp. 420-423

Feo, T.A.; Recende M.G.C. & Smith S.H. (1994). A Greedy Randomized Adaptive Search Procedure for Maximum Independent Set, *Operations Research*, Vol. 42, No. 5, pp. 860-878

Glover, F. (1989). Tabu Search - Part I, *ORSA Journal on Computing*, Vol. 1, pp. 190-206

Glover, F. (1990). Tabu Search - Part II, *ORSA Journal on Computing*, Vol. 2, pp. 4-32

Grotschel, M. & Holland, O. (1991). Solution of large-scale symmetric traveling salesman problems, *Mathematical Programming*, Vol. 51, pp. 141-202

Hooker, J.H. & Natraj, N.R. (1995). Solving a General Routing and Scheduling Problem by Chain Decomposition and Tabu Search, *Transportation Science*, Vol. 29, No. 1, pp. 30-44

Ingber, L. (1993). Simulated Annealing Practice versus Theory, *Journal of Mathl. Comput. and Modelling*, Vol. 18, No. 11, pp. 29-57

JLUG (2008). Benchmark - JLUG RC5-72 Cracking, *http://www.orange.co.jp/~masaki/rc572/*

Kanazawa, T. & Yasuda, K. (2004). Proximate Optimality Principle Based Tabu Search, *IEEJ Transactions on Electronics, Information and Systems*, Vol. 124, No. 3, pp. 912-920

Kirkpatrick, S.; Gelatt, C. D. & Vecchi, M. P. (1983). Optimization by Simulated Annealing, *Science*, Vol. 220, Num. 4598, pp. 671-680

Kolen, A. & Pesch, E. (1994). Genetic Local Search in Combinatorial Optimization, *Discrete Applied Mathematics*, Vol. 48, pp. 273-284

Kubota S.; Onoyama T.; Onayagi K. & Tsuruta S. (1999). Traveling Salesman Problem Solving Method fit for Interactive Repetitive Simulation of Large-scale Distribution Network, *Proc. of IEEE SMC'99*, pp. 533-538

Laporte, G. (1992). The Vehicle Routing Problem: An overview of exact and approximate algorithms, *European Journal of Operational Research*, Vol. 59, pp. 345-358

Lawer, E.; Lenstra, J.; Rinnony, K. & Shmoys, D. (1985). *The Traveling Salesman Problem: A Guided Tour of Combinatorial Optimization*, John Wiley & Sons, ISBN 0471904137

Lin, S. & Kernighan, B.W. (1972). An effective heuristic algorithm for the traveling salesman problem, *Operations Research*, Vol. 21, No. 2, pp. 498-516

Miki, M.; Hiroyasu, T. & Jitta, T. (2003). Adaptive Simulated Annealing for maximum temperature, *Proc. of IEEE International Conference on Systems, Man and Cybernetics 2003*, Vol. 1, pp. 20-25

Nagata, Y. & Kobayashi, S. (1999). The Proposal and Evaluation of a Crossover for Traveling Salesman Problems: Edge Assembly Crossover, *Journal of Japan Society for AI*, Vol. 14, No. 5, pp. 848-859

Nguyen, H.D.; Yoshihara, I.; Yamamori, K. & Yasunaga, M. (2007). Implementation of an Effective Hybrid GA for Large-Scale Traveling Salesman Problems, *IEEE Transactions on Systems, Man and Cybernetics*, Part. B, Vol. 37, Issue. 1, pp. 92-99

Onoyama, T.; Kubota, S.; Oyanagi, K. & Tsuruta, S. (2000). A Method for Solving Nested Combinatorial Optimization Problems, *Proc. of IEEE SMC2000*, pp. 340-345

Tamaki, H.; et al. (1994). A comparison study of genetic codings for the traveling salesman problem, *Proc. of the 1st IEEE Conference on Evolutionary Computation*, pp. 1-6

Tsai, H.; Yang, J.; Tsai, Y. & Kao, C. (2004). An evolutionary algorithm for large traveling salesman problems, *IEEE Transactions on Systems, Man and Cybernetics*, Part. B, Vol. 34, Issue. 4, pp. 1718-1729

Whiteley, D. & Starkweather, T. (1989). Scheduling Problem and Traveling Salesman: The Genetic Edge Recombination Operator, *Proc. of ICGA'89*, pp. 133-140

Yamamoto, Y. & Kubo, M. (1997). *Invitation to Traveling Salesman Problem*, Asakura Syoten, Tokyo

Yan, X.; Liu, H.; Yan, J. & Wu, Q. (2007). A Fast Evolutionary Algorithm for Traveling Salesman Problem, *Proc. of Third International Conference on Natural Computation (ICNC 2007)*, Vol. 4, pp. 85-90

Yanagiura, M. & Ibaraki, T. (2000). On Metaheuristic Algorithms for Combinatorial Optimization Problems, *Transactions of the IEICE*, Vol. J85-D-II, No. 8, pp. 3-25

10

An Efficient Solving the Travelling Salesman Problem: Global Optimization of Neural Networks by Using Hybrid Method

Yong-Hyun Cho
A School of Computer and Information Comm. Eng., Catholic University of Daegu
330, Kunrakri, Hayangup, Gyeongsan, Gyeongbuk, 712-702
Korea(South)

1. Introduction

The travelling salesman problem (TSP) is a problem in combinatorial optimization studied in operations research and theoretical computer science. Given a list of cities and their pair-wise distances, the task is to find a shortest possible tour that visits each city exactly once (Aarts & Laarhoven, 1985; Beale & Jackson, 1990; Bout & Miller, 1988; Cichock & Unbehaun, 1993; Lin, 1965; Zurada, 1992). The problem was first formulated as a mathematical problem in 1930 and is one of the most intensively studied problems in optimization. It is used as a benchmark for many optimization methods. Even though the problem is computationally difficult, a large number of heuristics and exact methods are known, so that some instances with tens of thousands of cities can be solved (Beale & Jackson, 1990; Freeman & Skapura, 1991; Lin, 1965).

The TSP has several applications even in its purest formulation, such as planning, logistics, and the manufacture of microchips. Slightly modified, it appears as a sub-problem in many areas, such as DNA sequencing. In these applications, the concept city represents, for example, customers, soldering points, or DNA fragments, and the concept distance represents travelling times or cost, or a similarity measure between DNA fragments (Beale & Jackson, 1990; Cichock & Unbehaun, 1993; Freeman & Skapura, 1991; Zurada, 1992). In many applications, additional constraints such as limited resources or time windows make the problem considerably harder.

In the theory of computational complexity, the decision version of TSP belongs to the class of NP-complete problems (Aarts & Laarhoven, 1985; Abe et al., 1992; Burke, 1994; Freeman & Skapura, 1991; Hopfield & Tank, 1985). Thus, it is assumed that there is no efficient algorithm for solving TSPs. In other words, it is likely that the worst case running time for any algorithm for TSP increases exponentially with the number of cities, so even some instances with only hundreds of cities will take many CPU years to solve exactly. The travelling salesman problem is regarded as difficult to solve. If there is a way to break this problem into smaller component problems, the components will be at least as complex as the original one. This is what computer scientists call NP-hard problems (Aarts & Laarhoven, 1985; Abe et al., 1992; Freeman & Skapura, 1991).

Many people have studied this problem. The easiest (and most expensive solution) is to simply try all possibilities. The problem with this is that for *n* cities you have *(n-1)!* possibilities. This means that for only 11 cities there are about 3.5 million combinations to try (Freeman & Skapura, 1991). In recent years, many algorithms for solving the TSP have been proposed (Cichock & Unbehaun, 1993; Dorigo et al., 1991; Goldberg, 1989; Lin & Kernighan, 1971; Mascato, 1989; Szu & Hartley, 1987). However, these algorithms sustain several disadvantages. First, some of these algorithms are not optimal in a way that the solution they obtain may not be the best one. Second, their runtime is not always defined in advance, since for every problem there are certain cases for which the computation time is very long due to unsuccessful attempts for optimization. They will often consistently find good solutions to the problem. These good solutions are typically considered to be good enough simply because they are the best that can be found in a reasonable amount of time. Therefore, optimization often takes the role of finding the best solution possible in a reasonable amount of time. There have been several types of approaches taken to solving the TSP [10-30] of the numerical methods and the neural networks (NNs) (Beale & Jackson, 1990; Cichock & Unbehaun, 1993; Freeman & Skapura, 1991; Goldberg, 1989; Zurada, 1992). Recently, NN is well suited for this type of problems.

An NN, also known as a parallel distributed processing network, is a computing paradigm that is loosely modeled after cortical structures of the brain (Beale & Jackson, 1990; Cichock & Unbehaun, 1993; Freeman & Skapura, 1991; Zurada, 1992). It consists of interconnected processing elements called nodes or neurons (Beale & Jackson, 1990; Zurada, 1992). NN, due to its massive parallelism, has been rigorously studied as an alternative to the conventional numerical approach for fast solving of the combinatorial optimization or the pattern recognition problems. The optimization is to find the neuron that lead to the energy minimum by applying repeatedly the optimization algorithm.

Hopfield model is energy-minimizing network, and is useful as a content addressable memory or an analog computer for solving combinatorial optimization problems (Abe et al., 1992; Abe, 1993, 1996; Aiyer et al., 1990; Andresol et al., 1997; Gall & Zissimopoulos 1999; Hegde et al., 1988; Sharbaro, 1994; Wilson & Pawley, 1988). Generally, Hopfield model may be operated in a discrete-time mode and continuous-time mode, depending on the model adopted for describing the neurons. The discrete-time mode is useful as a content addressable memory, and the continuous-time mode is also useful as an analog computer for solving combinatorial optimization problems. In formulating the energy function for a continuous-time Hopfield model, the neurons are permitted to have self-feedback loops. On the other words, a discrete-time Hopfield model is no self-feedback loops (Beale & Jackson, 1990; Cichock & Unbehaun, 1993; Freeman & Skapura, 1991).

Gradient-type NNs are generalized Hopfield model in which the computational energy decreases continuously in time loops (Beale & Jackson, 1990; Cichock & Unbehaun, 1993; Freeman & Skapura, 1991).. The continuous-time model is called the gradient-type model and converges to one of the stable minima in the state space. The evaluation of model is in the general direction of the negative gradient of energy function. Typically, the energy function is made equivalent to a certain objective function that needs to be minimized. The search for an energy minimum performed by gradient-type model corresponds to the search for a solution of an optimization problem loops (Beale & Jackson, 1990; Cichock & Unbehaun, 1993; Freeman & Skapura, 1991).

The major drawbacks of the continuous-time Hopfield model when it is used to solve some combinatorial problems, for instance, the TSP, are the non feasibility of the obtained solutions and the trial-and-error setting of the model parameters loops (Beale & Jackson, 1990; Bout & Miller, 1988; Cichock & Unbehaun, 1993; Freeman & Skapura, 1991). Most of the researches have been concentrated on the improvement of either the convergence speed or the convergence rate to the global minimum in consideration of the weight parameter of the energy function, etc. But there are few that try to solve both global convergence and speedup by simultaneously setting the initial neuron outputs (Baba, 1989; Biro et al., 1996; Gall & Zissimopoulos 1999; Gee & Prager, 1995; Heung, 2005).

This chapter proposes an efficient method for improving the convergence performances of the NN by applying a global optimization method. The global optimization method is a hybrid of a stochastic approximation (SA) (Styblinski & Tang, 1990) and a gradient descent method. The approximation value inclined toward a global escaping from a local minimum is estimated first by the stochastic approximation, and then the gradient-type update rule of Hopfield model is applied for high-speed convergence. The proposed method has been applied to the *7*- and *10*-city TSPs, respectively. We demonstrate the convergence performance to the conventional Hopfield model with randomized initial neuron outputs setting.

The rest of the chapter is organized as follows. The travelling salesman problem is introduced in section 2. Section 3 presents the Hopfield model for solving the TSP. Section 4 presents the method for estimating an initial value of optimization problems by using stochastic approximation. Section 5 describes how the proposed method can be applied for globally optimizing the neural network. Section 6 describes the experiments with the proposed global optimization method focusing on the TSP. The performance comparison of the experiment results with the Hopfield model is also given. Finally an outlook to future research activities is presented.

2. Travelling salesman problem

Generally, the optimization problems are typically posed in terms of finding the best way to do something, subject to certain constraints. When solving these problems with computers, often the only possible approach is to calculate every possible solution and then choose the best of those as the answer. Unfortunately, some problems have such large solution spaces that this is impossible to do. These are problems where the solution cannot be found in a reasonable time. These problems are referred to as NP-hard or NP-complete problems. In many cases, these problems are described in term of a cost function (Aarts & Laarhoven, 1985; Beale & Jackson, 1990; Cichock & Unbehaun, 1993; Freeman & Skapura, 1991).

One such problem is the TSP. The TSP describes a salesman who must travel between cities. The order in which he does so is unimportant, provided he visits each one during his trip, and finishes in his starting location. Each city is connected to other close by cities, or nodes. Each of those links between the cities has one or more weights (cost) attached. The cost describes how "difficult" it is to traverse this edge on the graph, and may be given, for example, by the cost of an airplane ticket or train ticket, or perhaps by the length of the edge, or time required for completing the traversal (Beale & Jackson, 1990; Bout & Miller, 1988; Cichock & Unbehaun, 1993; Lin, 1965; Zurada, 1992). The salesman wants to keep both the travel costs, as well as the distance he travels as low as possible. That is, the problem is to find the right sequence of cities to visit. The constraints are that all cities are visited, each is visited only once, and the salesman returns to the starting city at the end of the travel. The cost function to be minimized is the total distance or cost travelled in the course of the travel.

The TSP is computationally intensive if an exhaustive search is to be performed comparing all possible routes to find the best one (Freeman & Skapura, 1991). For an n-city trip, there are n! possible paths. Due to degeneracy, the number of distinct solutions is less than n!. The term distinct in this case refers to trips with different total distances. For a given trip, it does not matter which of the n cities is the starting location, in terms of the total distance traveled. This degeneracy reduces the number of distinct tours by a factor of n. Similarly, for a given trip, it does not also matter which of two directions the salesman travels. This fact further reduces the number of distinct trips by a factor of two. Thus, for n-city trip, there are n!/2n distinct tours to consider.

For a 5-city trip, there would be 120!/10=12 distinct trips-hardly a problem worthy of solution by a computer! A 10-city trip, however, has 3,628,800/20=181,440 distinct trips; a 30-city trip has over 4×10^{30} possibilities. Adding a single city to a trip results in an increase in the number of distinct trips by a factor of n. Thus, a 31-city trip requires that we examine 31 times as many trips as we must for a 30-city trip. The amount of computation time required by a digital computer to solve this problem grows exponentially with the number of cities.

There have been many approaches to solving the Traveling Salesman Problem. These approaches range from a simple heuristic algorithm to algorithms based on the physical workings of the human mind to those based on ant colonies (Andresol et al., 1997; Dorigo et al., 1991; Dorigo & Gambardella, 1997; Lin & Kernighan, 1971; Mascato, 1989; Szu & Hartley, 1987). These algorithms all have the same ultimate goal: in a graph with weighted edges, find the shortest Hamiltonian path (the path through all nodes with the smallest sum of edge weights). Unfortunately, this goal is very hard to achieve. The algorithms therefore settle for trying to accomplish two smaller goals: (1) to more quickly find a good solution and (2) to find a better good solution. A good solution is one that is close to being optimal and the best of these good solutions is, of course, the optimal solution itself. There have been several types of approaches taken to solving the TSP. They include heuristic approaches, memetic algorithms, ant colony algorithms, simulated annealing, genetic algorithms, neural networks, and various other methods for more specific variations of the TSP (Abe, 1993; Andresol et al., 1997; Dorigo et al., 1991; Dorigo & Gambardella, 1997; Lin & Kernighan, 1971; Mascato, 1989; Szu & Hartley, 1987; Xavier & Suykens, 2006; Mühlenbein, 1992).

These approaches do not always find the true optimal solution. Instead, they will often consistently find good solutions to the problem. These good solutions are typically considered to be good enough simply because they are the best that can be found in a reasonable amount of time. Therefore, optimization often takes the role of finding the best solution possible in a reasonable amount of time.

2.1 Heuristic algorithms

The heuristic means that a rule of thumb, simplification or educated guess that reduces or limits the search for solutions in domains that are difficult and poorly understood (Lin & Kernighan, 1971). Unlike algorithms, heuristics do not guarantee optimal, or even feasible, solutions and are often used with no theoretical guarantee. In contrast, an algorithm is defined as "a precise rule (or set of rules) specifying how to solve some problem" (Andresol

et al., 1997; Lin & Kernighan, 1971). To combine these together into a heuristic algorithm, we would have something like "a set of rules specifying how to solve some problem by applying a simplification that reduces the amount of solutions checked". In other words, the algorithm is the instructions for choosing the correct solution to the problem while the heuristic is the idea of how to shrink the list of possible solutions down to a reasonable size.
An example of a heuristic approach to the TSP might be to remove the most weighted edge from each node to reduce the size of the problem (Lin & Kernighan, 1971). The programmer in this situation may assume that the best solution would not have the most weighted edge. Upon close inspection, this heuristic may not actually give the best solution, maybe not even a feasible solution (if all of the most weighted edges from each node are connected with the same node) but it may be a calculated risk that the programmer takes (Lin & Kernighan, 1971).
The main idea of a heuristic approach to a problem is that, although there is exponential growth in the number of possible solutions to the problem, evaluating how good a solution is can be done in polynomial time.
In dealing with the TSP, the most common uses of heuristic ideas work with a local search. Similarly to the above example, the heuristic does not try to encompass every possibility of the problem at hand; instead it attempts to apply common sense to shrink the problem to a manageable size.
Perhaps the most-used local search heuristic that is applied to the TSP is the n-opt method developed by Lin and Kernighan (Andresol et al., 1997; Lin & Kernighan, 1971). It simply takes a random path and replaces n edges in it until it finds the best of those paths. This is typically done where n is set to *2* or *3* (Lin & Kernighan, 1971). These methods were applied to several different problems. Notably, they were able to find the optimal solutions for a *42*-city problem *4* out of *10* times and the optimal solution to a *48*-city problem *2* out of *10* times (Lin & Kernighan, 1971) (the *10* times in these were running concurrently so the optimum solution was found in each run of the program).

2.2 Simulated annealing

Simulated annealing is a method that is based on the cooling of a physical system (Kawabe et al., 2002; Szu & Hartley, 1987; Xavier et al., 2006). The general idea is that there is a temperature (T) and a cost function (H). In our case, the cost function is the sum of the weights of the edges in our circuit. In the beginning, there is a random solution to the problem. At each iteration, a change is proposed to this solution and that change is evaluated based on the cost function and the temperature. If the cost function decreases then the change is accepted. If the cost function does not decrease then the change is accepted or rejected based on the temperature. The higher the temperature, the better the chance that the change will be accepted. As time progresses, the temperature decreases and eventually there is no possibility for a change to occur without the cost function decreasing. Using this method, researchers were able to get to within two units of the optimal cost for problems up to a size of *100* (Xavier et al., 2006).

2.3 Neural networks

A neural network is a massively parallel distributed processor that has a natural propensity for storing experiential knowledge and making it available for use (Beale & Jackson, 1990; Bout & Miller, 1988; Cichock & Unbehaun, 1993; Freeman & Skapura, 1991; Lin, 1965; Zurada, 1992). It resembles the brain in two respects. One is that knowledge is acquired by the network through a learning process. Another is that interneuron connection strengths known as synaptic weights are used to store the knowledge. Basically, a neural network is made up of many independent units (neurons) and connections between them. The connections are given various weights based on a “learning process”. Based on the sum of the products of adjoining neurons and the weights of the connecting edges, each neuron finds a value. Additionally, if the value of one neuron changes then the values of all the adjoining neurons also change. This creates a ripple effect that can change the values of every neuron (although it could also change none of them).

An NN can be applied to a TSP with n cities (Beale & Jackson, 1990; Bout & Miller, 1988; Cichock & Unbehaun, 1993; Freeman & Skapura, 1991; Lin, 1965; Zurada, 1992). This is done by creating n^2 neurons. The output of each neuron ($V_{x,i}$) represents whether city x is visited as the i-th city in the sequence. It is a *1* if this is true or a *0* if it is not. Additionally, the amount d_{xy} is applied to the calculations as the distance between cities x and y.

2.4 Genetic algorithm

A genetic algorithm (GA) is based on the same idea as the theory of evolution (Goldberg, 1989; Mühlenbein, 1992). Basically, several random sets of parameters are applied to an algorithm and a fitness value is returned for each. Based on these fitness values, the best sets are mixed together and new sets are again applied to the algorithm until an optimal set of parameters is obtained. This effect is usually obtained by breaking the genetic algorithm into a few small parts. The main parts are the fitness function and the evolution function (Goldberg, 1989).

The evolution function produces a string of inputs (often a string of bits that are encodings of the input parameters) then asks the fitness function for a fitness value for that string. When several strings have been assigned a fitness value, the evolution function takes the best strings, mixes them together, sometimes throws in a "mutation" to the strings and then sends the results back as new input strings. The biological analogy is to a human’s genes. In fact, an input string is often called a chromosome and the bits in the string are referred to as genes.

The fitness function of a genetic algorithm takes in a string of inputs and runs them through the process that is being evaluated (Mühlenbein, 1992). Based on the performance of the inputs, the function returns a fitness value. In the case of the TSP, the fitness function returned the total length or weight of the path found. A GA has two main parts, an evolution function and a fitness function. In the case of the TSP, the parameters produced by the evolution function might be the order of the nodes through which the path will go. The fitness function in that same case would return the total length of the path found. The GA would then compare fitness values for each input string and assign priority to the ones that returns lower path lengths. Genetic algorithms and their applications to the TSP are described by Goldberg (Goldberg, 1989).

2.5 Memetic algorithms

A memetic algorithm (MA) is really a combination of several different techniques (Mascato, 1989). Generally, an MA can be thought of as an algorithm that combines local search heuristics with a crossover operator (the same type of mixing and matching that happens with a GA’s evolution function). Despite this, the difference between an MA and a GA is very distinct. As opposed to the fitness functions of GAs, MAs use a local search heuristic to determine how the parameter definitions will be modified each iteration. For example, an

MA might use simulated annealing to find a solution with some parameters and return that value to the crossover operator just like a GA would return a value from a fitness function. For this reason there are many other terms used to refer to MAs including hybrid genetic algorithms, parallel genetic algorithms, and genetic local search algorithms. The research in MAs was most notably conducted by Mascato (Mascato, 1989). Researchers such as Mühlenbein have shown MAs to be near-optimal with sizes at least as large as a *200*-city problem.

2.6 Ant colony algorithms

Ant-based algorithms are based on studies of ant colonies in nature (Dorigo et al., 1991; Dorigo & Gambardella, 1997). The main idea in these algorithms is that the behavior of each individual ant produces an emergent behavior in the colony. When applied to the TSP, individual agents ("ants") traverse the graph of the problem, leaving a chemical (pheromone) trail behind them. At each node it comes to, an ant must decide which edge to take to the next node. This is done by checking each edge for pheromone concentration and applying a probability function to the decision of which edge to choose. The higher the concentration of pheromone, the more likely the ant is to choose that edge. Also, to avoid stagnation in travel, the pheromone is given an evaporation rate so that in each iteration the pheromone loses a certain percentage on each edge. This method was researched originally by Dorigo, et al. (Dorigo et al., 1991). This method has been shown to do better than other algorithms on random *50*-city problems as well as finding the optimum solutions for problems with up to *100* cities (Dorigo & Gambardella, 1997).

3. Hopfield model for solving TSP information

In the most general case, NNs consist of a (often very high) number of neurons, each of which has a number of inputs, which are mapped via a relatively simple function to its output (Beale & Jackson, 1990; Bout & Miller, 1988; Cichock & Unbehaun, 1993; Freeman & Skapura, 1991; Lin, 1965; Zurada, 1992). Networks differ in the way their neurons are interconnected (topology), in the way the output of a neuron determined out of its inputs(propagation function) and in their temporal behavior(synchronous, asynchronous or continuous).

Ever since Hopfield and Tank (Hopfield & Tank, 1985) showed that the feedback neural network could be possibly used to solve combinatorial optimization problems such as the TSP, great efforts have been made to improve the performance. Most of the early work focused on ways to find valid solutions because of the disappointing results reported (Freeman & Skapura, 1991). While some researchers tried to find more appropriate parameters in the energy function (Aiyer et al., 1990; Baba, 1989; Biro et al., 1996; Burke, 1994; Gall & Zisssimopoulos, 1999; Gee & Prager, 1995; Hegde et al., 1988; Hopfield & Tank, 1985; Huang, 2005; Sharbaro, 1994; Wilson & Pawley, 1988), others hoped to get better energy functions (Baba, 1989). To date, research work has been extended to every aspect of the Hopfield model (Aarts & Laarhoven, 1985; Abe et al., 1992; Aiyer et al., 1990; Baba, 1989; Biro et al., 1996; Burke, 1994; Hegde et al., 1988; Hopfield & Tank, 1985; Sharbaro, 1994; Wilson & Pawley, 1988), and it is now clear how to correctly map problems onto the network so that invalid solutions never emerge. As for the quality of obtained solutions, while there are indications that the Hopfield model is solely suitable for solving Euclidean

TSPs of small size (Wilson & Pawley, 1988), some researchers argue it is unreasonable to take the TSP as the benchmark to measure the optimization ability of the Hopfield model (Sharbaro, 1994). According to that, the applicability of the Hopfield model to solve other optimization problems should not be ignored. By now, the Hopfield model has been successfully applied to many fields.

A key issue in the application of the Hopfield model is the choice of the weights1 in the energy function. Previous work addressing this problem is only concerned with the occasion for solving the TSP. The most successful and earliest work was conducted by Aiyer et al. (Aiyer et al., 1990). Using the eigenvalue analysis, they obtained values for the weights which make the network converge to very good solutions. Other works concerning on this problem include the technique of suppressing spurious states (Abe, 1993).

3.1 Hopfield model

Hopfield described a new way of modeling a system of neurons capable of performing computational tasks (Cichock & Unbehaun, 1993; Zurada, 1992). The Hopfield model emerged, initially as a means of exhibiting a content addressable memory (CAM). A general CAM must be capable of retrieving a complete item from the system's memory when presented with only sufficient partial information. Hopfield showed that his model was not only capable of correctly yielding an entire memory from any portion of sufficient size, but also included some capacity for generalization, familiarity recognition, categorization, error correction, and time-sequence retention (Hopfield & Tank, 1985).

The Hopfield model, as described in (Beale & Jackson, 1990; Zurada, 1992), comprises a fully interconnected system of n computational elements or neurons. Fig. 1 is a model of artificial neural network.

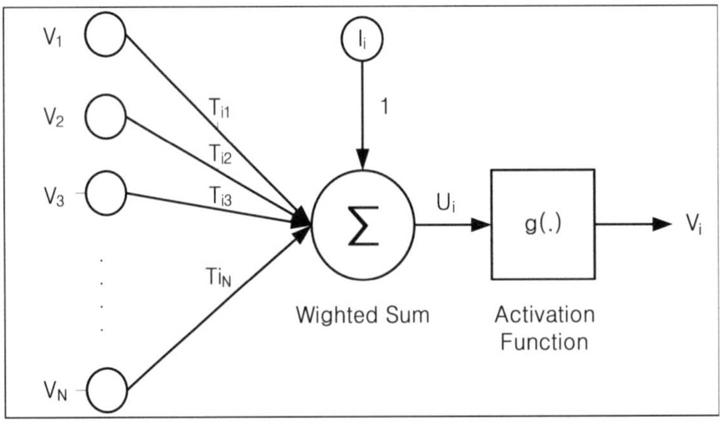

Fig. 1. Model of artificial neural network

In Fig. 1, Hopfield's original notation has been altered where necessary for consistency. The strength of the connection, or weight, between neuron i and neuron j is determined by T_{ij}, which may be positive or negative depending on whether the neurons act in an excitatory or inhibitory manner (Freeman & Skapura, 1991). The internal state of each neuron U_i is equivalent to the weighted sum of the external states of all connecting neurons. The external state of neuron i is given by Vi, with $0 \leq V_i \leq 1$. An external input, Ii, to each neuron i is also incorporated. The relationship between the internal state of a neuron and its output level in

this continuous Hopfield model is determined by an activation function $g_i(U_i)$, which is bounded below by 0 and above by 1.
Then the dynamics of each neuron can be given by a system of the differential eq. (1).

$$\frac{dU_i}{dt} = \sum_j T_{ij} V_j - \frac{U_i}{\tau} + I_i, \quad U_i = g_i^{-1}(V_i) \tag{1}$$

Where is a time constant, *Ii* is the external input(bias) of neuron *i*, and V_i and U_i are the output and input of neuron *i*. The relation g_i between the input U_i and the output V_i is characterized by a monotonically increasing function such as a sigmoid, or a piecewise linear function.
Hopfield model is a dynamic network (Beale & Jackson, 1990; Zurada, 1992), which iterates to converge from an arbitrary input state. The Hopfield model works as minimizing an energy function. The Hopfield model is single layer network which are fully interconnected. It is a weighted network where the output of the network is fed back and there are weights to each of this link. The fully connected Hopfield model is shown in following Fig. 2.

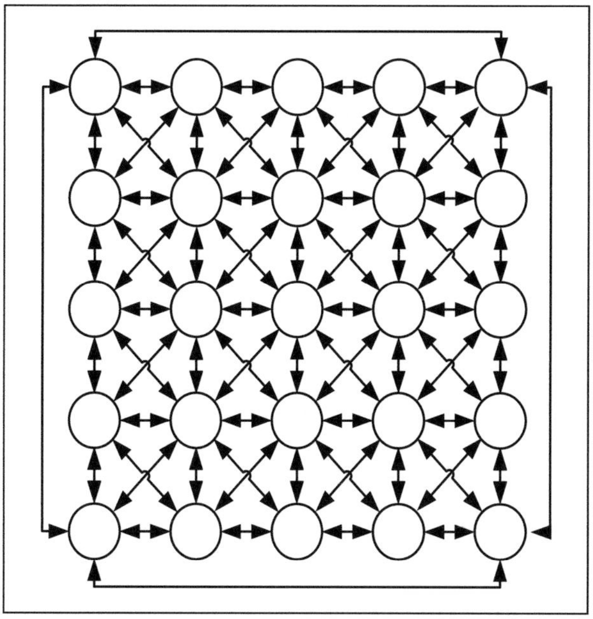

Fig. 2. Fully connected Hopfield model for 5-city TSP

As long as the neuron has a sufficiently high gain, the first term in (1) can be neglected. In that case, the Hopfield model has the Lyapunov energy function of eq. (2)

$$E = -\frac{1}{2}\sum_i \sum_j V_i T_{ij} V_j - \sum_i I_i V_i \tag{2}$$

And moreover we may note the following relations hold:

$$\frac{du_i}{dt} = -\frac{\partial E}{\partial V_i} \; and \; \frac{dE}{dt} \leq 0 \tag{3}$$

This means that the energy function monotonically decreases with the evolution of the network's state, and when the network reaches the final stable state, the energy function falls into a local minimum. The general method of applying the Hopfield model to solve optimization problems is to map the objectives and constraints involved in the problem into an energy function, and then obtain the neuron's dynamic equation by means of eq. (3).

3.2 Hopfield model to solve the TSP

The TSP is concerned with how to find a shortest closed path that travels each of n cities exactly once. In terms of the geometric structure of the distribution of the cities and the symmetry of distances between a pair of cities, the TSP can be classified into several categories (Aiyer et al., 1990; Baba, 1989; Biro et al., 1996; Burke, 1994; Gee & Prager, 1995; Hegde et al., 1988; Sharbaro, 1994; Wilson & Pawley, 1988).
The Hopfield model for the TSP is built of $n * n$ neurons. The network consists of n rows, containing n neurons according to Fig. 3.

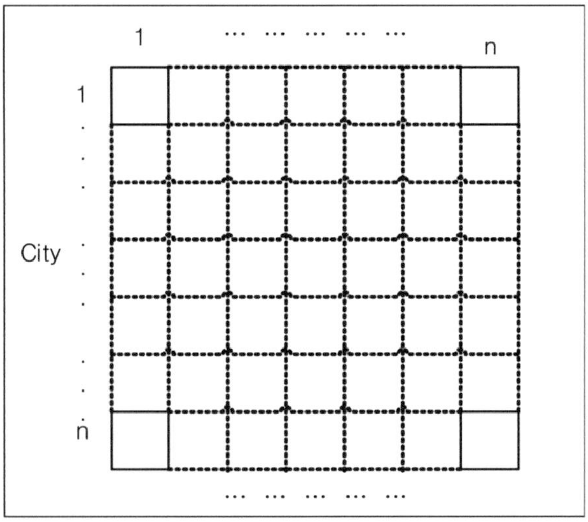

Fig. 3. The division of the network

All neurons have two subscripts. The first one defines the city number and the second one the position of the city in the tour. If a neuron in the stable state of the network, has the output signal $V_{x,i} = 1$, then it means that the city x should be visited in the stage i of the tour (Beale & Jackson, 1990; Zurada, 1992).
The energy function for mapping the TSP proposed by Hopfield is described by eq. (4)

$$E = \frac{A}{2}\sum_{x}\sum_{i}\sum_{j\neq i} V_{x,i}V_{x,j} + \frac{B}{2}\sum_{i}\sum_{x}\sum_{y\neq x} V_{x,i}V_{x,i} + \frac{C}{2}\left(\sum_{x}\sum_{i} V_{x,i} - n\right)^2 + \frac{D}{2}\sum_{x}\sum_{y\neq x}\sum_{i} d_{x,y}V_{x,i}(V_{y,i-1} + V_{y,i+1}) \quad (4)$$

Where $d_{x,y}$ is the distance from city x to city y, and the scaling parameters A, B, C, D are positive constants. The first and second term represents the constraint that at most one neuron of the array V is on fire at each row and column, respectively. The third term represents the constraint that the total number of neurons on fire is exactly n. The fourth term measures the tour length corresponding to a given tour, where the two terms inside the parenthesis stand for two neighboring visiting cities of $V_{x,i}$, implying the tour length is calculated twice. The energy function reaches a local minimum when the network is at a valid tour state.

With this formulation, the Hopfield model has the connection strengths and external input given as eq. (5) and eq. (6)

$$T_{xi,yi} = -\left\{ A\delta_{x,y}(1-\delta_{i.j}) + B(1-\delta_{x,y})\delta_{i,j} + C + D(\delta_{i,j-1} + \delta_{i,j+1})d_{x,y} \right\} \tag{5}$$

$$I_{x,i} = Cn \tag{6}$$

Where $\delta_{i,j}$ is equal to 1 $(i \neq j)$ or 0 (otherwise).

It is known that the Hopfield model formulation does not work well for the TSP since the network often converges to infeasible solutions. It has been widely recognized that the formulation is not ideal, even for problems other than the TSP. The nature of the energy function that the method utilizes causes infeasible solutions to occur most of the time. A number of penalty parameters which are an initial values of weights and neurons and the activation function, need to be fixed before each simulation of the network, yet the values of these parameters that will enable the network to generate valid solutions are unknown. The problem of optimally selecting these parameters is not trivial, and much work has been done to try to facilitate this process (Abe, 1993, 1996; Hegde et al., 1988; Lai & Coghill, 1994). Many other researchers believed that the Hopfield model's energy function needed to be modified before any progress would be made, and considerable effort has also been spent in this area.

4. Initial value estimation by stochastic approximation

We consider the following problem of global unconstrained optimization: minimize the multiextremal function $f(x) \in \boldsymbol{R}^{i}$, $x \in \boldsymbol{R}^{n}$, i.e.

$$\min_{x \in R^n} f(x) \tag{7}$$

A multiextremal function can be represented as a superposition of uniextremal function(i.e., having just one minimum) and other multiextremal function that add some noise to the uniextremal function. The objective of smoothing can be visualized as filtering out the noise and performing minimization on the smoothed uniextremal function, in order to reach the global minimum. In general, since the minimum of the smoothed uniextremal function does not coincide with the global function minimum, a sequence of minimization runs is required to zero in the neighborhood of global minimum (Styblinski & Tang, 1990). The smoothing process is performed by averaging $f(x)$ over some region of the parameter space $\boldsymbol{R}^{n}$ using a proper weighting (or smoothing) function $h^{\wedge}(x)$.

Let us introduce a vector of random perturbations $\eta \in \boldsymbol{R}^{n}$, and add η to x. The convolution function $f^{\sim}(x, \beta)$ is created as follows (Styblinski & Tang, 1990).

$$f^{\sim}(x,\beta) = \int_{R^n} h^{\wedge}(\eta,\beta) f(x-\eta) d\eta \tag{8}$$

Hence:

$$f^{\sim}(x,\beta) = E_\eta[f(x-\eta)] \tag{9}$$

Where $f^{\sim}(x, \beta)$ is the smoothed approximation to original function $f(x)$, and the kernel function $h^{\wedge}(\eta, \beta)$ is the probability density function(*pdf*) used to sample η. β controls the dispersion of $h^{\wedge}(\eta, \beta)$, i.e. the degree of $f(x)$, smoothing (Styblinski & Tang, 1990).
Note that $f^{\sim}(x, \beta)$ can be regarded as an averaged version of $f(x)$, weighted by $h^{\wedge}(\eta, \beta)$. $E_\eta[f(x-\eta)]$ is the expectation with respect to the random variable η.
Therefore an unbiased estimator $f^{\sim}(x, \beta)$ is the average:

$$f^{\sim}(x,\beta) = \frac{1}{N}\sum_{i=1} E_\eta[f(x-\eta^i)] \tag{10}$$

Where η is sampled with the *pdf* $h^{\wedge}(\eta, \beta)$.
The kernel function $h^{\wedge}(\eta, \beta)$ should have the following properties (Styblinski & Tang, 1990):

$$h^{\wedge}(\eta,\beta) = (\frac{1}{\beta^n}) \tag{11}$$

is piecewise differentiable with respect to η.

- $lim_{\beta\to 0}\, h^{\wedge}(\eta, \beta) = \delta(\eta)$ (Dirac delta function)
- $h^{\wedge}(\eta, \beta)$ is a pdf.

Under above the conditions, $lim_{\beta\to 0}\, f^{\sim}(x, \beta) = \int_{R^n} \delta(\eta)\, f(x - \eta)\, d\eta = f(x - 0) = f(x)$. Several *pdfs* fulfill above conditions, such as Gaussian, uniform, and Cauchy *pdfs*.
Smoothing is able to eliminate the local minima of $f^{\sim}(x, \beta)$, if β is sufficiently large. If $\beta \to 0$, then $f^{\sim}(x, \beta) \to f(x)$. This should actually happen at the end of optimization to provide convergence to the true function minimum (Styblinski & Tang, 1990). Formally, the optimization problem can be written as:

$$\min_{x\in R^n} f^{\sim}(x,\beta) \tag{12}$$

with $\beta \to 0$ as $x \to x^*$. Where x^* is the global minimum of original function $f(x)$. One class of methods to solve the modified problem Eq. (12), to be called large sample(LS) stochastic methods, can be characterized as follows: for each new point x, a large number of points sampled with the *pdf* $h^{\wedge}(\eta, \beta)$ (Eq. (11)) is used to estimate $f^{\sim}(x, \beta)$ and its gradient $\nabla_x f^{\sim}(x, \beta)$. The number of samples used should be sufficiently large to give small errors of the relevant estimators. Optimization and averaging are separated in LS methods. This is very inefficient (Styblinski & Tang, 1990).
Optimization and averaging can be combined into one iterative process, leading to much more efficient small-sample (SS) methods of stochastic programming. A large class of SS methods, called stochastic approximation, is applied to the function minimization or maximization (Styblinski & Tang, 1990). Their basic principle of operation is that only a small number of samples are used in each iteration to find the necessary estimators, but all the information is averaged over many steps.
In function minimization, SA methods create stochastic equivalent to the gradient methods of nonlinear programming. The advanced algorithms are proposed to estimate the gradient

$\nabla_x \tilde{f}(x, \beta)$. As the algorithm progresses, $\beta \rightarrow 0$, reducing the smoothing degree of the $f(x)$, and providing convergence to the true minimum. The SA algorithm implements a well-defined approximation to the conjugate gradient. The value x based on the smoothed function $\tilde{f}(x, \beta)$ is updated, as following,

$$\begin{aligned} \xi_k &= \nabla_x \tilde{f}(x_k, \beta) \\ S_k &= STEP \,/\, \|\xi_k\| \\ d_k &= (1-\rho_k)d_{k-1} + \rho_k \xi_k \;(0 \le \rho_k \le 1) \\ \rho_k &= (1-\rho_{k-1}) \,/\, (1+\rho_{k-1} - R) \\ x_{k+1} &= x_k - S_k d_k \end{aligned} \tag{13}$$

Where $k(1,2,\ldots,MAXITER)$ is the number of iterations, ξ is the gradient, S is a step size, d is the search direction, ρ is the gradient averaging coefficient of $\tilde{f}(x, \beta)$, and $R(0<R<1)$ is a constant controlling the rate of change of ρ_k. Therefore, we can find the global minimum of original function by iteratively performing one cycle of the SA optimization as $\beta \rightarrow 0$. This is called the stochastic approximation with smoothing (SAS) (Styblinski & Tang, 1990).

Fig. 4 is the flow chart of SA algorithm. In this Fig. 4, each new value x is performed in the direction $S_k d_k$, where d_k is a convex combination of the previous direction d_{k-1} and a new gradient ξ_k. Especially R is responsible for the rate of change of ρ_k, that is, it modifies the search direction d_k and provides a suitable amount of inertia of gradient direction.

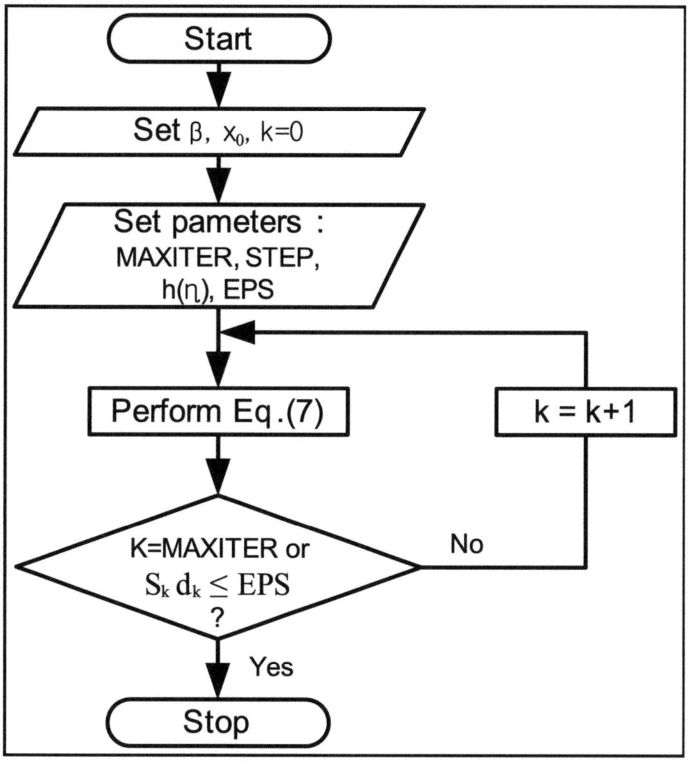

Fig. 4. Flowchart of stochastic approximation

Fig. 5 is the flow charts of SAS algorithm that repeatedly performs the SA algorithm according to a sequence: $\{\beta_0, \beta_1, ...\} \to 0$. We can get the global minimum by using the SAS algorithm based on specific sequences $\{\beta\}$ and $\{NMAX\}$. It turned out that the final solutions were not very sensitive to a specific choice of theses sequences based on rough heuristic criteria such as: low problem dimensionality requires a smaller number of function evaluations, β should be large at the beginning of optimization (to determine the approximate position of the global minimum), and small at the end of optimization (for precision) (Styblinski & Tang, 1990).
We consider the function $f(x) = x^4 - 16x^2 + 5x$ as an example (Styblinski & Tang, 1990). This function is continuous and differentiable, and it has two distinct minima as shown in Fig. 6. The smoothed $f^{\tilde{}}(x, \beta)$ is plotted to different values of $\beta \to 0(\{5, 4, 3, 2, 1, 0.001, 0.0\})$ and $MAXITER=100$ for uniform *pdf*. We can show that minimize the smoothed function $f^{\tilde{}}(x, \beta)$ with $\beta \to 0$ as $x \to x^*$.
As shown in Fig. 6, the smoothed functional $f^{\tilde{}}(x, \beta)$ is an uniextremal function having one minimum x_I from $\beta = 5$ to $\beta = 3$. That is, smoothing is able to eliminate the local minima of $f^{\tilde{}}(x, \beta)$, if β is sufficiently large. If $\beta \to 0$, then $f^{\tilde{}}(x, \beta) = f(x)$. We can also find out that the minimum x_I of uniextremal function inclines toward the global minimum x^* of the original function $f(x)$ in Fig. 6.
On the other hand, the simulated annealing is often explained in terms of the energy that particle has at any given temperature (Kwabe et al., 2002; Szu & Hartley, 1987; Xavier et al., 2006). A similar explanation can be given to the smoothed approximation approach discussed. Perturbing x can be viewed as adding some random energy to a particle which x

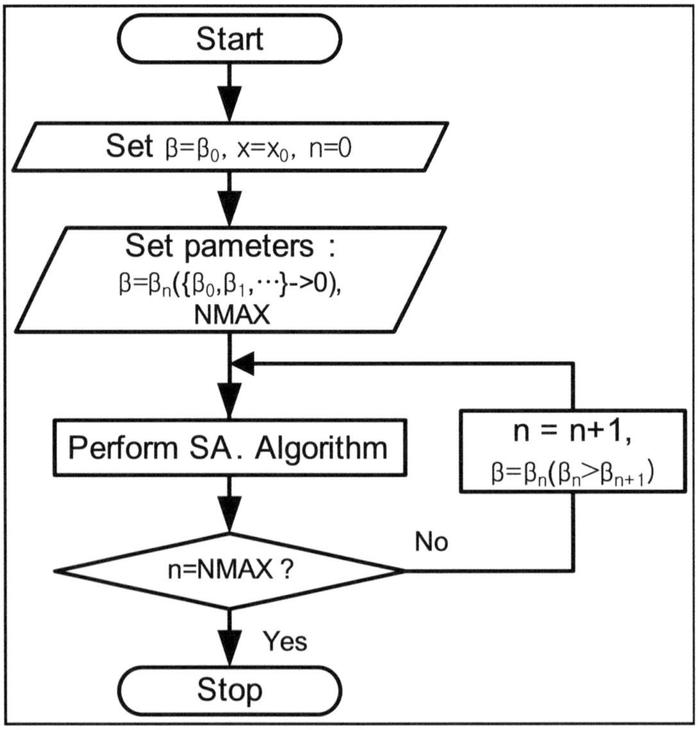

Fig. 5. Flowchart of stochastic approximation with smoothing

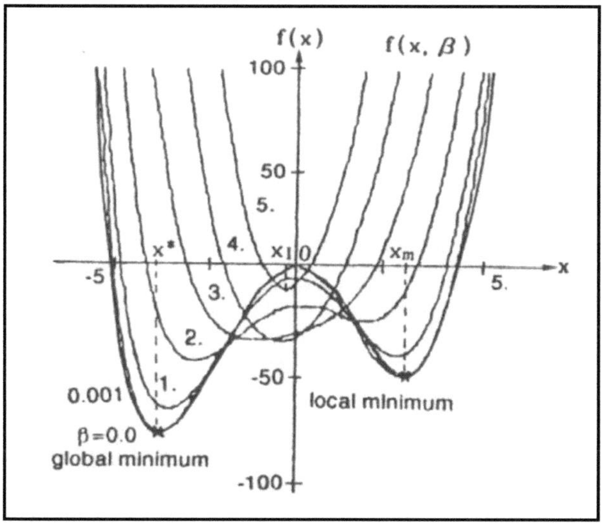

Fig. 6. Smoothed function $f^{\sim}(x, \beta)$ to β values

represents. The larger the β, the larger the energy (i.e., the larger the temperature in the simulated annealing), and also the broader the range of x changes. Reducing β for the smoothed approximation corresponds to temperature reduction in the simulated annealing. Although the global minimum can be found by repeatedly applying SA according to a sequence: $\{\beta_0, \beta_1, \ldots\} \rightarrow 0$, there are a few problems as follows: a specific sequences and a parameters should be determined heuristically in each iterations, and, due to its stochastic process, its convergence speed is rather slower than that of the deterministic algorithm and sometimes results in approximate solution.

For this reason, SAS is the stochastic algorithm as the simulated annealing. The stochastic algorithms guarantee that converges to the global minimum, but their convergence speed is lower than that of the deterministic algorithms. In order to solve the limitation of convergence speed, we present a new optimization method that combines advantages of both the stochastic algorithm and the deterministic algorithm. That is, we propose a hybrid method of SA algorithm and gradient descent algorithm. SA algorithm is previously applied to estimate an initial value leading to the global minimum, and the gradient descent algorithm is also applied for high-speed convergence. In Fig. 6, if we utilize the minimum x_l as an initial value of gradient descent algorithm, the global minimum of original function can be quickly and correctly looked for rather than that find by repeatedly applying the SA according to a sequences $\{\beta\}$.

Fig. 7 is the flow chart of proposed method. If the other minima exist between x_f (minimum of original function by using the gradient descent algorithm) and global minimum x^*, x^* can be find out by repeatedly applying the proposed method.

5. Neural network optimization by the proposed method

The basic idea in this paper is that, in applying the SA, if we initially choose a large β, we can get an uniextremal smoothed function $f^{\sim}(x, \beta)$, the minimum value x_l of which can approximately point out the hill side value of the global minimum well. Comparing optimization of functions with NNs, minimization of the function $f(x)$ to variable x are much the same as the minimization of energy function $E(\boldsymbol{V})$ to neuron outputs $\boldsymbol{V}$.

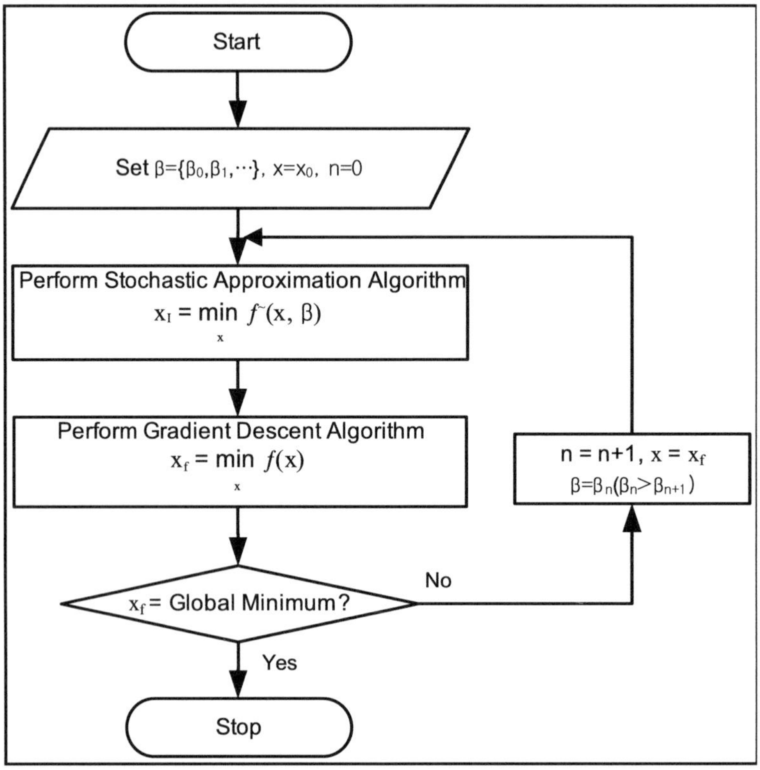

Fig. 7. Flowchart of the proposed method

Accordingly, we apply the proposed method to optimize the neural network. The update rule of Hopfield model is used in optimization as a gradient descent algorithm and operated in batch mode. SA algorithm is previously applied to estimate an initial neuron outputs leading to the global minimum, and then the update rule of Hopfield model is also applied for high-speed convergence. The neural network will be quickly optimized and clearly guaranteed that converges to a global minimum in state space if we go about it like this.

Therefore, the proposed hybrid algorithm using the SA and the update rule of Hopfield model can be detailed as follows:

Step 1. Define the energy function *E(**V**)* for the given problems.

$$E(\mathbf{V}) = -(1/2)\Sigma_i \Sigma_j T_{ij} V_i V_j - \Sigma_i I_i V_I \tag{14}$$

Where T_{ij} denotes the weight value connecting the output of the j neuron with the input of the i neuron, I_i is the bias of i neuron, V_i and V_j are the outputs of i and j neurons, respectively.

Step 2. Calculate the smoothed gradient $\nabla_V E^{\sim}(\mathbf{V}, \beta)$ over the $E(\mathbf{V})$.

$$\begin{aligned}\nabla_V E^{\sim}(V,\beta) &= (1/2)(\beta/\eta)\left[E(V+\beta\eta) - E(V-\beta\eta)\right] = -(1/2)\eta^2 \sum_i \sum_j T_{ij}(V_i + V_j) - \eta^2 \sum_i I_i \\ &= -(1/2)\eta^2 \left[\left(\sum_i \sum_j T_{ij} V_i + \sum_i I_i\right) + \left(\sum_i \sum_j T_{ij} V_j\right) + \sum_i I_i) \right]\end{aligned} \tag{15}$$

Step 3. Set the randomized initial neuron outputs $\mathbf{V}_0$.

Step 4. Estimate the neuron outputs by performing SA with a large β according to the gradient $\nabla_V E^{\tilde{}}(\mathbf{V}, \beta)$.

Step 5. Perform the conventional update rule of Hopfield model using the neuron outputs estimated in Step 4.

Step 6. If the energy function $E(\mathbf{V})$ value by the step 5 is less than a tolerance limit EPV, then stop. Otherwise go to step 4.

6. Experimental results and discussions

The proposed method has been applied to the *7-* and *10-*city TSPs. TSP is one of the combinatorial optimization problems. For an n-city tour, there are $n!/2n$ distinct circuits to consider (Freeman & Skaoura, 1991).

Pentium *IV-2.8G* CPU has been used in experiments. The initial values of neuron outputs are randomly chosen in [$-0.5 \sim +0.5$] by using the random seeds, the output function in response to the net input of neuron is sigmoid function, and then the gain is chosen in *0.5*. The stopping rule is used in each experiment so as to terminate the calculation if all the outputs do not change any more or the energy function $E(\mathbf{V})$ becomes less than the tolerance limit $EPV=0.0001$. The initial dispersion control parameter $\beta_0=3.0$ and the smoothing function $h(\eta)$ with uniform *pdf* are chosen, respectively.

The experimental results for each example are shown in Table 1 and 4, where N_{HM}, and N_{SA} are the number of iterations of Hopfield model and SA algorithm, respectively. E_t is the final energy value in termination. t_{HM} and t_{PM} are the CPU time in [sec] of Hopfield model and proposed algorithm, respectively. In Table 2 and 4, x^{-} and σ are mean and standard deviation.

Fig. 8 shows the *7-* and *10-*city coordinates that are randomly generated, respectively. A (x, y) coordinates are the 2-dimensional city positions.

Table 1 shows the experimental results of *7*-city TSP to *10* random seeds. In case of Hopfield model, the constraints are satisfied at random seeds *5, 20,* and *30*, but the stopping rule is only satisfied in random seeds *5* and 20. The proposed method satisfies the stopping rule to

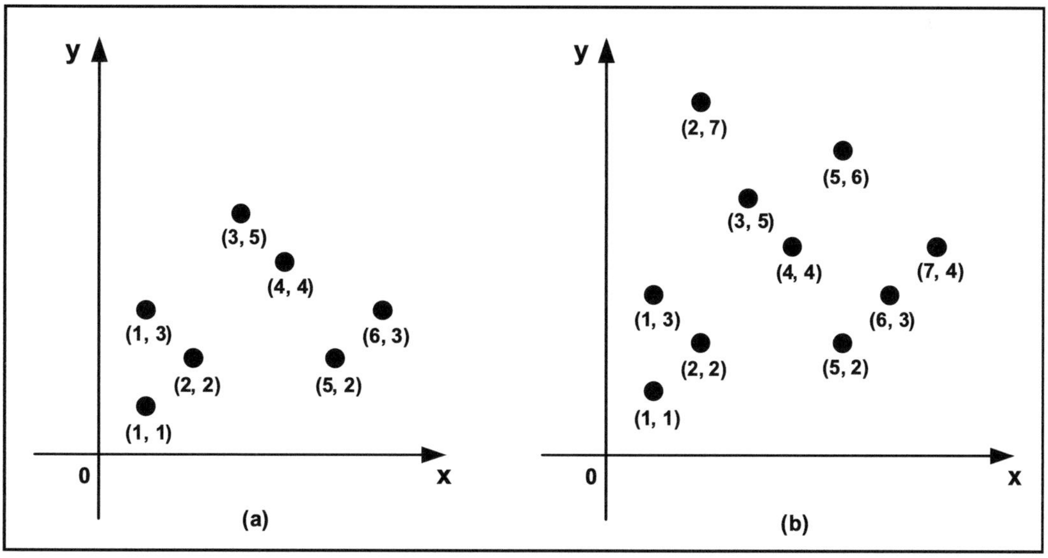

Fig. 8. *7*-city (a) and *10*-city (b) coordinates

Random seeds	Hopfield model			Proposed method		
	N_{HM}	E_t	t_{HM}	N_{SA}, N_{HM}	E_t	t_{PM}
0	241	0.0025 #	0.08	1, 287	0.0001	0.05
3	266	0.0021 #	0.07	1, 287	0.0001	0.05
5	298	0.0001	0.04	1, 287	0.0001	0.05
8	153	0.0023 #	0.04	1, 287	0.0001	0.05
10	325	0.0022 #	0.11	1, 287	0.0001	0.05
15	212	0.0018 #	0.06	1, 287	0.0001	0.05
20	337	0.0001	0.06	1, 287	0.0001	0.05
30	315	0.0014 #	0.05	1, 287	0.0001	0.05
50	182	0.0024 #	0.03	1, 287	0.0001	0.05
100	248	0.0019 #	0.08	1, 287	0.0001	0.05

Table 1. Experimental results of *7*-city TSP(# : non-convergence)

all *10* trials. The Hopfield model shows the faster convergence than the proposed method in case of the random seed *5*. This result shows that the deterministic rule of steepest descent may converge fast if the initial point is happen to be set near the global minimum. But there are few systematic methods that guarantee this initial point setting. The convergence rate by proposed method is *5* times and its convergence speed (time) is some higher than that of Hopfield model in case of successful convergence. We can also know that one cycle of SA takes more time than that of Hopfield model. Compared with the update rule of Hopfield model, SA is by reason of stochastic algorithm. But the SA algorithm is executed by a number of iteration in the proposed method.

Table 2 represents the experimental results of *7*-city TSP to *100* trials. Especially, Table 2 shows the experimental results that satisfy the stopping rule. N, t, and P_r are the number of iterations, the CPU time, and convergence ratio. As seen, the convergence rate by the proposed method is about *2.3* times and its convergence speed (time) is about *1.2* times higher than that of Hopfield model, respectively. The experimental results show that the convergence performances of proposed method are superior to that of Hopfield model with randomized initial neuron outputs setting. The standard deviation of proposed method is lower than that of Hopfield model. It means that the proposed method is less affected by the initial outputs setting than Hopfield model.

Table 3 shows the experimental results of *10*-city TSP to *10* random seeds. In case of Hopfield model, the constraints are satisfied at random seeds *3, 5,* and *30*, but the stopping rule is only satisfied in random seed *3*. The proposed method satisfies the stopping rule to all *10* trials as seen Table 1. The convergence rate by proposed algorithm is *10* times, and its convergence speed (time) is about *1.9* times higher than that of Hopfield model in case of successful convergence. We can also know that one cycle of SA algorithm takes more time than that of Hopfield model in this Table 3.

Table 4 also represents the experimental results of 10-city TSP to 100 trials. Table 4 also shows the experimental results that satisfy the stopping rule. As seen, the convergence rate Table 1 shows the experimental results of *7*-city TSP to *10* random seeds. In case of Hopfield model, the constraints are satisfied at random seeds *5, 20,* and *30*, but the stopping rule is only satisfied in random seeds *5* and 20. The proposed method satisfies the stopping rule to

N, t	Hopfield model		Proposed method	
	$x^{\sim}$	σ	$x^{\sim}$	σ
N	338.4	112.5	288	0
t	0.06	0.02	0.05	0
P_r(%)	43		100	

Table 2. Experimental results of *7*-city TSP to *100* trials

Random seeds	Hopfield model			Proposed method		
	N_{HM}	E_t	t_{HM}	N_{SA}, N_{HM}	E_t	t_{PM}
0	889	0.0043 #	1.16	2, 640	0.0001	0.44
3	793	0.0001	0.82	2, 640	0.0001	0.44
5	1470	0.0023 #	0.95	2, 640	0.0001	0.44
8	488	0.0174 #	0.61	2, 640	0.0001	0.44
10	1108	0.0128 #	1.50	2, 640	0.0001	0.44
15	697	0.0205 #	0.78	2, 640	0.0001	0.44
20	738	0.0223 #	0.52	2, 640	0.0001	0.44
30	1377	0.0016 #	0.86	2, 640	0.0001	0.44
50	1136	0.0102 #	0.73	2, 640	0.0001	0.44
100	508	0.0097 #	0.65	2, 640	0.0001	0.44

Table 3. Experimental results of 10-city TSP(# : non-convergence)

N, t	Hopfield model		Proposed method	
	$x^{\sim}$	σ	$x^{\sim}$	σ
N	1052.42	364.5	642	0
t	0.73	0.25	0.43	0
P_r(%)	19		100	

Table 4. Experimental results of 10-city TSP to 100 trials

Table 1 shows the experimental results of *7*-city TSP to *10* random seeds. In case of Hopfield model, the constraints are satisfied at random seeds *5, 20,* and *30,* but the stopping rule is only satisfied in random seeds *5* and 20. The proposed method satisfies the stopping rule to Compared Table 2(*7*-city) with Table 4(*10*-city), the Hopfield model is more difficult to set initial outputs for proving a good convergence as the problem size becomes larger. But the proposed method is less affected by the initial outputs setting and so gives relatively better results than the Hopfield model. Consequently, the convergence rate and speed by proposed method is higher than that of Hopfield model with randomized initial weights setting.

7. Conclusions

This paper proposes a global optimization of neural network by applying a hybrid method, which combines a stochastic approximation with a gradient descent. The approximation

point inclined toward a global escaping from a local minimum is estimated first by applying the stochastic approximation, and then the update rule of Hopfield model is applied for high-speed convergence.
The proposed method is applied to the *7*- and *10*-city TSPs, respectively. The experimental results show that the proposed method has superior convergence performances to the conventional method that performs the update rule of Hopfield model with randomized initial neuron outputs setting. Especially, the proposed method is less affected by the initial outputs setting and so gives relatively better results than the Hopfield model as the prom size becomes larger.
Our future research is to solve on a large scale combinatorial optimization problems by using neural networks of the proposed method.

8. References

Aarts, E. H. L. & Laarhoven, P. J. M. (1985). Statistical Cooling: A General Approach to Combinatorial Optimization Problems. *Philips Journal of Research 40*, pp.193–226

Abe, S.; Kawami, J. & Hirasawa, K. (1992). Solving Inequality Constrained Combinatorial Optimization Problems by the Hopfield Neural Networks. *Neural Networks*, Vol. 5, pp. 663–670

Abe, S. (1993). Global Convergence and Suppression of Spurious States of the Hopfield Neural Networks. *IEEE Trans. on Circuits Syst.*, Vol. 40, No. 4, pp. 246-257

Abe, S. (1996). Convergence Acceleration of the Hopfield Neural Network by Optimizing Integration Step Sizes. *IEEE Trans. on System., Man, and Cybernetics-Part B.*, Vol. 26, No. 1, pp. 194-201

Aiyer, S. V.; Niranjan, M. & Fallside, F. (1990). A Theoretical Investigation into the Performance of the Hopfield Model. *IEEE Trans. on Neural Networks*, Vol.1, No.2, pp.204-215

Andresol, R.; Gendreau, M. & Potvin, J. Y. (1997). *A Hopfield-Tank Neural Network Model for the Generalized Traveling Salesman Problem, in Meta-Heuristics: Advances and Trends in Local Search Paradigms for Optimization*, S. Voss et al. (eds.), Kluwer Academic Publishers, Boston

Baba, N. (1989). A New Approach for Finding the Global Minimum of Error Function of Neural Networks. *IEEE Trans. on Neural Networks*, Vol.2, pp.367-373

Beale, R. & Jackson, T. (1990). *Neural Computing: An Introduction*, IOP Publishing Ltd., Bristol, U.K.

Biro, J.; Koronkai, Z. & Tron, T. (1996). A Noise Annealing Neural Network for Global Optimization. *ICNN'1996*, Vol.1, pp. 513-518

Bout, D. E. & Miller, T. K. (1988). A Traveling Salesman Objective Function That Works. *ICNN-88*, pp. 299-303

Burke, L. I. (1994). Adaptive Neural Networks for the Traveling Salesman Problem: Insights from Operations Research. *Neural Networks*, Vol. 7, pp. 681–690

Cichock, A. & Unbehaun, R. (1993). *Neural Networks for Optimization and Signal Processing*, John-Wiley & Sons, New York

Dorigo, M.; Maniezzo, V. & Colorni, A. (1991). The Ant System: An Autocatalytic Optimizing Process. *Technical Report no. 91-016 Revised*, Politecnico di Milano, Italy

Dorigo, M. & Gambardella, L. (1997). Ant Colonies for the Traveling Salesman Problem. *Bio Systems*, Vol. 43, pp. 73-81

Freeman, J. A. & Skapura, D. M. (1991). *Neural Networks : Algorithms, Applications, and Programming Techniques*, Addison-Wesley Pub. Co., New York

Gall, A. L. & Zissimopoulos, V. (1999). Extended Hopfield Models for Combinatorial Optimization. *IEEE Trans. on Neural Networks*, Vol.10, No.1, pp.72-80

Gee, A. H. & Prager, R. W. (1995). Limitations of Neural Networks for Solving Traveling Salesman Problems. *IEEE Trans. on Neural Networks*, Vol. 6, pp. 280–282

Goldberg, D. (1989). *Genetic Algorithms in Search, Optimization & Machine Learning*, Addison Wesley

Hegde, S. U. ; Sweet, J. L. & Levy, W. B. (1988). Determination of Parameters in a Hopfield/Tank Computational Network. *ICNN-88*, pp.291-298

Hopfield, J. J. & Tank, D. W. (1985). Neural Computation of Decisions in Optimization Problems. *Biological Cybernetics*, Vol. 52, pp.141-152

Huang, X. (2005). A New Kind of Hopfield Networks for Finding Global Optimum. *IJCNN'05*, Foster City, USA, Vol.2, pp. 764-769

Kawabe, T.; Ueta, T. & Nishio, Y. (2002). Iterative Simulated Annealing for Hopfield Neural Network. *International Journal of Modelling and Simulation, Marina del Rey, USA*, pp. *353-409*

Lai, W.K. & Coghill, G. G. (1994). Initializing the Continuous Hopfield Net. *Proc. ISCAS*, pp. 4640-4644

Lin, S. (1965). Computer Solutions of the Traveling Salesman Problem. *Bell Syst. Journal*, Vol. 44, pp.2245-2269

Lin, S. & Kernighan, B. W. (1971). An Effective Heuristic Algorithm for the Traveling Salesman Problem. *Oper. Res.* 21, pp. 498-516

Mascato, P. (1989). On Evolution, Search, Optimization, Genetic Algorithms and Martial Arts : Towards Memetic Algorithms. *Caltech Concurrent Computation program*, pp. 158-179

Mühlenbein, H. (1992). Parallel Genetic Algorithms in Combinatorial Optimization. *Computer Science and Operations Research*, pp. 441-456

Sharbaro, D. (1994). A Stability Criterion for Hopfield Networks Based on Popov Theorem," *Proc. IJCNN*, pp. 4567-4570

Styblinski, M. A. & Tang, T.S. (1990). Experiments in Nonconvex Optimization: Stochastic Approximation with Function Smoothing and Simulated Annealing. *IEEE Trans. on Neural Networks*, Vol.3, pp.467-483

Szu, H. & Hartley, R. (1987). Fast Simulated Annealing. *Physics Letters*, Vol. 122, pp.157-162

Wilson, G. V. & Pawley, G. S. (1988). On the Stability of the TSP Problem Algorithm of Hopfield and Tank," *Biological Cybernetics*, Vol. 58, pp. 63-70

Xavier, S. S.; Suykens, J. A. K.; Vandewalle, J. & Bolle, D. (2006). Coupled Simulated Annealing for Continuous Global Optimization. *Internal Report 06-07*, ESAT-SISTA, K.U.Leuven (Leuven, Belgium)

Zurada, J. M. (1992). *Introduction to Artificial Neural Systems*, West Pub. Co., New York

11

Recurrent Neural Networks with the Soft 'Winner Takes All' Principle Applied to the Traveling Salesman Problem

Paulo Henrique Siqueira, Maria Teresinha Arns Steiner and Sérgio Scheer
Federal University of Paraná
Curitiba, Paraná,
Brazil

1. Introduction

This work shows the application of Wang's Recurrent Neural Network with the "Winner Takes All" (WTA) principle to solve the classic Operational Research problem called the Traveling Salesman Problem. The upgrade version proposed in this work for the 'Winner Takes All' principle is called soft, because the winning neuron is updated with only part of the activation values of the other competing neurons.

The problems in the TSPLIB (Traveling Salesman Problem Library - Reinelt, 1991) were used to compare the soft version with the 'Winner Takes All' hard version and they show improvement in the results using the 'Winner Takes All' soft version in most of the problems tested.

The implementation of the technique proposed in this paper uses the parameters of Wang's Neural Network for the Assignment problem (Wang, 1992; Hung & Wang, 2003) using the 'Winner Takes All' principle to form Hamiltonian circuits (Siqueira *et al.* 2007) and can be used for both symmetric and asymmetric Traveling Salesman Problems. The 2-opt technique is used to improve the routes found with the proposed Neural Network, thus becoming a technique that is competitive to other Neural Networks.

Other heuristic techniques have been developed recently to solve the Traveling Salesman Problem, and the work of Misevičius *et al.* (2005) shows the use of the ITS (Iterated Tabu Search) technique with a combination of intensification and diversification of solutions for the TSP. This technique is combined with the 5-opt and errors are almost zero in almost all of the TSPLIB problems tested.

The work of Wang *et al.* (2007) shows the use of Particle Swarm to solve the TSP with the use of the fraction (quantum) principle to better guide the search for solutions. The authors make comparisons with Hill Climbing, Simulated Annealing and Tabu Search, and show in a 14-cities case that the results are better than those of the other techniques.

In the area of Artificial Neural Networks, an interesting technique can be found in the work of Massutti & Castro (2009), who use a mechanism to stabilize winning neurons and the centroids of the groups of cities for the growing and pruning the network. The authors show modifications in the Rabnet's (real-valued antibody network) parameters for the Traveling Salesman Problem and comparisons made with TSPLIB problems solved by other techniques show that the Rabnet has better results.

Créput & Koukam (2007) show a hybrid technique with self-organizing maps (SOM) and evolutionary algorithms to solve the TSP, called Memetic Neural Network (MSOM). The results of this technique are compared with the CAN (Co-Adaptive Network) technique, developed by Cochrane & Beasley (2003), in which both have results that are regarded as satisfactory.
The Efficient and Integrated Self-Organizing Map (EISOM) was proposed by Jin *et al.* (2003), where a SOM network is used to generate a solution where the winning neuron is replaced by the position of the midpoint between the two closest neighboring neurons. The results presented by the authors show that the EISOM has better results than the Simulated Annealing and the ESOM network (Leung *et al.*, 2004).
The Modified Growing Ring Self-Organizing Map (MGSOM) presented in the work of Bai *et al.* (2006) shows some changes in the adaptation, selection of the number of neurons, the network's initial weights and the winning neurons indexing functions, as well as the effects of these changes on the order of cities for the TSP. The MGSOM technique is easy to implement and has a mean error of 2.32% for the 12 instances of the TSPLIB.
The work of Yi *et al.* (2009) shows an elastic network with the introduction of temporal parameters, helping neurons in the motion towards the cities' positions. Comparisons with problems from the TSPLIB solved with the traditional elastic network show that it is an efficient technique to solve the TSP, with smaller error and less computational time than the other elastic networks.
In Li *et al.* (2009) a class of Lotka-Volterra neural networks is used to solve the Traveling Salesman Problem with the application of global inhibitions, analyzing the stability of the proposed neural network by means of equilibrium points. The results are analyzed and compared with several experiments where the equilibrium status of this network represents a feasible solution to the Traveling Salesman Problem.
The work of Hammer *et al.* (2009) shows a review of the most recent works in the area of Recurrent Neural Networks, including discussions about new paradigms, architectures and processing structures of these networks. The authors show the works of Recurrent Neural Networks applied in solving various Operational Research problems, such as the Traveling Salesman Problem, Quadratic Programming problems, training of Support Vector Machines and Winner Takes All.
This work is divided into four sections besides this introduction. In section 2 are shown Wang's Recurrent Neural Network and the soft 'Winner Takes All' technique applied to the Traveling Salesman Problem. Section 3 shows the comparative results and Section 4 the conclusions.

2. Wang's neural network with the soft winner takes all principle

The mathematical formulation of the Traveling Salesman Problem is the same of the Assignment problem (1) - (4), with the additional constraint (5) that ensures that the route starts and ends in the same city.

$$\text{Minimize } C = \sum_{i=1}^{n}\sum_{j=1}^{n} c_{ij}x_{ij} \tag{1}$$

$$\text{Subject to } \sum_{i=1}^{n} x_{ij} = 1 \text{, } j = 1,\dots, n \tag{2}$$

$$\sum_{j=1}^{n} x_{ij} = 1, i = 1,..., n \quad (3)$$

$$x_{ij} \in \{0, 1\}, i, j = 1,..., n \quad (4)$$

$$\tilde{x} \text{ forms a Hamiltonian circuit,} \quad (5)$$

where c_{ij} and x_{ij} are respectively the cost and decision variables associated with the assignment of vertex i to vertex j in the Hamiltonian circuit. The objective function (1) minimizes costs. The set of constraints (2) and (3) ensure that each city will be visited only once. Constraints (4) ensure the condition of integrality of the binary variables x_{ij}, and vector $\tilde{x}$ represents the sequence of a Traveling Salesman's route.

To obtain a first approximation for the TSP, Wang's Recurrent Neural Network is applied to the Assignment Problem, this is, the solution satisfies constraints (1) - (4), which can be written in matrix form (Hung & Wang, 2003):

$$\text{Minimize } C = c^T x \quad (6)$$

$$\text{Subject to } Ax = b \quad (7)$$

$$x_{ij} \in \{0, 1\}, i, j = 1,..., n \quad (8)$$

where c^T is the vector with dimension n^2, which contains all of the cost matrix's lines in sequence, vector x contains the n^2 x_{ij} decision variables and vector b contains the number 1 in all of its positions. Matrix A has dimension $2n \times n^2$, with the following format:

$$A = \begin{bmatrix} I & I & \dots & I \\ B_1 & B_2 & \dots & B_n \end{bmatrix}$$

where I is the identity matrix with dimension n and each matrix B_i contains zeroes in all of its positions, with exception of the i-th line that contains "1" in all of its positions.

A Wang's Recurrent Neural Network is defined by the following differential equation (Wang, 1992; Hung & Wang, 2003):

$$\frac{du_{ij}(t)}{dt} = -\eta \sum_{k=1}^{n} x_{ik}(t) - \eta \sum_{l=1}^{n} x_{lj}(t) + \eta \theta_{ij} - \lambda c_{ij} e^{-\frac{t}{\tau}} \quad (9)$$

where x_{ij} = g (u_{ij} βt)), the equilibrium status of this network is a solution to the Assignment Problem (Wang, 1997) and function g is the sigmoid function with parameter β:

$$g(u) = \frac{1}{1 + e^{-\beta u}}. \quad (10)$$

The threshold is the vector of size n^2 $\theta = A^T b$, which has the value "2" in all of its positions. Parameters η, λ and τ are constant and empirically chosen (Hung & Wang, 2003). Parameter η penalizes violations of constraints (2) and (3). Parameters λ and τ control the minimization of the objective function (1). Considering $W = A^T A$, Wang's Neural Network's matrix form is the following:

$$\frac{du(t)}{dt} = -\eta(Wx(t) - \theta) - \lambda c e^{-\frac{t}{\tau}}, \tag{11}$$

The method proposed in this paper uses the "Winner Takes All" principle, which accelerates the convergence of Wang's Recurrent Neural Network, in addition to solve problems that appear in multiple solutions or very close solutions (Siqueira *et al.*, 2008).
The adjustment of parameter λ was done using the standard deviation between the coefficients of the rows in the problem's costs matrix and determining the vector

$$\overline{\lambda} = \eta\left(\frac{1}{\delta_1}, \frac{1}{\delta_2}, \ldots, \frac{1}{\delta_n}\right), \tag{12}$$

where δ_i is the standard deviation of row i of costs matrix c (Smith *et al.*, 2007).
The adjustment of parameter τ uses the third term of the definition of Wang's Neural Network (9), as follows: when $c_{ij} = c_{\max}$, term $-\lambda_i c_{ij} \exp(-t/\tau_i) = k_i$ must satisfy $g(k_i) \cong 0$, this is, x_{ij} will bear the minimum value (Siqueira *et al.*, 2007), considering $c_{ij} = c_{\max}$ and $\lambda_i = 1/\delta_i$, where $i = 1, \ldots, n$, τ is defined by:

$$\tau_i = \frac{-t}{\ln\left(\frac{-k_i}{\lambda_i c_{\max}}\right)}. \tag{13}$$

After a certain number of iterations, term $Wx(t) - \theta$ of equation (10) has no substantial alterations, thus ensuring that constraints (2) and (3) are almost satisfied and the 'Winner Takes All' method can be applied to establish a solution for the TSP.
The soft 'Winner Takes All' (SWTA) technique is described in the pseudo-code below, where the following situations occur with respect to parameter α:

- when $\alpha = 0$, the WTA update is nonexistent and Wang's Neural Network updates the solutions for the Assignment Problem with no interference;
- when $\alpha = 1$, the update is called hard WTA, because the winner gets all the activation of the other neurons and the losers become null. The solution is feasible for the TSP;
- in the other cases, the update is called soft WTA and the best results are found with $0.25 \leq \alpha \leq 0.9$.

Pseudo-code for the Soft 'Winner Takes All' (SWTA) technique

Choose the maximum number of routes r_{max}.
{
While $r < r_{max}$
  {
  While $Wx(t) - \theta > \phi$ *(where* $0 \leq \phi \leq 2$*):*
    Find a solution x for the Assignment Problem using Wang's Neural Network.
  }
  Make $\overline{x} = x$ *and* $m = 1$;
  Choose a line k from decision matrix $\overline{x}$;
  Make $p = k$ *and* $\tilde{x}(m) = k$;
  {

While $m < n$:

Find $\bar{x}_{kl} = \text{argmax}\{\bar{x}_{ki}, i = 1, \ldots, n\}$;

Do the following updates:

$$\bar{x}_{kl} = \bar{x}_{kl} + \frac{\alpha}{2}\left(\sum_{i=1}^{n} x_{il} + \sum_{j=1}^{n} x_{kj}\right) \tag{14}$$

$$\bar{x}_{kj} = (1-\alpha)\bar{x}_{kj}, \; j = 1,\ldots, n, \; j \neq l, \; 0 \leq \alpha \leq 1 \tag{15}$$

$$\bar{x}_{il} = (1-\alpha)\bar{x}_{il}, \; i = 1,\ldots, n, \; i \neq k, \; 0 \leq \alpha \leq 1 \tag{16}$$

Make $\tilde{x}(m+1) = l$ *and* $m = m + 1$;
to continue the route, make $k = l$.

}

Make $\bar{x}_{kp} = \bar{x}_{kp} + \frac{\alpha}{2}\left(\sum_{i=1}^{n} x_{ip} + \sum_{j=1}^{n} x_{kj}\right)$ *and* $\tilde{x}(n+1) = p$;

determine the cost of route C;

{

If $C < C_{min}$, *then*

Make $C_{min} = C$ *and* $x = \bar{x}$.

}

$r = r + 1$.

}

2.1 Example illustrating the SWTA technique applied to the TSP

Consider the 10-cities problem proposed in the work of Hopfield & Tank (1985). Considering $\alpha = 0.7$ and the parameters defined by equations (12) and (13), after 32 iterations Wang's Neural Network shows the following solution for the Assignment Problem:

$$\bar{x} = \begin{pmatrix} 0 & 0.017 & \overline{\underline{0.914}} & 0.028 & 0.004 & 0.001 & 0.015 & 0.002 & 0.007 & 0.015 \\ 0.02 & 0 & 0.077 & 0.001 & 0 & 0 & 0 & 0 & 0.002 & 0.801 \\ 0.018 & 0.977 & 0 & 0.003 & 0 & 0 & 0 & 0 & 0.001 & 0.001 \\ 0.919 & 0.001 & 0.002 & 0 & 0.065 & 0.001 & 0.001 & 0 & 0 & 0 \\ 0.007 & 0 & 0 & 1.038 & 0 & 0.022 & 0.007 & 0.001 & 0 & 0 \\ 0.003 & 0 & 0 & 0.001 & 0.021 & 0 & 0.94 & 0.033 & 0.002 & 0.002 \\ 0.014 & 0 & 0 & 0.001 & 0.81 & 0.045 & 0 & 0.027 & 0.007 & 0.007 \\ 0.003 & 0 & 0 & 0 & 0.001 & 0.971 & 0.026 & 0 & 0.026 & 0.016 \\ 0.007 & 0.001 & 0.001 & 0 & 0 & 0.002 & 0.007 & 0.886 & 0 & 0.055 \\ 0.016 & 0.003 & 0.001 & 0 & 0 & 0.002 & 0.009 & 0.019 & 1.069 & 0 \end{pmatrix}$$

A city must be chosen so that the TSP's route can be formed, in this case city 1, this is, $p = k = 1$. Element $l = 3$ satisfies $\bar{x}_{kl} = \bar{x}_{13} = \text{argmax}\{\bar{x}_{1i}, i = 1, \ldots, n\}$, this is, the traveling salesman makes his route leaving city 1 towards city 3. Using equations (14)-(16), the elements in line 1 and column 3 are updated resulting in matrix $\overline{x}$:

$$\overline{x} = \begin{pmatrix} 0 & 0.005 & \underline{\overline{1.294}} & 0.008 & 0.001 & 0 & 0.005 & 0.001 & 0.002 & 0.004 \\ 0.02 & 0 & 0.023 & 0.001 & 0 & 0 & 0 & 0 & 0.002 & 0.801 \\ 0.018 & \underline{\overline{0.977}} & 0 & 0.003 & 0 & 0 & 0 & 0 & 0.001 & 0.001 \\ 0.919 & 0.001 & 0.001 & 0 & 0.065 & 0.001 & 0.001 & 0 & 0 & 0 \\ 0.007 & 0 & 0 & 1.038 & 0 & 0.022 & 0.007 & 0.001 & 0 & 0 \\ 0.003 & 0 & 0 & 0.001 & 0.021 & 0 & 0.94 & 0.033 & 0.002 & 0.002 \\ 0.014 & 0 & 0 & 0.001 & 0.81 & 0.045 & 0 & 0.027 & 0.007 & 0.007 \\ 0.003 & 0 & 0 & 0 & 0.001 & 0.971 & 0.026 & 0 & 0.026 & 0.016 \\ 0.007 & 0.001 & 0 & 0 & 0 & 0.002 & 0.007 & 0.886 & 0 & 0.055 \\ 0.016 & 0.003 & 0 & 0 & 0 & 0.002 & 0.009 & 0.019 & 1.069 & 0 \end{pmatrix}$$

In order to continue the route, update $k = l = 3$ is done and element $l = 2$ satisfies the condition in which $\overline{x}_{kl} = \overline{x}_{32} = \text{argmax}\{\overline{x}_{3i}, i = 1, \ldots, n\}$. Proceeding this way, we obtain the matrix $\overline{x}$ in the form:

$$\overline{x} = \begin{pmatrix} 0 & 0.005 & \underline{\overline{1.294}} & 0.008 & 0.001 & 0 & 0.005 & 0.001 & 0.002 & 0.004 \\ 0.006 & 0 & 0.023 & 0 & 0 & 0 & 0 & 0 & 0.002 & \underline{\overline{0.87}} \\ 0.005 & \underline{\overline{0.993}} & 0 & 0.001 & 0 & 0 & 0 & 0 & 0 & 0 \\ \underline{\overline{1.296}} & 0 & 0.001 & 0 & 0.019 & 0 & 0 & 0 & 0 & 0 \\ 0.002 & 0 & 0 & \underline{\overline{1.064}} & 0 & 0.007 & 0.002 & 0 & 0 & 0 \\ 0.001 & 0 & 0 & 0 & 0.006 & 0 & \underline{\overline{0.984}} & 0.01 & 0.001 & 0.001 \\ 0.004 & 0 & 0 & 0 & \underline{\overline{0.877}} & 0.013 & 0 & 0.008 & 0.002 & 0.002 \\ 0.001 & 0 & 0 & 0 & 0 & \underline{\overline{1.022}} & 0.008 & 0 & 0.008 & 0.005 \\ 0.002 & 0 & 0 & 0 & 0 & 0.001 & 0.002 & \underline{\overline{0.941}} & 0 & 0.017 \\ 0.005 & 0.001 & 0 & 0 & 0 & 0.001 & 0.003 & 0.006 & \underline{\overline{1.476}} & 0 \end{pmatrix},$$

which is the solution in Fig. 1, at a cost of 2.7518 and a mean error of 2.27%.

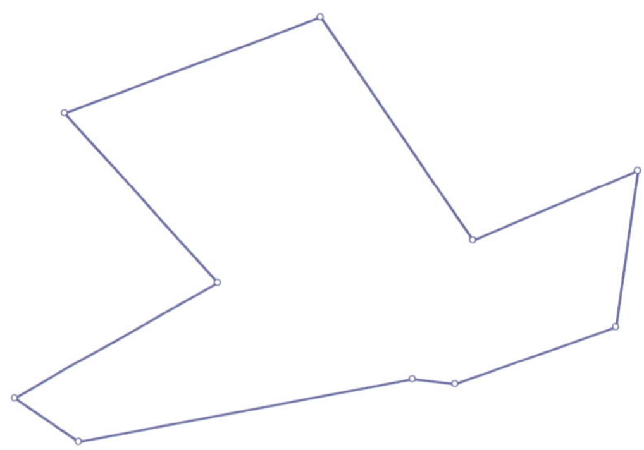

Fig. 1. Solution for the 10-cities problem of Hopfield & Tank, with cost 2.7518 and mean error 2.27%

The solution to the SWTA is once again applied to Wang's Neural Network and after other 13 iterations the following solution is found:

$$\overline{x}=\begin{pmatrix} 0 & 0.017 & 0.023 & 0.92 & 0.004 & 0.001 & 0.015 & 0.002 & 0.007 & 0.015 \\ 0.02 & 0 & 1.071 & 0.001 & 0 & 0 & 0 & 0 & 0.002 & 0.003 \\ 0.879 & 0.072 & 0 & 0.003 & 0 & 0 & 0 & 0 & 0.001 & 0.001 \\ 0.027 & 0.001 & 0.002 & 0 & 0.981 & 0.001 & 0.001 & 0 & 0 & 0 \\ 0.007 & 0 & 0 & 0.067 & 0 & 0.896 & 0.007 & 0.001 & 0 & 0 \\ 0.003 & 0 & 0 & 0.001 & 0.022 & 0 & 0.939 & 0.033 & 0.002 & 0.002 \\ 0.014 & 0 & 0 & 0.001 & 0.006 & 0.045 & 0 & 0.945 & 0.007 & 0.008 \\ 0.003 & 0 & 0 & 0 & 0.001 & 0.036 & 0.026 & 0 & 0.903 & 0.016 \\ 0.007 & 0.001 & 0.001 & 0 & 0 & 0.002 & 0.007 & 0.025 & 0 & 0.978 \\ 0.015 & 0.806 & 0.001 & 0 & 0 & 0 & 0.009 & 0.019 & 0.061 & 0 \end{pmatrix}$$

Using the SWTA technique an approximation to the optimal solution is found:

$$\overline{x}=\begin{pmatrix} 0 & 0.005 & 0.007 & \underline{1.298} & 0.001 & 0 & 0.005 & 0.001 & 0.002 & 0.005 \\ 0.006 & 0 & \underline{1.091} & 0 & 0 & 0 & 0 & 0 & 0.001 & 0.001 \\ \underline{1.247} & 0.022 & 0 & 0.001 & 0 & 0 & 0 & 0 & 0 & 0 \\ 0.008 & 0 & 0.001 & 0 & \underline{1.004} & 0 & 0 & 0 & 0 & 0 \\ 0.002 & 0 & 0 & 0.02 & 0 & \underline{0.955} & 0.002 & 0 & 0 & 0 \\ 0.001 & 0 & 0 & 0 & 0.007 & 0 & \underline{0.983} & 0.011 & 0.001 & 0.001 \\ 0.004 & 0 & 0 & 0 & 0.002 & 0.014 & 0 & \underline{1.001} & 0.002 & 0.002 \\ 0.001 & 0 & 0 & 0 & 0 & 0.011 & 0.008 & 0 & \underline{0.96} & 0.005 \\ 0.002 & 0 & 0 & 0 & 0 & 0.001 & 0.002 & 0.008 & 0 & \underline{1.01} \\ 0.005 & \underline{1.158} & 0 & 0 & 0 & 0 & 0.001 & 0.006 & 0.018 & 0 \end{pmatrix},$$

which is shown in Fig. 2.

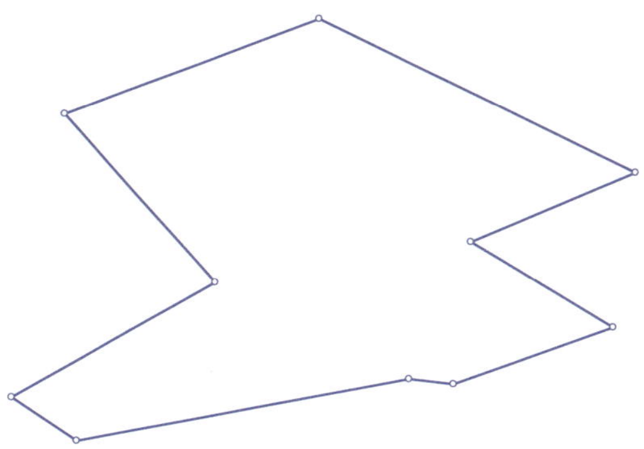

Fig. 2. Optimal solution for the 10-cities problem of Hopfield & Tank, cost 2.69

Applying the same SWTA technique to the 30-random-cities problem of Lin & Kernighan (1973), the solutions are shown below, where Fig. 3a shows the solution with cost 4.37 and 2.58% mean error, and Fig. 3b shows the optimal solution with cost 4.26

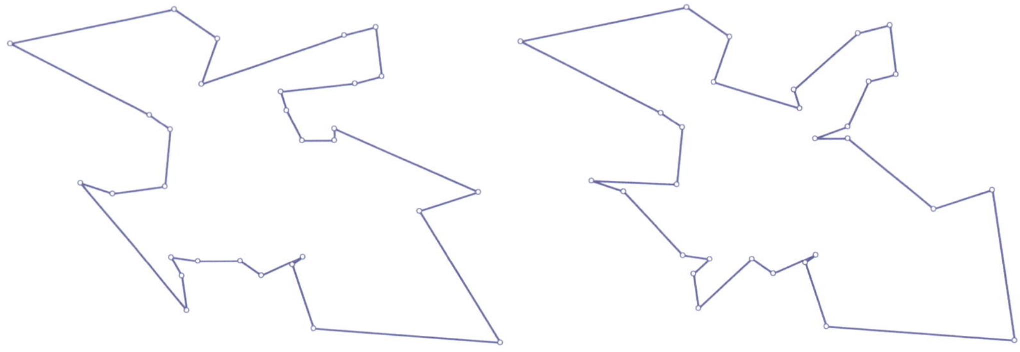

(a) (b)

Fig. 3. Solutions for the 10-random-cities problem of Hopfield & Tank: (a) cost 4.37 and 2.58% mean error; (b) optimal solution with cost 4.26

3. Results

The technique proposed in this paper, Soft Winner Takes All applied to Wang's Recurrent Neural Network, was used to solve 36 symmetric and 19 asymmetric problems from the TSPLIB (Traveling Salesman Problem Library) database. The results were compared with results from both the Hard Winner Takes All technique (Siqueira *et al.*, 2008) and from similar techniques published in the literature.

3.1 TSPLIB symmetric problems

Table 1 and Table 2 shows the comparison between the Soft and Hard WTA techniques, where the results of applying Wang's Neural Network with Soft WTA and the 2-opt (SWTA2) route improving technique in the final solutions have mean error ranging between 0 and 4.50%. The results without the application of the 2-opt (SWTA) vary between 0 and 14.39% and are better in almost all problems tested when compared to results obtained with the Hard WTA technique, and 95% confidence intervals (CI) for the mean were computed on the basis of standard deviations (SD) over 60 runs. Fig. 4 shows a comparison between the Soft and Hard WTA techniques applied to 36 problems from the TSPLIB, showing the best and worst results found with each technique.

Table 2 shows that from the 36 problems tested, only 6 have better results with the Hard WTA with 2-opt technique: att532, kroA200, u159, kroA150, pr124 and rd100. The best solutions with the Hard WTA technique without the 2-opt technique outweigh the results with the Soft WTA technique in only 3 problems: lin318, u159 and pr124.

Fig. 4 shows that from the 36 problems tested, 14 have the worst results with higher costs with the Soft WTA technique than with the Hard WTA: rd100, a280, ch130, bier127, kroA100, kroC100, kroE100, brazil58, pr107, eil51, gil262, lin318, fl417 and rat575.

In addition to comparing the technique proposed in this paper with the results of the TSPLIB with the Hard WTA technique, the results were compared with the following techniques:

- KNIESG method (Kohonen Network Incorporating Explicit Statistics Global) which uses statistical methods to determine the weights of neurons in a Self-Organizing Map, where all cities are used for the dispersion of neurons (Aras *et al.*, 1999);

TSP name	n	Optimal solution	Average error (%)							
			HWTA				SWTA			
			Best	Mean	SD	CI (95%)	Best	Mean	SD	CI (95%)
eil51	51	430	**1.16**	1.16	0.00	[1.16, 1.16]	0.47	1.59	0.78	[1.40, 1.79]
brazil58	58	16156	2.90	2.90	0.00	[2.90, 2.90]	**1.81**	2.65	1.18	[2.35, 2.94]
st70	70	678.6	2.71	3.55	0.64	[3.39, 3.71]	**1.68**	1.97	0.46	[1.86, 2.09]
eil76	76	545.4	1.03	2.00	0.76	[1.81, 2.20]	**0**	1.27	0.98	[1.02, 1.51]
kroA100	100	21282	3.68	4.22	0.58	[4.07, 4.36]	**3.05**	3.73	0.96	[3.49, 3.98]
kroB100	100	22141	8.27	8.54	0.25	[8.48, 8.60]	**4.73**	6.12	1.12	[5.83, 6.40]
kroC100	100	20749	5.20	5.20	0.01	[5.20, 5.21]	**3.35**	4.10	1.13	[3.81, 4.38]
kroD100	100	21294	8.57	8.85	0.47	[8.73, 8.97]	**4.64**	4.73	0.11	[4.71, 4.76]
kroE100	100	22068	6.18	6.37	0.25	[6.31, 6.44]	**4.07**	5.41	1.29	[5.09, 5.74]
rd100	100	7910	6.83	7.00	0.19	[6.95, 7.04]	**6.27**	7.02	1.28	[6.70, 7.34]
eil101	101	629	**3.02**	6.09	2.40	[5.49, 6.70]	**3.02**	5.86	1.32	[5.54, 6.20]
lin105	105	14383	4.33	5.41	0.83	[5.20, 5.62]	**3.70**	3.91	0.24	[3.85, 3.97]
pr107	107	44303	3.14	3.14	0.00	[3.14, 3.14]	**1.65**	2.89	0.77	[2.69, 3.08]
pr124	124	59030	**0.33**	1.44	1.22	[1.13, 1.75]	2.39	2.77	0.30	[2.69, 2.84]
bier127	127	118282	4.22	4.45	0.37	[4.35, 4.54]	**3.11**	5.14	1.61	[4.73, 5.55]
ch130	130	6110	5.06	5.97	0.83	[5.76, 6.18]	**4.52**	5.99	1.37	[5.64, 6.33]
pr136	136	96772	5.99	6.28	0.45	[6.16, 6.39]	**5.06**	5.66	0.55	[5.52, 5.80]
gr137	137	69853	9.09	9.14	0.13	[9.11, 9.18]	**6.65**	8.01	0.99	[7.76, 8.26]
kroA150	150	26524	8.85	9.53	0.98	[9.28, 9.78]	**8.50**	8.87	0.50	[8.74, 9.00]
kroB150	150	26130	7.33	8.43	0.92	[8.20, 8.67]	**6.80**	7.31	0.52	[7.17, 7.44]
pr152	152	73682	3.23	3.26	0.02	[3.25, 3.26]	**3.22**	3.23	0.00	[3.23, 3.23]
u159	159	42080	**6.33**	7.16	1.29	[6.84, 7.49]	6.40	7.57	1.07	[7.30, 7.84]
rat195	195	2323	5.55	6.63	1.37	[6.29, 6.98]	**5.42**	5.90	0.35	[5.81, 5.99]
d198	198	15780	10.43	10.75	0.31	[10.68, 10.83]	**6.86**	7.33	0.57	[7.18, 7.47]
kroA200	200	29368	8.95	10.57	1.42	[10.21, 10.93]	**8.03**	8.84	0.91	[8.61, 9.07]
tsp225	225	3859	7.64	8.40	0.92	[8.16, 8.63]	**5.73**	7.25	1.56	[6.86, 7.65]
gil262	262	2378	8.20	8.73	0.58	[8.58, 8.87]	**7.65**	8.33	0.86	[8.11, 8.55]
a280	280	2586	12.14	12.22	0.12	[12.19, 12.25]	**9.98**	12.01	1.96	[11.51, 12.50]
lin318	318	42029	**8.35**	8.50	0.16	[8.46, 8.54]	8.97	10.00	0.97	[9.75, 10.25]
fl417	417	11861	10.11	9.62	0.31	[9.54, 9.70]	**9.05**	10.02	1.10	[9.74, 10.30]
pr439	439	107217	**9.39**	10.95	1.17	[10.66, 11.25]	**9.39**	10.30	0.85	[10.09, 10.51]
pcb442	442	50783	9.16	10.50	2.01	[9.99, 11.01]	**8.76**	10.05	0.95	[9.81, 10.30]
att532	532	87550	14.58	14.83	0.34	[14.74, 14.91]	**9.10**	9.96	0.87	[9.74, 10.18]
rat575	575	6773	10.03	10.46	0.53	[10.33, 10.59]	**9.86**	10.73	0.59	[10.58, 10.88]
u724	724	41910	16.85	16.85	0.00	[16.85, 16.85]	**10.18**	10.56	0.44	[10.45, 10.67]
pr1002	1002	259045	15.66	15.91	0.30	[15.83, 15.99]	**14.39**	15.11	0.65	[14.95, 15.28]

Table 1. Comparisons between the results of 36 symmetric instances from the TSPLIB with the Hard WTA (HWTA) and Soft WTA (SWTA) techniques.

TSP name	n	Optimal solution	Average error (%)							
			HWTA2				SWTA2			
			best	Mean	SD	CI (95%)	Best	Mean	SD	CI (95%)
eil51	51	430	**0**	0.31	0.41	[0.21, 0.41]	**0**	0.09	0.21	[0.04, 0.15]
brazil58	58	16156	**0**	0.41	0.52	[0.28, 0.54]	**0**	0.30	0.51	[0.18, 0.43]
st70	70	678.6	**0**	0.14	0.28	[0.07, 0.21]	**0**	0.14	0.26	[0.08, 0.21]
eil76	76	545.4	**0**	0.12	0.28	[0.05, 0.19]	**0**	0.37	0.65	[0.21, 0.54]
kroA100	100	7910	0.84	2.12	1.18	[1.82, 2.42]	**0**	0.47	0.81	[0.26, 0.67]
kroB100	100	21282	0.71	1.47	0.72	[1.28, 1.65]	**0.47**	1.76	0.97	[1.52, 2.01]
kroC100	100	22141	**0**	0.29	0.40	[0.19, 0.39]	**0**	0.73	0.88	[0.51, 0.95]
kroD100	100	20749	0.73	1.23	0.58	[1.08, 1.38]	**0.59**	0.89	0.41	[0.78, 0.99]
kroE100	100	21294	0.84	1.65	0.83	[1.44, 1.86]	**0.32**	1.74	2.25	[1.77, 2.31]
rd100	100	22068	**0.08**	0.49	0.50	[0.36, 0.61]	0.49	1.48	0.90	[1.25, 1.71]
eil101	101	629	0.48	1.63	1.35	[1.29, 1.97]	**0.16**	0.95	1.20	[0.65, 1.26]
lin105	105	14383	0.20	0.73	0.77	[0.53, 0.93]	**0**	1.46	1.33	[1.13, 1.80]
pr107	107	44303	**0**	0.53	0.93	[0.29, 0.76]	**0**	0.11	0.15	[0.07, 0.14]
pr124	124	59030	**0**	0.45	0.82	[0.24, 0.66]	0.09	0.98	1.08	[0.71, 1.25]
bier127	127	118282	0.37	1.08	0.65	[0.92, 1.24]	**0.25**	1.55	1.03	[1.29, 1.81]
ch130	130	6110	1.39	1.85	0.72	[1.67, 2.03]	**0.80**	2.14	1.30	[1.81, 2.47]
pr136	136	96772	1.21	1.25	0.05	[1.24, 1.26]	**0.58**	1.18	0.48	[1.06, 1.30]
gr137	137	69853	2.07	2.96	1.83	[2.50, 3.42]	**0.21**	1.38	1.75	[0.94, 1.82]
kroA150	150	26524	**1.17**	2.35	1.21	[2.04, 2.65]	1.39	2.77	1.30	[2.44, 3.10]
kroB150	150	26130	2.16	3.48	1.22	[3.18, 3.79]	**1.48**	3.77	2.27	[3.20, 4.35]
pr152	152	73682	**0**	0.00	0.00	[0.00, 0.00]	**0**	0.51	1.01	[0.25, 0.76]
u159	159	42080	**0**	0.51	0.79	[0.31, 0.71]	0.79	1.71	0.86	[1.49, 1.93]
rat195	195	2323	3.32	3.95	1.11	[3.67, 4.24]	**2.71**	3.24	0.65	[3.08, 3.41]
d198	198	15780	1.22	1.95	1.25	[1.64, 2.27]	**0.73**	0.81	0.11	[0.78, 0.83]
kroA200	200	29368	**0.62**	6.02	5.87	[4.54, 7.51]	0.75	1.37	0.65	[1.20, 1.53]
tsp225	225	3859	2.54	3.10	0.66	[2.94, 3.27]	**1.06**	1.75	0.96	[1.51, 1.99]
gil262	262	2378	2.90	3.57	0.96	[3.32, 3.81]	**1.89**	3.02	1.31	[2.69, 3.35]
a280	318	42029	4.02	4.07	0.10	[4.04, 4.09]	**2.01**	2.87	1.02	[2.61, 3.13]
lin318	280	2586	1.90	2.38	0.84	[2.16, 2.59]	**1.89**	3.25	1.35	[2.91, 3.59]
fl417	417	11861	1.58	1.96	0.46	[1.85, 2.08]	**1.43**	1.61	0.32	[1.53, 1.69]
pr439	439	107217	2.39	3.26	0.84	[3.05, 3.48]	**1.99**	3.23	1.43	[2.86, 3.59]
pcb442	442	50783	2.87	3.18	0.52	[3.05, 3.32]	**2.79**	3.63	0.97	[3.39, 3.88]
att532	532	87550	**1.28**	1.91	1.22	[1.60, 2.22]	1.48	2.12	0.92	[1.89, 2.35]
rat575	575	6773	4.98	5.89	0.96	[5.65, 6.14]	**4.50**	5.33	0.78	[5.13, 5.53]
u724	724	41910	6.28	6.53	0.35	[6.44, 6.62]	**4.06**	4.47	0.51	[4.34, 4.60]
pr1002	1002	259045	4.68	5.58	0.72	[5.40, 5.76]	**4.39**	5.24	1.20	[4.94, 5.55]

Table 2. Comparisons between the results of 36 symmetric instances from the TSPLIB with the Hard WTA with 2-opt (HWTA2) and Soft WTA with 2-opt (SWTA2) techniques.

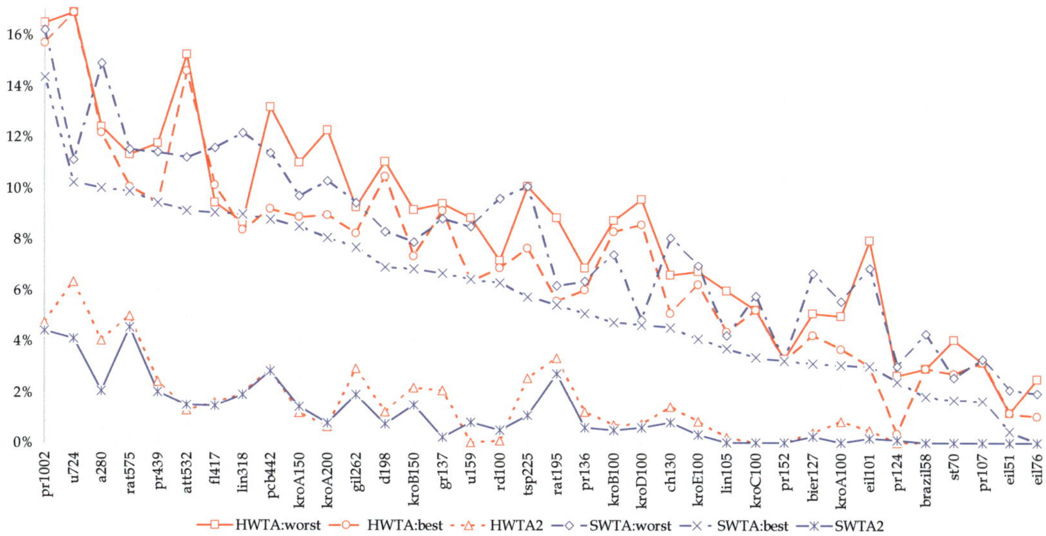

Fig. 4. Comparison between the results of the Hard WTA (HWTA) and Soft WTA (SWTA) techniques for 36 symmetrical problems from the TSPLIB

- the KNIESL technique, which consists of a local version of KNIESG, where only some cities are used for the neurons dispersion phase;
- in the Efficient and Integrated Self-Organizing Method (EISOM), a SOM network is used to generate a solution in which the winning neuron is substituted by the position of the mid-point between the two closest neighboring neurons (Jin *et al.*, 2003);
- the Co-Adaptive Network (CAN), which uses the idea of cooperation among neighboring neurons and uses a number of neurons that is higher than the number of cities in the problem (Cochrane & Beasley, 2003);
- the Real-Valued Antibody Network (RABNET), which uses a mechanism to stabilize the winning neurons and the centroids of the groups of cities for growth and pruning of the network (Massutti & Castro, 2009);
- the Modified Growing Ring Self-Organizing Network (MGSOM) incorporates other initialization methods for the weights in the network, with other adaptation parameters proposed for the SOM network and other indexing forms for the order of cities (Bai *et al.*, 2006);
- the MSOM, which consists in a hybrid technique with Self-Organizing Maps (SOM) and evolutionary algorithms to solve the TSP, called Memetic Neural Network (Créput & Kouka, 2007); and
- the technique of building a decision tree with minimum amplitude to choose the candidate cities for path exchange with the Lin-Kernighan of 2 up to 5-opt techniques (Kelsgaun, 2000).

The comparisons are shown in Table 3, where 16 of the 24 problems tested have better results with the technique proposed using the 2-opt route improving technique.

The order of computational complexity of the proposed technique is $O(n^2 + n)$ (Wang, 1997), considered competitive when compared with the complexity of Self-Organizing Maps, which have an $O(n^2)$ complexity (Leung *et al.*, 2004).

TSP name	Average error (%)									
	5OPT	**KNIESG**	**KNIESL**	**EISOM**	**MGSOM**	**RABNET**	**CAN**	**MSOM**	**SWTA**	**SWTA2**
eil51	0.85	2.86	2.86	2.56	1.40	0.56	0.94	1.64	0.47	**0**
st70	0.61	2.33	1.51	-	1.18	-	0.89	0.59	1.68	**0**
eil76	0.2	5.48	4.98	-	3.38	**0**	2.04	1.86	**0**	**0**
rd100	**0.16**	2.62	2.09	-	1.17	0.91	1.19	0.43	6.27	0.49
kroA100	1.65	-	-	-	-	0.24	0.57	0.18	3.05	**0**
kroB100	1.42	-	-	-	-	0.91	1.53	0.62	4.73	**0.47**
kroC100	1.35	-	-	-	-	0.80	0.80	0.30	3.35	**0**
kroD100	0.72	-	-	-	-	**0.38**	0.80	0.61	4.64	0.59
eil101	0.27	5.63	4.66	3.59	-	1.43	1.11	2.07	3.02	**0.16**
lin105	0.06	1.29	1.98	-	0.03	**0**	**0**	**0**	3.70	**0**
pr107	10.78	0.42	0.73	-	0.17	-	0.18	0.14	1.65	**0**
pr124	1.67	0.49	0.08	-	-	-	2.36	**0**	2.39	0.09
bier127	0.73	3.08	2.76	-	1.09	0.58	0.69	1.25	3.11	**0.25**
ch130	0.58	5.63	4.66	-	-	**0.57**	1.13	0.80	4.52	0.80
pr136	0.96	5.15	4.53	-	2.15	-	3.93	0.73	5.06	**0.58**
kroA150	0.88	-	-	1.83	-	**0.58**	1.55	1.75	8.50	1.40
pr152	2.1	1.29	0.97	-	0.74	-	0.74	1.07	3.23	**0**
rat195	**1.35**	11.92	12.24	-	5.98	-	4.69	4.69	5.42	2.71
kroA200	1.07	6.57	5.72	1.64	1.97	0.79	0.92	**0.70**	8.03	0.75
lin318	**0.35**	-	-	2.05	-	1.92	2.65	3.48	8.97	1.89
pcb442	**0.62**	10.45	11.07	6.11	8.58	-	5.88	3.57	8.76	2.79
att532	**0.99**	6.80	6.74	3.35	-	-	4.24	3.29	9.10	1.48
rat575	**0.74**	-	-	2.18	-	4.05	4.89	4.31	9.86	4.50
pr1002	**0.9**	-	-	4.82	-	-	4.18	4.75	14.39	4.39
mean	4.50	1.29	4.22	3.29	2.32	1.00	2.16	1.78	5.13	1.04

Table 3. Comparisons between the results of 24 symmetric problems from the TSPLIB with the techniques: Soft WTA (SWTA), Soft WTA with 2-opt (SWTA2), 5-OPT (decision tree with minimum amplitude of 2 up to 5-opt), KNIESG (Kohonen Network Incorporating Explicit Global Statistics), KNIESL (Kohonen Network Incorporating Explicit Statistics Local), EISOM (Efficient and Integrated SOM), MGSOM (Modified Growing Ring SOM), RABNET (Real-valued Antibody Network), CAN (Co-Adaptive Network) and MSOM (Memetic SOM)

Fig. 5a shows the best result found with the Soft WTA technique for the 1002-cities problem, by Padberg and Rinaldi, and Figure 5b shows the best result found with the same technique with the 2-opt route improvement. In Fig. 6 are the best results for drilling problem fl417 by Reinelt. In Fig. 7 are shown the best results for the of 439-cities problem by Padberg and Rinaldi.

Fig. 8 and 9 show the comparison between the best results for Wang's Recurrent Neural Network with the Hard and Soft WTA techniques for drilling problems d198 (Reinelt) and pcb442 (Groetschel, Juenger and Reinelt), respectively. Fig. 10 show the best result found with the Soft WTA technique for 399-cities problem of Parana, Brazil, where the optimal solution to this problem is 7,086,615.

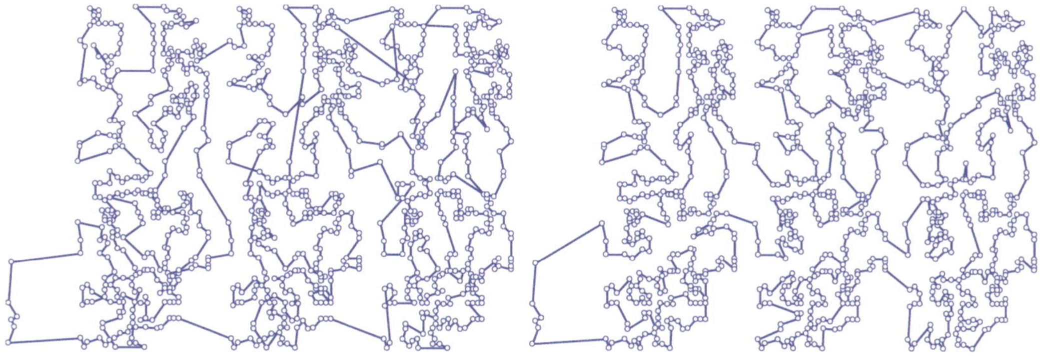

(a) (b)

Fig. 5. Example of the pr1002 problem with the application of Wang's Neural Network: (a) with Soft WTA and average error of 14.39%, (b) with Soft WTA and 2-opt improvement with average error of 4.39%

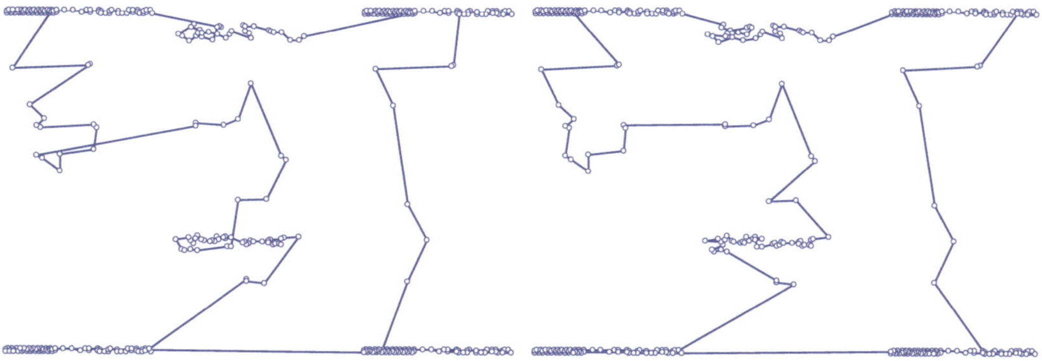

(a) (b)

Fig. 6. Example of the fl417 problem with the application of Wang's Neural Network: (a) with Soft WTA and average error of 9.05%, (b) with Soft WTA and 2-opt improvement with average error of 1.43%

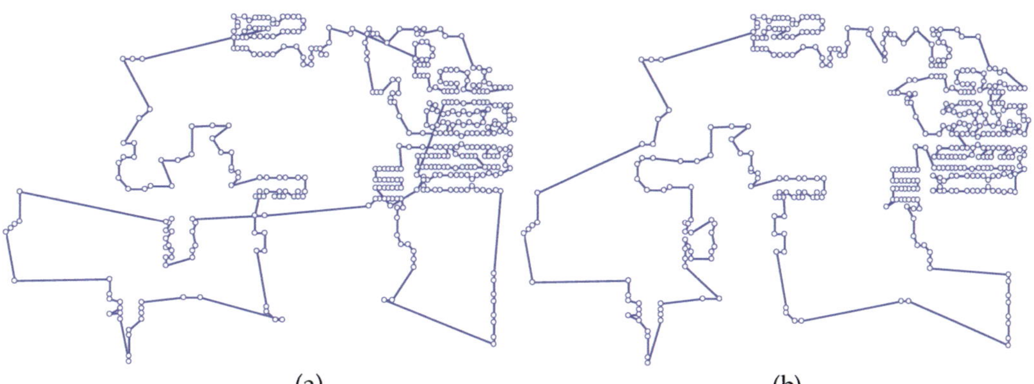

(a) (b)

Fig. 7. Example of the pr439 problem with the application of Wang's Neural Network: (a) with Soft WTA and average error of 9.39%, (b) with Soft WTA and 2-opt improvement with average error of 1.99%

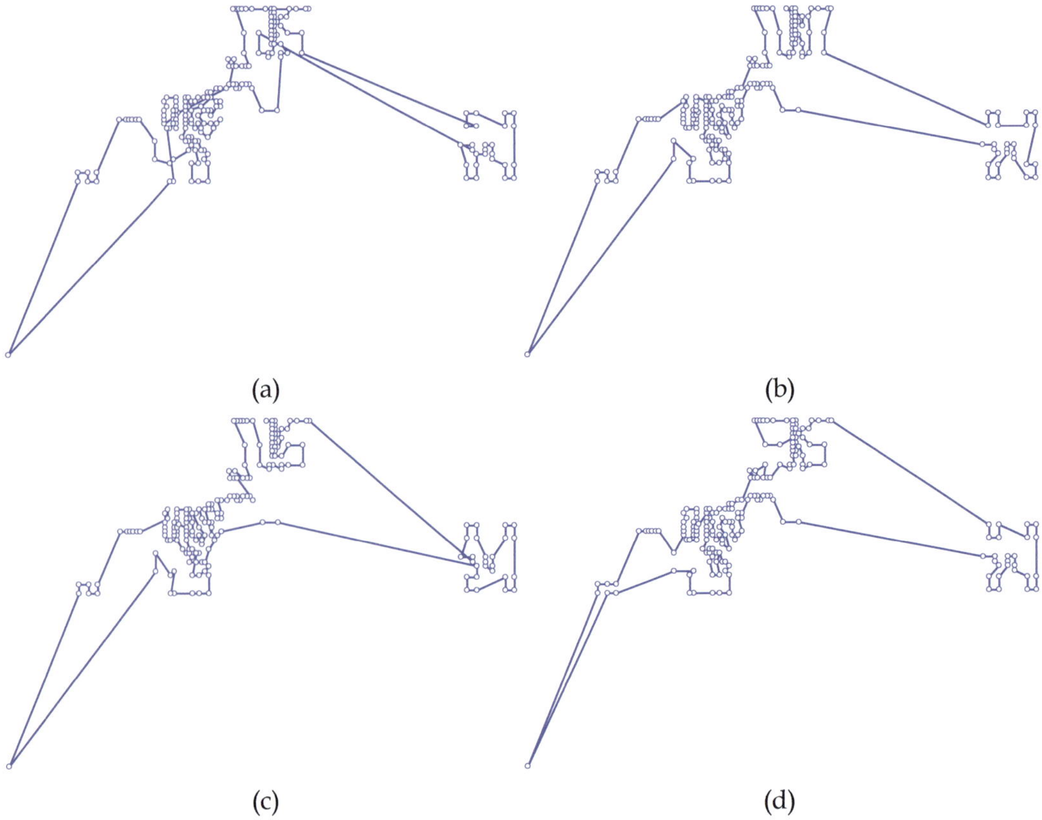

Fig. 8. Example of the d198 problem with the application of Wang's Neural Network: (a) with Hard WTA and average error of 10.43%, (b) with Hard WTA and 2-opt improvement with average error of 1.22% (c) with Soft WTA and average error of 6.86%, (d) with Soft WTA and 2-opt improvement with average error of 0.73%

3.2 Asymmetric problems from the TSPLIB

Table 4 and Table 5 shows the comparison between the Hard and Soft WTA techniques applied to asymmetric problems from the TSPLIB and demonstrates that the Soft WTA technique exceeds or equals the Hard WTA technical in all problems using 2-opt technique. The average error of the Soft WTA technique with 2-opt (SWTA2) varies between 0 and 10.56%, and with the Hard WTA technique with 2-opt (HWTA2) this error varies between 0 and 16.14%. The 95% confidence intervals for the mean were computed on the basis of standard deviations (sd) over 60 runs.

Fig. 11 shows a comparison between the Soft and Hard WTA techniques, showing the best and worst results from each asymmetric problem from the TSPLIB.

The techniques compared with the TSP asymmetric problems are described in the work of Glover *et al.* (2001):

- the Karp-Steele Path method (KSP) and the General Karp-Steele (GKS) method start with a cycle by removing paths and placing new ones to find a Hamiltonian cycle. The difference between these methods is that the GKS uses all vertices in the cycle to change paths.

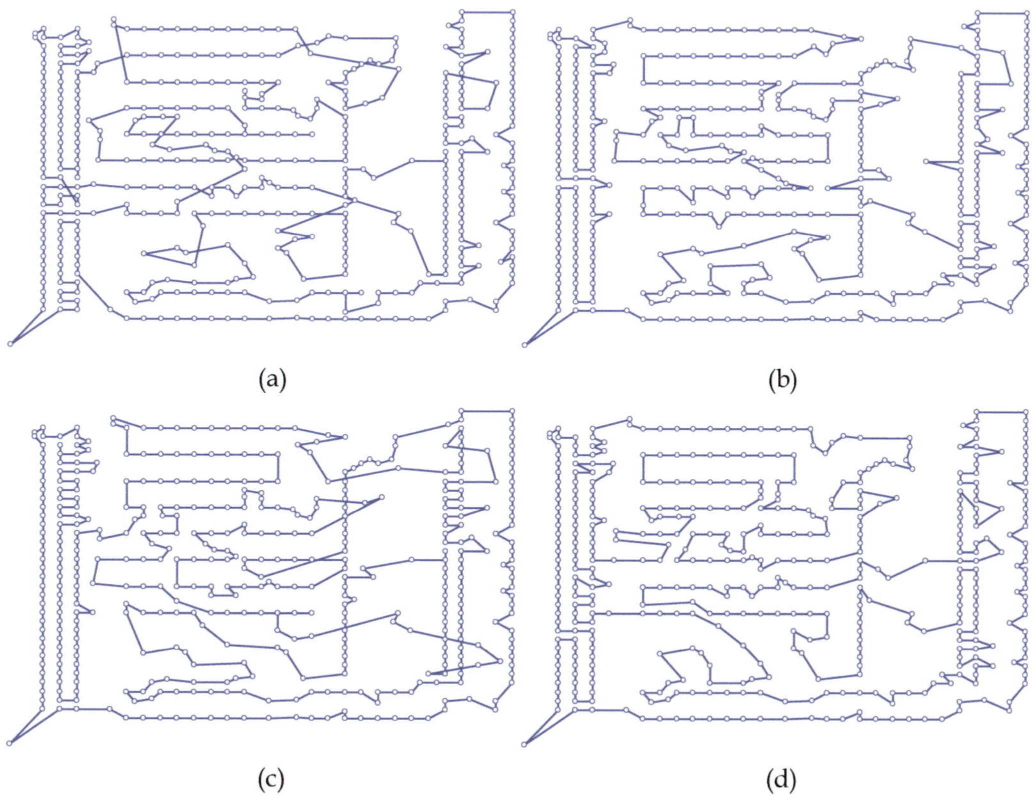

Fig. 9. Example of the pcb442 problem with the application of Wang's Neural Network: (a) with Hard WTA and average error of 9.16%, (b) with Hard WTA and 2-opt improvement with average error of 2.87%, (c) with Soft WTA and average error of 8.76%, (d) with Soft WTA and 2-opt improvement with average error of 2.79%

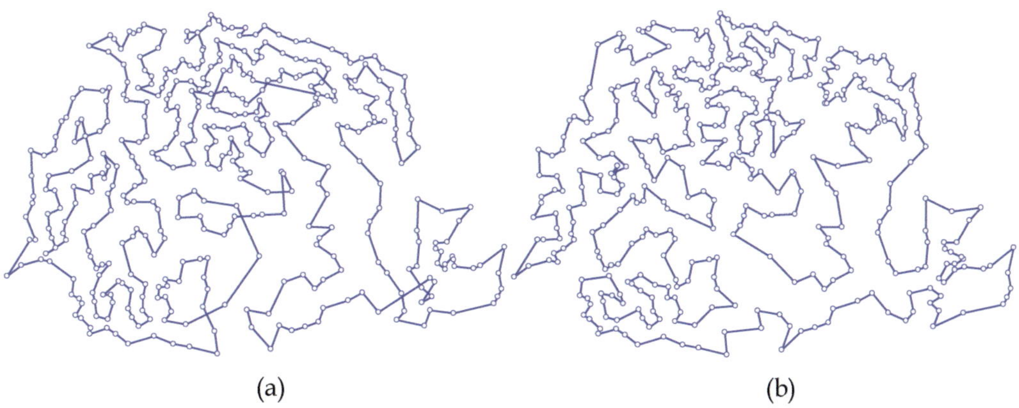

Fig. 10. Example of 399-cities problem of Paraná, Brazil (a) with Soft WTA and average error of 10.14%, and (b) with Soft WTA and 2-opt improvement with average error of 4.43%

TSP name	n	Optimal solution	Average error (%)							
			HWTA				SWTA			
			Best	**Mean**	**SD**	**CI (95%)**	**Best**	**Mean**	**SD**	**CI (95%)**
br17	17	39	**0**	0.73	1.25	[0.42, 1.05]	**0**	0.00	0.00	[0.00, 0.00]
ftv33	33	1286	**0**	5.26	0.77	[5.06, 5.45]	**0**	3.63	1.64	[3.22, 4.05]
ftv35	35	1473	3.12	4.84	1.33	[4.51, 5.18]	**0.61**	4.14	3.18	[3.34, 4.95]
ftv38	38	1530	3.73	3.77	0.03	[3.76, 3.78]	**2.94**	5.85	2.13	[5.32, 6.39]
pr43	43	5620	0.29	0.41	0.07	[0.39, 0.43]	**0.20**	0.28	0.06	[0.26, 0.29]
ftv44	44	1613	2.60	3.44	0.92	[3.21, 3.67]	**2.23**	5.29	2.64	[4.62, 5.95]
ftv47	47	1776	**3.83**	6.64	2.18	[6.09, 7.20]	5.29	7.32	2.86	[6.60, 8.04]
ry48p	48	14422	5.59	5.99	0.44	[5.88, 6.10]	**2.85**	4.16	0.91	[3.93, 4.40]
ft53	53	6905	**2.65**	3.04	0.30	[2.96, 3.11]	3.72	5.09	1.53	[4.70, 5.47]
ftv55	55	1608	11.19	8.00	3.23	[7.18, 8.81]	**2.11**	5.02	2.91	[4.29, 5.76]
ftv64	64	1839	2.50	2.50	0.00	[2.50, 2.50]	**1.41**	2.00	0.55	[1.86, 2.14]
ft70	70	38673	1.74	2.79	1.01	[2.53, 3.04]	**1.70**	1.94	0.27	[1.87, 2.01]
ftv70	70	1950	8.77	7.61	1.96	[7.11, 8.10}	**4.10**	8.01	3.16	[7.21, 8.81]
kro124p	124	36230	7.66	9.24	1.44	[8.88, 9.61]	**7.27**	8.25	1.00	[8.00, 8.50]
ftv170	170	2755	12.16	13.72	1.24	[13.41, 14.03]	**10.56**	12.63	2.34	[12.04, 13.22]
rbg323	323	1326	16.14	16.24	0.16	[16.20, 16.28]	**3.02**	3.19	0.27	[3.12, 3.26]
rbg358	358	1163	12.73	17.52	4.54	[16.37, 18.67]	**5.76**	7.57	2.26	[6.99, 8.14]
rbg403	403	2465	4.71	4.71	0.00	[4.71, 4.71]	**3.53**	3.93	0.66	[3.76, 4.10]
rbg443	443	2720	8.05	8.05	0.00	[8.05, 8.05]	**2.98**	3.33	0.55	[3.19, 3.47]

Table 4. Comparisons between the results of the 20 asymmetric problems from the TSPLIB for the techniques Hard WTA (HWTA) and Soft WTA (SWTA).

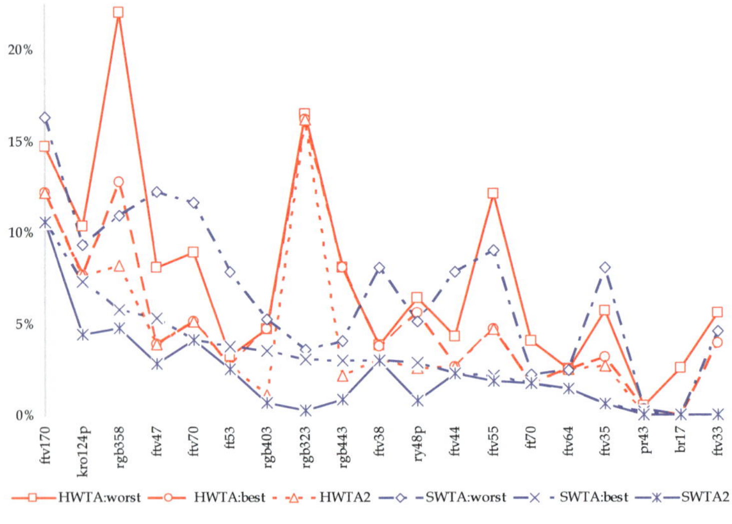

Fig. 11. Comparison between the results of the Hard WTA (HWTA) and Soft WTA (SWTA) techniques for the 19 asymmetric problems from the TSPLIB

TSP name	*n*	Optimal solution	Average error (%)							
			HWTA2				SWTA2			
			Best	**Mean**	**SD**	**CI (95%)**	**Best**	**Mean**	**SD**	**CI (95%)**
br17	17	39	**0**	0.00	0.00	[0.00, 0.00]	**0**	0.00	0.00	[0.00, 0.00]
ftv33	33	1286	**0**	2.68	2.13	[2.14, 3.22]	**0**	1.64	2.08	[1.12, 2.17]
ftv35	35	1473	3.12	3.22	1.28	[2.90, 3.54]	**0.61**	1.85	2.48	[1.22, 2.48]
ftv38	38	1530	3.01	3.71	0.37	[3.62, 3.81]	**2.94**	4.86	2.66	[4.19, 5.54]
pr43	43	5620	0.05	0.09	0.05	[0.07, 0.10]	**0**	0.16	0.17	[0.12, 0.21]
ftv44	44	1613	2.60	3.21	1.36	[2.87, 3.56]	**2.23**	4.23	1.89	[3.75, 4.71]
ftv47	47	1776	3.83	4.35	1.04	[4.09, 4.61]	**2.82**	5.38	2.43	[4.76, 5.99]
ry48p	48	14422	1.24	2.82	0.57	[2.67, 2.96]	**0.76**	1.65	1.31	[1.32, 1.98]
ft53	53	6905	2.65	3.21	0.58	[3.06, 3.36]	**2.49**	2.79	0.46	[2.67, 2.90]
ftv55	55	1608	6.03	5.97	1.65	[5.55, 6.39]	**1.87**	2.31	0.93	[2.08, 2.55]
ftv64	64	1839	2.50	3.50	1.73	[3.06, 3.94]	**1.41**	1.73	0.34	[1.65, 1.82]
ft70	70	38673	1.74	1.74	0.00	[1.74, 1.74]	**1.70**	2.19	0.34	[2.05, 2.33]
ftv70	70	1950	8.56	7.54	2.70	[6.85, 8.22]	**4.10**	7.32	4.98	[6.06, 8.58]
kro124p	124	36230	7.66	8.19	1.18	[7.89, 8.48]	**4.36**	4.94	1.29	[4.61, 5.26]
ftv170	170	2755	12.16	14.03	2.71	[13.34, 14.71]	**10.56**	11.23	1.32	[10.89, 11.56]
rbg323	323	1326	16.14	16.34	0.16	[16.30, 16.38]	**0.23**	1.71	1.29	[1.38, 2.03]
rbg358	358	1163	8.17	8.91	1.36	[8.57, 9.25]	**4.73**	6.29	1.55	[5.90, 6.69]
rbg403	403	2465	4.71	1.54	0.41	[1.44, 1.65]	**0.65**	0.91	0.33	[0.83, 1.00]
rbg443	443	2720	2.17	3.93	3.95	[2.94, 4.93]	**0.85**	0.91	0.06	[0.90, 0.93]

Table 5. Comparisons between the results of the 19 asymmetric problems from the TSPLIB for the techniques Hard WTA with 2-opt (HWTA2) and Soft WTA with 2-opt (SWTA2).

- the Path Recursive Contraction method (PRC) forms an initial cycle, removing sub-cycles to find a Hamiltonian cycle
- the Contraction of Paths (COP) heuristic is a combination of the GKS and PRC techniques;
- the Random Insertion (RI) heuristic starts with two vertices, inserting a vertex not yet chosen, creating a cycle. This procedure is repeated to create a route that contains all vertices;
- the Greedy heuristic (GR) choose the smallest path in the graph, contracts this path to create a new graph, maintaining this procedure up to the last path, forming a route.

Table 6 shows that the technique proposed in this paper has equal or better results than the techniques mentioned in 11 of the 19 tested asymmetric problems from the TSPLIB: br17, ftv33, ftv35, pr43, ftv44, ry48p, ft53, ftv55, ftv64, ft70 and kro124p.

Considering the techniques without the 2-opt improvement, Fig. 11 shows that the best solutions for the Hard WTA technique are better than the Soft WTA in only 3 problems: ftv47, ft70 and ft53. A great improvement can also be seen with the Soft WTA technique in the quality of the solutions for problems rgb443, rgb323 and rgb358.

The worst solutions for problems ftv35, ftv38, ftv44, ftv47, ft53, ftv70, ftv170 and rgb403 with the Soft WTA technique have higher costs than those found with the Hard WTA.

TSP name	Average error (%)							
	GR	RI	KSP	GKS	PRC	COP	SWTA	SWTA2
br17	102.56	**0**	**0**	**0**	**0**	**0**	**0**	**0**
ftv33	31.34	11.82	13.14	8.09	21.62	9.49	**0**	**0**
ftv35	24.37	9.37	1.56	1.09	21.18	1.56	**0.61**	**0.61**
ftv38	14.84	10.20	1.50	**1.05**	25.69	3.59	2.94	2.94
pr43	3.59	0.30	0.11	0.32	0.66	0.68	0.20	**0**
ftv44	18.78	14.07	7.69	5.33	22.26	10.66	**2.23**	**2.23**
ftv47	11.88	12.16	3.04	**1.69**	28.72	8.73	5.29	2.82
ry48p	32.55	11.66	7.23	4.52	29.50	7.97	2.85	**0.76**
ft53	80.84	24.82	12.99	12.31	18.64	15.68	3.72	**2.49**
ftv55	25.93	15.30	3.05	3.05	33.27	4.79	2.11	**1.87**
ftv64	25.77	18.49	3.81	2.61	29.09	1.96	**1.41**	**1.41**
ft70	14.84	9.32	**1.88**	2.84	5.89	1.90	4.10	4.10
ftv70	31.85	16.15	3.33	2.87	22.77	1.85	**1.70**	**1.70**
kro124p	21.01	12.17	16.95	8.69	23.06	8.79	7.27	**4.36**
ftv170	32.05	28.97	2.40	**1.38**	25.66	3.59	10.56	10.56
rbg323	8.52	29.34	**0**	**0**	0.53	**0**	3.02	0.23
rbg358	7.74	42.48	**0**	**0**	2.32	0.26	5.76	4.73
rbg403	0.85	9.17	**0**	**0**	0.69	0.20	3.53	0.65
rbg443	0.92	10.48	**0**	**0**	**0**	**0**	2.98	0.85
mean	25.80	15.07	4.14	2.94	16.39	4.30	3.17	2.22

Table 6. Comparisons between the results of the 19 asymmetric problems from the TSPLIB with the techniques Soft WTA (SWTA), Soft WTA with 2-opt (SWTA2) Random Insertion (RI), Karp-Steele Path (KSP), General Karp-Steele path (GKS), Path Recursive Contraction (PRC), Contraction or Path (COP) and Greedy heuristic (GR).

7. Conclusions

This paper presents a modification in the application of the 'Winner Takes All' technique in Wang's Recurrent Neural Network to solve the Traveling Salesman Problem. This technique is called Soft 'Winner Takes All', because the winning neuron receives only part of the activation of the other competing neurons.

The results were compared with the Hard 'Winner Takes All' variation, Self-Organizing Maps and the Path insertion and removal heuristics, showing improvement in most of the problems tested from the TSPLIB. The average errors for symmetric problems were between 0 and 4.50%, and for the asymmetric ones, between 0 and 10.56%.

The proposed technique was implemented with the 2-opt route improvement and the results shown in this study were compared both with and without the 2-opt technique.

8. References

Aras, N.; Oommen, B.J. & Altinel, I.K. (1999). The Kohonen network incorporating explicit statistics and its application to the traveling salesman problem. *Neural Networks*, Vol. 12, No. 9, November 1999, pp. 1273-1284, ISSN 0893-6080

Bai, Y.; Zhang, W. & Jin, Z. (2006). An new self-organizing maps strategy for solving the traveling salesman problem, *Chaos, Solitons and Fractals*, Vol. 28, No. 4, May 2006, pp. 1082–1089, ISSN 0960-0779

Cochrane, E.M. & Beasley, J.E. (2003). The Co-Adaptive Neural Network Approach to the Euclidean Travelling Salesman Problem. *Neural Networks*, Vol. 16, No. 10, December 2003, pp. 1499-1525, ISSN 0893-6080

Créput, J.C. & Koukam, A. (2009). A memetic neural network for the Euclidean travelling salesman problem. *Neurocomputing*, Vol. 72, No. 4-6, January 2009, pp. 1250-1264, ISSN 0925-2312

Glover, F.; Gutin, G.; Yeo, A. & Zverovich, A. (2001). Construction heuristics for the asymmetric TSP. *European Journal of Operational Research*, Vol. 129, No. 3, March 2001, pp. 555-568, ISSN 0377-2217

Hammer, B.; Schrauwen, B. & Steil, J.J. (2009), Recent advances in efficient learning of recurrent networks, *Proceedings of ESANN'2009 - European Symposium on Artificial Neural Networks - Advances in Computational Intelligence and Learning*, pp. 213-226, ISBN 2-930307-09-9, Bruges (Belgium), April 2009, D-side public., Bruges

Hopfield, J.J.. & Tank, D.W. (1985). "Neural" computation of decisions in optimization problems, *Biological cybernetics*, Vol. 52, No. 3, July 1985, pp. 141-152, ISSN 0340-1200

Hung, D.L. & Wang, J. (2003). Digital Hardware realization of a Recurrent Neural Network for solving the Assignment Problem. *Neurocomputing*, Vol. 51, Abril 2003, pp. 447-461, ISSN 0925-2312

Jin, H.D.; Leung, K.S.; Wong, M.L. & Xu, Z.B. (2003). An Efficient Self-Organizing Map Designed by Genetic Algorithms for the Traveling Salesman Problem. *IEEE Transactions On Systems, Man, And Cybernetics - Part B: Cybernetics*, Vol. 33, No. 6, December 2003, pp. 877-887, ISSN 1083-4419

Kelsgaun, K. (2000). An effective implementation of the Lin-Kernighan traveling salesman heuristic. *European Journal of Operational Research*, Vol. 126, No. 1, October 2000, pp. 106-130, ISSN 0377-2217

Leung, K.S.; Jin, H.D. & Xu, Z.B. (2004). An expanding self-organizing neural network for the traveling salesman problem. *Neurocomputing*, Vol. 62, December 2004, pp. 267-292, ISSN 0925-2312

Li, M.; Yi, Z. & Zhu, M. (2009). Solving TSP by using Lotka-Volterra neural networks, *Neurocomputing*, Vol. 72, No. 16-18, October 2009, pp. 3873-3880, ISSN 0925-2312

Lin, S. & Kernighan, B.W. (1973). An effective heuristic algorithm for the traveling-salesman problem. *Operations Research*, Vol. 21, No. 2, March-April 1973, pp. 498-516, ISSN 0030-364X

Masutti, T.A.S. & Castro, L.N. (2009). A self-organizing neural network using ideas from the immune system to solve the traveling salesman problem. *Information Sciences*, Vol. 179, No. 10, April 2009, pp. 1454-1468, ISSN 0020-0255

Misevičius, A.; Smolinskas, J. & Tomkevičius A. (2005). Iterated Tabu Search for the Traveling Salesman Problem: new results. *Information Technology And Control*, Vol. 34, No. 4, 2005, pp. 327-337, ISSN 1392-124X

Reinelt, G. (1991). TSPLIB – A traveling salesman problem library. *ORSA Journal on Computing*, Vol. 3, No. 4, 1991, pp. 376-384, ISSN 0899-1499

Siqueira, P.H.; Steiner, M.T.A. & Scheer, S. (2007). A new approach to solve the Traveling Salesman Problem. *Neurocomputing*, Vol. 70, No. 4-6, January 2007, pp. 1013-1021, ISSN 0925-2312

Siqueira, P.H.; Scheer, S. & Steiner, M.T.A. (2008). A Recurrent Neural Network to Traveling Salesman Problem. In: *Travelling Salesman Problem*, Greco, F. (Ed.), pp. 135-156, In-the, ISBN 978-953-7619-10-7, Croatia

Wang, J. (1992). Analog Neural Network for Solving the Assignment Problem. *Electronic Letters*, Vol. 28, No. 11, May 1992, pp. 1047-1050, ISSN 0013-5194

Wang, J. (1997). Primal and Dual Assignment Networks. *IEEE Transactions on Neural Networks*, Vol. 8, No. 3, May 1997, pp. 784-790, ISSN 1045-9227

Wang, Y.; Feng, X.Y.; Huang, Y.X.; Pu, D.B.; Liang, C.Y. & Zhou, W.G. (2007). A novel quantum swarm evolutionary algorithm and its applications, *Neurocomputing*, Vol. 70, No. 4-6, January 2007, pp. 633-640, ISSN 0925-2312

Yi, J.; Yang, G.; Zhang, Z. & Tang, Z. (2009). An improved elastic net method for travelling salesman problem, *Neurocomputing*, Vol. 72, No. 4-6, January 2009, pp. 1329-1335, ISSN 0925-2312

12

A Study of Traveling Salesman Problem Using Fuzzy Self Organizing Map

Arindam Chaudhuri[1] and Kajal De[2]
[1]*NIIT University, Neemrana,*
[2]*Netaji Subhas University, Kolkata,*
India

1. Introduction

Traveling Salesman Problem (TSP) is classical and most widely studied problem in Combinatorial Optimization **(Applegate D. L. et al., 2006)**. It has been studied intensively in both Operations Research and Computer Science since 1950s as a result of which a large number of techniques were developed to solve this problem. Much of the work on TSP is not motivated by direct applications, but rather by the fact that it provides an ideal platform for study of general methods that can be applied to a wide range of Discrete Optimization Problems. Indeed, numerous direct applications of TSP bring life to research area and help to direct future work. The idea of problem is to find shortest route of salesman starting from a given city, visiting n cities only once and finally arriving at origin city. The investigation question which arises is:

In what order should the cities be visited such that the distance traveled is minimized?

TSP is represented by complete edge-weighted graph $G=(V,E)$ with V being set of $n=|V|$ nodes or vertices representing cities and $E \subseteq V \times V$ being set of directed edges or arcs. Each arc $(i,j) \in E$ is assigned value of length d_{ij} which is distance between cities i and j with $i,j \in V$. TSP can be either asymmetric or symmetric in nature. In case of asymmetric TSP, distance between pair of nodes i,j is dependent on direction of traversing edge or arc i.e. there is at least one arc (i,j) for which $d_{ij} \neq d_{ji}$. In symmetric TSP, $d_{ij} = d_{ji}$ holds for all arcs in E. The goal in TSP is thus to find minimum length Hamiltonian Circuit **(Cormen T. H. et al., 2001)** of graph, where Hamiltonian Circuit is a closed path visiting each of n nodes of G exactly once. Thus, an optimal solution to TSP is permutation π of node indices $\{1,.......,n\}$ such that length $f(\pi)$ is minimal, where $f(\pi)$ is given by,

$$f(\pi) = \sum_{i=1}^{n-1} d_{\pi(i)\pi(i+1)} + d_{\pi(n)\pi(1)}$$

TSP is NP-hard problem as the search space is huge viz. $n!$ Thus, it is not possible to check all solutions for city sets with many thousands of cities **(Korte B. H. & Vygen J., 2008)**. Hence, a fast and effective heuristic method is needed. Based on a deterministic approach, the world record setting TSP solution is by **(Applegate D. L. et al.,1995)** which has solved instances as large as 24,978 cities to optimality. Trying to solve the course of exponentials parallel implementations of TSP were realized **(Christof T. & Reinelt G., 1995)**. However, for practicability reasons specifically for large numbers of cities, heuristic approaches for solving TSP are very popular, which try to produce an optimal or close to optimal solution. It arises as sub-problem in many transportation and logistic applications **(Chaudhuri A., 2007)**, for example the problem of arranging school bus routes to pick up children in a district. This application is of important significance to TSP since it provides motivation for Merrill Flood one of the pioneers of TSP research in 1940s. A second application from 1940s involved transportation of farming equipment from one location to another leading to mathematical studies by P. C. Mahalanobis and R. J. Jessen. More recent applications involve scheduling of service call at cable firms, delivery of meals to homebound persons, scheduling of stacker cranes in warehouses, routing of trucks for parcel post pickup etc. Although transportation applications are most natural setting for TSP, simplicity of the model has led to many interesting applications in other areas. A classic example is scheduling of machine to drill holes in circuit boards where holes to be drilled are cities and cost of travel is the time it takes to move the drill head from one hole to next.

TSP has some direct importance, since quite a lot of practical applications can be put in this form. It also has theoretical significance in Complexity Theory **(Garey M. & Johnson D., 1990)** since TSP is one of the classes of NP-Complete Combinatorial Optimization Problems **(Korte B. H. & Vygen J., 2008)** which are difficult optimization problems where the set of feasible solutions or trial solutions which satisfy constraints of problem but are not necessarily optimal is finite, though usually very large set. The numbers of feasible solutions grow as some combinatorics factor such as $n!$ where, n characterizes size of the problem. It has often been the case that progress on TSP **(Laporte G., 2010)** has led to the progress on many Combinatorial Optimization Problems. In this way, TSP is an ideal stepping stone for study of Combinatorial Optimization Problems.

Although many optimal algorithms exist for solving TSP it has been realized that it is computationally infeasible to obtain optimal solution to the problem. For large-size problem **(Cormen T. H. et al., 2001)** it has been proved that it is almost impossible to generate an optimal solution within reasonable amount of time. Heuristics instead of optimal algorithms are thus extensively used to solve such problems **(Hansen M. P., 2000)**. Many heuristic algorithms give near optimal solutions to the problem which are used for practicability reasons specifically for large numbers of cities. Heuristic approaches **(Lin S. & Kernighan B. W., 1973)** for solving TSP are thus very popular which try to produce an optimal or close to optimal solution. The commonly used heuristic approaches are: (a) Greedy Algorithms; (b) 2-opt Algorithm; (c) 3-opt Algorithm; (d) Simulated Annealing; (e) Genetic Algorithms and (e) Artificial Neural Network (ANN). However, efficiencies vary from case to case and from size to size.

Generally the most common heuristic is ANN which are well suited for solving problems that are hard to catch in mathematical models. However, the usage and employment of ANN in such application domains is often dependent on tractability of processing costs. The problem domains for employment of ANN are increasing **(Haykin S., 2008)** and also problem themselves are getting larger and more complex **(Arbib M., 2003)**. This leads to larger networks consisting of huge numbers of nodes and interconnection links which results in exceeding costs for network specific operations such as evaluation and training. Especially the cost intensive training phase of ANN inherits a major drawback due to the situation that large numbers of patterns viz. input and target values are fed into the network iteratively. The effectiveness of ANN can be improved by deployment of Fuzzy Logic **(Jang J. S. R. et al., 1997)** which is a computational paradigm that generalizes classical two valued logic for reasoning under uncertainty. This is achieved by the notation of membership. Two things are accomplished by this viz. (i) ease of describing human knowledge involving vague concepts and (ii) enhanced ability to develop a cost-effective solution to real-world problem. Fuzzy Logic is thus is a multi-valued logic **(Zadeh L. A., 1994)** which is model less approach and clever disguise of Probability Theory. ANN and Fuzzy Logic are two complementary technologies. ANN can learn from data and feedback. However, understanding knowledge or pattern learned by ANN has been difficult. More specifically it is difficult to develop an insight about the meaning associated with each neuron and its weight. Hence, ANN are often viewed as black box approach. In contrast, Fuzzy Rule Based Models are easy to comprehend because it uses linguistic terms and structure of if then rules. Unlike ANN, Fuzzy Logic does not come with learning algorithm. Since ANN can learn, it is natural to merge two technologies. This merger creates a new term i.e. Neuro Fuzzy networks. A Neuro Fuzzy network thus describes a Fuzzy Rule Based Model using an ANN like structure.

In this chapter, Fuzzy Self Organizing Map (FSOM) **(Bezdek J. C., 1981; Kohonen T., 2001; Arbib M., 2003; Haykin S., 2008)** with one dimensional neighborhood is used to find optimal solution for symmetrical TSP. The solution generated by FSOM algorithm is improved by 2opt algorithm **(Aarts E. H. & Lenstra J. K., 2003)**. FSOM algorithm is compared with Lin-Kerninghan **(Lin S. & Kernighan B. W., 1973)** and Evolutionary algorithm **(Goldberg D. E., 1989; Deb K., 2001)** with enhanced edge recombination operator and self-adapting mutation rate. Experimental results indicate that FSOM 2opt hybrid algorithm generates appreciably better results compared to both Evolutionary and Lin-Kerninghan algorithms for TSP as number of cities increases. Some other optimization algorithms other than 2opt algorithm give better results. One of the best operators for TSP is enhanced edge recombination operator in comparison to permutation operators which are for other permutation problems. The chapter is structured as follows. In section 2 a brief survey of SOM is given. The next section illustrates FSOM. Section 4 describes the heuristic solution of TSP using FSOM and the corresponding mathematical characterization is given. In section 5 numerical results are presented along with an indepth run time analysis. Finally, in section 6 conclusions are given.

2. Self organizing map

SOM introduced by Teuvo Kohonen **(Kohonen T., 2001)** is an ANN that is trained using competitive, unsupervised learning **(Haykin S., 2008)** to produce low-dimensional discretized representation of input space of training samples called a map which preserves *topological* properties of input space. The development of SOM as neural model is motivated by distinct feature of human brain which is organized in many places in such a way that different sensory inputs are represented by *topologically ordered computational maps*. The output neurons of network compete among themselves to be activated or fired, with the result that only one output neuron or one neuron per group is on at one time. An output neuron that wins competition is called *winner takes all* or *winning* neuron **(Arbib M., 2003)**. SOM is thus useful for visualizing low-dimensional views of high-dimensional data which is identical to multi-dimensional scaling. They generally operate in two modes viz. training and mapping. Training builds map using input examples, which is a competitive process also called vector quantization. Mapping automatically classifies a new input vector.

In SOM neurons are placed at nodes of *lattice* which is usually one or two dimensional. The neurons become selectively tuned to various input patterns or classes of input patterns in course of competitive learning process. The locations of neurons so tuned become ordered with respect to each other in such way that a meaningful coordinate system for different input features is created over lattice **(Kohonen T., 2001)**. As a neural model, SOM provides a bridge between two levels of adaptation viz. (a) adaptation rules formulated at microscopic level of single neuron and (b) formation of experimentally better and physically accessible patterns of feature selectivity at microscopic level of neural layers.

The competitive learning algorithm of SOM is either based on *winner takes all* or *winner takes mode* approach. However, *winner takes most* strategy is most common. When input vector is presented, distance to each neuron's synaptic weights are calculated. The neuron whose weights are most correlated to current input vector is winner. Correlation is equal to scalar product of input vector and considered synaptic weights. Only winning neuron modifies its synaptic weights to the point presented by input pattern. Synaptic weights of other neurons do not change. The learning process is described by **(Arbib M., 2003)**:

$$W_i \leftarrow W_i + \eta(x - W_i) \text{ where, } i \in \{0.........number\ of\ neurons\},$$

W_i represents all synaptic weights of winning neuron, η is learning rate and x is current input vector. This simple algorithm can be extended giving more chance of winning to neurons that are rarely activated. The *winner takes most* has better convergence than *winner takes all* strategy. The difference is that many neurons in *winner takes most* strategy adapt their synaptic weights in single learning iteration only. In this case not only the winner but also its neighborhood adapts. The further neighboring neuron is from winner, smaller the modification which is applied to its weights. This adaptation process is described as **(Bishop C. M., 1995)**:

$$W_i \leftarrow W_i + \eta N(i,x)(x - W_i)$$

for all neurons i that belongs to winner's neighborhood. W_i stands for synaptic weights of neuron i and x is current input vector, η stands for learning rate and $N(i, x)$ is function that defines neighborhood. Classical SOM is created when function $N(i, x)$ is defined as **(Hertz J., Krogh A. & Palmer R. G., 1991)**:

$$N(i,x) = \{^{1\, for d(i,w) \leq \lambda}_{0\, for others}$$

where, $d(i,w)$ is euclidean distance between winning and i^{th} neuron and λ is neighborhood radius. To train SOM euclidean distance between input vector and all neural weights are calculated. Neuron that has shortest distance to input vector i.e. winner is chosen and its weights are slightly modified to direction represented by input vector. Then neighboring neurons are taken and their weights are modified in same direction. η and λ are multiplied with $\Delta\eta$ and $\Delta\lambda$ respectively during each learning iteration. These two last parameters are always less than one. Therefore, η and λ become smaller during learning process. At beginning SOM tries to organize itself globally and with following iterations it performs more and more local organization because learning rate and neighborhood gets smaller. Kohonen SOM is shown in Figure 1 **(Kohonen T., 2001)**. It maps input vectors of any dimension onto map with one, two or more dimensions. Input patterns which are similar to one another in input space are put close to one another in the map. The input vector is passed to every neuron. Kohonen SOM is made of vector or matrix of output neurons. If vector representation is chosen each neuron have two neighbors, one on left and other on right then it is called one-dimensional neighborhood as shown in Figure 2. If two-dimensional matrix representation is used neurons have 4 neighbors (viz. left, right, top and bottom). This is classical two dimensional neighborhood as shown in Figure 3. Instead of taking 4 nearest neurons 8 or more can be taken as shown in Figure 4. As many dimensions can be used as required viz. one, two, three or more dimensions. However, two dimensional neighborhood is most common.

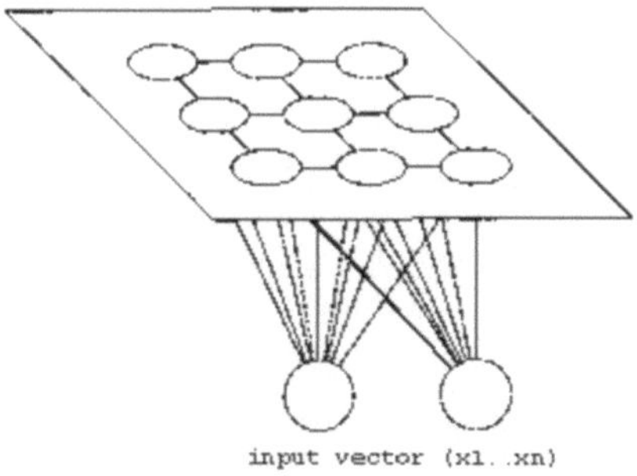

Fig. 1. Kohonen SOM with two dimensional neighborhood and input vector

Fig. 2. One dimensional neighborhood of Kohonen SOM

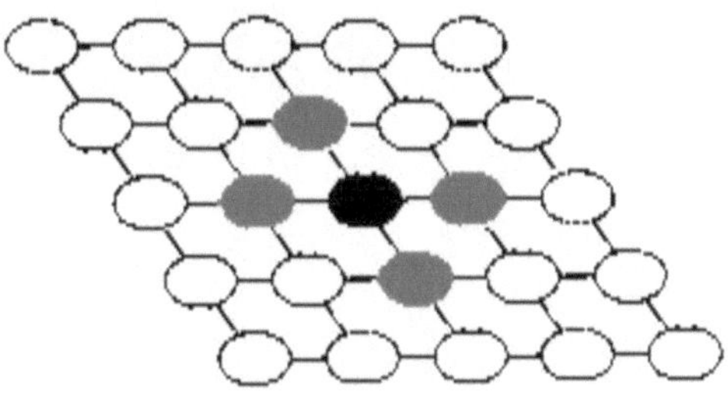

Fig. 3. Classical two dimensional neighborhoods

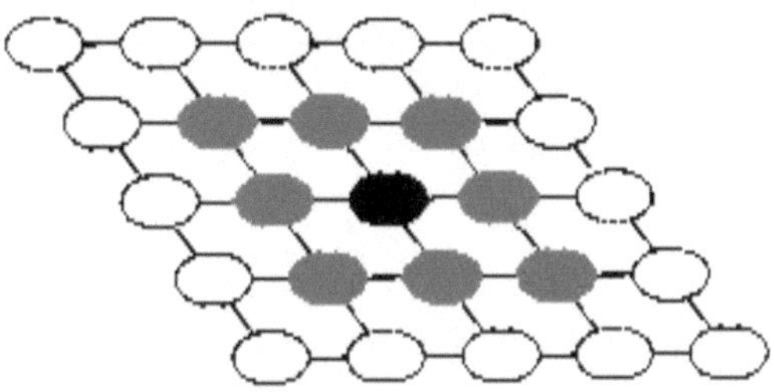

Fig. 4. Extended two dimensional neighborhood of Kohonen SOM

3. Fuzzy self organizing map

FSOM introduces the concept of membership function **(Bezdek J. C., 1981; Kohonen T., 2001; Arbib M., 2003; Haykin S., 2008)** in the theory of Fuzzy Sets to learning process. The membership R_{lj} of each pattern l to each neuron j is calculated and weight vector of each neuron is adjusted according to memberships of all patterns to the neuron. The learning algorithm is illustrated below. In FSOM some network parameters related to neighborhood in SOM are replaced with the membership function **(Bezdek J. C., 1981; Fritzke B., 1994; Kohonen T., 2001)**. Also the learning rate parameter is omitted. FSOM considers all input data at each iteration step. It is thus more effective at decreasing oscillations and avoiding dead units. FSOM used here is a combination of SOM and Fuzzy C Means (FCM) **(Bezdek J. C., 1981)** Clustering Algorithm.

3.1 Fuzzy C means clustering algorithm

FCM technique is a method of clustering which allows one piece of data to belong to two or more clusters. The method is developed by Dunn **(Dunn J. C.,1973)** and improved by Bezdek **(Bezdek J. C., 1981)** is frequently used in Pattern Recognition. It is based on minimization of the following objective function:

$$J_m = \sum_{i=1}^{N}\sum_{j=1}^{C} u_{ij}^m \,||\, x_i - c_j \,||^2 \;, 1 \le m < \infty$$

where, m is any real number greater than 1, u_{ij} is degree of membership of x_i in cluster j, x_i is i^{th} ith of d dimensional measured data, c_j is d dimension center of cluster and $||*||$ is any norm expressing similarity between any measured data and the center. FCM thus processes N vectors in d space as data input and uses them in conjunction with first order necessary conditions for minimizing FCM objective functional to obtain estimates for two sets of unknowns. Fuzzy partitioning is carried out through an iterative optimization of objective function with update of membership u_{ij} and cluster centers c_j by:

$$u_{ij} = \frac{1}{\sum_{k=1}^{C}\left(\frac{||x_i - c_j||}{||x_i - c_k||}\right)^{\frac{2}{m-1}}} \;, c_j = \frac{\sum_{i=1}^{N} u_{ij}^m \cdot x_i}{\sum_{i=1}^{N} u_{ij}^m}$$

This iteration will stop when $\max_{ij}\{|u_{ij}^{(k+1)} - u_{ij}^{(k)}|\} < \varepsilon$ where ε is termination criterion betweem 0 and 1 in k iteration steps. The procedure converges to a local minimum or a saddle point of J_m. The algorithm is composed of following steps:

a. Initialize the matrix $U = [u_{ij}]$ to $U^{(0)}$.
b. At k step calculate centre vectors $C^{(k)} = [c_j]$ with $U^{(k)}$,

$$c_j = \frac{\sum_{i=1}^{N} u_{ij}^m \cdot x_i}{\sum_{i=1}^{N} u_{ij}^m}$$

c. Update the matrices $U^{(k)}$ and $U^{(k+1)}$,

$$u_{ij} = \frac{1}{\sum_{k=1}^{C} \left(\frac{||x_i - c_j||}{||x_i - c_k||} \right)^{\frac{2}{m-1}}}$$

d. If $||U^{(k+1)} - U^{(k)}|| < \varepsilon$ then stop, otherwise goto step (b).

The data are bound to each cluster by means of membership function which represents the fuzzy behaviour of this algorithm. This is achieved by the matrix U whose factors are numbers between 0 and 1, and represent the degree of membership between data and centers of clusters. In FCM approach as the same given datum does not belong exclusively to a well defined cluster, it is placed somewhere in the middle such that the membership function follows a smoother line to indicate that every datum may belong to several clusters with different values of membership coefficient.

FCM is generalized in many ways **(Bezdek J. C., 1981)** such as, the memberships includes possibilities; prototypes have evolved from points to linear varieties to hyper-quadrics to shells to regression functions; the distance includes Minkowski (non-inner product induced) and hybrid distances. There are many relatives of FCM for dual problem called relational FCM which is useful when data are not object vectors but relational values viz. similarities between pairs of objects. There are also many acceleration techniques for FCM as well as very large versions of FCM that utilize both progressive sampling and distributed clustering. Many techniques use FCM clustering to build Fuzzy rule bases for Fuzzy Systems design. Numerous applications of FCM exist **(Arbib M., 2003; Haykin S., 2008)** virtually in every major application area of clustering.

3.2 FSOM learning algorithm

In ANN structure, each output neuron directly corresponds to a city in network of cities **(Haykin S., 2008)**. The number of output neurons used to describe the cities is generally arbitrary. However, if number of neurons is equal to number of cities the problem gets simplified. The more the number of neurons, the greater is accuracy of model. The number of output neurons needed for good accuracy depends on complexity of the problem. The more complex the problem, more output neurons are required. The number of output neurons is manually selected. The weight W connects input vector components and output neurons. The weight vectors are of same dimensions as sample vectors. The weight components are initialized randomly and adjusted gradually using self organizing learning algorithm and ultimately a mapping is done from input to output. Let M denote number of input patterns, N number of input vector components and K number of output neurons. The learning algorithm consists of the following steps **(Bezdek J. C., 1981)**:

a. Randomize weights for all neurons.
b. Input all patterns $X_l = \{X_{l1}, \ldots\ldots\ldots\ldots, X_{lN}\}, l = 1, \ldots\ldots\ldots, M$ .Take one random input pattern and calculate euclidean distances from each pattern X_l to all output neurons.

$$d_{lj}(t) = \sqrt{\sum_{i=1}^{N} (X_{li} - W_{ij}(t))^2} ; l = 1, \ldots\ldots\ldots, M, j = 1, \ldots\ldots\ldots, K.$$

c. Compute memberships of each pattern to all neurons **(Tao T., Gan J. R. & Yao L. S., 1992)**.

$$R_{lj}(t)=\frac{\{d_{lj}(t)\}^{-2}}{\sum_{m=1}^{K}\{d_{lm}(t)\}^{-2}};l=1,........,M,j=1,.........,K$$

d. Find winning neuron and neighbors of winner.
e. Adjust synaptic weights of each neuron according to computed memberships.

$$W_{ij}(t+1)=W_{ij}(t)+\frac{\sum_{l=1}^{M}R_{lj}(t)(X_{li}-W_{ij}(t))}{\sum_{l=1}^{M}R_{lj}(t)}$$

f. Reduce values of parameters η and λ.
g. Determine stability condition of network.

$$\max\{|W_{ij}(t+1)-W_{ij}(t)|\}<\varepsilon$$
$$1\leq i\leq N$$
$$1\leq j\leq K$$

If the stability condition is satisfied or predefined number of iterations is achieved, then learning process terminates, otherwise go to Step (b) for another loop of learning. From above learning procedure, it is observed that FSOM eases the difficulty of selecting network parameters. In above learning procedure, weights are adjusted only once in each learning loop and features of all input samples are taken into consideration once weights are adjusted **(Arbib M., 2003)**. Thus, learning speed and estimation accuracy are greatly improved.

4. Heuristic solution for traveling salesman problem by fuzzy self organizing map

Most interesting results of self-organization (Dittenbach M. et al., 2000; Kohonen T., 2001; Junfei Q. et al., 2007) are achieved in networks that have two dimensional input vectors and two dimensional neighborhoods. In this case input to network consists of two values viz. x and y which represent a point in two dimensional space. This kind of network can map two dimensional objects in such a way that a mesh which covers this object is created. This process is illustrated in Figure 5. Each example consists of six squares. First one shows the object that should be learned. The second square illustrates network just after randomization of all neural weights. Following squares describe the learning process. It is to be noted that each neuron or a circle represents a point whose coordinates are equal to neuron's weights. These figures illustrate that Kohonen ANN is powerful self-organizing and clustering tool. However, it is also possible to create network with one dimensional neighborhood and two dimensional inputs (Arbib M., 2003). Learning process of this is shown in Figure 6. It is observed that this network tries to organize its neurons in such a

way that a relatively short route between all neurons emerges. These experiments are stimulus to build system based on one-dimensional FSOM that would solve TSP problems **(Xu W. & Tsai W. T., 1991; Burke L. I., 1994; Sentiono R., 2001)**.
To solve TSP problem a one dimensional network is created. If the weights of neuron is equal to some city's coordinates the neuron represents that city. In other words a neuron and a city are assigned to each other and there is a one-to-one mapping **(Haykin S., 2008)** between set of cities and set of neurons. All neurons are organized in a vector. This vector represents sequence of cities that must be visited. However, some modifications need to be done before FSOM is able to fully solve this problem. This is because the real valued neural weights are never exactly equal to coordinates of cities. To solve the problem an algorithm that modifies FSOM solution to a valid one is created. Positions of cities and neurons may not equal. However, adequate neural weights and cities coordinates are very close to each other. An algorithm that modifies neural weights so that they equal to cities coordinates is applied. These weights are modified in such a way to restore one-to-one mapping assumed at beginning. If neuron A is assigned to a city B it means that weights of neuron A are equal to coordinates of city B. After applying this algorithm a good and fast solution is obtained. However, it is not locally optimal **(Applegate D. L. et al.,2006; Laporte G., 2010)**. Thus it needs to be optimized using well known 2opt algorithm **(Aarts E. H. & Lenstra J. K., 2003)**. In this case 2opt works fast even for large amount of cities because current solution is already good. Usually 2opt does not change the solution a lot as shown in the Figure 7. The 2opt algorithm is based on one simple rule which selects a part of the tour, reverses it and inserts back in the cycle. If new tour is shorter than original cycle, then it is replaced. The algorithm stops when no improvement can be done. For example if there is a cycle (A, B, C, D, E, F) and a path (B, C, D) is reversed, then new cycle is: (A, D, C, B, E, F). After 2opt optimization the solution is locally optimal as shown in Figure 8. FSOM optimal training parameters are chosen adequately to number of cities to achieve best results **(Arbib M., 2003; Haykin S., 2008)**. It is found empirically that good training parameters are as follows:

a. For 200 cities: $\eta = 0.5$, $\Delta\eta = 0.9667$, $\Delta\lambda = 0.966$
b. For 700 cities: $\eta = 0.6$, $\Delta\eta = 0.9665$, $\Delta\lambda = 0.9664$
c. For 1200 cities: $\eta = 0.8$, $\Delta\eta = 0.9662$, $\Delta\lambda = 0.9666$

In every case the number of iterations is set to 25000.

5. Numerical simulation

In the quest of finding solution to TSP problem **(Applegate D. L. et al., 2006)** using FSOM following two types of tests are done:

a. Using city sets taken from TSPLIB **(Reinelt G., 1991)** in which there are already some optimal solutions present
b. Using randomly chosen cities

TSPLIB city sets are hard to solve because in many cases the cities are not chosen randomly as shown in Figures 9 and 10. Generally larger city sets consist of small patterns. City set shown in Figure 10 consists of two different patterns and each of them is used nine times. Thus, optimal tour is identical in each one of these smaller patterns shown in Figure 10 top. FSOM tries to figure out a unique tour in each of the smaller pattern shown in Figure 10 bottom. The testing process using randomly chosen cities is more objective. It is based on Held-Karp Traveling Salesman bound **(Johnson D. S. et al., 2000)**. An empirical relation for expected tour length is:

$$L = k\sqrt{nR}$$

where L is expected tour length, n is a number of cities, R is an area of square box on which cities are placed and k is an empirical constant. For $n \geq 100$ value of k is:

$$k = 0.70805 + \frac{0.52229}{\sqrt{n}} + \frac{1.31572}{n} - \frac{3.07474}{n\sqrt{n}}$$

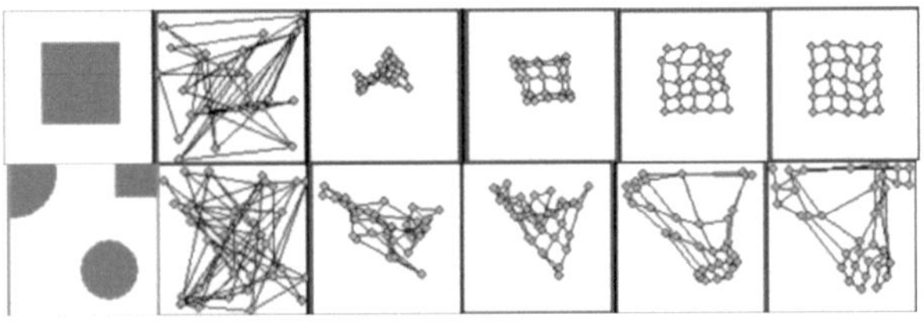

Fig. 5. Self-organization of network with two dimensional neighborhoods

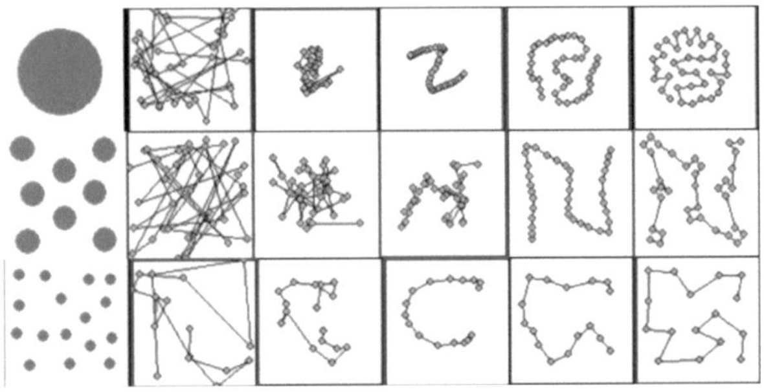

Fig. 6. Self-organization of network with one dimensional neighborhood

The three random city sets viz. 200, 700, 1200 cities are used in this experiment; square box edge length is restricted to 500. All statistics for FSOM are generated after 75 runs on each city set. When number of iterations is taken as 100, the average results did not show any considerable difference. Better results are obtained on increasing the number of iterations. FSOM generates a tour in relatively short time, such as 225 cities set is solved in 254 ms and 1000 cities set in less than 2 seconds. The average tour lengths for city sets up to 2000 cities are comparatively better than optimum. FSOM thus generates solutions that are noticeably good from optimal tour. FSOM is compared with the Evolutionary Algorithm **(Goldberg D. E., 1989; Deb K., 2001)**. Evolutionary Algorithm uses enhanced edge recombination operator **(Rahendi N. T A. & Atoum J., 2009)** and steady state survivor selection where always the worst solution is replaced with tournament parent selection where tournament size depends on number of cities and population size. Scramble mutation is used here. The optimal mutation rate depends on number of cities and state of evolution. Therefore, self-adapting mutation rate is used. Every genotype has its own mutation rate **(Michalewicz Z., 1996)** which is modified in a similar way as in evolution strategies. This strategy adapts mutation rate to number of cities and evolution state automatically, so it is not needed to check manually which parameters are optimal for each city set. Evolution stops when population converges **(Goldberg D. E., 1989)**. Population size is set to 1000 **(Michalewicz Z., 1996)**. With smaller populations, Evolutionary Algorithm did not work that well. When Evolutionary Algorithm stopped, its best solution is optimized by 2opt algorithm. The results for FSOM, Evolutionary Algorithm and 2opt Algorithm are shown in the Table 1. For Evolutionary Algorithm there are 20 runs of algorithm for sets EIL51, EIL101 and RAND100. For other sets Evolutionary Algorithm is run twice. The optimum solutions for instances taken from TSPLIB are already present there and optimum solutions for random instances are calculated from empirical relation described above.

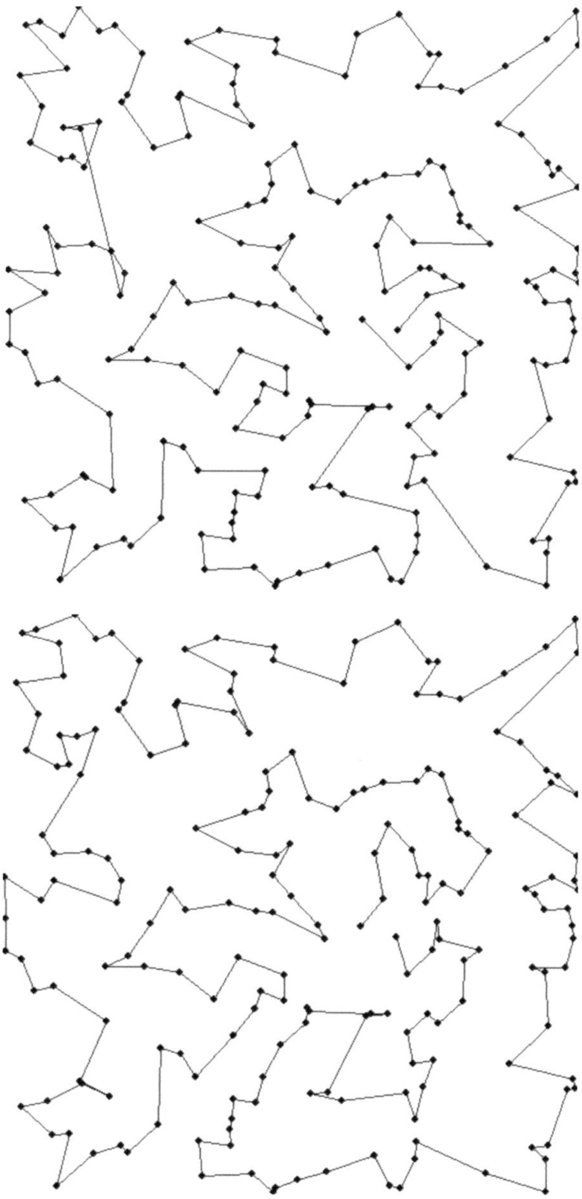

Fig. 7. Self Organizing Map solution without 2opt optimization (top). There are two local loops on left. First and last neuron can be seen in the middle. They are not connected in figure but distance between them is also computed. The same solution improved by 2opt (bottom). Loops on left have been erased. Additional changes can be observed

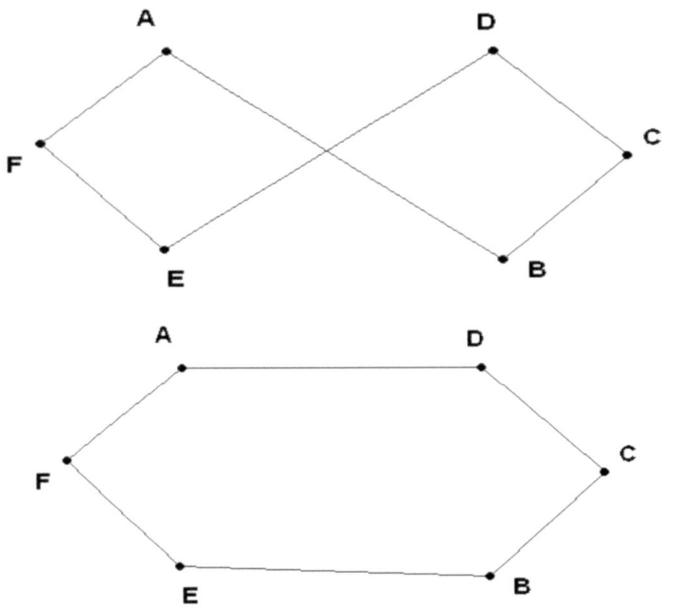

Fig. 8. 2opt optimization. If there is a cycle (A, B, C, D, E, F) and path (B, C, D) is reversed, then new cycle is (A, D, C, B, E, F).

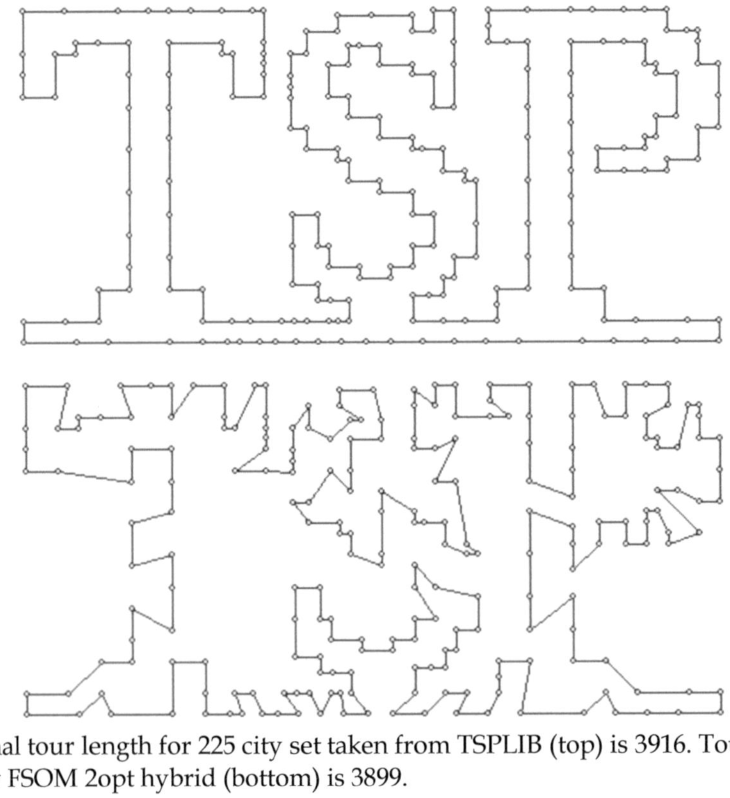

Fig. 9. Optimal tour length for 225 city set taken from TSPLIB (top) is 3916. Tour length generated by FSOM 2opt hybrid (bottom) is 3899.

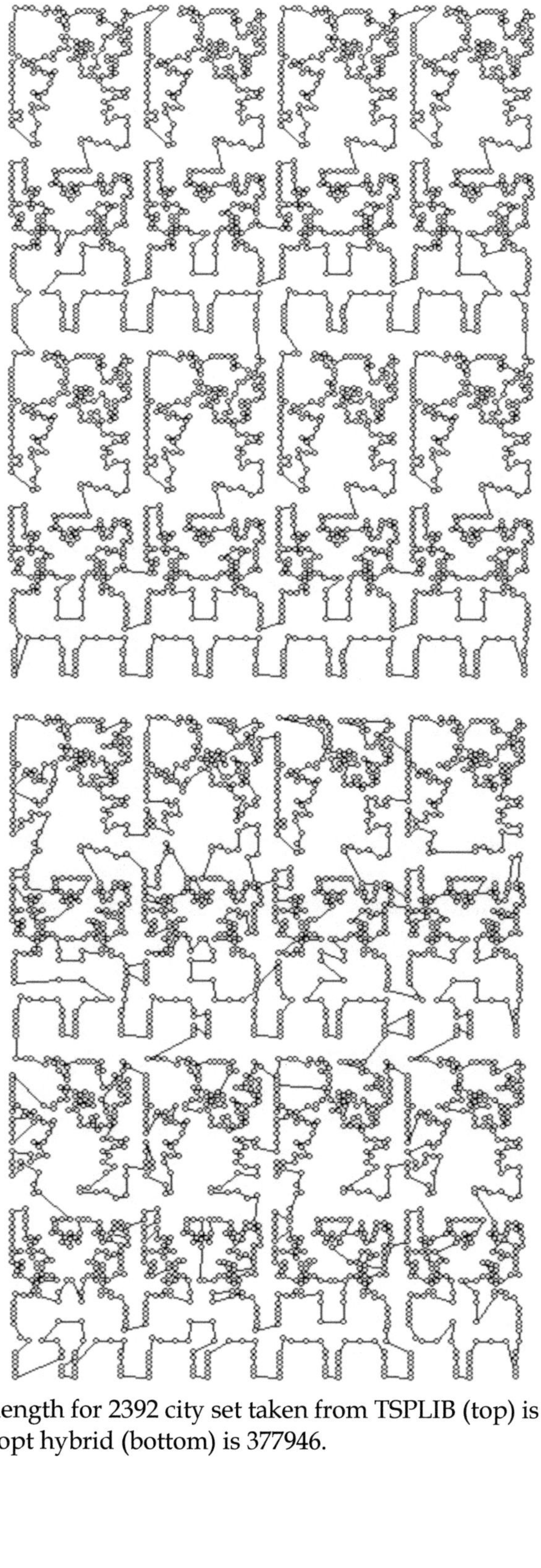

Fig. 10. Optimal tour length for 2392 city set taken from TSPLIB (top) is 378037. Tour length generated by FSOM 2opt hybrid (bottom) is 377946.

The experiments show that Evolutionary Algorithm **(Goldberg D. E., 1989; Deb K., 2001)** finds better solutions for instances with up to 100 cities. Both average and best results are better than FSOM. For city sets with 50 or less, Evolutionary Algorithm finds optimum in every execution. The results for 225 cities are nearly comparable for both algorithms. However, for larger amount of cities viz. 442 and more FSOM yields better solutions. With more number of cities search space increases significantly and Evolutionary Algorithm needs bigger population size. For TSP225 with population size of 1000 Evolutionary Algorithm result is 4044, but when population size is expanded to 3000 a tour with length 3949 is found which is comparable to FSOM solution. This underlines the fact that when Evolutionary Algorithm is used one can always expand population size **(Michalewicz Z., 1996)**, so the algorithm has greater chance of achieving good results. However, algorithm is much slower then.
It is interesting to compare FSOM algorithm to other Non-Evolutionary approaches **(Chaudhuri A., 2007)**. One of the best TSP algorithms which is appreciably fast is Lin-Kerninghan Algorithm **(Lin S. & Kernighan B. W., 1973)**. The algorithm is run 20 times on each city set. Average results and times are shown in Table 2 which indicate that Lin-Kerninghan is comparable to that of FSOM. There is no considerable difference in time for small 51-city instance which is 0.012 seconds for Lin-Kerninghan and 0.024 seconds for FSOM. On other hand, for 2392-city instance Lin-Kerninghan needed just 0.719 seconds and FSOM required almost 7 seconds. This is because FSOM is optimized by 2opt which is the slowest part of this algorithm. When average results are compared it can be easily seen that Lin-Kerninghan is superior in all cases. The higher is number of cities, bigger the difference between both algorithms. FSOM is also used to generate initial population for Evolutionary Algorithm. Such initialization takes only a fraction of time needed for Evolutionary Algorithm to finish because FSOM is fast algorithm. In this case, Evolutionary Algorithm tends to converge much faster and finally it did not improve the best solution generated by FSOM alone. It seems that all initial solutions are very similar to each other, thus population diversity is low and so the Evolutionary Algorithm lost all exploration abilities.

6. Conclusion

The experimental results indicate that FSOM 2opt hybrid algorithm generates appreciably better results compared to both Evolutionary and Lin Kerninghan Algorithm for TSP as number of cities increases. There are some parameters such as $\eta, \Delta\eta$, $\Delta\lambda$ that can be optimized. Experiments with other Self Organizing networks should be performed and gaussian neighborhood and conscience mechanism can be applied which can improve TSP solutions generated by ANN **(Christof T. & Reinelt G., 1995)**. Some other optimization algorithms may be used other than 2opt algorithm which gives better results. There are many algorithms that solve permutation problems. Evolutionary Algorithms have many different operators that work with permutations. Enhanced edge recombination is one of the best operators for TSP **(Goldberg D. E., 1989; Deb K., 2001)**. However, it is proved that other permutation operators which are worse for TSP than enhanced edge recombination are actually better for other permutation problems like warehouse or shipping scheduling applications **(Korte B. H. & Vygen J., 2008)**. Therefore, it might be possible that FSOM 2opt hybrid might work better for other permutation problems than for TSP.

Instances	Optimum	FSOM			Evolutionary Algorithm			2opt Algorithm		
		Average Result	Best Result	Best Time	Average Result	Best Result	Best Time	Average Result	Best Result	Best Time
EIL51	426	435	428	0.024	428.2	426	10	537	524	1.44
EIL101	629	654	640	0.069	653.3	639	75	869	789	2.96
TSP225	3916	3909	3899	0.254		4044	871		4679	6.7
PCB442	50778	50635	50537	0.407		55657	10395		56686	12.37
PR1002	259045	259024	259010	1.999		286908	25639		292069	29
PR2392	378037	377969	377946	7.967						
RAND200	3851.81	3844	3769	0.131	3931.4	3822	69.6	4344	4037	5.9
RAND700	8203.73	8199	8069	0.824		9261	11145		14116	17.8
RAND1200	11475.66	11469	11437	2.311		12858	56456		24199	37

Table 1. Comparison of FSOM, Evolutionary Algorithm and 2opt Algorithm

Instances	Optimum	Lin Kerninghan	
		Average Result	Average Time
EIL51	426	427.4	0.012
EIL101	629	640	0.039
PCB442	50778	51776.5	0.137
PR2392	378037	389413	0.719

Table 2. Results for Lin-Kerninghan Algorithm

7. References

Applegate, D. L., Bixby, R. E., Chvâtal, V. & Cook, W. J. (1995). *Finding cuts in TSP (A preliminary report)*,Technical Report DIMACS 95-05, Rutgers University, Piscataway, New Jersey.

Applegate, D. L., Bixby, R. E., Chvâtal, V. & Cook, W. J. (2006). *The Traveling Salesman Problem: AComputational Study*, Princeton University Press, Princeton, New Jersey.

Arbib, M. (2003). *The Handbook of Brain Theory and Neural Networks*, Second Edition, The MIT Press, Cambridge, Massachusettes.

Aarts, E. H. & Lenstra, J. K. (2003). *Local Search in Combinatorial Optimization*, Princeton University Press, Princeton, New Jersey.

Bezdek, J. C. (1981). *Pattern Recognition with Fuzzy Objective Function Algorithms*, Plenum Press, New York.

Bishop, C. M. (1995). *Neural Networks for Pattern Recognition*, Clarendon Press, Oxford.

Burke, L. I. (1994). Neural Methods for the Traveling Salesman Problem: Insights from Operations Research. *Neural Networks*, Vol. 7, No. 4, pp. 681–690.

Chaudhuri, A. (2007). A Dynamic Algorithm for looking Traveling Salesman Problem as a Fuzzy Integer Linear Programming Problem in an optimal way. *Proceedings of International Conference on Information Technology*, Haldia Institute Technology, India, Vol. 1, pp. 246–251.

Christof, T. & Reinelt, G. (1995). Parallel Programming and Applications, In: *Parallel Cutting Plane Generation for TSP*, P. Fritzson, L. Finmo, (Editors), pp. 163–169, IOS Press.

Cormen, T. H., Leiserson, C. E., Rivest, R. L. & Stein, C. (2001). *Introduction to Algorithms*, Second Edition, MIT Press Cambridge, Massachusetts.

Deb, K. (2001). *Multi-Objective Optimization using Evolutionary Algorithms*, John Wiley and Sons, New York.

Dittenbach, M., Merkel, D. & Rauber, A. (2000). The growing Hierarchical Self Organizing Map. *Proceedings of the International Joint Conference on Neural Networks*, vol. VI, pp.15–19.

Dunn, J. C. (1973). A Fuzzy relative of ISODATA Process and its use in detecting compact well separated Clusters. Journal of Cybernetics, Vol. 3, pp. 32-57.

Fritzke, B. (1994). Growing Cell Structure — A Self Organizing Neural Network for Unsupervised and Supervised Learning. *Neural Networks*, Vol. 7, No. 9, pp. 1441–1460.

Garey, M. & Johnson, D. (1990). *Computers and Intractability: A Guide to the Theory of NP-Completeness*, W. H. Freeman and Company, San Francisco.

Goldberg, D. E. (1989). *Genetic Algorithms in Search, Optimization and Machine Learning*, Reading, Mass, Addison Wesley.

Hansen, M. P. (2000). Use of Substitute Scalarizing Functions to Guide a Local Search Based Heuristics: The Case of MOTSP. *Journal of Heuristics*, Vol. 6, No. 3, pp. 419–431.

Haykin, S. (2008). *Neural Networks and Learning Machines*, Third Edition, Prentice Hall.

Hertz, J., Krogh, A. & Palmer, R. G. (1991). *Introduction to the Theory of Neural Computation*, Addison Wesley, Massachuttes.

Jang, J. S. R., Sun, C. T., Mizutani, E. (1997). *Neuro-Fuzzy and Soft Computing. A Computational Approach to Learning and Machine Intelligence*, Prentice Hall.

Johnson, D. S., McGeoch, L. A. & Rothberg, E. E. (2000). Asymptotic Experimental Analysis for the Held-Karp Traveling Salesman Bound. *Proceedings of ACM-SIAM symposium on Discrete Algorithms*.

Junfei Q., Honggui, H. & Yanmei, J. (2007). An Adaptive Growing Self Organizing Fuzzy Neural Network. *Proceedings of 5th International Conference on Wavelet Analysis and Pattern Recognition 2007*, pp. 711–715.

Kohonen, T. (2001). *Self-Organizing Maps*, Third Edition, Springer Verlag, Berlin.

Korte, B. H. & Vygen, J. (2008). *Combinatorial Optimization: Theory and Algorithms*, Algorithms and Combinatorics, Fourth Edition, Springer Verlag.

Laporte, G. (2010). A Concise Guide to Traveling Salesman Problem. *Journal of the Operational Research Society*, Vol. 61, No. 1, pp. 35–40.

Lin S., Kernighan B. W. (1973). An effective Heuristic for Traveling Salesman Problem. *Operations Research*, Vol. 21, pp. 498–516.

Michalewicz, Z. (1996). *Genetic Algorithms + Data Structures = Evolution Programs*, Springer Verlag.

Rahendi, N. T A. & Atoum, J. (2009). Solving the Traveling Salesman Problem using New Operators in Genetic Algorithms. *American Journal of Applied Sciences*, Vol. 6, No. 8, pp. 1586–1590.

Reinelt G. (1991). TSPLIB - A Traveling Salesman Problem Library. *ORSA Journal on Computing*, Vol. 3, pp. 376–384.

Sentiono R. (2001). Feed-forward Neural Network Construction using Cross Validation. *Neural Computation*, Vol. 13, No. 12, pp. 2865–2877.

Tao T., Gan J. R. & Yao L. S. (1992). Application of Fuzzy Neural Computing in Circuit Partitioning. *Chinese Journal of Compuing*, Vol. 15, No. 9, pp. 640–647.

Xu, W. & Tsai, W. T. (1991). Effective Neural Algorithm for the Traveling Salesman Problem. *Neural Networks*, Vol. 4, No. 2, pp. 193–205.

Zadeh, L. A. (1994). Fuzzy Logic, Neural Networks and Soft Computing. *Communications of the ACM*, Vol. 37, No. 3, pp. 77–84.

13

Hybrid Metaheuristics Using Reinforcement Learning Applied to Salesman Traveling Problem

Francisco C. de Lima Junior[1], Adrião D. Doria Neto[2] and Jorge Dantas de Melo[3]
University of State of Rio Grande do Norte,
Federal University of Rio Grande do Norte Natal - RN,
Brazil

1. Introduction

Techniques of optimization known as metaheuristics have achieved success in the resolution of many problems classified as NP-Hard. These methods use non deterministic approaches that reach very good solutions which, however, don't guarantee the determination of the global optimum. Beyond the inherent difficulties related to the complexity that characterizes the optimization problems, the metaheuristics still face the dilemma of exploration/exploitation, which consists of choosing between a greedy search and a wider exploration of the solution space. A way to guide such algorithms during the searching of better solutions is supplying them with more knowledge of the problem through the use of a intelligent agent, able to recognize promising regions and also identify when they should diversify the direction of the search. This way, this work proposes the use of Reinforcement Learning technique - Q-learning Algorithm (Sutton & Barto, 1998) - as exploration/exploitation strategy for the metaheuristics GRASP (Greedy Randomized Adaptive Search Procedure) (Feo & Resende, 1995) and Genetic Algorithm (R. Haupt & S. E. Haupt, 2004). The GRASP metaheuristic uses Q-learning instead of the traditional greedy-random algorithm in the construction phase. This replacement has the purpose of improving the quality of the initial solutions that are used in the local search phase of the GRASP, and also provides for the metaheuristic an adaptive memory mechanism that allows the reuse of good previous decisions and also avoids the repetition of bad decisions. In the Genetic Algorithm, the Q-learning algorithm was used to generate an initial population of high fitness, and after a determined number of generations, where the rate of diversity of the population is less than a certain limit L, it also was applied to supply one of the parents to be used in the genetic crossover operator. Another significant change in the hybrid genetic algorithm is an interactive/cooperative process, where the Q-learning algorithm receives an additional update in the matrix of Q-values based on the current best solution of the Genetic Algorithm. The computational experiments presented in this work compares the results obtained with the implementation of traditional versions of GRASP metaheuristic and Genetic Algorithm, with those obtained using the proposed hybrid methods. Both algorithms had been applied successfully to the symmetrical Traveling Salesman Problem, which was modeled as a Markov decision process.

2. Theoretical foundation

2.1 GRASP metaheuristic

The Metaheuristic Greedy Randomized Adaptive Search Procedure - GRASP (Feo & Resende, 1995), is a multi-start iterative process, where each iteration consists of two phases: constructive and local search. The constructive phase builds a feasible solution, whose neighbourhood is investigated until a local minimum is found during the local search phase. The best overall solution is kept as the final solution.

Each iteration of the construction phase let the set of candidate elements be formed by all elements that can be incorporated in to the partial solution under construction without destroying its feasibility. The selection of the next element for incorporation is determined by the evaluation of all candidate elements according to a greedy evaluation function $g(c)$, where c is a candidate element to compose the solution.

The evaluation of the elements by function $g(c)$ leads to the creation of a restricted candidate list - *RCL* formed by the best elements, i.e., those whose incorporation to the current partial solution results in the smallest incremental cost (this is the greedy aspect of the algorithm in the minimization case). Once the selected element is incorporated into the partial solution, the candidate list is updated and the incremental costs are revaluated (this is the adaptive aspect of the heuristic).

The probabilistic aspect of GRASP is given by the random choice of one of the elements of the *RCL*, not necessarily the best, except in the case of the *RCL*, which has unitary size. In this case, the selection criterion is reduced to the greedy criterion. The improvement phase typically consists of a local search procedure aimed at improving the solution obtained in the constructive phase, since this solution may not represent a global optimum.

In GRASP metaheuristics, it is always important to use a local search to improve the solutions obtained in the constructive phase. The local search phase works in an iterative way, replacing successively the current solution by a better one from its neighbourhood. Thus, the success of the local search algorithm depends on the quality of the neighbourhood chosen (Feo & Resende, 1995). This dependence can be considered a disadvantage of the GRASP metaheuristic.

The GRASP metaheuristic presents advantages and disadvantages:

Advantages:

- Simple implementation: greedy algorithm and local search;
- Some parameters require adjustments: restrictions on the candidate list and the number of iterations.

Disadvantages:

- It depends on good initial solutions: since it is based only on randomization between iterations, each iteration benefits from the quality of the initial solution;
- It does not use memory of the information collected during the search.

This work explores the disadvantages of the GRASP metaheuristic replacing the random-greedy algorithm of the constructive phase by constructive algorithms that use the Q-learning algorithm as an exploitation/exploration strategy aimed at building better initial solutions. The pseudo code of the traditional GRASP algorithm is presented in the Fig. 1, where *D* corresponds to the distance matrix for the *TSP* instances, α_g[1] is the control parameter of the restricted candidate list - *RCL*, and *Nm* the maximal number of interactions.

Algorithm 1 Traditional GRASP Algorithm

```
procedure GRASP(D, α_g, Nm)
    f(S*) ← +∞
    while i ≤ Nm do
        S ← RandomGreedy(D, α_g)
        S' ← LocalSearch(S, Near(S))
        if f(S') < f(S*) then
            S* = S'
        end if
        i ← i + 1
    end while
    return S*
end procedure
```

Fig. 1. Traditional GRASP Algorithm

In the GRASP metaheuristic, the restricted candidate list, specifically the α_g parameter, is practically the only parameter to be adjusted. The effect of the choice of α_g value, in terms of quality solution and diversity during the construction phase of the GRASP, is discussed by Feo and Resende (Feo & Resende, 1995). Prais and Ribeiro (Prais & Ribeiro, 1998) proposed a new procedure called reactive GRASP, for which the α_g parameter of the restricted candidate list is self-adjusted according to the quality of the solution previously found.

In the reactive GRASP algorithm, the α_g value is randomly selected from a discreet set containing *m* predetermined feasible values:

$$\Psi = \left\{ \alpha_g^1, \ldots, \alpha_g^m \right\} \tag{1}$$

The use of different α_g values at different iterations allows the building of different Restrict Candidate Lists - *RCL*, possibly allowing the generation of distinct solutions that would not be built through the use of a single fixed α_g value.

The choice of α_g in the set Ψ is made using a probability distribution p_i, $i=1,\ldots,m$, which is periodically updated by the so-called absolute qualification rule (Prais & Ribeiro, 1998), which is based on the average value of the solutions obtained with each α_g value and is computed as follows:

$$q_i = \frac{(F(S^*))^\delta}{A_i} \tag{2}$$

for all $i=1,\ldots,m$, where $F(S^*)$ is the value of the overall best solution already found and δ is used to explore the updated values of probability p_i. Using q_i, the probability distribution is given by:

---

1 The index g is used here to differ from the αg parameter used in the Q-learning algorithm in this paper.

$$p_i = q_i \Big/ \sum_{j=1}^{m} q_j \tag{3}$$

In this paper, the reactive GRASP is presented as a more robust version of the traditional GRASP algorithm, and its performance will be compared with the new method proposed.

2.2 Genetic algorithm

Genetic algorithms (GA) are based on a biological metaphor: they see the resolution of a problem as a competition among a population of evolving candidate problem solutions. A "fitness" function evaluates each solution to decide whether it will contribute to the next generation of solutions. Then, through analogous operations to gene transfer in sexual reproduction, the algorithm creates a new population of candidate solutions. At the beginning of a run of a genetic algorithm, a large population of random chromosomes is created. Each one, when decoded, will represent a different solution to the problem at hand. Some of the advantages of a GA (R. Haupt & S. E. Haupt, 2004) include the following:

- It optimizes with continuous or discrete variables;
- Does not require derivative information;
- Simultaneously searches through wide sampling of the cost surface;
- Deals with a large number of variables and is well suited for parallel computers;
- Optimizes variables with extremely complex cost surfaces (they can jump out of a local minimum);
- Provides a list of optimum variables, not just a single solution;
- May encode the variables so that the optimization is done with the encoded variables; and
- Works with numerically generated data, experimental data, or analytical functions.

A typical genetic algorithm presents the following operators:

- Crossover - this operator is used to vary the population of the chromosomes from one generation to the next. It selects the two fittest chromosomes in the population and produces a number of offspring. There are several crossover techniques; in this work, we will use the one-point crossover.
- Selection - this operator replicates the most successful solutions found in a population at a rate proportional to their relative quality, which is determined by the fitness function. In this paper we will use the roulette wheel selection technique for this operator.
- Mutation - used to maintain genetic diversity from one generation of a population of chromosomes to the next. It selects a position of an offspring chromosome with small probability and changes the value based on the problem model; for example, in this work, the mutation operator modifies the offspring chromosome simply by changing the position of a gene.

The pseudo code of the standard genetic algorithm is summarized in the Fig. 2, where *Tc* is the crossover rate or parameter that determines the rate at which the crossover operator is applied, *Tm* is the equivalent for the mutation rate, *Tp* is the population size (number of chromosomes) and *MaxG* the number of generations used in the experiment.

Algorithm 2 Genetic Algorithm

```
procedure GENETIC(Tc, Tm, Tp, MaxG)
    Pop ← GeneratePopulation(Tp)
    Pop ← Evaluation(Pop)
    for i = 1...MaxG do
        Pop ← Selection(Pop)
        With probability Tc do:
        Pop ← Crossover(Pop)
        With probability Tm do:
        Pop ← Mutation(Pop)
    end for
    return the best solution in Pop
end procedure
```

Fig. 2. Traditional Genetic Algorithm

2.3 Reinforcement learning

The reinforcement learning is characterized by the existence of an agent which should learn the behaviours through trial-and-error interactions in a dynamic environment. In the interaction process the learner agent, at each discrete time step t receives from the environment some denominated representation state. Starting from state $s_t \in S$ (S is the set of possible states), the learner agent chooses an action $a_t \in A$ (A is the set of actions available in state s_t). When the learner agent chooses an action, receives a numerical reward r_{t+1}, which represent the quality of the action selected and the environment response to that action presenting s_{t+1}, a new state of the environment.

The agent's goal is to maximize the total reward it receives along the process, so the agent has to exploit not only what it already knows in order to obtain the reward, but also explore the environment in order to select better action in the future (Sutton & Barto, 1998).

There are some classes of methods for solving the reinforcement learning problem, such as: Dynamic Programming, Monte Carlo methods and Temporal-difference learning. Each of these methods presents its characteristics. Dynamic programming methods are well developed mathematically, but require a complete and accurate model of the environment. Monte Carlo methods require no model and are very simple conceptually, but are not suited for step-by-step incremental computation. Temporal-difference methods do not require a complete model and are fully incremental, but it's more complex to mathematical analysis. Based in the characteristics and need of the problem in hand, this work will use a well-know Temporal-difference technique denominated Q-learning algorithm, which will be presented in details in the next section.

2.3.1 The Q-learning algorithm

Not all reinforcement learning algorithms need a complete modelling of the environment. Some of them do not need to have all the transition probabilities and expected return values for all the transitions of the possible environmental states. This is the case of the reinforcement learning techniques based on temporal differences (Sutton & Barto, 1998). One of these techniques is the well-known Q-learning algorithm (Watkins, 1989), considered one of the most important breakthroughs in reinforcement learning, since its convergence for optimum Q-values does not depend on the policy applied. The updated expression of the Q value in the Q-learning algorithm is:

$$Q(s,a) = (1-\alpha_q)Q(s,a) + \alpha_q[r + \gamma \max_{a \in A} Q(s',a)] \tag{4}$$

where s is the current state, a is the action carried out in the state s, r is the immediate reward received for executing a in s, s' is the new state, γ is a discount factor ($0 \leq \gamma \geq 1$), and α_q, ($0 < \alpha_q < 1$) is the learning factor.

An important characteristic of this algorithm is that the choice of actions that will be executed during the iterative process of function Q can be made through any exploration/exploitation criterion, even in a random way. A widely used technique for such a choice is the so-called *ε-greedy* exploration, which consists of an agent to execute the action with the highest Q value with probability $1\text{-}\varepsilon$, and choose a random action with probability ε.

The Q-learning was the first reinforcement learning method to provide strong proof of convergence. Watkins showed that if each pair state-action is visited an infinite number of times and with an adjusted value, the value function Q will converge with probability 1 to Q^*. The pseudo code of the Q-learning algorithm is presented in the Fig. 3, where, r is the reward matrix, ε is the parameter of the *ε-greedy* police.

Algorithm 3 Q-learning Algorithm

```
procedure QLEARNING(r, α_q, ε, γ, NEp)
    Initialize Q(s, a)
    repeat
        Initialize s
        repeat
            Select a using the ε − greedy rule
            Observe the values of r and s'
            Q(s, a) ← Update(Q(s, a))  ▷ (Eq. 3)
            s = s'
        until number of episodes = NEp
    until the convergence is gotten
    return Q(s, a)
end procedure
```

Fig. 3. Q-learning Algorithm

3. Proposed hybrid methods

Metaheuristics are approximate methods that depend on good exploration/exploitation strategies based on previous knowledge of the problem and are can guide the search for an optimum solution in order avoiding local minimum. Good strategies (or good heuristics) alternate adequately between exploration and exploitation. In other words they maintain the balance between these two processes during the search for an optimum solution. The methods presented here are hybrid since they use a well-known reinforcement learning method - Q-learning algorithm - as an exploration/exploitation mechanism for GRASP and genetic algorithm metaheuristics (Lima, F. C., et al., 2007).

The Fig. 4, presents a framework of the proposed hybrid methods:

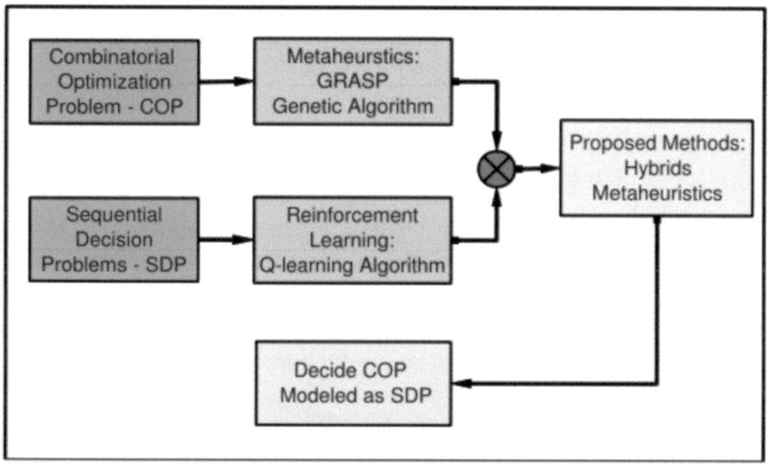

Fig. 4. Framework of the proposed hybrid methods.

The proposed methods in this section are applied to solve the symmetric traveling salesman problem - *TSP* and are modelled as a Reinforced Learning Problem.

3.1 The traveling salesman problem modeled as a sequential decision problem

The traveling salesman problem can be described as a sequential decision process, represented by the quintuplet $M=\{T, S, A, R, P\}$, in at least two different ways. For example, consider a model where the set of states S is the set of all possible solutions for *TSP* (Ramos et al, 2003). The model in this study has a high-dimensional inconvenience S, since *TSP* has a higher number of possible solutions in the symmetric case $(n-1)!/2$.

An alternative to model *TSP* as a sequential decision problem is to consider that S is formed by all the cities to solve *TSP*. In this new model, the cardinality of S is equal to the instance size of the problem. This lowers the risk of S suffering the "curse of dimensionality". In this study *TSP* is modelled as a sequential decision problem based on this second alternative.

To better understand the proposed model, consider an example of *TSP* with 5 cities shown in graph $G(V, E, W)$ of Fig. 5. V is the set of vertices, E is the set of arcs between the vertices and W is the weight associated to each arc. In graph $G(V,E,W)$, a_{12} corresponds to visiting the "city" s_2 derived from s_1, and the values associated to each arc (number between parentheses) corresponds to the distance between the "cities".

Considering graph $G(V,E,W)$, the quintuplet $M = \{T, S, A, R, P\}$, representing a sequential decision process, can be defined by *TSP* as follows:

- T: The set of decision instants is denoted by $T = \{1, 2, 3, 4, 5\}$, where the cardinality of T corresponds to the number of cities that compose a route to *TSP*.
- S: The set of states is represented by $S = \{s_1, s_2, s_3, s_4, s_5\}$, where each state s_i, $i=1,\dots,5$ corresponds to a city[2] at a route to *TSP*.
- A: The set of possible actions is denoted by:

[2] From this point onwards the expression "city" or "cities" indicates the association between a city of *TSP* and a state (or states) from the environment.

$$A = A(s_1) \cup A(s_2) \cup A(s_3) \cup A(s_4) \cup A(s_5)$$

$$A = \{a_{12}, a_{13}, a_{14}, a_{15}\} \cup \{a_{21}, a_{23}, a_{24}, a_{25}\} \cup \{a_{31}, a_{32}, a_{34}, a_{35}\} \cup \{a_{41}, a_{42}, a_{43}, a_{45}\} \cup \{a_{51}, a_{52}, a_{53}, a_{54}\}$$

$$A = \{a_{12}, a_{13}, a_{14}, a_{15}, a_{21}, a_{23}, a_{24}, a_{25}, a_{31}, a_{32}, a_{34}, a_{35}, a_{41}, a_{42}, a_{43}, a_{45}, a_{51}, a_{52}, a_{53}, a_{54}\} \tag{5}$$

It is important to emphasize that owing to the restriction of *TSP*, some actions may not be available when constructing a solution. To understand it more clearly, consider the following partial solution for *TSP*:

$$Sol_p : s_2 \rightarrow s_3 \rightarrow s_5 \tag{6}$$

where the decision process is in the decision instant *3* and state s_5. In this case the actions available are $A(s_5)=\{a_{51}, a_{54}\}$, since the "cities" s_2 (action choice a_{52}) and s_3 (action choice a_{53}) are not permitted to avoid repetitions in the route.

- R: S × A → ℜ: Expected Return. In TSP, elements rij are calculated using the distance between the "cities" si and sj. The return should be a reward that encourages the choice of "city" sj closest to si. Since TSP is a minimization problem, a trivial method to calculate the reward is to consider it inversely proportional to the traveling cost between the cities. That is:

$$r_{ij} = \frac{1}{d_{ij}} \tag{7}$$

where $d_{ij} > 0$ is a real number that represents the distance from "city" s_i to "city" s_j. Using the weights from the graph in Fig. 5, R is represented by:

$$R = \begin{bmatrix} 0 & 1/4 & 1/6 & 1/7 & 1/3 \\ 1/4 & 0 & 1/3 & 1/9 & 1/10 \\ 1/6 & 1/3 & 0 & 1/2 & 1/8 \\ 1/7 & 1/9 & 1/2 & 0 & 1/5 \\ 1/3 & 1/10 & 1/8 & 1/5 & 0 \end{bmatrix} \tag{8}$$

- P: S × A × S → [1, 0]: The function that defines the probability transition between states s∈S, where the elements pij(sj|si, aij) correspond to the probability of reaching "city" sj when in "city" si and choosing action aij. The values of pij are denoted by:

$$p_{ij}(s_j \mid s_i, a_{ij}) = \begin{cases} 1 & \text{if } s_j \text{ not visited} \\ 0 & \text{otherwise} \end{cases} \tag{9}$$

The quintuplet *M = {T, S, A, R, P}* defined in the graph of the Fig. 5. can be defined with no loss of generality for a generic graph *G(V, E, W)*, (with $|V|=N$) where a Hamiltonian cycle of cardinality *N* is found.
An optimum policy for *TSP*, given generic graph *G(V, E, W)*, should determine the sequence of visits to each "city" s_i, $i=1, 2,...,N$ to achieve the best possible sum of returns. In this case, the problem has a finite-time horizon, sets of states, and discrete and finite actions.

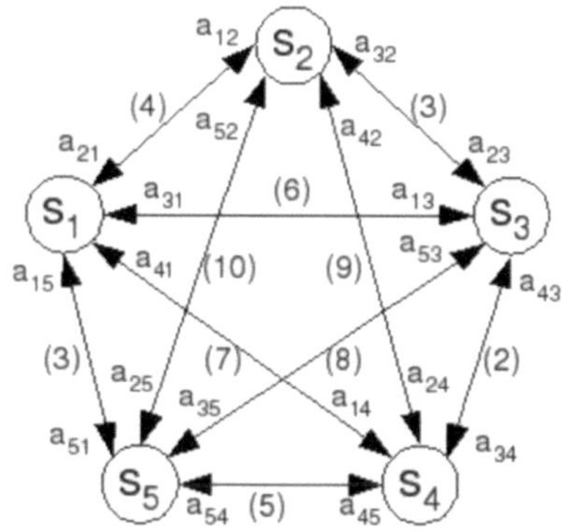

Fig. 5. Complete Graph, instance of the *TSP* with 5 cities.

3.2 The Markov property

In a sequential decision process, the environmental response in view of the action choice at any time *t+1* depends on the history of events at a time before *t+1*. This means that the dynamic of environmental behaviour will be defined by complete probability distribution (Sutton & Barto, 1998):

$$P_{ss'}^{a} = \Pr\{s_{t+1} = s', r_{t+1} = r \mid s_t, a_t, r_t, s_{t-1}, a_{t-1}, r_{t-1}, \ldots, s_1, a_1, r_1, s_0, a_0\} \quad (10)$$

where *Pr* represents the probability of s_{t+1} being s', for all *s, a, r,* states, actions and past reinforcements $s_t, a_t, r_t, \ldots, r_1, s_0, a_0$.

However, if the sequential process obeys the Markov property, the environmental response at *t+1* only depends on information for state *s* and action *a* available at *t*. In other words the environment dynamic is specified by:

$$P_{ss'}^{a} = \Pr\{s_{t+1} = s', r_{t+1} = r \mid s_t, a_t\} \quad (11)$$

which qualifies it as a Markov decision process - *MDP* (Puterman, 1994).

In the traveling salesman problem, an action is chosen (deciding which city to place on the route under construction) from state s_t (the actual city in the route under construction) based on the instance between this city and the others. It is important to note that, to avoid violating the restriction imposed by *TSP* (not to repeat cities on the route), actions that would lead to states already visited should not be available in state s_t. In this context, *TSP* is a Markov decision process since all the information necessary to make the decision at *t* is available at state s_t. A list of actions not chosen during route construction could be included in state s_t to provide information on the actions available in the state.

The Markov property is fundamentally important in characterizing the traveling salesman problem as a reinforcement learning task, since the convergence of methods used in this study depends on its verification in the proposed model.

The restriction imposed on *TSP* creates an interesting characteristic in the Markov decision process associated to the problem. The fact that the sets of available actions *A(s)* for state *s* at each time instant *t* vary during the learning process, implies changes in the strategies for choosing actions in any state s_t. This means that modifications will occur in the politics used during the learning process. Fig. 6 demonstrates this characteristic.

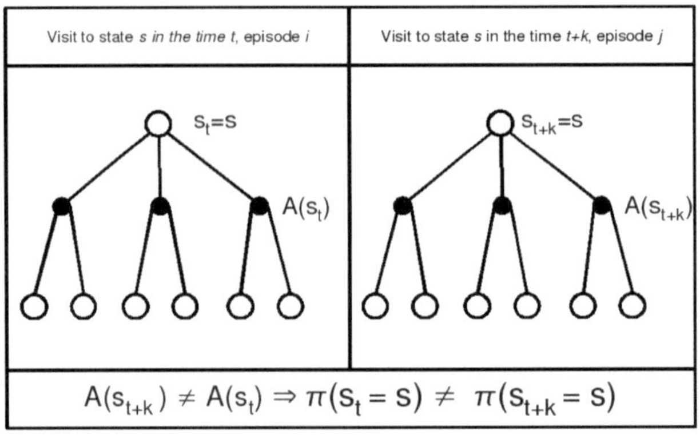

Fig. 6. Changes in the number of actions available during the decision process.

To understand more clearly, consider the following partial solution for *TSP*: The chart in Fig. 6, can be interpreted as follows: A route to *TSP* is constructed in each episode of the learning process. During construction of a route to *TSP*, at each decision instant *t*, a state is visited $s \in S$ and an action choice $a \in A$ is made. Since the set *A(s)* of actions available for state *s* varies along time, in an episode *i* the set of actions available for state s_t at instant *t* can be different of the actions available in the same state *s* at time instant *t+k* and episode *j*. This confirms that the Markov decision process associated to the traveling salesman problem can be modelled has a non-stationary policy.

3.3 The Q-learning algorithm implemented

Since the methods presented in this section use Q-learning, this section presents details such as: action selection policies and convergence of the algorithm when applied to the proposed problem.

3.3.1 Action selection policies for the Q-learning algorithm

When solving a reinforcement learning Problem, an action selection policy aims to determine the behaviour of the agent so that it alternates adequately between using obtained knowledge and acquiring new knowledge. This optimizes the exploration/exploitation process of the search space. More than one action selection policy is used for Q-learning to determine which policy is most appropriate to implement the proposed hybrid methods.

- The *ε-greedy* policy chooses the action with the highest expected value, compatibility defined by *(1-ε)* and random action with a probability of *ε*. Mathematically, given the matrix of Q-values *Q(s, a)*, the greedy action *a** is obtained for state *s* as follows:

$$
\begin{aligned}
a^* &= \max_{a \in A(s)} Q(s,a) \\
\pi(s,a^*) &= 1 - \varepsilon + \frac{\varepsilon}{|A(s)|} \\
\pi(s,a) &= \frac{\varepsilon}{|A(s)|} \quad \forall a \in A(s) - \{a^*\}
\end{aligned}
\tag{12}
$$

where $|A(s)|$ corresponds to the number of possible actions from s, and ε is the control parameter between greed and randomness. The restriction in Eq. 12 allows Q-learning to explore the state space of the problem and is needed to find the optimum control policy.

- The *Adaptive ε-greedy* Policy is similar to the *ε-greedy* policy described. In other words, it allows the action with the highest expected value to be chosen, with probability defined by $(1 - \varepsilon)$ and a random action with probability ε. It is different and also "Adaptive", since the value of ε suffers exponential decay calculated by:

$$\varepsilon = \max\left\{v_i, v_f.b^k\right\} \tag{13}$$

where k is the episode counter of Q-learning, b is the closest value of 1 and $v_i < v_f \in [0,1]$. The algorithm initially uses high values for ε (close to v_f) and, as the value of k increases, choice ε is directed to lower values (closer to v_i). The objective is to allow more random choices to be made and to explore more the greedy aspect as the number of episodes increases.

- Based on *Visitor Count* Policy chooses the action based on a technique called Reinforcement Comparison (Sutton & Barto, 1998). In this technique actions are chosen based on the principle that actions followed by large rewards are preferred to those followed by small rewards. To define a ``large reward'', a comparison is made with a standard reward known as a reference reward.

The objective of the proposed policy is similar to the reinforcement comparison technique. However, choosing preferred actions is based on the visitor count to the states affected by these actions. That is, the most visited states indicate preferred actions in detriment to actions that lead to states with a lower number of visits. When the preference measurement for actions is known, the probability of action selection can be determined as follows:

$$\pi_t(a) = P_r\left\{a_t = a\right\} = \frac{e^{p_{t-1}(a)}}{\sum_b e^{p_{t-1}(b)}} \tag{14}$$

where $\pi_t(a)$ denotes the probability of selecting action a at step t and $p_t(a)$ is the preference for action a at time t. This is calculated by:

$$p_{t+1}(a_t) = p_t(a_t) + \beta(N_v(s, a_t) / N_{Ep}) \tag{15}$$

where s is the state affected by selecting action a at step t, $N_v(s, a_t)$ is the number of visits to state s, NEp is the total number of episodes and $\beta \in [0,1]$ is the control parameter that considers the influence level of preferred actions.

An experiment was carried out to compare the policies tested using *10* instances of *TSP* available in *TSPLIB* library (TSPLIB, 2010) and the results for the three policies tested simultaneously considering the value of the function and processing time, the *adaptive ε-greedy* policy had the best performance. This policy will be used in the version of the Q-learning algorithm implemented in this work.

3.4 The GRASP learning method

In GRASP metaheuristics the exploration and exploitation processes occur at different moments. The constructive phase explores the space of viable solutions and the local search improves the solution constructed in the initial phase of exploiting the area. Despite the clear delimitation of roles, the two phases of GRASP metaheuristics work in collaboration. The good performance of local search algorithm varies with the neighbourhood chosen and depends substantially on the quality of the initial solution. (Feo & Resende, 1995).

This section presents a hybrid method using Q-learning algorithm in the constructive phase of GRASP metaheuristics. In traditional GRASP metaheuristics iteration is independent, in other words, actual iteration does not use information obtained in past iterations (Fleurent & Glover, 1999). The basic idea of this proposed method is to use the information from the Q-values matrix as a form of memory that enables good decisions to be made in previous iterations and avoids uninteresting ones. This facilitates the exploration and exploitation process.

Based on the results of using an isolated Q-learning algorithm to solve the small instances of *TSP*, the approach proposed may significantly improve metaheuristic performance in locating the global optimum.

In the GRASP-Learning method, the Q-learning algorithm is used to construct initial solutions for GRASP metaheuristic. A good quality viable solution is constructed at each iteration of the algorithm using information from the Q-values matrix. The Q-values matrix can then be used at each GRASP iteration as a form of adaptive memory to allow the past experience to be used in the future. The use of adaptive word means that at each iteration new information is inserted by using the matrix *Q*. This influences the constructive phase of the next iteration.

The Q-learning algorithm will therefore be implemented as a randomized greedy algorithm. The control between "greed" (Exploration) and "randomness" (Exploitation) is achieved using the parameter ε of the transition rule defined in equation *13*. The reward matrix is determined as follows:

$$R(s,a) = \frac{1}{d_{ij}} * N_v(s,a) \tag{16}$$

where $1/d_{ij}$ is the inverse distance between the two cities c_i and c_j (city c_i is represented by state s and city c_j by the state accessed by choosing action a), and $N_v(s,a)$ is the number of visits to the current state.

The procedure of the Q-learning algorithm proposed for the GRASP constructive phase applied to the symmetric TSP is:

A table of state-action values Q (Q-values matrix) initially receives a zero value for all items. An index of table Q is randomly selected to start the updating process and the index then becomes state s0 for Q-learning. State s_1 can be obtained from state s_0 using the *ε-greedy* adaptive transition rule of the following way:

- Randomly, selecting a new city of the route, or
- Using the maximum argument *Q* in relation to the previous state s_0.

Given states s_0 and s_1, the iteration that updates table *Q* begins using the equation *4*. The possibility of selecting a lower argument state through randomness ensures the method ability to explore other search areas. Table *Q* is obtained after a maximum number of episodes. The route to *TSP* is taken from this matrix. Constructing a solution for *TSP* after obtaining matrix Q is achieved as follows:

- Copy the data of matrix Q to auxiliary matrix Q_1;
- Select an index l that shows an initial line of table Q_1 (corresponding to the city at the start of the route)
- Starting from line l choose the line's greatest value, index c of this value is the column of the next city on the route.
- Attribute a null value to all the values of column c at Q_1, to ensure there is no repetition of cities on the route, repeating the basic restriction of *TSP*;
- Continue the process while the route is incomplete.

At each GRASP iteration the matrix Q is updated by executing the Q-learning algorithm. In other words, at the end of *Nmax* iterations Q-learning algorithm will have executed *Nmax*NEp* episodes, where *NEp* denotes the number of episodes executed for each iteration. Updating the Q-values matrix at each GRASP iteration improves the information quality collected throughout the search process. Fig. 7, shows a overview of the GRASP-Learning method.

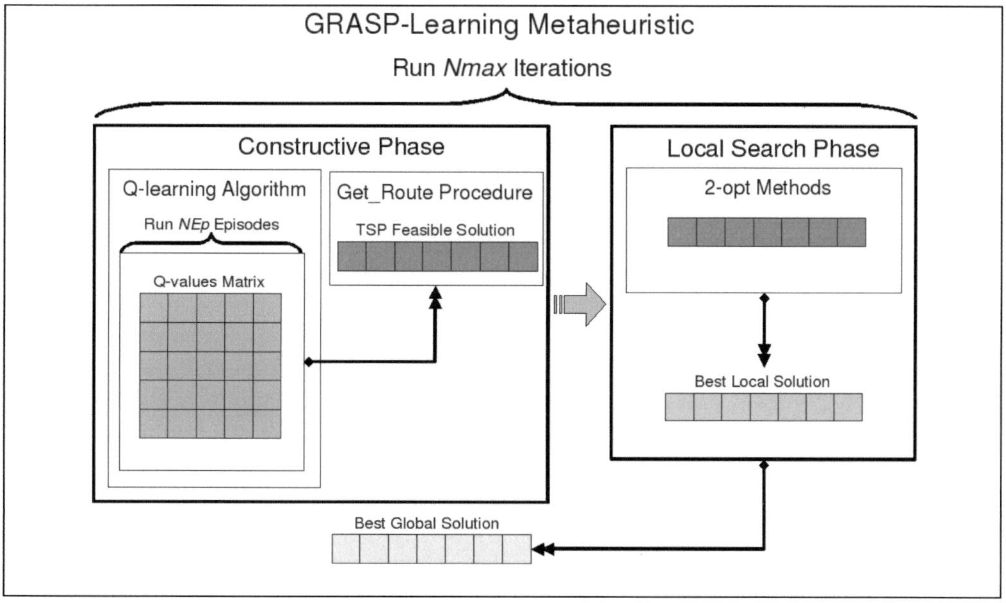

Fig. 7. Framework of the GRASP-Learning Method.

The local search phase in GRASP-Learning suffers no modifications. That is, it uses the same traditional GRASP algorithm that was implemented in this study as a descending method *2-Opt*. This local search technique only moves to a neighbouring solution if it improves in objective function. The Fig. 8, presents a simplified form of the pseudo code method GRASP-learning proposed.

When examining the pseudo code GRASP-Learning algorithm, significant modifications are seen in lines *3* and *5*. Function *MakeReward* in line *3* uses the distance matrix D to create a reward matrix, based on Equation *16*. In line *5* the function *Qlearning* returns a viable solution S for *TSP* and the updated Q-values matrix Q, which is used in the next iteration. The other aspects of GRASP-learning algorithm are identical to traditional GRASP metaheuristics.

Algorithm 4 GRASP-Learning Algorithm

```
procedure GRASP-LEARN(D, α, ε, γ, Nmax)
    f(S*) ← +∞
    R ← MakeReward(D)
    while i ≤ Nmax do
        [S, Q] ← Qlearning(R, α, ε, γ, Q)
        S' ← LocalSearch(S, Viz(S))
        if f(S') < f(S*) then
            S* = S'
        end if
        i ← i + 1
    end while
    return S*                          ▷ Best Solution
end procedure
```

Fig. 8. Pseudo code of GRASP-Learning Algorithm.

3.5 The cooperative genetic-learning algorithm

The hybrid genetic algorithm proposed in this section uses reinforcement learning to construct better solutions to the symmetric traveling salesman problem. The method main focus is the use the Q-learning algorithm to assist the genetic operators with the difficult task of achieving balance between exploring and exploiting the problem solution space. The new method suggests using the Q-learning algorithm to create an initial population of high fitness with a good diversity rate that also cooperates with the genetic operators.

In the learning process, the Q-learning algorithm considers using either the knowledge already obtained or choosing new unexplored search spaces. In other words, it has the characteristics of a randomized greedy algorithm. It is greedy owing to its use of the maximum value of *Q(s, a)* to choose action *a*, contributing to a greater return in state *s*, and randomized since it uses an action choice policy that allows for occasional visits to the other states in the environment. This behaviour allows Q-learning to significantly improve the traditional genetic algorithm.

As mentioned previously, the initial population of the proposed genetic algorithm is created by Q-learning algorithm. This is achieved by executing Q-learning with a determinate number of episodes (*NEp*). *Tp* chromosomes are then created using the matrix *Q* (Q-values matrix), where *Tp* is the population size. The choice criteria in the creation of each chromosome is the value of *Q(s, a)* associated to each gene so that the genes with the highest value of *Q(s, a)* are predominantly chosen in chromosome composition[3].

In addition to creating the initial population, the Q-learning algorithm cooperates with the genetic operators as follows:

- In each new generation, the best solution *S** obtained by the genetic operators is used to update the matrix of Q-values *Q* produced by the Q-learning algorithm in previous generations.
- After updating matrix *Q*, it is used in subsequent generations by the genetic algorithm. This iteration process rewards the state-action pairs that compose the

[3] A chromosome is an individual in the population (for example, a route to *TSP*), whereas a gene is each part that composes a chromosome (in *TSP* a city composes a route)

best solutions from the last generations. They receive an additional increment that identifies them as good decisions. Calculating the incremental value is based on the following theory:

- According to the model of *TSP* described in section 3.1, a solution for the model can be denoted by Fig. 9.

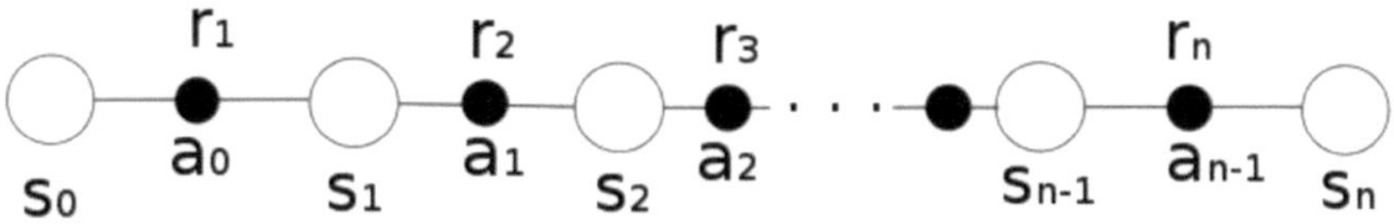

Fig. 9. *TSP* solution, modelled as a reinforcement learning Problem.

In the Fig. 9, the sequence of states, actions and rewards corresponds to a solution *S* constructed during an episode of Q-learning algorithm, where s_i, $i=0,\ldots,n$ is the current state and r_j, $j=1,\ldots,n$ is the immediate reward received by executing change s_i, for s_{i+1}. In this scenario, with solution S^*, the accumulated reward value R_i is easily calculated:

$$Q(s_0,s_1) = r_1 + r_2 + r_3 + \ldots + r_{n-1} + r_n = R_0$$

$$Q(s_1,s_2) = r_2 + r_3 + \ldots + r_{n-1} + r_n = R_1$$

$$\vdots$$

$$Q(s_{n-1},s_n) = r_n = R_n \tag{17}$$

- As mentioned in section 2.3, the Q-learning algorithm uses equation 4 in its updating process. However, since the value of R_i for solution S^* is already known, the incremental value proposed here can be calculated using:

$$Q(s_i,a_i) = Q(s_i,a_i) + \theta\left[R_i - Q(s_i,a_i)\right] \tag{18}$$

where a_i is the action of leaving state s_i and choosing to go to state s_{i+1}, and θ is a parameter that considers the importance of incremental value based on the number of visits to each state, denoted by:

$$\theta = N_v(s_i,a_i) / NEp \tag{19}$$

where, N_v is the number of visits to state-action pair (s_i, a_i), e *NEp* represents the number of episodes parameter of the Q-learning algorithm.

Fig. 10, shows a overview of the cooperative Genetic-learning method used.

The genetic operators were implemented identically to the traditional genetic algorithm, using a "dependent" spinner for selection. This allows each individual to be chosen proportionally to their value in the fitness function. The crossover of two points was used for the crossover operator. The mutation operator consists of a change in position between two cities on a route. The pseudo code shown in the Fig. 11 summarizes the method described.

The changes proposed in the Cooperative Genetic-learning algorithm that modify the traditional genetic algorithm can be seen in the pseudo code of lines *3, 7, 8, 9* and *15*. In line *3* the function *GeneratePop* executes Q-learning algorithm and creates the initial population.

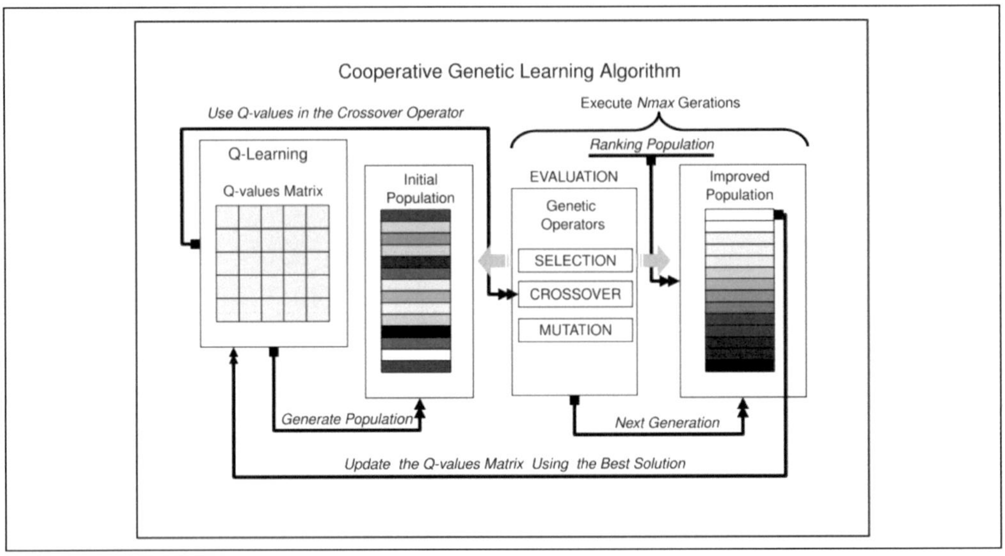

Fig. 10. Framework of the Cooperative Genetic-learning.

Algorithm 5 Cooperative Genetic-learning Algorithm

1: **procedure** CG-LEARN$(Tc, Tm, Tp, MaxG, L)$
2: $Q \leftarrow QLearning(R, \alpha_q, \epsilon, \gamma, NEp)$
3: $Pop \leftarrow GeneratePop(Q, Tp)$
4: $Pop \leftarrow evaluate(Pop)$
5: **for** $i = 1...MaxG$ **do**
6: $Pop \leftarrow Select(Pop)$
7: **if** $Div(Pop) < L$ **then**
8: $CQ \leftarrow GetCromo(Q, 1)$
9: $Pop \leftarrow Crossover(Pop, CQ, Tc)$
10: **else**
11: $Pop \leftarrow Crossover(Pop, Tc)$
12: **end if**
13: $Pop \leftarrow Mutation(Pop, Tm)$
14: $Pop \leftarrow SortPop(Pop)$
15: $Q \leftarrow UpdateQ(Q, Pop[1])$
16: **end for**
17: **return** Best solution Pop
18: **end procedure**

Fig. 11. Pseudo code of Cooperative Genetic-learning Algorithm

In line *7* the diversification rate of the population is compared with limit *L*. If the limit *L* is lower (less than *20%*), the crossover operator will use a chromosome from an extra execution of the Q-learning algorithm (line 9). In line 15 the matrix of Q-values Q is updated using information from the best solution of the current population.

The hybrid methods described in this section are modified versions of GRASP metaheuristics and genetic algorithms. Modifications used the Q-learning algorithm as an

intelligent strategy for exploration and/or exploitation of space solutions of the symmetric traveling salesman problem.
In GRASP metaheuristics, modifications use Q-learning algorithm to construct its initial solutions. According to (Feo & Resende, 1995), one of the disadvantages of traditional GRASP metaheuristics is the independence of its iterations. That is, the algorithm does not keep information on the history of solutions found in past iterations. These authors cite the good quality of the initial solution, as one of the factors that contribute to the success of a local search algorithm. The proposed use of Q-learning algorithm as an exploratory starting point for the GRASP metaheuristic, as described here, overcomes both deficiencies of the traditional method cited by (Feo & Resende, 1995). This is owing to the fact that Q-learning algorithm can produce good quality initial solutions and uses its Q-values matrix as a form of adaptive memory, allowing good decisions made in the past to be repeated in the future.
In relation to the genetic algorithm, the proposed method (cooperative Genetic-learning) used the Q-learning algorithm to create an initial population. A good quality initial population was achieved, both in the value of its objective function and diversity level. Another important innovation proposed in this method was the cooperation between Q-learning algorithm and the genetic operators.
Tests were carried out with two distinct versions of the genetic hybrid algorithm to determine the importance of the proposed cooperation in the algorithm. One test used the cooperative process and the other did not. The results are presented in the next section.

4. Experimental results

Before presenting the computational results it is important to note that the experiments carried out do not aim to find an optimum solution for *TSP*. Their objective is to compare the performance of traditional methods with the new methods proposed. There was no concern regarding the quality of entrance parameters during the experiments. All the algorithms were executed under the same condition, that is, the same number of iterations and identical values for the common adjustable parameters were used.
Tests were carried out using 10 instances of the *TSPLIB* library (TSPLIB, 2010), on a desktop computer with: 2.8 *Ghz*, 2 Gb of RAM memory and Linux operating system. Processing time was measured in seconds. Since the algorithms are nondeterministic, the results are a mean of *30* executions for each instance.
The information about instances used in the experiment is presented in Table 1:

Instance Name	Description	Best value
gr17	City problem (Groetschel)	2085.00
bays29	Bavaria (street distance)	2020.00
swiss42	Switzerland (Fricker)	1273.00
gr48	City problem (Groetschel)	5046.00
berlin52	Locations in Berlin (Germany)	7542.00
pr76	City problem (Padberg/Rinaldi)	108158.00
gr120	Germany (Groetschel)	6942.00
ch150	City problem (Churritz)	6528.00
si175	Vertex TSP (M. Hofmeister)	21407.00
a280	Drilling problem (Ludwig)	2579.00

Table 1. Information about TSPLIB instances utilized.

4.1 Comparison of the performance of the GRASP metaheuristics implemented

This section compares the results obtained with the computational implementation of GRASP metaheuristics, reactive GRASP and the new method proposed GRASP-Learning. All the algorithms were executed under the same parameter conditions. The values of adjustable parameters are listed in Table 2.

Instance	All	GRASP	Reactive GRASP	GRASP-Learning			
TSPLIB	Number Iterations	α	α	Episodes	α_q	γ	ε
gr17	300	0.8	*	10	0.9	1.0	*
bays29	300	0.8	*	10	0.9	1.0	*
swiss42	300	0.8	*	20	0.9	1.0	*
gr48	300	0.8	*	20	0.9	1.0	*
berlin52	300	0.8	*	50	0.9	1.0	*
pr76	300	0.8	*	100	0.9	1.0	*
gr120	300	0.8	*	100	0.9	1.0	*
ch150	300	0.8	*	150	0.9	1.0	*
si175	300	0.8	*	200	0.9	1.0	*
a280	300	0.8	*	200	0.9	1.0	*

Table 2. Adjustable parameters for the metaheuristics GRASP (*Adaptive parameters)

When examining Table 2, it is important to understand the parameters α of reactive GRASP and ε of GRASP-Learning. Both are self-adjustable values that vary at interval *[0, 1]*. Another important observation is that the parameters α (traditional and reactive version) are not equal to the parameter α_q of GRASP-Learning. In other words, parameter α is used to control the indices of "greed" and randomness in traditional GRASP and reactive GRASP. Parameter α_q is the coefficient of learning Q-learning algorithm used in the hybrid GRASP version.

The values listed in Table 3 correspond to the mean of *30* executions obtained with *10* instances of the symmetric traveling salesman (objective function value, the processing time in seconds). Fig. 12 and Fig. 13 compare the three versions of metaheuristics used, considering the objective function value and processing time, respectively. Data shown in graphs were normalized to improve their visualization and understanding.

The objective function values were normalized by the known optimum value at each instance of *TSPLIB* and the processing time was normalized by the mean execution time of each metaheuristic for each instance, this is calculated by Equation *20*.

$$M_i = \left(\sum_{j=1}^{m} T_{ij} \right) / m \ \forall i = 1,2,\ldots,n$$

$$TN_{ij} = T_{ij} / M_i \tag{20}$$

where, n is the number of instances used in the experiment, m is the number of algorithms tested. T_{ij} is the processing time for instance i executing algorithm j, and TN_{ij} is the value of normalized time for instance i executing algorithm j.

TSPLIB Instance	TSPLIB Optimal	Traditional GRASP		Reactive GRASP		GRASP Learning	
Name	Value	Value	Time	Value	Time	Value	Time
gr17	2085.00	2085.00	25.30	2085.00	21.07	2085.00	17.03
bays29	2020.00	2085.63	112.41	2060.50	103.96	2030.30	46.34
swiss42	1273.00	1441.43	373.62	1385.07	354.05	1281.40	84.64
gr48	5046.00	5801.77	559.81	5454.17	532.62	5442.77	127.41
berlin52	7542.00	8780.73	752.37	8420.93	599.10	8053.60	156.36
pr76	108159.00	140496.00	1331.51	131380.33	1724.84	129707.33	719.65
gr120	6942.00	10553.61	5000.10	8773.33	5945.75	8540.47	2443.82
Ch150	6528.00	10785.59	11167.91	9304.40	12348.96	7012.93	1753.29
si175	21407.00	25733.07	21509.92	23646.14	12803.00	22700.35	8830.08
a280	2579.00	5799.77	40484.48	4244.19	37075.25	2991.30	8442.40

Table 3. Performance of GRASP, reactive GRASP and GRASP-Learning Metaheuristics

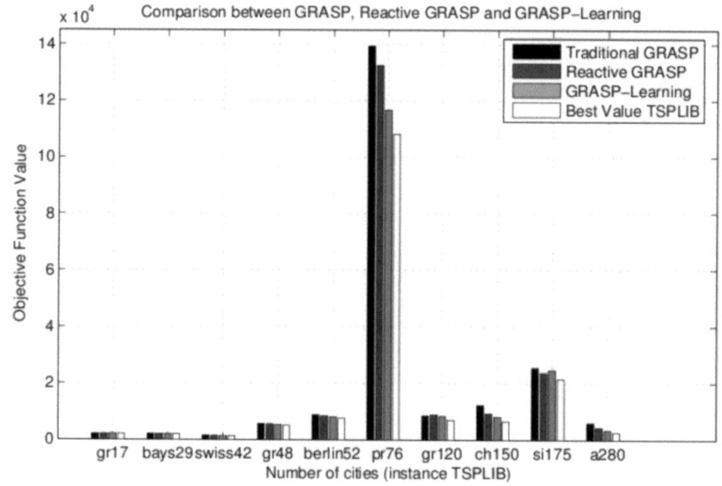

Fig. 12. Traditional GRASP, Reactive GRASP and GRASP-learning (Objective Function)

Upon analysis, the results in Table 6 show that the metaheuristic GRASP-Learning had better mean results than the traditional GRASP metaheuristic. It even performed better than reactive GRASP, the improved version of traditional GRASP metaheuristics. The results for objective function achieved with the hybrid method were better than those achieved using the traditional method. In the worst case, a tie occurred since all versions found the optimum instance *gr17*. In the best case, the new method showed a cost reduction of *48.42 %* (instance *a280*).

The hybrid method achieved very competitive results when compared to reactive GRASP. It performed better in most instances for objective function values and decreased the cost of instance *a280* by *29.52%*.

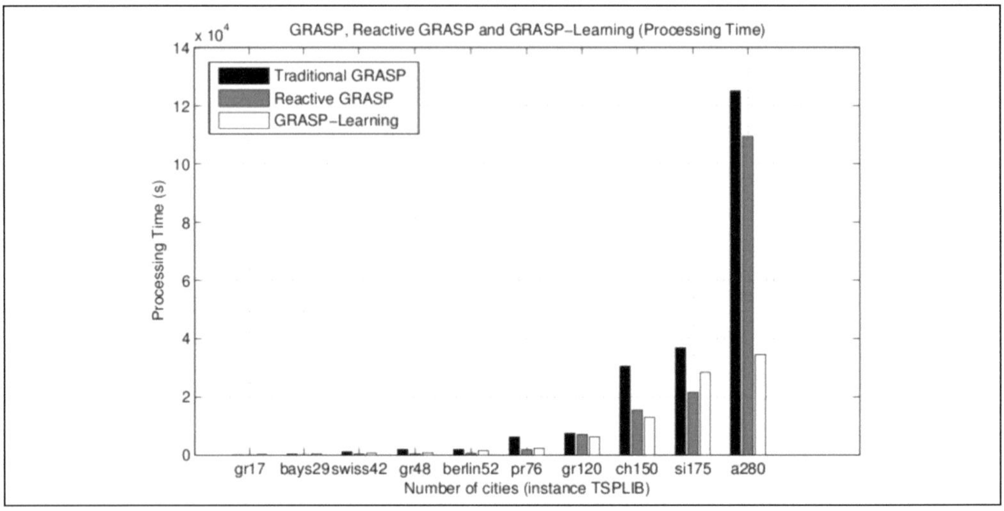

Fig. 13. Traditional GRASP, Reactive GRASP and GRASP-learning (Processing Time)

When comparing the processing time results, the advantage of the GRASP-Learning metaheuristic is even clearer. When compared with traditional GRASP, it achieved a decrease in processing time of *32.69%* for instance *gr17* (worst case) and *84.30%* for instance *ch150* (best case). In comparison with reactive GRASP, the hybrid method achieved *19.17%* for instance *gr17* in the worst case and *85.80* in the best case (instance *ch150*).

The best processing time results using the GRASP-Learning metaheuristic were achieved owing to the good quality of initial solutions created in the constructive phase of Q-learning algorithm. Since the metaheuristic started with good quality solutions, it was able to accelerate the local search. The GRASP-Learning metaheuristic also has the advantage of using the memory between iterations. This means that the quality of the initial solution is improved at each iteration, based on the information in the Q-values matrix, which is updated at each iteration by the Q-learning algorithm. It is important to note that good results are expressed as the instances grow, since greater the instance of *TSP*, the greater the difficulty level of a solution. Therefore, the advantage of Q-learning algorithm to generate good initial solutions is a consequence of the use of the matrix of q-values as a mechanism of adaptive memory.

4.2 Performance comparison of the genetic algorithms implemented

The experimental results for all versions of the genetic algorithms used were achieved using the same entrance parameters. These values are shown in Table 4.

The Table 5 shows the mean obtained with *30* executions for each version of the genetic algorithms.

The charts in the Fig. 14 and Fig. 15 compare the three versions of algorithms tested (traditional genetic, Genetic-learning, cooperative Genetic-learning) considering objective function value and processing time, respectively. Graph data were normalized in a similar form to the process used in GRASP metaheuristics. That is, the objective function value was normalized by the optimum value of each instance of *TSPLIB* and the processing time was normalized by the mean execution time of each algorithm for each instance, as described in Equation *20*.

TSPLIB Instance	All Genetic Algorithms				Genetic Learning Algorithm			
Name	Number of Generations	Tc	Tm	Tp	Number of Episodes	α_q	γ	ε
gr17	1000	0.7	0.2	100	500	0.8	1	*
bays29	1000	0.7	0.2	100	500	0.8	1	*
swiss42	1000	0.7	0.2	100	500	0.8	1	*
gr48	1000	0.7	0.2	100	500	0.8	1	*
berlin52	1000	0.7	0.2	100	500	0.8	1	*
pr76	1500	0.7	0.2	100	1000	0.8	1	*
gr120	2000	0.7	0.2	100	1000	0.8	1	*
ch150	2000	0.7	0.2	100	2000	0.8	1	*
si175	2000	0.7	0.2	100	2000	0.8	1	*
a280	2000	0.7	0.2	100	2000	0.8	1	*

Table 4. Adjustable parameters for the Genetics algorithms (*Adaptive parameters)

TSPLIB Instance	TSPLIB Optimal	Traditional Genetic Algorithm		Genetic Learning Algorithm		Cooperative Genetic Learning Algorithm	
Name	Value	Value	Time	Value	Time	Value	Time
gr17	2085.00	2104.97	48.73	2087.37	48.03	2085.00	51.77
bays29	2020.00	2286.23	52.27	2252.13	52.24	2166.47	57.45
swiss42	1273.00	1614.20	54.52	1546.53	55.01	1457.73	63.66
gr48	5046.00	6839.77	55.99	5967.90	56.19	5744.90	66.59
berlin52	7542.00	10095.63	55.55	8821.93	55.68	8679.43	69.17
pr76	108159.00	189659.00	89.49	165281.67	95.36	132100.33	123.60
gr120	6942.00	16480.73	132.05	12205.87	140.41	8787.00	211.51
ch150	6528.00	19705.47	142.44	9612.33	153.26	8803.37	247.47
si175	21407.00	30860.97	151.86	29264.13	193.25	24818.03	285.86
a280	2579.00	13642.07	205.92	3852.67	274.55	3768.03	543.17

Table 5. Performance of Genetic, Genetic Learning and Cooperative Genetic-Learning.

When analyzing the experimental results, the Genetic-learning algorithms achieved better results for objective function value but not for processing time.

The result for objective function value is achieved owing to the good quality of the initial population generated by Q-learning algorithm and cooperative iteration of genetic operators with the Q-values matrix. The good performance of the objective function value is mainly noted as the instances grow. For example, when comparing the traditional genetic algorithm with cooperative Genetic-Learning improvement in the worst case is 0.95% (instance gr17) and in the best case 72.38% (instance a280).

The processing time of cooperative Genetic-learning algorithm is at a disadvantage to the other two versions since this version uses Q-learning algorithm in initial population construction and cooperation with the genetic operators. The time spent processing episodes *NEp* of Q-learning algorithm is added to the final execution time.

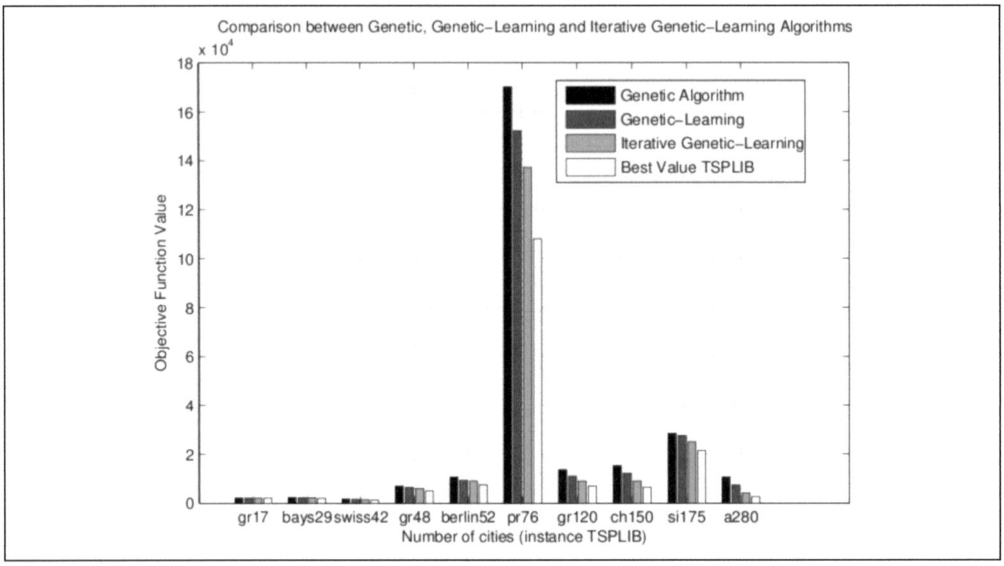

Fig. 14. Genetic, Genetic Learning and Cooperative Genetic-Learning. (Objective Function)

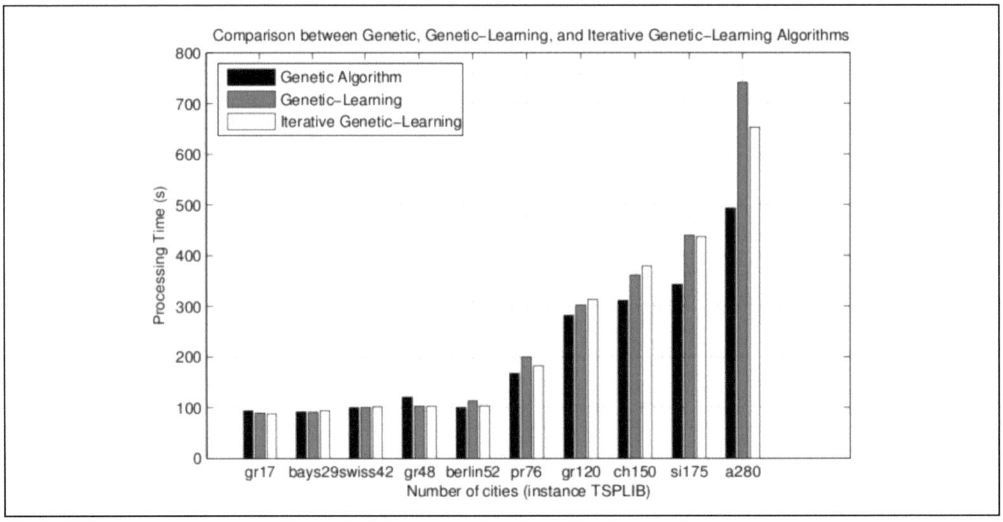

Fig. 15. Genetic, Genetic Learning and Cooperative Genetic-Learning. (Processing Time)

5. Conclusions

This section presents observations, conclusions and perspectives of this study. The text is subdivided into subsections according to the method proposed.

5.1 GRASP-learning method

The proposed method GRASP-Learning satisfies two requirements of GRASP metaheuristics: a good final performance based on good quality initial solutions and no memory mechanism between iterations.

Concerning the quality of initial solutions, using Q-learning algorithm to construct these olustions showed promising results for the objective function value and processing time.
The purpose of the randomized greedy Q-learning algorithm in the constructive phase of GRASP metaheuristic is not only to provide good initial solutions, but also a form of adaptive memory. This allows good decisions made in past iterations to be repeated in the future. The adaptive memory mechanism is implemented using information from the Q-values matrix created by Q-learning algorithm. The term adaptive memory is used since the Q-values matrix is updated at each episode of Q-learning. This incorporates the experience achieved by the learning agent in each update.
The GRASP-learning metaheuristic achieved better results than traditional GRASP and reactive GRASP when comparing general performance. In relation to processing time, good performance by GRASP-Learning is especially noted as the instances grow. This is confirmed by the fact that the hybrid method, traditional GRASP and reactive GRASP are only different in the constructive phase. Also, the partially greedy algorithm used in GRASP and reactive GRASP has complexity O(n2), while Q-learning algorithm has complexity O(NEp*n) where NEp is the number of episodes and n the instance size. Since updating the Q-values during execution of GRASP-learning is cumulative (in *k* iterations of algorithm GRASP-learning, *k*NEp* episodes of Q-learning are executed), the algorithm can be parameterized with a relatively small value of *NEp*. Based on the complexity orders of the algorithms, Q-learning outperforms the partially greedy algorithm as the instances grow.
Another important aspect that confirms the lower processing time of the hybrid method is the good quality of initial solutions constructed by Q-learning algorithm, since the GRASP metaheuristic starting with good initial solutions had an accelerated local search.

5.2 Genetic learning algorithm

The hybrid genetic algorithm proposed in this study showed very significant results, mainly in its cooperative version. Updating the Q-values matrix with elite solutions from each population produced a significant improvement in performance, especially in objective function values. The traditional version achieved better processing time results. This was expected since the traditional version constructed a randomized initial population. Learning versions use Q-learning algorithm; therefore, the execution time of the episodes is added to their processing time. Despite the non-significant processing time results, the Genetic-learning algorithm appreciably improved the objective function value. This was already substantial when comparing the quality of initial populations (see Subsection 4.2) since the population created by Q-learning algorithm achieved better quality (better Fitness) and an equal diversification rate for larger instances.
This method also contributes through the mutual cooperation between Q-learning algorithm and the genetic operators that exchange information throughout the evolution process. This cooperation offers a range of possibilities for the parallel implementation of these algorithms, for example by using a cooperative/competitive strategy to solve the traveling salesman problem.

5.3 Future works

The methods proposed in this study are tested using only the symmetric traveling salesman problem. Although *TSP* is a classic combined optimization problem from which many other practical problems can be derived, applying the methods proposed here to other problems of this class requires careful modelling.

Another important factor for improvement concerns is the instance sizes in the test. For questions of speed in method validation, small and medium-size instances of *TSP* were used. Based on the developed studies and possible improvements, prospects exist for the following future works:

- Computational tests with instances of TSP with a higher number of cities to determine the behaviour of the methods proposed when using larger instances.
- Applying GRASP-Learning metaheuristic and Genetic-learning algorithm to other combinatorial optimization problems.
- Using parallel hybrids for the traveling salesman problem based on the hybrid methods proposed here. This study is currently being developed in a PhD thesis of *PPgEEC/UFRN* (Queiroz, J.P. et al., 2008) with very interesting results.
- Investigating the use of the reinforcement learning Q-learning algorithm to improve other metaheuristics.

6. References

Feo T. & M. Resende (1995). Greedy randomized adaptive search procedures, *Journal of Global Optimization*, Vol. 06, (March 1995), Page numbers (109 - 133) ISBN : 0925 - 5001

Fleurent, C. & Glover, F. Improved constructive multistart strategies for the quadratic assignment problem using adaptive memory, *Informs Journal on Computing* Vol. 11, No. 2, Spring 1999, pp. 198-204, DOI: 10.1287/ijoc.11.2.198.

Lima, F. C. & Melo J. D. & Doria Neto A. D. Using Q-learning Algorithm for Initialization of the GRASP metaheuristic and Genetic Algorithm, *International Joint Conference on Neural Networks (IJCNN), 2007, IEEE Proceedings of IJCNN 2007*, Florida, pages. 1243-1248, 2007.

M. Prais & C. Ribeiro(1998) Reactive GRASP: An application to a matrix decomposition problem in TDMA traffic assignment. Catholic University of Rio de Janeiro, Department of Computer Science, Rio de Janeiro, 1998.

Puterman M. L. Markov Decision Processes Discrete Stochastic Dynamic Programming, John Wiley e Sons, Inc, New York, USA, 1994.

Queiroz, J. P. & Lima, F.C. & Magalhaes R.M. & Melo, J. D. & Adriao, Doria Neto A. D. A parallel hybrid implementation using genetic algorithm, GRASP and Reinforcement Learning, *International Joint Conference on Neural Networks*, pages 2798-2803, 2008.

Ramos, I. C. O. & Goldbarg, M. C. & Goldbarg, E. F. G. & Doria Neto, A. D. & Farias, J. P. F. ProtoG Algorithm Applied to the Traveling Salesman Problem. In: *XXIII International Conference of the Chilean Computer Science Society: Computer Society, IEEE*, pages 23--30, Los Alamitos, 2003.

Randy, L. Haupt & Sue Ellen Haupt. *Pratical Genetic Algorithms*, Second edition, a John Wiley and Sons, Inc.,Publication, New Jersey, 2004.

Sutton, R.S. & Barto, A.G. *Reinforcement Learning: An Introduction*, MIT Press, Cambridge, MA,1998.

TSPLIB, on-line library,http://www.iwr.uni-heidelberg.de/groups/comopt/software/TSPLIB95/, accessed April 2010.

Watkins, Christopher J. C. Hellaby. *Learning from delayed rewards*, PhD thesis, Cambridge University, Cambridge, England 1989.

14

Predicting Parallel TSP Performance: A Computational Approach

Paula Fritzsche, Dolores Rexachs and Emilio Luque
DACSO, University Autonoma of Barcelona
Spain

1. Introduction

Faced with a scientific force and a critical need to solve large-scale and/or time-constrained problems, the industry reports that access to high-performance computing (HPC) capability is required now more than ever. Continued hardware and software advances, such as more powerful and lower-cost processors, have made it easier for scientists and engineers to install and use clusters / multi-cores and complete high-performance computing jobs.

In particular, the Traveling Salesman Problem (TSP) is one of the most famous problems (and the best one perhaps studied) in the field of the combinatorial optimization. In spite of the apparent simplicity of their formulation, the TSP is a complex solving problem and the complexity of its solution has been a continue challenge to the mathematicians for centuries. Not only the study of this problem has attracted people from mathematics but also many researchers of other fields like operations research, physics, biology, or artificial intelligence, and accordingly there is a vast amount of literature on it. On the other hand, not yet an effective polynomial-time algorithm is known for the general case. Many aspects of the problem still need to be considered and questions are still left to be answered satisfactorily.

A significant challenge is being able to predict TSP performance order. It is important to bear in mind, that the TSP conclusions drawn could eventually be applied to any TSP family problem. There are important cases of practical problems that can be formulated as TSP problems and many other problems are generalizations of this problem. Therefore, there is a tremendous need for predicting the performance order of TSP algorithms.

Measuring the execution time (performance) of a TSP parallel algorithm for all possible input values would allow answering any question about how the algorithm will respond under any set of conditions. Unfortunately, it is impossible to make all of these measurements. TSP performance depends on the number of cores used, the data size, as well as other parameters. Detecting the main other parameters that affect performance order is the real clue to obtain a good estimation. The issue of measuring performance for the TSP problem in practice and how to relate practical results to the theoretical analysis is addressed in this chapter as a knowledge discovery methodology.

The defined methodology for performance modelling begins by generating a representative sample of the full population of TSP instances and measuring their execution times. An interactive and iterative process explores data in search of patterns and/or relationships detecting the main parameters that affect performance. Knowing the main parameters which characterise time complexity, it becomes possible to suspect new hypotheses to

restart the process and to produce a subsequent improved time complexity model. Finally, the methodology predicts the performance order for new data sets on a particular parallel computer by replacing a numerical identification. The methodology arises out of the need to give an answer to a great number of problems that are normally set aside. Besides, this is a good starting point for understanding some facts related with the non-deterministic algorithms, particularly the data-dependents algorithms. Any minimum contribution in this sense represents a great advance due to the lack of general knowledge.
An Euclidean TSP implementation, called global pruning algorithm (***GP-TSP***), to obtain the exact TSP solution in a parallel machine has been developed and studied. It is used to analyze the influence of indeterminism in performance prediction, and also to show the usefulness of the methodology. It is a branch-and-bound algorithm which recursively searches all possible paths and prunes large parts of the search space by maintaining a global variable containing the length of the shortest path found so far. If the length of a partial path is bigger than the current minimal length, this path is not expanded further and a part of the search space is pruned. The ***GP-TSP*** execution time depends on the number of processors (***P***), the number of cities (***C***), and other parameters. As a result of our investigation, right now the sum of the distances from one city to the other cities (***SD***) and the mean deviation of SDs values (***MDSD***) are the numerical parameters characterizing the different input data beyond the number of cities.
Comparisons of experimental results with predictions have been quite promising. Therefore, the efficacy of the methodology proposed has been demonstrated. In addition to the prediction capability, an interesting and practical issue from this research has been discovered: how to select the *best* starting city. With this important and non-trivial selection, the time spent on evaluation has been dramatically reduced.
This chapter is organized as follows. The next section describes the Traveling Salesman Problem, their computational complexity and their applications in several fields. Besides, it provides detailed coverage of the ***GP-TSP*** parallel algorithm. Section 3 presents the knowledge discovery methodology to the problem of predicting the TSP performance. Section 4 focuses on the discovering process carried out to find the significant input parameters and building the ***GP-TSP*** prediction model. In addition, two outstanding experiments have been studied. Section 5 summarizes and draws the main conclusions of this chapter. Appendix A shows the specification of the parallel machine used along the experimentation stage. Appendix B shows the characteristics of a clustering tool used to discover internal data information.

2. Traveling Salesman Problem

The Traveling Salesman Problem (TSP) is one of the most famous problems (and the best one perhaps studied) in the field of combinatorial optimization. In spite of the apparent simplicity of its formulation, the TSP is a complex data-dependent problem. Not only the complexity of its solution has been a continue challenge to the researchers of several fields but also the prediction of its performance. Predicting TSP performance is vital due to there are many practical problems that can be formulated as TSP problems and others problems are generalizations of this problem.

2.1 Problem statement

The TSP for C cities is the problem of finding a tour visiting all the cities exactly once and returning to the starting city such that the sum of the distances between consecutive cities is minimized (TSP page, 2010). The requirement of returning to the starting city does not change the computational complexity of the problem.

2.2 Computational complexity

The TSP has been shown to be NP-hard (Karp, 1972). More precisely, it is complete for the complexity class (FP^{NP})[1], and the decision problem version is NP-complete. If an efficient algorithm is found for the TSP problem, then efficient algorithms could be found for all other problems in the NP-complete class. Although it has been shown that, theoretically, the Euclidean TSP is equally hard with respect to the general TSP (Garey et al., 1976), it is known that there exists a sub exponential time algorithm for it.

The most direct solution for a TSP problem would be to calculate the number of different tours through *C* cities. Given a starting city, it has *C-1* choices for the second city, *C-2* choices for the third city, etc. Multiplying these together it gets *(C-1)!* for one city and *C!* for the *C* cities. Another solution is to try all the permutations (ordered combinations) and see which one is cheapest. At the end, the order is also factorial of the number of cities. Briefly, the solutions which appear in the literature are quite similar.

The factorial algorithm's complexity motivated the research in two attack lines: exact algorithms or heuristics algorithms. The exact algorithms search for an optimal solution through the use of branch-and-bound, linear programming or branch-and-bound plus cut based on linear programming (Karp, 1972) techniques. Heuristics solutions are approximation algorithms that reach an approximate solution (close to the optimal) in a time fraction of the exact algorithm. TPS heuristics algorithms might be based on genetic and evolutionary algorithms (Tsai et al., 2002), simulated annealing (Pepper et al., 2002), Tabu search, neural networks (Aras et al., 2003), ant systems, among others.

2.3 Practical problems

The TSP often comes up as a subproblem in more complex combinatorial problems. The best known and important one of which is the vehicle routing problem, that is, the problem of determining for a fleet of vehicles which customers should be served by each vehicle and in what order each vehicle should visit the customers assigned to it (Christofides, 1985). Another similar example is the problem of arranging school bus routes to pick up the children in a school district. The TSP naturally arises in many transportation and logistics applications (TSP page, 2010).

Besides problems having the TSP structure occur in the analysis of the structure of crystals (Bland & Shallcross, 1989), in material handling in a warehouse (Ratliff & Rosenthal, 1983), in genome rearrangement (Sankoff & Blanchette, 1997), in phylogenetic tree construction (Korostensky & Gonnet, 2000), and predicting protein functions (Johnson & Liu, 2006), among others. Important practical computer science problems including the TSP structure appear in clustering of data arrays (Lenstra & Kan, 1975), in sequencing of jobs on a single machine (Gilmore & Gomory, 1964), in physical mapping problems (Alizadeh et al., 1993), in drilling of printed circuits boards (Duman, 2004).

---

[1] The class NP is the set of decision problems that can be solved by a non-deterministic Turing machine in polynomial time. FP means function problems.

2.4 Related problems

An equivalent formulation in terms of graph theory can be described. Given a complete weighted graph find a Hamiltonian cycle with the least weight. The vertices would represent the cities, the edges would represent the roads, and the weights would be the cost or distance of that road (Gutin & Punnen, 2006).

Another related problem consists of finding a Hamiltonian cycle in a weighted graph with the minimal length of the longest edge. This problem, known as the bottleneck traveling salesman problem, is really useful in transportation and logistics areas.

Related variations on the TSP include the resource constrained traveling salesman problem which has applications in scheduling with an aggregate deadline (Miller & Pekny, 1991). The prize collecting TSP (Balas, 1989) and the orienteering problem (Golden et al., 1987) are special cases of the resource constrained TSP. The problem of finding a tour of maximum length is the objective in MAX TSP (Barvinok et al., 2003). The maximum scatter TSP is the problem of computing a path on a set of points in order to maximize the minimum edge length in the path. It is motivated by applications in manufacturing and medical imaging (Arkin et al., 1996).

2.5 *GP-TSP* parallel algorithm

As a representative of the practical problems, a global pruning TSP algorithm (called *GP-TSP*), has been deeply studied. It obtains the exact TSP Euclidean solution in a parallel machine. For simplicity, the algorithm works with cities in R^2 instead of R^3 and uses the Euclidean distance due to it is the most straightforward way of computing distances between cities in a two-dimensional space. Nevertheless, the choice of the distance measure used (Euclidean, Manhattan, Chebychev, ...) is irrelevant. More over, it would be the same to work with an equivalent formulation in terms of graph theory. Therefore, the ideas of this article can be generalized.

The *GP-TSP* algorithm is indeed both useful and profitable to analyze the influence of indeterminism in performance prediction. It is a branch-and-bound algorithm which recursively search all possible paths. It follows the Master-Worker programming paradigm (Fritzsche, 2007). Each city is represented by two coordinates in the Euclidean plane. Considering *C* different cities, the Master defines a certain level *L* to divide the tasks. Tasks are the possible permutations of *C-1* cities in *L* elements. The granularity *G* of a task is the number of cities that defines the task sub-tree, this is $G = C - L$. At the execution start-up the Master sends the cities coordinates to every Worker.

A diagram of the possible permutations for five cities (**V**ienna, **G**raz, **L**inz, **B**arcelona, **M**adrid), considering the salesman starts and ends his trip at Vienna, can be seen in Figure 1. The Master can divide this problem into 1 task of level 0 or 4 tasks of level 1 or 12 tasks of level 2 for example. The tasks of the first level would be represented by the cities Vienna and Graz for the first task, Vienna and Linz for the second, followed by Vienna and Barcelona, and Vienna and Madrid. The requirement of returning to the starting city is without detracting from the generality. In this closed cycle the salesman may begin and end in the city who wants.

Knowing the latitude and longitude of two cities on the Earth, it is possible to determine the distance between them in kilometres. The table 1 lists the latitude and longitude of the five cities mentioned previously. Figure 2(a) shows a strictly lower triangular distance matrix where each box contains the Euclidean distance in kilometres between two cities.

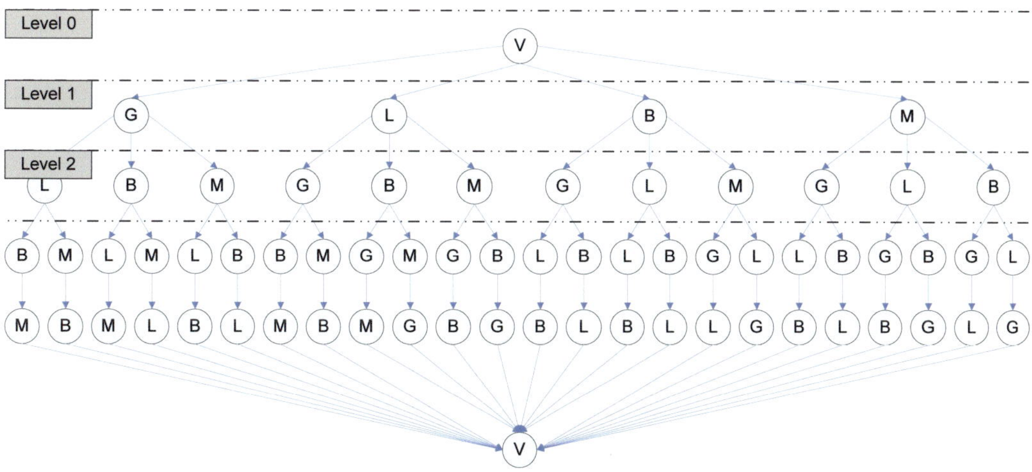

Fig. 1. Possible paths for the salesman considering five cities: **V**ienna, **G**raz, **L**inz, **B**arcelona, **M**adrid

	Latitude	*Longitude*
Barcelona	40° 26' north	3° 42' west
Graz	48° 13' north	16° 22' east
Linz	47° 05' north	15° 22' east
Madrid	48° 19' north	14° 18' east
Vienna	41° 18' north	2° 06' east

Table 1. Latitude and longitude of the five cities

Workers are responsible for calculating the distance of the permutations left in the task and sending to the Master the best path and distance of these permutations. One of the characteristics of the TSP is that once the distance for a path is superior to the already computed minimum distance it is possible to prune this path tree.
Figure 2(b) and Figure 2(c) exhibit the pruning processes for the *GP-TSP* algorithm where each arrow has the distance between the two cities it connects. Analyzing Figure 2(b), the total distance for the first followed path (in the left) is of 3845 km. The distance between Vienna and Barcelona on the second path (in the right) is already of 4737 km. It is then not necessary for the algorithm to keep calculating distances from the city Barcelona on because it is impossible to reach a better distance for this branch. Analyzing the other example, the total distance for the first followed path (in the left of Figure 2(c)) is of 3845 km. Then, the distance between Linz and Barcelona on the second path (in the right of Figure 2(c)) is already of 4839 km. Therefore, it is not necessary for the algorithm to keep calculating distances from the city Barcelona on.

3. TSP knowledge discovery methodology

The scientific experimental knowledge discovery methodology presented here is a first attempt to estimate the performance order of a TSP parallel algorithm. As well as the process of knowledge discovery is certainly not new, it is typical of the experimental

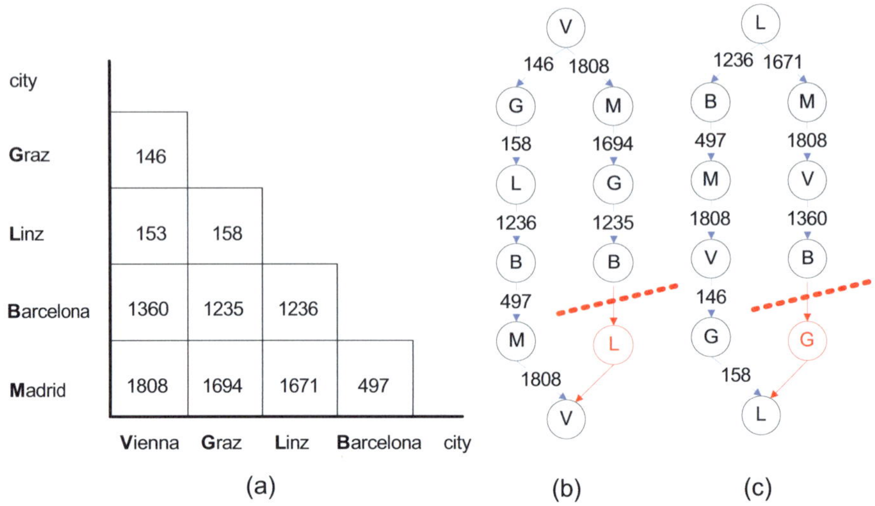

Fig. 2. (a) Matrix of Euclidean distances between cities (in km), (b)-(c) Two pruning processes in the *GP-TSP* algorithm

sciences. An experimental science is based on observation of performing repeated controlled experiments. Before computers were used to automate this process, people involved in math, physics or statistics were using probability techniques to model historical data.

The methodology consists of three main phases. First, the design and composition of experiments to define and improve the TSP asymptotic time complexity. Next, the validation of the built model. Finally, the definition of the TSP asymptotic time complexity.

3.1 Design and composition of experiments to define and improve the asymptotic time complexity

Foremost it is important understanding the application domain and the relevant prior knowledge, and analyzing their behavior step by step, in a deep way. It is a try-and-error method that requires specialists to manually or automatically identify the relevant parameters that can affect the execution time of the algorithm studied. Discovering the proper set of parameters is the basis to obtain a good capacity of prediction.

Designing a well-built experiment involves articulating a goal, choosing an output that characterizes an aspect of that goal and specifying the data that will be used in the study taking into account the worked hypotheses at that time. The experiments must provide a representative sample (a good training data set) first to measure the quality of the model / hypotheses and then to fit the model. After the necessary training data have been defined the TSP parallel algorithm studied must process each experiment obtaining a tour visiting and the execution time invested as output.

The term knowledge discovery in databases (KDD) refers to the process of analyzing data from different perspectives and summarizing it into useful information. Technically, KDD is the process of finding correlations or patterns among dozens of fields in large relational databases. A KDD process, a bold closed curve in Figure 3, involves data preparation, defining a study, reading the data and building a model, understanding the model, and finally predicting. It is an interactive and iterative process, surrounding numerous steps with many decisions that the end-user carries out (Groth, 1998).

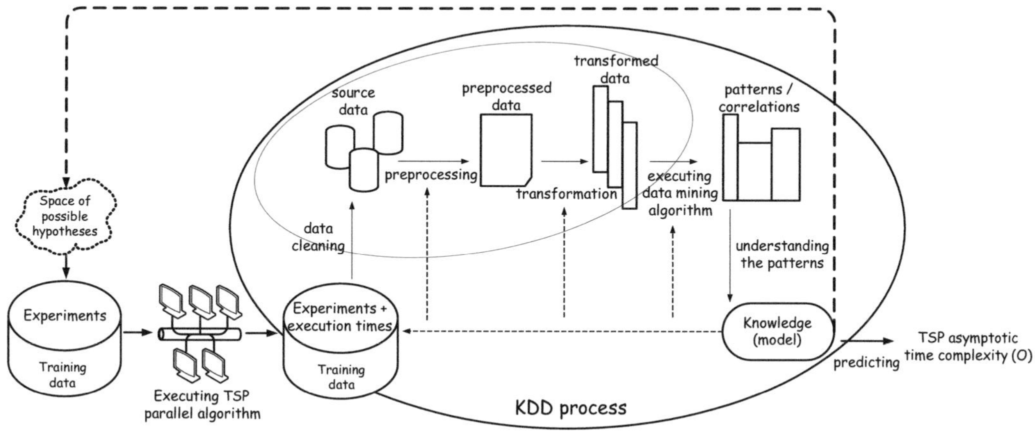

Fig. 3. Knowledge acquisition

Inside the KDD process, a gray closed curve in Figure 3, the stages of data preparation and defining a study surrounds both the decision of choosing between the data mining techniques (classification, regression, clustering, dependency modeling, summarization of data, or change and deviation detection), and also the selection of the data mining algorithm to apply according to the chosen technique.

Regarding the analysis of the problem, a clustering study could be performed to potentially identify groups. Clustering is the process of partitioning of a data set into subsets (clusters), so that the data in each subset (ideally) share some common trait (often proximity according to some defined distance measure). Therefore, a clustering data-mining tool through k-means algorithm analyzes the measured times and the main parameters values that affect performance in order to summarize these into a useful information. Knowing the main parameters which characterize time complexity, it becomes possible to suspect new hypotheses to restart the process and to produce a subsequent improved time complexity model.

Figure 3 shows the knowledge acquisition process which includes the design of experiments, the execution of the TSP parallel algorithm and the KDD process. There is no doubt that the design of experiments is directly related to the suspected hypotheses. The solid lines in Figure 3 represent the compulsory path to follow in the methodology and the dashed lines represent paths of refinement.

3.2 Validation of the model

A new data set is proposed to be able to validate the created model. Although the validation data set constitutes a hold-out sample, it has not been considered in the building of the model. This enables to estimate the error in the predictions without having the assumption that the execution times follow a particular distribution.

The analytical formulation, together a particular architecture, is used to make predictions for each experiment in the validation data. The quality analysis is a relevant issue in this stage and has to include interest measurements. The prediction for each experiment is then compared to the value of the dependent variable that was actually observed in the validation data obtaining the prediction error. Then the average of the square of these errors enables to compare different models and to assess the accuracy of the model in making predictions.

It is important to bear in mind that every stage in the design of experiments to obtain and improve the asymptotic time complexity is validated. Figure 4 exhibits the entire model validation phase.

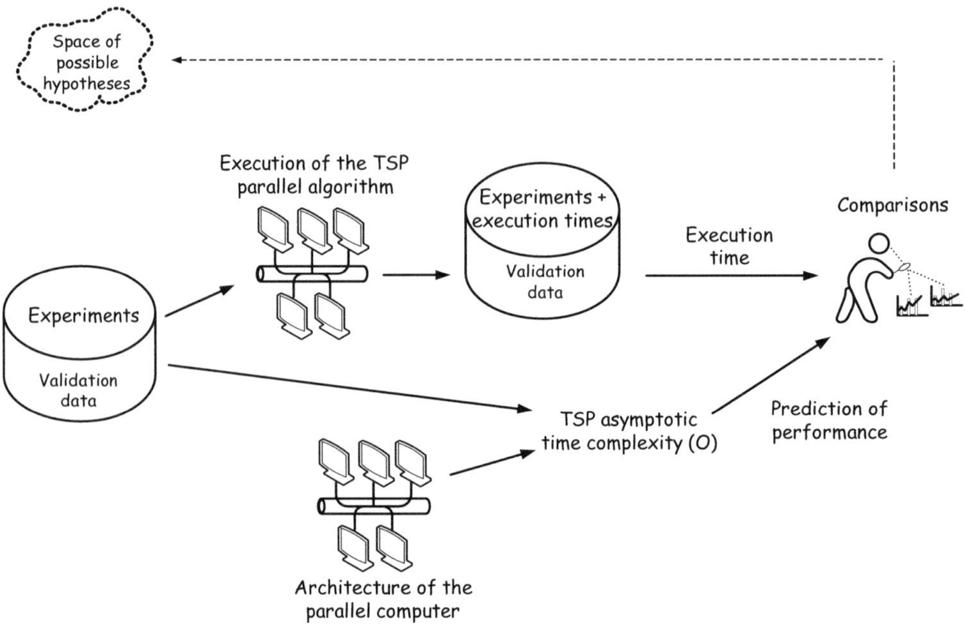

Fig. 4. Model validation phase

3.3 Definition of the asymptotic time complexity

The refined built model allows defining the asymptotic time complexity for the TSP parallel algorithm studied, Figure 5. Then the analytical formulation will be instanced with values coming from a new input data set and a particular parallel computer in order to give a prediction of performance.

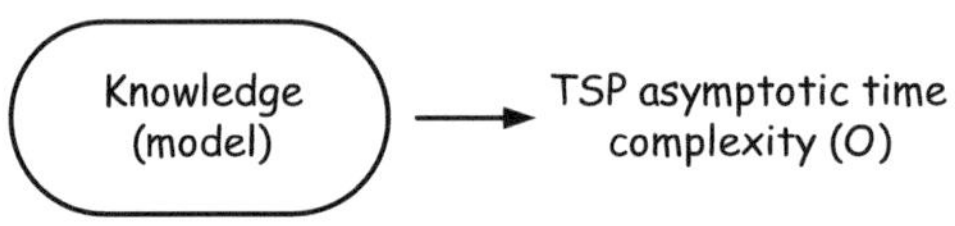

Fig. 5. The final definition of the TSP asymptotic time complexity

The entire TSP knowledge discovery methodology is shown in Figure 6. Every stage in the methodology defined can implicate a backward motion to previous steps in order to obtain extra or more precise information to fit the final model.

4. Analyzing the *GP-TSP* algorithm

Using simple experiments, varying one or two values at a time, it is possible to infer that time required for the parallel *GP-TSP* algorithm depends on certain parameters. Discovering these significant *GP-TSP* input parameters is the main issue of this section. Then, the prediction of *GP-TSP* performance order and two relevant experiments are analyzed.

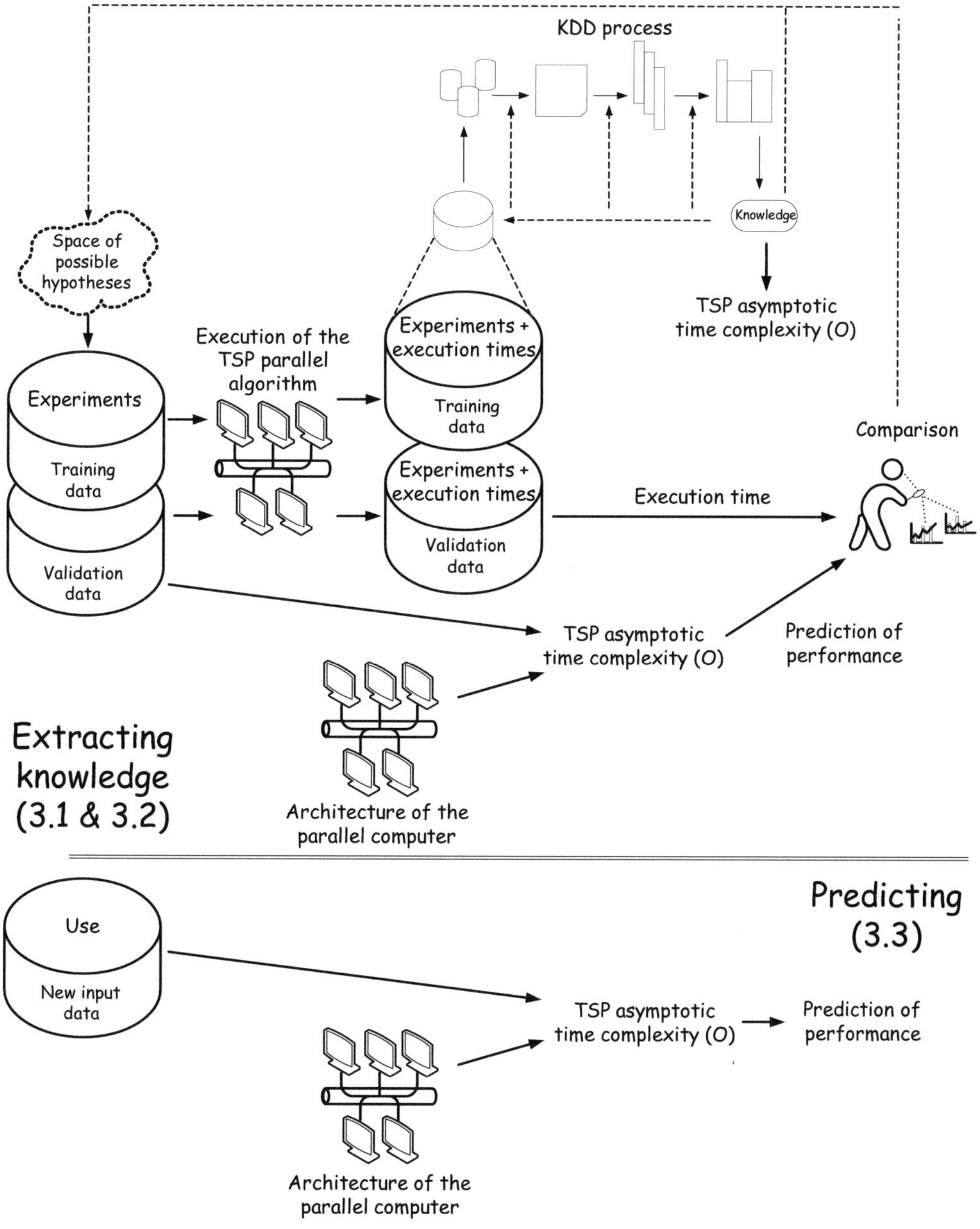

Fig. 6. Performance prediction using the knowledge discovery methodology

4.1 Discovering the significant GP-TSP input parameters

It is clear that the *GP-TSP* execution time depends on the number of processors (*P*), the number of cities (*C*), and *other parameters*. Discovering the *other parameters* is the key to obtain a good or an acceptable prediction of performance order. Undoubtedly, the knowledge discovery in databases process (KDD process) has been one of the most profitable stages in the scientific examination. A huge amount of data sets was processed with the only goal of finding

some common properties. First intuitions guided the different tests in order to determine the characteristics, the relationships, and the patterns between the data sets.
As a result of the investigation, right now the sum of the distances from one city to the other cities (*SD*) and the mean deviation of *SDs* values (*MDSD*) are the numerical parameters characterizing the different input data beyond the number of cities (*C*). But how these final parameters have been obtained? Next, it is described the followed way to discover the above mentioned dependencies (*SD* and *MDSD*) and the construction of a model.

4.1.1 First hypothesis → location of the cities (geographical pattern)

Given a number of cities with its pattern of distribution, the initial experiments have provided evidence that times required for the completion of the algorithm are dissimilar. In order to understand the general process, show its progress and results, it has been chosen an example data set to follow along this section. It consists of five different geographical patterns of fifteen cities each one (named $GPat_1$ to $GPat_5$) as it is shown in Figure 7.

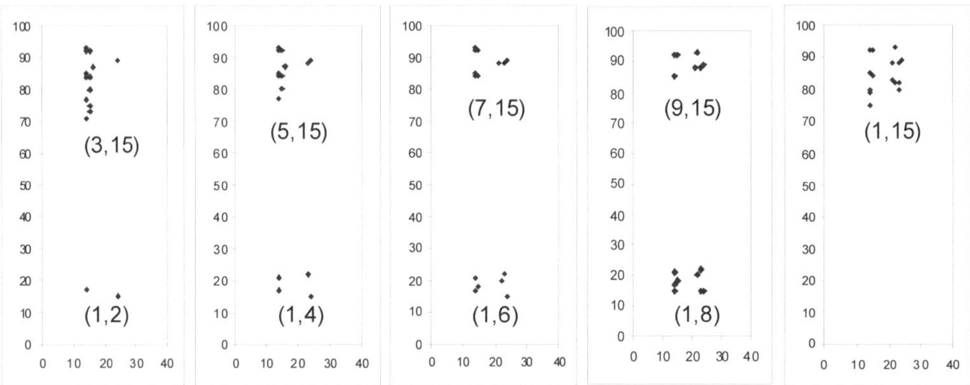

(a) $GPat_1$ (b) $GPat_2$ (c) $GPat_3$ (d) $GPat_4$ (e) $GPat_5$

Fig. 7. Five patterns defined for fifteen cities

The *GP-TSP* implementation receives the number of cities (*C*) and their coordinates ((x_1, y_1), …, (x_i, y_i), …, (x_C, y_C)), the level (*L*), and the number of processors (*P*) as input parameters. It behaves recursively searching all possible paths and applying the global pruning strategy whenever it is feasible and, finally, generating the minimal path and the time spent.
Table 2 shows the *GP-TSP* execution times (in sec.) by pattern (columns $GPat_1$ to $GPat_5$) and starting city (1...15) using only 8 nodes of the parallel machine described in Appendix A. It is important to observe the dispersion of times while maintaining constant the number of processors (*P*) and the number of cities (*C*).
Hence before continuing, there are two important concepts to refresh. The main goal of data mining is finding useful patterns and knowledge in data. Besides, clustering is one of the major data mining techniques, grouping objects together into clusters that exhibit internal cohesion (similar execution time) and external isolation. Therefore, in this work, clustering has been applied to discover the internal information and then to decrease the data-dependence. This general action has been done using the well-known k-means clustering algorithm (MacQueen, 1967) included in the Cluster-Frame tool; see Appendix B for extra information about the tool. With the idea of obtaining quite similar groups with respect to the groups (patterns) used at the beginning, *k* was fixed in five (*k* is the number of clusters).

The initial centroids (one for each cluster) were randomly selected by the clustering tool. Figure 8 shows the experiments by cluster in the Cluster-Frame environment.

	Geographical pattern (GPat)									
	1		2		3		4		5	
Starting city	*Time spent*	*Assigned cluster*	*Time spent*	*Assigned cluster*	*Time spent*	*Assigned cluster*	*Time spent*	*Assigned cluster*	*Time spent*	*Assigned cluster*
1	216.17	1	36.50	3	15.34	2	10.51	4	8.03	5
2	214.44	1	36.82	3	15.19	2	10.49	4	7.82	5
3	77.25	1	38.09	3	15.57	2	10.02	4	7.71	5
4	72.64	1	37.29	3	15.02	2	10.30	4	7.91	5
5	70.94	1	18.54	2	15.84	2	10.41	4	7.83	5
6	74.21	1	17.83	2	15.24	2	10.24	4	7.71	5
7	75.59	1	18.16	2	10.31	4	10.36	4	7.93	5
8	73.72	1	18.03	2	10.34	4	10.26	4	7.87	5
9	69.47	1	17.79	2	10.27	4	9.98	4	8.14	5
10	74.96	1	17.48	2	10.23	4	9.88	4	8.22	5
11	75.89	1	17.07	2	10.24	4	9.85	4	8.04	5
12	70.17	1	17.39	2	10.28	4	9.87	4	8.12	5
13	73.73	1	18.10	2	10.36	4	9.88	4	7.98	5
14	70.87	1	17.37	2	10.17	4	9.95	4	8.02	5
15	73.30	1	18.00	2	10.32	4	9.97	4	7.78	5
Mean	92.23		22.97		12.32		10.14		7.94	

Table 2. *GP-TSP* execution times (in sec.) and assigned cluster by k-means algorithm

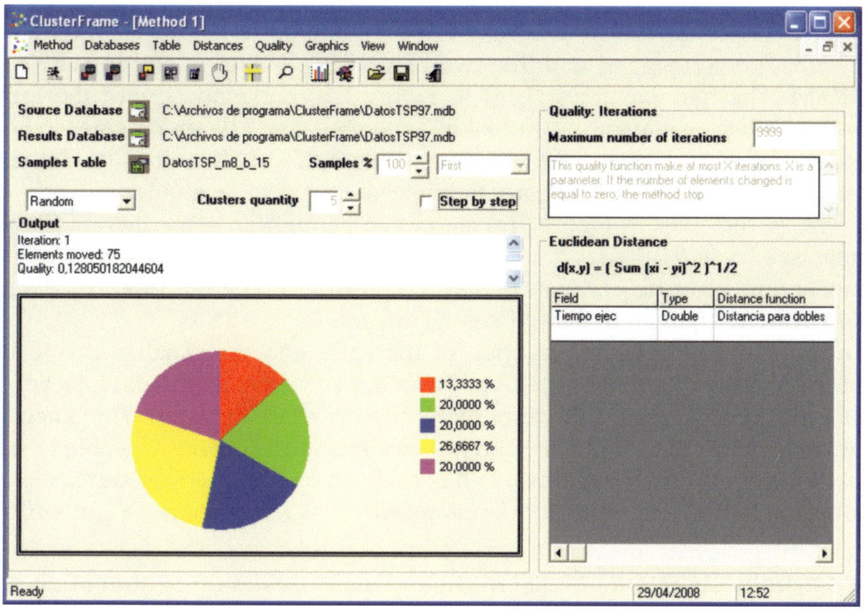

Fig. 8. Cluster-Frame environment

The k-means algorithm aims at minimizing a squared error function. In Equation (1), it is presented the widely used objective function with n data points and k disjoint subsets

$$\sum_{j=1}^{k}\sum_{i=1}^{n} | x_i^{(j)} - c_j |^2 \tag{1}$$

where $| x_i^{(j)} - c_j |^2$ is a chosen distance measure between a data point $x_i^{(j)}$ and the cluster centroid c_j. The entire function is an indicator of the distance of the n data points from their respective cluster centroids.
Table 2 show the assigned cluster for each experiment after executing k-means algorithm. For the clusters 1 to 5, the centroids values were 92.23 sec., 16.94 sec., 37.17 sec., 10.19 sec., and 7.94 sec., respectively.
The quality evaluation involves the validation of the above mentioned hypothesis. For each experiment, the assigned cluster was confronted with the defined graphic pattern previously. The percentage of hits expresses the capacity of prediction. A simple observation is that the execution times were clustered in a similar way to patterns fixed at starting, see Figure 7. In this example, the capacity of prediction was near of 75% (56 hits on 75 possibilities). There was a close relationship between the patterns and the execution times.
Conclusions: The initial hypothesis for the *GP-TSP* has been corroborated; the capacity of prediction has been greater than 75% for the full range of experiments worked. The remaining percentage has given evidence of the existence of other significant parameters. Therefore, a deep analysis of results revealed an open issue remained for discussion and resolution, the singular execution times by pattern. Another major hypothesis was formulated. At this stage, the asymptotic time complexity was defined as *O(P, C, pattern)*.

4.1.2 Second hypothesis → location of the cities and starting city

The example data set is the same used previously. Comparing each chart of Figure 7 with its corresponding column in Table 2 it is easy to infer some important facts. The two far cities (1, 2) in Figure 7(a) correspond with the two higher time values of starting city 1 and 2 in Table 2($GPat_1$). The four far cities (1, 4) in Figure 7(b) correspond with the four higher execution time values of starting city 1 to 4 in Table 2($GPat_2$). The six far cities in Figure 7(c) correspond with the six higher time values of Table 2($GPat_3$). The cities in Figure 7(d) are distributed among two zones; therefore, the times turn out to be similar enough, see Table 2($GPat_4$). Finally, the cities in Figure 7(e) are closed enough; in consequence, the times are quite similar, see Table 2($GPat_5$).
An additional important observation is that the mean of execution times by geographical pattern decreases as the cities approach, see again Table 2.
Conclusions: Without doubt, the location of the cities and the starting city (C_1) play an important role in execution times; the hypothesis has been corroborated. However, an open issue remained for discussion and resolution: how to relate a pattern (in general) with a numerical value which means execution time. This relationship would be able to establish a numerical characterization of patterns. On this basis, an original hypothesis was formulated. At this point, the *GP-TSP* asymptotic time complexity was redefined as $O(C, P, pattern, C_1)$.

4.1.3 Third hypothesis → sum of distances and mean deviation of sum of distances

What parameters could be used to quantitatively characterize different geographical patterns in the distribution of cities? In graph theory, the distance of a vertex p, $d(p)$, of such a connected graph G is defined by $d(p) = \Sigma\, d(p, q)$ where $d(p, q)$ is the distance between p and q and the summation extends over all vertices q of G. This measure is an inverse measure of centrality. Therefore, following the ideas previously mentioned, the sum of the distances from one city to the other cities (SD_j, as it is shown in Equation 2), and the mean deviation of *SDs* values (*MDSD*) are the worked inputs right now. As greater is the sum of the distances, the lower is the centrality.

$$\forall j: 1 \le j \le C \quad SD_j = \sum_{i=1}^{C} \sqrt{(x_j - x_i)^2 + (y_j - y_i)^2} \tag{2}$$

The *SD* value is an index time. If a j particular city is very remote of the others, its SD_j will be considerably greater to the rest and consequently its execution time will also grow. This can be observed in Table 3.

Why is it needed to consider *MDSD* in addition to *SD* as a significant parameter? Quite similar *SD* values from the same geographical pattern (same column) of Table 3 imply similar execution times. The SD_4 and SD_{10} values for the geographical pattern 1 are 230.11 and 234.84, respectively. Then, their execution times are similar 72.64 sec. and 74.96 sec. (labelled with the symbol ◊). Instead, this relation is not true considering similar *SD* values coming from different geographical patterns (different columns). The SD_3 value for geographical pattern 1 and the SD_{10} value for geographical pattern 2 are similar (315.51 and

	Geographical pattern (GPat)									
	1		2		3		4		5	
Starting city	*Time spent*	*SD*	*Time spent*	*SD*	*Time spent*	*SD*	*Time spent*	*SD*	*Time spent*	*SD*
1	216.17	853.94	36.50	746.10	15.34	664.60	10.51	643.75	8.03	148.74
2	214.44	887.44	36.82	740.49	15.19	649.14	10.49	635.54	7.82	104.16
3	*** 77.25**	*** 315.51**	38.09	820.63	15.57	707.70	10.02	555.70	7.71	141.15
4	**◊ 72.64**	**◊ 230.11**	37.29	789.80	15.02	678.07	10.30	599.99	7.91	103.35
5	70.94	226.88	18.54	345.83	15.84	643.65	10.41	611.45	7.83	111.79
6	74.21	244.56	17.83	330.76	15.24	638.04	10.24	595.58	7.71	102.81
7	75.59	276.09	18.16	369.56	10.31	467.99	10.36	592.68	7.93	111.28
8	73.72	294.62	18.03	383.38	10.34	490.55	10.26	639.61	7.87	147.14
9	69.47	233.53	17.79	370.10	10.27	491.52	9.98	574.23	8.14	123.19
10	**◊ 74.96**	**◊ 234.84**	*** 17.48**	*** 323.12**	10.23	446.48	9.88	578.78	8.22	172.52
11	75.89	259.19	17.07	332.87	10.24	477.42	9.85	544.61	8.04	124.64
12	70.17	234.22	17.39	325.19	10.28	449.03	9.87	534.91	8.12	131.68
13	73.73	306.99	18.10	383.11	10.36	504.79	9.88	530.72	7.98	109.78
14	70.87	239.19	17.37	327.02	10.17	451.21	9.95	574.97	8.02	124.96
15	73.30	295.27	18.00	372.00	10.32	494.09	9.97	534.36	7.78	96.29
MDSD		140.94		165.47		90.60		31.56		16.78

Table 3. *GP-TSP* execution times (in sec.) and sum of the distances from each starting city

323.12, respectively) but the execution times are completely dissimilar 77.25 sec. and 17.48 sec. (labelled with the symbol *). The reason is due to the different between the *MDSD* values of geographical pattern 1 and 2.

Conclusions: It is important to emphasize that the *GP-TSP* algorithm obtains good results of prediction. The asymptotic time complexity for the *GP-TSP* algorithm should be defined as *O(P, C, SD, MDSD)*. Another important fact has been reached beyond was originally sought. Choosing the *j* city which has minimum SD_j associated value, it is possible to obtain the exact TSP solution investing less amount of time. Much better results it would be reached if the algorithm begins considering the closer *L* cities to *j* city.

4.2 Predicting GP-TSP performance order

The *GP-TSP* has a time complexity of *O(P, C, SD, MDSD)*. The analytical formulation allows making predictions for a new data set on a particular parallel computer. Figure 9 shows the prediction framework.

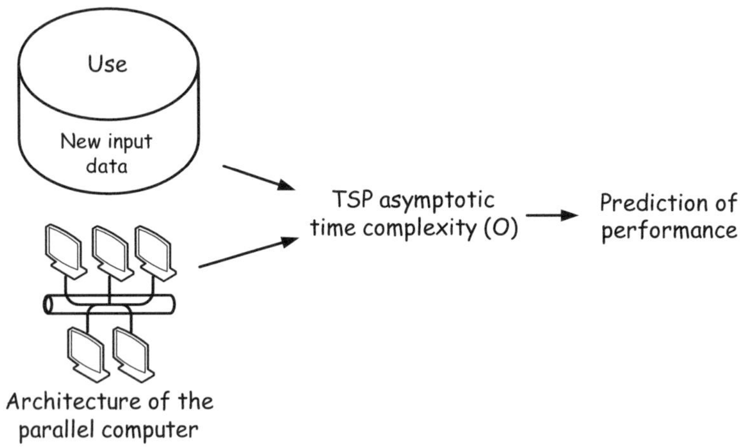

Fig. 9. The prediction of performance framework

4.3 Two relevant GP-TSP experiments

Additional TSP experiments have been performed to verify certain hypotheses. Some of them have shown how important is the geographical pattern of the cities instead of knowing their coordinates. Other experiments which follow a specific pattern have helped to confirm the strong compliance of our hypotheses. Due to the significance, these two groups of experiments were chosen to be developed in this section.

4.3.1 Importance of the geographical pattern

Making geometric transformations (shifting, scaling, and rotation) to well-known patterns is without no doubt a trivial test. This is an excellent case study for understanding the importance of geographical pattern. Applying each one of the transformations to a set of cities, similar execution times are expected executing the same algorithm. This leading to conclude, the time required to reach the solution of the *GP-TSP* algorithm is invariant to certain transformations into the geographical patterns.

The coordinates of a city shifted by Δx in the *x*-dimension and Δy in the *y*-dimension are given by

$$x' = x + \Delta x \qquad y' = y + \Delta y \tag{3}$$

where *x* and *y* are the original and *x′* and *y′* are the new coordinates.
The coordinates of a city scaled by a factor S_x in the *x*-direction and *y*-direction (the city is enlarged in size when S_x is greater than 1 and reduced in size when S_x is between 0 and 1) are given by

$$x' = xS_x \qquad y' = yS_y \tag{4}$$

The coordinates of a city rotated through an angle θ about the origin of the coordinate system are given by

$$x' = x\cos\theta + y\sin\theta \qquad y' = -x\sin\theta + y\cos\theta \tag{5}$$

An example set consisting of fifteen cities is chosen from the historical database. The execution times were obtained using 32 nodes of the parallel machine described in Appendix A. The shifting and rotation transformations are obtained interchanging *x*-coordinate by *y*-coordinate, and the scaling transformation dividing by 2 both coordinates. All these patterns are shown in Figure 10.

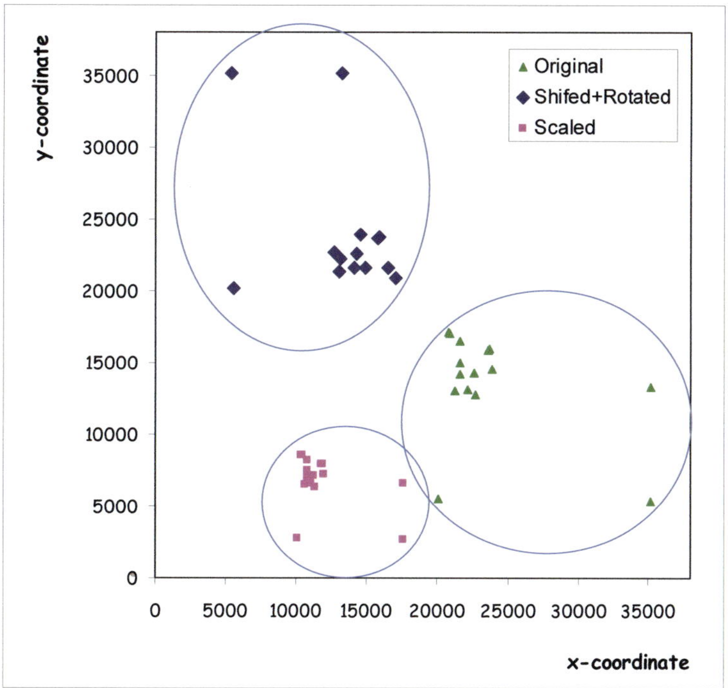

Fig. 10. A historical pattern consisting of fifteen cities. Besides, the same pattern shifted and rotated, and then the pattern scaled

Table 4 exhibits the execution times for the example set starting by each one of the cities. Analyzing the values by row, the historical execution times and the execution times of the geometric transformations for an experiment (row) are quite similar as it was to be expected. For all the experiments, the mean deviation was smaller than 2%.

Starting city	*Pattern*			*Mean deviation*
	Historical	*Shigted+Rotated*	*Scaled*	
1	46.25	48.52	47.30	0.78
2	100.30	105.60	102.77	1.81
3	73.48	76.34	74.52	1.04
4	32.92	34.52	33.75	0.54
5	30.83	31.96	31.35	0.39
6	30.49	31.92	31.22	0.48
7	31.77	33.00	32.21	0.45
8	30.10	31.06	30.43	0.35
9	31.08	32.13	31.92	0.42
10	30.98	32.24	31.60	0.42
11	29.94	31.09	30.36	0.42
12	30.33	31.53	30.85	0.42
13	31.45	32.82	32.14	0.46
14	32.67	33.44	32.53	0.37
15	32.49	33.49	32.89	0.36

Table 4. Comparison of execution times (in sec.) using 32 nodes for the three patterns plotted in Figure 9

4.3.2 Limit case

A singular case is to have the cities uniformly distributed in a circumference, see an example in Fig. 11. As the *MDSD* value will be near to 0, similar execution times are expected. The idea is considering a limit case in order to confirm the hypothesis with respect to the *MDSD* value and the geographical pattern.

Table 5 exhibits a comparative study of *GP-TSP* behaviour; the means and means deviations of execution times of different number of cities uniformly distributed in each circumference pattern are shown. The number of cities is between 15 and 25. As it can be appreciated in Table 5, there is a progressive increase in the mean times. For every circumference, the execution times were quite similar starting by each one of the cities. The mean deviations were smaller than 4%.

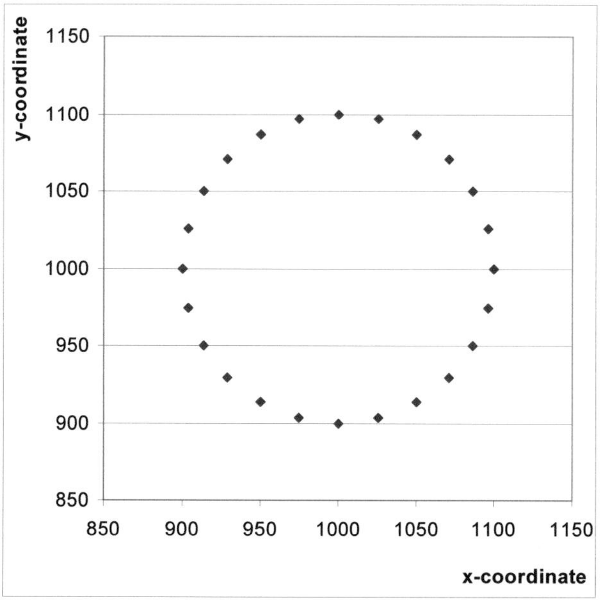

Fig. 11. A circumference pattern composed of 24 uniformly distributed cities

#Cities	*15*	*16*	*17*	*18*	*19*	*20*	*21*	22	23	24	25
Mean	12.71	17.47	23.42	32.93	42.95	54.94	68.67	129.53	367.29	1085.57	2957.15
Mean deviation	0.03	0.04	0.08	0.08	0.07	0.10	0.10	0.11	0.30	2.12	3.03

Table 5. Mean and mean deviation of execution times (in sec.) using 32 nodes by the number of cities that are present in each circumference pattern

5. Conclusions

This chapter introduces a knowledge discovery methodology to estimate the performance order of a hard data-dependent parallel algorithm that solves the traveling salesman problem. It is important to understand that the parallel performance achieved depends on several factors, including the application, the parallel computer, the data distribution, and also the methods used for partitioning the application and mapping its components onto the architecture.

Briefly, the general knowledge discovery methodology begins by designing a considerable number of experiments and measuring their execution times. A well-built experiment guides the experimenters in choosing what experiments actually need to be performed in order to provide a representative sample. A data-mining tool then explores these collected data in search of patterns and/or relationships detecting the main parameters that affect performance. Knowing the main parameters which characterise performance, it becomes possible to suspect new hypotheses to restart the process and to produce a subsequent improved time complexity model. Finally, the methodology predicts the performance order for new data sets on a particular parallel computer by replacing a numerical identification.

A TSP parallel implementation (called *GP-TSP*) has been deeply studied. The *GP-TSP* algorithm analyzes the influence of indeterminism in performance prediction, and also shows the usefulness and the profits of the methodology. Their execution time depends on the number of cities (*C*), the number of processors (*P*), and other parameters. As a result of the investigation, right now the sum of the distances from one city to the other cities (*SD*) and the mean deviation of *SDs* values (*MDSD*) are the numerical parameters characterizing the different input data beyond the number of cities. The followed way to discover this proper set of parameters has been exhaustively described.
The defined methodology for performance modelling is applicable to other related problems such as the knapsack problem, the graph partition, the bin packing, the motion planning, among others.

Appendix

A. Specification of the parallel machine

The execution has been reached with a 32 node homogeneous PC (Cluster Pentium IV 3.0GHz., 1Gb DDR-DSRAM 400Mhz., Gigabit Ethernet) at the Computer Architecture and Operating Systems Department, University Autonoma of Barcelona. All the communications have been accomplished using a switched network with a mean distance between two communication end-points of two hops. The switches enable dynamic routes in order to overlap communication.

B. Characteristics of Cluster-Frame environment

Cluster-Frame is a dynamic and open environment of clustering (Fritzsche, 2007). It permits the evaluation of clustering methods such as K-Means, K-Prototypes, K-Modes, K-Medoid, K-Means^{+}, K-Means^{++} for the same data set. Using Cluster-Frame, the results reached applying different methods and using several parameters can be analyzed and compared.

6. References

Alizadeh, F.; Karp, R.; Newberg, L. & Weisser, D. (1993). Physical mapping of chromosomes: A combinatorial problem in molecular biology. *Symposium on Discrete Algorithms*, pp. 371-381, ACM Press.

Aras, N.; Altinel, I. & Oommen, J. 2003. A kohonen-like decomposition method for the euclidean traveling salesman problem-knies/spl i.bar/decompose. *IEEE Transactions on Neural Networks*, Vol. 14, No.4, pp. 869–890.

Arkin, E.; Chiang, Y. ; Mitchell, J.; Skiena, S. & Yang, T. (1996). On the Maximum Scatter TSP, *In Proceedings of the 8th Annual ACM-SIAM Symposium on Discrete Algorithms (SODA 97)*, pp. 211-220, ACM New York.

Balas, E. (1989). The Prize Collecting Traveling Salesman Problem. *Networks,* Vol.19, pp. 621-636.

Barvinok, A.; Tamir, A.; Fekete, S.; Woeginger, G; Johnson, D. & Woodroofe, R. (2003). The Geometric Maximum Traveling Salesman Problem. *Journal of the ACM,* Vol.50, No.5, pp. 641-664.

Bland, R. & Shallcross, D. (1989). Large Traveling Salesman Problems Arising from Experiments in X-ray Crystallography: a Preliminary Report on Computation. Operations Research Letters, Vol.8, pp. 125-128.

Christofides, N. (1985). Vehicle Routing. *N. Christofides, A. Mingozzi, P. Toth, and C. Sandi, editors, Combinatorial Optimization,* pp. 315-338, Wiley, Chichester, UK.

Duman, E. & Or, I. (2004). Precedence constrained TSP arising in printed circuit board assembly. *International Journal of Production Research,* Vol.42, No.1, pp. 67-78, 1 January 2004, Taylor and Francis Ltd.

Fritzsche, P. (2007). ¿Podemos Predecir en Algoritmos Paralelos No-Deterministas?, *PhD Thesis, University Autonoma of Barcelona, Computer Architecture and Operating Systems Department,* Spain. http://caos.uab.es/

Garey, M.; Graham, R. & Johnson, D. (1976). Some NP-complete geometric problems, STOC '76: Proceedings of the eighth annual ACM symposium on Theory of computing, pp. 10-22, Hershey, Pennsylvania, United States, ACM, New York, NY, USA.

Gilmore, P. & Gomory, R. (1964). Sequencing a One-State-Variable Machine: A Solvable Case of the Traveling Salesman Problem. Operations Research, Vol.12, No.5, pp. 655-679.

Golden, B.; Levy, L. & Vohra, R. (1987). The Orienteering Problem. *Naval Research Logistics,* Vol.34, pp. 307-318.

Groth, R. (1998) Data mining: a hands-on approach for business professionals, Prentice Hall PTR.

Gutin, G. & Punnen, P. (2006). *The Traveling Salesman Problem and Its Variations,* Springer, 0-387-44459-9, New York.

Johnson, O. & Liu, J. (2006). *A Traveling Salesman Approach for predicting protein functions,* Source Code for Biology and Medicine, Vol.1, pp. 1-7.

Karp, R. (1972). Reducibility among combinatorial problems: In Complexity of Computer Computations. *Plenum Press,* pp. 85-103. New York.

Korostensky, C. & Gonnet, G. (2000). Using traveling salesman problem algorithms for evolutionary tree construction. *BIOINF: Bioinformatics,* Vol.16, No.7, pp. 619-627.

Lenstra, J. & Kan, A. (1975). Some simple applications of the Travelling Salesman Problem. Operations Research Quarterly, Vol.26, No.4, pp. 717-732.

Lilja, D. (2000). *Measuring computer performance: a practitioner's guide,* Cambridge University Press, ISBN: 0-521-64105-5, New York, NY, USA.

MacQueen, J. (1967). Some Methods for Classification and Analysis of MultiVariate Observations, *Proc. of the fifth Berkeley Symposium on Mathematical Statistics and Probability,* Vol.1, pp. 281-297, L. M. Le Cam and J. Neyman, University of California Press.

Miller, D. & Pekny, J. (1991). Exact Solution of Large Asymmetric Traveling Salesman Problems. *Science,* Vol.251, pp. 754-761.

Miller, R. & Boxer, L. (2005). *Algorithms Sequential and Parallel: A Unified Approach,* Charles River Media. Computer Engineering Series, 1-58450-412-9.

Pepper, J.; Golden, B. & Wasil, E. (2002). Solving the travelling salesman problem with annealing-based heuristics: a computational study. *IEEE Transactions on Man and Cybernetics Systems,* Part A, Vol. 32, No.1, pp. 72–77.

Ratliff, H. & Rosenthal, A. (1983). Order-Picking in a Rectangular Warehouse: A Solvable Case for the Traveling Salesman Problem. Operations Research, Vol.31, No.3, pp. 507-521.

Sankoff, D. & Blanchette, M. (1997). The median problem for breakpoints in comparative genomics, *Proceedings of the 3rd Annual International Conference on Computing and Combinatorics (COCOON'97)*, Vol.1276, pp. 251-264, New York.

Tsai, H.; Yang, J. & Kao, C. (2002). Solving traveling salesman problems by combining global and local search mechanisms, *Proceedings of the 2002 Congress on Evolutionary Computation (CEC'02)*, Vol.2, pp. 1290–1295.

TSP page (2010). http://www.tsp.gatech.edu/.

15

Linear Programming Formulation of the Multi-Depot Multiple Traveling Salesman Problem with Differentiated Travel Costs

Moustapha Diaby
University of Connecticut
USA

1. Introduction

The multiple traveling salesman problem (mTSP) is a generalization of the well-known traveling salesman problem (TSP; see Applegate *et al.*, 2006; Greco, 2008; Gutin and Punnen, 2007; or Lawler *et al.*, 1985)) in which each of $\mathfrak{c}$ cities must be visited by exactly one of $\mathfrak{s}$ ($1 < \mathfrak{s} < \mathfrak{c}$) traveling salesmen. When there is a single depot (or "base") for all the salesmen, the problem is called the *single depot* mTSP. On the other hand, when the salesmen are initially based at different depots, then the problem is referred to as the *multi-depot* mTSP (MmTSP). If the salesmen are required to return to their respective original bases at the end of the travels, the problem is referred to as the *fixed destination* MmTSP. When the salesmen are not required to return to their original bases, the problem is referred to as the *nonfixed destination* MmTSP. It is often also stipulated in the *nonfixed destination* MmTSP that the number of salesmen at a given depot at the end of the travels be the same as the number of salesmen that were initially there. Also, if there is no requirement that every salesman be activated, then fixed costs are (typically) associated with the salesmen and included in the cost-minimization objective of the problem, along with (or in lieu of) the usual total inter-site travel costs. More detailed discussions of these and other variations of the problem can be found in Bektas (2006), and Kara and Bektas (2006), among others.

Bektas (2006) discusses many contexts in which the mTSP has been applied including combat mission planning, transportation planning, print scheduling, satellite suveying systems design, and workforce planning contexts, respectively. More recent applications that are described in the literature include those of routing unmanned combat aerial vehicles (Shetty *et al.*, 2008), scheduling quality inspections (Tang *et al.*, 2007), scheduling trucks for the transportation of containers (Zhang *et al.*, 2010), and scheduling workforce (Tang *et al.*, 2007). Also, beyond these specific contexts, one can easily argue that most of the practical contexts in which the TSP has been applied could be more realistically modeled as mTSP's. Hence, the problem has a very wide range of applicability.

Mathematical Programming models that have been developed to solve the mTSP are reviewed in Bektas (2006). Additional formulations are proposed in Kara and Bektas (2006). Because of the complexity of the models, solution methods have been mostly heuristic approaches. The exact procedures are the cutting planes approach of Laporte and Norbert (1980), and the branch-and-bound approaches of Ali and Kennington (1986), Gavish and Srikanth (1986), and Gromicho *et al.* (1992), respectively (see Bektas, 2006). The heuristic approaches that have been developed are reviewed in Bektas (2006) and Ghufurian and Javadian (2010). They can be classified into two broad groups that we label as the "transformation-based" and the "direct" heuristics, respectively. The "transformation-based" heuristics consist of transforming the problem into a standard TSP on expanded graphs, and then using TSP heuristics to solve it (see Betkas, 2006). The "direct" heuristics tackle the problem in its natural form. They include evolutionary, genetic, k-opt, neural network, simulated annealing, and tabu search procedures, respectively (see Bektas, 2006, and Ghufurian and Javadian, 2010 for detailed discussions).

A general limitation of the existing literature is the fragmentation of models over the different types of mTSP's discussed above. In general, models developed for one type of mTSP cannot be applied in a straightforward manner to other types. Also, to the best of our knowledge, except for the VRP model of Christofides *et al.* (1981), and the *fixed destination* MmTSP Integer Programming (IP) model of Kara and Bektas (2006), none of the existing models can be extended in a straightforward manner to handle differentiated travel costs for the salesmen. Differentiated travel costs are more realistic in many practical situations however, such as in contexts of routing/scheduling vehicles for example, where there may be differing pay rates for drivers, vehicle types, and/or transportation modes.

In this chapter, we consider a generalization of the mTSP where there are differentiated intersite travel costs associated with the salesmen. There are several depots from which travels start (i.e., the problem considered is the MmTSP), the salesmen are required to return to their respective staring bases at the end of their travels (i.e., destinations are *fixed*), and the number of salesmen to be activated is a decision variable. We present a linear programming (LP) formulation of this problem. The complexity orders of the number of variables and the number of constraints of the proposed LP are $O\left(\mathfrak{c}^9 \cdot \mathfrak{s}^3\right)$ and $O\left(\mathfrak{c}^8 \cdot \mathfrak{s}^3\right)$, respectively, where $\mathfrak{c}$ and $\mathfrak{s}$ are the number of customer sites and the number of salesmen in the MmTSP instance, respectively. Hence, the model goes beyond the scope of the mTSP *per se*, to a re-affirmation of the equality of the computational complexity classes "*P*" and "*NP*." Also, the proposed model can be adjusted in a straightforward manner to accommodate *nonfixed destinations* and/or situations where it is required that all the salesmen be activated. It is therefore a more comprehensive model than existing ones that we know of (see Bektas (2006), and Kara and Bektas (2006)). In formulating our proposed LP, we first develop a bipartite network flow-based model of the problem. Then, we use a path-based modeling framework similar to that used in Diaby (2006b, 2007b, 2010a, and 2010b). The approach is illustrated with a numerical example.

Three reports (by a same author) with negative claims having some relation to the modeling approach used in this paper have been publicized through the internet (Hofman, 2006, 2007, and 2008b). These are the only such reports (and negative claims) that we know of. There is a counter-example claim in Hofman (2006) that has to do with the relaxation of the model in Diaby (2006b) suggested in Diaby (2006a) (see Diaby, 2006a, p. 20: "Proposition 6"). There is another counter-example claim (Hofman (2008b)) that pertains to a simplification of the model in Diaby (2007b) discussed in Diaby (2008). Indeed further checking revealed flawed developments in both of the papers against which these counter-example claims were made, specifically, "Proposition 6" for Diaby (2006a), and Theorem 25 and Corollary 26 for Diaby (2008). However, these are not aaplicable to the respective published, peer-reviewed papers dealing with the respective "full" models (Diaby(2006b), and Diaby (2007b)).Hence, the counter-example claims may have had some merit, but *only* for the relaxations to which they pertain. The claim in Hofman (2007) rests on the premise that an integral

polytope with an exponential number of vertices cannot be completely described using a polynomially-bounded number of linear constraints (see Hofman, 2007, p. 3). It is a well-established fact however, that the Assignment Polytope for example, is integral, has $n!$ extreme points (where n is the number of assignments), and is completely described by $2n$ linear constraints (see Burkard et al., 2007, pp. 24-26, and Schrijver, 1986, pp. 108-110, among others). Other contradictions of the premise of Hofman (2007) include the Transportation Polytope (see Bazaraa et al, 2010, pp. 513-535), and the general Min-Cost Network Flow Polytope (see Ahuja *et al.*, 1993, 294-449, or Bazaraa et al., 2010, pp. 453-493, for example). Characterizations of integral polytopes in general and additional examples (including some non-network flow-based ones) contradicting the premise of Hofman (2007) are discussed in Nemhauser and Wolsey, 1988, pp. 535-607, and Schrijver, 1986, pp. 266-338, among others. Hence, the foundations and implications of the claim in Hofman (2007) are in strong contradiction of well-established Operations Research knowledge.
It should be noted also that our overall approach consists essentially of developing an alternate linear programming reformulation of the Assignment Polytope (see Burkard et al., 2007, pp. 24-34) in terms of "complex flow modeling"variables we introduce (see section 4 of this chapter). Hence, the developments in Yannakakis (1991) in particular, are not applicable in the context of this work, since we do not deal with the TSP polytope *per se* (see Lawler et al., 1988, pp.256-261).
The plan of the chapter is as follows. Our BNF-based model of the MmTSP is developed in section 2. A path representation of the BNF-based solutions is developed in section 3. An Integer Programming (IP) model of the path representations in developed in section 4. A path-based LP reformulation of the BNF-based Polytope is developed in section 5. Our proposed overall LP model is developed model in section 6. Conclusions are discussed in section 7.

Definition 1 (*"MmTSP schedule"*) *We will refer to any feasible solution to the fixed destination MmTSP as a "MmTSP schedule."*

The following notation will be used throughout the rest of the chapter.

Notation 2 (General notation) *:*

1. $\mathfrak{d}$: Number of depot sites/nodes;
2. $\mathbb{D} := \{1,2,\ldots,\mathfrak{d}\}$ (index set for the depot sites);
3. $\mathfrak{c}$: Number of customer sites/nodes;
4. $\mathbb{C} := \{1,2,\ldots,\mathfrak{c}\}$ (index set for the customer sites);
5. $\mathfrak{s}$: Number of salesmen;
6. $\mathbb{S} := \{1,2,\ldots,\mathfrak{s}\}$ (index set for the salesmen);
7. $\forall p \in \mathbb{S}$, $\mathfrak{b}_p$: Index of the starting base (or initial depot) for salesman p $(\mathfrak{b}_p \in \mathbb{D})$;
8. $\forall p \in \mathbb{S}$, $\mathfrak{f}_p$: Fixed cost associated with the activation of salesman p;
9. $\forall p \in \mathbb{S}, \forall (i,j) \in (\mathbb{D} \cup \mathbb{C})^2$, $\mathfrak{c}_{pij}$: Cost of travel from site i to site j by salesman p;
10. A *MmTSP schedule* wherein salesman p visits m_p customers with $i_{p,k}$ being the kth customer visited will be denoted as the ordered set $((p,i_{p,k}) : p \in \overline{\mathbb{S}}, k = 1,\ldots,m_p)$, where $\overline{\mathbb{S}} \subseteq \mathbb{S}$ denotes the subset of activated salesmen;

11. $\mathbb{R}$: Set of real numbers;
12. For two column vectors $\mathbf{x}$ and $\mathbf{y}$, $\begin{pmatrix} \mathbf{x} \\ \mathbf{y} \end{pmatrix} = (\mathbf{x}^T, \mathbf{y}^T)^T$ will be written as "($\mathbf{x}$, $\mathbf{y}$)" (where $(\cdot)^T$denotes the transpose of $(\cdot)$), except for where that causes ambiguity;
13. For two column vectors $\mathbf{a}$ and $\mathbf{b}$, and a function or expression A having ($\mathbf{a}$, $\mathbf{b}$) as an argument, "A (($\mathbf{a}$, $\mathbf{b}$))" will be written as "A($\mathbf{a}$, $\mathbf{b}$)", except for where that causes ambiguity;
14. $\mathbf{x}_i$: i^{th} component of vector $\mathbf{x}$;
15. "$\mathbf{0}$" : Column vector (of comfortable size) that has every entry equal to 0;
16. "$\mathbf{1}$" : Column vector (of comfortable size) that has every entry equal to 1;
17. $Conv(\cdot)$: Convex hull of $(\cdot)$;
18. $Ext(\cdot)$: Set of extreme points of $(\cdot)$;
19. The notation "$\exists \ \langle i_1 \in A_1; \ \ldots; \ i_p \in A_p \rangle : \langle B_1; \ \ldots; \ B_q \rangle$" stands for "*There exists at least p objects with at least one from each* A_r $(r = 1, \ldots, p)$*, such that each expression* B_s $(s = 1, \ldots, q)$ *holds true.*" Where that does not cause ambiguity, the brackets (one or both sets) will be omitted.

Assumption 3 *We assume, without loss of generality (w.l.o.g.), that:*

1. $\mathfrak{c} \geq 5$;
2. $\mathfrak{d} \geq 1$;
3. $\forall j \in \mathbb{D}, \{p \in \mathbb{S} : \mathfrak{b}_p = j\} \neq \varnothing$;
4. $\forall p \in \mathbb{S}, \forall i \in \mathbb{C}, \mathfrak{e}_{pii} = \infty$;
5. $\forall p \in \mathbb{S}, \forall (i,j) \in \mathbb{D}^2, \mathfrak{e}_{pij} = \infty$
6. The set of cutomers/customer sites has been augmented with a fictitious customer/site, indexed as $\bar{\mathfrak{c}} := \mathfrak{c} + 1$, with $\mathfrak{e}_{p,\bar{\mathfrak{c}},\bar{\mathfrak{c}}} = 0$ for all $p \in \mathbb{S}$, $\mathfrak{e}_{p,i,\bar{\mathfrak{c}}} = \mathfrak{e}_{p,i,\mathfrak{b}_p}$ for all $(p,i) \in (\mathbb{S},\mathbb{C})$, and $\mathfrak{e}_{p,\bar{\mathfrak{c}},i} = \infty$ for all $(p,i) \in (\mathbb{S},\mathbb{C})$;
7. Fictitious customer site $\bar{\mathfrak{c}}$ can be visited multiple times by one or more of the traveling salesmen in any *MmTSP schedule*.

2. Bipartite network flow-based model of MmTSP schedules

The purpose of the bipartite network flow (BNF)-based model developed in this section is to simplify the exposition of the development of our overall LP model discussed in sections 5 and 6 of this chapter. However, as far as we know, it is a first such model for the MmTSP, and we believe it can also serve as the basis of good (near-optimal) heuristic procedures for solving large-scale (practical-sized) MmTSP's. We will first present the model. Then, we will illustrate it with a numerical example.

Notation 4 :

1. $\overline{\mathbb{C}} := \mathbb{C} \cup \{\bar{\mathfrak{c}}\} = \mathbb{C} \cup \{\mathfrak{c} + 1\}$
2. $\forall p \in \mathbb{S}, \mathbb{T}_p := \{1, \ldots, \mathfrak{c}\}$ (index set for the order (or "times") of visits for salesman p);

3. $\forall p \in \mathbb{S}, \forall i \in \overline{\mathbb{C}}, \forall t \in \mathbb{T}_p$, $x_{p,i,t}$ denotes a non-negative variable that is greater than zero iff i is the tth customer to be visited by salesman p.

Definition 5 ("BNF-based Polytope") *Let* $P_1 := \{x \in \mathbb{R}^{\mathfrak{s}\mathfrak{c}\bar{\mathfrak{c}}} : x$ *satisfies (1)-(6)*$\}$, *where (1)-(6) are specified as follows:*

$$\sum_{p\in\mathbb{S}}\sum_{t\in\mathbb{T}_p} x_{p,i,t} = 1; \quad i \in \mathbb{C} \tag{1}$$

$$\sum_{p\in S}\sum_{t\in\mathbb{T}_p} x_{p,\bar{\mathfrak{c}},t} = (\mathfrak{s}-1)\mathfrak{c}; \tag{2}$$

$$\sum_{i\in\overline{\mathbb{C}}} x_{p,i,t} = 1; \quad p \in \mathbb{S},\ t \in \mathbb{T}_p \tag{3}$$

$$x_{p,\bar{\mathfrak{c}},t-1} - x_{p,\bar{\mathfrak{c}},t} \leq 0; \quad p \in \mathbb{S},\ t \in \mathbb{T}_p : t > 1 \tag{4}$$

$$x_{pit} \in \{0,1\}; \quad p \in \mathbb{S},\ i \in \mathbb{C},\ t \in \mathbb{T} \tag{5}$$

$$x_{p,\bar{\mathfrak{c}},t} \geq 0; \quad p \in \mathbb{S},\ t \in \mathbb{T}_p \tag{6}$$

We refer to $Conv(P_1)$ *as the "Bipartite Network Flow (BNF)-based Polytope."*

Theorem 6 *There exists a one-to-one mapping of the points of* P_1 *(i.e., the extreme points of the BNF-based Polytope) onto the MmTSP schedules.*

Proof. It is trivial to verify that a unique point of P_1 can be constructed from any given *MmTSP schedule* and vice versa.
The *BNF*-based formulation is illustrated in Example 7.

Example 7 ***Fixed destination MmTSP with:***

- $\mathfrak{d} = 2,\ \mathbb{D} = \{1,2\}$;
- $\mathfrak{s} = 2,\ \mathbb{S} = \{1,2\},\ \mathfrak{b}_1 = 1, \mathfrak{b}_2 = 2$;
- $\mathfrak{c} = 5,\ \mathbb{C} = \{1,2,3,4,5\}$;
  BNF tableau form of the BNF-based formulation (where entries in the body are "technical coefficients," and entries in the margins are "right-hand-side values"):

	salesman "1"					*salesman "2"*					
time of visit, t =	1	2	3	4	5	1	2	3	4	5	*"Demand"*
customer "1"	1	1	1	1	1	1	1	1	1	1	1
customer "2"	1	1	1	1	1	1	1	1	1	1	1
customer "3"	1	1	1	1	1	1	1	1	1	1	1
customer "4"	1	1	1	1	1	1	1	1	1	1	1
customer "5"	1	1	1	1	1	1	1	1	1	1	1
customer "6"	1	1	1	1	1	1	1	1	1	1	5
"Supply"	1	1	1	1	1	1	1	1	1	1	—

- *Illustrations of Theorem 6:*
- *Illustration 1:*
Let the MmTSP schedule be: $((1,1),(1,3),(1,2),(2,5),(2,4))$.

The unique point of P_1 corresponding to this schedule is obtained by setting the entries of x as follows:

$$\forall (i,t) \in (\overline{\mathbb{C}}, \mathbb{T}_1),\ x_{1,i,t} = \begin{cases} 1 & \text{if } (i,t) \in \{(1,1),(3,2),(2,3),\{6,4),(6,5)\} \\ 0 & \text{otherwise} \end{cases}$$

$$\forall (i,t) \in (\overline{\mathbb{C}}, \mathbb{T}_2),\ x_{2,i,t} = \begin{cases} 1 & \text{if } (i,t) \in \{(5,1),(4,2),(6,3),\{6,4),(6,5)\} \\ 0 & \text{otherwise} \end{cases}$$

This solution can be shown in tableau form as follows (where only non-zero entries of x are shown):

	salesman "1"					*salesman "2"*				
time of visit, t =	1	2	3	4	5	1	2	3	4	5
customer "1"	1									
customer "2"			1							
customer "3"		1								
customer "4"							1			
customer "5"						1				
customer "6"				1	1			1	1	1

- Illustration 2:
Let $x \in P_1$ be as follows:

$$\forall (i,t) \in (\overline{\mathbb{C}}, \mathbb{T}_1),\ x_{1,i,t} = \begin{cases} 1 & \text{for } (i,t) \in \{(6,1),(6,2),(6,3),\{6,4),(6,5)\} \\ 0 & \text{otherwise} \end{cases}$$

$$\forall (i,t) \in (\overline{\mathbb{C}}, \mathbb{T}_2),\ x_{2,i,t} = \begin{cases} 1 & \text{for } (i,t) \in \{(3,1),(5,2),(1,3),\{4,4),(2,5)\} \\ 0 & \text{otherwise} \end{cases}$$

The unique MmTSP schedule corresponding to this point is $((2,3),(2,5),(2,1),(2,4),(2,2))$.

3. Path representation of BNF-based solutions

In this section, we develop a path representation of the extreme points of the *BNF-based Polytope* (i.e., the points of P_1). The framework for this representation is the multipartite digraph, $G = (V, A)$, illustrated in Example 10. The nodes of this graph correspond to the variables of the *BNF*-based formulation (i.e., the "cells" of the *BNF*-based tableau). The arcs of the graph represent (roughly) the inter-site movements at consecutive *times of travel*, respectively.

Definition 8

1. The set of nodes of *Graph G* that correspond to a given pair $(p,k) \in (\mathbb{S}, \mathbb{T}_p)$ is referred to as a *stage* of the graph;
2. The set of nodes of *Graph G* that correspond to a given customer site $i \in \overline{\mathbb{C}}$ is referred to as a *level* of the graph.

For the sake of simplicity of exposition, we perform a sequential re-indexing of the stages of the graph and formalize the specifications of the nodes and arcs accordingly, as follows.

Notation 9 (Graph formalization)

1. $n := \mathfrak{s} \cdot \mathfrak{c}$ (Number of stages of *Graph G*);
2. $\overline{R} := \{1, \ldots, n\}$ (Set of stages of *Graph G*);
3. $R := \overline{R} \backslash \{n\}$ (Set of stages of *Graph G* with positive-outdegree nodes);
4. $\forall\, p \in \mathbb{S}, \underline{\mathfrak{r}}_p := ((p-1)\mathfrak{c} + 1)$ (Sequential re-indexing of stage $(p,1)$);
5. $\forall\, p \in \mathbb{S}, \overline{\mathfrak{r}}_p := p \cdot \mathfrak{c}$ (Sequential re-indexing of stage $(p, \mathfrak{c})$);
6. $\forall\, r \in S, \mathfrak{p}_r := \max\{p \in \mathbb{S} : \underline{\mathfrak{r}}_p \leq r\}$ (Index of the salesman associated with stage r);
7. $V := \{(i,r) : i \in \overline{\mathbb{C}}, r \in \overline{R}\}$ (Set of nodes/vertices of *Graph G*);
8. $\forall\, r \in \overline{R};\ i \in \overline{\mathbb{C}}$,
$$F_r(i) := \begin{cases} \overline{\mathbb{C}} \backslash \{i\} & \text{for } r < n;\ i \in \mathbb{C}; \\ \{\overline{\mathfrak{c}}\} & \text{for } r < \overline{\mathfrak{r}}_{\mathfrak{p}_r};\ i = \overline{\mathfrak{c}} \\ \overline{\mathbb{C}} & \text{for } \overline{\mathfrak{r}}_{\mathfrak{p}_r} = r < n;\ i = \overline{\mathfrak{c}} \\ \varnothing & \text{for } r = n \end{cases}$$
(Forward star of node (i,r) of *GraphG*);
9. $\forall\, r \in \overline{R};\ i \in \overline{\mathbb{C}}$,
$$B_r(i) := \begin{cases} \varnothing & \text{for } r = 1 \\ \{j \in \overline{\mathbb{C}} : i \in F_{r-1}(j)\} & \text{for } r > 1 \end{cases}$$
(Backward star of node (i,r) of *Graph G*);
10. $A := \{(i,r,j) \in (\overline{\mathbb{C}}, R, \overline{\mathbb{C}}) :\ j \in F_r(i)\}$ (Set of arcs of *Graph G*).

The notation for the multipartite graph representation is illustrated in Example 10 for the MmTSP instance of Example 7.

Example 10 *The multipartite graph representation of the MmTSP of Example 7 is summarized as follows:*

-$n = 2 \times 5 = 10$; $\overline{R} = \{1,2,\ldots,10\}$; $R = \{1,\ldots,9\}$;
- Stage indices for the salesmen:

Salesman, p	First stage, $\underline{\mathfrak{r}}_p$	Last stage, $\overline{\mathfrak{r}}_p$
1	1	5
2	6	10

- Salesman index for the stages:

Stage, r	Salesman index, $\mathfrak{p}_r$
$r \in \{1,2,3,4,5\}$	1
$r \in \{6,7,8,9,10\}$	2

- Forward stars of the nodes of *Graph G*:

Level, i	Stage, r									
	1	2	3	4	5	6	7	8	9	10
$i=1$	$\overline{C}\setminus\{1\}$	$\overline{C}\setminus\{1\}$	$\overline{C}\setminus\{1\}$	$\overline{C}\setminus\{1\}$	$\overline{C}\setminus\{1\}$	$\overline{C}\setminus\{1\}$	$\overline{C}\setminus\{1\}$	$\overline{C}\setminus\{1\}$	$\overline{C}\setminus\{1\}$	$\varnothing$
$i=2$	$\overline{C}\setminus\{2\}$	$\overline{C}\setminus\{2\}$	$\overline{C}\setminus\{2\}$	$\overline{C}\setminus\{2\}$	$\overline{C}\setminus\{2\}$	$\overline{C}\setminus\{2\}$	$\overline{C}\setminus\{2\}$	$\overline{C}\setminus\{2\}$	$\overline{C}\setminus\{2\}$	$\varnothing$
$i=3$	$\overline{C}\setminus\{3\}$	$\overline{C}\setminus\{3\}$	$\overline{C}\setminus\{3\}$	$\overline{C}\setminus\{3\}$	$\overline{C}\setminus\{3\}$	$\overline{C}\setminus\{3\}$	$\overline{C}\setminus\{3\}$	$\overline{C}\setminus\{3\}$	$\overline{C}\setminus\{3\}$	$\varnothing$
$i=4$	$\overline{C}\setminus\{4\}$	$\overline{C}\setminus\{4\}$	$\overline{C}\setminus\{4\}$	$\overline{C}\setminus\{4\}$	$\overline{C}\setminus\{4\}$	$\overline{C}\setminus\{4\}$	$\overline{C}\setminus\{4\}$	$\overline{C}\setminus\{4\}$	$\overline{C}\setminus\{4\}$	$\varnothing$
$i=5$	$\overline{C}\setminus\{5\}$	$\overline{C}\setminus\{5\}$	$\overline{C}\setminus\{5\}$	$\overline{C}\setminus\{5\}$	$\overline{C}\setminus\{5\}$	$\overline{C}\setminus\{5\}$	$\overline{C}\setminus\{5\}$	$\overline{C}\setminus\{5\}$	$\overline{C}\setminus\{5\}$	$\varnothing$
$i=6$	$\{6\}$	$\{6\}$	$\{6\}$	$\{6\}$	$\overline{C}$	$\{6\}$	$\{6\}$	$\{6\}$	$\{6\}$	$\varnothing$

- Backward stars of the nodes of *Graph G*:

Level, i	*Stage*, r									
	1	2	3	4	5	6	7	8	9	10
$i=1$	$\varnothing$	$C\setminus\{1\}$	$C\setminus\{1\}$	$C\setminus\{1\}$	$C\setminus\{1\}$	$\overline{C}\setminus\{1\}$	$C\setminus\{1\}$	$C\setminus\{1\}$	$C\setminus\{1\}$	$C\setminus\{1\}$
$i=2$	$\varnothing$	$C\setminus\{2\}$	$C\setminus\{2\}$	$C\setminus\{2\}$	$C\setminus\{2\}$	$\overline{C}\setminus\{2\}$	$C\setminus\{2\}$	$C\setminus\{2\}$	$C\setminus\{2\}$	$C\setminus\{2\}$
$i=3$	$\varnothing$	$C\setminus\{3\}$	$C\setminus\{3\}$	$C\setminus\{3\}$	$C\setminus\{3\}$	$\overline{C}\setminus\{3\}$	$C\setminus\{3\}$	$C\setminus\{3\}$	$C\setminus\{3\}$	$C\setminus\{3\}$
$i=4$	$\varnothing$	$C\setminus\{4\}$	$C\setminus\{4\}$	$C\setminus\{4\}$	$C\setminus\{4\}$	$\overline{C}\setminus\{4\}$	$C\setminus\{4\}$	$C\setminus\{4\}$	$C\setminus\{4\}$	$C\setminus\{4\}$
$i=5$	$\varnothing$	$C\setminus\{5\}$	$C\setminus\{5\}$	$C\setminus\{5\}$	$C\setminus\{5\}$	$\overline{C}\setminus\{5\}$	$C\setminus\{5\}$	$C\setminus\{5\}$	$C\setminus\{5\}$	$C\setminus\{5\}$
$i=6$	$\varnothing$	$\overline{C}$	$\overline{C}$	$\overline{C}$	$\overline{C}$	$\overline{C}$	$\overline{C}$	$\overline{C}$	$\overline{C}$	$\overline{C}$

- Graph illustration: *Graph G*

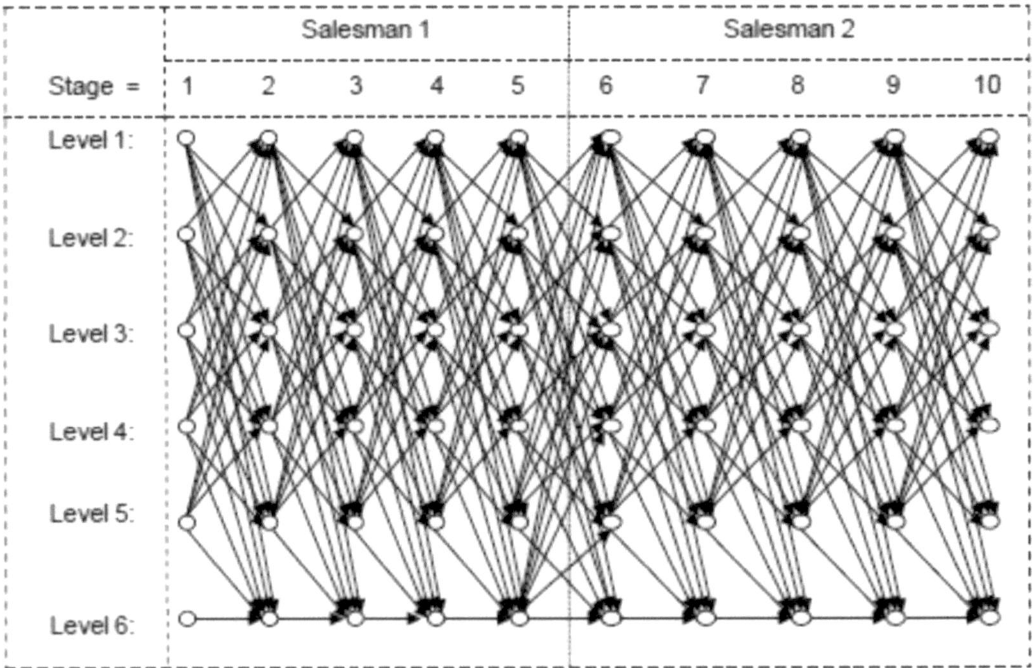

Definition 11 ("*MmTSP-path-in-G*")

1. We refer to a path of *Graph G* that spans the set of *stages* of the graph (i.e., a walk of length $(n-1)$ of the graph) as a *through-path* of the graph;

2. We refer to a *through-path* of *Graph G* that is incident upon each level of the graph pertaining to a customer site in $\mathbb{C}$ at exactly one node of the graph as a "*MmTSP-path-in-G*" (plural: "*MmTSP-paths-in-G*"); that is, a set of arcs, $((i_1,1,i_2),(i_2,2,i_3),...,(i_{n-1},n-1,i_n)) \in A^{n-1}$, is a *MmTSP-path-in-G* iff $(\forall t \in \mathbb{C}, \exists\ p \in \overline{R}:\ i_p = t$, and $\forall (p,q) \in (\overline{R},\overline{R}\backslash\{p\}) : (i_p,i_q) \in \mathbb{C}^2$, $i_p \neq i_q)$.

An illustration of a *MmTSP-path-in-G* is given in Figure 1 for the MmTSP instance of Example 7. The *MmTSP-path-in-G* that is shown on the figure corresponds to the *MmTSP schedule:* $((1,1),(1,3),(1,2),(2,5),(2,4))$.

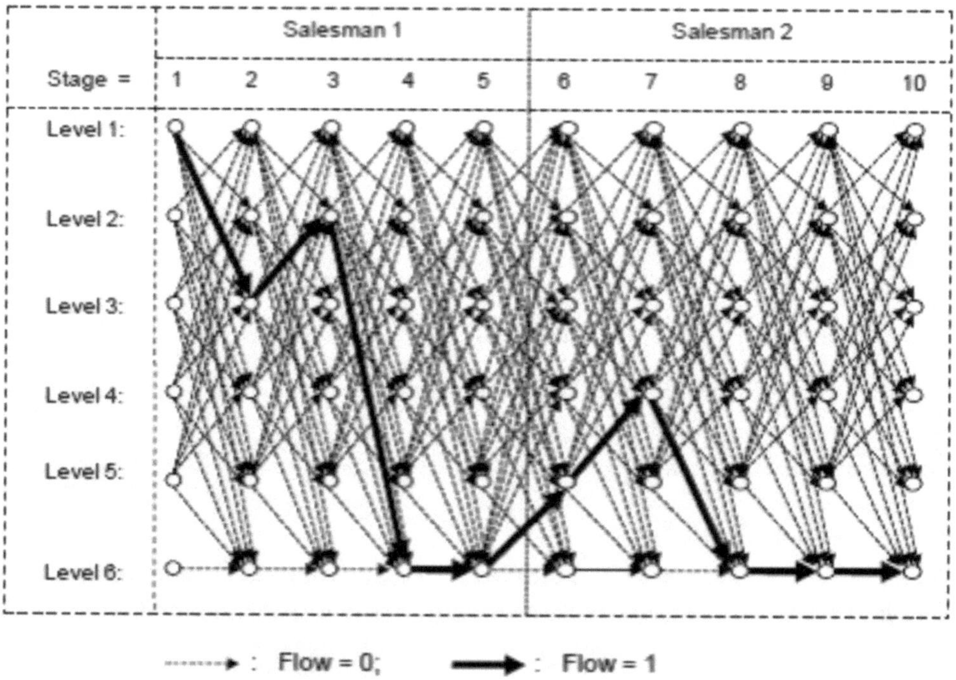

Fig. 1. Illustration of a *MmTSP-path-in-G*

Theorem 12 *The following statements are true:*

(*i*) There exists a one-to-one mapping between the *MmTSP-paths-in-G* and the extreme points of the *BNF-based Polytope* (*i.e.*, the points of P_1);

(*ii*) There exists a one-to-one mapping between the *MmTSP-paths-in-G* and the *MmTSP schedules*.

Proof. The theorem follows trivially from definitions.

Theorem 13 *A given MmTSP-path-in-G cannot be represented as a convex combination of other MmTSP-paths-in-G.*

Proof. The theorem follows directly from the fact that every *MmTSP-path-in-G* represents an extreme flow of the standard shortest path network flow polytope associated with *Graph G*,

$$W := \left\{ w \in [0,1]^{|A|} : \sum_{i \in \overline{\mathbb{C}}} \sum_{j \in F_1(i)} w_{i,1,j} = 1; \right.$$

$$\left. \sum_{j \in F_r(i)} w_{irj} - \sum_{j \in B_r(i)} w_{j,r-1,i} = 0,\ r \in R \backslash \{1\},\ i \in \overline{\mathbb{C}} \right\}$$

(where w is the vector of flow variables associated with the arcs of *Graph G*) (see Bazaraa *et al.*, 2010, pp. 619-639).

Notation 14 *We denote the set of all MmTSP-paths-in-G as* Ω*; i.e.,*

$$\Omega := \Big\{ ((i_1,1,i_2),(i_2,2,i_3),...,(i_{n-1},n-1,i_n)) \in A^{n-1} : \ (\forall\, t \in \mathbb{C},\ \exists\, p \in \overline{R} : \ i_p = t);$$
$$\Big(\forall\ (p,q) \in (\overline{R}, \overline{R} \backslash \{p\}) : (i_p, i_q) \in \mathbb{C}^2,\ i_p \neq i_q \Big) \Big\}.$$

4. Integer programming model of the path representations

Notation 15 ("Complex flow modeling" variables) *:*

1. $\forall (p,r,s) \in R^3 : r < s < p$, $\forall (i,j,k,t,u,v) \in (\overline{\mathbb{C}}, F_r(i), \overline{\mathbb{C}}, F_s(k), \overline{\mathbb{C}}, F_p(u))$, $z_{(irj)(kst)(upv)}$ denotes a non-negative variable that represents the amount of flow in *Graph G* that propagates from arc (i,r,j) on to arc (k,s,t), via arc (u,p,v); $z_{(irj)(kst)(upv)}$ will be witten as $z_{(i,r,j)(k,s,t)(u,p,v)}$ whenever needed for clarity.
2. $\forall (r,s) \in R^2 : r < s$, $\forall (i,j,k,t) \in (\overline{\mathbb{C}}, F_r(i), \overline{\mathbb{C}}, F_s(k))$, $y_{(irj)(kst)}$ denotes a non-negative variable that represents the total amount of flow in *Graph G* that propagates from *arc* (i,r,j) on to *arc* (k,s,t); $y_{(irj)(kst)}$ will be witten as $y_{(i,r,j)(k,s,t)}$ whenever needed for clarity.

The constraints of our Integer Programming (IP) reformulation of P_1 are as follows:

$$\sum_{i \in \overline{\mathbb{C}}} \sum_{j \in F_1(i)} \sum_{t \in F_2(j)} \sum_{v \in F_3(t)} z_{(i,1,j)(j,2,t)(t,3,v)} = 1 \tag{7}$$

$$\sum_{v \in B_p(u)} z_{(irj)(kst)(v,p-1,u)} - \sum_{v \in F_p(u)} z_{(irj)(kst)(upv)} = 0;$$
$$p,r,s \in R : r < s < p-1;\ i \in \overline{\mathbb{C}};\ j \in F_r(i);\ k \in \overline{\mathbb{C}};\ t \in F_s(k);\ u \in \overline{\mathbb{C}} \tag{8}$$

$$\sum_{v \in B_p(u)} z_{(irj)(v,p-1,u)(kst)} - \sum_{v \in F_p(u)} z_{(irj)(upv)(kst)} = 0;$$
$$p,r,s \in R : r+1 < p < s;\ i \in \overline{\mathbb{C}};\ j \in F_r(i);\ k \in \overline{\mathbb{C}};\ t \in F_s(k);\ u \in \overline{\mathbb{C}} \tag{9}$$

$$\sum_{v\in B_p(u)} z_{(v,p-1,u)(irj)(kst)} - \sum_{v\in F_p(u)} z_{(upv)(irj)(kst)} = 0;$$
$$p,r,s \in R: 1 < p < r < s;\ i \in \overline{\mathbb{C}};\ j \in F_r(i);\ k \in \overline{\mathbb{C}};\ t \in F_s(k);\ u \in \overline{\mathbb{C}} \quad (10)$$

$$y_{(irj)(kst)} - \sum_{u\in\overline{\mathbb{C}}} \sum_{v\in F_p(u)} z_{(irj)(kst)(upv)} = 0;$$
$$p,r,s \in R: r < s < p;\ i \in \overline{\mathbb{C}};\ j \in F_r(i);\ k \in \overline{\mathbb{C}};\ t \in F_s(u) \quad (11)$$

$$y_{(irj)(upv)} - \sum_{k\in\overline{\mathbb{C}}} \sum_{t\in F_s(k)} z_{(irj)(kst)(upv)} = 0;$$
$$p,r,s \in R: r < s < p;\ i \in \overline{\mathbb{C}};\ j \in F_r(i);\ u \in \overline{\mathbb{C}};\ v \in F_p(u) \quad (12)$$

$$y_{(kst)(upv)} - \sum_{i\in\overline{\mathbb{C}}} \sum_{j\in F_r(i)} z_{(irj)(kst)(upv)} = 0;$$
$$p,r,s \in R: r < s < p;\ k \in \overline{\mathbb{C}};\ t \in F_s(k);\ u \in \overline{\mathbb{C}};\ v \in F_p(u) \quad (13)$$

$$y_{(irj)(kst)} - \sum_{\substack{p\in R:\\ p<r}} \sum_{v\in F_p(u)} z_{(upv)(irj)(kst)} - \sum_{\substack{p\in R:\\ r<p<s}} \sum_{v\in F_p(u)} z_{(irj)(upv)(kst)}$$
$$- \sum_{\substack{p\in R:\\ s<p}} \sum_{v\in B_{p+1}(u)} z_{(irj)(kst)(vpu)} = 0;$$
$$r,s \in R: r < s;\ i \in \overline{\mathbb{C}};\ j \in F_r(i);\ k \in \overline{\mathbb{C}};\ t \in F_s(k);\ u \in \mathbb{C}\backslash\{i,j,k,t\} \quad (14)$$

$$\sum_{k\in\overline{\mathbb{C}}\backslash\{j\}} \sum_{t\in F_{r+1}(k)} y_{(irj)(k,r+1,t)} = 0; \quad r \in R\backslash\{n-1\};\ i \in \overline{\mathbb{C}};\ j \in F_r(i) \quad (15)$$

$$\sum_{\substack{(r,s)\in R^2:\\ s>r}} \sum_{j\in F_r(i)} \sum_{k\in B_{s+1}(i)} y_{(irj)(ksi)} + \sum_{\substack{(r,s)\in R^2:\\ s>r}} \sum_{j\in F_r(i)} \sum_{k\in F_s(i)} y_{(irj)(isk)} +$$
$$\sum_{\substack{(r,s)\in R^2:\\ s>r}} \sum_{j\in B_{r+1}(i)} \sum_{k\in B_{s+1}(i)} y_{(jri)(ksi)} + \sum_{\substack{(r,s)\in R^2:\\ s>r+1}} \sum_{j\in B_{r+1}(i)} \sum_{k\in F_s(i)} y_{(jri)(isk)} = 0;$$
$$i \in \mathbb{C} \quad (16)$$

$$y_{(irj)(kst)} \in \{0,1\};\ r,s \in R : r < s;\ (i,\ j,\ k,\ t) \in (\overline{\mathbb{C}},\ F_r(i),\ \overline{\mathbb{C}},\ F_s(k)) \tag{17}$$

$$z_{(irj)(kst)(upv)} \in \{0,1\};\ p,r,s \in R : r < s < p;$$
$$(i,\ j,\ k,\ t,\ u,\ v) \in (\overline{\mathbb{C}},\ F_1(i),\ \overline{\mathbb{C}},\ F_s(k),\ \overline{\mathbb{C}},\ F_p(u)). \tag{18}$$

One unit of flow is initiated at stage *1* of *Graph G* by constraint (7). Constraints (8), (9), and (10) are extended Kirchhoff Equations (see Bazaraa *et al.*, 2010, pp. 454) that ensure that all flows initiated at stage *1* propagate onward, to stage n of the graph, in a connected and balanced manner. Specifically, the total flow that traverses both of two given arcs (i,r,j) and (k,s,t) (where $s > r$) and also enters a given node (u,p) is equal to the total flow that traverses both arcs and also leaves the node. Constraints (8), (9) and (10) enforce this condition for "downstream" nodes relative to the two arcs (i.e., when $p > s$), "intermediary" nodes (i.e., when $r < p < s$), and "upstream" nodes (i.e., when $p < r$), respectively. Constraints (11), (12), and (13) ensure the consistent accounting of the flow propagation amount between any given pair of arcs of *Graph G* across all the stages of the graph. We refer to constraints (14) as the "*visit requirements*"constraints. They stipulate that the total flow on any given arc of *Graph G* must propagate on to every *level* of the graph pertaining to a non-fictitious customer site, or be part of a flow propagation that spans the levels of the graph pertaining to non-fictitious customer sites. Constraints (15) ensure that the initial flow propagation from any given arc of *Graph G* occurs in an "unbroken" fashion. Finally, constraints (16) stipulate (in light of the other constraints) that no part of the flow from *arc* (i,r,j) of *Graph G* can propagate back onto level i of the graph if i pertains to a non-fictitious customer site or onto level j if j pertains to a non-fictitious customer site.

The correspondence between the constraints of our path-based IP model above and those of *Problem BNF* are as follows. Constraints (1) and (2) of *Problem BNF* are "enforced" (i.e., the equivalent of the condition they impose is enforced) in the path-based IP model by the combination of constraints (7), (14), and (16). Constraints (3) of *Problem BNF* are enforced through the combination of constraints (7)-(10) of the path-based IP model. Finally, constraints (4) of the *BNF-based* model are enforced in the path-based IP model through the structure of *Graph G* itself (since travel from the fictitious customer site to a non-fictitious customer site is not allowed for a given salesman). Hence, the "complicating" constraints of the BNF-based model are handled only implicitly in our path-based IP reformulation above.

Remark 16 *Following standard conventions, any y- or z-variable that is not used the system (7)-(18) (i.e., that is not defined in Notation 15) is assumed to be constrained to equal zero throughout the remainder of the chapter.*

Definition 17

1. Let $Q_I := \{(y,z) \in \mathbb{R}^m : (y,z)\ satisfies\ (7)\text{-}(18)\}$, where m is the number of variables in the system (7)-(18). We refer to $Conv(Q_I)$ as the "IP Polytope;"
2. We refer to the linear programming relaxation of Q_I as the "LP Polytope," and denote it by Q_L; i.e., $Q_L := \{(y,z) \in \mathbb{R}^m : (y,z)$ satisfies (7)-(16), and $\mathbf{0} \leq (y,\ z) \leq \mathbf{1}\}$, where m is the number of variables in the system (7)-(16).

Theorem 18 *The following statements are true for Q_I and Q_L:*

(i) The number of variables in the system (7)-(16) is $O\left(\mathfrak{c}^9 \cdot \mathfrak{s}^3\right)$;

(ii) The number of constraints in the system (7)-(16) is $O\left(\mathfrak{c}^8 \cdot \mathfrak{s}^3\right)$.

Proof. Trivial.

Theorem 19 $(y,z) \in Q_I \iff$ *There exists exactly one n-tuple* $(i_r \in \overline{\mathbb{C}}, r = 1,\ldots,n)$ *such that:*
(i)

$$z_{(arb)(csd)(epf)} = \begin{cases} 1 & \textit{for } p,r,s \in R : r < s < p;\ (a,b,c,d,e,f) = (i_r, i_{r+1}, i_s, i_{s+1}, i_p, i_{p+1}) \\ 0 & \textit{otherwise} \end{cases}$$

(ii)

$$y_{(arb)(csd)} = \begin{cases} 1 & \textit{for } r,s \in R : r < s;\ (a,b,c,d) = (i_r, i_{r+1}, i_s, i_{s+1}) \\ 0 & \textit{otherwise} \end{cases}$$

(iii) $\forall\, t \in \mathbb{C}, \exists p \in \overline{R} : i_p = t;$
(iv) $\forall\, (p,q) \in (\overline{R}, \overline{R}\backslash\{p\}),\ (i_p, i_q) \in \mathbb{C}^2 \Longrightarrow i_p \neq i_q.$

Proof. Let $(y,z) \in Q_I$. Then, given (17)-(18):
$(a) \Longrightarrow$:

$(a.1)$ Constraint (7) $\Longrightarrow$There exists exactly one 4-tuple $(i_r \in \overline{\mathbb{C}}, r = 1,\ldots,4)$ such that:

$$z_{(i_1,1,i_2)(i_2,2,i_3)(i_3,3,i_4)} = 1 \tag{19}$$

Condition (i) follows directly from the combination of (19) with constraints (8)-(10).

$(a.2)$ Condition (ii) follows from the combination of condition (i) with constraints (11)-(13), and constraints (15).

$(a.3)$ Condition (iii) follows from the combination of conditions (i) and (ii) with constraints (14).

$(a.4)$ Condition (iv) follows from the combination of Conditions (i) and (ii) with constraints (16).

$(b) \Longleftarrow$: Trivial.

Theorem 20 *The following statements hold true:*

(i) There exists a one-to-one mapping between the points of Q_I and the *MmTSP-paths-in-G*;

(ii) There exists a one-to-one mapping between the points of Q_I, and the extreme points of the *BNF-based polytope* (i.e., the points of P_1);

(iii) There exists a one-to-one mapping between the points of Q_I and the *MmTSP schedules.*

Proof. Conditions (i) follows directly from the combination of Theorem 19 and Definition 11.2. Conditions (ii) and (iii) follow from the combination of condition (i) with Theorem 12.

Definition 21 *Let* $(y,z) \in Q_I$. *Let* $(i_r \in \overline{\mathbb{C}},\ r = 1,\ldots,n)$ *be the n-tuple satisfying Theorem 19 for* (y,z). *We refer to the solution to Problem BNF corresponding to* (y,z) *as the "MmTSP schedule corresponding to* (y,z),*" and denote it by the ordered set* $\mathcal{M}(y,z) := \left((\mathfrak{p}_r, i_r),\ r \in \overline{R} : i_r \neq \overline{\mathfrak{c}}\right)$.

5. Linear programming reformulation of the *BNF-based Polytope*

Our linear programming reformulation of the *BNF-based Polytope* consists of Q_L. We show that every point of Q_L is a convex combination of points of Q_I, thereby establishing (in light of Theorems 13 and 20) the one-to-one correspondence between the extreme points of Q_L and the points of Q_I.

Theorem 22 (*Valid constraints*) *The following constraints are valid for Q_L:*
(i) $\forall (r,s,t) \in R^3 : r < s < t,$

$$\sum_{i_r \in \overline{\mathbf{C}}} \sum_{j_r \in F_r(i_r)} \sum_{i_s \in \overline{\mathbf{C}}} \sum_{j_s \in F_s(i_s)} \sum_{i_t \in \overline{\mathbf{C}}} \sum_{j_t \in F_t(i_t)} z_{(i_r,r,j_r)(i_s,s,j_s)(i_t,t,j_t)} = 1$$

(ii) $\forall (r,s) \in R^2 : r < s,$

$$\sum_{i_r \in \overline{\mathbf{C}}} \sum_{j_r \in F_r(i_r)} \sum_{i_s \in \overline{\mathbf{C}}} \sum_{j_s \in F_s(i_s)} y_{(i_r,r,j_r)(i_s,s,j_s)} = 1$$

Proof. (i) *Condition* (i). First, note that by constraint (7), condition (i) of the theorem holds for $(r,s,t) = (1,2,3)$.
Now, assume $1 < r < s < t$. Then, we have:

$$\begin{aligned}
&\sum_{i_r \in \overline{\mathbf{C}}} \sum_{j_r \in F_r(i_r)} \sum_{i_s \in \overline{\mathbf{C}}} \sum_{j_s \in F_s(i_s)} \sum_{i_t \in \overline{\mathbf{C}}} \sum_{j_t \in F_t(i_t)} z_{(i_r,r,j_r)(i_s,s,j_s)(i_t,t,j_t)} \\
&= \sum_{i_r \in \overline{\mathbf{C}}} \sum_{j_r \in F_r(i_r)} \sum_{i_s \in \overline{\mathbf{C}}} \sum_{j_s \in F_s(i_s)} y_{(i_r,r,j_r)(i_s,s,j_s)} \quad \text{(Using (11))} \\
&= \sum_{i_r \in \overline{\mathbf{C}}} \sum_{j_r \in F_r(i_r)} \sum_{i_s \in \overline{\mathbf{C}}} \sum_{j_s \in F_s(i_s)} \sum_{i_1 \in \overline{\mathbf{C}}} \sum_{j_1 \in F_1(i_1)} z_{(i_1,1,j_1)(i_r,r,j_r)(i_s,s,j_s)} \quad \text{(Using (13))} \\
&= \sum_{i_1 \in \overline{\mathbf{C}}} \sum_{j_1 \in F_1(i_1)} \sum_{i_s \in \overline{\mathbf{C}}} \sum_{j_s \in F_s(i_s)} \sum_{i_r \in \overline{\mathbf{C}}} \sum_{j_r \in F_r(i_r)} z_{(i_1,1,j_1)(i_r,r,j_r)(i_s,s,j_s)} \quad \text{(Re-arranging)} \\
&= \sum_{i_1 \in \overline{\mathbf{C}}} \sum_{j_1 \in F_1(i_1)} \sum_{i_s \in \overline{\mathbf{C}}} \sum_{j_s \in F_s(i_s)} y_{(i_1,1,j_1)(i_s,s,j_s)} \quad \text{(Using (12))} \\
&= \sum_{i_1 \in \overline{\mathbf{C}}} \sum_{j_1 \in F_1(i_1)} \sum_{i_s \in \overline{\mathbf{C}}} \sum_{j_s \in F_s(i_s)} \sum_{i_2 \in \overline{\mathbf{C}}} \sum_{j_2 \in F_2(i_2)} z_{(i_1,1,j_1)(i_2,2,j_2)(i_s,s,j_s)} \quad \text{(Using (12))} \\
&= \sum_{i_1 \in \overline{\mathbf{C}}} \sum_{j_1 \in F_1(i_1)} \sum_{i_2 \in \overline{\mathbf{C}}} \sum_{j_2 \in F_2(i_2)} \sum_{i_s \in \overline{\mathbf{C}}} \sum_{j_s \in F_s(i_s)} z_{(i_1,1,j_1)(i_2,2,j_2)(i_s,s,j_s)} \quad \text{(Re-arranging)} \\
&= \sum_{i_1 \in \overline{\mathbf{C}}} \sum_{j_1 \in F_1(i_1)} \sum_{i_2 \in \overline{\mathbf{C}}} \sum_{j_2 \in F_2(i_2)} y_{(i_1,1,j_1)(i_2,2,j_2)} \quad \text{(Using (11))} \\
&= \sum_{i_1 \in \overline{\mathbf{C}}} \sum_{j_1 \in F_1(i_1)} \sum_{i_2 \in \overline{\mathbf{C}}} \sum_{j_2 \in F_2(i_2)} \sum_{i_3 \in \overline{\mathbf{C}}} \sum_{j_3 \in F_3(i_3)} z_{(i_1,1,j_1)(i_2,2,j_2)(i_3,3,j_3)} \quad \text{(Using (11))} \\
&= 1 \quad \text{(Using (7))}.
\end{aligned}$$

(ii) Condition (ii) of the theorem follows directly from the combination of condition (i) and constraints (11)-(13).

Lemma 23 *Let* $(y,z) \in Q_L$. *The following holds true:*

$$\forall r \in R : r \leq n-3, \ \forall (i_r, i_{r+1}, i_{r+2}, i_{r+3}) \in (\overline{\mathbb{C}}, F_r(i_r), \overline{\mathbb{C}}, F_{r+2}(i_{r+2})),$$

$$y_{(i_r,r,i_{r+1})(i_{r+2},r+2,i_{r+3})} > 0 \Longleftrightarrow \begin{cases} (i) \ i_{r+2} \in F_{r+1}(i_{r+1}); \\ and \\ (ii) \ z_{(i_r,r,i_{r+1})(i_{r+1},r+1,i_{r+2})(i_{r+2},r+2,i_{r+3})} > 0. \end{cases} \tag{20}$$

Proof. For $r \in R$, constraints (12) for $s = r+1$ and $p = r+2$ can be written as:

$$y_{(i_r,r,i_{r+1})(i_{r+2},r+2,i_{r+3})} - \sum_{k \in \overline{\mathbb{C}}} \sum_{t \in F_{r+1}(k)} z_{(i_r,r,i_{r+1})(k,r+1,t)(i_{r+2},r+2,i_{r+3})} = 0$$
$$\forall (i_r, i_{r+1}, i_{r+2}, i_{r+3}) \in (\overline{\mathbb{C}}, F_r(i_r), \overline{\mathbb{C}}, F_{r+2}(i_{r+2})). \tag{21}$$

Constraints (11)-(13), and (15) $\Longrightarrow$

$$\forall (i_r, i_{r+1}, i_{r+2}, i_{r+3}, k, t) \in (\overline{\mathbb{C}}, F_r(i_r), \overline{\mathbb{C}}, F_{r+2}(i_{r+2}), \overline{\mathbb{C}}, \overline{\mathbb{C}}),$$
$$z_{(i_r,r,i_{r+1})(k,r+1,t)(i_{r+2},r+2,i_{r+3})} > 0 \Longrightarrow (k = i_{r+1}, \text{ and } t = i_{r+2}). \tag{22}$$

Using (22), (21) can be written as:

$$y_{(i_r,r,i_{r+1})(i_{r+2},r+2,i_{r+3})} - z_{(i_r,r,i_{r+1})(i_{r+1},r+1,i_{r+2})(i_{r+2},r+2,i_{r+3})} = 0$$
$$\forall (i_r, i_{r+1}, i_{r+2}, i_{r+3}) \in (\overline{\mathbb{C}}, F_r(i_r), \overline{\mathbb{C}}, F_{r+2}(i_{r+2})). \tag{23}$$

Condition (ii) of the equivalence in the lemma follows directly from (23).
Condition (i) follows from Remark 16 and the fact that $z_{(i_r,r,i_{r+1})(i_{r+1},r+1,i_{r+2})(i_{r+2},r+2,i_{r+3})}$ is not defined if $i_{r+2} \notin F_{r+1}(i_{r+1})$.

Notation 24 ("Support graph" of (y,z)) *For* $(y,z) \in Q_L$:

1. The sub-graph of *Graph G* induced by the positive components of (y,z) is denoted as:

$$\overline{G}(y,z) := (\overline{V}(y,z), \overline{A}(y,z)),$$

where:

$$\overline{V}(y,z) := \left\{ (i,1) \in V : \sum_{j \in F_1(i)} \sum_{t \in F_2(j)} y_{(i,1,j)(j,2,t)} > 0 \right\} \cup$$
$$\left\{ (i,r) \in V : 1 < r < n; \sum_{a \in \overline{\mathbb{C}}} \sum_{b \in F_1(a)} \sum_{j \in F_r(i)} y_{(a,1,b)(irj)} > 0 \right\} \cup$$
$$\left\{ (i,n) \in V : \sum_{a \in \overline{\mathbb{C}}} \sum_{b \in F_1(a)} \sum_{j \in B_n(i)} y_{(a,1,b)(j,r-1,i)} > 0 \right\}; \tag{24}$$

$$\overline{A}(y,z) := \left\{ (i,1,j) \in A : \sum_{t \in F_2(j)} y_{(i,1,j)(j,2,t)} > 0 \right\} \cup$$
$$\left\{ (i,r,j) \in A : r > 1; \sum_{a \in \overline{\mathbb{C}}} \sum_{b \in F_1(a)} y_{(a,1,b)(irj)} > 0 \right\}. \tag{25}$$

2. The set of arcs of $\overline{G}(y,z)$ originating at stage r of $\overline{G}(y,z)$ is denoted $\mathcal{A}_r(y,z)$;
3. The index set associated with $\mathcal{A}_r(y,z)$ is denoted $\Lambda_r(y,z) := \{1,2,\ldots,|\mathcal{A}_r(y,z)|\}$. For simplicity $\Lambda_r(y,z)$ will be henceforth written as Λ_r;
4. The νth arc in $\mathcal{A}_r(y,z)$ is denoted as $a_{r,\nu}(y,z)$. For simplicity $a_{r,\nu}(y,z)$ will be henceforth written as $a_{r,\nu}$;
5. For $(r,\nu) \in (R,\Lambda_r)$, the tail of $a_{r,\nu}$ is labeled $\bar{t}_{r,\nu}(y,z)$; the head of $a_{r,\nu}$ is labeled $\overline{h}_{r,\nu}(y,z)$. For simplicity, $\bar{t}_{r,\nu}(y,z)$ will be henceforth written as $\bar{t}_{r,\nu}$, and $\overline{h}_{r,\nu}(y,z)$, as $\overline{h}_{r,\nu}$;
6. Where that causes no confusion (and where that is convenient), for $(r,s) \in R^2 : s > r$, and $(\rho,\sigma) \in (\Lambda_r,\Lambda_s)$, "$y_{(i_{r,\rho},r,j_{r,\sigma})(i_{s,\sigma},s,j_{s,\sigma})}$" will be henceforth written as "$y_{(r,\rho)(s,\sigma)}$." Similarly, for $(r,s,t) \in R^3$ with $r < s < t$ and $(\rho,\sigma,\tau) \in (\Lambda_r,\Lambda_s,\Lambda_t)$, "$z_{(i_{r,\rho},r,j_{r,\rho})(i_{s,\sigma},s,j_{s,\sigma})(i_{t,\tau},t,j_{t,\tau})}$" will be henceforth written as "$z_{(r,\rho)(s,\sigma)(t,\tau)}$;"
7. $\forall (r,s) \in R^2 : s \geq r+2$, $\forall (\rho,\sigma) \in (\Lambda_r,\Lambda_s)$, the set of arcs at stage $(r+1)$ of $\overline{G}(y, z)$ through which flow propagates from $a_{r,\rho}$ onto $a_{s,\sigma}$ is denoted:
$$I_{(r,\rho)(s,\sigma)}(y,z) := \{\lambda \in \Lambda_{r+1} : z_{(r,\rho)(r+1,\lambda)(s,\sigma)} > 0\};$$
8. $\forall (r,s) \in R^2 : s \geq r+2$, $\forall (\rho,\sigma) \in (\Lambda_r,\Lambda_s)$, the set of arcs at stage $(s-1)$ of $\overline{G}(y, z)$ through which flow propagates from $a_{r,\rho}$ onto $a_{s,\sigma}$ is denoted:
$$J_{(r,\rho)(s,\sigma)}(y,z) := \{\mu \in \Lambda_{s-1} : z_{(r,\rho)(s-1,\mu)(s,\sigma)} > 0\}.$$

Remark 25 *Let $(y,z) \in Q_L$. An arc of G is included in $\overline{G}(y,z)$ iff at least one of the flow variables (or entries of (y,z)) associated with the arc (as defined in Notation 15) is positive.*

Theorem 26 *Let $(y,z) \in Q_L$. Then,*

$$\forall\ (r,s) \in R^2 : s \geq r+2,\ \forall (\rho,\sigma) \in (\Lambda_r,\Lambda_s),$$
$$(\ (i)\ \ y_{(r,\rho)(s,\sigma)} > 0 \Longleftrightarrow I_{(r,\rho)(s,\sigma)}(y,z) \neq \varnothing;$$
$$(ii)\ \ y_{(r,\rho)(s,\sigma)} > 0 \Longleftrightarrow J_{(r,\rho)(s,\sigma)}(y,z) \neq \varnothing;$$
$$(iii)\ \ y_{(r,\rho)(s,\sigma)} = \sum_{\lambda \in I_{(r,\rho)(s,\sigma)}(y,z)} z_{(r,\rho)(r+1,\lambda)(s,\sigma)} = \sum_{\mu \in J_{(r,\rho)(s,\sigma)}(y,z)} z_{(r,\rho)(s-1,\mu)(s,\sigma)}\ ).$$

Proof. The theorem follows directly from the combination of constraints (12) and constraints (15).

Definition 27 ("Level-walk-in-(y,z)") *Let $(y,z) \in Q_L$. For $(r,s) \in R^2 : s \geq r+2$, we refer to the set of arcs, $\{a_{r,v_r}, a_{r+1,v_{r+1}}, \ldots, a_{s,v_s}\}$, of a* walk *of $\overline{G}(y,z)$ as a "level-walk-in-(y,z) from (r,v_r) to (s,v_s)" (plural: "level-walks-in-(y,z) from (r,v_r) to (s,v_s)") if $\forall (g,p,q) \in R^3 : r \leq g < p < q \leq s$, $z_{(g,v_g)(p,v_p)(q,v_q)} > 0$.*

Notation 28 *Let $(y,z) \in Q_L$. $\forall (r,s) \in R^2 : s \geq r+2$, $\forall (\rho,\sigma) \in (\Lambda_r, \Lambda_s)$,*

1. The set of all *level-walks-in-(y,z) from (r,ρ) to (s,σ)* is denoted $\mathcal{W}_{(r,\rho)(s,\sigma)}(y,z)$;
2. The index set associated with $\mathcal{W}_{(r,\rho)(s,\sigma)}(y,z)$ is denoted $\Pi_{(r,\rho)(s,\sigma)}(y,z) := \{1, 2, \ldots, \left|\mathcal{W}_{(r,\rho)(s,\sigma)}(y,z)\right|\}$;
3. The kth element of $\mathcal{W}_{(r,\rho)(s,\sigma)}(y,z)$ $(k \in \Pi_{(r,\rho)(s,\sigma)}(y,z))$ is denoted $\mathcal{P}_{(r,\rho),(s,\sigma),k}(y,z)$;
4. $\forall k \in \Pi_{(r,\rho)(s,\sigma)}(y,z)$, the $(s-r+2)$-tuple of customer site indices included in $\mathcal{P}_{(r,\rho),(s,\sigma),k}(y,z)$ is denoted $\mathcal{C}_{(r,\rho),(s,\sigma),k}(y,z)$; i.e., $\mathcal{C}_{(r,\rho),(s,\sigma),k}(y,z) := (\bar{t}_{r,i_{r,k}}, \ldots, \bar{t}_{s+1,i_{s+1,k}})$, where the $(p,i_{p,k})$'s index the arcs in $\mathcal{P}_{(r,\rho),(s,\sigma),k}(y,z)$, and $\bar{t}_{s+1,i_{s+1,k}} := \bar{h}_{s,i_{s,k}}$.

Theorem 29 *Let $(y,z) \in Q_L$. The following holds true:*
$\forall (r,s) \in R^2 : s \geq r+2$, $\forall (\rho,\sigma) \in (\Lambda_r, \Lambda_s)$,

$$y_{(r,\rho)(s,\sigma)} > 0 \Longleftrightarrow \begin{cases} (i)\ \mathcal{W}_{(r,\rho)(s,\sigma)}(y,z) \neq \varnothing; and \\ (ii)\ \forall p \in R : r < p < s,\ \forall v_p \in \Lambda_p, \\ z_{(r,\rho)(p,v_p)(s,\sigma)} > 0 \Longleftrightarrow \exists\, k \in \Pi_{(r,\rho)(s,\sigma)}(y,z) : a_{p,v_p} \in \mathcal{P}_{(r,\rho),(s,\sigma),k}(y,z). \end{cases}$$

Proof. First, note that it follows directly from Lemma 23 that the theorem holds true for all $(r,s) \in R^2$ with $s = r+2$, and all $(v_r, v_s) \in (\Lambda_r, \Lambda_s)$.
$(a) \Longrightarrow$:
Assume there exists an integer $\omega \geq 2$ such that the theorem holds true for all $(r,s) \in R^2$ with $s = r + \omega$, and all $(v_r, v_s) \in (\Lambda_r, \Lambda_s)$. We will show that the theorem must then also hold for all $(r,s) \in R^2$ with $s = r + \omega + 1$, and all $(v_r, v_s) \in (\Lambda_r, \Lambda_s)$.
Let $(p,q) \in R^2$ with $q = p + \omega + 1$, and $(\alpha,\beta) \in (\Lambda_p, \Lambda_q)$ be such that:

$$y_{(p,\alpha)(q,\beta)} > 0. \tag{26}$$

$(a.1)$ Relation (26) and Theorem 26$\Longrightarrow$

$$I_{(p,\alpha)(q,\beta)}(y,z) \neq \varnothing. \tag{27}$$

It follows from (27), Definition 24.7, and constraints (13) that:

$$\forall \lambda \in I_{(p,\alpha)(q,\beta)}(y,z),\ y_{(p+1,\lambda)(q,\beta)} > 0. \tag{28}$$

By assumption (since $q = (p+1) + \omega$), (28) $\Longrightarrow$

$$(a.1.1)\ \forall \lambda \in I_{(p,\alpha)(q,\beta)}(y,z),\ \mathcal{W}_{(p+1,\lambda)(q,\beta)}(y,z) \neq \varnothing;\ \text{and} \tag{29a}$$

$$(a.1.2)\ \forall \lambda \in I_{(p,\alpha)(q,\beta)}(y,z),\ \forall t \in R : p+1 < t < q,\ \forall \tau \in \Lambda_t,$$
$$z_{(p+1,\lambda)(t,\tau)(q,\beta)} > 0 \Longleftrightarrow \exists\, i \in \Pi_{(p+1,\lambda)(q,\beta)}(y,z) : a_{t,\tau} \in \mathcal{P}_{(p+1,\lambda)(q,\beta),i}(y,z). \tag{29b}$$

$(a.2)$ Relation (26) and Theorem 26 $\Longrightarrow$

$$J_{(p,\alpha)(q,\beta)}(y,z) \neq \varnothing. \tag{30}$$

It follows from (30), Definition 24.8, and constraints (11) that:

$$\forall \mu \in J_{(p,\alpha)(q,\beta)}(y,z),\ y_{(p,\alpha)(q-1,\mu)} > 0. \tag{31}$$

By assumption (since $(q-1) = p + \omega$), (31) $\Longrightarrow$

$$(a.2.1)\ \forall \mu \in J_{(p,\alpha)(q,\beta)}(y,z),\ \mathcal{W}_{(p,\alpha)(q-1,\mu)}(y,z) \neq \varnothing;\ \text{ and} \tag{32a}$$

$$\begin{aligned}&(a.2.2)\ \forall \mu \in J_{(p,\alpha)(q,\beta)}(y,z),\ \forall t \in R : p < t < q-1,\ \forall \tau \in \Lambda_t,\\ &z_{(p,\alpha)(t,\tau)(q-1,\mu)} > 0 \Longleftrightarrow \exists\, k \in \Pi_{(p,\alpha)(q-1,\mu)}(y,z) : a_{t,\tau} \in \mathcal{P}_{(p,\alpha)(q-1,\mu),k}(y,z).\end{aligned} \tag{32b}$$

$(a.3)$ Constraints (11)-(14) and Theorem 26.*iii* $\Longrightarrow$

$$\begin{aligned}&(a.3.1)\ \forall \mu \in \Lambda_{q-1},\ \exists\, \langle \lambda \in I_{(p,\alpha)(q,\beta)}(y,z);\ i \in \Pi_{(p+1,\lambda)(q,\beta)}(y,z)\rangle :\\ &\qquad \Big\langle a_{q-1,\mu} \in \mathcal{P}_{(p+1,\lambda)(q,\beta),i}(y,z)\Big\rangle;\ \text{ and}\end{aligned} \tag{33a}$$

$$\begin{aligned}&(a.3.2)\ \forall \lambda \in \Lambda_{p+1},\ \exists\, \langle \mu \in J_{(p,\alpha)(q,\beta)}(y,z);\ k \in \Pi_{(p,\alpha)(q-1,\mu)}(y,z)\rangle :\\ &\qquad \Big\langle a_{p+1,\lambda} \in \mathcal{P}_{(p,\alpha)(q-1,\mu),k}(y,z)\Big\rangle.\end{aligned} \tag{33b}$$

$(a.4)$ From the combination of (33a), (33b), constraints (9), and constraints (14), we must have that:

$$\begin{aligned}&\exists\, \langle \lambda \in I_{(p,\alpha)(q,\beta)}(y,z);\ i \in \Pi_{(p+1,\lambda)(q,\beta)}(y,z);\ \mu \in J_{(p,\alpha)(q,\beta)}(y,z);\ k \in \Pi_{(p,\alpha)(q-1,\mu)}(y,z)\rangle :\\ &\Big\langle \forall t \in R : p < t < q,\ \forall \tau \in \Lambda_t : a_{t,\tau} \in \mathcal{P}_{(p+1,\lambda)(q,\beta),i}(y,z),\ z_{(p,\alpha)(t,\tau)(q,\beta)} > 0;\\ &\ \Big(\mathcal{P}_{(p+1,\lambda)(q,\beta),i}(y,z)\backslash\{a_{q,\beta}\}\Big) = \Big(\mathcal{P}_{(p,\alpha)(q-1,\mu),k}(y,z)\backslash\{a_{p,\alpha}\}\Big) \neq \varnothing\Big\rangle.\end{aligned} \tag{34}$$

(In words, (34) says that there must exist *level-walks-in-(y,z) from* $(p+1,\lambda)$ to (q,β), and *level-walk-in-(y,z) from* (p,α) to $(q-1,\beta)$ that "overlap" at intermediary stages between $(p+1)$ and $(q-1)$ (inclusive)).
$(a.5)$ Let $\lambda \in I_{(p,\alpha)(q,\beta)}(y,z)$, $i \in \Pi_{(p+1,\lambda)(q,\beta)}(y,z)$, $\mu \in J_{(p,\alpha)(q,\beta)}(y,z)$, and $k \in \Pi_{(p,\alpha)(q-1,\mu)}(y,z)$ be such that they satisfy (34). Then, it follows directly from definitions that

$$\overline{P} := \{a_{p,\alpha}\} \cup \mathcal{P}_{(p+1,\lambda)(q,\beta),i}(y,z) = \{a_{q,\beta}\} \cup \mathcal{P}_{(p,\alpha)(q-1,\mu),k}(y,z) \tag{35}$$

is a *level-walk-in-(y,z) from* (p,α) *to* (q,β).
Hence, we have that $\mathcal{W}_{(p,\alpha)(q,\beta)}(y,z) \neq \varnothing$.
(b) $\Longleftarrow$: Follows directly from definitions and constraints (12).

Theorem 30 *Let* $(y,z) \in Q_L$*. Then,* $\forall(\alpha,\beta) \in (\Lambda_1,\Lambda_{n-1}) : y_{(1,\alpha)(n-1,\beta)} > 0$*, the following are true:*
(i) $\mathcal{W}_{(1,\alpha)(n-1,\beta)}(y,z) \neq \varnothing$*, and* $\Pi_{(1,\alpha)(n-1,\beta)}(y,z) \neq \varnothing$;
(ii) $\forall k \in \Pi_{(1,\alpha)(n-1,\beta)}(y,z)$, $\mathcal{C}_{(1,\alpha)(n-1,\beta),k}(y,z) \supseteq \mathbb{C}$;
(iii) $\forall k \in \Pi_{(1,\alpha)(n-1,\beta)}(y,z)$, $\forall(p,q) \in (\overline{R},\overline{R}\backslash\{p\})$,
$\Big((i_p,i_q) \in \mathcal{C}_{(1,\alpha)(n-1,\beta),k}(y,z))^2$*, and* $(i_p,i_q) \neq (\overline{\mathfrak{c}},\overline{\mathfrak{c}})\Big) \Longrightarrow i_p \neq i_q$.

Proof.
Condition (i) follows from Theorem 29.
Condition (ii) follows from constraints (14).
Condition (iii) follows from the combination of condition (i) and constraints (16).

Definition 31 ("MmTSP-path-in-(y,z)") *Let* $(y,z) \in Q_L$. $\forall(\nu_1,\nu_{n-1}) \in (\Lambda_1,\Lambda_{n-1})$*, a level-walk-in-*$(y,z)$ from $(1,\nu_1)$ to $(n-1,\nu_{n-1})$ *is referred to as a "MmTSP-path-in-*(y,z) (from $(1,\nu_1)$ to $(n-1,\nu_{n-1})$)*" (plural: "MmTSP -paths-in-*(y,z) (from $(1,\nu_1)$ to $(n-1,\nu_{n-1})$))*."*

Theorem 32 (Equivalences for *MmTSP-paths-in-(y,z)*) *For* $(y,z) \in Q_L$:

(i) Every *MmTSP-path-in-*(y,z) corresponds to exactly one *MmTSP-path-in-G;*

(ii) Every *MmTSP-path-in-*(y,z) corresponds to exactly one extreme point of the *BNF-based Polytope;*

(iii) Every *MmTSP-path-in-*(y,z) corresponds to exactly one point of Q_I;

(iv) Every *MmTSP-path-in-*(y,z) corresponds to exactly one *MmTSP schedule.*

Proof. Condition (i) follows from Definition 11.2 and Theorem 30. Conditions $(ii)-(iv)$ follow from the combination of condition (i) with Theorem 20.

Theorem 33 *Let* $(y,z) \in Q_L$*. The following hold true:*
(i) $\forall r \in R$, $\forall \rho \in \Lambda_r$,

$$\exists \Big\langle \alpha \in \Lambda_1;\ \beta \in \Lambda_{n-1};\ \iota \in \Pi_{(1,\alpha)(n-1,\beta)}(y,z) \Big\rangle :\ a_{r,\rho}\ \in\ \mathcal{P}_{(1,\alpha),(n-1,\beta),\iota}(y,z).$$

(ii) $\forall(r,s) \in R^2 : r < s$, $\forall \rho \in \Lambda_r;\ \sigma \in \Lambda_s$,

$$y_{(r,\rho)(s,\sigma)} > 0 \Longleftrightarrow \exists \Big\langle \alpha \in \Lambda_1;\ \beta \in \Lambda_{n-1};\ \iota \in \Pi_{(1,\alpha)(n-1,\beta)}(y,z) \Big\rangle :$$
$$(a_{r,\rho},a_{s,\sigma}) \in \mathcal{P}^2_{(1,\alpha),(n-1,\beta),\iota}(y,z);$$

(iii) $\forall(r,s,t) \in R^3 : r < s < t$, $\forall \rho \in \Lambda_r$, $\forall \sigma \in \Lambda_s$, $\forall \tau \in \Lambda_t$,

$$z_{(r,\rho)(s,\sigma)(t,\tau)} > 0 \Longleftrightarrow \exists \Big\langle \alpha \in \Lambda_1;\ \beta \in \Lambda_{n-1};\ \iota \in \Pi_{(1,\alpha)(n-1,\beta)}(y,z) \Big\rangle :$$
$$(a_{r,\rho},a_{s,\sigma},a_{t,\tau}) \in \mathcal{P}^3_{(1,\alpha),(n-1,\beta),\iota}(y,z).$$

Proof. The theorem follows directly from Theorem 29.

Theorem 34 ("Convex independence" of *MmTSP-paths-in-(y,z)*) *Let* $(y,z) \in Q_L$*. A given MmTSP-path-in-*(y,z) *cannot be represented as a convex combination of other MmTSP-paths-in-*(y,z)*.*

Proof. The theorem follows directly from the combination of Theorems 13 and 32.

Definition 35 ("Weights" of *MmTSP-paths- in-(y,z)*) *Let* $(y,z) \in Q_L$*. For* $(\alpha,\beta) \in (\Lambda_1, \Lambda_{n-1})$ *such that* $y_{(1,\alpha)(n-1,\beta)} > 0$*, and* $k \in \Pi_{(1,\alpha)(n-1,\beta)}(y,z)$*, we refer to the quantity*

$$\omega_{\alpha\beta k}(y,z) := \min_{\substack{(r,s,t)\in R^3: r<s<t; \\ (\rho,\sigma,\tau) \in (\Lambda_r,\Lambda_s,\Lambda_t):\ (a_{r,\rho},\, a_{s,\sigma},\, a_{t,\tau}) \in \mathcal{P}^3_{(1,\alpha),(n-1,\beta),k}(y,z)}} \left\{ z_{(r,\rho)(s,\sigma)(t,\tau)} \right\} \tag{36}$$

as the "weight" of (MmTSP-path-in-(y,z)) $\mathcal{P}_{(1,\alpha),(n-1,\beta),k}(y,z)$.

Lemma 36 *Let* $(y,z) \in Q_L$*. The following holds true:*
(i) $\forall (r,s,t) \in R^3 : r < s < t, \forall (v_r, v_s, v_t) \in (\Lambda_r, \Lambda_s, \Lambda_t)$,

$$z_{(r,v_r)(s,v_s)(t,v_t)} \geq \sum_{\alpha\in\Lambda_1} \sum_{\beta\in\Lambda_{n-1}} \sum_{\substack{\iota\in\Pi_{(1,\alpha)(n-1,\beta)}(y,z): \\ (a_{r,v_r},\, a_{s,v_s},\, a_{t,v_t})\in\mathcal{P}^3_{(1,\alpha),(n-1,\beta),\iota}(y,z)}} \omega_{\alpha\beta\iota}(y,z);$$

(ii) $\forall (r,s) \in R^2 : r < s, \forall (v_r, v_s) \in (\Lambda_r, \Lambda_s)$,

$$y_{(r,v_r)(s,v_s)} \geq \sum_{\alpha\in\Lambda_1} \sum_{\beta\in\Lambda_{n-1}} \sum_{\substack{\iota\in\Pi_{(1,\alpha)(n-1,\beta)}(y,z): \\ (a_{r,v_r},\, a_{s,v_s})\in\mathcal{P}^2_{(1,\alpha),(n-1,\beta),\iota}(y,z)}} \omega_{\alpha\beta\iota}(y,z).$$

Proof. The theorem follows directly from the combination of Theorem 33, Theorem 34 and the flow conservations implicit in constraints (11)-(13) (see Bazaraa *et al.*, 2006, pp. 453-474).

Theorem 37 *Let* $(y,z) \in Q_L$*. The following holds true:*
(i) $\forall (r,s,t) \in R^3 : r < s < t, \forall (v_r, v_s, v_t) \in (\Lambda_r, \Lambda_s, \Lambda_t)$,

$$z_{(r,v_r)(s,v_s)(t,v_t)} = \sum_{\alpha\in\Lambda_1} \sum_{\beta\in\Lambda_{n-1}} \sum_{\substack{\iota\in\Pi_{(1,\alpha)(n-1,\beta)}(y,z): \\ (a_{r,v_r},\, a_{s,v_s},\, a_{t,v_t})\in\mathcal{P}^3_{(1,\alpha),(n-1,\beta),\iota}(y,z)}} \omega_{\alpha\beta\iota}(y,z).$$

(ii) $\forall (r,s) \in R^2 : r < s, \forall (v_r, v_s) \in (\Lambda_r, \Lambda_s)$,

$$y_{(r,v_r)(s,v_s)} = \sum_{\alpha\in\Lambda_1} \sum_{\beta\in\Lambda_{n-1}} \sum_{\substack{\iota\in\Pi_{(1,\alpha)(n-1,\beta)}(y,z): \\ (a_{r,v_r},\, a_{s,v_s})\in\mathcal{P}^2_{(1,\alpha),(n-1,\beta),\iota}(y,z)}} \omega_{\alpha\beta\iota}(y,z).$$

Proof.
(i) Let $(r,s,t) \in R^3 : r < s < t$.
From the combination of constraints (7)-(10) and Theorems 22 and 34, we have:

$$\sum_{\rho\in\Lambda_r} \sum_{\sigma\in\Lambda_s} \sum_{\tau\in\Lambda_t} z_{(r,\rho)(s,\sigma)(t,\tau)} = \sum_{\alpha\in\Lambda_1} \sum_{\beta\in\Lambda_{n-1}} \sum_{\iota\in\Pi_{(1,\alpha)(n-1,\beta)}(y,z)} \omega_{\alpha\beta\iota}(y,z) = 1 \tag{37}$$

Using Theorem 33, we have:

$$\sum_{\alpha\in\Lambda_1}\sum_{\beta\in\Lambda_{n-1}}\sum_{\iota\in\Pi_{(1,\alpha)(n-1,\beta)}(y,z)}\omega_{\alpha\beta\iota}(y,z) = \sum_{\rho\in\Lambda_r}\sum_{\sigma\in\Lambda_s}\sum_{\tau\in\Lambda_t}\sum_{\alpha\in\Lambda_1}\sum_{\beta\in\Lambda_{n-1}}\sum_{\substack{\iota\in\Pi_{(1,\alpha)(n-1,\beta)}(y,z):\\(a_{r,\rho},\, a_{s,\sigma},\, a_{t,\tau})\in\mathcal{P}^3_{(1,\alpha),(n-1,\beta),\iota}(y,z)}}\omega_{\alpha\beta\iota}(y,z) \quad (38)$$

Combining (37) and (38), we have:

$$\sum_{\rho\in\Lambda_r}\sum_{\sigma\in\Lambda_s}\sum_{\tau\in\Lambda_t}\left(z_{(r,\rho)(s,\sigma)(t,\tau)} - \sum_{\alpha\in\Lambda_1}\sum_{\beta\in\Lambda_{n-1}}\sum_{\substack{\iota\in\Pi_{(1,\alpha)(n-1,\beta)}(y,z):\\(a_{r,\rho},\, a_{s,\sigma},\, a_{t,\tau})\in\mathcal{P}^3_{(1,\alpha),(n-1,\beta),\iota}(y,z)}}\omega_{\alpha\beta\iota}(y,z)\right) = 0. \quad (39)$$

Condition (i) of the theorem follows directly from the combination of (39) and Lemma 36.*i*.
(*ii*) Let $(r,s)\in R^2 : s > r$.
From the combination of constraints (7)-(13) and Theorems 22 and 34, we have:

$$\sum_{\rho\in\Lambda_r}\sum_{\sigma\in\Lambda_s} y_{(r,\rho)(s,\sigma)} = \sum_{\alpha\in\Lambda_1}\sum_{\beta\in\Lambda_{n-1}}\sum_{\iota\in\Pi_{(1,\alpha)(n-1,\beta)}(y,z)}\omega_{\alpha\beta\iota}(y,z) = 1 \quad (40)$$

Using Theorem 33, we have:

$$\sum_{\alpha\in\Lambda_1}\sum_{\beta\in\Lambda_{n-1}}\sum_{\iota\in\Pi_{(1,\alpha)(n-1,\beta)}(y,z)}\omega_{\alpha\beta\iota}(y,z) = \sum_{\rho\in\Lambda_r}\sum_{\sigma\in\Lambda_s}\sum_{\alpha\in\Lambda_1}\sum_{\beta\in\Lambda_{n-1}}\sum_{\substack{\iota\in\Pi_{(1,\alpha)(n-1,\beta)}(y,z):\\(a_{r,\rho},\, a_{s,\sigma})\in\mathcal{P}^2_{(1,\alpha),(n-1,\beta),\iota}(y,z)}}\omega_{\alpha\beta\iota}(y,z) \quad (41)$$

Combining (40) and (41), we have:

$$\sum_{\rho\in\Lambda_r}\sum_{\sigma\in\Lambda_s}\left(y_{(r,\rho)(s,\sigma)} - \sum_{\alpha\in\Lambda_1}\sum_{\beta\in\Lambda_{n-1}}\sum_{\substack{\iota\in\Pi_{(1,\alpha)(n-1,\beta)}(y,z):\\(a_{r,\rho},\, a_{s,\sigma})\in\mathcal{P}^2_{(1,\alpha),(n-1,\beta),\iota}(y,z)}}\omega_{\alpha\beta\iota}(y,z)\right) = 0. \quad (42)$$

The theorem follows directly from the combination of (42) and Lemma 36.*ii*.

Theorem 38

(*i*) $(y,\, z)\in Q_L \iff (y,z)$ corresponds to a convex combination of *MmTSP-paths-in-G* with coefficients equal to the weights of the corresponding *MmTSP-paths-in-(y,z)*;

(*ii*) $(y,\, z)\in Q_L \iff (y,z)$ corresponds to a convex combination of extreme points of the *BNF Polytope* with coefficients equal to the weights of the corresponding *MmTSP-paths-in-(y,z)*;

(*iii*) $(y, z) \in Q_L \iff (y,z)$ corresponds to a convex combination of *MmTSP schedules* with coefficients equal to the weights of the corresponding *MmTSP-paths-in-(y,z)*.

Proof. The theorem follows directly from Definition 35 and the combination of Theorems 34, and 37.

Theorem 39 *The following hold true:*

(*i*) $Ext(Q_L) = Q_I$;

(*ii*) $Q_L = Conv(Q_I)$;

Proof. The theorem follows directly from the combination of Theorems 32, 34, and 38.

6. Linear Programming formulation of the MmTSP

6.1 Reformulation of the travel costs

We will now discuss the costs associated with the arcs of *Graph G* (or, equivalently, with the variables of the BNF-based model), and the objective function costs to apply over Q_L, respectively.

Notation 40 (Reformulated travel costs)

1. $\forall r \in R, \forall (i,j) \in \overline{\mathfrak{C}}^2 : (i,r,j) \in A,$

$$\overline{\delta}_{irj} := \begin{cases} f_{\mathfrak{p}_r} + \mathfrak{e}_{\mathfrak{p}_r,\mathfrak{b}_{\mathfrak{p}_r},i} + \mathfrak{e}_{\mathfrak{p}_r,i,j} & \text{if } (r = \underline{\mathfrak{r}}_p;\ i \neq \overline{\mathfrak{c}}); \\ 0 & \text{if } ((r = \underline{\mathfrak{r}}_p;\ i = \overline{\mathfrak{c}}) \text{ or } (\overline{\mathfrak{r}}_p = r = n-1;\ i = j = \overline{\mathfrak{c}})); \\ \mathfrak{e}_{\mathfrak{p}_r,i,j} & \text{if } ((\underline{\mathfrak{r}}_p < r < \overline{\mathfrak{r}}_p) \text{ or } (\overline{\mathfrak{r}}_p = r < n-1;\ i = \overline{\mathfrak{c}})); \\ \mathfrak{e}_{\mathfrak{p}_r,i,\mathfrak{b}_{\mathfrak{p}_r}} & \text{if } ((\overline{\mathfrak{r}}_p = r < n-1;\ i \in \mathfrak{C}) \text{ or } (\overline{\mathfrak{r}}_p = r = n-1;\ i \neq \overline{\mathfrak{c}};\ j = \overline{\mathfrak{c}})); \\ \mathfrak{e}_{\mathfrak{p}_r,i,j} + \mathfrak{e}_{\mathfrak{p}_r,j,\mathfrak{b}_{\mathfrak{p}_r}} & \text{if } (\overline{\mathfrak{r}}_p = r = n-1;\ i \neq \overline{\mathfrak{c}};\ j \neq \overline{\mathfrak{c}}). \end{cases}$$

(Reformulated travel costs for the arcs of *Graph G*);

2. $\forall (p,r,s) \in R^3 : r < s < p, \forall (u,v,i,j,k,t) \in (\overline{\mathfrak{C}}, F_r(i), \overline{\mathfrak{C}}, F_s(k), \overline{\mathfrak{C}}, F_p(u)),$

$$\delta_{(irj)(kst)(upv)} := \begin{cases} \overline{\delta}_{irj} + \overline{\delta}_{kst} + \overline{\delta}_{upv} & \text{if } (r = 1;\ s = 2;\ p = 3); \\ \overline{\delta}_{upv} & \text{if } (r = 1;\ s = 2;\ p > 3); \\ 0 & \text{otherwise.} \end{cases}$$

(Reformulated travel costs for the "complex flow modeling" variables).

Example 41 *Consider the MmTSP of Example 7:*

Let the original costs be:

- *Salesman "1":*
  - $\mathfrak{f}_1$ *= 80*
  - *Inter-site travel costs:*

	$\mathfrak{b}_1$	1	2	3	4	5
$\mathfrak{b}_1$	–	18	16	9	21	15
1	18	–	24	14	14	7
2	4	6	–	21	17	13
3	20	18	3	–	14	28
4	14	27	13	5	–	8
5	29	6	8	16	22	–

- *Salesman "2":*
  - $\mathfrak{f}_2 = 90$
  - *Inter-site travel costs:*

	$\mathfrak{b}_2$	1	2	3	4	5
$\mathfrak{b}_2$	–	27	8	5	28	13
1	22	–	21	24	16	11
2	3	11	–	15	14	10
3	18	3	12	–	7	28
4	19	1	17	20	–	6
5	16	24	17	9	20	–

The costs to apply to the arcs of Graph G are illustrated for $i = 4$, $j \in \{3,6\}$, and $r \in \{1,2,5,9\}$, as follows:

	$r=1$	$r=2$	$r=5$	$r=9$
$j=3$	$80+21+5=106$	5	14	$20+18=38$
$j=6$	$80+21+14=115$	14	14	19

6.2 Overall linear program

Theorem 42 *Let:*

$$\vartheta(y,z) := \delta^T \cdot z + \mathbf{0}^T \cdot y$$

$$= \sum_{(p,r,s)\in R^3 : p<r<s} \sum_{i\in\overline{\mathbb{C}}} \sum_{j\in F_r(i)} \sum_{k\in\overline{\mathbb{C}}} \sum_{t\in F_s(k)} \sum_{u\in\overline{\mathbb{C}}} \sum_{v\in F_p(u)} \delta_{(irj)(kst)(upv)} z_{(irj)(kst)(upv)}$$

Then, for $(y,z) \in Ext(Q_L)$, $\vartheta(y,z)$ accurately accounts the cost of the MmTSP sschedule corresponding to (y,z).

Proof. From Theorem 39,

$$(y,z) \in Ext(Q_L) \Longleftrightarrow (y,z) \in Q_I$$

Now, using Theorem 19, it can be verified directly that for $(y,z) \in Q_I$, $\vartheta(y,z)$ accurately accounts the total of cost of the *MmTSP schedule* corresponding to (y,z), $\mathcal{M}(y,z)$ (see Definition 21).

Theorem 43 *The following statements are true of basic feasible solutions (BFS) of*

$$Problem\ LP : \min\{\vartheta(y,z) :\ (y,z) \in Q_L\}$$

and MmTSP schedules:

(i) Every BFS of *Problem LP* corresponds to a *MmTSP schedule;*

(ii) Every *MmTSP schedule* corresponds to a BFS of *Problem LP;*

(iii) The mapping of BFS's of *Problem LP* onto *MmTSP schedule* is surjective.

Proof. Statements (i) and (ii) of the theorem follow directly from the combination of Theorem 39 and the correspondence between BFS's of LP models and extreme points of their associated polyhedra (see Bazaraa *et al.*, 2010, pp. 94-104). Statement (iii) follows from the primal degeneracy of *Problem LP* (see Nemhauser and Wolsey, 1988, p. 32).

Corollary 44 *Problem LP solves the MmTSP.*

7. Conclusions

We have developed a first linear programming (LP) formulation of the multi-depot multiple traveling salesman problem. The computational complexity order of the number of variables and the number of constraints of our proposed LP are $O(\mathfrak{c}^9 \cdot \mathfrak{s}^3)$ and $O(\mathfrak{c}^8 \cdot \mathfrak{s}^3)$, respectively, where $\mathfrak{c}$ and $\mathfrak{s}$ are the number of customer sites and the number of salesmen in the *MmTSP* instance, respectively. Hence, our development represents a new re-affirmation of the important "$P = NP$" result. With respect to solving practical-sized problems, the major limitation of our LP model is its very-large-scale nature. However, we believe that to the extend that the solution method for the proposed model can be streamlined along the lines of procedures for special-structured LP (see Ahuja *et al.*, 1993, pp 294-449; Bazaraa *et al.*, 2010, pp. 339-392, 453-605; Desaulniers *et al.*, 2005; and Ho and Loute, 1981; for examples), it may eventually become possible to solve large-sized problems to optimality or near-optimality. The summary of one idea we are currently pursuing for such a streamlining is as follows: (i) Use a column generation/Dantzig-Wolfe decomposition framework where constraints (15)-(16) of our proposed model are handled implicitly, constraints (11)-(14) are "convexified" into the Master Problem (MP), and columns of the overall problem are generated using the "complex flow modeling" constraints (7) and (8)-(10); (ii) Manage size further by using revised simplex (see Bazaraa *et al.*, 2010, pp. 201-233) in solving the MP; (iii) Adapt the threaded-indexing method for solving the Assignment Problem (see Barr *et al.*, 1977; Cunningham, 1976; Golver and Klingman, 1970, 1973; and Glover *et al.*, 1972, 1973) using the correspondence between Basic Feasible Solutions (BFS's) of the Assignment Problem and BFS's of our model to streamline pivoting operations and to avoid degenerate pivots.

8. References

[1] Ahuja, R.K., T.L. Magnanti, and J.B. Orlin (1993). *Network Flows: Theory, Algorithms, and Applications.* Prentice Hall, Upper Saddle River, NJ.

[2] Ali, A.I., and J.L. Kennington (1986). The asymmetric m-traveling salesmen problem: a duality based branch-and-bound algorithm. *Discrete Applied Mathematics* 13, pp. 259-276.

[3] Applegate, D.L., R.E. Bixby, V. Chvátal, and W.J. Cook (2006). *The Traveling Salesman Problem: A Computational Study.* Princeton University Press, Princeton, NJ.

[4] Barr, R.S., F. Glover, and D. Klingman (1977). The alternating basis algorithm for assignment problems. *Mathematical Programming* 13, pp. 1-13.

[5] Bazaraa, M.S., J.J. Jarvis, and H.D. Sherali (2010). *Linear Programming and Network Flows.* Wiley, New York, NY.

[6] Bazaraa, M.S., H.D. Sherali, and C.M. Shetty (2006). *Nonlinear Programming: Theory and Algorithms.* Wiley, New York, NY.

[7] Bektas, T. (2006). The multiple traveling salesman problem: an overview of formulations and solution procedures. *Omega* 34, pp. 209-219.

[8] Burkard, R.E., M. Dell'Amico, and S. Martello (2009). *Assignment Problems.* SIAM, Phildelphia, PA.

[9] Carter, A.E., and C.T. Ragsdale (2009).

[10] Cunningham, W.H. (1976). A network simplex method. *Mathematical Programming* 11, pp. 105-116.

[11] Desaulniers, G., J. Desrosiers, and M.M. Salomon, eds. (2005). *Column Generation.*

Springer Science and Business Media, New York, NY.

[12] Desrosiers, J., and M.E. Lübbecke (2005). A primer in column generation. In G. Desaulniers, J. Desrosiers, and M.M. Salomon, eds., *Column Generation,* Springer Science and Business Media, New York, NY, pp. 1-32.

[13] Diaby, M. (2008). A $O(n\hat{}8)\times$ $O(n\hat{}8)$ Linear Programming Model of the Traveling Salesman Problem. Unpublished (Available: http://arxiv.org/PS_cache/arxiv/pdf/0803/0803.4354v1.pdf).

[14] Diaby, M. (2006a). Equality of the Complexity Classes P and NP: A Linear Programming Formulation of the Quadratic Assignment Problem. Unpublished (Available: http://arxiv.org/abs/cs/0609004v4.pdf).

[15] Diaby, M. (2010a). Linear programming formulation of the set partitioning problem. *International Journal of Operational Research* 8:4, pp. 399-427.

[16] Diaby, M. (2010b). Linear programming formulation of the vertex coloring problem. *International Journal of Mathematics in Operational Research* 2:3, pp. 259-289.

[17] Diaby, M. (2006b). On the Equality of Complexity Classes P and NP: Linear Programming Formulation of the Quadratic Assignment Problem. *Proceedings of the IMECS 2006,* Hong Kong, China, pp. 774-779.

[18] Diaby, M. (2007b). The Traveling Salesman Problem: A Linear Programming Formulation. *WSEAS Transactions on Mathematics* 6:6, pp. 745-754.

[19] Garey, M.R. and D.S. Johnson, *Computers and Intractability: A Guide to the Theory of NP-Completeness* (Freeman, San Francisco, 1979).

[20] Gavish, B., and K. Srikanth (1986). An optimal solution method for large-scale multiple traveling salesman problems. *Operations Research* 34, pp. 698-717.

[21] Ghafurian, S., and N. Javadian (2010). An ant colony algorithm for solving fixed destination multi-depot multiple traveling salesman problem. *Applied Soft Computing* (forthcoming).

[22] Glover, F., D. Karney, and D. Klingman (1972). The augmented predecessor index method for locating stepping-stone paths and assigning dual prices in distribution problems. *Transportation Science* 6:2, pp. 171-179.

[23] Glover, F., and D. Klingman (1973). A note on the computational simplifications in solving generalized transportation problems. *Transportation Science* 7:4, pp. 351-361.

[24] Glover, F., and D. Klingman (1970). Locating stepping-stone paths in distribution problems via the predecessor index method. *Transportation Science* 4:2, pp. 351-361.

[25] Glover, F., D. Klingman, and J. Stutz (1973). Extentions of the augmented predecessor index method to generalized network flow problems. *Transportation Science* 7:4, pp. 377-384.

[26] Greco, F., ed (2008). *Traveling Salesman Problem.* Intech, Vienna, Austria.

[27] Gromicho, J., J. Paixã, I. Branco (1992). Exact solution of multiple traveling salesman problems. In Mustafa Akgül et al., eds. *Combinatorial Optimization.* NATO ASI Series: F82. Springer, Berlin.

[28] Gutin, G., and A.P. Punen, eds (2007). *The Traveling Salesman Problem and Its Variations.* Springer, New York, NY.

[29] Ho, J.E., Loute, E. (1981). An advanced implementation of the Dantzig-Wolfe algorithm for linear programs. *Mathematical Programming* 20, pp. 303-326.

[30] Hofman, R. (2006). Report on article: P=NP: Linear programming formulation of the Traveling Salesman Problem. Unpublished (Available: http://arxiv.org/abs/cs/0610125).

[31] Hofman, R. (2008b). Report on article: The Traveling Salesman Problem: A Linear Programming Formulation. Unpublished (Available: http://arxiv.org/abs/0805.4718).

[32] Hofman, R. (2007). Why Linear Programming cannot solve large instances of NP-complete problems in polynomial time. Unpublished (Available: http://arxiv.org/abs/cs/0611008).

[33] Huisman, D., R. Jans, M. Peters, and A.P.M. Wagelmann (2005). Combining column generation and Lagrangean relaxation. In G. Desaulniers, J. Desrosiers, and M.M. Salomon, eds. *Column Generation.* Springer Science and Business Media, New York, NY, pp. 247-270.

[34] Kara, I., and T. Bektas (2006). Integer linear programming formulations of multiple traveling salesman problems and its variations. *European Journal of Operational Research* 174, pp. 1449-1458.

[35] Karp, R.M., (1972). Reducibility among combinatorial problems. In R.E. Miller and J.W. Thatcher, eds. *Complexity of Computer Computations.* Plenum Press, New York, NY, pp. 85-103.

[36] Laporte, G., and Y. Nobert (1980). A cutting planes algorithm for the *m*-salesmen problem. *Journal of the Operational Research Society* 31, pp. 1017-1023.

[37] Lawler, E.L., J.K. Lenstra, A.H.G. Rinnooy Kan, and D.B. Shmoys, eds (1985). *The Traveling Salesman Problem: A Guided Tour of Combinatorial Optimization.* Wiley, New York, NY.

[38] Nemhauser, G.L. and L.A. Wolsey (1988). *Integer and Combinatorial Optimization.* Wiley, New York, NY.

[39] Papadimitriou, C.H. and K. Steiglitz, *Combinatorial Optimization: Algorithms and Complexity* (Prentice-Hall, Englewood Cliffs, 1982).

[40] Schrijver, A. (1986). *Theory of Linear and Integer Programming.* Wiley, New York, NY.

[41] Yannakakis, M. (1991). Expressing combinatorial optimization problems by linear programming. *Journal of Computer and System Sciences* 43:3, pp. 441-466.

16

A Sociophysical Application of TSP: The Corporate Vote

Hugo Hernández-Saldaña
Universidad Autónoma Metropolitana at Azcapotzalco
Mexico

1. Introduction

The relevance of the Traveling Salesman Problem (TSP), or the Traveling Salesperson Problem, is large and an indication of that it is the fact the present book is not the first(Applegate et al., 2006; Lawler et al., 1985; Gutin & Punnen, 2007). In this chapter we do not define the problem, neither offer new and faster way of solution, we present, instead, an application of TSP to sociophysics. The specific problem we deal here is to offer a dynamical explanation to the vote distribution of some corporations, i.e. the corporate vote. Recently, this distribution was described for the ruling party in Mexico during the majority of the XX century. With the arrival of the new millennium such a party became opposition, but it keep part of the organization which gave it a large power during seven decades. In reference (Hernández-Saldaña, 2009) the distribution of votes of this political party during the new millennium elections was described very well by the so called daisy models of rank r (Hernández-Saldaña et al., 1998). However, the physical origins of these models makes hard to establish a direct link with a socio-political phenomena. In order to explore a solution to this problem a TSP approach was proposed in (Hernández-Saldaña, 2009) and analyzed in (Hernández-Saldaña et al., 2010). In the present chapter we offer an integrated and detailed exposition of the subject.

In recent years the analysis of the distribution of votes from the point of view of statistical physics has been of interest. The analysis include the proportional vote in Brazil (Filho et al., 1999; 2003; Bernardes et al., 2002; Lyra et al., 2003); India and Brazil (Araripe et al., 2006); India and Canada (Sinha & Pan, 2006); Mexico (Morales-Matamoros et al., 2006) and Indonesia (Situngkir, 2004). A statistical analysis of election in Mexico (Báez et al., 2010) and Russia (Sadovsky & Gliskov, 2007) has been realized. Several models appeared in order to understand why we vote as we do (Fortunato & Castellano, 2007) or a study of the spatial correlations of the voting patterns (Borghesi & Bouchaud, 2010). The analysis of this problem is only one aspect of two new branches in physical sciences: the sociophysics and the econophysics. For an illuminating exposition of the former topic see the book of P. Ball (Ball, 2004), and for the latter consult the book of R.N. Mantegna (Mantegna & Stanley, 2000).

But, how to use TSP to model votes?. The idea is compare the statistical properties of the number of votes obtained for a political party in each cabin with the distance between cities in a TSP. The way to compare pears(votes) with apples(distances) is to map them to new variables where their statistical properties could be compared. Such a process is named, for historical reason, unfolding and we shall devote subsection 3.1 to explain carefully how this is performed. The idea is to measure in a dimensionless variable with density one. This approach has been successful analyzing fluctuation properties in a large set of problems,

mainly in the spectra of quantum systems with a chaotic classical counterpart. One of the relevant aspects was to find universal features in the fluctuation which depends only of large symmetries present in the system, like the existence of time invariance or not. In fact this statistical approach, named Random Matrix Theory, is currently successful and with an increasing number of applications, see Refs. (Brody et al., 1981; Mehta, 2004; Guhr et al., 1998) for explanation.
The TSP has not been absent of such approach, in reference (Méndez-Sánchez et al., 1996) an attempt to find universal properties of the quasi-optimal paths of TSP on an *ensemble* of randomly distributed cities was performed. However no RMT fluctuations have been found, but a fitting with a novel model, named daisy model of rank r was found in a posterior work (Hernández-Saldaña et al., 1998). This model raised in the frame of the statistical analysis of spectra of disordered systems at the transition from metal to insulator, i.e. a localization transition of the system quantum states. This model shall be describe below, since in one of its version, the rank 2 reproduces the statistical properties of the quasi-optimal paths in TSP and, describes some cases of the corporate vote distributions.
Since in the present chapter we are concern to statistical properties of quasi-optimal paths, the way and the time we obtain such a solutions is irrelevant. The results presented here have been obtained using simulated annealing according to (Press et al., 2007).
The rest of the chapter is organized as follows: In the next section we describe the TSP models we use to compare with the corporate vote. In the same chapter we discuss about the importance of the initial distribution of cities taken as an example actual country maps. In section 3 we develop the statistical measures we shall use. In section 4 we explain how the daisy models are built up as well as the electoral data. We compare all the models and data in section 5. We summarize the results and offer some conclusions in section 6.

2. Models and initial conditions

In order to enlighten the corporate vote we use two models (Hernández-Saldaña et al., 2010), both depart from a master square lattice of size b in the Euclidean space (x,y), i.e. the intersection are localized at (nb,mb), with n and m integers. The cities shall be positioned in the intersection surroundings according to a probability distribution of width σ, $\mathcal{P}(\sigma)$ centered at (nb,mb). Hence, the position of the cities is

$$x_i = nb + p_i \tag{1}$$
$$y_i = mb + q_i, \tag{2}$$

being (p_i,q_i) selected from the distribution $\mathcal{P}(\sigma)$, which have zero mean. Up to now, the particular distribution is arbitrary. We choose as our model I an uniform one of total width $2\sigma_s$ and as the model II a Gaussian one of standard deviation σ_g. We shall use this parameter in order to obtain a transition from the square lattice for $\sigma_s = \sigma_g = 0$ to a map which looks like a randomly distributed cities map.
As it shall be clear when we discuss the nearest neighbour distribution, the important feature in this transition appears when the distribution width is large enough in order to admit a distribution overlap between nearest sites, i.e., when $\sigma_s = \sigma_g = b/2$ (see figure 1).
In order to obtain enough statistics we consider an *ensemble* of maps. In the present work we use 500 maps of 32×31 cities. The quasi-optimal paths is obtained using simulated annealing (Press et al., 2007). In figure 2 we present four realizations for different values of σ and for both models.

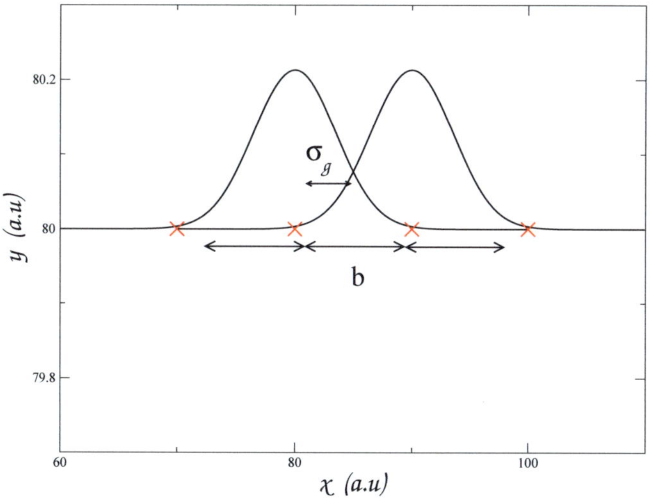

Fig. 1. Schematic construction of models I and II. In the figure we consider model II. The Gaussians are centered at red cross sites and cites are selected from the distribution.

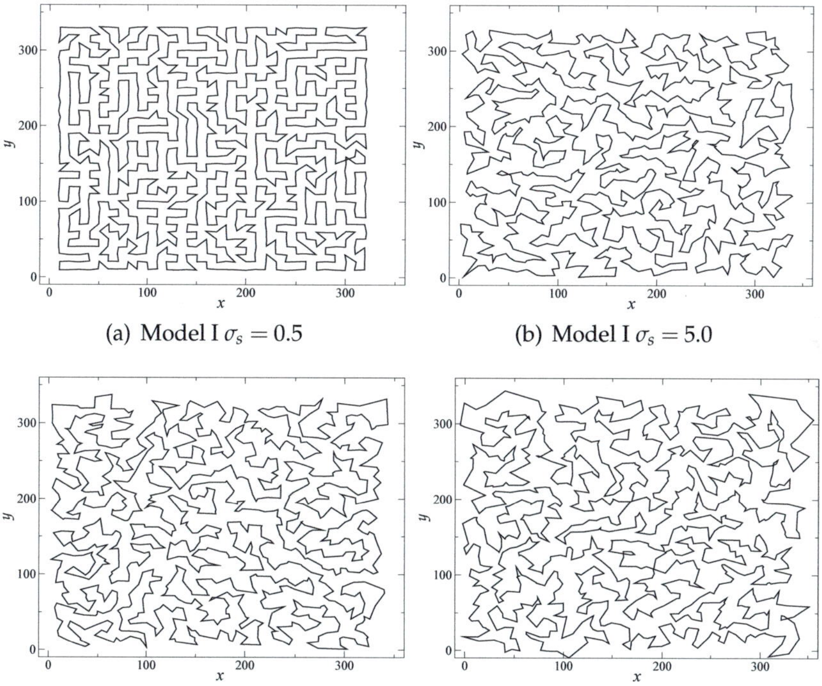

(a) Model I $\sigma_s = 0.5$

(b) Model I $\sigma_s = 5.0$

(c) Model II $\sigma_g = 5.0$

(d) Model II $\sigma_g = 8.5$

Fig. 2. Realizations of maps for both models with the parameter values indicated.

The statistical properties of distances between cities in the quasi-optimal path will be the point of comparison with votes for a corporate party. Note that this simple models are based on *standard* TSP, the peculiarity resides in the initial city distributions used for the calculations. This point is important since the initial set of cities, even in actual distribution of cities, rules what kind of distances distributions could appear. If the initial distribution of cities has no large distances the quasi-optimal path can not create them. In reference (Hernández-Saldaña et al., 2010) the distribution of cities was done and a large dependence of the country was found. Here we present a sample made for 16 countries with data taken from (Applegate et al., 2006). In figure 3 we present the histogram of all the possible distances in the maps. Even when all the countries, exception of Tanzania and Oman, present almost the same power law behaviour at the beginning, the tail and the bulk in the histograms present large variations, from exponential, like Sweden, to large fluctuations like Canada and China. The distribution of normalized distances (or unfolded) with the procedure described below shows similar fluctuations (see figure 1 and 2 in (Hernández-Saldaña et al., 2010)). The search of universal properties in the TSP of actual countries is important even when figure 3 shows large fluctuations.

3. Statistical properties

The statistical characterization we used is commonly named spectral analysis since it is applied to spectra of quantum, optical or acoustical systems. But, for completeness, we add here a wide explanation about it together with some computational details usually not considered in the literature. The applications of this statistical analysis is completely general, see references (Bohigas, 1991; Guhr et al., 1998; Mehta, 2004) for a general introduction.

3.1 Unfolding

The statistical analysis starts with a crucial step: separate the fluctuating properties from the secular ones in the data. This procedure fulfills two goals. First one, we take into account that the data could have a non constant density and a smooth variation could exist. The second goal is to have normalized fluctuations that can be compared between different members of an ensemble or even between different systems. This aspect played a crucial role in the analysis

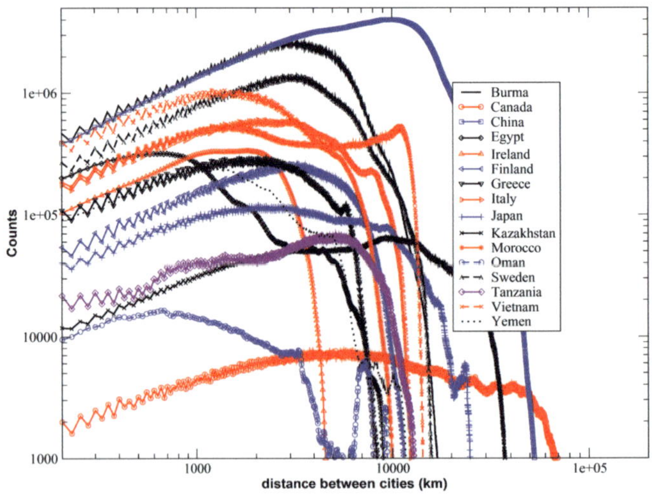

Fig. 3. Histogram of distances between cities for the countries shown in the inset. The data have been taken from (Applegate et al., 2006). Notice that all the countries, except Tanzania and Oman, start with a power law.

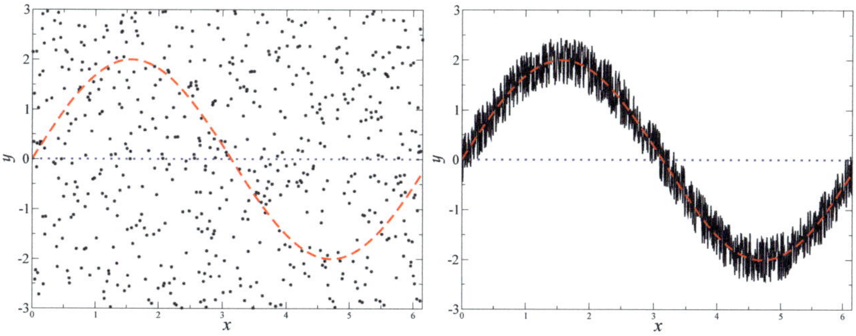

(a) Uniformly random (b) Random on a sine function

Fig. 4. Different averages of a random sequence, in (a) an uniformly random signal is shown in stars, its average is zero (blue dotted line). In (b) a signal with arithmetical average equal to zero, but with fluctuation around $2\sin(x)$, in red dashed line. The units are arbitrary.

of quantum chaotic systems and several of its applications. Including TSP and electoral processes. This procedure is called, for historical reasons, unfolding.
It is common to consider fluctuations, or the statistics like the variance, of a sequence which present a constant average or density like the presented in figure 4(a) in stars. In that case it is clear that the variance, for instance, is calculated in the usual way. However, there exists a large number of cases where the average is not longer constant but a smooth function like a polynomial or a sine function. In figure 4(b) we show this case. The arithmetical average is the same as in the previous case and indicated in dotted blue line, but the fluctuations, in fact, are around a sine function (red dashed line) and they are what we wish to analyze. That is clear that in the latter case the true average is a function and not longer a single number. In fact, an arithmetical analysis says that the function $\langle y \rangle(x) = 0$ is a good result in both cases and the variance is smaller in case (b). A simple view of the data shows how wrong is this procedure and what we require to analyze are the fluctuations around the sine function.
The nature of the average function depends on the particular system and could have different forms and contributions. A common example is the case of the quantum energy levels, E_i, in a Hamiltonian system where there exists a good approximation to the average density. In such a case the density is well represented by the Weyl formulae,

$$\langle \rho(E) \rangle = \frac{1}{(2\pi\hbar)^d} \int \delta(H - E) \mathrm{d}p \mathrm{d}q. \tag{3}$$

Where $\delta(\cdot)$ is the Dirac delta function, H corresponds to the Hamiltonian of d degrees of freedom and the integral is perform on all the phase space variables (p,q). The basic quantum area is represented by $\hbar$, the Planck's constant. This approximation is valid in the semiclassical limit. Even in the case where the system dynamics is well established an accurate calculation of the average is a delicate task (Guhr et al., 1998).
It is customary to deal with the integrated density $\mathcal{N}(E)$ instead of the density itself and the split is denoted as

$$\mathcal{N}(E) = \mathcal{N}_{Secular}(E) + \mathcal{N}_{fluctuations}(E). \tag{4}$$

As we explained previously, a second goal is to compare fluctuations of several members of an ensemble or even different systems. The reason, as we shall see below, is after unfolding the new variables will have mean equal to one. In the case where the system has a constant

density this procedure can be performed by dividing the spectrum by the density. In fact, the name itself "unfolding" comes from the density of energy in nuclear systems: For complex nuclei, the density is almost a semicircle and the idea is to *unfold it* to create a new, constant, density. Notice that this procedure is *always* of local character.
Now, we proceed to explain carefully how the unfolding is performed for distances in the TSP, however, *mutatis mutandis*, the present explanation can be applied to quantum energy levels, acoustic resonances, votes, DNA basis distances, etc. In order to perform the separation of equation (4) we require the analogue of the spectrum E_i, which is ordered as

$$E_1 < E_2 < E_3 < \cdots < E_k < \cdots . \tag{5}$$

Hence we consider the cumulative of lengths for a quasi-optimal tour, $d_k = \sum_{i=1}^{k} l_i$ with $l_i = \sqrt{(x_i - x_{i-1})^2 + (y_i - y_{i-1})^2}$. The cities are positioned at the points (x_i, y_i) and the cumulative lengths are ordered in increasing index. Notice that in this case the tour is periodic but in the case of energies not. The density of d's (or of energies) is defined as

$$\rho(d) = \sum_k \delta(d - d_k), \tag{6}$$

The corresponding cumulative, or integrated, density is

$$\mathcal{N}(d) = \sum_k \Theta(d - d_k), \tag{7}$$

with $\Theta(x)$, the Heaviside or step function. This creates a staircase function with the pair of numbers (d_k, k) and an example is shown in figure5(b). The secular part could be evaluated by a polynomial fitting of degree n. Numerical experience shows better results if, instead starting at $\mathcal{N}(d_1) = 1$ we start at one half (see figure 5)(Bohigas, 1991).
We shall perform the statistical analysis on the variable transformed as

$$\xi_k = \mathcal{N}_{Secular}(d_k), \tag{8}$$

The secular part depends on the particular system taken into account or if we are considering a particular window. Notice that this transformation makes the mean level spacing to be unity, i.e. $\Delta \equiv \langle \xi_k - \xi_{k-1} \rangle = 1$. The new variables are expressed in units of mean level spacing.
The analysis is performed on windows of different size, this kind of analysis is always of local character. The polynomial fitted does not produce a good match in the window extremes (see figure 5(a)) hence, the extreme data are not considered for the statistical analysis. It is convenient to divide the data set in three parts and use only the middle third of the data. In order to avoid a data loss, the window is moved from third to third in order to only loss the extremes of the whole data. The subsets of data ${\xi_k}^i$ of window i are considered as members of an *ensemble* and the statistics will consider averaging on these subsets, i.e., an *ensemble* average. We shall return to this point later. In figure 5 we show a fitting on a large window of a very complex set of data (the quasi-optimal path obtained for Sweden). The larger the window the larger the polynomial degree used to fit it, hence, it is important to consider smaller windows in case the integrated density presents similar long range fluctuations. For practical purposes we consider no less than 300 data per window in order to keep 100 fitted data. Another important question is which degree in the polynomial must be considered. A large value of n could consider part of the fluctuations as the secular term. The answer is not trivial and requires of knowledge of the system itself. Any way, it is important to look directly

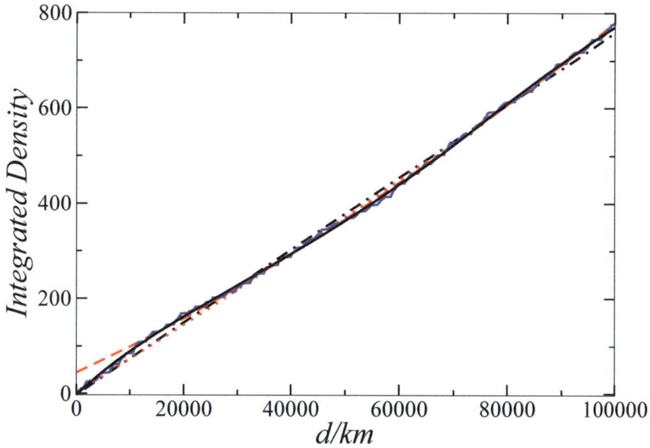

Fig. 5. Integrated density $\mathcal{N}(d)$ calculated for the quasi-optimal path obtained for Sweden (blue histogram) and different polynomial fittings. We plot a window from 0 to 100000 *km* in the length variable d. The fitting was performed in the window from $d = 10000$ to 100000 *km*. The linear approach is shown in black dot-dash line, the 2nd order in red dotted line, the 3rd order in dashed red line and the 4th order polynomial in black line. Note that even the fourth degree polynomial does not fit at all this large window but follows nicely the general shape.

the data fitting and do not believe the correlation coefficient value a priori(see figure 4). Many statistical estimators could give false results.
An important point is the integrated density could involve large numbers and we can loss accuracy in the fitting. A way to solve it is to use the translational invariance of the data and translate the windows to the origin each time. Since we are interested in differences of ξ_k this translation does

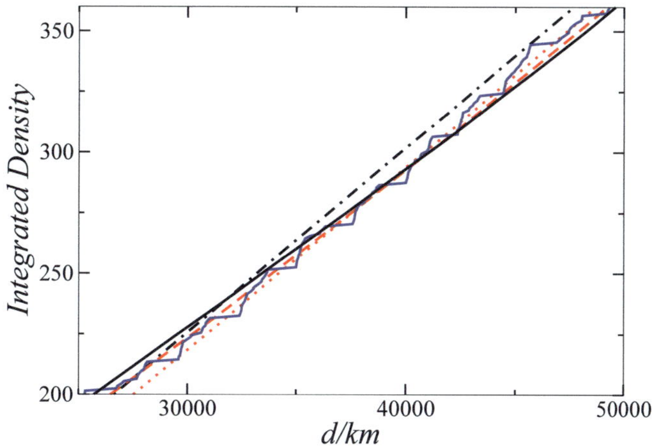

Fig. 6. A close up to previous figure, in order to see the fitted polynomial. Notice the staircase structure.

3.2 Fluctuations

Given the new sequence

$$\xi_1 < \xi_2 < \xi_3 < \cdots < \xi_k < \cdots < \xi_N, \tag{9}$$

we shall characterize their statistical properties. The probability of have a value at ξ_1 and $\xi_1 + \mathrm{d}\xi_1$, another between ξ_2 and $\xi_2 + \mathrm{d}\xi_2$ and, in general a number between ξ_k and $\xi_k + \mathrm{d}\xi_k$, is

$$P(\xi_1, \cdots, \xi_N)\mathrm{d}\xi_1 \cdots \mathrm{d}\xi_N, \tag{10}$$

regardless the labelling. Hence the statistical properties are characterized by the n-point correlation function,

$$R_n(\xi_1, \cdots, \xi_n) = \frac{N!}{(N-n)!} \int P(\xi_1, \cdots, \xi_N)\mathrm{d}\xi_{n+1} \cdots \mathrm{d}\xi_N. \tag{11}$$

However, for practical purposes, in the literature it is considered two measures, the nearest-neighbor distribution $p(1,s)$ and the number variance $\Sigma^2(L)$. The first one is the probability to have a separation $s_i = \xi_i - \xi_{i-1}$ between s and $s + \mathrm{d}s$ and measures short range correlations. The latter is the variance of the number of levels in a box of size L and measures long range correlations. Several other statistics could be used, like Fourier transform, skewness, kurtosis and the n-th neighbor distribution width. For larger explanation, the reader could see references (Bohigas, 1991; Guhr et al., 1998; Mehta, 2004).

The nearest-neighbour distribution is built up by a histogram of $s_i = \xi_i - \xi_{i-1}$. The mean value is, by construction, one. Since, in general, we are considering an analysis on windows which are taken as statistically equivalent, the final distribution is an average on the distributions of all the windows, i.e., we consider an *ensemble* average. However could be possible to build up an ensemble of systems, as those considered in model I and II, this average is considered in a natural way. In both cases we consider the average of all the distributions, say the $p(1;s)$ of each window or system.

In a similar way the n-th neighbour distribution is measured in the variable $s_i = \xi_{i+n} - \xi_i$. The number variance is calculated directly counting the number of level or numbers in boxes of size L and considering the variance. In order to obtain theoretical predictions it is useful to consider the 2-level cluster function $Y_2(s)$, defined as

$$Y_2(s) = 1 - R_2(s). \tag{12}$$

Where $R_2(s)$ is the two point correlation function as defined in (11). This function can be evaluated if we have information about the neighbours distribution for all order, i.e.,

$$R_2(s) = \sum_{n=1}^{\infty} p(n;s). \tag{13}$$

Using equations (12) and (13) we can obtain the number variance by

$$\Sigma^2(L) = L - 2\int_0^L \mathrm{d}s(L-s)Y_2(s). \tag{14}$$

Hence, if we know all the n-th neighbour distribution it is possible to calculate an analytical expression for Σ^2. Even when we shall not use the Σ^2 statistics for comparison with the electoral results is useful to calculate it. In figure 7 we show the result for several values of the TSP models and the asymptotic behavior in daisy models, where the grow is $\sim L/(r+1)$. The correlations are slightly different but all them remain linear.

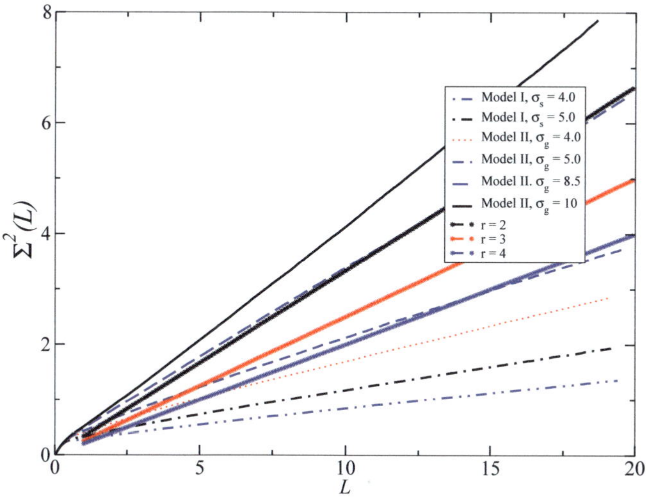

Fig. 7. Number variance Σ^2 for the models and values indicated in the inset. For the daisy models only the asymptotic values are reported.

4. Electoral data and daisy models

4.1 The electoral data

The electoral data were taken from the Mexican electoral authorities official web page (Instituto Federal Electoral, 2006) and they can be obtained on request as well. We consider three elections in the new millennium: the federal elections in 2000, 2003 and 2006. The selection was made since, in the three cases, the corporate party, the Partido Revolucionario Institucional (PRI), arrived as opposition with only their corporate members (in fact, this party loose the presidential election in 2000). This offer the opportunity to explore the corporate vote only. Additionally, the database of the last elections are available in electronic format. Analysis on different Mexican elections is matter of current research.

Federal elections in Mexico are organized by the Instituto Federal Electoral (IFE) and they are made by direct vote. In such an election, people choose the republic president and the members of both chambers. The country is divided in electoral districts and the cabins are localized according to the number of registered electors. Each cabin admits a maximum of 750 votes, except the special cabin which could admit a larger number of votes. Such cabins are devoted to people who have the right to vote but who are in transit or live in a different place where they are registered for electoral matters. The number of cabins in whole country is around 117,000.

The distribution of votes is built up by counting in how many cabins exists 1 vote, 2 votes and so on and considering a histogram of them. In symbols, be n_i the number of votes in cabin i, built the sequence x_i by

$$x_{i+1} = x_i + n_{i+1}, \tag{15}$$

and define $x_1 = n_1$. The corresponding histograms for the crude data can be seen in reference (Hernández-Saldaña, 2009). In order to obtain the statistical properties the unfolding must be done, however, a natural way to order the votes counts like in (9) is not obvious or, even, does not exist. This is clear since the order of cabins is assigned alphabetically into the database (Instituto Federal Electoral, 2006) and with no relation to the social or political distribution of votes of this particular party. Hence, the density of vote could vary tremendously or,

even, could not exist in the database. A way to handle this problem and in order to break the geographical correlations is to consider a randomization of the votes and construct an ordered sequence like in equation (9). Clearly, this new sequence should have an uniform distribution and we can use it in order to unfold the sequence since its density is constant. Notice that the transformed nearest neighbour distribution of votes is the mapped vote n_i to the unfolded new variable s_i. This procedure gives only information about the nearest neighbour distribution and it puts limits to our analysis. However, opens the research of a natural order in the vote being it geographical, corporative, social, etc.
In TSP the problem does not appear since the quasi optimal path offers a natural way to make the ordering. In the case of actual cities maps, however, the unfolding must be carefully performed since there exists a lot of variations (Hernández-Saldaña et al., 2010).

4.2 Daisy model of rank r

The daisy model is constructed by retaining each $r+1$ level in a sequence of random numbers increasingly ordered as in (9). Since the original sequence of numbers have the nth-neighbour distribution given by

$$p(n;s) = \frac{s^{n-1}}{(n-1)!}\exp(-s), \tag{16}$$

and being $n = 1$ the first or nearest neighbour, the new sequence has the $(r+1)n$th-neigbours distribution. But is must be renormalized in order to recover the standard average values, i.e.

$$\int_0^\infty sp(n;s)\mathrm{d}s = n. \tag{17}$$

With the appropriate change of variable we obtain the nth-neighbour distribution for the daisy model of rank r:

$$p_r(n;s) = \frac{(r+1)^{(r+1)n}}{\Gamma((r+1)n)}s^{(r+1)n-1}\exp\left(-(r+1)s\right). \tag{18}$$

Where $\Gamma(\cdot)$ is the gamma function. See reference (Hernández-Saldaña et al., 1998) for the whole derivation. The name of the models becomes clear for the case of rank $r = 1$: Here we label each level in the sequence ξ_i, one with the label "she loves me" and the next with the label "she loves me not". Since we are optimistic we retain only the love sequence. Meanwhile the rank 1 model applies to the metal to insulator transition the rank 2 fits very well the TSP with an ensemble of randomly distributed cities (Hernández-Saldaña et al., 1998).

5. Results

We can compare the nearest neighbour distribution $p(s)$ obtained from model I and II with the electoral results. The comparison is done on three cases: the presidential election of 2006, the senators election in 2000 and the low chamber election in 2006. The selection was done in order to present different cases. We shall use the notation $p(s)$ instead of $p(1;s)$ for shortand. The TSP models were built up on rectangles of size $b = 10$ km and 500 maps of 32×31 cities. The $p(s)$ for 2006 presidential election is presented in figure 8 in black histogram. The daisy model of rank 3, in black dashed line, presents a remarkable fitting to the distribution main bulk. The explicit expression for this daisy model is

$$p_3(s) = \frac{4^4}{3!}s^3\exp(-4s). \tag{19}$$

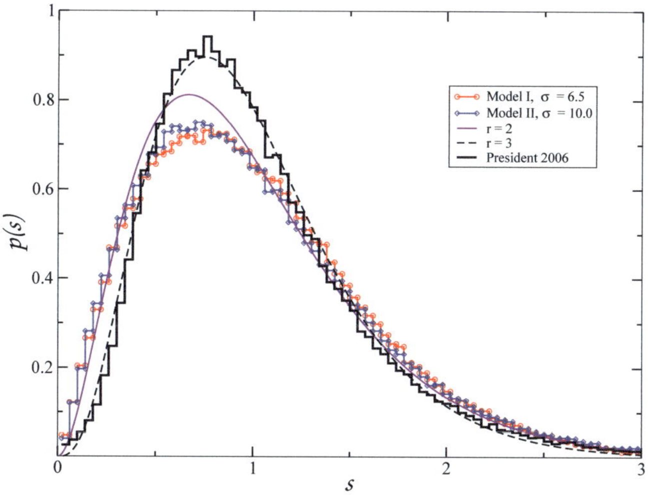

Fig. 8. Nearest neighbour distribution for the Presidential election in 2006 compared with models I and II and daisy models. The parameter values are indicated in the inset. Notice that the daisy model of rank 3 fits remarkably well the vote distribution. The variable s is expressed in mean spacings units, see subsection 3.1 for explanation.

However the tail does not longer fit, being fitted instead by a rank 2 daisy (see figure 9). Neither model I or II could fit the distribution bulk, but the tail is well fitted from widths, σ, departing from $\sigma_s \sim 6.5$ (in red line with circles) and $\sigma_g \sim 8.5$ (in blue line with diamonds)) for the respective model. The numerical exploration in both model shows that the decay reaches a limit compatible with an $\exp(-3s)$ decay (see figure 9). This limit corresponds to the daisy model of rank 2,

$$p_2(s) = \frac{3^3}{2!} s^2 \exp(-3s), \tag{20}$$

and it is compatible with a TSP with cities selected from an uniform random distribution (Hernández-Saldaña et al., 1998). As we have noticed before, for this values of σ we have overlapping city distributions, since for model I this start at $\sigma_s = b/2$ and for model II at $\sigma_g = b/2$, the distributions centers are two standard deviations apart.
Hence, a tail compatible with slower decay ~ 3 does not appear in the analyzed electoral data. It will be interesting to analyze the data for the incoming election in 2012. In the case of our models, model II presents slower decay for values larger than $3b$.
Referring the fit at the beginning of the vote distribution, we compare with other σ values for both models, see figure 10. For model I, maps with a $\sigma_s \approx 2.75$ fit well, meanwhile for model II the value is $\sigma_g = 3.5$ and the close up is reported in figure 11. As a general feature, the TSP models presented here are unable to produce a distribution with a start different from a power law of order 2 for values of σ larger than $\sim b/2$. Hence, this models do not reproduce this feature present in both, the electoral data and in the daisy models.
The rest of the comparisons are reported in figures 12 and 13. For the case of Low chamber election during 2006, figure 12, the value of the fitting parameters at the tail are compatible with $b/2$ and rank 3 daisy model. The values are $\sigma_s \approx 3.90$ and $\sigma_g \approx 4.75$. For the distribution beginning the values are equal to those reported for Presidential election in 2006. In the case of Senator in 2000, figure 13, the tail is fitted by $r = 4$ and $\sigma_s \approx 3.13$ and $\sigma_g = 3.5$. The beginning of the vote distribution presents a linear grow that makes it incompatible with all the models

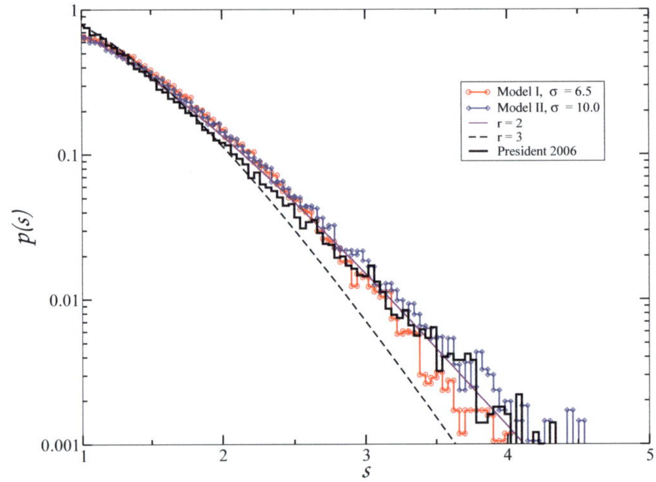

Fig. 9. Same as previous figure but in semilog scale. Notice that daisy of rank 3 does not fit the tail, it is better fitted by rank 2 daisy and for models I and II with the values indicated in the inset.

presented here. Notwithstanding such a result appears clearly as a deviation into the crude data reported previously in (Hernández-Saldaña, 2009).
From the analysis it is clear the correct tail for electoral results requires some overlapping between the initial cities distribution. The model II, the Gaussian one, presents a better fitting in all the cases. The TSP models fails in to obtain correctly the maxima of the distribution. This fail is common in all the cases and that happens even in the case of daisy models. It is a truism that the maxima and the average in a probability distribution are not the same. Since the distribution is normalized a different value of position of maxima causes a different rate decay at the tail. Hence, a search on new TSP models which could present a different

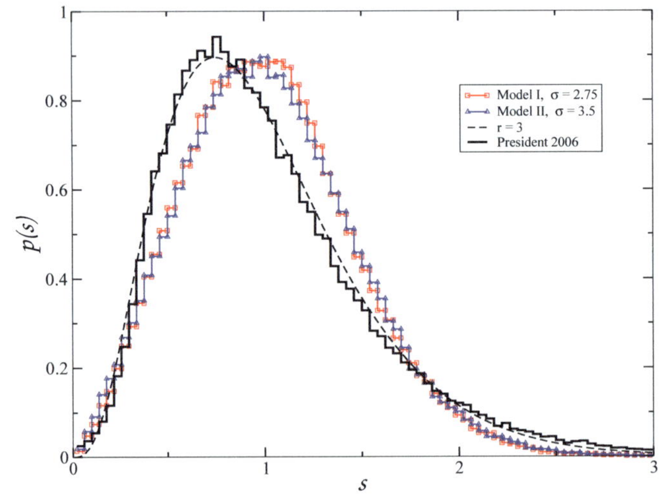

Fig. 10. Nearest neighbour distribution for the Presidential election in 2006 compared with models I and II and daisy models in order to fit the distribution at the beginning. The parameter values are indicated in the inset.

position of the maxima could give a better fitting of electoral data. A remarkable exception is Presidential case in 2006.

In reference to the long range correlation for the TSP models they grow linearly, but with a slope that slightly differs from daisy models. It is important to remark that long range correlations are extremely sensitive to unfolding procedure, but knowledge of longer correlations than first neighbour helps to understand the dynamics. Such has been the experience in quantum chaos and recently in the study of DNA sequences.

As a final point for this section is in reference to the reliability of electoral data. Even when we assume a fair play election and that the data are correctly collected and expressed, such a phenomenon is of a large complexity. One, which can be determined, is the self consistency in the data. In the Mexican 2006 election such a reliability is unclear (Báez et al., 2010) and must be taken into account when the analysis is performed. The 2006 data for the corporate party was particularly clear since they were, by far, the third position in the whole election. Many of the usual allies that sum their vote to this party were split with the two other large parties.

6. Conclusion

In this chapter we expose an application of TSP to a socio-political problem: explain the distribution of votes of a corporate party. The link between TSP and vote processes is made considering the distances between cities as the amount of votes received for a party in a cabin. In order to compare their statistical properties we perform a deconvolution process in order to separate the fluctuation from the average properties, such a procedure is called unfolding. The comparison was made for the nearest neighbour distribution of the unfolded variables. The corporate vote distribution for Mexican elections of 2000, 2003 and 2006 show that the distribution presents an exponential decay and start with a power law. These distributions are well described by a daisy model of rank r but there is not a clear interpretation for these models and the vote distribution. However, since the TSP with a cities distribution randomly selected is well described by a daisy model or frank 2, we decide to explore this option. To this end, we consider two TSP models with different initial cities distribution. We start with a square master lattice with a probability distribution centered in the intersection. The city

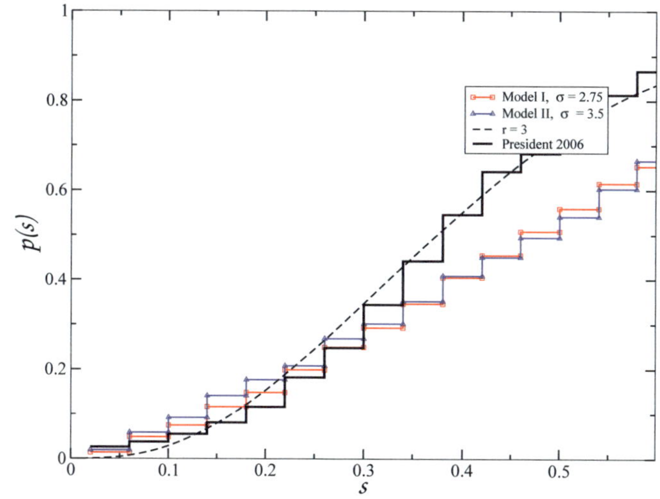

Fig. 11. Same as previous figure. The TSP models does not fit departing from $s \approx 0.35$

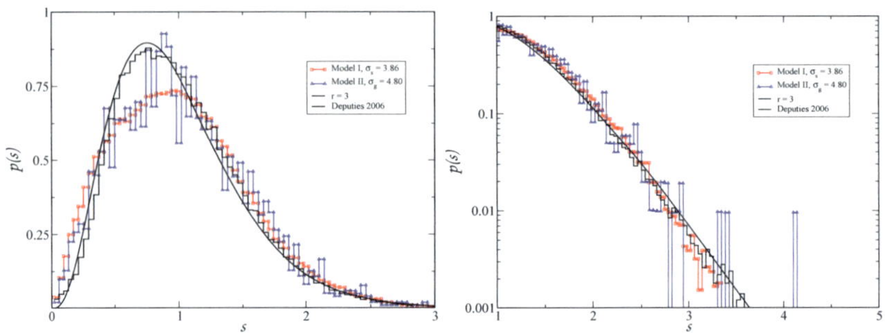

(a) Linear scale. (b) Semi-log scale.

Fig. 12. Nearest neighbour distribution for the cases indicated in the inset. (a) Linear scale and (b) the semilog scale in order to show the behaviour at the tail.

location is selected from this probability distribution. We use two models, model I consists of an uniform distribution of total width $2\sigma_s$ and, as model II, a Gaussian distribution of width σ_g. Both models present a transition from a distribution of cities, departing from a square lattice for $\sigma = 0$ to a distribution of cities that resembles one selected randomly. For large enough width both models reproduce the rank 2 daisy model tail.
With this two models we analyzed the electoral problem. The result obtained shows that the tail behavior could be described by such a models but the behaviour for small distances is not. The vote data best situated for analysis is the federal election in 2006. For the Presidential election of 2006, the extreme case, the decaying behaviour is well fitted by the models and the rank 2 daisy model. For an intermediate case, as it is represented by the Deputy and Senator elections in 2006 the model reproduces the tail by width values that are near from the value $b/2$, being b the size of the master square lattice. In all the vote distribution of 2006 the small distance behaviour is well described by our models with width of the order of $(3/5)b$.
The problem in the description for small distances with our models is that they present a limit for the beginning of the distribution. This limit appears when the width of the models admits overlapping of the different sites in the master lattice. This limit appears not only in our model but in actual cities distribution(see figure 3). If this behaviour is universal or not it is matter of current research.

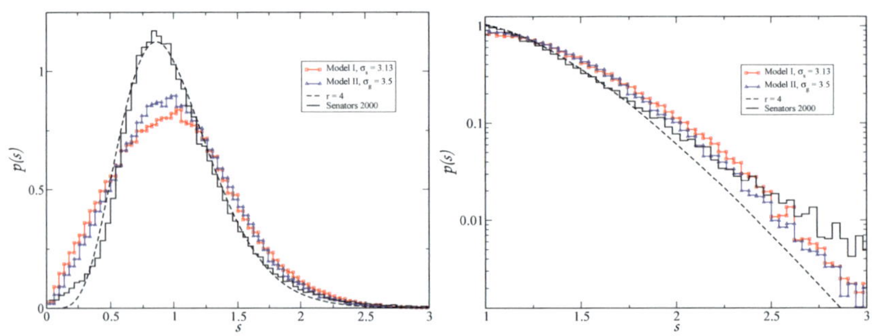

(a) Linear scale. (b) Semi-log scale.

Fig. 13. Nearest neighbour distribution for the cases indicated in the inset. (a) Linear and (b) semilog scales in order to show the behaviour at the tail.

The existence of overlapping or not in the models becomes crucial in the description. This could be interpreted, in the vote case, as the corporate party having a similar distribution of voters in each cabin instead of single agents. In terms of a political description this means that agents of the party (the members of a national syndicate like the elementary school teachers, for instance) have a sphere of influence (with their relatives, for instance). This kind of behaviour has been observed, see (Crespo, 2008). How far this analogy goes is matter of current research and opens new questions about how we vote, beyond of the opinion models currently investigated by (Fortunato & Castellano, 2007), for instance. The peculiarities and deviations in the actual data can be taken into account. In the case of 2000 elections all the vote distributions presented a linear grow for small number of votes. This behaviour could not be explained by the models, this is a characteristic of such election. The electoral data itself can be noisy and subject to a lot of influences no related to fair-game. To this subject see (Crespo, 2008; Báez et al., 2010).
Even when the distribution of votes of the corporate party are better described by daisy models than the presented models of TSP, the latter offers a better dynamical insight of the voters behaviour. The search of new TSP models that present a better description of the actual data is open as well as models that reproduce the dynamics of the corporate vote. Human societies are complex, indeed, but simple models are discovering and enlightening features that could be explanation of the large consequences of our every day behaviour.

7. Acknowledgements

We thank support from PROMEP 2115/35621, Mexican agency.

8. References

Applegate, D. L., Bixby, R. E., Chvatal, V. & Cook, W. (2006). *The Traveling Salesman Problem: A Computational Study*, Princeton Univ. Press, U.S.A.

Araripe, L., Costa-Filho, R., Herrmann, H. & Andrade-Jr, J. (2006). Plurality voting: the statistical laws of democracy in Brazil, *Int. J. Mod. Phys. C* Vol. 17: 1809.

Báez, G., Hernández-Saldaña, H. & Méndez-Sánchez, R. (2010). On the reliability of electoral processes: the mexican case. `arxiv:physics/0609114v2`.

Ball, P. (2004). *Critical mass*, Farrar, Straus and Giroux, London U.K.

Bernardes, A., Stauffer, D. & Kertész, J. (2002). Election results and the Sznajd model on Barabási network, *Eur. Phys. J. B* Vol. 25: 123–127.

Bohigas, O. (1991). Random matrices and chaotic dynamics, *in* A. V. . J. Z.-J. M.-J. Giannoni (ed.), Chaos and Quantum physics. Les Houches, session LII, 1989, North-Holland, Amsterdam, pp. 87–200.

Borghesi, C. & Bouchaud, J.-P. (2010). Partial correlations in vote statistics: a diffusive field model for decision-making, *Eur. Phys. J. B* Vol. 75: 395404.

Brody, T. A., Flores, J., French, J., Pandey, A. & Wong, S. S. M. (1981). Random-matrix physics: spectrum and strength fluctuations, *Rev Mod. Phys.* Vol. 53(3): 385–480.

Crespo, J. A. (2008). *2006: Hablan las actas. Las debilidades de la autoridad electoral mexicana*, Debate, Mexico.

Filho, R. C., Almeida, M., Andrade, J. & Moreira, J. (1999). Scaling behavior in a proportional voting process, *Phys. Rev. E* Vol. 60: 1067–1068.

Filho, R. C., Almeida, M. & Jr., J. A. (2003). Brazilian elections: voting for a scaling democracy, *Physica A* Vol. 322: 698–700.

Fortunato, S. & Castellano, C. (2007). Scaling and universality in proportional elections, *Phys. Rev. Lett.* Vol. 99: 138701–138704.

Guhr, T., Müller-Groeling, A. & Weidenmüller, H. (1998). Random matrix theories in quantum physics: Common concepts, Phys. Rep. Vol. 229: 189–425.

Gutin, G. & Punnen, A. P. (2007). *The Traveling Salesman Problem and its variations*, Springer, New York.

Hernández-Saldaña, H. (2009). On the corporate votes and their relation with daisy models, *Physica A* Vol. 388: 2699–2704.

Hernández-Saldaña, H., Flores, J. & Seligman, T. (1998). Semi-poisson statistics and beyond, *Physical Review E* Vol 60: 449–452.

Hernández-Saldaña, H., Gómez-Quezada, M. & Hernández-Zapata, E. (2010). Statistical distributions of quasi-optimal paths in the traveling salesman problem: the role of the initial distribution of cities, *Rev. Mex Phys. S* Accepted paper: 6 pages. arxiv.org: [cond-mat.stat-mech] 1003.3913.

Instituto Federal Electoral, I. F. E. (2006). Cómputo distrital de las elecciones federales de 2006. www.ife.org.mx.

Lawler, E. L., Lenstra, J. K., Kan, A. H. G. R. & Shmoy, D. B. (1985). *The Traveling Salesman Problem: A Guided Tour of Combinatorial Optimization*, Wiley, U.S.A.

Lyra, M., Costa, U., Filho, R. C. & Andrade, J. (2003). Generalized Zipf's law in proportional voting processes, *Europhys. Lett.* Vol. 62: 131.

Mantegna, R. N. & Stanley, H. E. (2000). *An introduction to Econophysics*, Cambridge Univ. Press, U.K.

Mehta, M. L. (2004). *Random Matrices*, Elsevier, Amsterdam.

Méndez-Sánchez, R., Valladares, A., Flores, J., Seligman, T. & Bohigas, O. (1996). Universal fluctuations of quasi-optimal paths of the travelling salesman problem, *Physica A* Vol.232: 554–562.

Morales-Matamoros, O., Martínez-Cruz, M. & Tejeida-Padilla, R. (2006). Mexican voter network as a dynamic complex system, *50th Annual Meeting of the ISSS*.

Press, W. H., Teukolsky, S. A., Vetterling, W. T. & Flannery, B. P. (2007). *Numerical Recipes. The art of scientific computation*, Cambridge Univ. Press, U.K.

Sadovsky, M. & Gliskov, A. (2007). Towards the typology of elections at Russia. arXiv:0706.3521 [physics.soc-ph].

Sinha, S. & Pan, R. (2006). How a hit is born: the emergence of popularity from the dynamics of collective choice, *in* A. C. B.K. Chakrabarti, A. Chakraborti (ed.), Econophysics and Sociophysics: Trends and Perspectives, Wiley-VCH, Berlin, pp. 417–447. arXiv:0704.2955 [physics.soc-ph].

Situngkir, H. (2004). Power-law signature in Indonesian legislative election 1999 and 2004. arXiv:nlin/0405002.

17

Some Special Traveling Salesman Problems with Applications in Health Economics

Liana Lupşa[1], Ioana Chiorean[1], Radu Lupşa[1] and Luciana Neamţiu[2]

[1]*Babeş-Bolyai University*
[2]*Cancer Institute Ion Chiricuţă*
Romania

1. Introduction

Starting from a practical *Health Economics* problem (the optimal planning of visits for a given medical registrar to its allocated cities, for selection and registration of eligible patients to be included in the regional non-communicable diseases registries for a specified type of chronic disease) we construct a mathematical model. We show that this model can be seen as a new generalization of the following problems: Prize Collecting Traveling Salesman Problem, Simple Cycle Problem, Capacitated Prize-Collecting Traveling Salesman Problem or Orienteering Problem.

Our purpose is that of finding a cycle, belonging to a directed graph, with a given number of vertices (nodes), among which one is fixed, so that the total bonus (which varies in time) is maximized and the total costs (transport costs plus accommodation costs) are minimized. A boundary condition must also be satisfied.

In contrast to the known generalizations of the Traveling Salesman Problem, the originality of our approach relies on three ideas:

- the fact that the exact number of cycle vertices is fixed,
- the bonus depends not only on the visited vertex, but also on the visiting time, that is, on the position of the vertex along the cycle, and
- the goal is expressed by a vector, with two components (bonus and cost).

The solving of the problem reduces to the determination of a lexicographic max-min non-dominant cycle, the choice of the lexicographic order being determined by the initial health economics problem.

It is important to mention that we do not just analyze the problem from a theoretical point of view, but also from a practical one, therefore we propose two algorithms: a Greedy algorithm and an exact one. They both generate good solutions. Unfortunately, the exact algorithm becomes slower as the number of vertices increases. That is, as in (Trobec et al., 2009), we also analyze the possibility of using parallel calculus for improving the execution time.

We are interested in continuing the research, focused on other health economics problems, whose mathematical model can be seen as a generalization of the classical Traveling Salesmen Problem.

2. The medical motivational background

During the last years, many studies belonging to a field known as *Health Economics Research*, have been developed. The term includes a multitude of issues related to the management of pharmaceutical products and of medical activities, from an optimization perspective. In this context, several major issues arise:

- finding new treatments with increased effectiveness and with little costs;
- making the treatment to be carried out to a patient as bearable as possible (little inconvenience, fewer side effects);
- detecting, in early stages, the disease, since it is known that healing is safer, faster and less expensive as the disease is diagnosed sooner;
- monitoring a chronic disease both for determining its objective causes, and for understanding its evolution trend, in order to anticipate correctly the necessary treatment costs;
- finding those treatments which may keep the patient's life quality at a high level, but with lower costs (usually constrained to fit into a given budget), in chronic diseases, when returning to the normal health state is impossible;
- preventing infectious diseases, by controlling the possible contacts, isolating the sick persons, and, in some cases vaccinating them.

The basic idea behind pharmacoeconomics studies is: *to win as a good health as possible with the smallest amount of money*. Therefore, in these studies which consider a treatment by its results reported to the cost, some ratios are generated, called indices. Among them, we recall ICER, INB, and NHB. It is clear that, in order to draw a conclusion closer to reality on the costs and effectiveness of a treatment, it is necessary to apply it to a sufficient number of patients. As a result, costs and effects will be replaced by average costs, average effects, respectively. The need of averages leads to the necessity of using results from mathematical statistics. Hence, if in their early phases, the pharmacoeconomics studies highlighted the treatment effects and identified the costs involved in applying it (the actual cost of the drugs used, their application costs, costs of the medical advices), nowadays these studies have been starting to use advanced mathematical tools like Probability Theory, Bayesian Analysis, Markov Processes and Multi-Criteria Optimization. We recall (Briggs & Sculpher, 1998; Briggs et al., 2006; Fayers, 1997) and (Willan & Briggs, 2006) as main reference works related to pharmacoeconomics studies, works that use the indices mentioned above.
Because health budgets are not unlimited, whatever the country, the health economics problems are, in most cases, optimization problems which get a multi-criteria character (see, for example, (Lupsa, 1999; 2000a;b; Tigan et al., 2001; Grosan et al., 2005; 2007)). Other works, as (Canfelt et al., 2004; Kang & Lagakos, 2007; Chiorean et al, 2008; Lupsa et al, 2008; Neamtiu, 2008; 2009), contain mathematical models which were built by using Bayesian Analysis, Markov Processes or Dynamic Optimization.
The aim of this chapter is to present an approach to a health-economics problem, using in its solving variants of the Traveling Salesman Problem. The problem was raised during the optimization process of the data collection for the cancer registry at the North-West Regional Cancer Registry (Romania). The research is sustained by a multidisciplinary consortium in the framework of CRONIS project (contract no. 11-003/2007, developed under PN II national R&D programme, financed by the Romanian Government).

3. The problem of medical registrars

To organize regional non-communicable diseases registries for a specified type of chronic disease (cancer, diabetes, cardiovascular), registrars (persons with specialized training who register data) must visit, at certain interval of times, the medical units subordinated (clinics, hospitals, etc.) for selection and registration of eligible patients to be included in the register. More precisely, registrars, based on medical documentation, have to decide whether a case should be registered or not, and, in the first situation, to specify, beside the patient's personal data, some disease-related remarks, remarks that are coded. For example, for cancer, the registration and coding rules are well established and standardized (see (World Health Organization, 1991)).

Knowing those medical units which are subordinated to a registrar, the problem is to plan the days in which he has to make the registrations at every medical unit. The maximum number of registrations that he/she can make in one day is known, as well as the fact that, in one day, he/she visits one medical unit, due to the fact that these units are in different locations (cities). The number of patients whose medical records have to be investigated is variable, it increases from one day to another. Specifically, every morning, in the stack of processed medical records, new ones are added. One makes the assumption that, at the very beginning, the number of existing medical records is known and also its growth rate, depending of time. In this paper we assume that the rate is constant, and equal to the monthly average number of new files. Planning should be such that the number of medical records left unchecked (from all the files gathered until the end of the period) to be as low as possible, and also the total costs (which include transportation costs plus subsistence and accommodation costs) to be as low as possible. The registrar may remain for several days to record documents in one medical unit. He/she can move from one unit to another or return to the base, case in which he/she is obliged to remain a day there.

The following data are known:

- n, the number of hospitals, numbered from 1 to n; with 0 being numbered the hospital to which the registrar belongs; it is the location where he starts the early registration period and where he must return at the end of the recording process;
- p, the number of days corresponding to the time period when the registration is made;
- c_{ij}, transport costs from hospital i to hospital j, for any $i, j \in \{0,1,\ldots,n\}, i \neq j$;
- q, maximum number of medical records that can be investigated by the registrar in a day;
- d_i, accommodation costs per night if remains to sleep overnight in the area corresponding to hospital i (if it coincides with the place where hospital 0 is located, we have obviously $d_i = 0$);
- f_i, estimated number of medical records that can exist in hospital i at the beginning of the work;
- r_i, the growth rate, from day to day, of the number of medical records;
- s, daily subsistence if, in that day, the registrar is located in another location than that where the hospital to which he belongs is;
- δ, the working number of hours/days.

We use the notation $T = \{1,\ldots,p\}$.

One of the difficulties in solving this problem is the fact that there are hospitals where the number of medical records to be processed exceeds the processing capacity of the registrar in a day. In that case, he has to work more than a day at that site and we must decide which is better for him, to stay over night there or to go back home and return the next day. Another difficulty arises from the fact that the total number of medical records to be processed at a site increases from one day to the next. To treat these difficulties, we introduce dummy (fictive) hospitals, as it will be seen next.

Let us consider hospital i. The total number of unprocessed medical records that exist until the morning of day k is $f_i + (k-1)r_i$. To process the files collected until the morning of the last day (the p-th day), it would be necessary m_i working days, where

$$m_i = \begin{cases} \dfrac{f_i + (p-1)r_i}{q}, \text{ if } \dfrac{f_i + (p-1)r_i}{q} \in \mathbb{N}, \\ \left[\dfrac{f_i + (p-1)r_i}{q}\right] + 1, \text{ if } \dfrac{f_i + (p-1)r_i}{q} \notin \mathbb{N}. \end{cases} \tag{1}$$

Therefore, for the sake of simplicity, we consider that, instead of hospital i, we have m_i hospitals, denoted by $i_1,\ldots,i_{m_i}$. All the files of these hospitals come from the hospital i; the number of files in these hospitals will vary in time, but none of them will exceed the maximum number of files that can be processed in one day. More precisely, the moment when, at the hospital i_h, q files have been gathered for processing, the subsequent files are considered to be at hospital i_{h+1}; when for hospital i_{h+1}, q files are gathered, the next ones are sent to hospital i_{h+2}, etc.

We denote by $g_{i_h,k}$ the number of files to be processed, existing in hospital i_h in the day $k \in T$. This is equal to

$$g_{i_h,k} = \begin{cases} f_i + (k-1)r_i, \text{ if } h = 1, f_i + (k-1)r_i \leqq q, \\ q, \text{ if } h = 1, f_i + (k-1)r_i > q, \\ 0, \text{ if } 1 < h, f_i + (k-1)r_i - (h-1)q \leqq 0, \\ f_i + (k-1)r_i - (h-1)q, \text{ if } 1 < h, 1 \leqq f_i + (k-1)r_i - (h-1)q \leqq q, \\ q, \text{ if} 1 < h, f_i + (k-1)r_i - (h-1)q > q. \end{cases} \tag{2}$$

The distance between any two dummy hospitals generated by hospital i is equal to d_i (instead of transport, the accommodation has to be paid), and the distance between any dummy hospital i_h and hospital k, $k \neq i$, is equal to the distance between hospital i and hospital k. Then, the following relation holds:

$$c_{i_h,k} = \begin{cases} c_{ik}, \forall\, h \in \{1,\ldots,m_i\}, k \in \{0,1,\ldots,n\} \setminus \{i\}, \\ d_i, \forall\, h \in \{1,\ldots,m_i\}, k \in \{i_1,\ldots,i_m\}, i_h \neq k. \end{cases} \tag{3}$$

Following this transformation, the problem size increases by increasing the number of hospitals, but the problem is simplified by the fact that every day, the registrar can examine all existing files in any of the hospitals where he arrives. We denote by m the number of new hospitals resulting by performing this transformation (i.e. $m = m_1 + \cdots + m_n$).

We continue to denote by c_{ik} the transport costs between any two hospitals i and k, $i \neq k$. Since there may be days when the registrar does not work in the subordinated hospitals, we introduce more p dummy hospitals, numbered $m+1,\ldots,m+p$.

The transport costs for the new hospitals are defined by

$$c_{ik} = \begin{cases} 0, \text{ if } i,k \in \{m+1,\ldots,m+p\}, i \neq k, \\ c_{0k}, \text{ if } i \in \{m+1,\ldots,m+p\}, k \in \{1,\ldots,m\}, \\ 0, \text{ if } i = 0, k \in \{m+1,\ldots,m+p\}, \\ c_{i0}, \text{ if } i \in \{1,\ldots,m\}, k \in \{m+1,\ldots,m+p\}. \end{cases} \tag{4}$$

Every day, the number of existing medical records in the location $m+1,\dots,m+p$ is equal to 0, hence we have

$$g_{ij} = 0, \forall i \in \{m+1,\dots,m+p\}, j \in \{1,\dots,p\}.$$

The accommodation costs will be also equal to 0, so

$$d_i = 0, \forall i \in \{m+1,\dots,m+p\}.$$

Because, under the new conditions, the registrar will not stay more than one day in a hospital, we attach the subsistence costs to the hospital. More precisely, we define the numbers s_i, $i \in \{1,\dots,m+p\}$, by $s_i := s$, if the hospitals i and 0 are not at the same location and $s_i := 0$ otherwise.

Hence, after making these changes, we consider that we have $m+p+1$ hospitals, from 0 to $m+p$, with 0 being the "home" hospital (the registrar's home). The following data are known:

- transport costs between any two locations $i,k \in \{0,1,\dots,m+p\}, i \neq k$, denoted by c_{ik},
- number of medical records that can be processed in the hospital i in every day $j \in T$, denoted by g_{ij},
- the accommodation cost, d_i, and the subsistence cost, s_i, according to the area where the hospital i is located.

Example. Let us take $n=3$, $p=4$, $q=10$, $e=14$, $d_1=3$, $d_2=7$, $d_3=2$, $s=1$,

$$C = \begin{bmatrix} 0 & 5 & 7 & 3 \\ 5 & 0 & 2 & 4 \\ 7 & 2 & 0 & 6 \\ 3 & 4 & 6 & 0 \end{bmatrix},$$

$$f_1 = 20,\ f_2 = 15,\ f_3 = 1,\ r_1 = 2,\ r_2 = 1,\ r_3 = 3.$$

According with the previous specification, we work with $m = 3+2+1$ and $p = 4$. In total, 10 hospitals, plus the "home" hospital, 0. The transport costs between any two hospitals are given in the table 1.

	S_0	S_1	S_2	S_3	S_4	S_5	S_6	S_7	S_8	S_9	S_{10}
S_0	0	5	5	5	7	7	3	0	0	0	0
S_1	5	0	0	0	2	2	4	5	5	5	5
S_2	5	0	0	0	2	2	4	5	5	5	5
S_3	5	0	0	0	2	2	4	5	5	5	5
S_4	7	2	2	2	0	0	6	7	7	7	7
S_5	7	2	2	2	0	0	6	7	7	7	7
S_6	3	4	4	4	6	6	0	3	3	3	3
S_7	0	5	5	5	7	7	3	0	0	0	0
S_8	0	5	5	5	7	7	3	0	0	0	0
S_9	0	5	5	5	7	7	3	0	0	0	0
S_{10}	0	5	5	5	7	7	3	0	0	0	0

Table 1. Transportation costs table

The medical records matrix will be

$$G = \begin{bmatrix} 10 & 10 & 10 & 10 \\ 10 & 10 & 10 & 10 \\ 0 & 2 & 4 & 6 \\ 10 & 10 & 10 & 10 \\ 5 & 6 & 7 & 8 \\ 1 & 4 & 7 & 10 \\ 0 & 0 & 0 & 0 \\ 0 & 0 & 0 & 0 \\ 0 & 0 & 0 & 0 \\ 0 & 0 & 0 & 0 \end{bmatrix}.$$

The new vectors d and s will be

$$d = (3,3,3,7,7,2,0,0,0,0),$$

$$s = (1,1,1,1,1,1,0,0,0,0).$$

Our purpose is to obtain a planning for the registrar (this means to specify, for every day $j \in T$, the hospital where the registrar should go) such as the number of medical records that are processed to be as large as possible, and the costs involved in transportation, accommodation and subsistence to be as low as possible. The following assumptions are made:

1) If in the day j, $j \in T$, the registrar works at the hospital i, $i \in \{1,\ldots,m+p\}$, then in the following night he/she sleeps in the city where hospital i is located. Therefore, the total costs for that day contain the transportation costs from the location where the registrar worked in the previous day and the city i, the accommodation costs for one night in locality i, (equal to d_i) and the subsistence costs for locality i (equal to s_i).
2) The departure of the registrar is soon enough, so that, after reaching the destination, he may work δ hours.
3) The first day, the registrar leaves from hospital 0.
4) The registrar returns to hospital 0 only in the morning of day $p+1$.
5) One day, the registrar works exactly in one hospital.
6) In every hospital the registrar works at most one day.
7) The available amount of money which can be spent for the entire action is equal to e and it includes also the costs of returning to hospital 0 in the day $p+1$.

4. A mathematical model for the problem of medical registrars

In order to generate the mathematical model, we introduce the binary variables x_{ij}, $i \in \{1,\ldots,m+p\}$, $j \in \{1,\ldots,p\}$, where

$$\begin{cases} x_{ij} = 1, \text{ if in day } j \text{ the registrar is in hospital } i, \\ x_{ij} = 0, \text{ if not.} \end{cases} \tag{5}$$

Conditions 3)-5) imply that

$$\sum_{i=1}^{m+p} x_{ij} = 1, \; \forall j \in \{1,\ldots,p\}. \tag{6}$$

Condition 4) implies

$$\sum_{j=1}^{p}\sum_{i=1}^{m+p} x_{ij} = p. \tag{7}$$

Condition 6) means that

$$\sum_{j=1}^{p} x_{ij} \leqq 1,\ \forall\, i \in \{1,\ldots,m+p\}. \tag{8}$$

Considering the hypotheses 1) and 3), the first day costs will be

$$\sum_{k=1}^{m+p} (c_{0k} + d_k + s_k)x_{k1}.$$

According to hypothesis 4), the costs of returning to hospital 0 in day $p+1$ are

$$\sum_{k=1}^{m+p} c_{k0}x_{kp}.$$

According to 1), the costs for a day $j \in \{2,\ldots,p\}$ are

$$\sum_{i=1}^{m+p}\sum_{k=1,k\neq i}^{m+p} c_{ik}x_{i,j-1}x_{kj} + \sum_{k=1}^{m+p}(d_k + s_k)x_{k,j}.$$

Then, the hypothesis 7) implies

$$\sum_{k=1}^{m+p} c_{0k}x_{k1} + \sum_{j=2}^{p}\left(\sum_{i=1}^{m+p}\sum_{k=1,k\neq i}^{m+p} c_{ik}x_{i,j-1}x_{kj}\right) + \tag{9}$$

$$+\sum_{j=1}^{p}\sum_{k=1}^{m+p}(d_k + s_k)x_{kj} + \sum_{k=1}^{m+p} c_{k0}x_{kp} \leqq e.$$

The set of matrices $X = [x_{ij}] \in \{0,1\}^{(m+p)\times p}$ which verify (6), (7) and (8) will be denoted by $\mathcal{X}$. The set of matrices $X = [x_{ij}] \in \mathcal{X}$ which verify in addition the condition (8), will be denoted by $\tilde{X}$.

As the registrar may process in one day all existing files in a location, he will do so. Therefore, considering that, in one day $j \in T$, he can be in one location, the number of medical records processed that day will be equal to

$$\sum_{i=1}^{m+p} g_{ij}x_{ij},$$

and the total number of processed medical records is equal to

$$\sum_{j=1}^{p}\sum_{i=1}^{m+p} g_{ij}x_{ij}.$$

The number of medical records that would be gathered at the end of the period is equal to

$$\sum_{i=1}^{m+p} \max\{g_{ij}\,|\, j \in \{1,\ldots,p\}\}.$$

The two objective functions are:
- F_f, which denotes the total processed medical records, i.e. $F_f : \{0,1\}^{(m+p)\times p} \to \mathbb{R}$,

$$F_f(X) = \sum_{i=1}^{m+p} \sum_{j=1}^{p} g_{ij} x_{ij}, \tag{10}$$

for all $X = [x_{ij}] \in \{0,1\}^{(m+p)\times p}$ and
- F_c, which denotes the total cost, i.e. $F_c : \{0,1\}^{(m+p)\times p} \to \mathbb{R}$,

$$F_c(X) = \sum_{k=1}^{m+p} c_{0k} x_{k1} + \sum_{j=2}^{p} \sum_{i=1}^{m+p} \sum_{k=1,k\neq i}^{m+p} c_{ik} x_{i,j-1} x_{kj} + \sum_{j=1}^{p} \sum_{k=1}^{m+p} (d_k + s_k) x_{kj} + \sum_{k=1}^{m+p} c_{k0} x_{kp}, \tag{11}$$

for all $X = [x_{ij}] \in \{0,1\}^{(m+p)\times p}$.
The corresponding mathematical model for the Registrar Problem is the *Max-min Lexicographical Optimization Problem* with the objective function $F = (F_f, F_c) : \{0,1\}^{(m+p)\times p} \to \mathbb{R}^2$, whose scalar components are given by (10), (11), and the feasible set is $\tilde{S}$,

$$\tilde{S} = \{X \in \{0,1\}^{(m+p)\times p} \,|\, \text{satisfies the conditions}\,(6),(7),(8),(9)\}, \tag{12}$$

Hence, our problem, denoted by (PB), is the following:

$$\begin{cases} \begin{pmatrix} F_f(X) & = & \displaystyle\sum_{i=1}^{m+p} \sum_{j=1}^{p} g_{ij} x_{ij} \\ F_c(X) & = & \displaystyle\sum_{k=1}^{m+p} (c_{0k} + d_k + s_k) x_{k1} \\ & + & \displaystyle\sum_{j=2}^{p} \sum_{i=1}^{m+p} \sum_{k=1,k\neq i}^{m+p} c_{ik} x_{i,j-1} x_{kj} \\ & + & \displaystyle\sum_{j=2}^{p} \sum_{k=1}^{m+p} (d_k + s_k) x_{kj} + \sum_{k=1}^{m+p} c_{k0} x_{kp} \end{pmatrix} \to lex - \max - \min \\ \displaystyle\sum_{i=1}^{m+p} x_{ij} = 1,\ \forall\, j \in \{1,\ldots,p\}, \\ \sum_{j=1}^{p} x_{ij} \leqq 1,\ \forall\, i \in \{1,\ldots,m+p\}, \\ \displaystyle\sum_{k=1}^{m+p} (c_{0k} + d_k + s_k) x_{k1} + \sum_{j=2}^{p} \sum_{i=1}^{m+p} \sum_{k=1,k\neq i}^{m+p} c_{ik} x_{i,j-1} x_{kj} + \\ \quad + \displaystyle\sum_{j=2}^{p} \sum_{k=1}^{m+p} (d_k + s_k) x_{kj} + \sum_{k=1}^{m+p} c_{k0} x_{kp} \leqq e, \\ x_{ij} \in \{0,1\},\ \forall\, i\{1,\ldots,m+p\},\, j \in \{1,\ldots,p\}. \end{cases}$$

Using an appropriate change of variables, the problem (PB) may be transformed in a linear one. It is easy to notice that, if $x,y,z \in \{0,1\}$, then we have $z = x \cdot y$ if and only if z is the unique solution of the system

$$\begin{cases} x + y - z \leqq 1 \\ -x - y + 2z \leqq 0 \\ z \in \{0,1\}. \end{cases} \tag{13}$$

So, for each $j \in \{2,\dots,p\}$, $i \in \{1,\dots,m+p\}$ and $k \in \{1,\dots,m+p\}$, $k \neq i$, we introduce the binary variable

$$z_{ijk} := x_{i,j-1} \cdot x_{kj} \tag{14}$$

and the corresponding conditions

$$\begin{aligned} & x_{i,j-1} + x_{kj} - z_{ijk} \leqq 1, \\ & -x_{i,j-1} - x_{kj} + 2z_{ijk} \leqq 0, \\ & z_{ijk} \in \{0,1\}. \end{aligned}$$

Then the problem (PB) can be rewritten as

$$\begin{cases} \left(\begin{array}{lcl} F_f(X) & = & \sum\limits_{i=1}^{m+p} \sum\limits_{j=1}^{p} g_{ij} x_{ij} \\ F_c(X) & = & \sum\limits_{k=1}^{m+p} (c_{0k} + d_k + s_k) x_{k1} \\ & + & \sum\limits_{j=2}^{p} \sum\limits_{i=1}^{m+p} \sum\limits_{k=1, k\neq i}^{m+p} c_{ik} z_{ijk} \\ & + & \sum\limits_{j=2}^{p} \sum\limits_{k=1}^{m+p} (d_k + s_k) x_{kj} + \sum\limits_{k=1}^{m+p} c_{k0} x_{kp} \end{array} \right) \to lex - \max - \min \\ \sum\limits_{i=1}^{m+p} x_{ij} = 1, \forall j \in \{1,\dots,p\}, \\ \sum_{j=1}^{p} x_{ij} \leqq 1, \forall i \in \{1,\dots,m+p\}, \\ \sum\limits_{k=1}^{m+p} (c_{0k} + d_k + s_k) x_{k1} + \sum\limits_{j=2}^{p} \sum\limits_{i=1}^{m+p} \sum\limits_{k=1,k\neq i}^{m+p} c_{ik} z_{ijk} + \sum\limits_{j=2}^{p} \sum\limits_{k=1}^{m+p} (d_k + s_k) x_{kj} + \\ \quad + \sum\limits_{k=1}^{m+p} c_{k0} x_{kp} \leqq e, \\ x_{i,j-1} + x_{kj} - z_{ijk} \leqq 1, \forall j \in \{2,\dots,p\}, i \in \{1,\dots,m+p\}, k \in \{1,\dots,m+p\}, k \neq i, \\ -x_{i,j-1} - x_{kj} + 2z_{ijk} \leqq 0, \forall j \in \{2,\dots,p\}, i \in \{1,\dots,m+p\}, k \in \{1,\dots,m+p\}, k \neq i, \\ x_{ij} \in \{0,1\}, \forall i \{1,\dots,m+p\}, j \in \{1,\dots,p\}, \\ z_{ijk} \in \{0,1\}, \forall j \in \{2,\dots,p\}, i \in \{1,\dots,m+p\}, k \in \{1,\dots,m+p\}, k \neq i. \end{cases}$$

This problem can be solved by using any of the algorithms for solving pseudo-boolean linear optimization problems (see, for example (Hammer & Rudeanu, 1968; Crama, 1989)). But, it can be seen as a special type of the Prize Collecting Traveling Salesman Problem or as a special type of the Simple Cycle Problem, as it will be shown in the next section.

5. Max-min lexicographical traveling salesman problem with objective function depending on a parameter

Let m and p be natural numbers, $m \neq 0$, and let e, g_{ij}, a_{kj}, b_{ik}, c_{kj}, d_{ik}, $i \in \{1,\dots,m+p\}$, $j \in \{1,\dots,p\}$, $k \in \{1,\dots,m+p\}$, $k \neq i$, be positive real numbers.
By $\mathcal{X}$ we denote the set of the matrices $X = [x_{ij}]$ with $m+p$ rows and p columns, whose elements satisfy the following three conditions:

$$\sum_{i=1}^{m+p} x_{ij} = 1, \forall j \in \{1,\dots,p\}, \tag{15}$$

$$\sum_{j=1}^{p} x_{ij} \leqq 1, \forall\, i \in \{1,\ldots,m+p\}, \tag{16}$$

$$x_{ij} \in \{0,1\}, \forall\, i \in \{1,\ldots,m+p\},\ j \in \{1,\ldots,p\}, \tag{17}$$

and by $\tilde{\mathcal{X}}$ the set of matrices of $\mathcal{X}$ which satisfies, in addition, the bounded condition

$$\sum_{j=1}^{p}\sum_{k=1}^{m+p} c_{kj}x_{kj} + \sum_{j=2}^{p}\sum_{i=1}^{m+p}\sum_{k=1,k\neq i}^{m+p} d_{ik}x_{i,j-1}x_{kj} \leqq e. \tag{18}$$

Let us remark that from (15) we obtain

$$\sum_{i=1}^{m+p}\sum_{j=1}^{p} x_{ij} = p. \tag{19}$$

Then, from (16) it follows that there are p distinct indices $i_1,\ldots,i_p \in \{1,\ldots,m+p\}$ such that

$$\sum_{j=1}^{p} x_{i_k,j} = 1, \forall\, k \in \{1,\ldots,p\},$$

and

$$\sum_{j=1}^{p} x_{ij} = 0, \forall\, i \in \{1,\ldots,m+p\} \setminus \{i_1,\ldots,i_p\}.$$

Let us define the vector function $F = (F_1, F_2) : \mathcal{X} \to \mathbb{R}^2$, where

$$F_1(X) = \sum_{i=1}^{m+p}\sum_{j=1}^{p} g_{ij}x_{ij}, \forall\, X \in \mathcal{X}, \tag{20}$$

$$F_2(X) = \sum_{j=1}^{p}\sum_{k=1}^{m+p} a_{kj}x_{kj} + \sum_{j=2}^{p}\sum_{i=1}^{m+p}\sum_{k=1,k\neq i}^{m+p} b_{ik}x_{i,j-1}x_{kj}, \forall\, X \in \mathcal{X}. \tag{21}$$

The problem (PB) can be see as a special case of the pseudo-boolean lexicographical max-min optimization problem with the objective function F and the set of feasible solution equal to $\tilde{\mathcal{X}}$, i.e., the problem:

$$(PBG)\quad \begin{cases} \begin{pmatrix} \sum\limits_{i=1}^{m+p}\sum\limits_{j=1}^{p} g_{ij}x_{ij} \\ \sum\limits_{j=1}^{p}\sum\limits_{k=1}^{m+p} a_{kj}x_{kj} + \sum\limits_{j=2}^{p}\sum\limits_{i=1}^{m+p}\sum\limits_{k=1,k\neq i}^{m+p} b_{ik}x_{i,j-1}x_{kj} \end{pmatrix} \to lex-\max-\min \\ \sum\limits_{i=1}^{m+p} x_{ij} = 1, \forall\, j \in \{1,\ldots,p\}, \\ \sum\limits_{j=1}^{p} x_{ij} \leqq 1, \forall\, i \in \{1,\ldots,m+p\}, \\ \sum\limits_{j=1}^{p}\sum\limits_{k=1}^{m+p} c_{kj}x_{kj} + \sum\limits_{j=2}^{p}\sum\limits_{i=1}^{m+p}\sum\limits_{k=1,k\neq i}^{m+p} d_{ik}x_{i,j-1}x_{kj} \leqq e, \\ x_{ij} \in \{0,1\}, \forall\, i\{1,\ldots,m+p\}, j \in \{1,\ldots,p\}. \end{cases}$$

We show how the problem (PBG) can be modeled as a new special type of the Prize Collecting Traveling Salesman Problem, or as a new special type of the Simple Cycle Problem. We name it *max-min lexicographical Traveling Salesman Problem with objective function depending on a parameter*, and we denote it as *lex max-min BTSPPF*.
To this purpose, let us consider the following complete directed graph $G = (V, E)$, where

$$V = \{0, 1, \ldots, m+p\}$$

and

$$E = \{(i,k) \,|\, i \in V, k \in V, k \neq i\}.$$

Let $\mathcal{C}$ be the set of all cycles with the following properties:

- contain vertex 0,
- apart from vertex 0, they contain exactly p distinct vertices.

Note that each cycle $C \in \mathcal{C}$ may be described by a $p+2$-dimensional vector $(0, u_1, \ldots, u_p, 0)$, which indicates the order in which the vertices follow one other in the cycle. Since this vector always contains 0 on the first and on the last position, the useful information is given by the p-dimensional vector $u = (u_1, \ldots, u_p)$, called *descriptor vector* or *the vector which describes the cycle* C.
For instance, for $m = 5$, $p = 3$, the cycle through the vertices 0, 1, 4, 2 and again 0 is described by the vector $u = (1,4,2)$. Similarly, $u = (1,5,4)$ describes the cycle consisting in the vertices 0, 1, 5 , 4 and returning to 0.

Remark 5.1 *The vector $u = (u_1, \ldots, u_p) \in \mathbb{R}^p$ describes a cycle from $\mathcal{C}$, if and only if the following two conditions are fulfilled:*

i1) $u_j \in \{1, \ldots, m+p\}$, for all $j \in \{1, \ldots, p\}$;

i2) for all $k, h \in \{1, \ldots, p\}$, $k \neq h$, we have $u_k \neq u_h$.

In the following, we use the function $sign : \mathbb{R} \to \{-1, 0, 1\}$,

$$\text{sign} r = \begin{cases} 0, \text{ if } r = 0, \\ 1, \text{ if } r > 0, \\ -1, \text{ if } r < 0. \end{cases} \tag{22}$$

Remark 5.2 *If $u = (u_1, \ldots, u_p)$ is the descriptor vector of a cycle in $\mathcal{C}$, then the following conditions hold:*

i) For every $j \in \{1, \ldots, p\}$, there exists a unique $h_j \in \{1, \ldots, m+p\}$ such that $h_j = u_j$ and, therefore, if $h \in \{1, \ldots, m+p\}$, we have

$$(1 - sign(|u_j - h|)) = \begin{cases} 1, \text{ if } h = h_j, \\ 0, \text{ if } h \neq h_j. \end{cases} \tag{23}$$

ii) $\sum\limits_{h=1}^{m+p} (1 - sign(|h - u_j|)) = 1.$

iii) For every $i \in \{1, \ldots, m+p\}$, there is at most an index $j_i \in \{1, \ldots, p\}$ such that $i = u_{j_i}$.

Remark 5.3 *If $X = [x_{ij}] \in \mathcal{X}$, then for every $j \in \{1,\dots,p\}$, the following statements hold:*

i) there exists a unique index $h_j \in \{1,\dots,m+p\}$ such that $x_{h_j,j} = 1$ and we have $x_{hj} = 0$, for all $h \in \{1,\dots,m+p\} \setminus \{h_j\}$;

ii) $\sum_{h=1}^{m+p} hx_{hj} = h_j$.

Theorem 5.4 *a) If $X = [x_{ij}] \in \mathcal{X}$, then the vector $u = (u_1,\dots,u_p)$, where*

$$u_j = \sum_{i=1}^{m+p} ix_{ij}, \forall j \in \{1,\dots,p\}, \tag{24}$$

is a descriptor of a cycle in $\mathcal{C}$.
b) If the vector $u = (u_1,\dots,u_n)$ is a descriptor of a cycle in $\mathcal{C}$, then the matrix $X = [x_{ij}]$, with

$$x_{ij} = 1 - sign(|i - u_j|), \forall i \in \{1,\dots,m+p\}, j \in \{1,\dots,p\}, \tag{25}$$

verifies the conditions (15) - (17).

Proof. a) If $X = [x_{ij}] \in \mathcal{X}$, from Remark 5.3, we deduce that, for every $j \in \{1,\dots,p\}$, there is a unique $h_j \in \{1,\dots,m+p\}$ such that

$$\sum_{h=1}^{m+p} hx_{hj} = h_j.$$

Then, in view of (24), we have

$$u_j = h_j, \forall j \in \{1,\dots,p\}. \tag{26}$$

It follows that $u_j \in \{1,\dots,m+p\}$, for all $j \in \{1,\dots,p\}$.
There may not exist two distinct indices $j', j'' \in \{1,\dots,p\}$ such that $u_{j'} = u_{j''}$. Indeed, if we have $u_{j'} = u_{j''}$, then we get that $h_{j'} = h_{j''}$. Then, as $j' \neq j''$, we have

$$\sum_{h=1}^{m+p} hx_{hj'} + \sum_{h=1}^{m+p} hx_{hj''} = h_{j'} + h_{j''} > 1 + 1.$$

On the other hand, from (16), we obtain

$$\sum_{h=1}^{m+p} hx_{hj'} + \sum_{h=1}^{m+p} hx_{hj''} \leqq 1 + 1,$$

that contradicts the previous inequality.
Hence, the numbers $u_j, j \in \{1,\dots,p\}$, are p distinct elements in set $\{1,\dots,m+p\}$, so the vector u satisfies the conditions i) and ii) from Remark 5.1. Therefore, the vector $u = (u_1,\dots,u_p)$ is the descriptor of a cycle in $\mathcal{C}$.
b) Let us suppose that the vector $u = (u_1,\dots,u_p)$ is a descriptor of a cycle in $\mathcal{C}$. Let us consider $i \in \{1,\dots,m+p\}, j \in \{1,\dots,p\}$. Due to the fact that $|i - u_j| \geqq 0$, we have

$$\text{sign}(|i - u_j|) \in \{0, 1\},$$

which implies

$$x_{ij} = 1 - \text{sign}(|i - u_j|) \in \{1, 0\}.$$

Hence (17) holds. Based on Remark 5.2, for every $j \in \{1, \dots, p\}$ we have

$$\sum_{i=1}^{m+p} x_{ij} = 1,$$

so (15) takes place.

Let $i \in \{1, \dots, m+p\}$. From Remark 5.2, iii), it results that only the following two cases are possible:

a) There exists $j_i \in \{1, \dots, p\}$ such that $u_{j_i} = i$ and $u_j \neq i$, for all $j \in \{1, \dots, p\} \setminus \{j_i\}$; in this case we have

$$\sum_{j=1}^{p} x_{ij} = \sum_{j=1}^{p} (1 - \text{sign}(|i - u_j|)) = \sum_{j=1, j \neq j_i}^{p} (1 - 1) + (1 - \text{sign}(0)) = 1.$$

b) There is no $j \in \{1, \dots, p\}$ such that $u_j = i$; in this case

$$\sum_{j=1}^{p} x_{ij} = \sum_{j=1}^{p} (1 - \text{sign}(|i - u_j|)) = \sum_{j=1}^{p} (1 - 1) = 0.$$

In both cases (17) holds. $\diamond$

Corollary 5.5 *The following statements hold:*

i) If $X \in \tilde{\mathcal{X}}$ is a feasible solution to problem (PBG), then the vector $u = (u_1, \dots, u_p)$, where u_j is given by (24), for all $j \in \{1, \dots, p\}$, is the descriptor vector of a cycle in $\mathcal{C}$, cycle which verifies the condition

$$\sum_{j=1}^{p} c_{u_j, j} + \sum_{j=2}^{p} d_{u_{j-1}, u_j} \leqq e, \tag{27}$$

equivalent to

$$\sum_{j=1}^{p} \sum_{i=1}^{m+p} c_{ij} (1 - sign(|u_j - i|)) + \tag{28}$$

$$\sum_{j=2}^{p} \sum_{i=1}^{m+p} \sum_{k=1, k \neq i}^{m+p} d_{ik} (1 - sign(|u_{j-1} - i|))(1 - sign(|u_j - k|)) \leqq e.$$

ii) If $u = (u_1, \dots, u_p)$ describes a cycle in $\mathcal{C}$ for which condition (27) is verified, then the matrix $X = [x_{ij}]$, where x_{ij} is given by (25), is a feasible solution to problem (PBG).

Proof. i) Since $X = [x_{ij}]$ is a feasible solution to problem (PBG), the conditions (15)- (17) will be verified. Hence, based on Theorem 5.4, the vector $u = (u_1, \dots, u_p)$ describes a cycle in $\mathcal{C}$. Applying Remark 5.3 we deduce that for every $j \in \{1, \dots, p\}$ there is a unique $h_j \in \{1, \dots, m+p\}$ such that $x_{h_j, j} = 1$ and $x_{ij} = 0$, for all $i \in \{1, \dots, m+p\} \setminus \{h_j\}$. Then

$$\sum_{i=1}^{m+p} c_{ij} x_{ij} = c_{h_j, j}. \tag{29}$$

Also, for $i,k \in \{1,\ldots,m+p\}$ and $j \in \{2,\ldots,p\}$, we have

$$d_{ik}x_{i,j-1}x_{k,j} = \begin{cases} d_{h_{j-1},h_j}, \text{ if } i = h_{j-1},\ k = h_j \\ 0, \text{ if } i \neq h_{j-1}, \text{or } k \neq h_j. \end{cases} \tag{30}$$

From (29) and (30) we get

$$\sum_{j=1}^{p}\sum_{k=1}^{m+p} c_{kj}x_{kj} + \sum_{j=2}^{p}\sum_{i=1}^{m+p}\sum_{k=1,k\neq i}^{m+p} d_{ik}x_{i,j-1}x_{kj} = \sum_{j=1}^{p} c_{h_j,j} + \sum_{j=1}^{p-1} d_{h_{j-1},h_j}.$$

As X is a feasible solution to (PBG), inequality (18) holds. Therefore, from the previous equality, we get

$$\sum_{j=1}^{p} c_{h_j,j} + \sum_{j=1}^{p-1} d_{h_{j-1},h_j} \leqq e. \tag{31}$$

Taking into account condition ii) from Remark 5.3, for vector $u = (u_1,\ldots,u_p)$, where u_j is given by (24), we have

$$u_j = h_j, \text{ for any } j \in \{1,\ldots,p\}, \tag{32}$$

which, based on (31), implies that we have

$$\sum_{j=1}^{p} c_{u_j,j} + \sum_{j=2}^{p} d_{u_{j-1},u_j} \leqq e,$$

so (27) holds.
We will prove that (27) is equivalent to (28).
Let us consider $j \in \{1,\ldots,p\}$. From (32), successively, we get

$$\sum_{i=1}^{m+p} c_{ij}(1 - \text{sign}(|u_j - i|)) = c_{h_j,j}, \tag{33}$$

and

$$\sum_{i=1}^{m+p}\sum_{k=1,k\neq i}^{m+p} d_{ik}(1 - \text{sign}(|u_{j-1} - i|))(1 - \text{sign}(|u_j - k|)) = d_{h_{j-1},h_j}. \tag{34}$$

From (33) and (34), it results that, if (28) holds, then (27) also holds, and vice-versa. So, (28) is equivalent to (27).
ii) Let $u = (u_1,\ldots,u_n)$ be a vector which describes a cycle in $\mathcal{C}$ and verifies the condition (28). Consider also the matrix $X = [x_{ij}]$, with x_{ij} given by (25). From theorem 5.4, we know that X verifies (15)-(17). We still have to prove that the condition (18) holds. Let us consider $j \in \{1,\ldots,p\}$. Using (25), we get:

$$\sum_{i=1}^{m+p} c_{ij}x_{ij} = \sum_{i=1}^{m+p} c_{ij}(1 - \text{sign}(|i - u_j|)) = c_{u_j,j}. \tag{35}$$

Hence

$$\sum_{j=1}^{p}\sum_{i=1}^{m+p} c_{ij}x_{ij} = \sum_{j=1}^{p} c_{u_j,j}. \tag{36}$$

Also,

$$\sum_{j=1}^{p-1}\sum_{i=1}^{m+p}\sum_{k=1}^{m+p} d_{ik}x_{i,j-1}x_{k,j} = \sum_{j=1}^{p-1}\sum_{i=1}^{m+p}\sum_{k=1,k\neq i}^{m+p} d_{ik}(1-\mathrm{sign}(|i-u_j|)(1-\mathrm{sign}(|i-u_{j+1}|) \tag{37}$$

$$= \sum_{j=1}^{p-1} d_{u_j,u_{j+1}}.$$

From (36)-(37), taking into account (27), it results that (18) holds.$\diamond$
Let us denote by $\tilde{\mathcal{C}}$ the set of cycles from $\mathcal{C}$ which verify the condition (28), and let $U(\mathcal{C})$ be the set of vectors which describe the cycle in $\mathcal{C}$. On the set $U(\mathcal{C})$, we define the vector function $\tilde{F} = (\tilde{F}_1, \tilde{F}_2)$, where

$$\tilde{F}_1(u) = \sum_{j=1}^{p} g_{u_j,j},\ \forall\, u \in U(\mathcal{C}), \tag{38}$$

and

$$\tilde{F}_2(u) = \sum_{j=1}^{p} a_{u_j,j} + \sum_{j=2}^{p} b_{u_{j-1},u_j}, \forall\, u \in U(\mathcal{C}), \tag{39}$$

respectively.

Remark 5.6 *It is not difficult to prove that:*

i) If $X = [x_{ij}] \in \mathcal{X}$, and $u = (u_1, \ldots, u_p)$ is the vector whose components are defined by (24) for all $j \in \{1, \ldots, p\}$, then

$$F_1(X) = \tilde{F}_1(u); \tag{40}$$

ii) If $u = (u_1, \ldots, u_p) \in U(\mathcal{C})$, then, for the matrix $X = [x_{ij}]$ whose components are defined by (25), we have

$$\tilde{F}_2(u) = F_2(X). \tag{41}$$

We say that a cycle $C^0 \in \tilde{\mathcal{C}}$ is *lexicographical max-min non dominate with respect to the set $\tilde{\mathcal{C}}$* if there is no cycle $C \in \tilde{\mathcal{C}}$ such that:

$$\tilde{F}_1(C) > \tilde{F}_1(C^0), \text{ or } \tilde{F}_1(C) = \tilde{F}_1(C^0) \text{ and } \tilde{F}_2(C) < \tilde{F}_2(C^0).$$

The problem of finding a lexicographically max-min non dominated cycle with respect to set $\tilde{\mathcal{C}}$ will be denoted as (PG). We describe this problem as:

$$(PG)\quad \begin{cases} \begin{pmatrix} \sum_{j=1}^{p} g_{u_j,j} \\ \sum\limits_{j=1}^{p} a_{u_j,j} + \sum\limits_{j=2}^{p} b_{u_{j-1},u_j} \end{pmatrix} \rightarrow lex - \max - \min \\ \\ \sum\limits_{j=1}^{p} c_{u_j,j} + \sum\limits_{j=2}^{p} d_{u_{j-1},u_j} \leqq e, \\ u = (u_1, \ldots, u_p) \in U(\mathcal{C}). \end{cases} \tag{42}$$

By *optimal solution for* (PG) we understand each lexicographical max-min non dominated cycle with respect to set $\tilde{\mathcal{C}}$.

Corollary 5.7 *The following statements hold:*
i) If X is an optimal solution to problem (PBG), meaning that it is lex-max-min with respect to set $\mathcal{X}$, then the vector $u = (u_1, \ldots, u_p)$, where u_j is given by (24), for all $j \in \{1, \ldots, p\}$, describes a cycle which is lexicographical max-min with respect to set $\tilde{\mathcal{C}}$.
ii) If the vector $u = (u_1, \ldots, u_p)$ describes a cycle which is lexicographical max-min with respect to the set $\tilde{\mathcal{C}}$, then the matrix $X = [x_{ij}]$, where x_{ij} are given by (25), is an optimal solution to problem (PB), which means that it is a lexicographical max-min point according with set $\tilde{X}$.

Proof. Let $X = [x_{ij}]$ be a point that is lexicographical max-min non dominated with respect to the set $\tilde{X}$. Based on Consequence 5.5, the vector $u = (u_1, \ldots, u_n)$ is a feasible solution to problem (PG). Let us suppose that u is not a lexicographically max-min cycle with respect to the set $\tilde{\mathcal{C}}$. Two cases are possible:
Case I. There exists $C^* \in \tilde{\mathcal{C}}$ such that

$$\tilde{F}_1(u) < \tilde{F}_1(v), \tag{43}$$

where v denotes the vector which describes the circuit C^*. Based on Consequence 5.5, the matrix $Y = [y_{ij}]$, where y_{ij} are given by

$$y_{ij} = 1 - \text{sign}(|i - v_j|), \forall i, j \in \{1, \ldots, n\} \tag{44}$$

is a feasible solution to problem (PBG). Based on Remark 5.6, we have $F_1(Y) = \tilde{F}_1(v)$ and $F_2(Y) = \tilde{F}_2(v)$. Now, by taking into account (43), we get $F_1(Y) > F_1(X)$, which contradicts the hypothesis that X is an optimal solution to problem (PBG), which means that it is lexicographical max-min non dominated with respect to the set of feasible solutions to the problem. Since this is a contradiction, we deduce that there cannot exist a cycle $C^* \in \mathcal{C}$ such that (43) holds.
Case II. There exists $C^* \in \tilde{\mathcal{C}}$ such that

$$\tilde{F}_1(u) = \tilde{F}_1(v), \text{ but } \tilde{F}_2(u) > \tilde{F}_2(v), \tag{45}$$

where v is the descriptor vector of the cycle C^*. As in the previous case, we consider the matrix $Y = [y_{ij}]$ whose components are given by (44), matrix which is a feasible solution to problem (PBG). Based on Remark 5.6, we get that $F_1(X) = \tilde{F}_1(u)$, $\tilde{F}_2(u) = F_2(X)$ and $F_1(Y) = \tilde{F}_1(v)$, $\tilde{F}_2(v) = F_2(Y)$. Therefore, by taking into account (45), the following relations hold:

$$F_1(X) = F_1(Y) \text{ and } F_2(X) > F_2(Y),$$

which contradicts the hypothesis that X is a lexicographical max-min point with respect to the set of feasible solutions to problem (PBG). Similarly, ii) may be proved. ◇
From Theorem 5.4 and Consequences 5.5, 5.7, it results that solving the problem (PG) may be reduced to solving problem (PBG) and vice-versa. Therefore, the Registrar Problem consists in finding a cycle, C^0, which is lexicographical max-min non dominated with respect to the set $\tilde{\mathcal{C}}$.

6. The problem (PG) from general point of view

The (PG) problem can be seen, in terms of the Traveling Salesman Problem, as follows: a traveling salesman must take a tour through exactly p towns, at his choice among the $m + p$ given towns, and stays exactly one day in each town. The costs b_{ik} of going from town i to town k are also given, for all towns i and k, $i \neq k$. For each town i that is visited, the salesman gets a bonus g_{ij} that depends not only on the location i, but also on the day j he gets to that location. Also, for each visited location i, in days j, he pays a_{ij} for accommodation. The problem is that of finding a cycle so that the total bonus is maximized and the total costs (transport costs plus accommodation costs) are minimized. A boundary condition (18) must also be satisfied.

For this reason, the problem (PG) can be seen as a generalization of the following problems: Prize Collecting Traveling Salesman Problem, Simple Cycle Problem, Capacitated Prize-Collecting Traveling Salesman Problem or Orienteering Problem. Note that all these variants of the Traveling Salesman Problem allow that the cycle not to visit all the vertices of the graph.

The *Prize Collecting Traveling Salesman Problem* was posed in 1986 by E. Balas. A synthesis of the results on this topic and of the solving methods for this problem can be found in (Balas, 2002). In accordance with this paper, in the Prize Collecting Traveling Salesman Problem: *a salesman gets a prize w_k in every city k that he visits and pays a penalty c_l to every city l that he fails to visit. Traveling at cost c_{ij} between cities i and j our salesman wants to find a tour that minimizes his travel costs and penalties, subject to a lower bound w_0 on the amount of prize money he collects.*

In *Simple Cycle Problem* (see (Fischetti et al, 2002)), a complete undirected graph $G = (V, E)$ is given. A cost c_e is associated to each edge $e \in E$ and a prize p_n is associated to each node $n \in V$. The cost of a cycle C is given by the difference between the sum of all costs corresponding to the edges of this cycle and the sum of all prizes corresponding to the nodes of this cycle. The problem is to find a min-cost cycle of at least 3 vertices. A further requirement may be that a given vertex be part of the cycle.

Capacitated Prize-Collecting Traveling Salesman Problem is derived from simple cycle problem. For this problem, to each node it is assigned a *weight* and there is a further restriction that the sum of weights of visited vertices not to exceed a given maximum value.

In the case of the *Orienteering Problem* or *Selective Traveling Salesman Problem*, the transport costs assigned to all edges are zero, that is, $c_e = 0$, for all $e \in E$. In exchange, to each edge $e \in E$ it is assigned a positive value, a duration t_e, and it is required that the sum of durations for all visited edges not to exceed a given value.

All these problems can be seen as some variants or generalization of the Traveling Salesman Problem. Practically (see (Balas, 2002)) each situation involving decisions that affect the sequence in which various actions, tasks or operations are to be executed, has a traveling salesman problem aspect to it. We remember that in accordance with (Punnen, 2002) the *Traveling Salesman Problem* (TSP) is to find a routing of a salesman who starts from a home location, visits a prescribed set of cities and returns to the original location in such a way that the total distance traveled is minimum and each city is visited exactly once.

The differences between the above four TSP variants and the (PG) problem are:

- the fact that the exact number of cycle vertices is fixed,
- the bonus depends not only on the visited vertex, but also on the visiting time, that is, on the position of the vertex along the cycle;
- the goal is expressed by a vector, with two components (bonus and cost).

The authors of this work do not have knowledge of a paper discussing a TSP variant, where the bonus depends on the visiting time or where the exact number of vertices to be used is given (except, obviously, the case where all vertices are to be visited). These are new original topics, discussed in this work.

The subject of multi-criteria Traveling Salesman Problem, in a general context, is treated, for example, by (Ehrgott, 2005). To transfer the concept of optimal solutions to multi-criteria problems, the notion of Pareto curves was introduced
A Pareto curve is the set of Pareto points or, equivalent, efficient points.
Let $D \subseteq \mathbb{R}^n$ be a nonempty set, $f = (f_1, ..., f_p) : D \to \mathbb{R}^p$ a vectorial function, and $S \subseteq D$. A point $x \in S$ is said to be a max-efficient point of f with respect to S or a max-Pareto point of f with respect to S if there is no $y \in S$ such that

$$f_i(x) \leqq f_i(y), \forall i \in \{1, ..., p\} \text{ and } \sum_{i=1}^{p} f_i(x) < \sum_{i=1}^{p} f_i(y),$$

or, equivalent,

$$f_i(x) \leqq f_i(y), \forall i \in \{1, ..., p\} \text{ and there is } h \in \{1, ..., p\} \text{ such that } f_h(x) < f_h(y).$$

Unfortunately, Pareto curves cannot be computed efficiently in many cases because they are often of exponential size and NP-hard to compute even for otherwise easy optimization problems. Therefore, sometimes, one prefers to choose a point on this curve, point subject to some additional restriction which derives from the scalar components of the scope function. This point is, often, a maximum point of the weighted sum of these scalar components. In other cases, it is chosen to be a non-dominant point into a lexicographical ordering relation. This is exactly the situation presented in this paper.
There exist, also, papers which present possibilities to approximate the Pareto curve (see, for example (Warburton, 1987), (Angel et al., 2004) or (Manthey, 2009)).
The globally convex structure of Pareto curves in studied for example in (Borges & Hansen, 2001) and (Villagra et al., 2006).
We mention that, in (Feillet et al., 2005), the authors show that if, in the TSP, we consider that we have two objective functions, the profit and the cost, we obtain a bi-criteria TSP. According to the results of multi-criteria optimization, for solving bi-criteria TSP three cases are considered by the authors:
- Both objectives are combined in the objective function and the aim is to find a circuit that minimizes travel costs minus collected profit, i.e. the bi-criteria Traveling Salesman Problem may be seen as a prize collecting traveling salesman problem;
- The travel costs objective is stated as a constraint and the aim is to find a circuit that maximizes collected profit such that travel costs do not exceed a preset value, i.e. the bi-criteria Traveling Salesman Problem may be seen as a orienteering problem;
- The profit objective is stated as a constraint and the aim is to find a circuit that minimizes travel costs and whose collected profit is not smaller than a preset value, i.e. the bi-criteria Traveling Salesman Problem may be seen as a capacitated prize-collecting Traveling Salesman Problem.
However, the above transformations cannot be applied to our problem because the profit and the costs depending, in addition, on the time. Based on these considerations we choose to work with the lexicographic ordering. We remind that the idea to use the lexicographic ordering in a Traveling Salesman Problem was used in (Lupsa et al, 2008), where an application in health economics is also given.

7. Algorithms for solving problem (PG)

It is known that, for solving a route choice problem, techniques of branch and bound type are often used. Based on this technique, in the following, three algorithms are given for solving problem (PG): a greedy algorithm, a parallel approach algorithm and an exact algorithm.

7.1 A greedy algorithm

The algorithm 0.1 constructs a cycle, in a graph, with $p+1$ distinct vertices (vertex 0 plus other p) which satisfies the boundary condition (18). The algorithms signals the case where it is impossible to construct such a cycle. For its construction, one always goes to the branch where the growth of the first component, $\tilde{F}_1$, of the goal function, is the highest. If there are several possibilities of getting the same growth, then it favors that whose second component, $\tilde{F}_2$, is the lowest. In the algorithm, the p-dimensional vector u is used. If $\tilde{C} \neq \emptyset$, it becomes the descriptor vector of the optimal solution of problem (PG). Also, the following sets are used:
- V_j, that contains, at every iteration j, the candidate vertices to generate the cycle;
- V_j^*, that, at every iteration j, contains those vertices from V_j, whose corresponding coefficients from component $\tilde{F}_1$ of the scope function are maximum;

If the set V_j^* has more than one element, that vertex in the circuit will be chosen, for which we obtain a minimal increase in the value of $\tilde{F}_2$, the second component of the scope function. This can be fulfilled by using the real number r. The cost of the current circuit is stored in r_j. If when building a circuit we determine that the restriction on costs is not satisfied, the last added arc is abandoned, the output vertex being temporarily removed from the set of candidates.

Algorithm 0.1 The Greedy Algorithm.
input: the natural numbers m and p;
  the elements of matrices: $G=[g_{ij}]$, $i\in\{0,1,\ldots,m+p\}$, $j\in\{1,\ldots,p\}$;
  $A=[a_{ij}]$, $i\in\{0,1,\ldots,m+p\}$, $j\in\{1,\ldots,p\}$;
  $B=[b_{ik}]$, $i\in\{0,1,\ldots,m+p\}$, $k\in\{0,1,\ldots,m+p\}$;
  $C=[c_{ij}]$, $i\in\{0,1,\ldots,m+p\}$, $j\in\{1,\ldots,p\}$;
  $D=[d_{ik}]$, $i\in\{0,1,\ldots,m+p\}$, $k\in\{0,1,\ldots,m+p\}$;
output: ok — *true* if a solution exists
  u — the solution
algorithm:
  $u_k := 0, \forall k\in\{0,1,\ldots,p\}$;
  $r_0 := 0$;
  finish := *false*;
  $j := 1$;
  while not *finish* do
    $$V_j := \left\{x\in\{1,\ldots,m+p\}\setminus\{u_1,\ldots,u_{j-1}\}\,\middle|\, r_{j-1}+c_{x,j}+d_{u_{j-1},x}\leqq e\right\};$$
    if $V_j\neq\emptyset$ then
      $g^* := \max\{g_{x,j}\,|\,x\in V_j\}$;
      $V_j^* := \{x\in V_j\,|\,g_{x,j}=g^*\}$;
      $r^* := \min\{a_{x,j}+b_{u_{j-1},x}\,|\,x\in V_j^*\}$;
      $R^* := \{x\in V_j^*\,|\,a_{x,j}+b_{u_{j-1},x}=r^*\}$;
      choose $x\in R^*$;

```
                $u_j := x;$
                $r_j := r_{j-1} + c_{x,j} + d_{u_{j-1},x};$
                $j := j + 1;$
                if $j > p$ then
                        $ok := true$
                        $finish := true$
                end if
        else
                if $j = 1$ then
                        $ok := false$
                        $finish := true$
                end if
                $V_j := V_j \setminus \{u_{j-1}\};$
                $j := j - 1;$
        end if
    end while
end algorithm
```

It is possible to make a small change of this algorithm by introducing that vertex which minimizes the ratio between the growth of function $\tilde{F}_1$ and the growth of function $\tilde{F}_2$ relatively to the set of vertex that do not close the cycle; we mention, also, that the introduction of this vertex does not exceed the cost limit.

7.2 Parallel approach for the registrar route problem

The algorithm previously presented is a serial one, which means that it is perform with one processing unit, and depends on the number of hospitals that the registrar has to browse. A more general situation is when the graph is not complete, it means that the registrar may not move to each hospital, but only to some of them, let us say n. If this number is big enough, the serial execution will take a lot of time. In order to speed up and get faster the result, a parallel approach is more convenient. As in (Feilmeier, 1982) applications for high performance computing are given. If we use more than one processing unit, we may obtain the desired result approximately n times faster. We know that the registrar starts from node 0 and has to browse n different locations, being constrained by the restrictions of possible total cost.

The parallel algorithm is of "master-slave" type and has the following steps:

1. According to the graph of problem (PG), the algorithm generates the adjacent matrix, denoted by $E = [e_{ik}]$, where $e_{ik} = 1$,if in graph G there is an edge from i to k, and $e_{ik} = 0$ if not, for every $i,k \in \{0,\ldots,m+p\}$.
2. In the system work as many processors, as many figures 1 appear on the first row of matrix A. For instance, if five figures 1 appear on the first row, then five processors will work. Obviously, the maximum number of processors is n. Every processor will store a copy of the matrix E.
3. According with the adjacent matrix, every processor builds its own circuit and verifies the restrictions. If they are fulfilled, the processor memorizes the circuit and sends a message to the processor master. If one processor finds that there exist more than one admissible circuit, it gives a signal to the master processor, which will allocate another processor in charge with the new circuit.

4. Finally, the processor master will decide which circuit is optimal for problem (PG).

Generally, the parallel machine on which the following algorithm may be implemented is of SIMD type (Single Instruction stream, Multiple Data stream). Due to this fact, no communication among Slave processors is needed. They communicate only with the processor Master. Any type of network may be defined on the parallel machine (for the parallel calculus see, for example (Chiorean, 2000)). When the parallel network is defined by the program, every processor gets an identification number. The Processor Master receives 0, and all the other processors in the system receive numbers starting with 1.

Algorithm 0.2 ParPg

```
algorithm:
    Define_Network {determine the configuration of processors, get their Id's}
    if id = 0 then
        Generate_Adjacent_Matrix(G,E);{input graph, output matrix E}
        Determine_Number_of_Slaves (E,n);{n, equal to values of 1 that there are on the
            first row}
        Send_Message_to_Slaves(E){send matrix E in every processor Slave}
    else
        for i = 1 to n in parallel do
            Get_Message_from_Master(E);
            {copy matrix E from Master};
            Verify_Number_of_Cycles (E, nr);
            if nr ≧ 1 then
                for j = 1 to nr do
                    Verify_Restrictions_on_the_Cycle(E, j, finalvalues);
                    {every processor will work on the "nr" of cycles};
                    {in "finalvalue" memorizes the values of variables for
                    the objective function};
                    Memorize_Cycle (finalvalues,j,u);
                    {the corresponding circuit is kept in vector u};
                    Send_Message_to_Master(j,u);
                end for
            end if
        end for
    end if
    if id = 0 then
        Get_Message_from_Slaves(u){Master collects all the possible cycles}
    end if
    Determine_Optimum_cycles(final_u){Compares cycles and determines the optimum
    one, denoted "final_u"}
    Print(final_u)
end algorithm
```

Working this way, with more than one processor, the result is obtained n times faster, where n is the number of processors in the system.

7.3 An exact algorithm of the Little type

For solving the problem (PG), we built an exact but not polynomial algorithm, based on the branch and bound method as in (Little et al, 1963). For its construction, one always goes to the branch where the growth of the first component, $\tilde{F}_1$, of the goal function, is the highest. If there are several possibilities of getting the same growth, then it favors that whose second component, $\tilde{F}_2$, is the lowest. The bound is made by using two real improper numbers, bf and bc. These numbers are defined iteratively. In the beginning, $bf := 0$ and $bc := +\infty$. If we have at least a cycle, in the graph attached to our problem, then the value of the pair (bf, bc) is equal to the lexicographical max-min of the set of all such pair attached to the cycles which we have been obtain until this moment.

A finite sequence $(k_h, I_h, J_h, G^h, f_h, \gamma_h, \delta_h, w^h)_{h=1}^N$, where $N \leqq (m+p)\ldots(p+1)$, is built.

- k_h is a binary variable: it has the value 1 if the term h was not studied yet and the value 0 otherwise.
- G^h, is the work matrix in the h-th iteration.
- $u^h \in IR^p$ will be used for building the descriptor of a cycle.
- the numbers f_h and γ_h are equal to $\tilde{F}_1(u^h)$, $\tilde{F}_2(u^h)$, respectively, and there are computed iteratively.
- δ_h is equal to the value of right hand side term of bounded equation corresponding to u^h; it is also iteratively computed.
- The vector w^k is used to inhibit branching; its components are iteratively computed.

Algorithm 0.3 An Exact Algorithm
input: the natural numbers m and p;
 the elements of matrices: $G = [g_{ij}]$, $i \in \{0,1,\ldots,m+p\}$, $j \in \{1,\ldots,p\}$;
 $A = [a_{ij}]$, $i \in \{0,1,\ldots,m+p\}$, $j \in \{1,\ldots,p\}$;
 $B = [b_{ik}]$, $i \in \{0,1,\ldots,m+p\}$, $k \in \{0,1,\ldots,m+p\}$;
 $C = [c_{ij}]$, $i \in \{0,1,\ldots,m+p\}$, $j \in \{1,\ldots,p\}$;
 $D = [d_{ik}]$, $i \in \{0,1,\ldots,m+p\}$, $k \in \{0,1,\ldots,m+p\}$;
output:
algorithm:
 $I_1 := \{0,1,\ldots,m+p\}$;
 $J_1 := \{1,\ldots,p\}$;
 $t_1 := 1$;
 $n_1 := 0$;
 $u^1 := (u_0, u_1, \ldots, u_n) = (0,\ldots,0)$;
 $u^* := (0,\ldots,0) \in \mathbb{R}^{p+1}$;
 $f_1 := 0$;
 $\gamma_1 := 0$;
 $\delta_1 := 0$;
 $bf := 0$;
 $bc := +\infty$;
 $\forall i \in I_1, \forall j \in J_1, g_{ij}^1 := g_{ij}$;
 $\forall j \in J_1, w_j^1 := \max\{g_{ij}^1 | i \in I_1\}$;
 $h := 1$;
 $K := \{k \in \{1,\ldots,h\} | t_k = 1\}$;

while $K \neq \emptyset$ do
    $s := (\max\max\min)_{\text{lex}} \{(n_k, f_k, \gamma_k) \mid k \in K\}$;
    choose $k \in K$ such that $(n_k, f_k, \gamma_k) = s$;
    $j := n_k + 1$;
    $I^* := \{i \in I_k \mid \delta_k + c_{ij} + d_{u^k_{j-1}, i} > e\}$;
    if $I_k \setminus I^* = \emptyset$ then
        $t_k := 0$;
    else
        $\forall i \in I^*$, $g^k_{ij} := -\infty$;
        $w^k_j := \max\{g_{ij} \mid i \in I_k \setminus I^*\}$;
        if $f_k + \sum_{\alpha \in J_k} w^k_\alpha < bf$ then
            $t_k := 0$;
        else
            $M := \{i \in I_k \setminus I^* \mid g_{ij} = w^k_j\}$;
            $v := \max\{a_{ij} + b_{u_{j-1}, i} \mid i \in M\}$;
            $V := \{i \in M \mid a_{ij} + b_{u_{j-1}, i} = v\}$;
            choose $u^k_j \in V$;
            if $(I_k \setminus (I^* \cup \{u^k_j\}) \neq \emptyset)$ and

$$f_k + \sum_{\alpha=1\, \alpha > j}^{p} w^k_\alpha + \max\{g_{ij} \mid i \in I_k \setminus (I^* \cup \{u^k_j\})\} \geqq bf$$

            then
                $h := h + 1$;
                $t_h := 1$;
                $n_h := n_k$;
                $u^h := u^k$;
                $u^h_0 := 0$;
                $f_h := f_k$;
                $\gamma_h := \gamma_k$;
                $\delta_h := \delta_k$;
                $I_h := I_k \setminus I^*$;
                $J_h := J_k$;
                $\forall i \in I, \forall j \in J$, $g^h_{rs} := g^k_{rs}$;
                $g^h_{u_j, j} := -\infty$;
                $\forall r \in J \setminus \{j\}$, $w^h_r := w^k_r$;
                $w^h_j := \max\{g^h_{ij} \mid i \in I_k\}$;
            end if
            $f_k := f_k + g^k_{u^k_j, j}$;
            $\gamma_k := \gamma_k + a_{u^k_j, j} + b_{u^k_{j-1}, u^k_j}$;
            $\delta_k := \delta_k + c_{u^k_j, j} + d_{u^k_{j-1}, u^k_j}$;
            if $j = p$ then
                if $f_k \geqq bf$ then
                    $bf := f_k$;
                    $bc := \gamma_k$;

$u^* := (u_1^k, \ldots, u_p^k);$
end if
else
$h := h + 1;$
$t_h := 1;$
$n_h := n_k + 1;$
$u^h := u^k + u_j^k e^j;$
$f_h := f_k;$
$\gamma_h := \gamma_k;$
$\delta_h := \delta_k;$
$I_h := I_k \setminus \{u_j^k\};$
$J_h := J_k \setminus \{j\};$
$\forall i \in I, \forall j \in J, g_{rs}^h := g_{rs}^k;$
$\forall r \in I, g_{rj}^h := -\infty;$
$\forall s \in J, g_{u_j,s}^h := -\infty;$
$\forall r \in J \setminus \{j\}, w_r^h := w_r^k;$
$w_j^h := g_{u_j^k, j}^h;$
$t_k := 0;$
end if
end if
end if
$K := \{k \in \{1, \ldots, h\} | t_k = 1\};$
end while
if bf=0 then
output: the problem (PBG) is inconsistent;
else
output: u^* is an optimal solution of (PBG);
end if
end algorithm

The algorithm 0.3 is very easy to implement and it has been used on a number of test cases for determining the optimal route of the registrar. The output result is optimal.

8. References

Angel, E.; Bampis, E. & Gourvès, L. (2004). Approximating the Pareto curve with local search for the bi-criteria TSP(1,2) problem. *Theoretical Computer Science*, Vol. 310, no. 1-3, 135-146, ISSN 0304-3975

Balas, E. (2002). The Prize Collecting Traveling Salesman Problem and its Application, In: Traveling Salesman Problem and its Variations, Gutin, G. & Punnen, A. (Ed.), 663-695, Kluwer Academic Publishers, ISBN 1-4020-0664-0, Dordrecht

Borges, P.C. & Hansen, P.H. (2001). A study of global convexity for a multiple objective travelling salesman problem. In Ribeiro, C.C. & Hansen, P. (Ed.), *Essays and Surveys in Metaheuristics*, 129-150, Kluwer Academic Publishers, ISBN 978-0-7923-7520-3

Briggs, A. & Sculpher, M. (1998). An Introduction to Markov Modelling for Economic Evaluation. *Pharmacoeconomics*, Vol. 13, no. 4, 397-409, ISSN 1170-7690

Briggs, A.; Claxton, K. & Sculpher, M. (2006). *Decision Modelling for Health Economic Evaluation.*

Oxford University Press, ISBN 978-0-19-852662-9, Oxford

Canfelt, K.; Barnabas, R.; Patnik, J. & Bera, V. (2004). The predicted effect of changes in cervical screening practice in the U.K: results from a modelling study. *British Journal of Cancer*, Vol. 91, 530-536, 0007-0920

Chiorean, I. (2000). *Parallel Calculus* (in roumanian), Ed.Albastra, ISBN 973-9215-08-4, Cluj-Napoca

Chiorean, I.; Lupsa, L. & Neamtiu, L. (2008). Markov Models for the Simulation of Cancer Screening Process, In *International Conference on Numerical Analysis and Applied Mathematics proceedings*, 143-147, ISBN 978-0-7354-0576-9, Kos, Greece, September 2008, American Institute of Physics

Crama, Y. (1989) Recognition problems for special classes of polynomials in 0-1 variables. *Mathematical Programming*, Vol. 44, 139-155, ISSN 0025-5610

Ehrgott, M. (2005). Multicriteria Optimization, Second ed., Springer, ISBN 3-540-21398-8, Berlin Heidelberg New York

Eveden, D.; Harper, P.R.; Brailsford, S.C. & Harindra, V. (2005). System Dynamics modelling of Chlamydia infection for screening intervention planning cost-benefit estimation. *IMA Journal of Management Mathematics*, Vol. 16, no. 3, 265-279, ISSN 1471-678X

Fayers, P. M.; Ashby, D. & Parmer, M. K. B. (1997). Bayesian data monitoring in clinical trials, *Statistics in Medicine*, Vol. 16, 1413-1430, ISSN 0277-6715

Feillet, D.; Dejax, P. & Gendreau, M. (2005). Traveling Salesman Problems with Profits, Transportation Science, Vol. 39, May 2005, 188-205, ISSN 0041-1655

Feilmeier, M. (1982). Parallel numerical algorithms, In *Parallel Processing Systems*, Evans, D. (ed.), 285-338, Cambridge University Press, ISBN 0-521-24366-1, Cambridge

Fischetti, M.; Salazar-González, J.-J. & Toth, P. (2002). The Generalized Traveling Salesman and Orienteering Problems, In: Traveling Salesman Problem and its Variations, Gutin, G. & Punnen, A. (Ed.), 609-662, Kluwer Academic Publishers, ISBN 1-4020-0664-0, Dordrecht

Grosan, C.; Abraham, A.; Campian, R. & Ţigan, Şt. (2005). Evolution Strategies for Ranking Several Trigeminal Neuralgia Treatments, *Applied Medical Informatics*, Vol. 17, no. 3-4, 72-78, ISSN 103-443-015

Grosan, C.; Abraham, A. & Ţigan, Şt. (2007). Multicriteria programming in medical diagnosis and treatments, *Applied Soft Computing*, Vol. 8, no. 4 (September), 1407-1417, ISSN 1568-4946

Hammer (Ivănescu), P.L. & Rudeanu, S. (1968). Boolean Methods in Operations Research and Related Areas, Springer, ISBN 0387042911, Berlin

Kang, M. & Lagakos, St. W. (2007). Statistical methods for panel data from a semi-Markov process, with application to HPV, *Biostatistics*, Vol. 8, no. 2, 252-264, ISSN 1465-4644

Little, J.D.C.; Murty, K.G.; Sweeney & D.W.; Karel, K. (1963). An algorithm for the traveling salesman problem. *Operation Research*, Vol. 11, No. 6, November-December 1963, 972-989, ISSN 0160-5682

Lupşa, L. (1999) A Criterion for Caracterizing a Medical Treatment that Uses Multicriteria Programming in Pharmacoeconomics. In *Analysis, Functional Equations, Approximation and Convexity*. Editura Carpatica, 142-146, ISBN 979-97664-9-8, Cluj-Napoca

Lupşa, L. (2000) Multicriteria Programming Used in Medico-Economic Analysis of Treatment Protocols. In *Proceedings of the "Tiberiu Popoviciu" Itinerant Seminar of Functional Equations, Approximation and Convexity*. Editura SRIMA, 103-111, ISBN 973-98591-9-4,

Cluj-Napoca
Lupşa, L. (2000). The sort of a class of drugs using the balanced points methods. In *Séminaire de la Théorie de la Meilleure Approximation, Convexité et Optimisation*, Editura SRIMA 2000, 171-181, ISBN 973-99781-0-X, Cluj-Napoca
Lupşa, R.; Lupşa, L. & Neamtiu, L. (2008):.Optimal Model to Solve the Transport Model for Mammography Screening, 2008 IEEE International Conference on Automation, Quality and Testing, Robotics (AQTR 2008) THETA 16th edition proceedings, tome 3, pp. 139-142, ISBN 978-1-4244-2576-1, Cluj-Napoca
Manthey, B. (2009). On Approximating Multi-Criteria TSP, In *Symposium on Theoretical Aspects of Computer Science*, 637648, Freiburg, 2009, www.stacs-conf.org
Neamţiu, L. (2008). *Modeling and Decision in Health Economics* (in roumanian), Casa cărţii de ştiinţa, ISBN 978-973-133-380-9, Cluj-Napoca
Neanţiu, L. (2009). A Medical Resources Allocation Problem, *Results in Mathematics*, Vol. 53, nr. 3-4 (July), 341-348, ISSN 1422-6383
Punnen, A. P. (2002). The Traveling Salesman Problem: Applications, Formulation and Variations, In: Traveling Salesman Problem and its Variations, Gutin, G. & Punnen, (Ed.), 1-28, Kluwer Academic Publishers, ISBN 1-4020-0664-0, Dordrecht
Trobec, R.; Vajtersic, M. & Zinterhof, P. (eds) (2009). *Parallel Computing. Numerics, Applications, and Trends.* Springer, ISBN 978-1-84882-408-9, Dordrecht Heidelberg London New York
Ţigan, Şt.; Achimaş, A.; Coman, I.; Drugan, T. & Iacob, E. (2001). *Multifactorial Decisions* (in roumanian) . Editura SRIMA, ISBN 973-99781-3-4, Cluj-Napoca
Villagra, M.; Barán, B. & Gómez, O. (2006). Global Convexity in the Bi-Criteria Traveling Salesman Problem. In *Artificial Intelligence in Theory and Practice*, 217-226, Springer, ISBN 978-0-387-34654-0, Boston
Warburton, A. (1987). Approximation of Pareto optima in multiple-objective shortest path problems. *Operations Research*, Vol. 35, no. 1 (Jan-Feb.), 7079, ISSN 0030-364X
Willan, A. R. & Briggs, A. H. (2006). *Statistical Analysis of Cost-effectiveness Data.* John Wiley & Sons Ltd, ISBN 978-0-470-85626-0, Chichester
World Health Organization (1999). Cancer Registration: Principles and Methods, Jensen, O.M.; Parkon, D.M.; MacLennan, R.; Muir, C.S.; Skeet, R.G. eds., IARC Scientific Publications no. 95, ISBN 92-832-1195-2, Lyon